MANAGERIAL
ACCOUNTING

Linda Smith Bamber
University of Georgia

Karen Wilken Braun
Case Western Reserve University

Walter T. Harrison, Jr.
Baylor University

PEARSON

Prentice
Hall

Pearson Education International

AVP/Executive Editor: Jodi McPherson
VP/Publisher: Natalie Anderson
Director, Product Development: Pamela Hersperger
Editorial Project Manager: Rebecca Knauer
Editorial Assistant: Kate Horton
Marketing Manager: Andrew Watts
Marketing Assistant: Justin Jacob
Senior Managing Editor, Production: Cynthia Zonneveld
Production Project Manager: Melissa Feimer
Permissions Coordinator: Charles Morris
Senior Operations Supervision: Nick Sklitsis
AV Project Manager: Rhonda Aversa
Art Director: Anthony Gemmellaro
Cover Design: Anthony Gemmellaro
Composition: GEX Publishing Services
Full-Service Project Management: GEX Publishing Services

Credits and acknowledgments borrowed from other sources and reproduced, with permission, in this textbook appear on appropriate page within text and on page PC-1.

If you purchased this book within the United States or Canada you should be aware that it has been wrongfully imported without the approval of the Publisher or the Author.

Pearson Education LTD., London
Pearson Education Singapore, Pte. Ltd
Pearson Education, Canada, Ltd
Pearson Education–Japan
Pearson Education, Upper Saddle River, New Jersey

Pearson Education Australia PTY, Limited
Pearson Education North Asia Ltd
Pearson Educación de Mexico, S.A. de C.V.
Pearson Education Malaysia, Pte. Ltd.

10 9 8 7 6 5 4 3 2 1
ISBN-13: 978-0-13613284-4
ISBN-10: 0-13-613284-7

MyAccountingLab

For Instructors

MyAccountingLab is web-based, tutorial and assessment accounting software that not only gives students more "I Get It" moments, but gives instructors the flexibility to make technology an integral part of their course. It's also an excellent supplementary resource for students.

MyAccountingLab provides instructors with a rich and flexible set of course materials, along with course-management tools that make it easy to deliver all or a portion of your course online.

Powerful Homework and Test Manager

Create, import, and manage online homework assignments, quizzes, and tests. Create assignments from online exercises directly correlated to your textbook. Homework exercises include guided solutions and DemoDocs to help students understand and master concepts. You can choose from a wide range of assignment options, including time limits, proctoring, and maximum number of attempts allowed.

Comprehensive Gradebook Tracking

MyAccountingLab's online gradebook automatically tracks your students' results on tests, homework, and tutorials and gives you control over managing results and calculating grades. All MyAccountingLab grades can be exported to a spreadsheet program, such as Microsoft® Excel. The MyAccountingLab Gradebook provides a number of student data views and gives you the flexibility to weigh assignments, select which attempts to include when calculating scores, and omit or delete results for individual assignments.

Department-Wide Solutions

Get help managing multiple sections and working with Teaching Assistants using MyAccountingLab Coordinator Courses. After your MyAccountingLab course is set up, it can be copied to create sections or "member courses." Changes to the Coordinator Course ripple down to all members, so changes only need to be made once.

For Students

MyAccountingLab provides students with a personalized interactive learning environment, where they can learn at their own pace and measure their progress.

Interactive Tutorial Exercises

MyAccountingLab's homework and practice questions are correlated to the textbook, and they regenerate algorithmically to give students unlimited opportunity for practice and mastery. Questions include guided solutions, DemoDoc examples, and learning aids for extra help at point-of-use, and they offer helpful feedback when students enter incorrect answers.

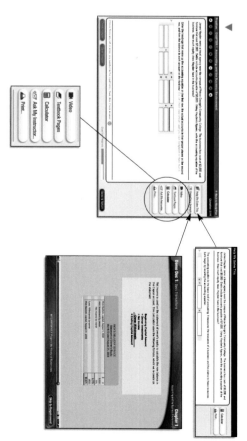

Study Plan for Self-Paced Learning

MyAccountingLab's study plan helps students monitor their own progress, letting them see at a glance exactly which topics they need to practice. MyAccountingLab generates a personalized study plan for each student based on his or her test results, and the study plan links directly to interactive, tutorial exercises for topics the student hasn't yet mastered. Students can regenerate these exercises with new values for unlimited practice, and the exercises include guided solutions and multimedia learning aids to give students the extra help they need.

View a guided tour of MyAccountingLab at http://www.myaccountinglab.com/support/tours.

How to Use MyAccountingLab

If you have not yet had a chance to explore the benefits of the MyAccountingLab (MAL) Web site, I would encourage you to log in now and see what a valuable tool it can be. MyAccountingLab is a terrific tool for helping you grasp the accounting concepts that you are learning. So what exactly is MyAccountingLab? MyAccountingLab is a homework management tool that allows you to complete homework online.

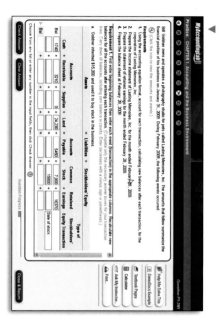

What is so great about completing the homework online, you might wonder?

Well, how about the ability to ask for and receive help *immediately* while you are working the problems? MAL allows you to click on a *Help Me Solve This* button at anytime while you are working the problem, and a pop-up window appears with tips to help you solve the specific part of the problem that you are working on. It is similar to having someone standing over your shoulder to help you—right in the middle of the problem—so that you can get through it and understand how to solve it.

MAL also has a button that you can click on that will open an *online version of the textbook*—it even takes you right to the section of the textbook that explains the topic related to the problem that you are working on.

Another great feature of MAL is the *Ask My Instructor...* button. If your instructor allows you to e-mail questions, you are able to send an e-mail to your instructor in which you can explain what you are having difficulties with. When your instructor receives the e-mail, there will be a link that will take the instructor right to the problem you were working on in MAL.

You will also find two different types of problems in MAL, *bookmatch* and *algorithmic* problems. The bookmatch problems are the exact problems right out of your textbook (your instructor must make these available in MAL). The algorithmic problems are identical to the ones in the textbook, except they have several variables that change in the problem every time it is selected. The algorithmic problems allow you to have an unlimited number of problems you can work in order to master the material. This means that you can see how to do a problem similar to the one in the book.

The other benefit of working the problems in MAL is that each problem is broken down into different parts. MAL gives you three attempts at working each part and then it fills in the correct answer. This allows you to learn from your mistakes as you go.

Support is always available for you online at:
http://www.myaccountinglab.com/support/student.html.

How to Maximize Your Time in MyAccountingLab

1. Read the textbook material.

2. Review the Demo Docs in your textbook and your study guide.

3. Work the algorithmic problems in MAL utilizing the *Help Me Solve This* hints as needed. If your instructor has not assigned any of the homework problems in MAL, you can access the algorithmic problems by clicking on the *Study Plan* button. Although it would be helpful to work all of the problems, you should focus on the problems that your instructor has assigned for each chapter, if any.

4. Rework any of the problems that you had difficulty understanding as many times as you need in order to achieve understanding. If you open the Study Plan, you can see which problems you had incorrect answers on.

5. Work the homework problems that were assigned by your instructor if any (either in MAL or from the textbook using paper and pencil).

6. In order to prepare for a quiz or exam using MAL, rework the algorithmic equivalent of any of the assigned homework. Additionally, if your instructor has made them available, you can access the *Sample Tests* in the *Take a Test* section. There is a sample pre-test and post-test available for every chapter in the text so you can focus on the chapters covered in your quiz or exam.

Overall, using MyAccountingLab can be a great benefit to you in this course. It provides immediate feedback while doing homework and is a great preparation for exams. We encourage you to try it and see how it can help you have a more successful course experience.

Brief Contents

Contents

8 Short-Term Business Decisions   439

9 Capital Investment Decisions and the Time Value of Money   495

To Michael in grateful appreciation
Linda Bamber

To Cory, Rachel, and Hannah who fill my life with joy
Karen Braun

To Billie Harrison who taught me to pursue excellence in all things
Tom Harrison

For professors whose greatest joy is hearing students say "I get it!"

Help your students achieve "I get it!" moments when you're with them AND when you're NOT. When you're there showing how to solve a problem in class, students "get it." When you're not there, they get stuck—it's only natural. That's where our system comes in, at these "they have the book, but they don't have you" moments. The *Managerial Accounting*, Demo Doc System provides the vehicle for you and your students to have more "I get it!" moments inside and outside of class.

Why the System Was Created

Introductory accounting students consistently tell us, "When doing homework, I get stuck trying to solve problems the way they were demonstrated in class." Instructors consistently tell us, "I have so much to cover in so little time; I can't afford to go backward and review homework in class." Those challenges inspired us to develop Demo Docs.

How the System Works

Demo Docs are comprehensive worked-through problems, available for several chapters of the *Managerial Accounting text,* to help students when they are trying to solve exercises and problems on their own. The idea is to help students duplicate the classroom experience outside of class. Entire problems that mirror end of chapter material are shown solved and annotated with explanations written in a conversational style, essentially imitating what an instructor might say if standing over a student's shoulder. In addition to the Demo Docs in the textbook, there are Demo Docs for every chapter in the Study Guide, in MyAccountingLab, and as a part of the instructor package for instructors to use in class.

- **In-Chapter Demo Docs** sit right after the extensive end-of-chapter material to help students recreate those "I get it" moments that before only you could provide.

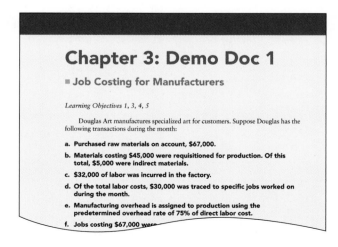

- **In-Study Guide Demo Docs** and **Flash Demo Docs** on CD are also available. These additional Demo Docs will assist in furthering students' understanding out of class. The Flash Demo Docs on CD that come with the Study Guide will meet the needs of differing learning styles by simulating a live tutor assisting with homework completion.

- **Flash Instructor Demo Docs**—The very same Demo Docs that your students will use to stay on top of the material and complete their homework are provided for you on CD for use in lecture. In theory, you will not need to prepare your own walk-through problems. You can simply use these to help students "get it" in your lecture.

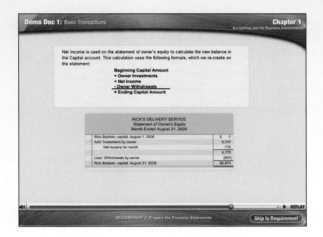

MyAccountingLab is about helping students at their teachable moment, whether that is 1:00 PM or 1:00 AM, because whenever you are not there, MyAccountingLab can be. It is packed with algorithmic problems and the exact same end of chapter material that you're used to assigning for homework. It includes a Demo Doc for the more complex exercises and problems that students can refer to as they work through the questions.

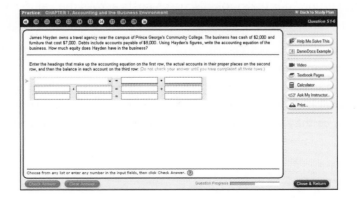

From the Authors

Our overall goal is to provide an *accessible and understandable* textbook that is accurate, engages students' interests, and provides students with ample opportunities to learn and practice the material. From our own experience, we know that students will stop reading a textbook if they think it's boring, too difficult, or too "wordy." Our aim is to avoid these potential pitfalls by providing a textbook that students feel comfortable picking up and reading on their own.

Accuracy

In addition to having the textbook accuracy checked by professionals, we previously created a Class Test Edition that was used by instructors from all regions of the country. Each instructor used the book in his or her class along with the supplements and submitted detailed feedback on each aspect of the *Managerial Accounting* program.

Engaging Students' Interests

- For the most part, we have placed each chapter's material in the context of a given company. This story-like setting provides a cohesive coverage of the material and helps to engage students' interests. Even non-accountants have told us that the stories have been very interesting, and made them want to continue reading.

- To further stimulate interest, we've presented the material in a variety of different business settings, including manufacturers, retailers, and service firms. Even when we use a manufacturing setting, our textbook discusses costs across the value chain, rather than only discussing costs incurred in the manufacturing process.

- Professors and students are often concerned with the "wordiness" of a textbook. To minimize this concern, we've taken a "middle of the road" approach: We avoid wordiness when it is not necessary, yet walk students, step-by-step, through the most difficult concepts and exhibits in the material. In other words, we are right there, holding the students' hands, as they tackle the most difficult aspects of managerial accounting.

Opportunities to Practice Material

- We believe the end-of-chapter assignment material should adequately address the material presented in the chapter and offer a broad selection of questions. We want professors to be able to choose the types of questions and difficulty level that is most appropriate for their unique student body. Therefore, each of our chapters contains 30 to 50 different end-of-chapter short exercises, exercises, and problems. Each question is titled and keyed to the learning objectives, so that professors can quickly select the questions they wish to use for homework and so that students have a cue to help them begin to solve the questions.

  - The short exercises are concise questions that address individual learning objectives. These short exercises can usually be answered in five minutes or less and allow students to gain confidence in their understanding of the material.

  - Once students gain confidence through the short exercises, they are ready to move on to the exercises, which require a deeper understanding of the learning objectives.

  - Finally, many students will be ready for the challenge of the problems, which require a more critical understanding of the material and more time to complete.

- In addition to the textbook, students have a variety of practice materials to choose from such as a Study Guide, a Companion Website, MyAccountingLab, and VangoNotes. Please see the Student Supplement section for detailed descriptions of these ancillaries.

Minimizing Confusion

- **Consistency** The entire package matters. Consistency in terminology and problem set-ups from one medium to another—Test Bank to Study Guide to Instructor's Edition—is critical to your success in the classroom. So when students ask "Where do the numbers come from?" they can go to our text *or* go online and see what to do. If it's worded one way in the text, you can count on it being worded the same way in the supplements.

- **Clutter-Free** This first edition is built on the premise of "Less Is More." Extraneous boxes and features, nonessential bells and whistles—they are all gone. We know that excess crowds out what really matters—the concepts, the problems, and the learning objectives. Instructors asked for fewer "features" in favor of less clutter and better cross-referencing, and Bamber, Braun, Harrison, *Managerial Accounting*, is delivering on that wish.

Instructor Supplements

Instructor's Edition Featuring Instructor Demo Docs
(ISBN 0-13-812979-7)

- **The Look of the Instructor's Edition** We've asked a lot of instructors how we can help them successfully implement new course-delivery methods (e.g., online) while maintaining their regular campus schedule of classes and academic responsibilities. In response, we developed a system of instruction for those of you who are long on commitment and expertise—but short on time and assistance.

  The primary goal of the Instructor's Edition is **ease of implementation, using any delivery method**—traditional, self-paced, or online. That is, the Instructor's Edition quickly answers for you, the professor, the question "What must the student do?" Likewise, the Instructor's Edition quickly answers for the student "What must I do?", offers time-saving tips with "best of" categories for in-class discussion, and strong examples to illustrate difficult concepts to a wide variety of students. The Instructor's Edition also offers a quick one-shot cross-reference at the exact point of importance with key additional teaching resources, so everything is in one place. The Instructor's Edition includes chapter summaries and outlines, lecture outlines and assignment grids, teaching tips, pitfalls for new students, 10 minute quizzes, and "best of" practices from instructors.

- **The Instructor's Edition Also Includes Instructor Demo Docs**

  In *Instructor Demo Docs,* we walk the students through how to solve a problem as if it were the first time they've seen it. There are no lengthy passages of text. Instead, bits of expository text are woven into the steps needed to solve the problem, in the exact sequence—for you to provide at the teachable *"I get it!"* moment. This is the point at which the student has a context within which he or she can understand the concept. We provide conversational text around each of the steps so the student stays engaged in solving the problem. We provide notes to the instructor for key teaching points around the Demo Docs, and "best of" practice tidbits before each *Instructor Demo Doc.*

  The *Instructor Demo Docs* are written with all of your everyday classroom realities in mind—and trying to save you time in prepping new examples each time your book changes. We keep the terminology consistent with the text, so there are no surprises for students as they try and work through a problem the first time.

Instructor's Resource Center CD (ISBN 0-13-812981-9)

The Instructor's Resource Center CD includes electronic files for the following ancillaries in various formats:

- **Solutions Manual** The Solutions Manual contains solutions to all end-of-chapter questions, including the Quick Check multiple-choice questions, short exercises, exercise sets, problems sets, decision cases, ethical issues, and team projects. Additionally, every page of the solutions manual is reproduced in acetate format for use on an overhead projector (ISBN 0-13-812978-9).

- **Test Item File and Alternate Test Item File** The Test Item File includes more than 1,000 questions.

- **TestGen** The TestGen test-generating software allows instructors to easily create custom tests by choosing questions from the test bank. Files are also available for course-management use in WebCT, Blackboard, and CourseCompass.

- **PowerPoints** These summarize and reinforce key text materials. They capture classroom attention with original problems and solved step-by-step exercises. These walk-throughs are designed to help facilitate classroom discussion and demonstrate where the numbers come from and what they mean to the concept at hand.

- **Classroom Response Systems (CRS)** CRS is an exciting new wireless polling technology that makes large and small classrooms even more interactive, because it enables instructors to pose questions to their students, record results, and display those results instantly. Students can easily answer questions using compact remote-control–type transmitters. Prentice Hall has partnerships with leading classroom response-systems providers and can show you everything you need to know about setting up and using a CRS system. Prentice Hall will provide the classroom hardware, text-specific PowerPoint slides in the IRCD, software, and support. Visit **www.prenhall.com/crs** to learn more.

- **E-Working Paper Solutions**

Instructor's Resource Center

www.prenhall.com/irc is where instructors can access a variety of print, media, and presentation resources available with this text in downloadable, digital format. Resources are also available for course management platforms such as Blackboard, WebCT, and CourseCompass.

After registering at the **www.prenhall.com/irc** site, instructors do not need to fill out any additional forms nor do they need to be able to recall multiple usernames and passwords in order to access new titles and/or editions. As a registered faculty member, instructors can log in directly to download resource files and receive immediate access and instructions for installing course management content to their campus server.

The Prentice Hall dedicated Technical Support team is ready to assist instructors with questions about the media supplements that accompany this text. Instructors can visit **http://247pearsoned.custhelp.com** for answers to frequently asked questions and toll-free user support phone numbers.

- All of the materials from *Managerial Accounting's* Instructor's Resource Center CD are available in the Instructor's Resource Center for download. The Instructor's Edition files are also available as well as other valuable resources. Instructors can also access these materials by visiting the book's Web site at **www.prenhall.com/bamber** and clicking on Instructor Resource Center.

Instructor Supplements

MyAccountingLab www.myaccountinglab.com

MyAccountingLab is Prentice Hall's online homework and assessment manager to help students "get" accounting through the power of practice. MyAccountingLab features a full e-book, Flash Demo Docs, instructor videos, and additional resources at the student's fingertips to aid learning. With MyAccountingLab, instructors can:

- Deliver all or a portion of the course online, whether the students are in a lab setting or working from home.
- Create and assign online homework and tests that are automatically graded and tightly correlated to the textbook.
- Manage students' results in a powerful online gradebook designed specifically for mathematics and statistics.
- Customize the course, depending on the syllabus and the students' needs.

Companion Website www.prenhall.com/bamber

The book's Companion Website contains the following:

- Self-study quizzes—an interactive study guide for each chapter
- E-Working papers that students can use to complete homework assignments for each chapter
- Student PowerPoints—for use as a study aid or note-taking guide
- Sample Flash Demo Doc

Online Courses with WebCT/Blackboard/CourseCompass

Prentice Hall offers a link to MyAccountingLab through the Bb and WebCT course management systems.

Student Supplements

Study Guide Including Demo Docs and E-Working Papers
(ISBN 0-13-812980-0)

Demo Docs are available in the study guide—in print and on CD in Flash so students can easily refer to them when they need them. The Study Guide also includes a summary overview of key topics and multiple-choice and short-answer questions and solutions for students to test their knowledge. Electronic working papers are included on the accompanying CD.

MyAccountingLab www.myaccountinglab.com

MyAccountingLab is Prentice Hall's online homework and assessment manager to help students "get" accounting through the power of practice. MyAccountingLab features a full e-book, Flash Demo Docs, instructor videos, and additional resources at the student's fingertips to aid learning. With MyAccountingLab, students can:

- Work through unlimited tutorial exercises correlated to the exercises in the textbook.
- Receive a personalized study plan to diagnose areas where practice is needed.
- Access a multimedia textbook with links to learning aids, such as animations and videos.
- View Demo Docs correlated right to the questions and places where students need help the most.

Companion Website www.prenhall.com/bamber

The book's Companion Website contains the following:

- Self-study quizzes—an interactive study guide for each chapter
- E-Working papers that students can use to complete homework assignments for each chapter
- Student PowerPoints—for use as a study aid or note-taking guide
- Sample Flash Demo Doc

VangoNotes.com

Students can study on the go with VangoNotes—chapter reviews from this text in downloadable MP3 format. Students can purchase VangoNotes for the entire textbook or for individual chapters. For each chapter, VangoNotes contains:

- **Big Ideas** The "need to know" for each chapter.
- **Key Terms** Audio "flashcards" to help students review key concepts and terms.
- **Rapid Review** A quick drill session—to use right before taking a test.

► Acknowledgments

We'd like to extend a special thank you to our reviewers, Class Test Supplement contributors and to all of our Class Test Edition participants who took the time to help us develop teaching and learning tools for Managerial Accounting courses to come. We value and appreciate your commitment, dedication, and passion for your students and the classroom:

Nasrollah Ahadiat *California State Polytechnic University*
Markus Ahrens *St. Louis Community College*
Vern Allen *Central Florida Community College*
Michael T. Blackwell *West Liberty State College*
Charles Blumer *St. Charles Community College*
Kevin Bosner *SUNY Genesco*
Anna Boulware *St. Charles Community College*
Nina E. Brown *Tarrant County College*
Helen Brubeck *San Jose State University*
Cheryl Copeland *California State University Fresno*
Patrick Cunningham *Dawson Community College*
Alan B. Czyzewski *Indiana State University*
Darlene K. Edwards *Bellingham Technical College*
Anita Ellzey *Harford Community College*
Jean Fornasieri *Bergen Community College*
Shirley Glass *Macomb Community College*
Sueann Hely *West Kentucky Community & Technical College*
Ken Koerber *Bucks County Community College*
Pamela Legner *College of DuPage*
Elliott Levy *Bentley College*
Lizbeth Matz *University of Pittsburgh at Bradford*
Florence McGovern *Bergen Community College*
Kitty O'Donnell *Onondaga Community College*
Deborah Pavelka *Roosevelt University*
Donald Reynolds *Calvin College*
Doug Roberts *Appalachian State University*
Christine Schalow *California State University, San Bernadino*
Tony Scott *Norwalk Community College*
David Skougstad *Metropolitan State College of Denver*
Gracelyn V. Stuart *Palm Beach Community College*
Iris Stuart *California State University, Fullerton*
Diane Tanner *University of North Florida*
Andy Williams *Edmonds Community College*

Feedback

Your authors and their book's product team would appreciate hearing from you! Let us know what you think about this textbook by writing to: college_marketing@prenhall.com. Please include "Feedback about Bamber, Managerial Accounting 1e" in the subject line.

About the Authors

Linda Smith Bamber holds the J.M. Tull Chair of Accounting at the J.M. Tull School of Accounting at the University of Georgia. She graduated summa cum laude from Wake Forest University, where she was a member of Phi Beta Kappa. She is a Certified Public Accountant, and received an Elijah Watt Sells Award as well as the North Carolina Bronze Medal for her performance on the CPA examination. Before returning to graduate school, Professor Bamber gained professional experience working in management accounting at R.J. Reynolds, Inc. She then earned an MBA from Arizona State University, and a Ph.D. from The Ohio State University.

Professor Bamber has received numerous teaching awards from The Ohio State University, the University of Florida, and the University of Georgia.

She has lectured in Canada and Australia, in addition to the U.S., and her research has appeared in numerous journals, including *The Accounting Review*, *Journal of Accounting Research*, *Journal of Accounting and Economics*, *Journal of Finance*, *Contemporary Accounting Research*, *Accounting Horizons*, *Issues in Accounting Education*, and *The CPA Journal*. She also developed the annotations for the *Annotated Instructor's Edition* of Horngren, Foster, and Datar's *Cost Accounting: A Managerial Emphasis*, Seventh, Eighth, and Ninth Editions.

A member of the Institute of Management Accounting, the American Accounting Association (AAA) and the AAA's Management Accounting Section and Financial Accounting and Reporting Section, Professor Bamber has chaired the AAA New Faculty Consortium and the AAA Competitive Manuscript Award Committees, served on the AAA Council, the AAA Research Advisory Committee, the AAA Nominations Committee, and numerous other AAA and section committees. She served as Associate Editor of *Accounting Horizons*, and as editor of *The Accounting Review*.

Karen Wilken Braun is currently a faculty member of the Weatherhead School of Management at Case Western Reserve University. From 1996 to 2004, Professor Braun was on the faculty of the J.M. Tull School of Accounting at the University of Georgia, where she received the Outstanding Accounting Teacher of the Year award from the UGA chapter of Alpha Kappa Psi.

Professor Braun is a Certified Public Accountant, a member of the American Accounting Association (AAA), and has published in *Contemporary Accounting Research*. She is also a member of the AAA's Management Accounting Section as well as the Teaching & Curriculum Section.

Dr. Braun received her Ph.D. from the University of Connecticut, where she was an AICPA Doctoral Fellow, a Deloitte & Touche Doctoral Fellow, and an AAA Doctoral Consortium Fellow. She received her B.A., summa cum laude, from Luther College, where she was a member of Phi Beta Kappa and received the Outstanding Accounting Student award from the Iowa Society of Certified Public Accountants.

She gained public accounting experience while working at Arthur Andersen & Co. and accumulated additional business and management accounting experience as Corporate Controller for Gemini Aviation, Inc.

Professor Braun and her husband, Cory, have two daughters, Rachel and Hannah. In her free time she enjoys playing tennis, gardening, skiing, hiking, and music.

Walter T. Harrison, Jr. is Professor Emeritus of Accounting at the Hankamer School of Business, Baylor University. He received his B.B.A. degree from Baylor University, his M.S. from Oklahoma State University, and his Ph.D. from Michigan State University.

Professor Harrison, recipient of numerous teaching awards from student groups as well as from university administrators, has also taught at Cleveland State Community College, Michigan State University, the University of Texas, and Stanford University.

A member of the American Accounting Association and the American Institute of Certified Public Accountants, Professor Harrison has served as Chairman of the Financial Accounting Standards Committee of the American Accounting Association, on the Teaching/Curriculum Development Award Committee, on the Program Advisory Committee for Accounting Education and Teaching, and on the Notable Contributions to Accounting Literature Committee.

Professor Harrison has lectured in several foreign countries and published articles in numerous journals, including *The Accounting Review, Journal of Accounting Research, Journal of Accountancy, Journal of Accounting and Public Policy, Economic Consequences of Financial Accounting Standards, Accounting Horizons, Issues in Accounting Education*, and *Journal of Law and Commerce*.

He is co-author of *Financial Accounting*, Sixth Edition, 2006 (with Charles T. Horngren), published by Prentice Hall. Professor Harrison has received scholarships, fellowships, and research grants or awards from PriceWaterhouse Coopers, Deloitte & Touche, the Ernst & Young Foundation, and the KPMG Foundation.

MANAGERIAL
ACCOUNTING

1 Introduction to Managerial Accounting

n 1988, Outback Steakhouse's cofounders decided to create a chain of four or five restaurants that would generate enough income to let them have a nice lifestyle, stay in the Tampa Bay area, and play golf. That was then; this is now. Outback Steakhouse Inc., currently owns over 900 steakhouses that operate in all 50 states and in 20 different countries. Outback also owns six other restaurant brands, including Carrabba's Italian Grill. Annual sales have topped $3.2 billion, and operating income is over $252 million. How did Outback become so successful? Part of the answer is managerial accounting. Outback won't invest in a new restaurant location unless the projected annual sales are at least double the initial cost of the

location's property, improvements, and equipment. Outback motivates restaurant managers by requiring them to buy into the property for $25,000 and sign a five-year contract. In exchange, the manager receives an annual base salary of $45,000 plus 10% of the location's cash flow, resulting in an average pay of $118,000. Outback's founders also decided that the cost of replacing overworked managers and employees would exceed profits from lunchtime business. So, they bucked the industry trend and open only for dinner. As a result, managers have incentives to ensure their restaurant is profitable and employee turnover is far lower than industry standards.

Sources: "Bounce of the Kangaroo," *Maddux Business Report*, September 2004, pp. 18–23; www.outbacksteakhouse.com; "Inside Outback," *Nation's Restaurant News*, March 27, 1995, pp. 51–69. ∎

Learning Objectives

1 Identify managers' four primary responsibilities

2 Distinguish financial accounting from managerial accounting

3 Describe organizational structure and the roles and skills required of management accountants within the organization

4 Describe the role of the Institute of Management Accountants (IMA) and use its ethical standards to make reasonable ethical judgments

5 Discuss trends in the business environment

6 Use cost-benefit analysis to make business decisions

As the Outback story shows, managers use accounting information for much more than preparing annual financial statements. They use managerial accounting (or management accounting) information to guide their actions and decisions, such as building a new restaurant. In this chapter, we'll introduce managerial accounting and discuss how managers use it to fulfill their duties. We will also explore how managerial accounting differs from financial accounting. Finally, we will discuss the business environment in which today's managers and management accountants operate.

Managerial Accounting: Information for Managers

1 Identify managers' four primary responsibilities

As you will see throughout the book, managerial accounting is very different from financial accounting. Financial accounting focuses on providing stockholders and creditors with the information they need to make investment and lending decisions. This information takes the form of financial statements: the balance sheet, income statement, statement of shareholders' equity, and statement of cash flows. Managerial accounting focuses on providing internal management with the information it needs to run the company efficiently and effectively. This information takes many forms depending on management's needs.

To understand the kind of information managers need, let's first look at their primary responsibilities.

Managers' Four Primary Responsibilities

Managerial accounting helps managers fulfill their four primary responsibilities, as shown in Exhibit 1-1: planning, directing, controlling, and decision making.

- **Planning** involves setting goals and objectives for the company and determining how to achieve them. For example, one of Outback's goals is to generate more sales. One strategy to achieve this goal is to open more restaurants, so management may plan to build and begin operating 25 new steakhouses next year. Managerial accounting translates these plans into **budgets**—the quantitative expression of a plan. Management analyzes the budgets before proceeding to determine whether its expansion plans make financial sense.

- **Directing** means overseeing the company's day-to-day operations. Management uses product cost reports, product sales information, and other managerial accounting reports to run daily business operations. Outback uses product sales data to determine which menu items are generating the most sales and then uses that information to adjust menus and marketing strategies.

- **Controlling** means evaluating the results of business operations against the plan and making adjustments to keep the company pressing toward its goals. Outback uses performance reports to compare each restaurant's actual performance against budget and then uses that *feedback* to take corrective actions if needed. If actual costs are higher than planned or actual sales are lower than planned, management may revise its plans or adjust operations. Perhaps the newly opened steakhouses are not generating as much income as budgeted. As a result, management may decide to increase local advertising to increase sales.

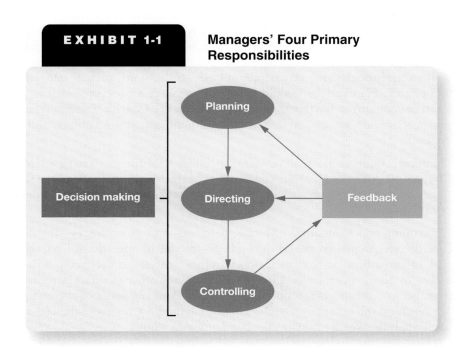

EXHIBIT 1-1   **Managers' Four Primary Responsibilities**

- Management is continually **making decisions** while it plans, directs, and controls operations. Outback must decide where to open new restaurants, which restaurants to refurnish, what prices to set for meals, what entrees to offer, and so forth. Because Outback is in business to generate profits for its stockholders, management must consider the financial impact of each of these decisions. Managerial accounting gathers, summarizes, and reports cost and revenue data relevant to each of these decisions.

A Road Map: How Does Managerial Accounting Fit In?

This book will show you how managerial accounting information helps managers fulfill their responsibilities. The rest of the text is organized around the following themes:

1. **Managerial Accounting Building Blocks**   Chapter 1 helps you understand more about the management accounting profession and today's business environment. Chapter 2 teaches you some of the language that is commonly used in managerial accounting. Just as musicians must know the notes to the musical scale, management accountants *and* managers must understand managerial accounting terms to effectively use managerial accounting information to run the business.

2. **Determining Unit Cost (Product Costing)**   How does a company decide how high to set its prices? It must first figure out how much it costs to make its product or deliver its service. Outback must calculate the cost of each item on the menu to set prices high enough to cover costs and generate a profit. This is tougher than it sounds. Outback's cost to prepare each meal includes more than just the cost of the ingredients. Outback's cost also includes the chefs' and servers' wages and benefits, restaurant lease payments, property taxes, utilities, business and alcohol licenses, and so forth. Chapters 3, 4, and 5 discuss how businesses determine their product costs. Once management knows its product costs, it uses that information for decision making, planning, directing, and controlling.

3. **Making Decisions**   Before Outback opened any restaurants, management determined how many meals it would have to serve just to break even—that is, just to cover costs. Management had to understand how costs behave before it could calculate a *breakeven* point. Chapters 6 and 7 discuss how costs behave, how to determine a breakeven point, and how managers use cost behavior knowledge to make good decisions and accurate forecasts. Then, Chapter 8 walks you through some very common business decisions, such as *outsourcing* and pricing. For example, should Outback outsource its desserts—that is, have another company make them? Many restaurants do. Chapter 9 shows you how managers decide whether to invest in new equipment, new locations, and new projects.

4. **Planning**   Budgets are management's primary tool for expressing its plans. Chapter 10 discusses all of the components of the *master budget* and the way a large company like Outback rolls its 900-plus steakhouse budgets into one corporate budget.

5. **Controlling and Evaluating**   Management uses *budget variances*—the difference between actual costs and the budget—to control operations. Chapters 10 and 11 show how management uses variance analysis to determine how and where to adjust operations. Chapter 12 discusses other evaluation tools that management uses to determine whether individual segments of the company are reaching the company's goals. Finally, Chapter 13 reviews financial statement analysis, which evaluates the company as a whole.

Managerial Accounting Versus Financial Accounting

 Distinguish financial accounting from managerial accounting

Managerial accounting information differs from financial accounting information in many respects. Exhibit 1-2 summarizes these differences. Take a few minutes to study the exhibit, and then we'll apply it to Outback.

EXHIBIT 1-2   Managerial Accounting Versus Financial Accounting

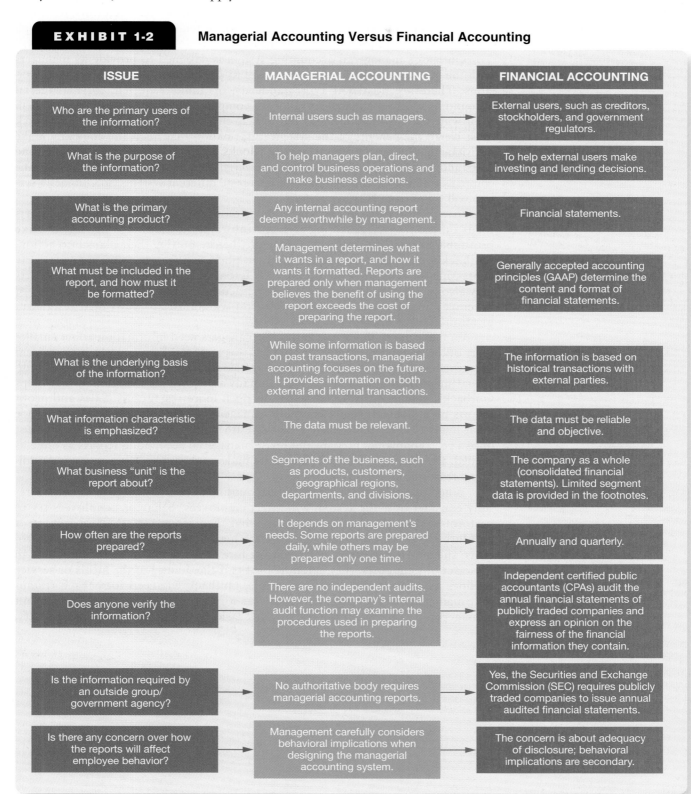

ISSUE	MANAGERIAL ACCOUNTING	FINANCIAL ACCOUNTING
Who are the primary users of the information?	Internal users such as managers.	External users, such as creditors, stockholders, and government regulators.
What is the purpose of the information?	To help managers plan, direct, and control business operations and make business decisions.	To help external users make investing and lending decisions.
What is the primary accounting product?	Any internal accounting report deemed worthwhile by management.	Financial statements.
What must be included in the report, and how must it be formatted?	Management determines what it wants in a report, and how it wants it formatted. Reports are prepared only when management believes the benefit of using the report exceeds the cost of preparing the report.	Generally accepted accounting principles (GAAP) determine the content and format of financial statements.
What is the underlying basis of the information?	While some information is based on past transactions, managerial accounting focuses on the future. It provides information on both external and internal transactions.	The information is based on historical transactions with external parties.
What information characteristic is emphasized?	The data must be relevant.	The data must be reliable and objective.
What business "unit" is the report about?	Segments of the business, such as products, customers, geographical regions, departments, and divisions.	The company as a whole (consolidated financial statements). Limited segment data is provided in the footnotes.
How often are the reports prepared?	It depends on management's needs. Some reports are prepared daily, while others may be prepared only one time.	Annually and quarterly.
Does anyone verify the information?	There are no independent audits. However, the company's internal audit function may examine the procedures used in preparing the reports.	Independent certified public accountants (CPAs) audit the annual financial statements of publicly traded companies and express an opinion on the fairness of the financial information they contain.
Is the information required by an outside group/government agency?	No authoritative body requires managerial accounting reports.	Yes, the Securities and Exchange Commission (SEC) requires publicly traded companies to issue annual audited financial statements.
Is there any concern over how the reports will affect employee behavior?	Management carefully considers behavioral implications when designing the managerial accounting system.	The concern is about adequacy of disclosure; behavioral implications are secondary.

Outback is a publicly traded company, so its financial accounting system must generate consolidated financial statements, in accordance with generally accepted accounting principles (GAAP), on an annual and quarterly basis. The annual financial statements, which are audited by independent certified public accountants (CPAs), objectively summarize the transactions that occurred between Outback and external parties during the previous year. Outback's financial statements are useful to its investors and creditors, but they do not provide management with enough information to run the company effectively.

Outback's managerial accounting system is designed to provide its managers with the accounting information they need to plan, direct, control and make decisions. There are no GAAP-type standards, or audits required, for managerial accounting. Outback's managers tailor the company's managerial accounting system to provide the information they need to help them make better decisions. Outback must weigh the benefits of the system (information that helps the company make decisions that increase profits) against the costs to develop and run the system. The costs and benefits of any particular managerial accounting system differ from one company to another. Different companies create different systems, so Outback's system will differ from Nissan's system.

In contrast to financial statements, most managerial accounting reports focus on the *future,* providing *relevant* information that helps managers make profitable business decisions. For example, before putting their plans into action, Outback's managers determine if their plans make sense by quantitatively expressing them in the form of budgets. Outback's managerial accounting reports may also plan for and reflect *internal* transactions, such as the daily movement of beverages and dry ingredients from central warehouses to individual restaurant locations.

To make good decisions, Outback's managers need information about smaller units of the company, not just the company as a whole. For example, management uses revenue and cost data on individual restaurants, geographical regions, and individual menu items to increase the company's profitability. Regional data helps Outback's management decide where to open more restaurants. Sales and profit reports on individual menu items help management choose menu items and decide what items to offer on a seasonal basis. Rather than preparing these reports just once a year, companies prepare and revise managerial accounting reports as often as needed. For example, Outback revises its budget when new menu items and additional restaurant locations are added.

When designing the managerial accounting system, management must carefully consider how the system will affect employees' behavior. Employees try to perform well on the parts of their jobs that the accounting system measures. If an Outback restaurant manager were evaluated only on her ability to control costs, she may use cheaper ingredients or hire less experienced servers. Although these actions cut costs, they can hurt profits if the quality of the meals or service declines as a result. As another example, Outback wants to focus each restaurant manager's attention on cash flow. As a result, Outback pays its restaurant managers a percentage of the restaurant's cash flows in addition to a base salary.

The Management Accountant Within the Organization

Let's look at how management accountants fit into the company's organizational structure, how their roles are changing, what skills they need to successfully fill their roles, and what their professional association is. We'll also discuss ethical standards.

3 Describe organizational structure and the roles and skills required of management accountants within the organization

Organizational Structure

Most corporations are too large to be governed directly by their stockholders. Therefore, stockholders elect a **board of directors** to oversee the company. Exhibit 1-3 shows a typical organizational structure, with the green boxes representing employees of the firm and the orange and blue boxes representing nonemployees.

The board meets only periodically, so they hire a **chief executive officer (CEO)** to manage the company on a daily basis. The CEO hires other executives to run various aspects of the organization, including the **chief operating officer (COO)** and the **chief financial officer (CFO)**. The COO is responsible for the company's operations, such as research and development (R&D), production, and distribution. The CFO is responsible for all of the company's financial concerns. The **treasurer** and the **controller** report directly to the CFO. The treasurer is primarily responsible for raising capital (through issuing stocks and bonds) and investing funds. The controller is usually responsible for general financial accounting, managerial accounting, and tax reporting.

The New York Stock Exchange requires that listed companies have an **internal audit function**. The role of the internal audit function is to ensure that the company's internal controls and risk management policies are functioning properly. The internal audit department reports directly to a subcommittee of the board of directors called the **audit committee**. The audit committee oversees the internal audit function as well as the annual audit of the financial statements by independent CPAs. Both the internal audit

EXHIBIT 1-3   **Typical Organizational Structure**

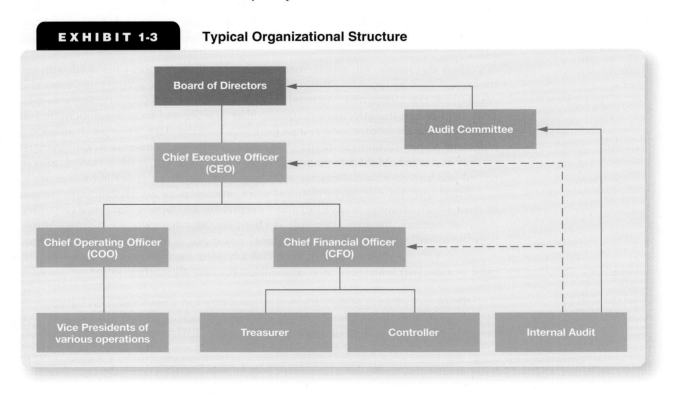

department and the independent CPAs report directly to the audit committee for one very important reason: to ensure that management will not intimidate them or bias their work. However, since the audit committee meets only periodically, it isn't practical for the audit committee to manage the internal audit function on a day-to-day basis. Therefore, the internal audit function also reports to a senior executive, such as the CFO or CEO, for administrative matters.

When you look at the organizational chart pictured in Exhibit 1-3, where do you think management accountants work? It depends on the company. Management accountants used to work in accounting departments and reported directly to the controller. Now, over half of management accountants are located throughout the company and work on cross-functional teams. **Cross-functional teams** consist of employees representing various functions of the company, such as R&D, design, production, marketing, distribution, and customer service. Cross-functional teams are effective because each member can address business decisions from a different viewpoint. These teams often report to various vice presidents of operations. Management accountants often take the leadership role in the teams. Here is what two managers had to say in a study about management accountants:[1]

> Finance (the management accountant) has a unique ability and responsibility to see across all the functions and try and make sense of them. They have the neat ability to be a member of all of the different groups (functions) and yet not be a member of any of them at the same time. (U.S. West)

> Basically the role of the financial person on the team is analyzing the financial impact of the business decision and providing advice. Does this make sense financially or not? (Abbott Laboratories)

The Changing Roles of Management Accountants

Technology has changed the roles of management accountants. Management accountants no longer perform routine mechanical accounting tasks. Computer programs perform those tasks. Yet, management accountants are in more demand than ever before. Company managers used to view management accountants as "scorekeepers" or "bean counters" because they spent most of their time recording historical transactions. Now, they view management accountants as internal consultants or business advisors.

Does this mean that management accountants are no longer involved with the traditional task of recording transactions? No. Management accountants must still ensure that the company's financial records adequately capture economic events. They help design the information systems that capture and record transactions and make sure that the information system generates accurate data. They use professional judgment to record nonroutine transactions and make adjustments to the financial records as needed. Management accountants still need to know what transactions to record and how to record them, but they let technology do most of the routine work.

Freed from the routine mechanical work, management accountants spend more of their time planning, analyzing, and interpreting accounting data and providing decision support. Because their role is changing, management accountants rarely bear the job title "management accountant" any more; managers often refer to them as business management support, financial advisors, business partners, or analysts. Here is what two management accountants have said about their jobs:[2]

> We are looked upon as more business advisors than just accountants, which has a lot to do with the additional analysis and forward-looking goals that we are setting. We spend more of our time analyzing and understanding our margins, our

---

[1, 2]*Counting More, Counting Less: The 1999 Practice Analysis of Management Accounting*, Institute of Management Accountants, Montvale, NJ, 1999.

prices, and the markets in which we do business. People have a sense of purpose; they have a real sense of "I'm adding value to the company." (Caterpillar, Inc.)

Accounting is changing. You're no longer sitting behind a desk just working on a computer, just crunching the numbers. You're actually getting to be a part of the day-to-day functions of the business. (Abbott Laboratories)

The Skills Required of Management Accountants

Because computers now do the routine "number crunching," do management accountants need to know as much as they did 20 years ago? The fact is, management accountants now need to know *more*! They have to understand what information management needs and how to generate that information accurately. Therefore, management accountants must be able to communicate with the computer/IT system programmers to create an effective information system. Once the information system generates the data, management accountants interpret and analyze the raw data and turn it into *useful* information management can use.[3]

Twenty years ago we would say, "Here are the costs and you guys need to figure out what you want to do with them." Now we are expected to say, "Here are the costs and this is why the costs are what they are, and this is how they compare to other things, and here are some suggestions where we could possibly improve." (Caterpillar, Inc.)

Today's management accountants need the following skills:[4]

- Solid knowledge of both financial and managerial accounting
- Analytical skills
- Knowledge of how a business functions
- Ability to work on a team
- Oral *and* written communication skills

The skills shown in Exhibit 1-4 are critical to these management accountants:

We're making more presentations that are seen across the division. So you have to summarize the numbers . . . you have to have people in sales understand what those numbers mean. If you can't communicate information to the individuals, then the information is never out there; it's lost. So, your communication skills are very important. (Abbott Laboratories)

Usually when a nonfinancial person comes to you with financial questions, they don't really ask the right things so that you can give them the correct answer. If they ask you for cost, well, you have to work with them and say, "Well, do you want total plant cost, a variable cost, or an accountable cost?" Then, "What is the reason for those costs?" Whatever they're using this cost for determines what type of cost you will provide them with. (Caterpillar, Inc.)

Chapter 2 explains these cost terms. The point here is that management accountants need to have a solid understanding of managerial accounting, including how different types of costs are relevant to different situations. Additionally, they must be able to communicate that information to employees from different business functions.

---

[3]*Counting More, Counting Less: The 1999 Practice Analysis of Management Accounting*, Institute of Management Accountants, Montvale, NJ, 1999.
[4]Gary Siegel and James Sorenson, *What Corporate America Wants in Entry-Level Accountants*, Institute of Management Accountants, Montvale, NJ, 1994.

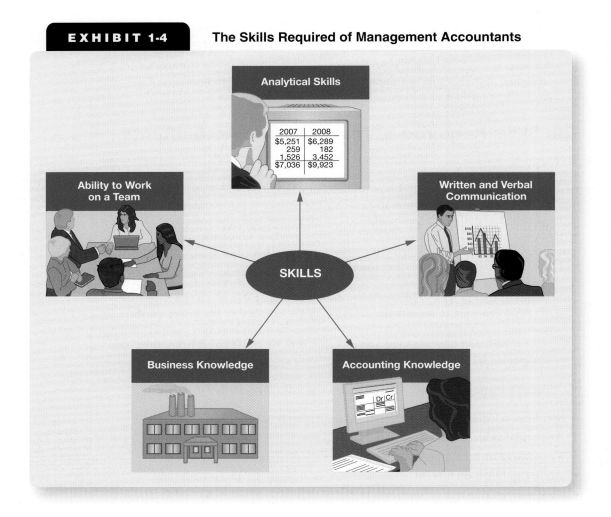

EXHIBIT 1-4   **The Skills Required of Management Accountants**

Average Salaries of Management Accountants

The average salaries of management accountants reflect their large skill set. Naturally, salaries will vary with the accountant's level of experience, his or her specific job responsibilities, and the size and geographical location of the company.[5] However, to give you a general idea, in 2007, a cost analyst with less than one year of experience could expect to earn between $35,250 and $42,250 at a medium-size company. With one to three years of experience, the average salary increased to $41,750–$52,250. With more experience, salaries ranged upward to approximately $80,500.[6] Accountants in leadership positions command even greater pay. For example, the CFO, controller, treasurer, and internal audit manager of a medium-size company can expect to earn annual salaries exceeding well over $100,000.

You can obtain more specific accounting and finance salary information in a yearly guide published by Robert Half International Inc. The guide also provides information on current hiring trends for accounting and finance professionals. To obtain a free copy of the *Salary Guide*, go to www.roberthalf.com.

---

[5]A medium-size company is defined as a company with annual sales ranging from $25 million to $250 million.
[6]*2007 Salary Guide, Accounting and Finance Salaries*, Robert Half International Inc., Menlo Park, CA.

Professional Association

The **Institute of Management Accountants (IMA)** is the professional association for management accountants. The goal of the IMA is to advance the managerial accounting profession primarily through certification, practice development, education, and networking. They also want to educate society about the role management accountants play in organizations. According to the IMA, about 85% of accountants work in organizations, performing the roles discussed earlier. The IMA publishes a monthly journal called *Strategic Finance*. (Prior to 1999, the journal was called *Management Accounting*; but as the role of management accountants changed, so did the journal's title.) The journal addresses current topics of interest to management accountants and helps them keep abreast of recent techniques and trends.

 Describe the role of the Institute of Management Accountants (IMA) and use its ethical standards to make reasonable ethical judgments

The IMA also issues two professional certifications: the **Certified Management Accountant (CMA)** and the **Certified Financial Manager (CFM)**. To become a CMA or CFM, you must pass a rigorous examination and maintain continuing professional education. The CMA exam focuses on managerial accounting topics similar to those discussed in this book, as well as economics and business finance. The CFM exam focuses on financial statement analysis, working capital policy, capital structure, business valuation, and risk management. While most employers do not require the CMA or CFM designation, management accountants bearing the CMA or CFM designation usually command higher salaries and obtain higher-level positions within the company. You can find out more about the IMA and the certifications it offers at its Web site: www.imanet.org.

Ethics

Management accountants continually face ethical challenges. The IMA has developed principles and standards to help management accountants deal with these challenges. The principles and standards remind us that society expects professional accountants to exhibit the highest level of ethical behavior. The IMA adopted a new *Statement on Ethical Professional Practice* in 2005, which requires management accountants to:

- Maintain their professional competence.
- Preserve the confidentiality of the information they handle.
- Uphold their integrity.
- Perform their duties with credibility.

These ethical standards are summarized in Exhibit 1-5, while the full *Statement of Ethical Professional Practice* appears in Exhibit 1-6.

To resolve ethical dilemmas, the IMA suggests that management accountants first follow their company's established policies for reporting unethical behavior. If the conflict is not resolved through the company's procedures, the management accountant should consider the following steps:

- Discuss the unethical situation with the immediate supervisor unless the supervisor is involved in the unethical situation. If so, notify the supervisor at the next higher managerial level. If the immediate supervisor involved is the CEO, notify the audit committee or board of directors.
- Discuss the unethical situation with an objective advisor, such as an IMA ethics counselor. The IMA offers a confidential "Ethics Hotline" to its members. Members may call the hotline and discuss their ethical dilemma. The ethics counselor will not provide a specific resolution but will clarify how the dilemma relates to the IMA's *Statement of Ethical Professional Practice* shown in Exhibit 1-6.
- Consult an attorney regarding legal obligations and rights.

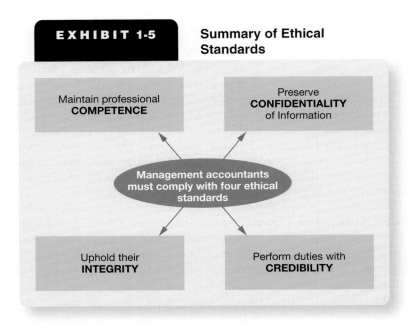

EXHIBIT 1-5 **Summary of Ethical Standards**

Maintain professional **COMPETENCE**

Preserve **CONFIDENTIALITY** of Information

Management accountants must comply with four ethical standards

Uphold their **INTEGRITY**

Perform duties with **CREDIBILITY**

Examples of Ethical Dilemmas

Unfortunately, the ethical path is not always clear. You may want to act ethically and do the right thing, but the consequences can make it difficult to decide what to do. Let's consider several ethical dilemmas in light of the *Statement of Ethical Professional Practice*:

Dilemma #1

Sarah Baker is examining the expense reports of her staff, who counted inventory at Top-Flight's warehouses in Arizona. She discovers that Mike Flinders has claimed but not included hotel receipts for over $1,000 of accommodation expenses. Other staff, who also claimed $1,000, did attach hotel receipts. When asked about the receipts, Mike admits that he stayed with an old friend, not in the hotel, but he believes that he deserves the money he saved. After all, the company would have paid his hotel bill.

By asking to be reimbursed for hotel expenses he did not incur, Flinders violated the IMA's integrity standards (conflict of interest in which he tried to enrich himself at the company's expense). Because Baker discovered the inflated expense report, she would not be fulfilling her ethical responsibilities of integrity and credibility if she allowed the reimbursement.

Dilemma #2

As the accountant of Entreé Computer, you are aware of your company's weak financial condition. Entreé is close to signing a lucrative contract that should ensure its future. To do so, the controller states that the company must report a profit this year (ending December 31). He suggests: "Two customers have placed orders that are really not supposed to be shipped until early January. Ask production to fill and ship those orders on December 31 so we can record them in this year's sales."

EXHIBIT 1-6	**IMA Statement of Ethical Professional Practice**

Members of IMA shall behave ethically. A commitment to ethical professional practice includes: overarching principles that express our values, and standards that guide our conduct.

Principles

IMA's overarching ethical principles include: Honesty, Fairness, Objectivity, and Responsibility. Members shall act in accordance with these principles and shall encourage others within their organizations to adhere to them.

Standards

A member's failure to comply with the following standards may result in disciplinary action.

I. Competence

Each member has a responsibility to:

1. Maintain an appropriate level of professional expertise by continually developing knowledge and skills.
2. Perform professional duties in accordance with relevant laws, regulations, and technical standards.
3. Provide decision support information and recommendations that are accurate, clear, concise, and timely.
4. Recognize and communicate professional limitations or other constraints that would preclude responsible judgment or successful performance of an activity.

II. Confidentiality

Each member has a responsibility to:

1. Keep information confidential except when disclosure is authorized or legally required.
2. Inform all relevant parties regarding appropriate use of confidential information. Monitor subordinates' activities to ensure compliance.
3. Refrain from using confidential information for unethical or illegal advantage.

III. Integrity

Each member has a responsibility to:

1. Mitigate actual conflicts of interest. Regularly communicate with business associates to avoid apparent conflicts of interest. Advise all parties of any potential conflicts.
2. Refrain from engaging in any conduct that would prejudice carrying out duties ethically.
3. Abstain from engaging in or supporting any activity that might discredit the profession.

IV. Credibility

Each member has a responsibility to:

1. Communicate information fairly and objectively.
2. Disclose all relevant information that could reasonably be expected to influence an intended user's understanding of the reports, analyses, or recommendations.
3. Disclose delays or deficiencies in information, timeliness, processing, or internal controls in conformance with organization policy and/or applicable law.

Institute of Management Accountants. Adapted with permission (2006).

The resolution of this dilemma is less clear-cut. Many people believe that following the controller's suggestion to manipulate the company's income would violate the standards of competence, integrity, and credibility. Others would argue that because Entreé Computer already has the customer orders, shipping the goods and recording the sale in December is still ethical behavior. You might discuss the available alternatives with the next managerial level or the IMA ethics hotline counselor.

Dilemma #3

As a new accounting staff member at Central City Hospital, your supervisor has asked you to prepare the yearly *Medicare Cost Report*, which the government uses to determine its reimbursement to the hospital for serving Medicare patients. The report requires specialized knowledge that you don't believe you possess. The supervisor is busy planning for the coming year and cannot offer much guidance while you prepare the report.

This situation is not as rare as you might think. You may be asked to perform tasks that you don't feel qualified to perform. The competence standard requires you to perform professional duties in accordance with laws, regulations, and technical standards; but laws and regulations are always changing. For this reason, the competence standard also requires you to continually develop knowledge and skills. CPAs and CMAs are required to complete annual continuing professional education (about 40 hours per year) to fulfill this responsibility. However, even continuing professional education courses will not cover every situation you may encounter.

In the Medicare cost report situation, advise your supervisor that you currently lack the knowledge required to complete the Medicare cost report. By doing so, you are complying with the competence standard that requires you to recognize and communicate any limitations that would preclude you from fulfilling an activity. You should ask for training on the report preparation and supervision by someone experienced in preparing the report. If the supervisor denies your requests, you should ask him to reassign the Medicare report to a qualified staff member.

Dilemma #4

> Your company is negotiating a large multiyear sales contract that, if won, would substantially increase the company's future earnings. At a dinner party over the weekend, your friends ask you how you like your job and the company you work for. In your enthusiasm, you tell them not only about your responsibilities at work but also about the contract negotiations. As soon as the words pop out of your mouth, you worry that you've said too much.

This situation is difficult to avoid. You may be so excited about your job and the company you work for that information unintentionally "slips out" during casual conversation with friends and family. The confidentiality standard requires you to refrain from disclosing information or using confidential information for unethical or illegal advantage. Was the contract negotiation confidential? If so, would your friends invest in company stock in hopes that the negotiations increase stock prices? Or were the negotiations public knowledge in the financial community? If so, your friends would gain no illegal advantage from the information. Recent cases, such as those involving Martha Stewart, remind us that insider trading (use of inside knowledge for illegal gain) has serious consequences. Even seemingly mundane information about company operations could give competitors an advantage. Therefore, it's best to disclose only information that is meant for public consumption.

Unethical Versus Illegal Behavior

Finally, is there a difference between unethical and illegal behavior? Not all unethical behavior is illegal, but all illegal behavior is unethical. For example, consider the competence standard. The competence standard states that management accountants have a responsibility to provide decision support information that is accurate, clear, concise, and timely. Failure to follow this standard is unethical but in most cases not illegal. Now, consider the integrity standard. It states that management accountants must abstain from any activity that might discredit the profession. A management accountant who commits an illegal act is violating this ethical standard. In other words, ethical behavior encompasses more than simply following the law. The IMA's ethical principles include honesty, fairness, objectivity, and responsibility—principles that are much broader than what is codified in the law.

Decision Guidelines

Outback made the following decisions in designing its managerial accounting system to provide managers with the information they need to run operations efficiently and effectively.

Decision	Guidelines
What information should management accountants provide? What is the primary focus of managerial accounting?	Managerial accounting provides information that helps managers plan, direct, and control operations and make better decisions; it has a: • *Future* orientation. • Focus on *relevance* to business decisions.
How do managers design a company's managerial accounting system that is not regulated by GAAP?	Managers design the managerial accounting system so that the benefits (from helping managers make wiser decisions) outweigh the costs of the system.
How should managers decide if their plans make financial sense? How do they decide if the company is operating according to plans?	Managers quantitatively express their plans in the form of budgets. They can analyze the budgets to determine whether the plans will be profitable. Once the plans have been put into place, managers compare actual results to plans and make adjustments where needed.
In designing the organizational structure, where should managers place management accountants?	In the past, most management accountants worked in isolated departments. Now, over 50% of management accountants are deployed throughout the company and work on cross-functional teams. Management must decide which structure best suits its needs.
What skills do management accountants need to possess?	Because of their expanding role within the organization, most management accountants need financial and managerial accounting knowledge, analytical skills, knowledge of how a business functions, ability to work on teams, and written and oral communication skills.
How should a management accountant resolve an ethical dilemma?	Consult the IMA's *Statement of Ethical Professional Practice* and the company's policies. The Statement offers guidance through overarching ethical principles (honesty, fairness, objectivity, and responsibility) and standards (competence, confidentiality, integrity, and credibility).

Summary Problem 1

1. Each of the following statements describes a responsibility of management. Match each statement to the management responsibility being fulfilled.

Statement	Management Responsibility
1. Identifying alternative courses of action and choosing among them	a. Planning
2. Running the company on a day-to-day basis	b. Decision making
3. Determining whether the company's units are operating according to plan	c. Directing
4. Setting goals and objectives for the company and determining strategies to achieve them	d. Controlling

2. Are the following statements more descriptive of managerial accounting or financial accounting information?
   a. Describes historical transactions with external parties
   b. Is not required by any authoritative body, such as the SEC
   c. Reports on the company's subunits, such as products, geographical areas, and departments
   d. Is intended to be used by creditors and investors
   e. Is formatted in accordance with GAAP

3. Each of the following statements paraphrases an ethical responsibility. Match each statement to the standard of ethical professional practice being fulfilled. Each standard may be used more than once or not at all.

Responsibility	Standard of Ethical Professional Practice
1. Don't disclose company information unless authorized to do so.	a. Competence
2. Continue to develop skills and knowledge.	b. Confidentiality
3. Don't bias the information and reports presented to management.	c. Integrity
4. If you don't have the skills to complete a task correctly, don't pretend you do.	d. Credibility
5. Avoid actual *and* apparent conflicts of interest.	

Solutions

Requirement 1

1. (b) Decision making
2. (c) Directing
3. (d) Controlling
4. (a) Planning

Requirement 2

a. financial accounting
b. managerial accounting
c. managerial accounting
d. financial accounting
e. financial accounting

Requirement 3

1. (b) Confidentiality
2. (a) Competence
3. (d) Credibility
4. (a) Competence
5. (c) Integrity

Today's Business Environment

5 Discuss trends in the business environment

The following chapters describe managerial accounting tools that managers use to plan, direct, and control operations and make business decisions. Before we turn to these tools, let's first consider recent trends that affect managers' decisions and the managerial accounting systems that support them. These trends include the Sarbanes-Oxley Act; the shifting economy; the rise of the global marketplace; time-based competition (including changes in information systems, electronic commerce, and just-in-time management); and total quality management.

Sarbanes-Oxley Act of 2002

As a result of recent corporate accounting scandals, such as those at Enron and WorldCom, the U.S. Congress enacted the **Sarbanes-Oxley Act of 2002 (SOX)**. The purpose of SOX is to restore trust in publicly traded corporations, their management, their financial statements, and their auditors. SOX enhances internal control and financial reporting requirements and establishes new regulatory requirements for publicly traded companies and their independent auditors. Publicly traded companies have spent millions of dollars upgrading their internal controls and accounting systems to comply with SOX regulations.

As shown in Exhibit 1-7, SOX requires the company's CEO and CFO to assume responsibility for the financial statements and disclosures. The CEO and CFO must certify that the financial statements and disclosures fairly present, in all material respects, the operations and financial condition of the company. Additionally, they must accept responsibility for establishing and maintaining an adequate internal control structure and procedures for financial reporting. The company must have its internal controls and financial reporting procedures assessed annually.

EXHIBIT 1-7 **Some Important Results of SOX**

CEO and CFO assume responsibility for the company's financial statements, internal control system, and procedures for financial reporting.

Audit committee must be independent and should include a financial expert.

Sarbanes-Oxley Act of 2002

New requirements for CPA firms, including limited non-audit services for audit clients and periodic quality review.

Stiffer imprisonment and monetary fines for white-collar crimes.

Source: http://fmcenter.aicpa.org/Resources/Sarbanes-Oxley+Act/Summary+of+the+Provisions+of+the +Sarbanes-Oxley+Act+of+2002.htm

SOX also requires audit committee members to be independent, meaning that they may not receive any consulting or advisory fees from the company other than for their service on the board of directors. In addition, at least one of the members should be a financial expert. The audit committee oversees not only the internal audit function but also the company's audit by independent CPAs.

To ensure that CPA firms maintain independence from their client company, SOX does not allow CPA firms to provide certain non-audit services (such as book-keeping and financial information systems design) to companies during the same period of time in which they are providing audit services. If a company wants to obtain such services from a CPA firm, it must hire a different firm to do the non-audit work. Tax services may be provided by the same CPA firm if preapproved by the audit committee. The audit partner must rotate off the audit engagement every five years, and the audit firm must undergo quality reviews every one to three years.

SOX also increases the penalties for white-collar crimes such as corporate fraud. These penalties include both monetary fines and substantial imprisonment. For example, knowingly destroying or creating documents to "impede, obstruct, or influence" any federal investigation can result in up to 20 years of imprisonment.[7] Since its enactment in 2002, SOX has significantly affected the internal operations of publicly traded corporations and their auditors. SOX will continue to play a major role in corporate management and the audit profession.

Shifting Economy

In the last century, North American economies have shifted away from manufacturing toward service. Service companies provide health care, communication, transportation, banking, and other important benefits to society. Service companies now make up the largest sector of the U.S. economy and employ 55% of the workforce. The U.S. Census Bureau expects services, especially technology and health care services, to be among the fastest-growing industries over the next decade. Even companies that traditionally carried out manufacturing, such as General Electric (GE), are shifting toward selling more services. It's easy to see why. In GE's jet engine business, services contribute only 30% of the revenues but generate two-thirds of the profit.

Managerial accounting has its roots in the industrial age of manufacturing. Most traditional managerial accounting practices were developed to fill the needs of manufacturing firms. However, since the U.S. economy has shifted away from manufacturing, managerial accounting has shifted, too. The field of managerial accounting has *expanded* to meet the needs of service and merchandising firms as well as manufacturers. For example:

1. Manufacturers still need to know how much each unit of their product costs to manufacture. In addition to using this information for inventory valuation and pricing decisions, manufacturers now use cost information to determine whether they should outsource production to another company or to an overseas location.

2. Service companies also need cost information to make decisions. They need to know the cost of providing a service rather than manufacturing a product. For example, banks must include the cost of servicing checking and savings accounts in the fees they charge customers. And hospitals need to know the cost of performing appendectomies to justify reimbursement from insurance companies and from Medicare.

---

[7]If you want to learn more about SOX, the AICPA provides a summary at http://fmcenter.aicpa.org/Resources/Sarbanes-Oxley+Act/Summary+of+the+Provisions+of+the+Sarbanes-Oxley+Act+of+2002.htm.

3. Retailers need to consider importing costs when determining the cost of their merchandise. Because many goods are now produced overseas rather than domestically, determining the cost of a product is often more difficult than it was in the past. Management accountants need to consider foreign currency translation, shipping costs, and import tariffs when determining the cost of imported products.

Competing in the Global Marketplace

The barriers to international trade have fallen over the past decades, allowing foreign companies to compete with domestic firms. Firms that are not world-class competitors will vanish from the global market. However, global markets provide competitive companies with great potential: Foreign operations account for over 35% of GE's revenues, over 40% of Amazon.com's revenues, and over 65% of Coca-Cola's and McDonald's revenues.

Manufacturers often move operations to other countries to be closer to new markets and less expensive labor. For example, Thomson SA, maker of GE's television sets, closed the world's largest TV factory in Bloomington, Indiana, and moved the work to Mexico to save an estimated $75 million a year in labor costs. Ford, General Motors, and DaimlerChrysler all built plants in Brazil to feed Brazil's car-hungry middle class. The same week Alcoa announced it was closing two plants in the United States, it spelled out plans to build a $1 billion plant in Iceland.

Globalization has several implications for managerial accounting:

1. Stiffer competition means managers need more accurate information to make wise decisions. For example, if Nokia overestimates the cost of its new cell phone, it may set prices too high and lose business to competitors.

2. Companies must decide whether to expand sales and/or production into foreign countries. Managers need estimates of the costs and benefits of international expansion.

3. Globalization fosters the transfer of management philosophy across international borders. Many U.S. companies now follow the just-in-time philosophy developed in Japan.

Time-Based Competition

The Internet, electronic commerce (e-commerce), and other new technologies speed the pace of business. Think about your last trip to the grocery store or Wal-Mart. Did you use the self-scanning checkout? Retailers install expensive self-scanning technology to give shoppers an alternative to standing in longer checkout lines. Some studies have shown that, on average, the self-scanning checkout process is really not faster. However, shoppers *perceive* the checkout time to be faster because they are actively engaged rather than passively standing in line. Businesses are doing whatever they can to shorten the time a customer has to wait for their order. Why? Because *time* is the latest competitive weapon in business.

Dell Computer commits to delivering your desktop computer within a week of receiving your order. Toyota says that it can make a car within five days of receiving a custom order. Sweden's Ericsson Radio Systems has increased on-time delivery from 20% to 99.98%—nearly perfect. How do they do it? By using advanced information systems, e-commerce, and just-in-time management.

Advanced Information Systems

Many small businesses use QuickBooks or Peachtree software to track their costs and to develop the information that owners and managers need to run the business. But large companies such as Fujitsu and Allstate Insurance are turning to **enterprise resource planning (ERP) systems** that can integrate all of a company's worldwide functions, departments, and data. ERP systems such as SAP, Oracle, and PeopleSoft gather company data into a centralized data warehouse. The system feeds the data into software for all of the company's business activities, from budgeting and purchasing to production and customer service.

Advantages of ERP systems include the following:

- Companies streamline their operations before mapping them into ERP software. Streamlining operations saves money.
- ERP helps companies respond quickly to changes. A change in sales instantly ripples through the ERP's purchases, production, shipping, and accounting systems.
- An ERP system can replace hundreds of separate software systems, such as different software in different regions, or different payroll, shipping, and production software.

ERP is expensive. Major installations cost Fujitsu and Allstate over $40 million. ERP also requires a large commitment of time and people. For example, Hershey Foods tried to shrink a four-year ERP project into two and one-half years. The result? The software did not map into Hershey Foods' operations, and it disrupted deliveries and hurt profits during the critical Halloween season.

E-commerce

To survive in a competitive, globally wired economy, companies use the Internet in everyday operations such as budgeting, planning, selling, and customer service. Imagine a salesclerk who can sell to thousands of customers at once. This clerk instantly provides every product, option, and price the company offers. It works 24 hours a day, 365 days a year, and never takes a break or vacation. This salesclerk is an e-commerce Web site!

Business-to-business e-commerce takes speed and efficiency to new levels. Imagine sitting in your office anywhere in the world. You enter Dell's Web site and customize the new computer you're buying. After you fill your virtual shopping cart, business-to-business software automates ordering, approval, and delivery.

Electronic purchases below specified dollar limits are often untouched by human hands, generate little if any paper, and avoid the time and cost of processing paperwork. Even the federal government is on the e-bandwagon. An electronic marketplace, E-Mall, allows buyers in the Department of Defense and other federal agencies access to 17 million items online. An order on E-Mall costs about $11 to process, while one placed by hand costs around $150.

Stop & Think...

Electronically billing customers is also becoming more popular. Analysts estimate that:

1. Companies save $7 per invoice by billing customers electronically.
2. The average large company issues 800,000 invoices a year.
3. The average cost of installing an e-billing system is $500,000. Should companies that issue 800,000 invoices a year consider e-billing?

Answer: Yes, these companies should consider e-billing. Comparing expected benefits to costs reveals significant expected net benefits from e-billing:

Expected benefits:	
800,000 invoices × $7 savings per invoice	$5,600,000
Expected costs:	
Installation of e-billing system	(500,000)
Net expected benefits	$5,100,000

Managers of Krispy Kreme's stores use the company's customized Web portal to plan production and order supplies. Weather news appears on the opening screen. Why? Because Krispy Kreme found that people buy more coffee and doughnuts when the weather is bad. This simple innovation helps managers forecast how many doughnuts to make. "I've seen a good 2 to 3 percent increase in profitability just from the portal," says the manager of a Miami-based store.[8]

Firms also use the Internet to tap into other companies' business processes. Companies that supply component parts to Dell use the Internet to look into Dell's production process through a customized virtual window. Each supplier sees the current demand for and inventory levels of the parts it supplies Dell. Access to real-time information that lets suppliers automate the size of the next day's order helps Dell cut order-to-delivery times and control costs.

E-commerce is an important means of **supply-chain management**, where companies exchange information with suppliers to reduce costs, improve quality, and speed delivery of goods and services from suppliers to the company itself and on to the customer. E-commerce also increases a firm's ability (and need) to use just-in-time management.

Just-in-Time Management

The costs of holding inventory can add up to 25% or more of the inventory's value. Money tied up in inventory cannot be used for other purposes. Inventory held too long becomes obsolete. Storing inventory costs money and takes up space that could be used to increase production. The just-in-time philosophy helps managers cut holding costs by speeding the transformation of raw materials into new, finished products. Let's see how it works.

Toyota generally gets credit for pioneering the **just-in-time (JIT)** philosophy, which means producing *just in time* to satisfy needs. Exhibit 1-8 shows that ideally, suppliers deliver materials for today's production in exactly the right quantities *just in time* to begin production and finished units are completed *just in time* for delivery to customers. This means that raw materials are not stored before production and that finished units are shipped directly to the customer when they are completed, rather than first being stored in a finished goods warehouse. By reducing the amount of inventory stored, JIT reduces storage costs (warehousing and associated security, utilities, and shrinkage costs) and handling costs (labor costs associated with storing and unstoring inventory). Firms adopting JIT report sharp reductions in inventory and related carrying costs.

JIT also cuts **throughput time**, the time between buying raw materials and selling finished products. For example, Dell Computer recently cut its throughput time from 17 days to fewer than 5 days. Why is this important? An article in *The Wall Street Journal* estimates that new technologies reduce the value of a completed PC by 1% *per week*.[9] Moving inventory quickly means that Dell can cut prices immediately when costs of component parts decline. Less inventory means that Dell can quickly incorporate new technologies and that more plant space is available for production.

Manufacturers adopting JIT have a limited safety stock of raw materials, so they depend on their suppliers to make on-time deliveries of perfect-quality materials. As noted earlier, Dell designed special Web pages for its major suppliers that give them a "virtual window" into Dell's operations. Suppliers use these windows to decide when and how much raw material to deliver to Dell.

Companies that adopt JIT strive for perfect quality because defects stop production lines. Firms that adopt JIT also commit to total quality management.

---

[8]Catherine Skip, "Hot Bytes, by the Dozen," *Newsweek*, April 28, 2003, p. 42.
[9]"Compaq Stumbles as PCs Weather New Blow," *Wall Street Journal*, March 9, 1998, p. B1.

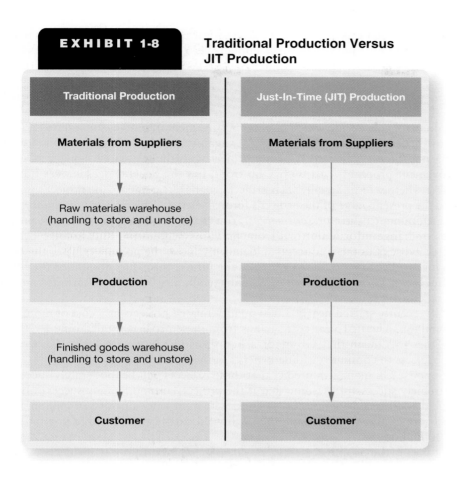

EXHIBIT 1-8 — Traditional Production Versus JIT Production

Total Quality Management

Companies must deliver high-quality goods and services to remain competitive. Hewlett-Packard and Ford in the United States, British Telecom in the United Kingdom, and Toyota in Japan view **total quality management (TQM)** as a key to succeeding in the global economy. The goal of TQM is to delight customers by providing them with superior products and services. Companies achieve this goal by improving quality and eliminating defects and waste.

In TQM, each business function examines its own activities and works to improve performance by continually setting higher goals. For example, Motorola wanted to reduce the time required to issue a purchase order. The TQM team of Motorola's purchasing department reduced the number of steps in handling a purchase order from 17 to 6, slashing average processing time from 30 minutes to 3.

ISO 9001:2000

Many firms want to demonstrate their commitment to continuous quality improvement. The International Organization for Standardization (ISO), made up of 146 member countries, has developed international quality management standards and guidelines. Firms may become ISO 9001:2000-certified by complying with the quality management standards set forth by the ISO and undergoing extensive audits of their quality management processes. The prestigious certification gives firms a competitive advantage in the global marketplace. Many companies will purchase supplies only from firms bearing the ISO 9001:2000 certification. To better understand the ISO's global impact, consider the following: by 2005, over 650,000 certificates had been issued to firms in 154 countries! The certification does not only apply to manufacturing firms. Service firms account for over 31% of all certificates issued. The American Institute of Certified Public Accountants was the first professional membership organization in the United States to earn the ISO 9001 certification.

Cost-Benefit Analysis

6 Use cost-benefit analysis to make business decisions

How do managers decide which quality improvement initiatives to undertake? They use **cost-benefit analysis**—weighing costs against benefits. Most decisions involve comparing the estimated costs of the project with the estimated benefits. Quality improvement programs cost money up front, but the benefits accrue over time. In deciding whether to undertake such projects, managers compare the project's present cost to the present value of the project's future benefits. (This is called *discounting* the future amounts to their *present values*. You may already be familiar with present value concepts and calculations from previous accounting and finance classes. Chapter 9 discusses these concepts in detail. For now, the present value of the benefits is given.) Because no one can foresee the future, the exact amount of the future benefits is not known. Let's see how managers adjust for this uncertainty in performing cost-benefit analysis.

GE recently started nearly 3,000 quality-related projects at a cost of more than $200 million. The first-year cost savings from these projects totaled only $170 million. Does this mean that GE made a bad decision? Not necessarily. GE expects these projects to continue yielding benefits in the future.

Suppose GE managers predict that these projects will be moderately successful or extremely successful. Assume that if the projects are moderately successful, they will yield additional benefits (cost savings) with a present value of $20 million. If the projects are extremely successful, they will yield extra benefits with a present value of $100 million.

Suppose the managers estimate a 60% chance that the projects will be extremely successful and a 40% chance that they will be moderately successful. In an uncertain environment, managers make decisions based on expected values. We compute expected values by multiplying the dollar value of each possible outcome by the probability of that outcome and then adding the results:

Outcome	Benefit	×	Probability	=	Expected Value
Extremely successful	$100 million	×	60% chance	=	$60 million
Moderately successful	20 million	×	40% chance	=	8 million
					$68 million

What does this $68 million mean? If GE faced this exact situation ten times, it would expect to get $100 million in extra benefits six times and only $20 million of additional benefits four times. The *average* extra benefits across the ten situations is $68 million.

Thus, the total benefits expected from GE's quality projects ($238 million, calculated as $170 million initial benefits + $68 million additional expected benefits) exceed the $200 million cost of the projects. This analysis suggests that GE's quality initiative was worthwhile.

Even after adopting quality programs, companies cannot "rest on their laurels." TQM requires that companies (and individual employees) continually look for ways to improve performance. This is the **continuous improvement** philosophy.

How do companies improve? Many businesses find that they can save money in the long run by spending more up front on *preventing* defects from occurring in the first place. Successful companies design and build quality into their products and services rather than depending on finding and fixing defects later. For example, by increasing the proportion of vehicles built right the first time from 50% to 70%, General Motors cut average warranty costs from roughly $1,600 to $1,000 per vehicle, in addition to reducing costs of rework and inspections.

Decision Guidelines

THE CHANGING BUSINESS ENVIRONMENT

Successful companies have to respond to changes in the business environment. Here are some of the key decisions managers consider to ensure that the company thrives in the future.

Decision	Guidelines
What companies need to comply with SOX?	Publicly traded companies must comply with SOX. Many of the law's specific requirements focus on implementing adequate internal controls and financial reporting procedures and maintaining independence from the company's auditors.
How do companies compete in a global economy?	They use advanced information systems; embrace e-commerce; and use supply-chain management, JIT, and TQM to compete more effectively. They consider becoming ISO 9001:2000-certified.
How do companies decide whether to undertake new projects such as international expansion, ERP, JIT, and TQM?	They use cost-benefit analysis. They compute the benefits of the project and compare them with the costs. They undertake the project if benefits exceed costs. They abandon the project if costs exceed benefits.
How do companies adjust the cost-benefit analysis if they do not know the exact amount of the benefit (or cost)?	They compute the expected value of the benefits (or costs) of each outcome as follows:

$$\begin{array}{ccccc} \text{Estimated} & & \text{Probability} & & \text{Expected} \\ \text{amount of} & \times & \text{of} & = & \text{value of} \\ \text{outcome} & & \text{outcome} & & \text{outcome} \end{array}$$

Then, they add the expected values across all possible outcomes.

Summary Problem 2

This summary review problem shows how you can apply cost-benefit analysis to a decision about international expansion.

EZ-Rider Motorcycles is considering whether to expand into Germany. If gas prices increase, EZ-Rider Motorcycles expects more interest in fuel-efficient transportation such as motorcycles. EZ-Rider Motorcycles is considering setting up a motorcycle assembly plant on the outskirts of Berlin.

EZ-Rider Motorcycles estimates it will cost €850,000 (850,000 euros) to convert an existing building to motorcycle production. Workers will need training, at a total cost of €65,000. The CEO of EZ-Rider Motorcycles, Dennis Popper, would have to spend a month in Berlin to organize the business and to establish relationships. He estimates the cost of this travel at €43,000.

Popper sees a 60% chance that the price of gasoline in Germany will increase significantly. If this increase occurs, he believes EZ-Rider Motorcycles can earn profits (before considering the costs in the preceding paragraph) with a present value of €1,624,000. However, if gas prices remain stable, Popper expects to earn profits with a present value of only about €812,000. He believes there is a 40% chance that gas prices will remain stable.

Requirements

1. What are the total costs of EZ-Rider Motorcycles' proposed expansion into Germany?

2. Compute the *expected value* of the benefits if EZ-Rider Motorcycles expands into Germany.

3. Do the benefits outweigh the costs of expanding into Germany? Explain.

Solution

Requirement 1
The total costs are as follows:

Conversion of building to manufacturing plant...........	€850,000
Workforce training	65,000
Popper's trip to Berlin	43,000
Total costs...	€958,000

Requirement 2
Expected value of the benefits is computed as follows:

Benefit	× Probability	=	Expected Value
€1,624,000	× 0.60	=	€ 974,400
812,000	× 0.40	=	324,800
			€ 1,299,200

The *expected value* of the benefits, or profits, is €1,299,200. This means that should EZ-Rider Motorcycles find itself in this exact situation many times, its average profits across all of the situations would be €1,299,200.

Requirement 3

Yes, the total expected benefits outweigh the costs of the expansion:

Total expected value of benefits of expansion (from requirement 2)...	€1,299,200
Total costs of expansion (from requirement 1).................................	958,000
Net benefits of expansion...	€ 341,200

Review Introduction to Managerial Accounting

■ Accounting Vocabulary

Audit Committee. (p. 33)
A subcommittee of the board of directors that is responsible for overseeing both the internal audit function and the annual financial statement audit by independent CPAs.

Board of Directors. (p. 33)
The body elected by shareholders to oversee the company.

Budget. (p. 29)
Quantitative expression of a plan that helps managers coordinate and implement the plan.

Certified Financial Manager (CFM). (p. 37)
A professional certification issued by the IMA to designate expertise in the areas of financial statement analysis, working capital policy, capital structure, business valuation, and risk management.

Certified Management Accountant (CMA). (p. 37)
A professional certification issued by the IMA to designate expertise in the areas of managerial accounting, economics, and business finance.

Chief Executive Officer (CEO). (p. 33)
The position hired by the board of directors to oversee the company on a daily basis.

Chief Financial Officer (CFO). (p. 33)
The position responsible for all of the company's financial concerns.

Chief Operating Officer (COO). (p. 33)
The position responsible for overseeing the company's operations.

Continuous Improvement. (p. 50)
A philosophy requiring employees to continually look for ways to improve performance.

Controller. (p. 33)
The position responsible for general financial accounting, managerial accounting, and tax reporting.

Controlling. (p. 29)
One of management's primary responsibilities; evaluating the results of business operations against the plan and making adjustments to keep the company pressing toward its goals.

Cost-Benefit Analysis. (p. 50)
Weighing costs against benefits to help make decisions.

Cross-Functional Teams. (p. 34)
Corporate teams whose members represent various functions of the organization, such as R&D, design, production, marketing, distribution, and customer service.

Decision Making. (p. 30)
One of management's primary responsibilities; identifying possible courses of action and choosing among them.

Directing. (p. 29)
One of management's primary responsibilities; running the company on a day-to-day basis.

Enterprise Resource Planning (ERP). (p. 46)
Software systems that can integrate all of a company's worldwide functions, departments, and data into a single system.

Institute of Management Accountants (IMA). (p. 37)
The professional organization that promotes the advancement of the management accounting profession.

Internal Audit Function. (p. 33)
The corporate function charged with assessing the effectiveness of the company's internal controls and risk management policies.

Just-In-Time (JIT). (p. 48)
A system in which a company produces just in time to satisfy needs. Suppliers deliver materials just in time to begin production, and finished units are completed just in time for delivery to customers.

Planning. (p. 29)
One of management's primary responsibilities; setting goals and objectives for the company and deciding how to achieve them.

Sarbanes-Oxley Act of 2002 (SOX). (p. 44)
A congressional act that enhances internal control and financial reporting requirements and establishes new regulatory requirements for publicly traded companies and their independent auditors.

Supply-Chain Management. (p. 48)
Exchange of information with suppliers to reduce costs, improve quality, and speed delivery of goods and services from suppliers to the company itself and on to customers.

Throughput Time. (p. 48)
The time between buying raw materials and selling finished products.

Treasurer. (p. 33)
The position responsible for raising the firm's capital and investing funds.

Total Quality Management (TQM). (p. 49)
A philosophy of delighting customers by providing them with superior products and services. Requires improving quality and eliminating defects and waste throughout the value chain.

■ Quick Check

1. Which of the following is *not* one of the four primary responsibilities of management?
   a. controlling
   b. costing
   c. directing
   d. planning

2. Which of the following about managerial accounting is *true*?
   a. GAAP requires managerial accounting.
   b. Internal decision makers use managerial accounting.
   c. CPAs audit managerial accounting reports.
   d. Managerial accounting reports are usually prepared on an annual basis.

3. Which of the following is *not* a characteristic of managerial accounting information?
   a. emphasizes relevance
   b. focuses on the future more than the past
   c. provides detailed information about parts of the company, not just the company as a whole
   d. emphasizes reliability

4. What company position is in charge of raising the firm's capital?
   a. director of internal audit
   b. controller
   c. COO
   d. treasurer

5. Which of the following statements is *true*?
   a. The COO reports to the CFO.
   b. The treasurer reports to the CEO.
   c. The internal audit department reports to the audit committee.
   d. The controller reports to the internal auditor.

6. To get a job as a management accountant in most companies, you must:
   a. join the IMA
   b. be certified as a CMA
   c. be certified as a CFM
   d. none of the above

7. In addition to accounting knowledge, management accountants must possess all of the following skills *except*:
   a. written communication skills
   b. knowledge of how a business functions
   c. computer programming skills
   d. analytical skills

8. A management accountant who refuses an expensive gift from a software salesperson meets the ethical standard of:
   a. credibility
   b. confidentiality
   c. integrity
   d. competence

9. Which of the following is not one of the provisions of the Sarbanes-Oxley Act of 2002?
   a. The company's auditors assume responsibility for the financial statements.
   b. The penalties (i.e., prison time and fines) for corporate fraud were increased.
   c. At least one audit committee member should be a financial expert.
   d. The CEO and CFO must certify that the financial statements fairly present the company's operations and financial condition.

10. All of the following tools help companies compete in today's market *except*:
   a. JIT
   b. KJD
   c. ERP
   d. TQM

Quick Check Answers

1. b 2. b 3. d 4. d 5. c 6. d 7. c 8. c 9. a 10. b

 For Internet Exercises, Excel in Practice, and additional online activities, go to this book's Web site at www.prenhall.com/bamber.

Assess Your Progress

■ Learning Objectives

1 Identify managers' four primary responsibilities

2 Distinguish financial accounting from managerial accounting

3 Describe organizational structure and the roles and skills required of management accountants within the organization

4 Describe the role of the Institute of Management Accountants (IMA) and use its ethical standards to make reasonable ethical judgments

5 Discuss trends in the business environment

6 Use cost-benefit analysis to make business decisions

■ Short Exercises

S1-1 Roles of managers *(Learning Objective 1)*
Describe the four primary roles of managers and the way they relate to one another.

S1-2 Contrast managerial and financial accounting *(Learning Objective 2)*
Your roommate, who plans to specialize in international business, is considering whether to enroll in the second principles of accounting course. She says, "I don't want to be an accountant, so why do I need a second accounting course? I just spent a whole term on financial accounting. Most of this second course focuses on managerial accounting, but how can that be so different from what I already learned in financial accounting?" Respond.

S1-3 Roles and skills of management accountants *(Learning Objective 3)*
Your friends call you a "bean counter" because you are taking an accounting class. Explain to them why they are wrong.

S1-4 Role of internal audit function *(Learning Objective 3)*
Explain what the role of the internal audit function is and why the internal audit function usually reports to the CEO or CFO and the audit committee.

S1-5 Importance of ethical standards *(Learning Objective 4)*
Explain why each of the four broad ethical standards in the IMA's *Statement of Ethical Professional Practice* is necessary.

S1-6 Violations of ethical standards *(Learning Objective 4)*
The IMA's *Statement of Ethical Professional Practice* (Exhibit 1-6) requires management accountants to meet standards regarding:

- Competence.
- Confidentiality.
- Integrity.
- Credibility.

continued . . .

Consider the following situations. Which guidelines are violated in each situation?

a. You tell your brother that your company will report earnings significantly above financial analysts' estimates.

b. You see that other employees take home office supplies for personal use. As an intern, you do the same thing, assuming that this is a "perk."

c. At a conference on e-commerce, you skip the afternoon session and go sightseeing.

d. You failed to read the detailed specifications of a new general ledger package that you asked your company to purchase. After it is installed, you are surprised that it is incompatible with some of your company's older accounting software.

e. You do not provide top management with the detailed job descriptions they requested because you fear they may use this information to cut a position from your department.

S1-7   Just-in-time management *(Learning Objective 5)*
Is JIT more appropriate for Amazon.com, a book, music, and electronics e-tailer, or Mouton-Rothschild, a French winemaker specializing in fine red wines? Explain.

S1-8   Cost-benefit analysis *(Learning Objective 6)*
Consider the cost-benefit analysis for GE's quality program discussed on page 50. Suppose GE's managers now estimate an 85% chance that the projects will yield an extra $20 million in benefits and a 15% chance that the projects will yield an extra $80 million. What is the expected value of the additional benefits *now*? Assuming that total costs remain at $200 million, and cost savings in the first year already amounted to $170 million, does this change your mind about whether the quality program was a worthwhile investment?

■ Exercises

E1-9   Managers' responsibilities *(Learning Objective 1)*
Categorize each of the following activities as to which management responsibility it fulfills: planning, directing, controlling, or decision making. Some activities may fulfill more than one responsibility.

a. Management conducts variance analysis by comparing budget to actual.

b. Management reviews hourly sales reports to determine the level of staffing needed to service customers.

c. Management decides to increase sales growth by 10% next year.

d. Management uses information on product costs to determine sales prices.

e. To lower product costs, management moves production to Mexico.

E1-10   Define key terms *(Learning Objectives 1, 2)*
Complete the following statements with one of the terms listed here. You may use a term more than once, and some terms may not be used at all.

Budget	Creditors	Managerial accounting	Planning
Controlling	Financial accounting	Managers	Shareholders

a. Companies must follow GAAP in their _____ systems.

b. Financial accounting develops reports for external parties such as _____ and _____ .

c. When managers evaluate the company's performance compared to the plan, they are performing the _____ role of management.

d. _____ are decision makers inside a company.

e. _____ provides information on a company's past performance to external parties.

f. _____ systems are not restricted by GAAP but are chosen by comparing the costs versus the benefits of the system.

g. Choosing goals and the means to achieve them is the _____ function of management.

h. _____ systems report on various segments or business units of the company.

i. _____ statements of public companies are audited annually by CPAs.

E1-11 **Classify roles within the organization** *(Learning Objective 3)*
Complete the following statements with one of the terms listed here. You may use a term more than once, and some terms may not be used at all.

Audit committee	Board of directors	CEO	CFO
Treasurer	Controller	Cross-functional teams	COO

a. The _____ and the _____ report to the CEO.

b. The internal audit function reports to the CFO or _____ and the _____.

c. The _____ is directly responsible for financial accounting, managerial accounting, and tax reporting.

d. The CEO is hired by the _____.

e. The _____ is directly responsible for raising capital and investing funds.

f. The _____ is directly responsible for the company's operations.

g. Management accountants often work with _____.

h. A subcommittee of the board of directors is called the _____.

E1-12 **Describe needed skills and knowledge** *(Learning Objective 3)*
A study by the IMA found that management accountants need skills and knowledge above and beyond pure accounting knowledge. Describe the set of skills and knowledge identified in the study and explain why they are important to the new role of management accountants.

E1-13 **Professional organization and certification** *(Learning Objective 4)*
Complete the following sentences:

a. The _____ is the professional association for management accountants.

b. The institute offers two types of certification: the _____ and _____.

c. The _____ exam focuses on managerial accounting topics, economics, and business finance.

d. The _____ exam focuses on financial statement analysis, business valuation, risk management, working capital policy, and capital structure.

e. The institute's monthly publication, called _____, addresses current topics of interest to management accountants.

f. The institute says that approximately _____ percent of accountants work in organizations rather than at CPA firms.

E1-14 **Ethical dilemma** *(Learning Objective 4)*

Mary Gonzales is the controller at Ditoro, a car dealership. She recently hired Cory Loftus as a bookkeeper. Loftus wanted to attend a class on Excel spreadsheets, so Gonzales temporarily took over Loftus's duties, including overseeing a fund for topping off a car's gas tank before a test drive. Gonzales found a shortage in this fund and confronted Loftus when he returned to work. Loftus admitted that he occasionally uses this fund to pay for his own gas. Gonzales estimated that the amount involved is close to $300.

Requirements

1. What should Gonzales do?
2. Would you change your answer to the previous question if Gonzales was the one recently hired as controller and Loftus was a well-liked, longtime employee who indicated that he always eventually repaid the fund?

E1-15 **Classify ethical responsibilities** *(Learning Objective 4)*

According to the IMA's *Statement of Ethical Professional Practice* (Exhibit 1-6), management accountants should follow four standards: competence, confidentiality, integrity, and credibility. Each of these standards contains specific responsibilities. Classify each of the following responsibilities according to the standard it addresses.

Responsibility:

1. Refrain from using confidential information for unethical or illegal advantage.
2. Maintain an appropriate level of professional expertise by continually developing knowledge and skills.
3. Communicate information fairly and objectively.
4. Recognize and communicate professional limitations that would preclude responsible judgment or successful performance of an activity.
5. Mitigate actual conflicts of interest. Regularly communicate with business associates to avoid apparent conflicts of interest. Advise all parties of any potential conflicts.
6. Provide decision support information and recommendations that are accurate, clear, concise, and timely.
7. Abstain from engaging in or supporting any activity that might discredit the profession.
8. Disclose all relevant information that could reasonably be expected to influence an intended user's understanding of the reports, analyses, or recommendations.
9. Inform all relevant parties regarding the appropriate use of confidential information. Monitor subordinates' activities to ensure compliance.
10. Perform professional duties in accordance with relevant laws, regulations, and technical standards.
11. Refrain from engaging in any conduct that would prejudice carrying out duties ethically.
12. Keep information confidential except when disclosure is authorized or legally required.
13. Disclose delays or deficiencies in information, timeliness, processing, or internal controls in conformance with organization policy and/or applicable law.

E1-16 **Define key terms** *(Learning Objectives 5, 6)*

Complete the following statements with one of the terms listed here. You may use a term more than once, and some terms may not be used at all.

E-commerce	Future value	Shift to service economy
ERP	JIT	Throughput time
Expected value	Present	TQM
Future	Present value	ISO 9001:2000

a. To account for uncertainty in the amounts of future costs and benefits, we compute the _____ by multiplying the probability of each outcome by the dollar value of that outcome.

b. To make a cost-benefit decision today, we must find the _____ of the costs and benefits that are incurred in the future.

c. The goal of _____ is to meet customers' expectations by providing them with superior products and services by eliminating defects and waste throughout the value chain.

d. Most of the costs of adopting ERP and JIT, expanding into a foreign market, or improving quality are incurred in the _____; but most of the benefits occur in the _____.

e. _____ is the time between buying raw materials and selling the finished products.

f. _____ serves the information needs of people in accounting as well as people in marketing and in the warehouse.

g. Firms adopt _____ to conduct business on the Internet.

h. Firms acquire the _____ certification to demonstrate their commitment to quality.

E1-17 **Summarize the Sarbanes-Oxley Act** *(Learning Objective 5)*

You just obtained an entry-level job as a management accountant. Other newly hired accountants have heard of the Sarbanes-Oxley Act of 2002 (SOX), but don't know much about it (they attended a different university). Write a short memo to your colleagues discussing the reason for SOX, the goal of SOX, and some of the specific requirements of SOX that will affect your company.

E1-18 **JIT cost-benefit analysis** *(Learning Objective 6)*

Land Shark manufactures snowboards. Shawn Mobbs, the CEO, is trying to decide whether to adopt JIT. He expects that in present-value terms, adopting JIT would save $97,000 in warehousing expenses and $46,000 in spoilage costs. Adopting JIT will require several one-time up-front expenditures: (1) $13,500 for an employee training program, (2) $37,000 to streamline the plant's production process, and (3) $8,000 to identify suppliers that will guarantee zero defects and on-time delivery.

Requirements

1. What are the total costs of adopting JIT?

2. What are the total benefits of adopting JIT?

3. Should Land Shark adopt JIT? Why or why not?

P1-19A Summarize managerial accounting and recent business trends *(Learning Objectives 1, 2, 3, 5)*

Your roommate is an engineering student who has developed a new marketable technology as part of her graduate studies. As soon as she finishes her degree, she intends to start her own company to manufacture and sell the technology. She has not taken any business classes but has begun to read business periodicals to develop some business savvy. She has several issues on which she would like your input. Discuss what you know about the following:

1. Your roommate feels confident about her abilities as the company's chief product engineer but questions whether she should manage the company herself. She wonders what her role as company manager would be.

2. She's heard of financial and managerial accounting and wonders if they are the same thing.

3. Because you are taking an accounting class, she asks you to explain how to structure the financial arm of a large organization.

4. Your roommate has high hopes for her company. She's already anticipating it to be publicly traded some day in the near future. She wants to know how SOX will affect her business.

5. The business magazines often mention TQM and the ISO. She wants to know more about TQM and the ISO 9001:2000 certification.

6. Your roommate also sees frequent references to JIT production. She would like to know what JIT is about and if she should consider adopting it.

7. Because she will sell the new technology to other companies rather than consumers, your roommate doesn't see the need to set up an electronic purchasing Web site. Explain to her why e-commerce is helpful even if she isn't selling directly to individual consumers.

P1-20A Ethical dilemmas *(Learning Objective 4)*

Kate Royer is the new controller for Simple Solutions, which develops and sells educational software. Shortly before the December 31 fiscal year-end, Matt Adams, the company president, asks Royer how things look for the year-end numbers. He is not happy to learn that earnings growth may be below 15% for the first time in the company's five-year history. Adams explains that financial analysts have again predicted a 15% earnings growth for the company and that he does not intend to disappoint them. He suggests that Royer talk to the assistant controller, who can explain how the previous controller dealt with this situation. The assistant controller suggests the following strategies:

a. Persuade suppliers to postpone billing until January 1.

b. Record as sales certain software awaiting sale that is held in a public warehouse.

c. Delay the year-end closing a few days into January of the next year so that some of next year's sales are included as this year's sales.

d. Reduce the allowance for bad debts (and bad debts expense).

e. Postpone routine monthly maintenance expenditures from December to January.

Which of these suggested strategies are inconsistent with IMA standards? What should Royer do if Adams insists that she follow all of these suggestions?

P1-21A ERP cost-benefit analysis *(Learning Objectives 5, 6)*

As CEO of Garrity Industries, Ron Greenwood knows it is important to control costs and to respond quickly to changes in the highly competitive boat-building industry. When IDG Consulting proposes that Garrity Industries invest in an ERP system, he forms a team to evaluate the proposal: the plant engineer, the plant foreman, the systems specialist, the human resources director, the marketing director, and the management accountant.

A month later, management accountant Mike Cobalt reports that the team and IDG estimate that if Garrity Industries implements the ERP system, it will incur the following costs:

a. $350,000 in software costs

b. $80,000 to customize the ERP software and load Garrity Industries' data into the new ERP system

c. $125,000 for employee training

The team estimates that the ERP system should provide several benefits:

a. More efficient order processing should lead to savings with a present value of $185,000.

b. Streamlining the manufacturing process so that it maps into the ERP system will create savings with a present value of $275,000.

c. Integrating purchasing, production, marketing, and distribution into a single system will allow Garrity Industries to reduce inventories, saving $220,000.

d. Higher customer satisfaction should increase sales, which, in turn, should increase the present value of profits by $150,000.

The team knows that because of complexity, some ERP installations are not successful. If Garrity Industries' system fails, there will be no cost savings and no additional sales. The team predicts that there is an 80% chance that the ERP installation will succeed and a 20% chance that it will fail.

Requirements

1. If the ERP installation succeeds, what is the dollar amount of the benefits?

2. Should Garrity Industries install the ERP system? Why or why not? Show your calculations.

P1-22A Continuation of P1-21A: revised probabilities *(Learning Objectives 5, 6)*

P1-21A asked you to perform a quantitative analysis to help Garrity Industries' managers decide whether to embark on the project. Now consider some qualitative factors in Garrity Industries' ERP project.

1. Why did Greenwood create a team to evaluate IDG's proposal? Consider each piece of cost-benefit information that management accountant Cobalt reported. Which person on the team is most likely to have contributed each item? (*Hint:* Which team member is likely to have the most information about each cost or benefit?)

2. Quantifying ERP benefits can be difficult. After further discussion, the team predicts that there is a 60% chance that the ERP installation will succeed and a 40% chance that it will fail. Should Garrity Industries still install the new ERP system?

P1-23A E-commerce cost-benefit analysis *(Learning Objectives 5, 6)*

Jones Corporation wants to move its sales order system to the Web. Under the proposed system, gas stations and other merchants will use a Web browser and, after typing in a password for the Jones Corporation Web page, will be able to check the availability and current price of various products and place an order. Currently, customer service representatives take dealers' orders over the phone; they record the information on a paper form, then manually enter it into the firm's computer system.

CFO Carrie Smith believes that dealers will not adopt the new Web system unless Jones Corporation provides financial assistance to help them purchase or upgrade their PCs. Smith estimates this one-time cost at $750,000. Jones Corporation will also have to invest $150,000 in upgrading its own computer hardware. The cost of the software and the consulting fee for installing the system will be $230,000. The Web system will enable Jones Corporation to eliminate 25 clerical positions. Smith estimates that the benefits of the new system's lower labor costs will have a present value of $1,357,000.

Requirements

Use a cost-benefit analysis to recommend to Smith whether Jones Corporation should proceed with the Web-based ordering system. Give your reasons, showing supporting calculations.

P1-24A Continuation of P1-23A: revised probabilities *(Learning Objectives 5, 6)*

Consider the Jones Corporation proposed entry into e-commerce in P1-23A. Smith revises her estimates of the benefits from the new system's lower labor costs. She now thinks there is a 40% chance of receiving the $1,357,000 in benefits and a 60% chance the benefits will be only $933,000.

Requirements

1. Compute the expected benefits of the Web-based ordering system.
2. Would you recommend that Jones Corporation accept the proposal?
3. Before Smith makes a final decision, what other factors should she consider?

■ Problems (Problem Set B)

P1-25B Summarize managerial accounting and recent business trends *(Learning Objectives 1, 2, 3, 5)*

One of your friends has taken a great interest in Australia and wants to import home décor items from Australia after college. He has not taken any business classes but has begun to read business newspapers and magazines to develop some business knowledge. He has several issues on which he would like your input. Discuss with him what you know about the following:

1. Your friend feels confident about his abilities to select marketable Australian home décor, but questions whether he should manage the company himself or hire someone to manage the company while he takes on the role of the chief buyer. He wonders what his role would be if he were the company manager as well.
2. He's heard of financial and managerial accounting and wonders if they are the same thing.
3. Because you are taking an accounting class, he asks you to explain how to structure the financial arm of a large organization.

4. Your friend has high hopes for his company. He foresees his business growing into a chain of home décor stores, similar to Pier 1 Imports or Cost Plus World Market. To grow the business to this level, he will have to take the company public. He wants to know how SOX will affect a publicly traded company.

5. The business magazines often mention TQM and the ISO. He wants to know if TQM and the ISO 9001:2000 certification apply only to manufacturers.

6. Your friend also sees frequent references to JIT production. First, he would like to know what JIT is. Second, he wonders if it would apply to his business.

7. Your friend wonders if he should invest in e-commerce or depend solely on sales generated by foot traffic into his "brick-and-mortar" retail stores.

P1-26B Ethical dilemmas *(Learning Objective 4)*

Kara Williams is the new controller for Paradise Platforms, a designer and manufacturer of sportswear. Shortly before the December 31 fiscal year-end, Lashea Lucas (the company president) asks Williams how things look for the year-end numbers. Lucas is not happy to learn that earnings growth may be below 10% for the first time in the company's five-year history. Lucas explains that financial analysts have again predicted a 12% earnings growth for the company and that she does not intend to disappoint them. She suggests that Williams talk to the assistant controller, who can explain how the previous controller dealt with this situation. The assistant controller suggests the following strategies:

a. Postpone planned advertising expenditures from December to January.

b. Do not record sales returns and allowances on the basis that they are individually immaterial.

c. Persuade retail customers to accelerate January orders to December.

d. Reduce the allowance for bad debts (and bad debts expense).

e. Paradise Platforms ships finished goods to public warehouses across the country for temporary storage until it receives firm orders from customers. As Paradise Platforms receives orders, it directs the warehouse to ship the goods to nearby customers. The assistant controller suggests recording goods sent to the public warehouses as sales.

Which of these suggested strategies are inconsistent with IMA standards? What should Williams do if Lucas insists that she follow all of these suggestions?

P1-27B TQM cost-benefit analysis *(Learning Objectives 5, 6)*

Winchendon Systems manufactures computer disk drives. It sells these disk drives to other manufacturers, which use them in assembling computers. Winchendon Systems is having trouble with its new DVD drive. About half the time, Winchendon Systems employees find defects while the disk drive is still on the production line. These drives are immediately reworked in the plant. Otherwise, Winchendon Systems' customers do not identify the problem until they install the disk drives they've purchased. Customers return defective drives for replacement under warranty. They have also complained that after they install the disk drive, the drive's connector (which plugs into the computer system board) often shakes loose while the computer is being assembled. The customers must then reassemble the computer after fixing the loose connection.

Winchendon Systems' CEO Jay Rich has just returned from a seminar on TQM. He forms a team to address these quality problems. The team includes the plant engineer, the production supervisor, a customer service representative, the marketing director, and the management accountant.

continued . . .

Three months later, the team proposes a major project to *prevent* these quality problems. Winchendon Systems' accountant Anna Crowe reports that implementing the team's proposal will require Winchendon Systems to incur the following costs over the next three months:

- $180,500 for Winchendon Systems' scientists to develop a completely new disk drive.
- $70,000 for the company's engineers to redesign the connector so that it better tolerates rough treatment.

The project team is unsure whether this investment will pay off. If the effort fixes the problem, Crowe expects that:

- A reputation for higher quality will increase sales, which, in turn, will increase the present value of profits by $200,000.
- Fewer disk drives will fail. The present value of the savings from fewer warranty repairs is $170,300.
- The plant will have fewer defective disk drives to rework. The present value of this savings is $100,200.

However, if this project is not successful, there will be no cost savings and no additional sales. The team predicts a 70% chance that the project will succeed and a 30% chance that it will fail.

Requirements

1. If the quality improvement project succeeds, what is the dollar amount of the benefits?
2. Should Winchendon Systems undertake this project? Why or why not? Show supporting calculations.

P1-28B **Continuation of P1-27B: revised probabilities** *(Learning Objectives 5, 6)*
P1-27B asked you to perform a quantitative analysis to help Winchendon Systems' managers decide whether to embark on the project. Now consider some qualitative factors in Winchendon Systems' quality improvement project.

1. Why did Rich create a team to address this quality problem rather than assigning the task to one person? Consider each piece of cost/benefit information reported by management accountant Crowe. Which person on the team is most likely to have contributed each item? (*Hint:* Which team member is likely to have the most information about each cost or benefit?)
2. Quantifying TQM benefits can be difficult. After further discussion, the team predicts that there is only a 50% chance that the proposal will succeed, and a 50% chance that it will fail. Should Winchendon Systems still implement the project?

P1-29B **Information system cost-benefit analysis** *(Learning Objectives 5, 6)*
Mountain Bank processes checks for smaller banks and insurance companies. When a customer complains that a check was not deposited to its account, a Mountain Bank clerk takes the complaint over the phone and fills out a paper form. The complaint form triggers a long search through piles of canceled checks in a warehouse to find the check in question. Mountain Bank then compares this check to its computer and paper records.

Mountain Bank is considering moving this process to the Web. When a customer has a question, an employee simply uses a Web browser and a password to access Mountain Bank's databases. The customer's employee pulls up a computerized image of the check in question to verify the amount and then queries Mountain Bank's databases to locate the mistake. If required, a credit to the customer's account can be issued immediately.

The Web-based system will require the bank to invest $83,000 in a new server and check-scanning equipment. eNow! Consultants will charge $110,000 for the software and consulting fees to get the system running. The system will also require increasing the bank's Internet capacity. The present value of this cost is $20,000.

Mountain Bank has identified two benefits of this project. First, several bank clerks freed from searching through stacks of canceled checks will be reassigned, which will lead to cost savings with a present value of $173,000. Second, the new system's additional capacity will enable Mountain Bank to accept more check-processing business, which should lead to additional profits with a present value of $43,200.

Requirements

Does a cost-benefit analysis justify the Web-based system? Explain why, showing supporting calculations.

P1-30B **Continuation of P1-29B: revised probabilities** *(Learning Objectives 5, 6)*

Consider the Mountain Bank project described in P1-29B. Mountain Bank has revised its estimates of additional profits the bank is likely to earn. There is an 80% chance that the bank will earn $43,200 in extra profits, but also a 20% chance the bank will earn $75,000.

Requirements

1. Compute the expected value of the benefits from the additional business.

2. Would you recommend that Mountain Bank accept the proposal? Give your reason, showing supporting calculations.

3. Are there other potential benefits not listed in P1-29B or P1-30B that may make the proposal more attractive to Mountain Bank?

Apply Your Knowledge

■ Decision Case

Case 1-31. Ethical standards *(Learning Objective 4)*

The IMA's *Statement of Ethical Professional Practice* (Exhibit 1-6) can be applied to more than just managerial accounting. It is also relevant to college students. Explain at least one situation that shows how each IMA standard is relevant to your experiences as a student. For example, the ethical standard of competence would suggest not cutting classes.

■ Ethical Issue

Issue 1-32. Ethical dilemma *(Learning Objective 4)*

Ricardo Valencia recently resigned his position as controller for Tom White Automotive, a small, struggling foreign car dealer in Austin, Texas. Valencia has just started a new job as controller for Mueller Imports, a much larger dealer for the same car manufacturer. Demand for this particular make of car is exploding, and the manufacturer cannot produce enough cars to satisfy demand. Each manufacturer's regional sales managers is given a certain number of cars. Each regional sales manager then decides how to divide the cars among the independently owned dealerships in the region. Because most dealerships can sell every car they receive, the key is getting a large number of cars from the manufacturer's regional sales manager.

Valencia's former employer, Tom White Automotive, received only about 25 cars a month. Consequently, the dealership was not very profitable.

Valencia is surprised to learn that his new employer, Mueller Imports, receives over 200 cars a month. Valencia soon gets another surprise. Every couple of months, a local jeweler bills the dealer $5,000 for "miscellaneous services." Franz Mueller, the owner of the dealership, personally approves the payment of these invoices, noting that each invoice is a "selling expense." From casual conversations with a salesperson, Valencia learns that Mueller frequently gives Rolex watches to the manufacturer's regional sales manager and other sales executives. Before talking to anyone about this, Valencia decides to work through his ethical dilemma by answering the following questions:

1. What is the ethical issue?
2. What are my options?
3. What are the possible consequences?
4. What should I do?

■ Team Project

Project 1-33. Interviewing a local company about e-commerce *(Learning Objective 5)*

Search the Internet for a nearby company that also has a Web page. Arrange an interview with a management accountant, a controller, or another accounting/finance officer of the company. Before you conduct the interview, answer the following questions:

1. What is the company's primary product or service?

2. Is the primary purpose of the company's Web site to provide information about the company and its products, to sell online, or to provide financial information for investors?

3. Are parts of the company's Web site restricted so that you need password authorization to enter? What appears to be the purpose of limiting access?

4. Does the Web site provide an e-mail link for contacting the company?

   At the interview, begin by clarifying your answers to questions 1 through 4 and ask the following additional questions:

5. If the company sells over the Web, what benefits has the company derived? Did the company perform a cost-benefit analysis before deciding to begin Web sales?

   Or

   If the company does not sell over the Web, why not? Has the company performed a cost-benefit analysis and decided not to sell over the Web?

6. What is the biggest cost of operating the Web site?

7. Does the company make any purchases over the Internet? What percentage?

8. How has e-commerce affected the company's managerial accounting system? Have the management accountant's responsibilities become more or less complex? more or less interesting?

9. Does the company use Web-based accounting applications such as accounts receivable or accounts payable?

10. Does the company use an ERP system? If so, does it view the system as a success? What have been the benefits? the costs?

    Prepare a report describing the results of your interview.

2 Building Blocks of Managerial Accounting

I n 1999, Nissan Motor Company had a problem. With no cash dividends and a net *loss* of over ¥684 billion yen (approximately $4.1 billion), CEO Carlos Ghosn knew he had to do something. In his words: "The *lack* of profit is like a fever. When your business is not profitable, that's a serious signal that something is wrong. Either the products are not right, or marketing is inefficient, or the cost base is too high—something is wrong. If you ignore a fever, you can get very sick. If you ignore unprofitability, the situation can only worsen." Ghosn launched the *Nissan Revival Plan* that turned the company around by designing and marketing new models, investing in new plant technologies, slashing supply costs, and emphasizing the company's most profitable products. Five years later, Nissan's annual operating income tops ¥861 billion yen (approximately $7.6 billion).

Nissan's operating margin is now the highest in the automotive industry, and it is paying its shareholders cash dividends at record levels.

Before Nissan could attack its problems, it had to know where its costs were incurred and whether it could control those costs by making different decisions. Was the company spending too much in production, using outdated equipment and technologies? Was it spending enough on designing new products that better met customers' needs and desires? Was it targeting the right audiences in its television advertising? In this chapter, we talk about many costs: costs that both managers and management accountants must understand to successfully run a business.

Sources: NissanUSA.com; Nissan-Global.com; and Nissan Motor Co., Ltd., Annual Reports 2002, 2003, 2004. ■

Learning Objectives

1 Distinguish among service, merchandising, and manufacturing companies

2 Describe the value chain and its elements

3 Distinguish between direct and indirect costs

4 Identify the inventoriable product costs and period costs of merchandising and manufacturing firms

5 Prepare the financial statements for service, merchandising, and manufacturing companies

6 Describe costs that are relevant and irrelevant for decision making

7 Classify costs as fixed or variable and calculate total and average costs at different volumes

So far, we have seen how managerial accounting provides information that managers use to run their businesses more efficiently. Managers must understand basic managerial accounting terms and concepts before they can use the information to make good decisions. This terminology provides the "common ground" through which managers and accountants communicate. Without a common understanding of these concepts, managers may ask for (and accountants may provide) the wrong information for making decisions. As you will see, different types of costs are useful for different purposes. Both managers and accountants must have a clear understanding of the situation and the types of costs that are relevant to the decision at hand.

Three Business Sectors and the Value Chain

Before we talk about specific types of costs, let's consider the three most common types of companies and the business activities in which they incur costs.

Service, Merchandising, and Manufacturing Companies

Organizations other than not-for-profits and governmental agencies are in business to generate profits for their owners. The primary means of generating that profit generally fall into one of three categories:

1 Distinguish among service, merchandising, and manufacturing companies

Service Companies

Service companies are in business to sell intangible services—such as health care, insurance, and consulting—rather than tangible products. Recall from the last chapter that service firms now make up the largest sector of the U.S. economy, providing jobs to over 55% of the workforce. For service companies such as eBay (online auction), H&R Block (tax return preparation), and Accountemps (temporary personnel services), salaries and wages often make up over 70% of their costs. Because service companies sell services, they generally don't have Inventory or Cost of Goods Sold accounts. Some service providers carry a minimal amount of supplies inventory; however, this inventory is used for internal operations—not sold for profit. In addition to labor costs, service companies incur costs to develop new services, advertise, and provide customer service.

Merchandising Companies

Merchandising companies such as Amazon.com, Wal-Mart, and Foot Locker resell tangible products they buy from suppliers. Amazon.com, for example, buys books, CDs, and DVDs and resells them to customers at higher prices than what it pays its own suppliers for these goods. Merchandising companies include retailers (such as Home Depot) and wholesalers. **Retailers** sell to consumers such as you. **Wholesalers,** often referred to as "middlemen," buy products in bulk from manufacturers, mark up the prices, and then sell those products to retailers. Because merchandising companies sell tangible products, they have inventory. Even merchandising companies that use just-in-time (JIT) systems have inventory; they just have *less* inventory than their non-JIT competitors. The cost of merchandise inventory is the cost merchandisers pay for the goods *plus* all costs necessary to get the merchandise in place and ready to sell, including freight-in costs and any import duties or tariffs. Because the entire inventory is ready for sale, a merchandiser's balance sheet usually reports just one inventory account called Inventory or Merchandise Inventory. Merchandisers also incur other costs to identify new products and locations for new stores, to advertise and sell their products, and to provide customer service.

Manufacturing Companies

Manufacturing companies use labor, plant, and equipment to convert raw materials into new finished products. For example, Nissan's production workers use the company's factories (plant and equipment) to transform raw materials such as steel and tires into high-performance automobiles. Manufacturers sell their products to retailers or wholesalers at a price that is high enough to cover their costs and generate a profit.

Because of their broader range of activities, manufacturers have three types of inventory (pictured in Exhibit 2-1):

EXHIBIT 2-1 Manufacturers' Three Types of Inventory

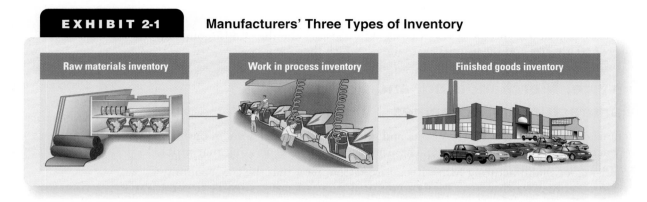

1. **Raw materials inventory:** *All raw materials used in manufacturing.* Nissan's raw materials include steel, glass, carpeting, tires, upholstery fabric, engines, and other automobile components. It also includes other physical materials used in the plant, such as machine lubricants and janitorial supplies.

2. **Work in process inventory:** *Goods that are partway through the manufacturing process but not yet complete.* At Nissan, the work in process inventory consists of partially completed vehicles.

3. **Finished goods inventory:** *Completed goods that have not yet been sold.* Nissan is in business to sell completed cars, not work in process. Manufacturers sell their finished goods inventory to merchandisers. Nissan, for example, sells its completed automobiles to retail dealerships. Some manufacturers, such as The Original Mattress Factory, sell their products directly to consumers.

Exhibit 2-2 summarizes the differences among service, merchandising, and manufacturing companies.

EXHIBIT 2-2 Service, Merchandising, and Manufacturing Companies

	Service Companies	Merchandising Companies	Manufacturing Companies
Examples	Advertising agencies Banks Law firms Insurance companies	Amazon.com Kroger Wal-Mart Wholesalers	Procter & Gamble DaimlerChrysler Dell Computer Nissan
Primary Output	Intangible services	Tangible products purchased from suppliers	New tangible products made as workers and equipment convert raw materials into new finished products
Type(s) of Inventory	None	Inventory (or Merchandise Inventory)	Raw materials inventory Work in process inventory Finished goods inventory

Stop & Think...

What type of company is Outback Steakhouse, Inc.?

Answer: Some companies don't fit nicely into one of the three categories discussed previously. Outback has some elements of a service company (it serves hungry patrons), some elements of a manufacturing company (its chefs convert raw ingredients into finished meals), and some elements of a merchandising company (it sells ready-to-serve bottles of wine and beer). Outback is really a hybrid of the three types of companies we just discussed.

As the "Stop & Think" shows, not all companies are strictly service, merchandising, or manufacturing firms. Recall from Chapter 1 that the U.S. economy is shifting more toward service. Many traditional manufacturers, such as General Electric (GE), have developed profitable service segments that provide much of their company's profits. General Motors now earns more from its financing and insurance operations than it does from car sales. Even merchandising firms are getting into the "service game" by selling extended warranty contracts on merchandise sold. Retailers offer extended warranties on products ranging from furniture and major appliances to sporting equipment and consumer electronics. While the merchandiser recognizes a liability for these warranties, the price charged to customers for the warranties greatly exceeds the company's cost of fulfilling its warranty obligations.

Which Business Activities Make Up the Value Chain?

2 Describe the value chain and its elements

Many people describe Nissan, Dell Computer, and Coca-Cola as manufacturing companies. But it would be more accurate to say that these are companies that *do* manufacturing. Why? Because companies that do manufacturing also do many other things. Nissan also conducts research to determine what type of new technology to integrate into next year's models. Nissan designs the new models based on its research and then produces, markets, distributes, and services the cars. These activities form Nissan's **value chain**—the activities that add value to products and services.

To set a selling price or to determine how profitable the Xterra model is, Nissan must know how much it costs to research, design, produce, market, distribute, and service the product. In other words, Nissan can't set selling prices high enough to *just* cover the costs of production. Pricing decisions require Nissan to calculate the *full cost* of the Xterra, including costs incurred across all six elements of the value chain pictured in Exhibit 2-3.

EXHIBIT 2-3   **The Value Chain**

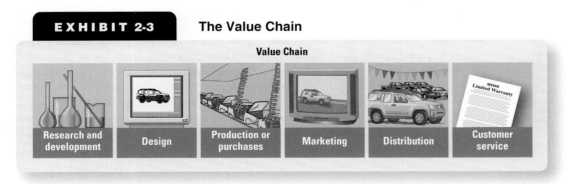

Research and Development (R&D): *Researching and developing new or improved products or services and the processes for producing them.* Nissan continually engages in researching and developing new technologies to incorporate in its vehicles (such as GPS systems, "smart keys," and automatic headlamps) and in its manufacturing plants (such as manufacturing robotics). Nissan's GREEN program aims at developing fuel cells for vehicles, new ultra-low emission vehicles, new hybrid vehicles, and better fuel economy on existing models. Nissan currently spends over ¥300 billion (approximately $2.6 billion) a year in R&D.

Design: *Detailed engineering of products and services and the processes for producing them.* Nissan's CEO describes design as the "interface between customers and the brand." Nissan's designers need to fulfill customers' desires for vehicle style, features, safety, and quality. Nissan's goal is to engineer its products to create "total customer satisfaction." (Nissan has embraced total quality management.) As a result, Nissan employs over 500 designers in North America and introduced 12 new models as part of its revival plan. Designers consider not only what the customers want but also how to mass-produce the vehicles. Because Nissan produces over 3 million vehicles per year, engineers must design production processes to be flexible (to allow for new features and models) and efficient. These initiatives cost a lot of money. Nissan's new technical center alone cost over $118 million to build. Despite these costs, new models and production designs were critical to Nissan's turnaround.

Production or Purchases: *Resources used to produce a product or service or to purchase finished merchandise intended for resale.* For a manufacturer such as Nissan, the production activity in the value chain includes the costs incurred to *make* the vehicles. These costs include raw materials (such as steel), plant labor (such as machine operators' wages and benefits), and manufacturing overhead (such as plant utilities and equipment depreciation). For a merchandiser such as Best Buy, this value-chain activity includes the cost of inventory, such as CDs, TVs, and PCs that the company buys to resell to customers. It also includes all costs associated with getting the inventory to the store ready for sale, including freight-in costs and any import duties and tariffs.

As part of Nissan's revival plan, it opened new manufacturing facilities, including a state-of-the-art facility in Canton, Mississippi. Nissan's new investments in plant and equipment cost over ¥377 billion (approximately $3.3 billion). These costs are part of the production stage of the value chain. Nissan was also able to cut some production costs. Nissan slashed purchasing costs over 20% by working with suppliers of major components, such as tires, engines, and steel. To cut costs through JIT production, some of Nissan's suppliers have moved their own manufacturing facilities right next door to Nissan's!

Marketing: *Promotion and advertising of products or services.* The goal of marketing is to create consumer demand for products and services. Nissan uses print advertisements in magazines and newspapers, billboards, and television advertising to market its vehicles. But Nissan's revival plan includes much more than simply advertising their new models. Part of its marketing effort was directed at the dealerships that sold its vehicles. Nissan worked with dealerships to make them more effective and attractive to consumers shopping for cars so that customers would "sense quality" when walking into a Nissan dealership's showroom. As a result, most dealerships improved their cosmetic appearance and interior layout.

Distribution: *Delivery of products or services to customers.* Nissan sells most of its vehicles through traditional dealerships. However, more customers are ordering "build-your-own" vehicles through Nissan's Web site. People who are willing to wait a short time can have the features they want rather than settle for one of the vehicles in stock at the local dealership. Forrester Research, an independent research firm specializing in the impact of technology on business and consumers, expects build-to-order car sales to account for 21% of all new car sales by 2010, up from 5% in 2001.[1] Nissan's distribution costs include the costs of shipping the vehicles to retailers and customers and the costs of setting up and administering Web-based sales portals. Other industries use different distribution mechanisms. Tupperware primarily sells its products through home-based parties. Amazon.com sells only through the Internet. Until recently, Lands' End sold only through catalogs and the Web. Now, it also distributes its products through Sears' retail outlets. WebVan tried, but failed, to create an online delivery-only grocery store.

Distribution

Customer Service: *Support provided for customers after the sale.* Nissan incurs substantial customer service costs, especially in connection with warranties on new car sales. Nissan generally warranties its vehicles for the first three years and/or 36,000 miles, whichever comes first. Nissan cut warranty costs by ¥41 million in 2004. How? Through total quality management (TQM). Nissan tests *every* vehicle rolling off the Canton plant production line before shipping it out. Nissan also emphasizes quality right from the start, beginning with R&D.

Customer service

Coordinating Activities Across the Value Chain

Many of the value-chain activities occur in the order discussed here. However, managers cannot simply work on R&D and not think about customer service until after selling the car. Rather, cross-functional teams work on R&D, design, production, marketing, distribution, and customer service simultaneously. As the teams develop new model features, they also plan how to produce, market, and distribute the redesigned vehicles. They also consider how the new design will affect warranty costs. Recall from the last chapter that management accountants typically participate in these cross-functional teams. Even at the highest level of global operations, Nissan used cross-functional teams to implement its revival plans.

The value chain in Exhibit 2-3 also reminds managers to control costs over the value chain as a whole. For example, Nissan spends more in R&D and product design to increase the quality of its vehicles, which, in turn, reduces customer service costs. Even though R&D and design costs are higher, the total cost of the vehicle—as measured throughout the entire value chain—is lower as a result of this tradeoff. Enhancing its reputation for high-quality products may also enable Nissan to increase sales or to charge higher selling prices.

The value chain applies to service and merchandising firms as well as manufacturing firms. For example, an advertising agency such as Saatchi & Saatchi incurs:

- *Design* costs to develop each client's ad campaign.
- *Marketing* costs to obtain new clients.
- *Distribution* costs to get the ads to the media.
- *Customer service* costs to address each client's concerns.

---

[1]Dave Hirshchman, "*Coming soon: built-to-order cars delivered in 10–15 days,*" *The Atlanta Journal Constitution*, March 25, 2001, p. Q1.

Determining the Costs to Serve a Customer or to Make a Product

How do companies such as eBay, Amazon.com, and Nissan determine how much it costs to serve a customer, fill an order, or produce an Xterra? Before we can answer this question, let's first consider some of the specialized language that accountants use when referring to costs.

3 Distinguish between direct and indirect costs

Cost Objects, Direct Costs, and Indirect Costs

A **cost object** is anything for which managers want a separate measurement of cost. Nissan's cost objects may include the following:

- Individual products (the Xterra, Pathfinder, and Altima)
- Alternative marketing strategies (sales through dealers versus built-to-order Web sales)
- Geographic segments of the business (United States, Europe, Japan)
- Departments (human resources, payroll, legal)

Costs are classified as either direct or indirect with respect to the cost object. A **direct cost** is a cost that can be traced to the cost object. For example, say the cost object is one Xterra. Nissan can trace the cost of tires to a specific Xterra; therefore, the tires are a direct cost of the vehicle. An **indirect cost** is a cost that relates to the cost object but cannot be traced to it. For example, Nissan incurs substantial cost to run the Xterra manufacturing plant, including utilities, property taxes, and depreciation on the plant and equipment. Nissan cannot build an Xterra without incurring these costs, so the costs are related to the Xterra. However, it's impossible to trace a specific amount of these costs to one Xterra. Therefore, these costs are indirect costs of an Xterra.

As shown in Exhibit 2-4, the same costs can be indirect with respect to one cost object yet direct with respect to another cost object. For example, plant and equipment

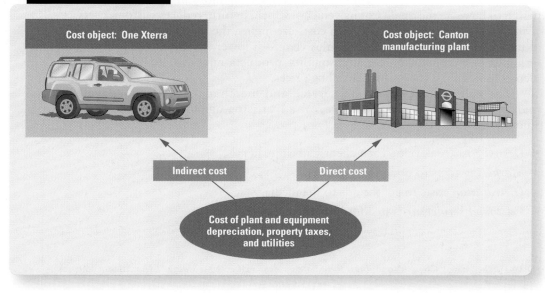

EXHIBIT 2-4 **The Same Cost Can Be Direct or Indirect, Depending on the Cost Object**

depreciation, property taxes, and utilities are indirect costs of an Xterra. However, if management wants to know how much it costs to run the Canton manufacturing plant, the plant becomes the cost object; so the same depreciation, tax, and utility costs are direct costs of the manufacturing facility. Whether a cost is direct or indirect depends on the specified cost object. In most cases, we'll be talking about a unit of product (such as one Xterra) as the cost object.

If a company wants to know the *total* cost attributable to a cost object, it must **assign** all direct *and* indirect costs to the cost object. Assigning a cost simply means that you are "attaching" a cost to the cost object. Why? Because the cost object caused the company to incur that cost. In determining the cost of an Xterra, Nissan assigns both the cost of the tires *and* the cost of running the manufacturing plant to the Xterras built at the plant. Nissan assigns direct costs to each Xterra by **tracing** those costs to specific units, or batches. However, because Nissan cannot trace indirect costs to specific units or batches, it must **allocate** these costs to the vehicles produced at the plant. We will discuss the allocation process in more detail in the next chapter; but for now, think of allocation as dividing up the indirect costs over all of the units produced, just as you might divide a pizza among friends. Exhibit 2-5 illustrates these concepts.

EXHIBIT 2-5   **Assigning Direct and Indirect Costs to Cost Objects**

Why is this terminology important? Because it helps managers understand how accountants arrive at cost figures. Direct costs are traced to cost objects so that managers and accountants are confident that the amount of direct cost assigned to a cost object is very accurate. For example, managers are confident in the tire cost assigned to one Xterra because they can *trace* a particular Xterra's four tires (plus a spare tire) back to a specific invoice. In contrast, indirect costs are *allocated* rather than traced; so the amount of indirect cost assigned to a cost object is more of an estimate. As a result, managers and accountants are less confident in the amount of indirect cost assigned each Xterra. Managers know the total amount of indirect costs from paying utility and tax bills and recording depreciation expense. However, the *division* of the total amount of indirect costs among the vehicles is less precise. Therefore, managers are less confident in the amount of indirect cost that should be assigned to the cost object (for example, the amount of utilities cost that should be assigned to a particular Xterra).

Identify the
inventoriable product
costs and period costs
of merchandising and
manufacturing firms

Product Costs for Internal Decision Making and External Reporting

Let's look more carefully at how companies determine the costs of one of the most common cost objects: products. As a manager, you'll want to focus on the products that are most profitable. But which products are these? To determine a product's profitability, you subtract the cost of the product from its selling price. But how do you calculate the cost of the product? Most companies use two different definitions of product costs: (1) full product costs for internal decision making and (2) inventoriable product costs for external reporting. Let's see what they are and how managers use each type of cost.

Full Product Costs for Internal Decision Making

Full product costs include the costs of *all resources used throughout the value chain*. For Nissan, the full product cost of a particular model is the total cost to research, design, manufacture, market, and distribute the model, as well as to service the customers who buy it. Before launching a new model, managers predict the full product costs of the vehicle to set a selling price that will cover *all costs* plus return a profit. Nissan also compares each model's sale price to its full cost to determine which models are most profitable. Perhaps Xterras are more profitable than Pathfinders. Marketing can then focus on advertising and promoting the most profitable models. We'll talk more about full costs in Chapter 8, where we discuss business decisions. For the next few chapters, we'll concentrate primarily on inventoriable product costs.

Inventoriable Product Costs for External Reporting

GAAP does not allow companies to use full product costs when reporting the cost of their inventories in the financial statements. For external reporting, GAAP allows only a *portion* of the full product cost to be treated as an inventoriable product cost. GAAP specifies which costs are inventoriable product costs and which costs are not. **Inventoriable product costs** include *only* the costs incurred during the "production or purchases" stage of the value chain (see Exhibit 2-6). Inventoriable product costs are treated as an asset (inventory) until the product is sold. When the product is sold, these costs are removed from inventory and expensed as cost of goods sold. Since inventoriable product costs include only costs incurred during the production or purchases stage of the value chain, all cost incurred in the *other* stages of the value chain must be expensed in the period in which they are incurred. Hence, we refer to R&D, design, marketing, distribution, and customer service costs as **period costs**. Period costs are often called "operating costs" or "selling, general, and administrative costs" (SG&A). Period costs are *never* part of an inventory asset account. Period costs are expensed in the period in which they are incurred.

Exhibit 2-6 shows that a company's full product cost has two components: inventoriable product costs (those costs treated as part of inventory until the product is sold) and period costs (those costs expensed in the current period regardless of when inventory is sold). GAAP requires this distinction for external financial reporting. Study the exhibit carefully to make sure you understand how the two components of full product costs—inventoriable product costs and period costs—affect the income statement and balance sheet.

Now that you understand the difference between inventoriable product costs and period costs, let's take a closer look at the costs that are inventoriable in merchandising and manufacturing companies. Inventoriable costs include only those costs incurred at the purchase stage in merchandising companies and at the production stage in manufacturing companies.

EXHIBIT 2-6   Full Product Costs, Inventoriable Product Costs, and Period Costs

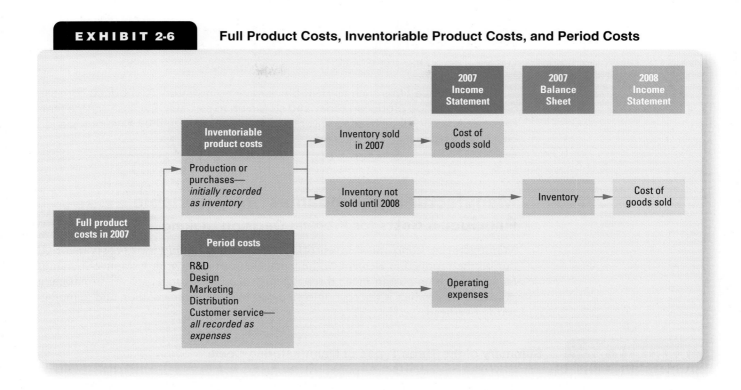

Merchandising Companies' Inventoriable Product Cost

Merchandising companies' inventoriable costs include *only* the cost of purchasing the inventory from suppliers plus any costs incurred to get the merchandise to the merchandiser's place of business and ready for sale. Typically, these additional costs include freight-in costs and import duties or tariffs, if any. Why does their inventory include freight-in charges? Think of the last time you purchased a shirt from a catalog such as J.Crew. The catalog may have shown the shirt's price as $30, but by the time you paid the shipping and handling charges, the shirt really cost you around $35. Likewise, merchandising companies pay freight charges to get the goods to their place of business (plus import duties if the goods were manufactured overseas). These charges become part of the cost of their inventory.

For instance, Home Depot's inventoriable costs include what the company paid for its store merchandise plus freight-in and import duty charges. Home Depot records these costs in an asset account—Inventory—until it *sells* the merchandise. Once the merchandise sells, it belongs to the customer, not Home Depot. Therefore, Home Depot takes the cost out of the inventory account and records it as an expense—the *cost of goods sold*. Home Depot expenses costs incurred in other elements of the value chain as period costs, such as employee salaries, advertising expenses, and store operating costs (for example, utilities and depreciation).

Some companies, such as Pier 1 Imports, refer to their cost of goods sold as "cost of sales." However, we use the more specific term *cost of goods sold* throughout the text because it more aptly describes the actual cost being expensed in the account—the inventoriable product cost of the goods themselves, not the total cost of making the sale (which would include selling and marketing costs).

Stop & Think...

What are the inventoriable costs for a service firm such as H&R Block?

Answer: Service firms such as H&R Block have no inventory of products for sale. Services cannot be produced today and stored up to sell later. Because service firms have no inventory, they have no inventoriable costs. Instead, they have only period costs that are expensed as incurred.

Manufacturing Companies' Inventoriable Product Cost

Manufacturing companies' inventoriable costs include *only* those costs incurred during the production element of the value chain. As shown in Exhibit 2-7, manufacturers such as Nissan incur three types of manufacturing costs when making a product (the product is the cost object): direct materials, direct labor, and manufacturing overhead.

EXHIBIT 2-7   **Summary of the Three Types of Manufacturing Costs**

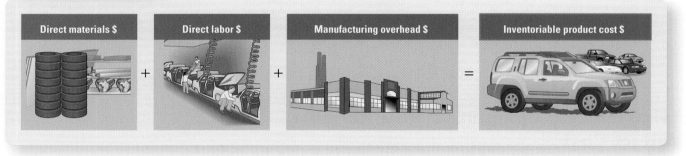

Direct Materials (DM)

Manufacturers convert raw materials into finished products. **Direct materials** are the *primary* raw materials that become a physical part of the finished product. Xterra's direct materials include steel, tires, engines, upholstery, carpet, and dashboard instruments such as the speedometer and odometer. Nissan can trace the cost of these materials (including freight-in and any other charges, such as import duties, necessary to obtain the materials) to specific units or batches of vehicles; thus, they are direct costs of the vehicles.

Direct Labor (DL)

Although many manufacturing facilities are highly automated, most still require some direct labor to convert raw materials into a finished product. **Direct labor** is the cost of compensating employees who physically convert raw materials into the company's products. At Nissan, direct labor includes the wages and benefits of assembly workers, machine operators, and technicians who assemble the parts and wire the electronics to build the completed vehicle. These costs are *direct* with respect to the cost object (the vehicle) because Nissan can *trace* the time each of these employees spends working on specific units or batches of vehicles.

Manufacturing Overhead (MOH)

The third production cost is manufacturing overhead. **Manufacturing overhead** includes all manufacturing costs other than direct materials and direct labor. Manufacturing overhead includes all *indirect* costs of production. Manufacturing overhead is also referred to as factory overhead because all of these costs relate to the factory. Manufacturers must incur these costs to produce their products; but because these costs are indirect, they can't be traced to individual units or batches. As a result, the amount of manufacturing overhead that should be assigned to each completed unit is more uncertain. The allocation process (discussed in Chapter 3) estimates the amount of manufacturing overhead to assign to each completed unit. As shown in Exhibit 2-8, manufacturing overhead includes indirect materials, indirect labor, and other indirect manufacturing costs.

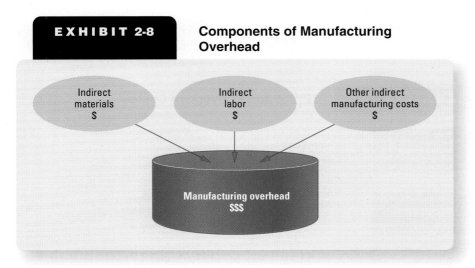

EXHIBIT 2-8　**Components of Manufacturing Overhead**

- **Indirect material** includes materials used in the plant that are not easily traced to individual units. For example, indirect materials often include janitorial supplies, oil and lubricants for the machines, and any physical components of the finished product that are inexpensive. For example, Nissan might treat the invoice sticker placed on each vehicle's window as an indirect material. Even though the cost of the sticker (about $0.10) *could* be traced to the vehicle, it wouldn't make much sense to do so. Why? Because the cost of tracing the sticker to the vehicle outweighs the benefit management receives from the increased accuracy of the information. Therefore, Nissan treats the cost of the sticker as indirect material, which becomes part of manufacturing overhead.

- **Indirect labor** includes the cost of all employees *in the plant* other than those employees directly converting the raw materials into the finished product. For example, at Nissan, indirect labor includes the salaries, wages, and benefits of plant forklift operators, plant security officers, plant janitors, and plant supervisors.

- **Other indirect manufacturing costs** include insurance and depreciation on the plant, plant equipment depreciation, plant property taxes, plant repairs and maintenance, and plant utilities. Indirect manufacturing costs have grown in recent years as manufacturers automate their plants. These costs continue to increase as manufacturers install the latest technology.

In summary, *manufacturing overhead includes only those indirect costs that are related to the manufacturing plant.* Insurance and depreciation on the *plant's* building and equipment are indirect manufacturing costs, so they are part of manufacturing overhead. In contrast, depreciation on *delivery trucks* is not a manufacturing cost. Delivery is part of the distribution element of the value chain, so its cost is a distribution expense (a period expense). Similarly, auto insurance for the sales force's vehicles is part of the marketing element of the value chain, so its cost is a marketing expense (a period expense). These two expenses are *not* part of *manufacturing* overhead because they do not relate to production at the plant.

Prime and Conversion Costs

Managers and accountants sometimes talk about certain combinations of manufacturing costs. As shown in Exhibit 2-9, **prime costs** refer to the combination of direct materials and direct labor. Prime costs used to be the primary costs of production. However, as companies have automated production with expensive machinery, manufacturing overhead has become a greater cost of production. **Conversion costs** refer to the combination of direct labor and manufacturing overhead. These are the costs of *converting* direct materials into finished goods.

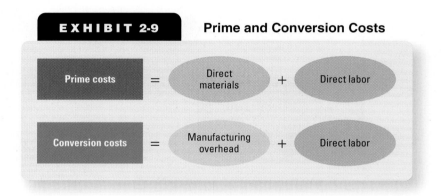

EXHIBIT 2-9   **Prime and Conversion Costs**

Prime costs = Direct materials + Direct labor

Conversion costs = Manufacturing overhead + Direct labor

Direct and Indirect Labor Compensation

The cost of direct and indirect labor includes more than the salaries and wages paid to the plant employees. The cost also includes company-paid fringe benefits such as health insurance, retirement plan contributions, payroll taxes, and paid vacations. These costs are very expensive. Health insurance premiums, which have seen double-digit increases for many years, often amount to $500 to $1,000 per month for *each* employee electing family coverage. Many companies also contribute an amount equal to 3% to 6% of their employees' salaries to company-sponsored retirement 401(k) plans. Employers must pay Federal Insurance Contributions Act (FICA) payroll taxes to the federal government for Social Security and Medicare, amounting to 7.65% of each employee's gross pay. In addition, most companies offer paid vacation and other benefits. Together, these fringe benefits usually cost the company an *additional* 35% beyond gross salaries and wages. Thus, an assembly-line worker who makes a $40,000 salary costs Nissan another $14,000 (= $40,000 × 35%) in fringe benefits. Believe it or not, for automobiles manufactured in the United States, the cost of health care assigned to the vehicle is greater than the cost of the steel in the vehicle! Throughout the remainder of this book, any references to wages or salaries also include the cost of fringe benefits.

Review: Inventoriable Product Costs or Period Costs?

Exhibit 2-10 summarizes the differences between inventoriable product costs and period costs for service, merchandising, and manufacturing companies. Study this exhibit carefully. When are such costs as depreciation, insurance, utilities, and property taxes inventoriable product costs? *Only* when those costs are related to the manufacturing plant. When those costs are related to nonmanufacturing activities such as R&D or marketing, they are treated as period costs. Service companies and merchandisers do no manufacturing, so they always treat depreciation, insurance, utilities, and property taxes as period costs. When you studied financial accounting, you studied nonmanufacturing firms. Therefore, salaries, depreciation, insurance, and taxes were always expensed.

EXHIBIT 2-10 **Inventoriable Product Costs and Period Costs for Service, Merchandising, and Manufacturing Companies**

	Inventoriable Product Costs	Period Costs
Accounting Treatment	• Initially recorded as inventory • Expensed only when inventory is sold	• Always recorded as an expense • Never considered part of inventory
Type of Company:		
Service company	• None	• All costs along the value chain • For example, salaries, depreciation expense, utilities, insurance, property taxes, and advertising
Merchandising company	• Purchases of merchandise • Freight-in; customs and duties	• All costs along the value chain *except* for the purchases element • For example, salaries, depreciation expense, utilities, insurance, property taxes, advertising, and freight-out
Manufacturing company	• Direct materials • Direct labor • Manufacturing overhead (including indirect materials, indirect labor, and other indirect manufacturing costs)	• All costs along the value chain *except* for the production element • For example, R&D; freight-out; all expenses for executive headquarters (separate from plant), including depreciation, utilities, insurance, and property taxes; advertising; and CEO's salary

Decision Guidelines

BUILDING BLOCKS OF MANAGERIAL ACCOUNTING

Dell engages in *manufacturing* when it assembles its computers, *merchandising* when it sells them on its Web site, and support *services* such as start-up and implementation services. Dell had to make the following types of decisions as it developed its accounting systems.

Decision	Guidelines

How do you distinguish among service, merchandising, and manufacturing companies? How do their balance sheets differ?	*Service companies:*
	• Provide customers with intangible services
	• Have no inventories on the balance sheet
	
	Merchandising companies:
	• Resell tangible products purchased ready-made from suppliers
	• Have only one category of inventory
	
	Manufacturing companies:
	• Use labor, plant, and equipment to transform raw materials into new finished products
	• Have three categories of inventory:
	  1. Raw materials inventory
	  2. Work in process inventory
	  3. Finished goods inventory

What business activities add value to companies?	All of the elements of the value chain, including: • R&D • Design • Production or Purchases • Marketing • Distribution • Customer Service
What costs should be assigned to cost objects such as products, departments, and geographic segments?	Both direct and indirect costs are assigned to cost objects. Direct costs are traced to cost objects, whereas indirect costs are allocated to cost objects.
Which product costs are useful for internal decision making, and which product costs are used for external reporting?	Managers use *full product costs* for product pricing and profitability decisions. However, GAAP requires companies to use only *inventoriable product costs* for external financial reporting.
What costs are inventoriable under GAAP?	• *Service companies:* No inventoriable product costs • *Merchandising companies:* Purchases and all costs of getting the merchandise to its place of business (for example, freight-in and import duties) • *Manufacturing companies:* Direct materials, direct labor, and manufacturing overhead
How are inventoriable product costs treated on the financial statements?	Inventoriable product costs are initially treated as assets (Inventory) on the balance sheet. These costs are expensed (as cost of goods sold) on the income statements when the products are sold.

Summary Problem1

Requirements

1. Classify each of the following business costs into one of the six value chain elements:
   a. Costs associated with warranties and recalls
   b. Cost of shipping finished goods to overseas customers
   c. Costs a pharmaceutical company incurs to develop new drugs
   d. Cost of a 30-second commercial during the Super Bowl
   e. Cost of making a new product prototype
   f. Cost of assembly labor used in the plant

2. For a manufacturing company, identify the following as either an inventoriable product cost or a period cost. If it is an inventoriable product cost, classify it as direct materials, direct labor, or manufacturing overhead.
   a. Depreciation on plant equipment
   b. Depreciation on salespeople's automobiles
   c. Insurance on plant building
   d. Marketing manager's salary
   e. Cost of major components of the finished product
   f. Assembly-line workers' wages
   g. Costs of shipping finished products to customers
   h. Forklift operator's salary

Solutions

Requirement 1

a. Customer service

b. Distribution

c. Research and Development

d. Marketing

e. Design

f. Production

Requirement 2

a. Inventoriable product cost; manufacturing overhead

b. Period cost

c. Inventoriable product cost; manufacturing overhead

d. Period cost

e. Inventoriable product cost; direct materials

f. Inventoriable product cost; direct labor

g. Period cost

h. Inventoriable product cost; manufacturing overhead

Inventoriable Product Costs and Period Costs in Financial Statements

5 Prepare the financial statements for service, merchandising, and manufacturing companies

The difference between inventoriable product costs and period costs is important because they are treated differently in the financial statements. All costs incurred in the production or purchases stage of the value chain are inventoriable product costs that remain in inventory accounts until the merchandise is sold—then, these costs become the cost of goods sold. However, costs incurred in all other areas of the value chain (R&D, design, marketing, distribution, and customer service) are period costs, which are expensed on the income statement in the period in which they are incurred. Keep these differences in mind as we review the financial statements of service firms (which have no inventory), merchandising companies (which purchase their inventory), and manufacturers (which make their inventory).

Service Companies

Service companies have the simplest accounting. Exhibit 2-11 shows the income statement of eNow!, a group of e-commerce consultants. The firm has no inventory and, thus, no inventoriable costs, so eNow!'s income statement has no Cost of Goods Sold. Rather, all of the company's costs are period costs, so they are shown grouped together under operating expenses.

EXHIBIT 2-11   **Service Company Income Statement**

eNOW!
Income Statement
Year Ended December 31, 2007

Revenues		$160,000
Operating expenses:		
Salary expense	$106,000	
Office rent expense	18,000	
Depreciation expense—furniture and equipment	3,500	
Marketing expense	2,500	
Total operating expenses		(130,000)
Operating income		$ 30,000

In this textbook, we always use "operating income" rather than "net income" as the bottom line on the income statement since internal managers are particularly concerned with the income generated through operations. To determine "net income," we would have to deduct interest expense and income taxes from "operating income" and add back interest income. In general, "operating income" is simply the company's income before interest and income taxes.

Merchandising Companies

In contrast with service companies, merchandisers' income statements feature Cost of Goods Sold as the major expense. Consider Apex Showrooms, a merchandiser of lighting fixtures. Apex's *only* inventoriable costs are for the purchase of chandeliers and track lights that it buys to resell, plus freight-in. Merchandisers such as Apex compute the Cost of Goods Sold as follows:[2]

Beginning inventory	$ 9,500	What Apex had at the beginning of the period
+ Purchases and freight-in	110,000	What Apex bought during the period
= Cost of goods available for sale	119,500	Total available for sale during the period
− Ending inventory.................	(13,000)	What Apex had left at the end of the period
= Cost of goods sold...............	$106,500	What Apex sold during the period

Exhibit 2-12 shows Apex's complete income statement, where we have highlighted the Cost of Goods sold computation. Notice that the Cost of Goods Sold is deducted from Sales Revenue to determine the company's gross profit. All operating expenses (period costs) are then deducted from gross profit to arrive at operating income.

EXHIBIT 2-12   **Merchandiser's Income Statement**

APEX SHOWROOMS
Income Statement
Year Ended December 31, 2007

Sales revenue		$150,000
Cost of goods sold:		
Beginning inventory......................................	$ 9,500	
Purchases and freight-in	110,000	
Cost of goods available for sale........................	119,500	
Ending inventory...	(13,000)	
Cost of goods sold		106,500
Gross profit		43,500
Operating expenses:		
Showroom rent expense	5,000	
Sales salary expense	4,000	9,000
Operating income..		$ 34,500

Manufacturing Companies

Exhibit 2-13 shows the income statement of Top-Flight, a manufacturer of golf equipment and athletic shoes. Compare its income statement with the merchandiser's income statement in Exhibit 2-12. The only difference is that the merchandiser (Apex) uses *purchases and freight-in* in computing Cost of Goods Sold, whereas the manufacturer (Top-Flight) uses the *cost of goods manufactured* (we've highlighted both in blue). Notice that the term **cost of goods manufactured** is in the past tense. It is the cost of manufacturing the goods that Top-Flight *finished producing during*

---

[2]To highlight the roles of beginning inventory, purchases, and ending inventory, we assume that Apex uses a periodic inventory system. However, even companies that use perpetual inventory systems during the year recalculate Cost of Goods Sold this way before preparing their annual financial statements.

2007. This is the manufacturer's cost to obtain new finished goods that are ready to sell. Thus, it is the counterpart to the merchandiser's *purchases*.

EXHIBIT 2-13	**Manufacturer's Income Statement**

TOP-FLIGHT
Income Statement
Year Ended December 31, 2007

Sales revenue		$65,000
Cost of goods sold:		
Beginning finished goods inventory	$ 6,000	
Cost of goods manufactured*	42,000	
Cost of goods available for sale	48,000	
Ending finished goods inventory	(8,000)	
Cost of goods sold		40,000
Gross profit		25,000
Operating expenses:		
Sales salary expense	3,000	
Delivery expense	7,000	10,000
Operating income		$15,000

*From the Schedule of Cost of Goods Manufactured in Exhibit 2-15.

Calculating the Cost of Goods Manufactured

The cost of goods manufactured summarizes the cost of activities that take place in a manufacturing plant over the period. Let's begin by reviewing these activities. Exhibit 2-14 reminds us that the manufacturer starts by buying direct materials, which are stored in Raw Materials Inventory until they are needed for production. During production, the company uses direct labor and manufacturing overhead to convert direct materials into a finished product.

These are all inventoriable product costs because they are related to manufacturing. All units being worked on are in Work in Process Inventory. When the units are completed, they move out of Work in Process Inventory into Finished Goods Inventory.

Finished goods are the only inventory that is ready to sell. The cost of the finished goods that the manufacturer sells becomes its Cost of Goods Sold on the income statement. Costs the manufacturer incurs in other (nonmanufacturing) elements of the value chain are operating expenses, or period costs, that are expensed in the period incurred. Exhibit 2-14 shows that these operating expenses are deducted from gross profit to obtain operating income.

Exhibit 2-15 shows how Top-Flight computes its cost of goods manufactured—the cost of the goods the plant *finished* during 2007. The computation of the cost of goods manufactured summarizes the activities and related costs incurred on Top-Flight's plant floor throughout 2007. For simplicity, we'll assume that Top-Flight's raw materials inventory contains only direct materials.[3]

---

[3]We assume that Top-Flight uses its indirect materials as soon as they are purchased rather than storing them in Raw Materials Inventory. In Chapter 3, we expand the discussion to include manufacturers who store indirect materials in the Raw Materials Inventory account until they are used in production.

| EXHIBIT 2-14 | **Manufacturing Company: Inventoriable Costs and Period Costs** |

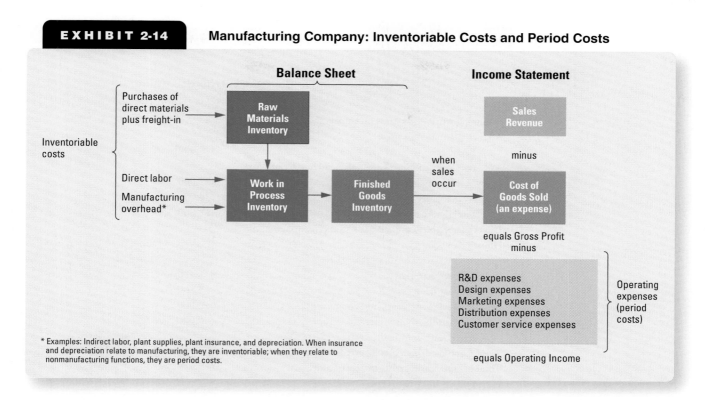

Exhibit 2-15 shows that Top-Flight begins 2007 with $2,000 of partially completed golf clubs and shoes that remained on the plant floor at the close of business on December 31, 2006.

During 2007, Top-Flight's production plant used $14,000 of direct materials, $19,000 of direct labor, and $12,000 of manufacturing overhead. The sum of these three costs ($45,000) represents the total manufacturing costs incurred during the year. Adding the total manufacturing costs incurred *during* the year ($45,000) to the *beginning* Work in Process Inventory balance ($2,000) gives the total manufacturing costs to account for ($47,000). This figure represents the total manufacturing cost assigned to *all* goods the plant worked on during the year. The plant finished most of these goods and sent them to Finished Goods Inventory, but some were not finished. By the close of business on December 31, 2007, Top-Flight had spent $5,000 on ending work in process inventory that lay partially complete on the plant floor.

The final step is to figure out the *cost of goods manufactured during 2007*— that is, the cost of the goods that Top-Flight *finished* during 2007. Of the $47,000 total manufacturing costs to account for during the year, $5,000 has been assigned to unfinished units in ending work in process inventory. That means the rest of the cost ($42,000) is assigned to units that were finished. Top-Flight's cost of goods manufactured for 2007 is $42,000 ($47,000 − $5,000).

EXHIBIT 2-15   Schedule of Cost of Goods Manufactured

TOP-FLIGHT
Schedule of Cost of Goods Manufactured
Year Ended December 31, 2007

Beginning work in progress inventory			$ 2,000
Add: Direct materials used			
Beginning raw materials inventory*	$ 9,000		
Purchases of direct materials including freight-in			
and any import duties	27,000		
Available for use	36,000		
Ending raw materials inventory	(22,000)		
Direct materials used		$14,000	
Direct labor		19,000	
Manufacturing overhead:			
Indirect materials	$ 1,500		
Indirect labor	3,500		
Depreciation—plant and equipment	3,000		
Plant utilities, insurance, and property taxes	4,000		
Manufacturing overhead		12,000	
Total manufacturing costs incurred during year			45,000
Total manufacturing costs to account for			47,000
Less: Ending work in process inventory			(5,000)
Costs of goods manufactured			$42,000

*For simplicity, we assume that Top-Flight's Raw Materials Inventory account contains only direct materials because the company uses indirect materials as soon as they are purchased. In Chapter 3, we expand the discussion to include manufacturers who store both direct and indirect materials in the Raw Materials Inventory account until they are used in production.

Flow of Costs Through Inventory Accounts

Exhibit 2-16 diagrams the flow of costs through Top-Flight's three inventory accounts. Notice how the final amount at each stage flows into the next stage. The format is the same for all three inventory accounts:

- Each inventory account starts with a beginning inventory balance.
- Top-Flight adds costs to each inventory account (it adds direct materials *purchased* to Raw Materials Inventory; it adds direct materials *used*, direct labor, and manufacturing overhead to Work in Process Inventory; and it adds the cost of goods manufactured to Finished Goods Inventory).
- Top-Flight subtracts the ending inventory balance to find out how much inventory passed through the account during the period *and on to the next stage*. At all stages, the flow of costs follows the flow of physical goods.

Take time to see how the Schedule of Cost of Goods Manufactured (Exhibit 2-15) captures the flow of costs through the Raw Materials and Work in Process Inventory accounts. The Income Statement (Exhibit 2-13) captures the flow of costs through the Finished Goods Inventory account. Some manufacturers combine the flow of costs through *all three* inventory accounts into one combined Schedule of Cost of Goods Manufactured and Cost of Goods Sold, and then show only the resulting Cost of Goods Sold figure on the income statement.

EXHIBIT 2-16 **Flow of Costs Through Top-Flight's Inventory Accounts**

Raw Materials Inventory		
Beginning inventory		$ 9,000
+ Direct materials purchased plus freight-in*		27,000
= Direct materials available for use		36,000
– Ending inventory		(22,000)
= Direct materials used*		$14,000

Work in Process Inventory		
Beginning inventory		$ 2,000
+ Direct materials used	$14,000	
+ Direct labor	19,000	
+ Manufacturing overhead	12,000	
Total manufacturing costs incurred during the year		45,000
= Total manufacturing costs to account for		47,000
– Ending inventory		(5,000)
= Cost of goods manufactured		$42,000

Finished Goods Inventory		
Beginning inventory		$ 6,000
+ Cost of goods manufactured		42,000
= Cost of goods available for sale		48,000
– Ending inventory		(8,000)
= Cost of goods sold		$40,000

*For simplicity, we assume that Top-Flight's Raw Materials Inventory account contains only direct materials because the company uses indirect materials as soon as they are purchased. In Chapter 3, we expand the discussion to include manufacturers who store both direct and indirect materials in the Raw Materials Inventory account until they are used in production.

Effects on the Balance Sheet

Now that we've looked at the income statement, let's turn our attention to the balance sheet. The only difference in the balance sheets of service, merchandising, and manufacturing companies relates to inventories. Exhibit 2-17 shows how the current asset sections of eNOW! (service company), Apex Showrooms (merchandising company), and Top-Flight (manufacturing company) might differ at the end of 2007. eNOW! has no inventory at all, Apex Showrooms has a single category of inventory, and Top-Flight has three categories of inventory (raw materials, work in process, and finished goods).

EXHIBIT 2-17 **Current Asset Sections of Balance Sheets**

eNOW! (SERVICE COMPANY)

Cash	$ 4,000
Accounts receivable	5,000
Prepaid expenses	1,000
Total current assets	$10,000

APEX SHOWROOMS (MERCHANDISING COMPANY)

Cash	$ 4,000
Accounts receivable	5,000
Inventory (Exhibit 2-12)	13,000
Prepaid expenses	1,000
Total current assets	$23,000

TOP-FLIGHT (MANUFACTURING COMPANY)

Cash		$ 4,000
Accounts receivable		5,000
Inventories:		
Raw materials inventory (Exhibit 2-15)	22,000	
Work in process inventory (Exhibit 2-15)	5,000	
Finished goods inventory (Exhibit 2-13)	8,000	
Total inventories		35,000
Prepaid expenses		1,000
Total current assets		$45,000

Other Cost Terms for Planning and Decision Making

So far in this chapter, we have discussed direct versus indirect costs and inventoriable product costs versus period costs. Now let's turn our attention to other cost terms that managers and accountants use when planning and making decisions.

 6 Describe costs that are relevant and irrelevant for decision making

Controllable Versus Uncontrollable Costs

As discussed in the chapter opening story, Nissan knew that it had to make changes if it was to stay in business. But what changes to make? Management had to distinguish controllable costs from uncontrollable costs. In the long run, most costs are **controllable**, meaning management is able to influence or change them. However, in the short run, companies are often "locked in" to certain costs arising from previous decisions. These are called **uncontrollable costs**. For example, Nissan had little or no control over the property tax and insurance costs of their existing plants. These costs were "locked in" when Nissan built its plants. Nissan could replace existing production facilities with different-sized plants in different areas of the world that might cost less to operate, but that would take time. To see immediate benefits, management had to change those costs that were controllable at present. For example, management could control costs of research and development, design, and advertising. Recall that Nissan's management chose to *increase* rather than decrease these costs! Management knew it would have to design and market new models to successfully compete. However, Nissan was able to *decrease* other controllable costs, such as the price paid for raw materials, by working with its suppliers. In short, management's plans to revitalize the company focused first on costs that were controllable in the short run.

Relevant and Irrelevant Costs

Decision making involves identifying various courses of action and then choosing among them. When managers make decisions, they focus on those costs and revenues that are relevant to the decision. For example, Nissan wanted to build a new state-of-the-art production facility. After considering alternative locations, management decided to build the facility in Canton, Mississippi. The decision was based on relevant information such as the **differential cost** of building and operating the facility in Canton versus building and operating the facility in other potential locations. Differential cost refers to the difference in cost between two alternatives.

Say you want to buy a new car. You narrow your decision to two choices: the Nissan Sentra or the Toyota Corolla. As shown in Exhibit 2-18, the Sentra you like costs $14,480, whereas the Corolla costs $15,345. Because sales tax is based on the sales price, the Corolla's sales tax is higher. However, your insurance agent quotes you a higher price to insure the Sentra ($365 per month versus $319 per month for the Corolla). All of these costs are relevant to your decision because they differ between the two cars. Other costs are not relevant to your decision. For example, both cars run on regular unleaded gasoline and have the same fuel economy ratings, so the cost of operating the vehicles is about the same. Likewise, you don't expect cost differences in servicing the vehicles because they both carry the same warranty and have received excellent quality ratings in *Consumer Reports*. Because you project operating and maintenance costs to be the *same* for both cars, these costs are irrelevant to your decision. In other words, they won't influence your decision either way. Based on your analysis, the differential cost is $1,825 in favor of the Corolla. Does this mean that you will choose the Corolla? Not necessarily. The Sentra may have some characteristics you like better, such as a particular paint color, more comfortable seating, or more trunk space. When making decisions, management must also consider qualitative factors (such as effect on employee morale) in addition to differential costs.

EXHIBIT 2-18   **Comparison of Relevant Information**

	Sentra	Corolla	Differential Cost
Car's price	$14,480	$15,345	($865)
Sales tax (8%) (rounded to the nearest dollar)	1,158	1,228	(70)
Insurance*	21,900	19,140	2,760
Total relevant costs	$37,538	$35,713	$1,825

*Over the five years (60 months) you plan to keep the car.

Another cost that is irrelevant to your decision is the cost you paid for the vehicle you currently own. Say you just bought a Ford F-150 pickup truck two months ago, but you've decided you need a small sedan rather than a pickup truck. The cost of the truck is a **sunk cost**. Sunk costs are costs that have already been incurred. Nothing you do now can change the fact that you already bought the truck. Thus, the cost of the truck is not relevant to your decision of whether to buy the Sentra versus the Corolla. The only thing you can do now is (1) keep your truck or (2) sell it for the best price you can get. Management often has trouble ignoring sunk costs when making decisions, even though they should. Perhaps they invested in a factory or a computer system that no longer serves the company's needs. Many times, new technology makes management's past investments in older technology look like bad decisions, even though they weren't at the time. Management should ignore sunk costs because its decisions about the future cannot alter decisions made in the past.

Fixed and Variable Costs

Managers cannot make good plans and decisions without first knowing how their costs behave. Costs generally behave as fixed costs or variable costs. We will spend all of Chapter 6 discussing cost behavior. For now, let's look just at the basics. **Fixed costs** stay constant in total over a wide range of activity levels. For example, let's say you decide to buy the Corolla, so your insurance cost for the year is $3,828 ($319 per month × 12 months). As shown in Exhibit 2-19, your insurance cost stays fixed whether you drive your car 0 miles, 1,000 miles, or 10,000 miles during the year.

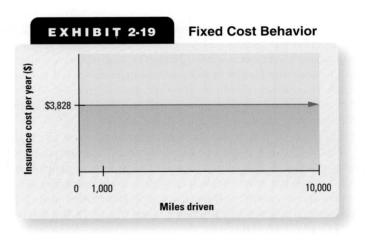

EXHIBIT 2-19   **Fixed Cost Behavior**

However, the total cost of gasoline to operate your car varies depending on whether you drive 0 miles, 1,000 miles, or 10,000 miles. The more miles you drive, the higher your total gasoline cost for the year. If you don't drive your car at all, you won't incur any costs for gasoline. Your gasoline costs are **variable costs**, as shown in Exhibit 2-20. Variable costs change in total in direct proportion to changes in volume. To accurately forecast the total cost of operating your Corolla during the year, you need to know which operating costs are fixed and which are variable.

---

7 Classify costs as fixed or variable and calculate total and average costs at different volumns

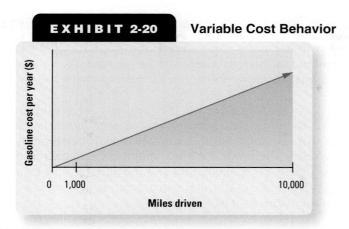

EXHIBIT 2-20   **Variable Cost Behavior**

How Manufacturing Costs Behave

Most companies have both fixed and variable costs. Manufacturing companies such as Nissan know that their direct materials are variable costs. The more cars Nissan makes, the higher its total cost for tires, steel, and parts. The behavior of direct labor is harder to characterize. Salaried employees are paid a fixed amount per year. Hourly wage earners are paid only when they work. The more hours they work, the more they are paid. Nonetheless, direct labor is generally treated as a variable cost because the more cars Nissan produces, the more assembly-line workers and machine operators it must employ. Manufacturing overhead includes both variable and fixed costs. For example, the cost of indirect materials is variable, while the cost of property tax, insurance, and straight-line depreciation on the plant and equipment is fixed. The cost of utilities is partially fixed and partially variable. Factories incur a certain level of utility costs just to keep the lights on. However, when more cars are produced, more electricity is used to run the production equipment. Exhibit 2-21 summarizes the behavior of manufacturing costs.

EXHIBIT 2-21   **The Behavior of Manufacturing Costs**

Calculating Total and Average Costs

Why is cost behavior important? Managers need to understand how costs behave to predict total costs and calculate average costs. In our example, we'll look at Nissan's total and average *manufacturing* costs; but the same principles apply to nonmanufacturing costs.

Let's say Nissan wants to predict the total cost of manufacturing 10,000 Xterras next year. To do so, Nissan must know its total fixed manufacturing costs and the variable cost of manufacturing each vehicle (direct material + direct labor + variable manufacturing overhead). Let's say total fixed manufacturing costs for the year at the Xterra plant are $20,000,000 and the variable cost of manufacturing each Xterra is $5,000. How much total manufacturing cost should Nissan budget for the year? Nissan calculates it as follows:

Total fixed cost + (Variable cost per unit × Number of units) = Total cost

$20,000,000 + ($5,000 per vehicle × 10,000 vehicles) = $70,000,000

What is the **average cost** of manufacturing each Xterra next year? It's the total cost divided by the number of units:

$$\frac{\text{Total cost}}{\text{Number of units}} = \text{Average cost per unit}$$

$$\frac{\$70,000,000}{10,000 \text{ vehicles}} = \$7,000 \text{ per vehicle}$$

If Nissan's managers decide they need to produce 12,000 Xterras instead, can they simply predict total costs as follows?

Average cost per unit × Number of units = Total cost???

$7,000 × 12,000 = $84,000,000???

No! They cannot! Why? *Because the average cost per unit is NOT appropriate for predicting total costs at different levels of output.* Nissan's managers should forecast total cost based on cost behavior:

Total fixed cost + (Variable cost per unit × Number of units) = Total cost

$20,000,000 + ($5,000 per vehicle × 12,000 vehicles) = $80,000,000

Why is the *correct* forecasted cost of $80 million less than the *faulty* prediction of $84 million? The difference stems from fixed costs. Remember, Nissan incurs $20 million of fixed manufacturing costs whether it makes 10,000 vehicles or 12,000 vehicles. As Nissan makes more Xterras, the fixed manufacturing costs are spread over more vehicles, so the average cost per vehicle declines. If Nissan ends up making 12,000 vehicles, the new average manufacturing cost per Xterra decreases as follows:

$$\frac{\text{Total cost}}{\text{Number of units}} = \text{Average cost per unit}$$

$$\frac{\$80,000,000}{12,000 \text{ vehicles}} = \$6,667 \text{ per vehicle (rounded)}$$

The average cost per unit is lower when Nissan produces more vehicles because it is using the fixed manufacturing costs more efficiently—taking the same $20 million of resources and making more vehicles with it.

> *The moral of the story: The average cost per unit is valid only at ONE level of output—the level used to compute the average cost per unit. Thus, NEVER use average costs to forecast costs at different output levels; if you do, you will miss the mark!*

Finally, a **marginal cost** is the cost of making *one more unit*. Fixed costs will not change when Nissan makes one more Xterra unless the plant is operating at 100% capacity (24 hours a day, 7 days a week, 365 days a year) and simply cannot make one more unit. (If that's the case, Nissan will need to incur additional costs to expand the plant.) So, the marginal cost of a unit is simply its variable cost.

As you have seen, management accountants and managers use specialized terms for discussing costs. They use different costs for different purposes. Without a solid understanding of these terms, managers are likely to make serious judgment errors.

Decision Guidelines

As a manufacturer, Dell needs to know how to calculate its inventoriable product costs for external reporting. Dell also needs to know many characteristics about its costs (that is, which are controllable, which are relevant to different decisions, which are fixed, and so forth) in order to plan and make decisions.

Decision	Guidelines
How do you compute cost of goods sold?	• *Service companies:* No cost of goods sold because they don't sell tangible goods • *Merchandising companies:* Beginning inventory + Purchases plus freight-in and import duties, if any = Cost of goods available for sale – Ending inventory = Cost of goods sold • *Manufacturing companies:* Beginning finished goods inventory + Cost of goods manufactured = Cost of goods available for sale – Ending finished goods inventory = Cost of goods sold
How do you compute the cost of goods manufactured for a manufacturer?	Beginning work in process inventory + Total manufacturing costs incurred during year (direct materials used + direct labor + manufacturing overhead) = Total manufacturing costs to account for – Ending work in process inventory = Cost of goods manufactured
How do managers decide which costs are relevant to their decisions?	Costs are relevant to a decision when they differ between alternatives and affect the future. Thus, *differential costs* are relevant, whereas *sunk costs* and costs that don't differ are not relevant.
How should managers forecast total costs for different production volumes?	To forecast total costs, managers should compute: $$\frac{\text{Total}}{\text{cost}} = \frac{\text{Total}}{\text{fixed costs}} + (\text{Variable cost per unit} \times \text{Number of units})$$ Managers should *not* use a product's *average cost* to forecast total costs because it will change as production volume changes. As production increases, the average cost per unit declines (because fixed costs are spread over more units).

Summary Problem 2

Requirements

1. Show how to compute cost of goods manufactured. Use the following amounts: direct materials used ($24,000), direct labor ($9,000), manufacturing overhead ($17,000), beginning work in process inventory ($5,000), and ending work in process inventory ($4,000).

2. Auto-USA spent $300 million in total to produce 50,000 cars this year. The $300 million breaks down as follows: The company spent $50 million on fixed costs to run its manufacturing plants and $5,000 of variable costs to produce each car. Next year, it plans to produce 60,000 cars using the existing production facilities.
   a. What is the current *average cost* per car this year?
   b. Assuming there is no change in fixed costs or variable costs per unit, what is the *total forecasted cost* to produce 60,000 cars next year?
   c. What is the *forecasted average cost* per car next year?
   d. Why does the average cost per car vary between years?

Solutions

Requirement 1
Cost of goods manufactured:

Beginning work in process inventory		$ 5,000
Add: Direct materials used	24,000	
Direct labor	9,000	
Manufacturing overhead	17,000	
Total manufacturing costs incurred during the period		50,000
Total manufacturing costs to account for		55,000
Less: Ending work in process inventory		(4,000)
Cost of goods manufactured		$51,000

Requirement 2

a. Total cost ÷ Number of units = Current average cost

   $300 million ÷ 50,000 cars = $6,000 per car

b. Total fixed costs + Total variable costs = Total projected costs

   $50 million + (60,000 cars × $5,000 per car) = $350 million

c. Total cost ÷ Number of units = Projected average cost

   $350 million ÷ 60,000 cars = $5,833 per car

d. The average cost per car decreases because Auto-USA will use the same fixed costs ($50 million) to produce more cars next year. Auto-USA will be using its resources more efficiently, so the average cost per unit will decrease.

Review Building Blocks of Managerial Accounting

Accounting Vocabulary

Allocate. (p. 79)
To assign an *indirect* cost to a cost object.

Assign. (p. 79)
To attach a cost to a cost object.

Average cost. (p. 98)
The total cost divided by the number of units.

Controllable Costs. (p. 92)
Costs that can be influenced or changed by management.

Conversion Costs. (p. 84)
The combination of direct labor and manufacturing overhead costs.

Cost Object. (p. 78)
Anything for which managers want a separate measurement of costs.

Cost of Goods Manufactured. (p. 89)
The manufacturing (or plant-related) cost of the goods that finished the production process this period.

Customer Service. (p. 77)
Support provided for customers after the sale.

Design. (p. 76)
Detailed engineering of products and services and the processes for producing them.

Differential Cost. (p. 95)
The difference in cost between two alternative courses of action.

Direct Cost. (p. 78)
A cost that can be traced to a cost object.

Direct Labor. (p. 82)
The cost of compensating employees who physically convert raw materials into the company's products; labor costs that are directly traceable to the finished product.

Direct Materials. (p. 82)
Primary raw materials that become a physical part of a finished product and whose costs are traceable to the finished product.

Distribution. (p. 77)
Delivery of products or services to customers.

Finished Goods Inventory. (p. 74)
Completed goods that have not yet been sold.

Fixed Costs. (p. 96)
Costs that stay constant in total despite wide changes in volume.

Full Product Costs. (p. 80)
The costs of all resources used throughout the value chain for a product.

Indirect Cost. (p. 78)
A cost that relates to the cost object but cannot be traced to it.

Indirect Labor. (p. 83)
Labor costs that are difficult to trace to specific products.

Indirect Materials. (p. 83)
Materials whose costs are difficult to trace to specific products.

Inventoriable Product Costs. (p. 80)
All costs of a product that GAAP requires companies to treat as an asset (inventory) for external financial reporting. These costs are not expensed until the product is sold.

Manufacturing Company. (p. 73)
A company that uses labor, plant, and equipment to convert raw materials into new finished products.

Manufacturing Overhead. (p. 83)
All manufacturing costs other than direct materials and direct labor. Also called factory overhead and indirect manufacturing cost.

Marginal Cost. (p. 99)
The cost of producing one more unit.

Marketing. (p. 76)
Promotion and advertising of products or services.

Merchandising Company. (p. 73)
A company that resells tangible products previously bought from suppliers.

Period Costs. (p. 80)
Operating costs that are expensed in the period in which they are incurred.

Prime Costs. (p. 84)
The combination of direct material and direct labor costs.

Production or Purchases. (p. 76)
Resources used to produce a product or service or to purchase finished merchandise intended for resale.

Raw Materials Inventory. (p. 74)
All raw materials (direct materials and indirect materials) not yet used in manufacturing.

Research and Development (R&D). (p. 76)
Researching and developing new or improved products or services or the processes for producing them.

Retailer. (p. 73)
Merchandising company that sells to consumers.

Service Company. (p. 73)
A company that sells intangible services rather than tangible products.

Sunk Cost. (p. 96)
A cost that has already been incurred.

Trace. (p. 79)
To assign a *direct* cost to a cost object.

Uncontrollable Costs. (p. 95)
Costs that cannot be changed or influenced in the short run by management.

Value Chain. (p. 75)
The activities that add value to a firm's products and services. Includes R&D, design, production or purchases, marketing, distribution, and customer service.

Variable Costs. (p. 96)
Costs that change in total in direct proportion to changes in volume.

Wholesaler. (p. 73)
Merchandising companies that buy in bulk from manufacturers, mark up the prices, and then sell those products to retailers.

Work in Process Inventory. (p. 74)
Goods that are partway through the manufacturing process but not yet complete.

■ Quick Check

1. Wal-Mart is a:
   a. service company
   b. retailer
   c. wholesaler
   d. manufacturer

2. Which is *not* an element of Nissan's value chain?
   a. administrative costs
   b. cost of shipping cars to dealers
   c. salaries of engineers who update car design
   d. cost of print ads and television commercials

3. For Nissan, which is a direct cost with respect to the Xterra?
   a. depreciation on plant and equipment
   b. cost of vehicle engine
   c. salary of engineer who rearranges plant layout
   d. cost of customer hotline

4. Which of the following is *not* part of Nissan's manufacturing overhead?
   a. insurance on plant and equipment
   b. depreciation on its North American corporate headquarters in Nashville
   c. plant property taxes
   d. plant utilities

5. In computing cost of goods sold, which of the following is the manufacturer's counterpart to the merchandiser's purchases?
   a. direct materials used
   b. total manufacturing costs incurred during the period
   c. total manufacturing costs to account for
   d. cost of goods manufactured

Questions 6, 7, and 8 refer to the following list. Suppose Nissan reports (in millions of dollars):

Beginning raw materials inventory	$ 6
Ending raw materials inventory	5
Beginning work in process inventory	2
Ending work in process inventory	1
Beginning finished goods inventory	3
Ending finished goods inventory	5
Direct labor	30
Purchases of materials	100
Manufacturing overhead	20

6. What is the cost of the materials that Nissan used (in millions)?
   a. 99
   b. 100
   c. 101
   d. 106

7. What is the cost of goods manufactured (in millions)?
   a. 149
   b. 150
   c. 151
   d. 152

8. What is the cost of goods sold (in millions)?
   a. 150
   b. 152
   c. 153
   d. 154

9. Which of the following is irrelevant to most business decisions?
    a. differential costs
    b. sunk costs
    c. variable costs
    d. qualitative factors

10. Which of the following is true?
    a. Total fixed costs increase as production volume increases.
    b. Total fixed costs decrease as production volume decreases.
    c. Total variable costs increase as production volume increases.
    d. Total variable costs stay constant as production volume increases.

Quick Check Answers

1. b 2. a 3. b 4. b 5. d 6. c 7. d 8. d 9. b 10. c

For Internet Exercises, Excel in Practice, and additional online activities, go to this book's Web site at www.prenhall.com/bamber.

Assess Your Progress

■ Learning Objectives

1 Distinguish among service, merchandising, and manufacturing companies

2 Describe the value chain and its elements

3 Distinguish between direct and indirect costs

4 Identify the inventoriable product costs and period costs of merchandising and manufacturing firms

5 Prepare the financial statements for service, merchandising, and manufacturing companies

6 Describe costs that are relevant and irrelevant for decision making

7 Classify costs as fixed or variable and calculate total and average costs at different volumes

■ Short Exercises

S2-1 **Indentify type of company from balance sheets** (*Learning Objective 1*)
The current asset sections of the balance sheets of three companies follow. Which company is a service company? Which is a merchandiser? Which is a manufacturer? How can you tell?

X-Treme		Y-Not?		Zesto	
Cash............	$ 2,500	Cash................	$3,000	Cash............	$ 2,000
Accounts receivable	5,500	Accounts receivable	6,000	Accounts receivable	5,000
Inventory.......	8,000	Prepaid expenses..........	500	Raw materials inventory.....	1,000
Prepaid expenses......	300	Total	$9,500	Work in process inventory.....	800
Total	$16,300			Finished goods inventory.....	4,000
				Total	$12,800

S2-2 **Identify types of companies and inventories** (*Learning Objective 1*)
Fill in the blanks with one of the following terms: *manufacturing, service, merchandising, retailer(s), wholesaler(s), raw materials inventory, merchandise inventory, work in process inventory, finished goods inventory, freight-in, the cost of merchandise.*
a. _____ companies generally have no inventory.
b. Boeing is a _____ company.
c. Merchandisers' inventory consists of _____ and _____.

d. _____ companies carry three types of inventories: _____,
_____, and _____.

e. Prudential Insurance Company is a _____ company.

f. Two types of _____ companies include _____ and _____.

g. Direct materials are stored in _____.

h. Sears is a _____ company.

i. Manufacturers sell from their stock of _____.

j. Labor costs usually account for the highest percentage of _____
companies' costs.

k. Partially completed units are kept in the _____.

S2-3 **Give examples of value chain functions** *(Learning Objective 2)*
Give an example of costs that E*TRADE (an online brokerage firm) might
incur in each of the six business functions in the value chain. Provide
another example that shows how E*TRADE might deliberately decide to
spend more money on one of the six business functions to reduce the costs
in other business functions.

S2-4 **Label value chain functions** *(Learning Objective 2)*
List the correct value chain element for each of the six business functions
described below.

a. Delivery of products and services

b. Detailed engineering of products and services and the processes for producing them

c. Promotion and advertising of product or services

d. Investigating new or improved products or services and the processes
for producing them

e. Support provided to customers after the sale

f. Resources used to make a product or obtain finished merchandise

S2-5 **Classify costs by value chain function** *(Learning Objective 2)*
Classify each of Hewlett-Packard's (HP's) costs as one of the six business
functions in the value chain.

a. Depreciation on Roseville, California, plant

b. Costs of a customer support center Web site

c. Transportation costs to deliver laser printers to retailers such as
Best Buy

d. Depreciation on research lab

e. Cost of a prime-time TV ad featuring the new HP logo

f. Salary of scientists at HP laboratories who are developing new printer
technologies

g. Purchase of plastic used in printer casings

h. Salary of engineers who are redesigning the printer's on-off switch

i. Depreciation on delivery vehicles

j. Plant manager's salary

S2-6   **Classify costs as direct or indirect** *(Learning Objective 3)*

Classify the following as direct or indirect costs with respect to a local Blockbuster store (the store is the cost object). In addition, state whether Blockbuster would trace or allocate these costs to the store.

a. Store utilities

b. The CEO's salary

c. The cost of the DVDs

d. The cost of national advertising

e. The wages of store employees

f. The cost of operating the corporate payroll department

g. The cost of Xbox, PlayStation, and Nintendo games

h. The cost of popcorn and candy sold at the store

S2-7   **Give examples of manufacturing costs** *(Learning Objective 4)*

Consider Marvin Windows' manufacturing plant. Give two examples of each of the following:

a. Direct materials

b. Direct labor

c. Indirect materials

d. Indirect labor

e. Other manufacturing overhead

S2-8   **Classify inventoriable and period costs** *(Learning Objective 4)*

Classify each of Georgia-Pacific's costs as either inventoriable product costs or period costs. Georgia-Pacific is a manufacturer of paper, lumber, and building material products.

a. Depreciation on the gypsum board plant

b. Purchase of lumber to be cut into boards

c. Life insurance on CEO

d. Salaries of scientists studying ways to speed forest growth

e. Cost of new software to track inventory during production

f. Cost of electricity at one of Georgia-Pacific's paper mills

g. Salaries of Georgia-Pacific's top executives

h. Cost of chemical applied to lumber to inhibit mold from developing

i. Cost of TV ads promoting environmental awareness

S2-9   **Classify a manufacturer's costs** *(Learning Objective 4)*

Classify each of the following costs as a period cost or an inventoriable product cost. If you classify the cost as an inventoriable product cost, further classify it as direct material (DM), direct labor (DL), or manufacturing overhead (MOH).

a. Depreciation on automated production equipment

b. Telephone bills relating to customer service call center

c. Wages and benefits paid to assembly-line workers in the manufacturing plant

d. Repairs and maintenance on factory equipment

e. Lease payment on administrative headquarters

f. Salaries paid to quality control inspectors in the plant

g. Property insurance—40% of building is used for sales and administration; 60% of building is used for manufacturing

h. Standard packaging materials used to package individual units of product for sale (for example, cereal boxes in which cereal is packaged)

S2-10 **Classify costs incurred by a dairy processing company** *(Learning Objective 4)*

Each of the following costs pertains to DairyPlains, a dairy processing company. Classify each of the company's costs as a period cost or an inventoriable product cost. Further classify inventoriable product costs as direct material (DM), direct labor (DL), or manufacturing overhead (MOH).

Cost	Period Cost or Inventoriable Product Cost?	DM, DL, or MOH?
1. Cost of milk purchased from local dairy farmers		
2. Lubricants used in running bottling machines		
3. Depreciation on refrigerated trucks used to collect raw milk from local dairy farmers		
4. Property tax on dairy processing plant		
5. Television advertisements for DairyPlains' products		
6. Gasoline used to operate refrigerated trucks delivering finished dairy products to grocery stores		
7. Company president's annual bonus		
8. Plastic gallon containers in which milk is packaged		
9. Depreciation on marketing department's computers		
10. Wages and salaries paid to machine operators at dairy processing plant		
11. Research and development on improving milk pasteurization process		

S2-11 **Determine total manufacturing overhead** *(Learning Objective 4)*

Snap's manufactures disposable cameras. Suppose the company's March records include the items described below. What is Snap's total manufacturing overhead cost in March?

Glue for camera frames	$ 250
Depreciation expense on company cars used by sales force	3,000
Plant depreciation expense	10,000
Interest expense	2,000
Company president's salary	25,000
Plant supervisor's salary	4,000
Plant janitor's salary	1,000
Oil for manufacturing equipment	25
Flashbulbs	50,000

S2-12 **Compute Cost of Goods Sold for a merchandiser** *(Learning Objective 5)*
Given the following information for Circuits Plus, an electronics e-tailer, compute the cost of goods sold.

Web site maintenance	$ 7,000
Delivery expenses	1,000
Freight-in	3,000
Import duties	1,000
Purchases	40,000
Ending inventory	5,500
Revenues	60,000
Marketing expenses	10,000
Beginning inventory	3,500

S2-13 **Prepare a retailer's income statement** *(Learning Objective 5)*
Salon Secrets is a retail chain specializing in salon-quality hair care products. During the year, Salon Secrets had sales of $38,230,000. The company began the year with $3,270,000 of merchandise inventory and ended the year with $3,920,000 of inventory. During the year, Salon Secrets purchased $23,450,000 of merchandise inventory. The company's selling, general, and administrative expenses totaled $6,115,000 for the year. Prepare Salon Secrets' income statement for the year.

S2-14 **Recalculate Cost of Goods Manufactured** *(Learning Objective 5)*
Turn to Exhibit 2-15. If direct material purchases and freight-in were $20,000 rather than $27,000, what would be the cost of direct materials used and the cost of goods manufactured? (Other costs remain the same as in Exhibit 2-15.)

S2-15 **Calculate direct materials used** *(Learning Objective 5)*
You are a new accounting intern at Sunny's Bikes. Your boss gives you the following information and asks you to compute the cost of direct materials used (assume that the company's raw materials inventory contains only direct materials).

Purchases of direct materials	$16,000
Import duties	1,000
Freight-in	200
Freight-out	1,000
Ending raw materials inventory	1,500
Beginning raw materials inventory	4,000

S2-16 **Compute Cost of Goods Manufactured** *(Learning Objective 5)*
Smith Manufacturing found the following information in their accounting records: $524,000 of direct materials used, $223,000 of direct labor, and $742,000 of manufacturing overhead. The Work in Process Inventory account had a beginning balance of $76,000 and an ending balance of $85,000. Compute the company's Cost of Goods Manufactured.

S2-17 **Consider relevant information** *(Learning Objective 6)*

You've been offered an entry-level marketing position at two highly respectable firms: one in Los Angeles, California, and one in Sioux Falls, South Dakota. What quantitative and qualitative information might be relevant to your decision? What characteristics about this information make it relevant?

S2-18 **Classify costs as fixed or variable** *(Learning Objective 7)*

Classify each of the following personal expenses as either fixed or variable. In some cases, your answer may depend on specific circumstances. If so, briefly explain your answer.

a. Apartment rental

b. Television cable service

c. Cost of groceries

d. Water and sewer bill

e. Cell phone bill

f. Health club dues

g. Bus fare

■ Exercises

E2-19 **Identify types of companies and their inventories** *(Learning Objective 1)*

Complete the following statements with one of the terms listed here. You may use a term more than once, and some terms may not be used at all.

Finished goods inventory	Inventory (merchandise)	Service companies
Manufacturing companies	Merchandising companies	Work in process inventory
Raw materials inventory	Wholesalers	Retailers

a. _____ produce their own inventory.

b. _____ typically have a single category of inventory.

c. _____ do not have tangible products intended for sale.

d. _____ resell products they previously purchased ready-made from suppliers.

e. _____ use their workforce and equipment to transform raw materials into new finished products.

f. _____ sell to consumers.

g. Swaim, a company based in North Carolina, makes furniture. Partially completed sofas are _____. Completed sofas that remain unsold in the warehouse are _____. Fabric and wood are _____.

h. For Kellogg's, corn, cardboard boxes, and waxed paper liners are classified as _____.

i. _____ buy in bulk from manufacturers and sell to retailers

E2-20 Classify costs along the value chain for a retailer *(Learning Objective 2)*
Suppose Kiwi Electronics incurred the following costs at its Charleston, South Carolina, store:

Research on whether store should sell satellite radio service	$ 400	Payment to consultant for advise on location of new store	$2,500
Purchases of merchandise	30,000	Freight-in	3,000
Rearranging store layout	750	Salespeople's salaries	4,000
Newspaper advertisements	5,000	Customer complaint department	800
Depreciation expense on delivery trucks	1,000		

Requirements

1. Use the following format to classify each cost according to its place in the value chain.

R&D	Design	Purchases	Marketing	Distribution	Customer Service

2. Compute the total costs for each value-chain category.
3. How much are the total inventoriable product costs?

E2-21 Classify costs along the value chain for a manufacturer *(Learning Objectives 2, 3)*
Suppose the cell phone manufacturer Harnum Electronics provides the following information for its costs last month (in hundreds of thousands):

Salaries of telephone salespeople	$ 5	Transmitters	$61
Depreciation on plant and equipment	65	Rearrange production process to accommodate new robot	2
Exterior case for phone	6	Assembly-line workers' wages	10
Salaries of scientists who developed new model	12	Technical customer support hotline	3
Delivery expense to customers via UPS	7	1-800 (toll-free) line for customer orders	1

Requirements

1. Use the following format to classify each cost according to its place in the value chain. (*Hint:* You should have at least one cost in each value-chain function.)

		Production					
R&D	Design of Products or Processes	Direct Materials	Direct Labor	Manufacturing Overhead	Marketing	Distribution	Customer Service

2. Compute the total costs for each value-chain category.
3. How much are the total inventoriable product costs?
4. How much are the total prime costs?
5. How much are the total conversion costs?

E2-22   **Classify costs as direct or indirect** *(Learning Objective 3)*

Classify each of the following costs as a *direct cost* or an *indirect cost* assuming the cost object is the produce department (fruit and vegetable department) of a local grocery store.

a.   Produce manager's salary

b.   Cost of the produce

c.   Store utilities

d.   Bags and twist ties provided to customers in the produce department for packaging fruits and vegetables

e.   Depreciation expense on refrigerated produce display shelves

f.   Cost of shopping carts and baskets

g.   Wages of checkout clerks

h.   Cost of grocery store's advertisement flyer placed in the weekly newspaper

i.   Store manager's salary

j.   Cost of equipment used to peel and core pineapples at the store

k.   Free grocery delivery service provided to senior citizens

l.   Depreciation on self-checkout machines

E2-23   **Define cost terms** *(Learning Objectives 3, 4)*

Complete the following statements with one of the terms listed here. You may use a term more than once, and some terms may not be used at all.

Prime costs	Cost objects	Inventoriable product costs
Assigned	Direct costs	Fringe benefits
Period costs	Assets	Cost of goods sold
Indirect costs	Conversion costs	Full product costs

a.   _____ can be traced to cost objects.

b.   _____ are expensed when incurred.

c.   _____ are the combination of direct materials and direct labor.

d.   Compensation includes wages, salaries, and _____.

e.   _____ are treated as _____ until sold.

f.   _____ include costs from only the production or purchases element of the value chain.

g.   _____ are allocated to cost objects.

h.   Both direct and indirect costs are _____ to _____.

i.   _____ include costs from every element of the value chain.

j.   _____ are the combination of direct labor and manufacturing overhead.

k.   _____ are expensed as _____ when sold.

l.   Manufacturing overhead includes all _____ of production.

E2-24 **Classify and calculate a manufacturer's costs** *(Learning Objectives 3, 4)*
An airline manufacturer incurred the following costs last month (in thousands of dollars):

a.	Airplane seats	$ 250
b.	Depreciation on administrative offices	60
c.	Assembly workers' wages	600
d.	Plant utilities	120
e.	Production supervisors' salaries	100
f.	Jet engines	1,000
g.	Machine lubricants	15
h.	Depreciation on forklifts	50
i.	Property tax on corporate marketing office	25
j.	Cost of warranty repairs	225
k.	Factory janitors' wages	30
l.	Cost of designing new plant layout	175
m.	Machine operators' health insurance	40
	TOTAL	$2,690

Requirements

1. If the cost object is an airplane, classify each cost as one of the following: direct material (DM), direct labor (DL), indirect labor (IL), indirect materials (IM), other manufacturing overhead (other MOH), or period cost. (*Hint:* Set up a column for each type of cost.) What is the total for each type of cost?
2. Calculate total manufacturing overhead costs.
3. Calculate total inventoriable product costs.
4. Calculate total prime costs.
5. Calculate total conversion costs.
6. Total period costs.

E2-25 **Prepare the current assest section of the balance sheet** *(Learning Objective 5)*
Consider the following selected amounts and account balances of Lawrence:

Cost of goods sold	$104,000	Prepaid expenses	$ 6,000
Direct labor	47,000	Marketing expense	30,000
Direct materials used	20,000	Work in process inventory	40,000
Accounts receivable	80,000	Manufacturing overhead	26,000
Cash	15,000	Finished goods inventory	63,000
Cost of goods manufactured	94,000	Raw materials inventory	10,000

Show how Lawrence reports current assets on the balance sheet. Not all data are used. Is Lawrence a service company, a merchandiser, or a manufacturer? How do you know?

E2-26   Prepare a retailer's income statement *(Learning Objective 5)*

Robbie Roberts is the sole proprietor of Pampered Pups, an e-tail business specializing in the sale of high-end pet gifts and accessories. Pampered Pups' sales totaled $987,000 during 2007. During the year, the company spent $56,000 on expenses relating to Web site maintenance; $22,000 on marketing; and $25,000 on wrapping, boxing, and shipping the goods to customers. Pampered Pups also spent $642,000 on inventory purchases and an additional $21,000 on freight-in charges. The company started the year with $17,000 of inventory on hand and ended the year with $15,000 of inventory. Prepare Pampered Pups' 2007 income statement.

E2-27   Compute direct materials used and cost of goods manufactured *(Learning Objective 5)*

Ivanhoe's Die-cuts is preparing its Cost of Goods Manufactured Schedule at year-end. Ivanhoe's accounting records show the following: The Raw Materials Inventory account had a beginning balance of $13,000 and an ending balance of $17,000. During the year, Ivanhoe purchased $58,000 of direct materials. Direct labor for the year totaled $123,000, while manufacturing overhead amounted to $152,000. The Work in Process Inventory account had a beginning balance of $21,000 and an ending balance of $15,000. Compute the Cost of Goods Manufactured for the year. (*Hint:* The first step is to calculate the direct materials used during the year. Model your answer after Exhibit 2-15.)

E2-28   Compute cost of goods manufactured and cost of goods sold *(Learning Objective 5)*

Compute the 2007 cost of goods manufactured and cost of goods sold for Goodrow Marine Company using the amounts described below. Assume that raw materials inventory contains only direct materials.

	Beginning of Year	End of Year		End of Year
Raw materials inventory	$25,000	$28,000	Insurance on plant....................	$ 9,000
Work in process inventory	50,000	35,000	Depreciation—plant building and equipment	13,000
Finished goods inventory........	18,000	25,000	Repairs and maintenance— plant.....................................	4,000
Purchases of direct materials.....		78,000	Marketing expenses.................	77,000
Direct labor...........................		82,000	General and administrative expenses.............................	29,000
Indirect labor		15,000		

E2-29   Continues E2-28: Prepare income statement *(Learning Objective 5)*

Prepare the 2007 income statement for Goodrow Marine Company in E2-28. Assume that the company sold 32,000 units of its product at a price of $12 each during 2007.

E2-30   Work backwards to find missing amounts *(Learning Objective 5)*

Super Sounds manufactures and sells a new line of MP3 players. Unfortunately, Super Sounds suffered serious fire damage at its home office. As a result, the accounting records for October were partially destroyed—and completely jumbled. Super Sounds has hired you to help figure out the missing pieces of the accounting puzzle. Assume that Super Sounds' raw materials inventory contains only direct materials.

continued . . .

Work in process inventory, October 31........................	$ 1,500
Finished goods inventory, October 1.............................	4,300
Direct labor in October..	3,000
Purchases of direct materials in October	9,000
Work in process inventory, October 1...........................	0
Revenues in October..	27,000
Gross profit in October..	12,000
Direct materials used in October..................................	8,000
Raw materials inventory, October 31............................	3,000
Manufacturing overhead in October	6,300

Requirement

Find the following amounts:

a. Cost of goods sold in October

b. Beginning raw materials inventory

c. Ending finished goods inventory
   (*Hint:* You may find Exhibits 2-15 and 2-16 helpful.)

E2-31 **Determine whether information is relevant** *(Learning Objective 6)*
Classify each of the following costs as relevant or irrelevant to the decision at hand and briefly explain your reason.

a. Cost of operating automated production machinery versus the cost of direct labor when deciding whether to automate production

b. Cost of computers purchased six months ago when deciding whether to upgrade to computers with a faster processing speed

c. Cost of purchasing packaging materials from an outside vendor when deciding whether to continue manufacturing the packaging materials in-house

d. The property tax rates in different locales when deciding where to locate the company's headquarters

e. The type of gas (regular or premium) used by delivery vans when deciding which make and model of van to purchase for the company's delivery van fleet

f. Depreciation expense on old manufacturing equipment when deciding whether to replace it with newer equipment

g. The fair market value of old manufacturing equipment when deciding whether to replace it with new equipment

h. The interest rate paid on invested funds when deciding how much inventory to keep on hand

i. The cost of land purchased three years ago when deciding whether to build on the land now or wait two more years

j. The total amount of the restaurant's fixed costs when deciding whether to add additional items to the menu

E2-32 **Describe other cost terms** (*Learning Objectives 6, 7*)
Complete the following statements with one of the terms listed here. You may use a term more than once, and some terms may not be used at all.

Differential costs	Irrelevant costs	Controllable costs
Marginal costs	Sunk costs	Average cost
Uncontrollable costs	Fixed costs	Variable costs

a. Managers cannot influence _____ in the short run.

b. Total _____ decrease when production volume decreases.

c. For decision-making purposes, costs that do not differ between alternatives are _____ .

d. Costs that have already been incurred are called _____ .

e. Total _____ stay constant over a wide range of production volumes.

f. The _____ is the difference in cost between two alternative courses of action.

g. The product's _____ is the cost of making one more unit.

h. A product's _____ and _____ , not the product's _____ , should be used to forecast total costs at different production volumes.

E2-33 **Classify costs as fixed or variable** (*Learning Objective 7*)
Classify each of the following costs as fixed or variable:

a. Thread used by a garment manufacturer

b. Property tax on a manufacturing facility

c. Yearly salaries paid to sales staff

d. Gasoline used to operate delivery vans

e. Annual contract for pest (insect) control

f. Boxes used to package breakfast cereal at Kellogg's

g. Straight-line depreciation on production equipment

h. Cell phone bills for sales staff—contract billed at $.03 cents per minute

i. Wages paid to hourly assembly-line workers in the manufacturing plant

j. Monthly lease payment on administrative headquarters

k. Commissions paid to the sales staff—5% of sales revenue

l. Credit card transaction fee paid by retailer—$0.20 per transaction plus 2% of the sales amount

m. Annual business license fee from city

n. Cost of ice cream sold at Baskin-Robbins

o. Cost of shampoo used at a hair salon

E2-34 **Compute total and average costs** (*Learning Objective 7*)
Apricot-Cola spends $1 on direct materials, direct labor, and variable manufacturing overhead for every unit (12-pack of soda) it produces. Fixed manufacturing overhead costs $5 million per year. The plant, which is currently operating at only 75% of capacity, produced 20 million units this year. Management plans to operate closer to full capacity next year, producing 25 million units. Management doesn't anticipate any changes in the prices it pays for materials, labor, and overhead.

continued . . .

a. What is the current total product cost (for the 20 million units), including fixed and variable costs?

b. What is the current average product cost per unit?

c. What is the current fixed cost per unit?

d. What is the forecasted total product cost next year (for the 25 million units)?

e. What is the forecasted average product cost next year?

f. What is the forecasted fixed cost per unit?

g. Why does the average product cost decrease as production increases?

■ Problems (Problem Set A)

P2-35A Classify costs along the value chain (*Learning Objectives 2, 4*)

Peach Cola produces a lemon-lime soda. The production process starts with workers mixing the lemon syrup and lime flavors in a secret recipe. The company enhances the combined syrup with caffeine. Finally, Peach dilutes the mixture with carbonated water.

Peach Cola incurs the following costs (in thousands):

Plant utilities	$ 750
Depreciation on plant and equipment	3,000
Payment for new recipe	1,000
Salt	25
Replace products with expired dates upon customer complaint	50
Rearranging plant layout	1,100
Lemon syrup	18,000
Lime flavoring	1,000
Production costs of "cents-off" store coupons for customers	600
Delivery truck drivers' wages	250
Bottles	1,300
Sales commissions	400
Plant janitors' wages	1,000
Wages of workers who mix syrup	8,000
Customer hotline	200
Depreciation on delivery trucks	150
Freight-in on materials	1,500
Total	$38,325

Requirements

1. Use the following format to classify each of these costs according to its place in the value chain. (*Hint:* You should have at least one cost in each value-chain function.)

R&D	Design of Products or Processes	Production			Marketing	Distribution	Customer Service
		Direct Materials	Direct Labor	Manufacturing Overhead			

2. Compute the total costs for each value-chain category.

3. How much are the total inventoriable product costs?

4. Suppose the managers of the R&D and design functions receive year-end bonuses based on meeting their unit's target cost reductions. What are they likely to do? How might this affect costs incurred in other elements of the value chain?

P2-36A **Prepare income statements** *(Learning Objective 5)*

Part One: In 2007, Amy Lee opened Amy's Pets, a small retail shop selling pet supplies. On December 31, 2007, her accounting records show the following:

Inventory on December 31, 2007	$10,250
Inventory on January 1, 2007	15,000
Sales revenue	54,000
Utilities for shop	2,450
Rent for shop	4,000
Sales commissions	2,300
Purchases of merchandise	27,000

Requirement

Prepare an income statement for Amy's Pets, a merchandiser, for the year ended December 31, 2007.

Part Two: Amy's Pets succeeded so well that Amy decided to manufacture her own brand of pet toys—Zippy Manufacturing. At the end of December 2008, her accounting records show the following:

Work in process inventory, December 31, 2008	$ 720
Finished goods inventory, December 31, 2007	0
Finished goods inventory, December 31, 2008	5,700
Sales revenue	105,000
Customer service hotline expense	1,000
Utilities for plant	4,600
Delivery expense	1,500
Sales salaries expense	5,000
Plant janitorial services	1,250
Direct labor	18,300
Direct material purchases	31,000
Rent on manufacturing plant	9,000
Raw materials inventory, December 31, 2007	13,500
Raw materials inventory, December 31, 2008	9,275
Work in process inventory, December 31, 2007	0

Requirements

1. Prepare a schedule of cost of goods manufactured for Zippy Manufacturing for the year ended December 31, 2008.

2. Prepare an income statement for Zippy Manufacturing for the year ended December 31, 2008.

continued . . .

3. How does the format of the income statement for Zippy Manufacturing differ from the income statement of Amy's Pets?

Part Three: Show the ending inventories that would appear on these balance sheets:

1. Amy's Pets at December 31, 2007
2. Zippy Manufacturing at December 31, 2008

P2-37A Fill in missing amounts (*Learning Objective 5*)

Certain item descriptions and amounts are missing from the monthly schedule of cost of goods manufactured below and the income statement of Rollins Manufacturing. Fill in the missing items.

ROLLINS MANUFACTURING COMPANY

_____ June 30, 2007

				$ 21,000
Beginning _____				
Add: Direct _____ :				
Beginning raw materials inventory	$ X			
Purchases of direct materials	51,000			
_____	78,000			
Ending raw materials inventory	(23,000)			
Direct _____		$ X		
Direct _____		X		
Manufacturing overhead		40,000		
Total _____ costs _____				166,000
Total _____ costs _____				X
Less: Ending _____				(25,000)
_____				$ X

ROLLINS MANUFACTURING COMPANY

_____ June 30, 2007

Sales revenue			$ X
Cost of goods sold:			
Beginning _____	$115,000		
_____	X		
Cost of goods _____	X		
Ending _____	X		
Cost of goods sold			209,000
Gross profit			254,000
_____ expenses:			
Marketing expense	99,000		
Administrative expense	X		154,000
_____ income			$ X

P2-38A **Identify relevant information** *(Learning Objective 6)*

You receive two job offers in the same big city. The first job is close to your parents' house, and they have offered to let you live at home for a year so you won't have to incur expenses for housing, food, or cable TV. This job pays $30,000 per year. The second job is far from your parents' house, so you'll have to rent an apartment with parking ($6,000 per year), buy your own food ($2,400 per year), and pay for your own cable TV ($600 per year). This job pays $35,000 per year. You still plan to do laundry at your parents' house once a week if you live in the city, and you plan to go into the city once a week to visit with friends if you live at home. Thus, the cost of operating your car will be about the same either way. In addition, your parents refuse to pay for your cell phone service ($720 per year), and you can't function without it.

Requirements

a. Based on this information alone, what is the net difference between the two alternatives (salary, net of relevant costs)?

b. What information is irrelevant? Why?

c. What qualitative information is relevant to your decision?

d. Assume that you really want to take Job #2, but you also want to live at home to cut costs. What new quantitative and qualitative information will you need to incorporate into your decision?

P2-39A **Calculate the total and average costs** *(Learning Objective 7)*

The owner of Pizza-Shack Restaurant is disappointed because the restaurant has been averaging 3,000 pizza sales per month, but the restaurant and wait staff can make and serve 5,000 pizzas per month. The variable cost (for example, ingredients) of each pizza is $2.00. Monthly fixed costs (for example, depreciation, property taxes, business license, and manager's salary) are $6,000 per month. The owner wants cost information about different volumes so that he can make some operating decisions.

Requirements

1. Fill in the chart below to provide the owner with the cost information he wants. Then use the completed chart to help you answer the remaining questions.

Monthly pizza volume	2,500	3,000	5,000
Total fixed costs	$	$	$
Total variable costs			
Total costs			
Fixed cost per pizza	$	$	$
Variable cost per pizza			
Average cost per pizza			
Sales price per pizza	$10.00	$10.00	$10.00
Average profit per pizza			

2. From a cost standpoint, why do companies such as Pizza-Shack Restaurant want to operate near or at full capacity?

continued . . .

3. The owner has been considering ways to increase the sales volume. He believes he could sell 5,000 pizzas a month by cutting the sales price from $10 a pizza to $9.50. How much extra profit (above the current level) would he generate if he decreased the sales price? (*Hint:* Find the restaurant's current monthly profit and compare it to the restaurant's projected monthly profit at the new sales price and volume.)

4. The owner's other idea is to advertise his restaurant on the local radio stations. If he keeps the sales price at $10 per pizza, the advertising agency says he'll have to spend $10,000 in advertising each month to increase monthly sales to 5,000 pizzas. How much extra profit (above the current level) would he generate if he kept the sales price at $10 per pizza but spent $10,000 per month on advertising? Which of the owner's ideas is most profitable?

5. The owner is surprised by your calculations. Because the current average profit per pizza is $6.00, he thought the restaurant would make $30,000 of income per month (before advertising costs) if it sold 5,000 pizzas at the normal $10 sales price. How did the owner arrive at this figure, and why is it wrong?

■ Problems (Problem Set B)

P2-40B Classify costs along the value chain (*Learning Objectives 2, 4*)

Suppose Apple Computer reported the following costs last month (all costs are in millions):

Payment to UPS for delivering PCs to customers............	$ 300
Cost of hard drives used...	4,700
Cost of Internet banner ads..	650
Plant janitors' wages	10
Wages of workers who assemble the PCs	1,500
Cost of customer hotline for troubleshooting problems	40
Wages of forklift drivers on the plant floor	25
Plant utilities	35
Cost of software loaded on computers	30
Depreciation on plant and equipment	300
Salaries of scientists working on next-generation laptops....	45
Insurance and taxes on plant property	40
Cost of oil used for conveyor belts and other plant equipment...	5
Payment to engineers redesigning the exterior case.........	20
Wages of sales associates taking phone orders................	50
Cost of circuit boards used...	5,500
Total	$13,250

1. Use the following format to classify each of these costs according to its place in the value chain. (*Hint:* You should have at least one cost in each value-chain function.)

R&D	Design of Products or Processes	Production			Marketing	Distribution	Customer Service
		Direct Materials	Direct Labor	Manufacturing Overhead			

2. Compute the total costs for each category.

3. How much are the total inventoriable product costs?

4. Suppose the managers of the R&D and design departments receive year-end bonuses based on meeting their department's target cost reductions. What are they likely to do? How might this affect costs incurred in other elements of the value chain?

P2-41B Prepare income statements (*Learning Objective 5*)

Part One: On January 1, 2007, Terri Shaw opened Golden Memories, a small retail store dedicated to selling picture frames, crafts, and art. On December 31, 2007, her accounting records show the following:

Store rent	$ 7,000
Sales salaries	4,500
Freight-in	550
Inventory on December 31, 2007	8,750
Sales revenue	90,000
Store utilities	1,950
Purchases of merchandise	36,000
Inventory on January 1, 2007	12,700
Advertising expense	2,300

Requirement

Prepare an income statement for Golden Memories, a merchandiser, for the year ended December 31, 2007.

continued . . .

Part Two: Golden Memories succeeded so well that Shaw decided to manufacture her own special brand of picture frames, to be called Madeline Manufacturing. At the end of December 2009, her accounting records show the following:

Finished goods inventory, December 31, 2009	$ 2,000
Work in process inventory, December 31, 2009	1,750
Raw materials inventory, December 31, 2009	7,750
R&D for graphic designs	3,700
Sales commissions	4,000
Utilities for plant	2,000
Plant janitorial services	750
Direct labor	20,000
Direct material purchases	32,000
Rent on plant	11,000
Finished goods inventory, December 31, 2008	0
Depreciation expense on delivery truck	2,500
Depreciation expense on plant equipment	3,500
Work in process inventory December 31, 2008	0
Sales revenue	126,450
Customer warranty refunds	1,500
Raw materials inventory, December 31, 2008	13,000

Requirements

1. Prepare a schedule of cost of goods manufactured for Madeline Manufacturing for the year ended December 31, 2009.
2. Prepare an income statement for Madeline Manufacturing for the year ended December 31, 2009.
3. How does the format of the income statement for Madeline Manufacturing differ from the income statement of Golden Memories?

Part Three: Show the ending inventories that would appear on these balance sheets:

1. Golden Memories at December 31, 2007
2. Madeline Manufacturing at December 31, 2009

P2-42B Fill in missing amounts *(Learning Objective 5)*

Certain item descriptions and amounts are missing from the monthly schedule of cost of goods manufactured and income statement of Pace Manufacturing Company. Fill in the missing items.

PACE MANUFACTURING COMPANY

_____ April 30, 2007

_____ work in process inventory			$ 15,000
Add: Direct materials used:			
_____ materials _____	$ X		
_____ of direct materials	65,000		
_____	75,000		
_____ materials _____	(23,000)		
Direct _____		$ X	
Direct _____		68,000	
Manufacturing overhead		X	
Total _____ costs _____			X
Total _____ costs _____			175,000
Less: _____ work in process inventory			X
_____			$150,000

PACE MANUFACTURING COMPANY

_____ April 30, 2007

_____ revenue		$450,000
_____:		
Beginning _____	$ X	
_____	X	
Cost of goods _____	X	
Ending _____	(67,000)	
Cost of goods sold		X
_____		243,000
_____ expenses:		
Marketing expenses	X	
Administrative expenses	$64,000	X
_____		$ 76,000

P2-43B Identify relevant information *(Learning Objective 6)*

You receive two job offers in the same big city. The first job is close to your parents' house, and they have offered to let you live at home for a year so you won't have to incur expenses for housing, food, or cable TV. This job pays $45,000 per year. The second job is far away from your parents' house, so you'll have to rent an apartment with parking ($10,000 per year), buy your own food ($3,000 per year), and pay for your own cable TV ($700 per year). This job pays $50,000 per year. You still plan to do laundry at your parents' house once a week if you live in the city, and you plan to go into the city once a week to visit with friends if you live at home. Thus, the cost of operating your car will be about the same either way. In addition, your parents refuse to pay for your cell phone service ($720 per year), and you can't function without it.

continued . . .

Requirements

a. Based on this information alone, what is the net difference between the two alternatives (salary, net of relevant costs)?

b. What information is irrelevant? Why?

c. What qualitative information is relevant to your decision?

d. Assume that you really want to take Job #2, but you also want to live at home to cut costs. What new quantitative and qualitative information will you need to incorporate into your decision?

P2-44B **Calculate total and average costs** *(Learning Objective 7)*

The owner of Gabe's Deli restaurant is disappointed because the restaurant has been averaging 4,000 sandwich sales per month, but the restaurant can make and serve 6,000 sandwiches per month. The variable cost (for example, ingredients) of each sandwich is $1.25. Monthly fixed costs (for example, depreciation, property taxes, business license, manager's salary) are $6,000 per month. The owner wants cost information about different volumes so that he can make some operating decisions.

Requirements

1. Fill in the chart below to provide the owner with the cost information he wants. Then use the completed chart to help you answer the remaining questions.

Monthly sandwich volume	3,000	4,000	6,000
Total fixed costs	$	$	$
Total variable costs			
Total costs			
Fixed cost per sandwich	$	$	$
Variable cost per sandwich			
Average cost per sandwich			
Sales price per sandwich	$6.00	$6.00	$6.00
Average profit per sandwich			

2. From a cost standpoint, why do companies such as Gabe's Deli want to operate near or at full capacity?

3. The owner has been considering ways to increase the sales volume. He believes he could sell 6,000 sandwiches a month by cutting the sales price from $6.00 a sandwich to $5.50. How much extra profit (above the current level) would he generate if he decreased the sales price? (*Hint:* Find the deli's current monthly profit and compare it to the deli's projected monthly profit at the new sales price and volume.)

4. The owner's other idea is to advertise his restaurant on the local radio stations. If he keeps the sales price at $6 per sandwich, the advertising agency says he'll have to spend $4,000 in advertising each month to increase monthly sales to 6,000 sandwiches. How much extra profit (above the current level) would he generate if he kept the sales price at $6 per sandwich but spent $4,000 per month on advertising? Which of the owner's two ideas is most profitable?

5. The owner is surprised by your calculations. Because the current average profit per sandwich is $3.25, he thought the restaurant would make $19,500 of income per month (before advertising costs) if it sold 6,000 sandwiches at the normal $6.00 sales price. How did the owner arrive at this figure, and why is it wrong?

Apply Your Knowledge

▪ Decision Case

Case 2-45. Determine ending inventory balances *(Learning Objective 5)*

PowerBox designs and manufactures switches used in telecommunications. Serious flooding throughout North Carolina affected PowerBox's facilities. Inventory was completely ruined, and the company's computer system, including all accounting records, was destroyed.

Before the disaster recovery specialists clean the buildings, Annette Plum, the company controller, is anxious to salvage whatever records she can to support an insurance claim for the destroyed inventory. She is standing in what is left of the accounting department with Paul Lopez, the cost accountant.

"I didn't know mud could smell so bad," Paul says. "What should I be looking for?"

"Don't worry about beginning inventory numbers," responds Annette. "We'll get them from last year's annual report. We need first-quarter cost data."

"I was working on the first-quarter results just before the storm hit," Paul says. "Look, my report's still in my desk drawer. But all I can make out is that for the first quarter, material purchases were $476,000 and that direct labor, manufacturing overhead (other than indirect materials), and total manufacturing costs to account for were $505,000, $245,000, and $1,425,000, respectively. Wait, and cost of goods available for sale was $1,340,000."

"Great," says Annette. "I remember that sales for the period were approximately $1.7 million. Given our gross profit of 30%, that's all you should need."

Paul is not sure about that, but decides to see what he can do with this information. The beginning inventory numbers are as follows:

- Raw materials, $113,000
- Work in process, $229,000
- Finished goods, $154,000

He remembers a schedule he learned in college that may help him get started.

Requirements

1. Exhibit 2-16 resembles the schedule Paul has in mind. Use it to determine the ending inventories of raw materials, work in process, and finished goods.

2. Draft an insurance claim letter for the controller, seeking reimbursement for the flood damage to inventory. PowerBox's insurance representative is Gary Streer, at Industrial Insurance, 1122 Main Street, Hartford, CT 06268. The policy number is #3454340-23. PowerBox's address is 5 Research Triangle Way, Raleigh, NC 27698.

3 Job Costing

Despite intense competition in the technology sector, Dell continues to gain market share and increase profits while rivals such as IBM struggle. How does Dell do it? Cutting costs is one way. Using management accounting information to decide how to cut costs gives Dell a 10% to 15% cost advantage over its competitors.

To pinpoint cost-cutting opportunities, Dell first figures out how much it costs to assemble a computer. Dell's workers build each computer to a specific customer order, which is called a *job*. Dell's *job costing* system traces direct materials (such as CD-ROMs and hard drives) and direct labor (such as assembly-line labor) to each job. Then, Dell allocates indirect manufacturing overhead costs (such as depreciation on the plant) to each job. The sum of the job's direct materials, direct labor, and manufacturing overhead is its total manufacturing cost.

Dell compiles this cost information for each product into a *cost package* spreadsheet that is available online to all of Dell's managers. Managers throughout the company need to know how much it costs to assemble desktops, laptops, and servers to make vital business decisions such as these:

- Identifying opportunities to cut costs of different products
- Setting selling prices that will lead to profits for each product
- Determining which products are the most profitable and therefore deserve the most sales emphasis

Managers also need costs to prepare Dell's financial statements to determine the following:

- Cost of goods manufactured and cost of goods sold for the income statement
- Inventory for the balance sheet

Sources: S. Lohr, "Dell's Results Match Those of a Year Ago," *New York Times*, May 17, 2002, p. C5; G. McWilliams, "Lean Machine: How Dell Fine-Tunes Its PC Pricing to Gain Edge in Slow Market," *Wall Street Journal*, June 8, 2001, p. A1; G. McWilliams, "Mimicking Dell, Compaq to Sell Its PCs Directly," *Wall Street Journal*, November 11, 1998, p. B1; E. Bangeman, CNN.com, January 18, 2005; B. Breen, FastCompany.com, November 2004, iss. 88, p. 86; and J. Emigh, eweek.com, November 15, 2005. ■

Learning Objectives

1 Distinguish between job costing and process costing

2 Summarize a job's cost and use it to make business decisions

3 Account for manufacturing materials and labor

4 Account for manufacturing overhead

5 Account for completion and sales of finished goods and close manufacturing overhead

6 Use job costing at a service firm as a basis for billing clients

The Dell story shows why you need to know how much it costs to produce a product whether you plan a career in marketing, engineering, production, general management, or finance. Dell's marketing team needs to know how much it costs to assemble a computer to set the selling price high enough to cover costs and provide a profit. Engineers study the materials, labor, and manufacturing overhead that go into each computer to pinpoint new cost-cutting opportunities. Production managers who know how much it costs to assemble a motherboard can decide whether it is more profitable for Dell to assemble motherboards itself or to *outsource* (buy) them from a supplier. General managers who know Dell's cost to make desktops, laptops, and servers can identify the most profitable products and guide marketing to boost sales of those products. And the accounting department uses product costs to figure the cost of goods sold and inventory for the financial statements.

Because it is so important for managers in all areas of the business to know how much it costs to make each product, in this chapter and the next, we show you how to determine these costs.

Full Product Costs: A Brief Overview

First, let's review some key points about product costs. In Chapter 2, you learned that managers make certain decisions (such as setting sale prices) based on *full product costs* from all elements of the value chain: R&D, design, production or purchases, marketing, distribution, and customer service.

Recall that full product costs have two components: inventoriable product costs and period costs (also called noninventoriable costs). Inventoriable product costs are from the third element of the value chain in Exhibit 3-1: production for manufacturers and purchases for merchandisers. They are called inventoriable costs because in addition to serving as one of the six building blocks for computing full product costs, these are the costs that GAAP requires companies to use in computing inventory and cost of goods sold for the balance sheet and income statement. Most of Chapters 3 and 4 focus on how companies determine these inventoriable product costs. However, we'll also explain how the noninventoriable costs from the other five elements of the value chain can be assigned to products or services. By adding noninventoriable costs to inventoriable costs, managers can build up full product costs to make their internal decisions.

With this big picture in mind, let's see how companies such as Dell, Boeing, and Kellogg's determine the costs of making computers, airplanes, and cornflakes.

EXHIBIT 3-1   **The Value Chain, Inventoriable Costs, and Noninventoriable Costs**

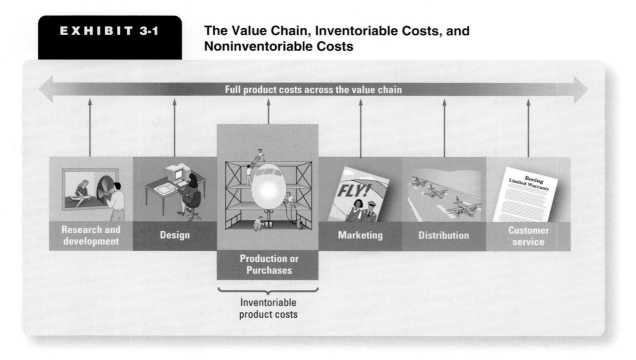

How Much Does It Cost to Make a Product? Two Approaches

1 Distinguish between job costing and process costing

Dell traces the cost of direct materials such as hard drives to the computers in which they are installed. But indirect costs, such as depreciation on the plant, cannot be traced directly to an individual computer because Dell cannot determine exactly how much depreciation a particular computer "caused." The existence of these indirect costs means that we cannot determine the precise cost of a specific product. Instead, companies use one of two product costing systems that *average* costs across products:

- Process costing
- Job costing

As the name suggests, *process costing* focuses on accumulating costs for each production process. *Job costing* accumulates costs for each individual job. Let's see how each works.

Process Costing

Process costing is used by companies that produce large numbers of identical units in a continuous fashion through a series of uniform production steps or processes. For example, Pace Foods uses two processes to make picante sauce: (1) chopping vegetables and (2) mixing and bottling. First, Pace accumulates the costs incurred in the chopping process. Next, the company averages the costs of the chopping process over all units passing through the process. Then, Pace accumulates the costs incurred in the mixing and bottling process and averages the costs of the mixing and bottling process over all units passing through that process. If Pace spent $50,000 to mix and bottle 100,000 bottles of picante sauce, the mixing and bottling cost per bottle would be:

$$\text{Cost per bottle of mixing and bottling picante sauce} = \frac{\$50,000}{100,000 \text{ bottles}} = \$0.50$$

To get the total manufacturing cost of a bottle of picante sauce, Pace would add the $0.50 mixing and bottling cost to the cost per bottle of the chopping process. Each bottle of picante sauce is identical to every other bottle, so each bears the same average cost.

Other industries and companies that use process costing include:

- Oil refining—Texaco
- Food and beverages—Kellogg's
- Consumer paper products—Kimberly-Clark

Exhibit 3-2 shows that process costing is not limited to manufacturers. Service companies such as banks use it to determine the cost of processing customer transactions. Merchandisers such as granaries use process costing to determine the storage cost for each bushel of grain. We consider process costing in detail in Chapter 4.

EXHIBIT 3-2	Job and Process Costing in Service, Merchandising, and Manufacturing Companies		
	Service	Merchandising	Manufacturing
Job costing:	Law firms (cases) Health-care providers (patients) Marketing firms (campaigns) Accounting firms (clients)	E-tailers such as Amazon.com Mail-order catalog companies such as L.L.Bean	Commercial building construction Custom furniture Aircraft manufacturers
Process costing:	Banks (process customer deposit transactions)	Granaries (distribute tons of identical grains)	Paper mills Mining operations Textile mills

Job Costing

Job costing assigns costs to a specific unit or to a small batch of products that passes through production as a distinct identifiable job. Each job is a separate cost object. Different jobs can vary considerably in materials, labor, and manufacturing overhead costs, so job costing accumulates these costs separately for each individual job. We focus on job costing in this chapter.

Job costing is common in industries that produce goods to meet customers' specifications. Dell custom-builds each personal computer based on the exact components the customer orders. Since each PC is unique, Dell treats each order as a unique job. Dell uses job costing to keep track of the cost of producing each separate job. Job costing would also be used by Boeing (airplanes), custom-home builders (unique houses), high-end jewelers (unique jewelry), and custom furniture and drapery manufacturers.

However, job costing is not confined to manufacturers. Exhibit 3-2 shows that service providers such as hospitals and physicians, law firms, accounting firms, and marketing firms all use job costing to determine the cost of serving their clients. The job cost is used as a basis for determining how much to bill each client. The last section of this chapter is devoted to illustrating job costing in a service firm. Finally, merchandisers such as Amazon.com can use job costing to determine the cost of meeting each customer's order.

Keep the following in mind: companies use job costing when different jobs vary widely in:

- The resources and time required
- The complexity of the production process

Because the jobs are so different, it would not be reasonable to assign them equal costs. Therefore, the cost of each job is compiled separately. Exhibit 3-3 summarizes the key differences between job and process costing.

Summarizing a Job's Cost and Using It to Make Business Decisions

As we've just seen, companies use job costing if they produce unique products or provide unique services. Often times, job costing begins with a customer order for a unique product, such as an order for a customized laptop computer at Dell or an

 2 Summarize a job's cost and use it to make business decisions

	EXHIBIT 3-3	Differences Between Job and Process Costing

	Job Costing	Process Costing
Cost object:	Job	Process
Outputs:	Single units or small batches with large difference between jobs	Large quantities of identical units
Extent of averaging:	Less averaging—costs are averaged over the small number of units in a job (often 1 unit in a job)	More averaging—costs are averaged over the many identical units that pass through the process

order placed by Delta Airlines for five Boeing 747s. However, at other manufacturers, job costing begins with a preset production schedule. Production schedules are based on expected demand for the company's various products at various points throughout the year. For example, at a furniture manufacturer, the production schedule for the month might indicate that 100 recliners, 1,000 chairs, and 500 sofas of particular styles and colors should be manufactured during the month in order to meet expected demand from different furniture retailers. These pieces of furniture would then be sold to various furniture retailers after they are produced.

In this chapter, we will see how job costing is used at E-Z-Boy Furniture, a manufacturer of recliners, chairs, and sofas. We will follow Job 293, a batch of ten recliners, through E-Z-Boy's job costing system. By the end, we will see that Job 293's total job cost ($1,220) is the sum of:

Job 293 Job Cost Record	
Direct materials	$ 500
Direct labor	$ 400
Manufacturing overhead	$ 320
Total job cost	$1,220
Units	÷ 10
Average cost per unit	$ 122

- The direct materials used on the job ($500)
- The direct labor used on the job ($400)
- Manufacturing overhead allocated to the job ($320)

Notice that the job cost includes all three types of manufacturing costs that we discussed in Chapter 2. A **job cost record** documents the direct materials, direct labor, and manufacturing overhead costs assigned to each individual job. A summarized version is shown above. The company starts the job cost record when it starts the job. When the job is complete, the total cost accumulated on the job cost record is averaged over the 10 units in the batch to yield an average cost of $122 per recliner ($1,220 ÷ 10).

The job's cost, as shown in the job cost record, becomes E-Z-Boy's basis for valuing inventory and cost of goods sold. Managers also use the job cost as a basis for controlling costs (that is, once they know how much it costs to produce a job, they can work on producing similar jobs more efficiently, if possible). The job cost is also the starting point for setting sales prices: E-Z-Boy's sales price must be high enough to cover the cost of manufacturing each recliner ($122), help pay for E-Z-Boy's period costs, and generate a profit for the company.

For example, to determine a sales price for each recliner, E-Z-Boy may use **cost-plus pricing**; that is, E-Z-Boy may start with the cost of manufacturing each recliner and then add a markup to help cover period costs and generate a profit for the company. For example, say E-Z-Boy sets its estimated sales price as 150% over manufacturing job cost. The sales price E-Z-Boy hopes to achieve is $305 per recliner, calculated as follows:

Average manufacturing cost per unit +	Mark-up	= Estimated sales price
$122	+ ($122 × 150%) =	$305

This is an estimated sales price because we haven't considered whether E-Z-Boy's customers are willing to pay $305 per recliner. While this may seem like a substantial markup, remember that E-Z-Boy's job cost ($122 per recliner) includes only manufacturing costs. E-Z-Boy will also incur other costs along the value chain associated with this job (for example, design of the recliners, marketing, freight-out, and customer service). So, E-Z-Boy needs to set its sales price high enough to cover these other costs as well as generate a profit.

To get a more accurate idea of what the sales price of each product should be, E-Z-Boy could expand its job costing system to include noninventoriable costs as well as manufacturing costs. We'll discuss this extension toward the end of the chapter. We'll also discuss pricing in more detail in Chapter 8. But for now, keep in mind that companies often use the job cost as a *starting point* for developing pricing and for developing bids for customized jobs.

Now that you have a basic understanding of what costs are included in a job and how the job cost can be used, let's look at how the job costs flow through the accounting records.

An Overview of How Job Costs Flow Through the Accounts

As E-Z-Boy incurs costs for the job, it adds them to the job cost record. For jobs that the company has started but not yet finished, the job cost records form the subsidiary ledger for the general ledger account: Work in Process Inventory. Recall that a subsidiary ledger provides the supporting details of a general ledger account. Most general ledger accounts—including all inventory accounts—have subsidiary ledgers. When E-Z-Boy finishes a job, it totals the costs on the job cost record and transfers the total cost out of Work in Process Inventory and into Finished Goods Inventory, as shown in Exhibit 3-4.

If the entire job is sold to one customer, E-Z-Boy moves the entire cost of the job out of Finished Goods Inventory and into Cost of Goods Sold, as shown in Exhibit 3-4. However, what if E-Z-Boy sells the recliners one at a time to various customers? In this case, every time one of the recliners from Job 293 is sold, E-Z-Boy moves the average unit cost of the recliner ($122) out of Finished Goods Inventory and into Cost of Goods Sold. The cost of unsold units stays in Finished Goods Inventory until the units are sold. Exhibit 3-4 summarizes how the costs of the jobs flow from Work in Process Inventory into Finished Goods Inventory and finally into Cost of Goods Sold.

In the next sections, we'll show you the documents that are used to track the flow of costs to Job 293. We'll also explain the journal entries that E-Z-Boy would make to accumulate its manufacturing costs and assign them to the jobs it works on, such as Job 293.

EXHIBIT 3-4   **Flow of Costs Through the Accounts in a Job Costing System**

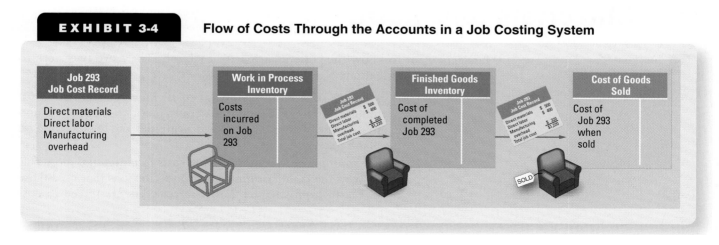

Data Set for E-Z-Boy Job Costing Illustration

The following data set summarizes E-Z-Boy's transactions for 2009. We will explain the accounting for these transactions step-by-step. For simplicity, we will show summary journal entries for the entire year. In practice, however, companies record these transactions more frequently: daily or even on a real-time basis.

1.	Materials purchased on account (direct and indirect materials)	$320,000
2.	Direct materials used for manufacturing	285,000
	Indirect materials used for manufacturing	40,000
3.	Manufacturing wages incurred (total of both direct and indirect labor itemized below)	335,000
4.	Direct labor on jobs	250,000
	Indirect labor to support manufacturing	85,000
5.	Depreciation on plant and equipment	50,000
6.	Plant utilities incurred	20,000
7.	Prepaid plant insurance expired	5,000
8.	Plant property taxes incurred	10,000
9.	Manufacturing overhead allocated to jobs	200,000
10.	Cost of goods manufactured	740,000
11.	Sales on account	996,000
	Cost of goods sold (unadjusted)	734,000

Each numbered transaction listed above is keyed to later journal entries so that you can refer to this data set as needed. We also will assume that E-Z-Boy had the following inventories on January 1, 2009, the beginning of its fiscal year:

Raw materials inventory (lumber, padding, fabric, nails, and so forth)	$20,000
Work in process inventory (partially completed recliners from five jobs)	29,000
Finished goods inventory (unsold recliners from completed jobs)	12,000

Job Costing: Accounting for Materials and Labor

 Account for manufacturing materials and labor

Managers want to know the costs incurred for each job. There are two steps to obtaining this information:

> STEP 1: *Accumulate the manufacturing costs incurred for all jobs.* Accumulate total purchases of materials, labor costs incurred, and manufacturing overhead costs (such as utilities and depreciation on the plant and equipment).
>
> STEP 2: *Assign appropriate amounts of these costs to individual jobs.* This step assigns the manufacturing costs to specific jobs that used those costs. Recall from Chapter 2 that direct costs are traced to cost

objects, while indirect costs are allocated to cost objects. In job costing, each individual job is a cost object. Therefore, **cost tracing** is used to assign direct materials and direct labor costs to jobs, while **cost allocation** is used to assign manufacturing overhead to jobs. **Cost assignment** is a general term that refers to both (1) tracing direct costs to cost objects and (2) allocating indirect costs to cost objects.

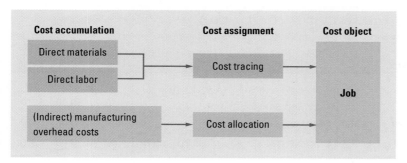

Accounting for Materials

Recall from Chapter 2 that direct and indirect materials are *descriptions* of different types of materials—they are not general ledger accounts. Most manufacturers, like E-Z-Boy, accumulate the cost of direct *and* indirect materials in the Raw Materials Inventory account until the company uses the materials in production.[1]

Purchasing Materials

E-Z-Boy *accumulates* the costs of the materials it purchases during the year by making the following journal entry (data from E-Z-Boy Data Set):

1.		Raw Materials Inventory	320,000	
		Accounts Payable		320,000
		(to record purchases of raw materials)		

Journal entry (1) is similar to the way a merchandiser such as Home Depot records purchases (under the perpetual method). Entry 1 *accumulates* materials costs but does not *assign* them. E-Z-Boy cannot assign the costs to specific jobs until it *uses* the materials on those jobs.

Raw Materials Inventory is a general ledger control account that is supported by a detailed subsidiary ledger. The subsidiary ledger is made up of individual materials records for each type of raw material E-Z-Boy has on hand. For example, the *lumber* record in Exhibit 3-5 shows that E-Z-Boy *received* 20 units of lumber at $9 each on July 23 and then used 10 units on July 24.

As shown in Exhibit 3-6, together, the materials records form the subsidiary ledger for the Raw Materials Inventory account. See how the balances in the individual materials records (lumber, padding, upholstery fabric, and so forth) sum to the general ledger balance in the Raw Materials Inventory account ($1,170). Exhibit 3-6 shows the balance on July 24; but of course, this balance will change daily as materials are purchased and used.

---

[1]To simplify in Chapter 2, we assumed that Top-Flight's Raw Materials Inventory account contained only direct materials.

EXHIBIT 3-5   Materials Record

Materials Record   E-Z-Boy

Item No. B-220   Description Lumber

Date	Received Units	Received Cost	Received Total Cost	Used Mat. Req. No.	Used Units	Used Cost	Used Total Cost	Balance Units	Balance Cost	Balance Total Cost
7-20								30	$9.00	$270
7-23	20	$9.00	$180					50	9.00	450
7-24				334	10	$9.00	$90	40	9.00	360

EXHIBIT 3-6   Raw Materials Inventory Subsidiary Ledger

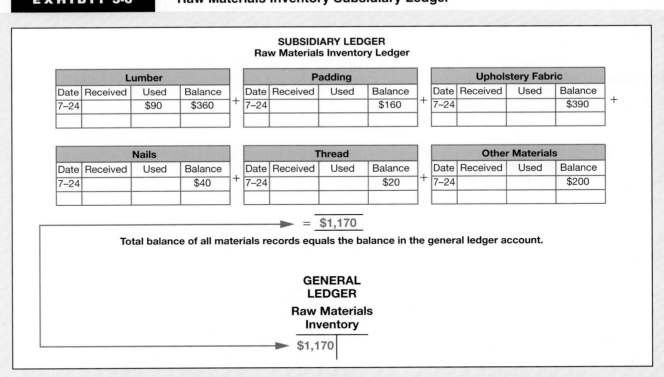

SUBSIDIARY LEDGER
Raw Materials Inventory Ledger

Lumber
Date	Received	Used	Balance
7-24		$90	$360

Padding
Date	Received	Used	Balance
7-24			$160

Upholstery Fabric
Date	Received	Used	Balance
7-24			$390

Nails
Date	Received	Used	Balance
7-24			$40

Thread
Date	Received	Used	Balance
7-24			$20

Other Materials
Date	Received	Used	Balance
7-24			$200

= $1,170

Total balance of all materials records equals the balance in the general ledger account.

GENERAL LEDGER

Raw Materials Inventory

$1,170

Using Materials

Now, let's see what E-Z-Boy does when production is ready to *use* materials. For both direct and indirect materials, the production team completes a **materials requisition** to request the transfer of materials from Raw Materials Inventory to the production floor so work can begin. Exhibit 3-7 shows E-Z-Boy's materials requisition for the 10 units of lumber needed to make ten recliner chairs for Job 293.

EXHIBIT 3-7   **Materials Requisition**

MATERIALS REQUISITION NO. 334

E–Z–Boy

Date 7–24   **Job No.** 293

Item no.	Item	Quantity	Unit cost	Amount
B-220	Lumber	10	$9.00	$90

See how E-Z-Boy traces the cost of lumber used from the materials requisition (Exhibit 3-7) to the "Direct Materials" section of the job cost record for Job 293 in Exhibit 3-8. Follow the $90 cost of the lumber from the lumber materials record (Exhibit 3-5) to the materials requisition (Exhibit 3-7) to the job cost record in Exhibit 3-8. All of the dollar amounts in these exhibits show E-Z-Boy's *costs*—not the prices at which E-Z-Boy sells its products.

Technology simplifies the way companies keep track of materials. Few companies track the movement of materials "by hand" as we saw in Exhibits 3-5, 3-7, and 3-8. Rather, they scan bar-coded materials to electronically capture the receipt (purchase) of raw materials, the use of direct materials on specific jobs, and the use of indirect materials in the plant. We show "hard copies" of E-Z-Boy's materials records, materials requisitions, and job cost records. However, most companies maintain these records as electronic files.

EXHIBIT 3-8   **Direct Materials Entry on Job Cost Record**

JOB COST RECORD

E–Z–Boy

Job No. 293
Customer Name and Address Macy's New York City
Job Description 10 Recliner Chairs

Date Promised	7–31	Date Started	7–24	Date Completed		

Date	Direct Materials		Direct Labor		Manufacturing Overhead Allocated		
	Requisition Numbers	Amount	Labor Time Record Numbers	Amount	Date	Rate	Amount
7–24	334	$90					

Overall Cost Summary
Direct Materials ....$
Direct Labor ....
Manufacturing Overhead
        Allocated ....

| Totals | | | | | Total Job Cost ....$ | | |

Recording the Cost of Direct and Indirect Materials Used

Journal entry (1) debited Raw Materials Inventory for the costs of all materials E-Z-Boy *purchased*—whether direct or indirect. Thus, when E-Z-Boy *uses* materials (whether direct or indirect), it *credits* Raw Materials Inventory.

But what account does E-Z-Boy *debit* when it uses the materials? The answer depends on the type of material used. To *assign* the cost of *direct materials* used, such as lumber and upholstery fabric, E-Z-Boy *debits* the Work in Process Inventory account in the general ledger. Recall that the job cost records form the subsidiary ledger for Work in Process Inventory, just like the materials records form the subsidiary ledger for Raw Materials Inventory. *Therefore, every time a cost is posted to a job cost record, the cost must also be debited to Work in Process Inventory.*

However, E-Z-Boy cannot trace the costs of *indirect materials* such as machine lubricants, janitorial supplies, and thread to a specific job. This means that E-Z-Boy cannot record indirect materials on any of the specific job cost records that underlie the general ledger Work in Process Inventory account. So, it cannot debit Work in Process Inventory. Instead, it debits indirect materials costs to a separate account, called Manufacturing Overhead, in the general ledger.

Recall from Chapter 2 that manufacturing overhead includes all manufacturing costs *other than* direct materials and direct labor. The Manufacturing Overhead account is simply a *temporary* account that companies use to *accumulate* all indirect manufacturing costs until the company can allocate these costs to specific jobs. Later in this chapter, we'll show how E-Z-Boy allocates indirect manufacturing costs *out* of Manufacturing Overhead and *into* specific jobs in Work in Process Inventory. For now, keep this distinction in mind: *Indirect manufacturing costs, such as indirect materials used, are not debited **directly** to Work in Process Inventory. Instead, they are accumulated in the Manufacturing Overhead account.*

E-Z-Boy works on many jobs during the year. The summary journal entry to *assign* the cost of the direct and indirect materials that E-Z-Boy used in all of its jobs during 2009 is (data from E-Z-Boy Data Set):

2.	Work in Process Inventory (for direct materials used on jobs)	285,000	
	Manufacturing Overhead (for indirect materials used in the factory)	40,000	
	Raw Materials Inventory		325,000
	(*to record the use of direct and indirect materials*)		

We can summarize the flow of materials costs through the T-accounts as follows (the numbers in parentheses refer to the journal entry numbers):

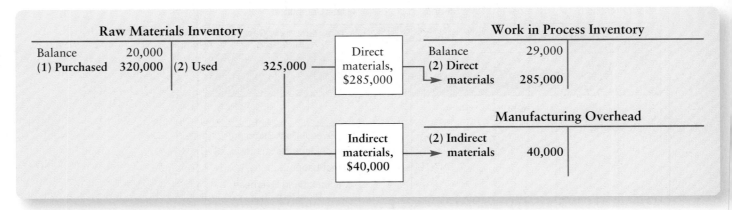

Accounting for Manufacturing Labor

When E-Z-Boy accounted for materials, it did the following:

1. Accumulated all materials purchased in the Raw Materials Inventory account.

2. Assigned the following:
   - The cost of *direct* materials used to individual jobs in Work in Process Inventory.
   - The cost of *indirect* materials used to Manufacturing Overhead.

E-Z-Boy uses the same two basic steps to account for manufacturing labor. First, E-Z-Boy accumulates all manufacturing labor—both direct and indirect—in a general ledger account called Manufacturing Wages. E-Z-Boy uses this temporary account to "store" payroll costs incurred (including wages, salaries, *and* fringe benefits) until it can properly assign the costs. The total amount of manufacturing payroll costs is determined from personnel and payroll records: fixed amounts for salaried workers and varying amounts for hourly wage earners, depending on the number of hours they worked. E-Z-Boy *accumulates* the total actual labor costs incurred during 2009 by making the following summary journal entry (data from E-Z-Boy Data Set):

3.	Manufacturing Wages	335,000	
	Wages Payable		335,000
	(*to record manufacturing labor costs incurred*)		

Next, E-Z-Boy *assigns* the manufacturing labor costs as follows:

- The cost of *direct* labor to individual jobs in Work in Process Inventory
- The cost of *indirect* labor to Manufacturing Overhead

How does E-Z-Boy figure out the amount of direct labor cost to *assign* to individual jobs? Each direct laborer fills out a **labor time record** for each job he or she works on. The labor time record in Exhibit 3-9 identifies the employee (Jay Barlow), the amount of time he spent on Job 293 (7 hours and 30 minutes), and the labor cost charged to the job ($60 = 7½ hours × $8 per hour). Exhibit 3-9 shows a "hard copy" example of E-Z-Boy's labor time record. Most manufacturers have automated this process by having production employees insert their identification cards into computer terminals set up on the plant floor. This system captures each employee's direct labor time and cost for a job without using paper documents. Any paid downtime that is not spent working on specific jobs is considered indirect labor.

EXHIBIT 3-9 **Labor Time Record**

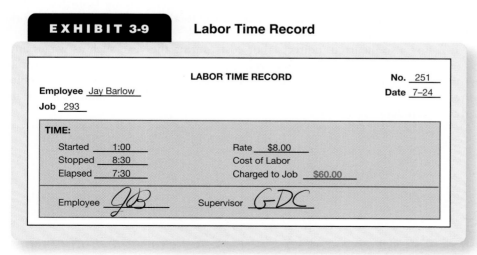

For each job, E-Z-Boy totals the labor time records to trace, or *assign*, the direct labor cost to that job. Exhibit 3-10 shows how E-Z-Boy adds the direct labor cost to the job cost record. The "labor time record numbers" show that on July 24, three employees worked on Job 293. Labor time record 251 is Jay Barlow's, from Exhibit 3-9. Labor time records 236 and 258 (not shown) indicate that two other employees also worked on Job 293. The job cost record shows that E-Z-Boy assigned Job 293 a total of $150 of direct labor costs for the three employees' work on July 24 ($60 from Jay Barlow's labor time record and the remainder from the other two employees' records).

EXHIBIT 3-10   **Direct Labor Entry on Job Cost Record**

JOB COST RECORD   E-Z-Boy

Job No. 293
Customer Name and Address Macy's New York City
Job Description 10 Recliner Chairs

Date Promised	7–31	Date Started	7–24	Date Completed		
	Direct Materials		**Direct Labor**		**Manufacturing Overhead Allocated**	
Date	Requisition Numbers	Amount	Labor Time Record Numbers	Amount	Date	Rate	Amount
7–24	334	$90	236 251 258	$40 60 50 $150	Overall Cost Summary Direct Materials ....$ Direct Labor .... Manufacturing Overhead Allocated		
Totals					Total Job Cost ....$		

Recall that the job cost records form the subsidiary ledger for the general ledger account Work in Process Inventory. Therefore, the total direct labor costs traced to all of the individual jobs E-Z-Boy worked on during the period (as recorded on job cost records such as Exhibit 3-10) must equal the total direct labor debits to Work in Process Inventory.

E-Z-Boy also incurred indirect labor costs during the year, such as wages and benefits for factory maintenance workers, quality control inspectors, and janitorial personnel. E-Z-Boy cannot trace indirect labor to specific jobs; therefore, it debits indirect labor costs to Manufacturing Overhead (just as it debited indirect materials used to Manufacturing Overhead).

The summary journal entry to *assign* total direct and indirect labor costs that E-Z-Boy incurred during 2009 (data from E-Z-Boy Data Set) is:

4.	Work in Process Inventory (for direct labor used on jobs)	250,000	
	Manufacturing Overhead (for indirect labor used in the factory)	85,000	
	Manufacturing Wages		335,000
	(*to assign direct and indirect labor costs*)		

In the following T-accounts, notice how the journal entry brings the balance in the (temporary) Manufacturing Wages account to zero.

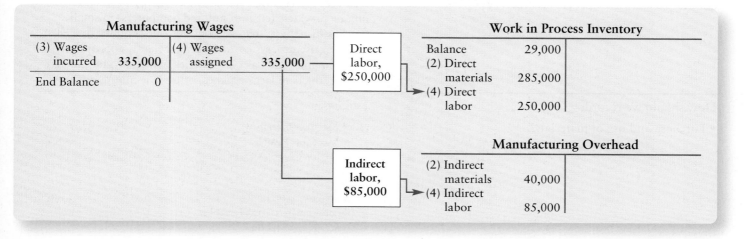

Stop & Think...

How can E-Z-Boy's managers use the raw materials inventory subsidiary ledger (Exhibit 3-6), labor time records (Exhibit 3-9), and job cost records (Exhibit 3-10) to run the company more effectively and efficiently?

Answer: Managers can use the *raw materials inventory subsidiary ledger* to see when lumber, nails, thread, and other materials are running low so they can reorder.

Managers use *labor time records* to control labor costs. Suppose E-Z-Boy pays an employee for 7½ hours of work per day. Summing the time recorded on all of her labor time records for the day should yield a total of 7½ hours worked. If not, the manager should find out how the employee spent any time unaccounted for. By showing how much time employees spend on each job, labor time records and job cost records help managers determine whether employees are working efficiently. If they spend longer than expected on a job, that job may not yield a profit.

Engineers study the detailed materials and labor charges on the *job cost records* to see if they can use materials and labor more efficiently. If a job's costs exceed its budget, E-Z-Boy may be able to use the job cost record to negotiate a price increase with the customer. E-Z-Boy's managers must do a better job controlling costs on future jobs (or raise the sales price on similar jobs) to ensure that the company remains profitable.

Decision Guidelines

JOB COSTING: ACCOUNTING FOR MATERIALS AND LABOR

Dell uses a job costing system that assigns manufacturing costs to each individual computer Dell that assembles. These guidelines explain some of the decisions Dell made in designing its system to trace direct materials and labor.

Decision	Guidelines
Should we use job or process costing?	Dell uses *job costing* because the company produces unique products (custom-tailored computers) in small batches (usually a "batch" contains one computer). Dell does not use *process costing* because that is appropriate for companies such as oil refineries, which produce identical products in large batches, often in a continuous flow.

How should we record:

- Purchase and use of materials?

Purchase:

Raw Materials Inventory	XX	
Accounts Payable		XX

Use:

Work in Process Inventory	XX	
(for direct materials used on jobs)		
Manufacturing Overhead	XX	
(for indirect materials used in factory)		
Raw Materials Inventory		XX

- Incurrence and assignment of labor?

Incurred:

Manufacturing Wages	XX	
Wages Payable		XX

Assigned:

Work in Process Inventory	XX	
(for direct labor used on jobs)		
Manufacturing Overhead	XX	
(for indirect labor used in factory)		
Manufacturing Wages		XX

Summary Problem 1

Ecosphere Associates in Tucson, Arizona, produces ecospheres—self-sustaining enclosed glass spheres that include water, algae, tiny shrimp, and snails. Suppose Ecosphere Associates has the following transactions:

a. Purchased raw materials on account, $35,000.

b. Production requisitioned materials costing $30,000. Of this total, $3,000 were indirect materials.

c. Labor time records show that direct labor of $22,000 and indirect labor of $4,000 were incurred (but not yet paid).

Requirements
Prepare journal entries for each transaction.

Solution

a.	Raw Materials Inventory	35,000	
	Accounts Payable		35,000
	(to record purchase of raw materials)		

When materials are purchased on account:

- Debit Raw Materials Inventory for the *cost* of the materials.

- Credit Accounts Payable to record the liability (the amount owed) to suppliers for the cost of the materials.

b.	Work in Process Inventory	27,000	
	Manufacturing Overhead	3,000	
	Raw Materials Inventory		30,000
	(to record use of direct materials on jobs and use of		
	indirect materials in the factory)		

When materials are requisitioned (used) in production, we record the movement of materials out of Raw Materials Inventory and into production:

- Debit Work in Process Inventory for the cost of the *direct* materials used on jobs (in this case, $27,000—the $30,000 total materials requisitioned less the $3,000 indirect materials).

- Debit Manufacturing Overhead for the cost of the *indirect* materials used in the factory.

- Credit Raw Materials Inventory for the cost of both direct and indirect materials moved out of the raw materials storage area and into production.

c.	Manufacturing Wages	26,000	
	Wages Payable		26,000
	(to record manufacturing labor costs incurred)		

To record total labor costs actually incurred ($22,000 + $4,000):

- Debit Manufacturing Wages.
- Credit Wages Payable to record the liability for wages incurred but not paid.

Work in Process Inventory	22,000	
Manufacturing Overhead	4,000	
Manufacturing Wages		26,000
(to assign direct and indirect labor costs)		

To assign the labor costs:

- Debit Work in Process Inventory for the cost of the *direct* labor used on jobs.
- Debit Manufacturing Overhead for the cost of the *indirect* labor used in the factory.
- Credit Manufacturing Wages for the cost of both direct and indirect labor.

This zeros out the temporary Manufacturing Wages account.

Job Costing: Accounting for Manufacturing Overhead

In the first half of the chapter, you learned how manufacturers accumulate materials and labor costs and then assign the appropriate amounts to individual jobs. The cost of indirect materials and indirect labor used in the plant was assigned to the Manufacturing Overhead account. In this part of the chapter, you'll see how E-Z-Boy accumulates other indirect manufacturing costs (such as utilities and plant depreciation) and then allocates some manufacturing overhead to each job worked on during the year.

4 Account for manufacturing overhead

Accumulating Other Indirect Manufacturing Costs

In a job costing system, *all* indirect manufacturing costs are *debited* to the Manufacturing Overhead account. We have already debited this account for the indirect materials used in the plant (journal entry 2) and the indirect labor used in the plant (journal entry 4). Journal entries 5 through 8 record other indirect manufacturing costs incurred by E-Z-Boy during the year: depreciation on plant and equipment, plant utilities, plant insurance, and plant property taxes. Each journal entry is keyed to the data given in the E-Z-Boy Data Set. The account titles in parentheses indicate the underlying records in the Manufacturing Overhead subsidiary ledger.

5.	Manufacturing Overhead (Depreciation—Plant and Equipment)	50,000	
	Accumulated Depreciation—Plant and Equipment		50,000
6.	Manufacturing Overhead (Plant Utilities)	20,000	
	Accounts Payable		20,000
7.	Manufacturing Overhead (Plant Insurance)	5,000	
	Prepaid Insurance—Plant		5,000
8.	Manufacturing Overhead (Plant Property Taxes)	10,000	
	Property Taxes Payable		10,000

E-Z-Boy debits the actual manufacturing overhead costs (such as indirect materials; indirect labor; and depreciation, utilities, insurance, and property taxes related to the plant) to Manufacturing Overhead as they occur throughout the year. By the end of the year, the Manufacturing Overhead account has accumulated *all of the actual manufacturing overhead costs as debits:*

Manufacturing Overhead	
(2) Indirect materials	40,000
(4) Indirect labor	85,000
(5) Depreciation—plant and equipment	50,000
(6) Plant utilities	20,000
(7) Plant insurance	5,000
(8) Plant property taxes	10,000
Total manufacturing overhead cost	210,000

> ### Stop & Think...
>
> How can E-Z-Boy's managers use the Manufacturing Overhead subsidiary ledger to control manufacturing overhead costs?
>
> **Answer:** Managers plan the amount of each manufacturing overhead item, such as plant-related depreciation, utilities, and insurance. If actual costs differ from planned costs, the managers find out why. For example, why are plant utilities higher than expected? Did utility rates increase? Was there a delay in installing more energy-efficient machinery? Answers to those questions may help managers control (reduce) utility costs. If utility costs have increased for reasons beyond the company's control, management may have to increase selling prices to cover the higher utility costs.

Allocating Manufacturing Overhead to Jobs

You have seen how E-Z-Boy *accumulates* manufacturing overhead costs in the accounting records. But how does it *assign* manufacturing overhead costs to individual jobs? Manufacturing overhead includes a variety of costs that E-Z-Boy cannot trace to individual jobs. For example, it is impossible to say how much of the cost incurred to cool the plant is related to Job 293. Yet, manufacturing overhead costs are as essential to producing a job as direct materials and direct labor. So, E-Z-Boy must find some way to assign, or allocate, these costs to specific jobs.

Choose a Manufacturing Overhead Allocation Base

The key to assigning indirect manufacturing costs to jobs is to identify a manufacturing overhead allocation base. The **allocation base** is a common denominator that links indirect manufacturing overhead costs to the cost objects. Ideally, the allocation base is the cost driver of manufacturing overhead costs. As the term implies, a **cost driver** is the primary factor that causes a cost. For example, in many companies, manufacturing overhead costs rise and fall with direct labor costs. In this case, accountants use direct labor costs or direct labor hours as the allocation base. The more direct labor a job uses, the more manufacturing overhead cost allocated to the job.

But labor is less important in companies that use automated production, such as Nissan. Equipment depreciation, maintenance costs, and utilities costs change with the number of machine hours used. These companies often use machine hours as the allocation base. The important point is that the cost allocation base should be the primary driver of the manufacturing overhead costs.

For simplicity, we'll assume that E-Z-Boy uses only one allocation base—direct labor cost—to assign manufacturing overhead costs to jobs. Chapter 5 relaxes this assumption. There, we'll see how companies use a method called *activity-based costing* to identify multiple allocation bases that more accurately link indirect costs with the jobs that caused those costs. Because activity-based costing is a straightforward extension of the single allocation base method, it is important to develop a solid understanding of the simpler system we describe here.

Calculate the Predetermined Manufacturing Overhead Rate

To get the most accurate allocation, E-Z-Boy would have to wait until the total amount of the manufacturing overhead cost is known at the end of the year. But managers making pricing, inventory management, and other decisions today cannot wait that long for product cost information. So, E-Z-Boy develops an estimated manufacturing overhead allocation rate at the beginning of the year, using estimated data for the *entire* year. This **predetermined manufacturing overhead rate**—sometimes called the **budgeted manufacturing overhead rate**—is computed as follows:

$$\text{Predetermined manufacturing overhead rate} = \frac{\text{Total estimated manufacturing overhead costs}}{\text{Total estimated quantity of the manufacturing overhead allocation base}}$$

A key point is that both the numerator and the denominator are estimated *before* the year begins (actual manufacturing overhead costs and the actual quantity of the manufacturing overhead allocation base are not known until after the end of the period). Throughout the year, companies use this predetermined rate to allocate manufacturing overhead to individual jobs. This allows managers to generate timely product cost information, which they use to determine pricing and to make other decisions as well as to generate monthly and quarterly financial statements.

Let's see how this works for E-Z-Boy. Recall that E-Z-Boy has chosen to use direct labor cost as its manufacturing overhead allocation base. Before the year begins, E-Z-Boy estimates the total manufacturing overhead costs in 2009 to be $220,000 and total direct labor cost to be $275,000. E-Z-Boy takes many factors into consideration when making these estimates: last year's costs, changes in production plans, changes in labor contracts, inflation rate, and so forth. E-Z-Boy calculates its predetermined manufacturing overhead rate as follows:

$$\text{Predetermined manufacturing overhead rate} = \frac{\text{Total estimated manufacturing overhead costs}}{\text{Total estimated quantity of the manufacturing overhead allocation base}}$$

$$= \frac{\$220,000 \text{ of estimated manufacturing overhead costs}}{\$275,000 \text{ of estimated direct labor cost}}$$

$$= 0.80, \text{ or } 80\% \text{ of direct labor cost}$$

Allocate Manufacturing Overhead to Individual Jobs

Once E-Z-Boy has calculated its predetermined manufacturing overhead rate for the year, it uses that rate to allocate manufacturing overhead to *every* job it works on during 2009. The amount of manufacturing overhead allocated to each job is determined as follows:

$$\text{Manufacturing overhead allocated to a job} = \text{Predetermined manufacturing overhead rate} \times \text{Actual quantity of the allocation base used by the job}$$

Let's allocate manufacturing overhead to E-Z-Boy's Job 293. The job cost record shown in Exhibit 3-11 indicates that a total of $400 of direct labor cost was traced to Job 293 (notice that after our July 24 posting in Exhibit 3-10, more direct labor cost was incurred on July 25 and 28 to finish the job). E-Z-Boy can now compute the amount of manufacturing overhead to allocate to Job 293 as follows:

$$\text{Manufacturing overhead allocated to Job 293} = 80\% \text{ of direct labor cost} \times \$400$$
$$= \$320$$

After E-Z-Boy has determined the amount of manufacturing overhead to allocate—$320—it posts it to the job cost record. The completed job cost record for Job 293 (Exhibit 3-11) shows the total job cost of $1,220: $500 in direct materials, $400 in direct labor, and $320 of allocated manufacturing overhead. The total job cost is averaged over the 10 units in the job, yielding an average manufacturing cost per recliner of $122 ($1,220 ÷ 10).

EXHIBIT 3-11 **Manufacturing Overhead Entry on Job Cost Record**

JOB COST RECORD

E–Z–Boy

Job No. 293

Customer Name and Address Macy's New York City

Job Description 10 Recliner Chairs

Date Promised	7–31	Date Started	7–24	Date Completed		7–29
	Direct Materials		**Direct Labor**		**Manufacturing Overhead Allocated**	
Date	Requisition Numbers	Amount	Labor Time Record Numbers	Amount	Date	Rate	Amount
7–24	334	$ 90	236, 251, 258	$150	7–29	80% of Direct Labor Cost	$320
25	338	180	264, 269, 273, 291	200		Overall Cost Summary	
28	347	230	305	50		Direct Materials ....$ 500	
						Direct Labor.....................400	
						Manufacturing Overhead Allocated....................320	
Totals		$500		$400		Total Job Cost............$1,220	
						Number of units in job ....÷ 10	
						Cost per unit $122	

Exhibit 3-12 summarizes the six steps to allocating manufacturing overhead. Review this exhibit before continuing.

E-Z-Boy would have repeated Steps 5 and 6 (in Exhibit 3-12) to allocate some manufacturing overhead to *every* job it worked on during the year. Each time manufacturing overhead is allocated to a particular job and posted on the job sheet, the company makes a journal entry to *assign* the cost to the job in Work in Process Inventory and to allocate that cost *out of* Manufacturing Overhead.

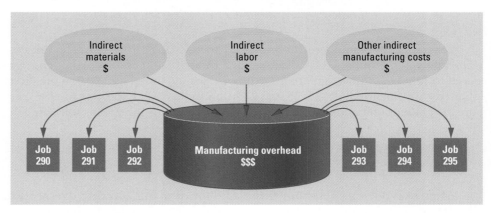

Rather than showing every journal entry made during the year to assign overhead, we will show you the summary entry for *all jobs* worked on during the year. Recall from E-Z-Boy's Data Set that the company incurred a *total* of $250,000 of

EXHIBIT 3-12   **Steps in Allocating Manufacturing Overhead**

Companies follow six steps in allocating manufacturing overhead costs. Steps 1–4 are completed *before* the year begins. Steps 5 and 6 are completed as jobs are produced throughout the year.

1. Estimate the total manufacturing overhead cost for the year.
2. Identify the manufacturing overhead cost allocation base. This should be the cost driver of the manufacturing overhead costs. Many companies use direct labor cost, direct labor hours, or machine hours.
3. Estimate the total quantity of the manufacturing overhead allocation base for the year.
4. Compute the *predetermined* manufacturing overhead rate using estimated information as follows:

$$\text{Predetermined manufacturing overhead rate} = \frac{\text{Total estimated manufacturing overhead costs (from Step 1)}}{\text{Total estimated quantity of the manufacturing overhead allocation base (from Step 3)}}$$

5. Obtain *actual* quantities of the manufacturing overhead allocation base used by individual jobs as the year unfolds.
6. Allocate manufacturing overhead cost to jobs as follows:

$$\begin{array}{c}\text{Manufacturing} \\ \text{overhead allocated} \\ \text{to a job}\end{array} = \begin{array}{c}\text{Predetermined} \\ \text{manufacturing} \\ \text{overhead rate}\end{array} \times \begin{array}{c}\text{Actual quantity of} \\ \text{the allocation base} \\ \text{used by the job}\end{array}$$

direct labor cost during 2009. Since manufacturing overhead is allocated at a rate of 80% of direct labor cost, the *total* amount of overhead allocated to *all* jobs is $200,000 (= 80% × $250,000). The summary journal entry to allocate manufacturing overhead to Work in Process Inventory is:

9.	Work in Process Inventory	200,000	
	Manufacturing Overhead		200,000
	(to assign manufacturing overhead to every job worked on		
	during the year)		

When Is Manufacturing Overhead Allocated to Jobs?

At what point in time does a company allocate manufacturing overhead? The answer depends on the company's accounting software. Companies with simple software wait to allocate manufacturing overhead until a job is complete, as E-Z-Boy did. When the job is complete, managers know the quantity of the allocation base that the job has used (Job 293 used a total of $400 of direct labor cost), so they can make one journal entry to allocate manufacturing overhead based on this usage ($400 × 80% = $320). If the period end falls before the job is complete, managers need to allocate some manufacturing overhead to the job based on the direct labor cost incurred by the job to that point.

Companies with more sophisticated software automatically allocate manufacturing overhead every time some of the allocation base is posted to the job. For example, if E-Z-Boy's software was more sophisticated, every time $1.00 of direct labor cost was posted to one of E-Z-Boy 's jobs, the computer system would automatically post $0.80 ($1.00 × 80%) of manufacturing overhead to the same job.

Review of Manufacturing Overhead T-account

The flow of manufacturing overhead through the T-accounts follows. Notice again how *actual* manufacturing overhead costs are recorded as *debits* to the Manufacturing Overhead account, while allocations are recorded as *credits* to the same account.

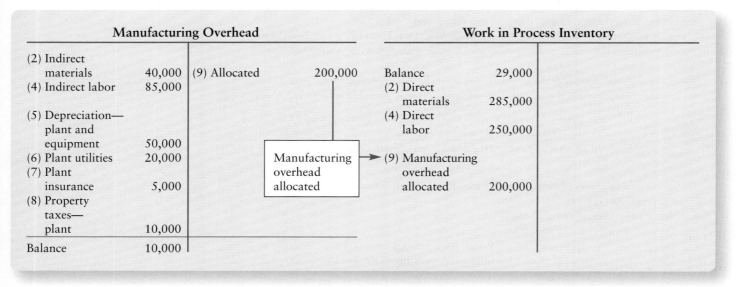

After allocation, a $10,000 debit balance remains in the Manufacturing Overhead account. This means that E-Z-Boy's *actual* manufacturing overhead costs exceed the manufacturing overhead *allocated* to Work in Process Inventory. We say that E-Z-Boy's Manufacturing Overhead is *underallocated*. We'll discuss how to correct this problem in the next section.

Stop & Think...

Now that E-Z-Boy's managers know that the manufacturing cost is $122 per recliner (see Exhibit 3-11), what decisions can they make?

Answer:

1. *Pricing:* Marketing must price the recliners considerably above the $122 man-ufacturing cost to cover R&D, design, marketing, distribution, and customer service costs, as well as profits.

2. *Product emphasis:* Using profit calculations (selling price minus cost), E-Z-Boy's top management can design operations and marketing strategy to focus on the most profitable products.

3. *Cost control:* Engineers can study the detailed cost information to identify opportunities to cut costs below $122. Production managers can compare the $122 cost per recliner with the budgeted cost to evaluate worker effi-ciency, material usage efficiency, and other factors.

4. *Outsourcing:* Management can compare the $122 cost to make the recliner versus the cost of buying a similar recliner from a subcontractor. (For exam-ple, Teva outsources production of its footwear to companies in China; Teva's management focuses on design and marketing.)

5. *Valuing inventory:* Finance and accounting can use the $122 cost per recliner to value the job as inventory (before it is sold) and as cost of goods sold (after the sale).

Accounting for Completion and Sale of Finished Goods and Closing Manufacturing Overhead

Now you know how to accumulate direct materials, direct labor, and manufacturing overhead and then assign those costs to individual jobs. To complete the process, we must account for the completion and sale of finished goods and then close Manufacturing Overhead at the end of the period to adjust for any underallocation or overallocation.

5 Account for completion and sales of finished goods and close manufacturing overhead

Accounting for Completion and Sale of Finished Goods

Once a job is complete, it is no longer a "work in process." As completed jobs leave the plant floor, E-Z-Boy moves the cost of the completed job out of Work in Process Inventory and into Finished Goods Inventory. This flow of costs is shown in Exhibit 3-4. From E-Z-Boy's Data Set, we see that the cost of all jobs completed during the year (cost of goods manufactured) was $740,000. The summary entry to record the completion of all jobs during the year and their movement into the finished goods storage area follows:

10.	Finished Goods Inventory	740,000	
	Work in Process Inventory		740,000
	(to record the completion of jobs)		

When E-Z-Boy sells furniture, it makes the usual perpetual inventory system journal entries for recording sales and cost of goods sold (data from E-Z-Boy Data Set):

11.	Accounts Receivable	996,000	
	Sales Revenue		996,000
	Cost of Goods Sold	734,000	
	Finished Goods Inventory		734,000
	(to record the sale and release of inventory)		

The key T-accounts for E-Z-Boy's manufacturing costs now show the following:

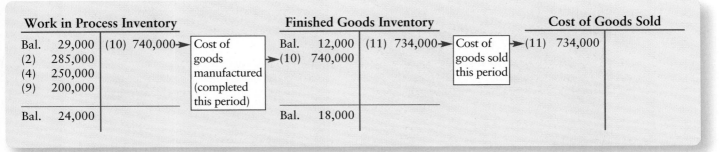

The Work in Process Inventory T-account summarizes what happens on the manufacturing plant floor. Notice that the Work in Process Inventory T-account also summarizes the Schedule of Cost of Goods Manufactured: E-Z-Boy starts the period

with a beginning inventory of jobs that were started but not finished last period ($29,000). During the current period, the plant uses direct materials ($285,000) and direct labor ($250,000) and manufacturing overhead is allocated to the jobs passing through the plant floor ($200,000). Some jobs are completed, and their costs are transferred out to Finished Goods Inventory ($740,000). We end the period with other jobs started but not finished during this period ($24,000).

Closing Manufacturing Overhead at Year-End

Recall that Manufacturing Overhead is simply a temporary account for accumulating indirect manufacturing costs until E-Z-Boy can assign those costs to specific jobs. During the year, E-Z-Boy debits Manufacturing Overhead for the manufacturing overhead costs the company actually incurred and credits Manufacturing Overhead for amounts allocated to Work in Process Inventory. The total debits rarely equal the total credits. Why? Because E-Z-Boy allocates manufacturing overhead to jobs using a *predetermined* allocation rate that represents the *expected* relation between manufacturing overhead costs and the allocation base.

In our example, the $10,000 debit balance of Manufacturing Overhead shown on page 152 is called **underallocated manufacturing overhead** because E-Z-Boy allocated *less* manufacturing overhead to Work in Process Inventory ($200,000) than it actually incurred ($210,000). **Overallocated manufacturing overhead** is just the opposite. The manufacturing overhead allocated to Work in Process Inventory is *more* than the amount of manufacturing overhead costs actually incurred. A credit balance in the Manufacturing Overhead account occurs when a company allocates *more* manufacturing overhead to Work in Process Inventory than it incurs. These relationships are shown in Exhibit 3-13.

EXHIBIT 3-13 **Underallocated and Overallocated Manufacturing Overhead**

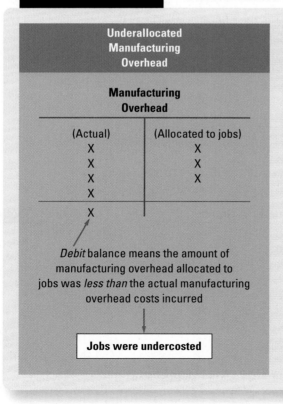
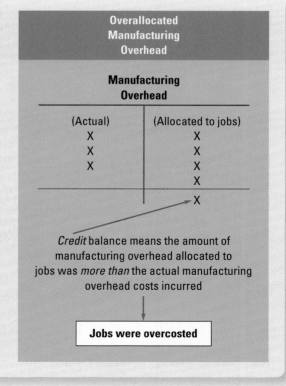

Because the Manufacturing Overhead account still has a balance at year-end, E-Z-Boy must close it. Accountants accomplish two goals by closing the Manufacturing Overhead account:

1. They "zero out" the account because it is a temporary account that is not part of the financial statements.

2. They "correct" for the overallocation or underallocation of manufacturing overhead.

How do accountants close this account? E-Z-Boy's Manufacturing Overhead account has a *debit* balance of $10,000, so they *credit* Manufacturing Overhead $10,000 to bring the account balance to zero. What account do they debit? Most accountants debit Cost of Goods Sold. Therefore, E-Z-Boy would make the following journal entry:

12.	Cost of Goods Sold	10,000	
	Manufacturing Overhead		10,000
	(to close cost of goods sold and correct for underallocation)		

To see why E-Z-Boy debited cost of goods sold, you need to understand how E-Z-Boy underallocated manufacturing overhead. E-Z-Boy *expected* to incur 2009 manufacturing overhead at the predetermined rate of:

$$\frac{\$220,000 \text{ } expected \text{ manufacturing overhead costs}}{\$275,000 \text{ } expected \text{ direct labor costs}} = 80\%$$

Without a crystal ball to foretell the future, it would be surprising if *actual* costs and *actual* quantities of the allocation base—which are not known until the end of the year—exactly matched the expected amounts that E-Z-Boy used to compute the predetermined rate at the beginning of the year. At the end of 2009, E-Z-Boy's *actual* manufacturing overhead rate turns out to be:

$$\frac{\$210,000 \text{ } actual \text{ manufacturing overhead costs}}{\$250,000 \text{ } actual \text{ direct labor costs}} = 84\%$$

At the beginning of the year, E-Z-Boy *underestimated* the manufacturing overhead rate, expecting it to be only 80%.

Because the predetermined rate was *less* than the actual rate, E-Z-Boy allocated too *little* manufacturing overhead cost to every job. In other words, every job worked on in 2009 was *undercosted*. To correct this error, E-Z-Boy should *increase* the cost of these jobs. Most of the jobs that E-Z-Boy made during the year have already been sold, so the cost of the jobs is already in the Cost of Goods Sold account. Because E-Z-Boy has *undercosted* the jobs during the year, Cost of Goods Sold is *undercosted*. E-Z-Boy makes a correction by *increasing* the Cost of Goods Sold, as done in journal entry 12. However, if a substantial number of jobs have not yet been sold (they are still in inventory), companies will allocate the correction between Cost of Goods Sold, Finished Goods Inventory, and Work in Process Inventory. This allocation method is discussed in more advanced accounting textbooks. For our purposes, we will always assume that most jobs worked on during the year have been sold; therefore, the correction should be made to Cost of Goods Sold.

Companies with more sophisticated software are able to recost each job worked on during the year. The software automatically corrects each job at the end of the year using the *actual* manufacturing overhead rate. This gives managers a better idea of the actual gross profit they earned on each job rather than the gross profit previously reported using the predetermined overhead rate. This helps managers as they plan for similar jobs the following year. Also, managers will examine the reasons for the underallocation or overallocation of manufacturing overhead. Was it due primarily to errors in cost estimation? Or was it due primarily to differences in production activity? By understanding the cause(s), managers should be better able to pinpoint their estimates for the coming year.

By making journal entry 12, the following T-accounts show that E-Z-Boy has accomplished two goals: (1) the Manufacturing Overhead account is now closed (zero balance) and (2) Cost of Goods Sold is increased to correct for undercosting the jobs produced and sold throughout the year:

Manufacturing Overhead				Cost of Goods Sold		
Actual	210,000	Allocated (9)	200,000	(11)	734,000	
		Closing (12)	10,000 →	Closing (12)	10,000	
Balance	0			Balance	744,000	

Exhibit 3-14 summarizes the accounting for manufacturing overhead:

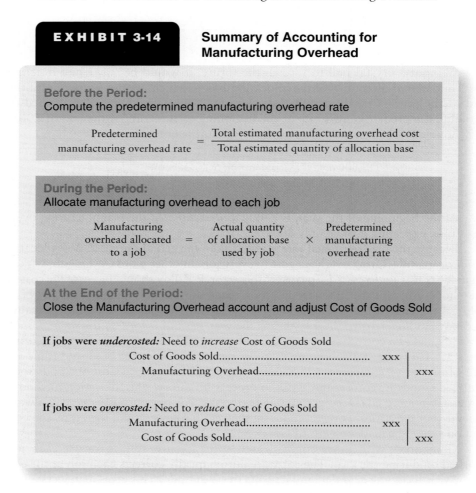

EXHIBIT 3-14 **Summary of Accounting for Manufacturing Overhead**

Before the Period:
Compute the predetermined manufacturing overhead rate

$$\text{Predetermined manufacturing overhead rate} = \frac{\text{Total estimated manufacturing overhead cost}}{\text{Total estimated quantity of allocation base}}$$

During the Period:
Allocate manufacturing overhead to each job

$$\text{Manufacturing overhead allocated to a job} = \text{Actual quantity of allocation base used by job} \times \text{Predetermined manufacturing overhead rate}$$

At the End of the Period:
Close the Manufacturing Overhead account and adjust Cost of Goods Sold

If jobs were *undercosted:* Need to *increase* Cost of Goods Sold

Cost of Goods Sold	xxx	
Manufacturing Overhead		xxx

If jobs were *overcosted:* Need to *reduce* Cost of Goods Sold

Manufacturing Overhead	xxx	
Cost of Goods Sold		xxx

Stop & Think...

Suppose E-Z-Boy's actual manufacturing overhead costs were $180,000 rather than $210,000.

1. What would the actual manufacturing overhead rate have been?
2. Would manufacturing overhead have been underallocated or overallocated?
3. What journal entry would you make to close the Manufacturing Overhead account?

Answers

1. The actual manufacturing overhead rate would have been:

$$\frac{\$180,000 \ actual \ \text{manufacturing overhead costs}}{\$250,000 \ actual \ \text{direct labor costs}} = 72\%$$

2. The predetermined manufacturing overhead rate (80%) is *higher* than the actual manufacturing overhead rate (72%). In this case, each job would have been *overcosted*. And Manufacturing Overhead would have been *overallocated* by $20,000, as shown in this T-account:

Manufacturing Overhead			
Actual	180,000	Allocated	200,000
		Balance	20,000

3. The jobs E-Z-Boy worked on during the year were allocated too much manufacturing overhead. Accordingly, the jobs in Cost of Goods Sold were *overcosted*; so, the correction should decrease (credit) Cost of Goods Sold and debit Manufacturing Overhead (to zero it out) as shown in the following journal entry:

Manufacturing Overhead	20,000	
Cost of Goods Sold		20,000
(to close manufacturing overhead and correct for overallocation)		

Overview of Job Costing in a Manufacturing Company

In this section, we will review E-Z-Boy's T-accounts, discuss the impact of technology on job costing, and discuss how manufacturers can expand their job costing systems to include noninventoriable (period) costs as well as manufacturing costs.

A Review of E-Z-Boy's T-accounts

Exhibit 3-15 provides an overview of E-Z-Boy's job costing system. Each entry is keyed to 1 of the 12 transactions described throughout the chapter (amounts in thousands). Study this exhibit carefully.

Review the flow of costs through the general ledger accounts and note the following:

- Material and labor costs are split between direct costs (traced directly to specific jobs in Work in Process Inventory) and indirect costs (first accumulated in Manufacturing Overhead and then allocated to jobs in Work in Process Inventory).
- The Work in Process Inventory account summarizes the transactions that occurred on the floor of the manufacturing plant—direct materials are converted into finished products through the use of direct labor and manufacturing overhead.
- When jobs are completed, their cost is moved out of Work in Process Inventory and into Finished Goods Inventory. The cost of goods manufactured ($740,000) represents the total cost of all jobs completed during the year.
- *Debits* to the Manufacturing Overhead account represent *actual* manufacturing overhead costs incurred during the year. *Credits* to the Manufacturing Overhead account represent *allocations* of manufacturing overhead to jobs in Work in Process Inventory. At year-end, E-Z-Boy closes the balance in the Manufacturing Overhead account ($10,000 underallocation) to Cost of Goods Sold. After closing, the balance in Manufacturing Overhead is zero.
- Manufacturing Wages, like Manufacturing Overhead, is a temporary account (used to accumulate labor costs until those costs are assigned), which does not show up on the financial statements.
- E-Z-Boy shows the three inventory accounts (Raw Materials, Work in Process, and Finished Goods) on its balance sheet. E-Z-Boy shows the Cost of Goods Sold on its income statement.

The T-accounts shown in Exhibit 3-15 are general ledger control accounts. Behind each general ledger account appear three examples of subsidiary accounts that underlie the general ledger control account.

How Information Technology Has Changed Job Costing

The flow of costs through the T-accounts and the journal entries apply to systems ranging from simple manual costing to sophisticated ERP systems. The main difference is the source of data. In traditional systems, sources include material requisitions, labor time records, and job cost records like those described. These documents can be paper-based or automated.

In contrast, highly automated systems may have no physical source documents. Employees use bar codes to record materials used and scan identification cards to

EXHIBIT 3-15 **Job costing: Flow of Costs Through E-Z Boy's Accounts (amounts in thousands)**

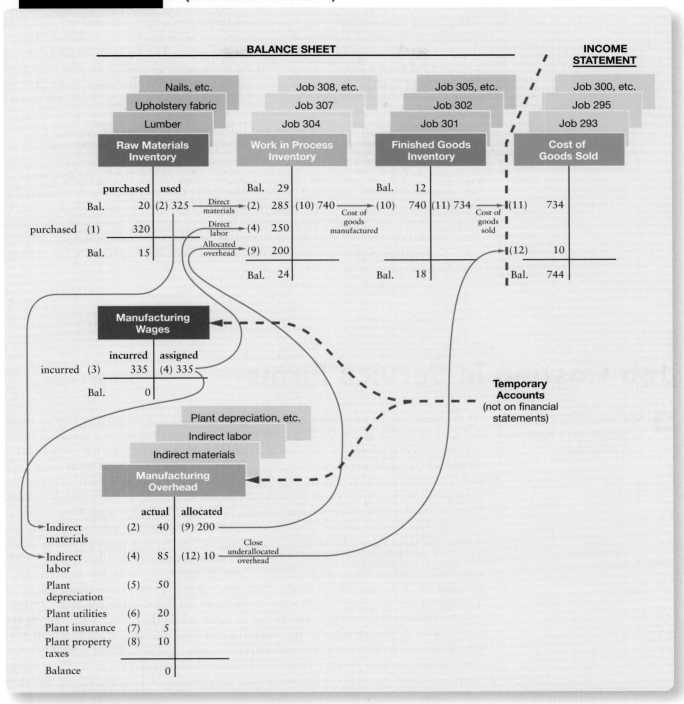

record their labor time. The software immediately tracks these material and labor costs to the specific job and updates the general ledger accounts (for example, Raw Materials Inventory, Work in Process Inventory, Manufacturing Wages, and Manufacturing Overhead). ERP systems may not store data in the form of separate job cost records. But when employees enter the job number, the system quickly tallies costs assigned to the job so far. Even in sophisticated ERP systems, however, the cost flows and journal entries are identical to those described for E-Z-Boy.

Noninventoriable Costs in Manufacturing Companies

Job costing in manufacturing companies has traditionally focused on assigning *manufacturing* costs (*inventoriable* costs) to jobs. This is why our E-Z-Boy illustration focuses on assigning only manufacturing costs. The focus on manufacturing costs arises because GAAP require that the accounting records treat only inventoriable costs as assets. Costs incurred in other elements of the value chain (period costs) are not assigned to products for external reporting but, instead, are treated as expenses.

Managers often want to know the full (total) cost of a product or a job, not just the inventoriable cost. The same principles of tracing direct costs and allocating indirect costs (using predetermined allocation rates) apply to noninventoriable period costs incurred in other elements of the value chain: R&D, design, marketing, distribution, and customer service. Managers can add these noninventoriable (period) costs to inventoriable costs to build the full cost of the product or job to guide internal decisions, such as setting long-run average sale prices. However, these noninventoriable costs are assigned to products (or jobs) *only for internal decision making*. Noninventoriable costs are not assigned to products for external reporting.

Job Costing in Service Firms

6 Use job costing at a service firm as a basis for billing clients

At the beginning of this chapter, we said that job costing is commonly used at many service firms, such as law firms, accounting firms, marketing firms, consulting firms, and health-care providers. At service firms, the work performed for each client is considered a separate job. Because they have no inventory, service firms incur only period costs (operating expenses). However, their managers still need to know the costs of different jobs in order to make decisions, such as how much to bill a client. We now illustrate how service firms assign period costs to individual jobs.

The law firm of Barnett Associates considers each client a separate job. Barnett Associates' most significant cost is direct labor—attorneys' time spent on clients' cases. The firm also incurs general operating costs, such as office rent, office support staff, and office supplies. These are the indirect costs of serving all of the law firm's clients.

Let's first consider how service firms trace direct labor to individual jobs. For automated services such as Web site design and information technology consulting, employees simply enter the client number when they start working on the client's job. Software records the time elapsed until the employee signs off that job. When the service is not automated, employees typically fill out a weekly labor time record, or time sheet. Exhibit 3-16 shows Attorney Teresa Fox's time record for the week of June 10. On it, we see that she devoted 14 hours to Client 367 during the week.

Fox's salary and benefits total $100,000 per year. Assuming a 40-hour workweek and 50 workweeks in each year, Fox has 2,000 available work hours per year (50 weeks × 40 hours per week). Barnett Associates' hourly cost rate of employing Teresa Fox is:

$$\text{Hourly cost rate to the employer} = \frac{\$100,000 \text{ per year}}{2,000 \text{ hours per year}} = \$50 \text{ per hour}$$

| EXHIBIT 3-16 | Labor Time Record |

Barnett Associates		M	T	W	Th	F
Name _Teresa Fox_	8:00–8:30	367	520	415	367	415
	8:30–9:00					
Employee Time Record	9:00–9:30					
Week of ___6/10___	9:30–10:00					
	10:00–10:30			367		
Weekly Summary	10:30–11:00					
Client # Total hours	11:00–11:30	520				
	11:30–12:00	520				
367 14	12:00–1:00					
415 13	1:00–1:30	520	367	367	520	415
520 13	1:30–2:00			367		
	2:00–2:30			415		
	2:30–3:00					
	3:00–3:30					
	3:30–4:00					
	4:00–4:30					
	4:30–5:00					

Fox is the only attorney who served Client 367, so the direct labor cost traced to the Client is calculated as follows:

14 hours × $50 per hour = $700 of direct labor

However, the law firm needs to know the *total* costs of serving clients, not just the direct labor cost. So, the law firm also allocates its indirect costs to individual client jobs. The law firm develops a predetermined indirect cost allocation rate following the same six-step approach shown in Exhibit 3-12.

1. **Estimate the total indirect costs.**

Before the fiscal year begins, Barnett estimates the total indirect costs that will be incurred in the coming year:

Office rent	$190,000
Office supplies, telephone, Internet access, and copier lease	10,000
Office support staff	70,000
Maintaining and updating law library for case research	25,000
Advertisements in the Yellow Pages	3,000
Sponsorship of the symphony	2,000
Total indirect costs	$300,000

2. **Identify a cost allocation base.**

Barnett uses direct labor hours as the allocation base because the number of hours that attorneys work on clients' cases is the main driver of indirect costs.

3. **Estimate the total quantity of the indirect cost allocation base.**

Barnett estimates that its attorneys will work 10,000 direct labor hours in 2009.

4. **Compute the predetermined indirect cost allocation rate.**

To find the indirect allocation rate, divide Step 1 by Step 3:

$$\text{Predetermined indirect cost allocation rate} = \frac{\$300,000 \text{ expected indirect costs}}{10,000 \text{ expected direct labor costs}}$$

$$= \$30 \text{ per direct labor hour}$$

5. **Obtain the actual quantity of the cost allocation base used by individual jobs.**

Exhibit 3-16 shows that Client 367 required 14 direct labor hours during the week of June 10.

6. **Allocate indirect costs to jobs.**

Client 367 is allocated indirect costs as follows:

$$\begin{array}{ccc} \text{Indirect} & \text{Predetermined} & \text{Actual quantity of} \\ \text{costs allocated} = & \text{indirect cost} \times & \text{the allocation base} \\ \text{to a job} & \text{allocation rate} & \text{used by the job} \end{array}$$

$$= \$30/\text{hour} \times 14 \text{ direct labor hours}$$

$$= \$420$$

Now, Barnett can determine the total job cost of serving Client 367 during the week. The total job cost is the sum of the direct labor traced to the client plus the indirect operating costs allocated to the client. Notice that materials such as office supplies are such an insignificant cost that they are considered part of the indirect costs. Therefore, there is no separate cost category for direct materials, as there is at a manufacturer. To summarize, the total costs assigned to Client 367 for the week of June 10, 2009, are:

Direct costs: 14 hours × $50/hour	$ 700
Indirect costs: 14 hours × $30/hour	420
Total costs...	$1,120

Since this is a service firm, there are no inventory accounts. Therefore, no journal entries are needed to move these costs through any inventory or cost of goods sold accounts. However, the law firm still uses the job costing system to calculate the cost of serving each client. This cost is used as a basis for billing its clients. For example, Barnett may set its billing rate to achieve a 25% profit over its costs. To achieve this profit, Barnett would bill Client 367 (for work performed during the week of June 10) as follows:

$$\begin{array}{l} \text{Job cost} + \text{Mark-up for profit} = \text{Amount to bill client} \\ \$1,120 + (\$1,120 \times 25\%) = \$1,400 \end{array}$$

As you have just seen, job costing in service firms is very similar to job costing at manufacturers. Direct costs are traced to jobs, while indirect costs are allocated to jobs. The job cost is then used as a basis for making management decisions.

Decision Guidelines

JOB COSTING

Dell pioneered the assemble-to-order PC production process. To determine the cost of its computers, Dell uses a job costing system that treats each individual computer as a separate cost object. In designing its job costing system, Dell made decisions such as these, in addition to those listed in the midchapter "Decision Guidelines" on pages 143–144.

Decision	Guidelines
Who should have access to product cost information?	All of Dell's managers have access to product cost information. *Marketing* uses it to set selling prices that cover costs and contribute to profits. *Top management* uses it to identify the most profitable products so it can focus on increasing sales of those products. *Engineers* study product costs to identify opportunities for further cost cuts. *Production* managers use product cost information to evaluate how efficiently assembly-line employees are working. *Finance and accounting* use product costs to figure inventory for the balance sheet and cost of goods sold for the income statement.
Are utilities, insurance, property taxes, and depreciation manufacturing overhead? operating expenses?	These costs are part of manufacturing overhead *only* when they are incurred in the manufacturing plant. If not related to manufacturing, they are operating expenses. For example, if related to the research lab, they are R&D expenses. If related to executive headquarters, they are administrative expenses. If related to distribution centers, they are distribution expenses. These are all operating expenses, not manufacturing overhead.

How should we record *actual* manufacturing overhead costs?

Manufacturing Overhead	XXX	
Accumulated Depreciation—		
Plant and Equipment		XX
Prepaid Insurance—Plant and		
Equipment		XX
Utilities Payable (or Accounts		
Payable) and so forth		XX

How should we compute a predetermined manufacturing overhead rate?

$$= \frac{\text{Total estimated manufacturing overhead cost}}{\text{Total estimated quantity of allocation base}}$$

How should we record allocation of manufacturing overhead to individual jobs?

Work in Process Inventory	XX	
Manufacturing Overhead		XX

How much manufacturing overhead should be allocated to each job?

Actual quantity of the manufacturing overhead allocation base used by the job	×	Predetermined manufacturing overhead rate

How do we close Manufacturing Overhead at the end of the period?   Close directly to Cost of Goods Sold, assuming most jobs have already been sold.

continued . . .

Decision	Guidelines
Why should companies allocate noninventoriable costs to jobs?	Managers need total product costs for internal decisions (such as setting selling prices). For external reporting, they assign only inventoriable costs to jobs.
How does job costing at a service firm work?	Job costing at a service firm is very similar to job costing at a manufacturing company. The main difference is that the company is allocating indirect period costs (rather than manufacturing costs) to each client. In addition, since there are no Inventory or Cost of Goods Sold accounts, no journal entries are needed to move these costs through the system.
When providing services, how is employees' direct labor traced to individual jobs?	Automated software directly captures time that employees spend on a client's job, or employees fill out a labor time record.

Summary Problem 2

StarZ manufactures skateboards. The company has a highly automated production process, so it allocates manufacturing overhead based on machine hours. StarZ expects to incur $240,000 of manufacturing overhead costs and to use 4,000 machine hours during 2009.

At the end of 2008, StarZ reported the following inventories:

Raw Materials Inventory..	$20,000
Work in Process Inventory	17,000
Finished Goods Inventory	11,000

During January 2009, StarZ actually used 300 machine hours and recorded the following transactions:

a. Purchased materials on account, $31,000.

b. Used direct materials, $39,000.

c. Manufacturing labor cost incurred was $40,000.

d. Manufacturing labor was 90% direct labor and 10% indirect labor.

e. Used indirect materials, $3,000.

f. Incurred other manufacturing overhead, $13,000 (credit Accounts Payable).

g. Allocated manufacturing overhead for January 2009.

h. Cost of completed skateboards, $99,000.

i. Sold skateboards on account, $172,000; cost of skateboards sold, $91,400 (StarZ uses a perpetual inventory system).

Requirements

1. Compute StarZ's predetermined manufacturing overhead rate for 2009.

2. Record the transactions in the general journal.

3. Post the inventory balances and transactions to the following accounts:

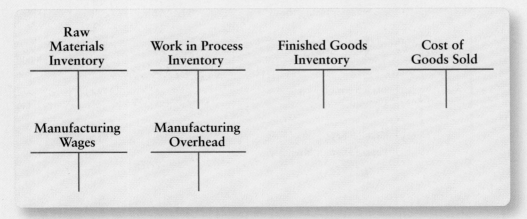

4. Record the journal entry to close the ending balance of Manufacturing Overhead. Post your entry to the T-accounts.

5. What are the ending balances in the three inventory accounts and Cost of Goods Sold?

Solution

Requirement 1

$$\text{Predetermined manufacturing overhead rate} = \frac{\text{Total estimated manufacturing overhead costs}}{\text{Total estimated quantity of allocation base}}$$

$$= \frac{\$240,000}{4,000 \text{ machine hours}}$$

$$= \$60/\text{machine hour}$$

Requirement 2

Journal entries:

a.		Raw Materials Inventory	31,000	
		Accounts Payable		31,000
b.		Work in Process Inventory	39,000	
		Raw Materials Inventory		39,000
c.		Manufacturing Wages	40,000	
		Wages Payable		40,000
d.		Work in Process Inventory ($40,000 × 0.90)	36,000	
		Manufacturing Overhead ($40,000 × 0.10)	4,000	
		Manufacturing Wages		40,000
e.		Manufacturing Overhead	3,000	
		Raw Materials Inventory		3,000
f.		Manufacturing Overhead	13,000	
		Accounts Payable		13,000
g.		Work in Process Inventory (300 × $60)	18,000	
		Manufacturing Overhead		18,000
h.		Finished Goods Inventory	99,000	
		Work in Process Inventory		99,000
i.		Accounts Receivable	172,000	
		Sales Revenue		172,000
		Cost of Goods Sold	91,400	
		Finished Goods Inventory		91,400

Requirement 3
Post the transactions:

Raw Materials Inventory				Work in Process Inventory				Finished Goods Inventory				Cost of Goods Sold			
Bal.	20,000	(b)	39,000	Bal.	17,000	(h)	99,000	Bal.	11,000	(i)	91,400	(i)	91,400		
(a)	31,000	(e)	3,000	(b)	39,000			(h)	99,000						
Bal.	9,000			(d)	36,000			Bal.	18,600						
				(g)	18,000										
				Bal.	11,000										

Manufacturing Wages				Manufacturing Overhead			
(c)	40,000	(d)	40,000	(d)	4,000	(g)	18,000
Bal.	0			(e)	3,000		
				(f)	13,000		
				Bal.	2,000		

Requirement 4
Close Manufacturing Overhead:

	Cost of Goods Sold		2,000	
	Manufacturing Overhead			2,000

Manufacturing Overhead				Cost of Goods Sold			
(d)	4,000	(g)	18,000	(i)	91,400		
(e)	3,000		2,000		2,000		
(f)	13,000						
Bal.	0			Bal.	93,400		

Requirement 5
Ending Balances:

Raw Materials Inventory (from Requirement 3).....................................	$ 9,000
Work in Process Inventory (from Requirement 3)	11,000
Finished Goods Inventory (from Requirement 3)	18,600
Cost of Goods Sold (from Requirement 4)	93,400

Review Job Costing

Accounting Vocabulary

Allocation Base. (p. 148
A common denominator that links indirect costs to cost objects (such as jobs or production processes). Ideally, the allocation base is the primary cost driver of the indirect cost.

Cost Allocation. (p. 137)
Assigning indirect costs (such as manufacturing overhead) to cost objects (such as jobs or production processes).

Cost Assignment. (p. 137)
A general term that refers to both tracing direct costs and allocating indirect costs to cost objects.

Cost Driver. (p. 148)
The primary factor that causes a cost.

Cost-Plus Pricing. (p. 134)
Setting the estimated sales price at an amount equal to manufacturing cost plus a markup to help cover period costs and generate a profit for the company.

Cost Tracing. (p. 137)
Assigning direct costs (such as direct materials and direct labor) to cost objects (such as jobs or production processes) that used those costs.

Job Cost Record. (p. 134)
The document that accumulates the direct materials, direct labor, and manufacturing overhead costs assigned to each individual job.

Job Costing. (p. 133)
The system for assigning costs to a specific unit or to a small batch of products or services that (1) pass through production steps as a distinct identifiable job and (2) can vary considerably in materials, labor, and overhead costs.

Labor Time Record. (p. 141)
Identifies the employee, the amount of time spent on a particular job, and the labor cost charged to the job; a record used to assign direct labor cost to specific jobs.

Materials Requisition. (p. 138)
Request for the transfer of both direct and indirect materials from Raw Materials Inventory to the production floor.

Overallocated Manufacturing Overhead. (p. 154)
The manufacturing overhead allocated to Work in Process Inventory is more than the amount of manufacturing overhead costs actually incurred.

Predetermined Manufacturing Overhead Rate. (p. 149)
An estimated manufacturing overhead allocation rate computed at the beginning of the year, calculated as the total estimated manufacturing overhead costs divided by the total estimated quantity of the manufacturing overhead allocation base. Also called the **budgeted manufacturing overhead rate**.

Process Costing. (p. 132)
System for assigning costs to large numbers of identical units that usually proceed in a continuous fashion through a series of uniform production steps or processes.

Underallocated Manufacturing Overhead. (p. 156)
The manufacturing overhead allocated to Work in Process Inventory is less than the amount of manufacturing overhead costs actually incurred.

■ Quick Check

1. Would the advertising agency Saatchi & Saatchi use job or process costing? What about a Georgia-Pacific paper mill?
   a. Saatchi & Saatchi—job costing
      Georgia-Pacific—job costing
   b. Saatchi & Saatchi—job costing
      Georgia-Pacific—process costing
   c. Saatchi & Saatchi—process costing
      Georgia-Pacific—job costing
   d. Saatchi & Saatchi—process costing
      Georgia-Pacific—process costing

2. When Dell *uses* direct materials, it *traces* the cost by debiting:
   a. Raw Materials Inventory
   b. Direct Materials
   c. Manufacturing Overhead
   d. Work in Process Inventory

3. When Dell *uses* indirect materials, it *assigns* the cost by debiting:
   a. Raw Materials Inventory
   b. Indirect Materials
   c. Manufacturing Overhead
   d. Work in Process Inventory

4. When Dell *uses* direct labor, it *traces* the cost by debiting:
   a. Direct Labor
   b. Manufacturing Wages
   c. Manufacturing Overhead
   d. Work in Process Inventory

Questions 5, 6, 7, and 8 are based on the following information. Assume that Dell's Austin, Texas, plant allocates manufacturing overhead based on machine hours. Suppose Dell budgeted 10 million machine hours and $90 million of manufacturing overhead costs. Finally, assume that Dell actually used 12 million machine hours and incurred the following actual costs (in millions):

Indirect labor	$10
Depreciation on plant	47
Machinery repair	15
Direct labor	75
Plant supplies	5
Plant utilities	8
Advertising	35
Sales commissions	25

5. What is Dell's predetermined manufacturing overhead rate?
   a. $9.00/machine hour
   b. $7.50/machine hour
   c. $0.13/machine hour
   d. $0.11/machine hour

6. What is Dell's actual manufacturing overhead cost (in millions)?
   a. $85
   b. $120
   c. $160
   d. $220

7. How much manufacturing overhead would Dell allocate (in millions)?
   a. $85
   b. $90
   c. $108
   d. $220

8. What entry would Dell make to close the Manufacturing Overhead account (in millions)?

a.	Manufacturing Overhead	5	
	Cost of Goods Sold		5
b.	Manufacturing Overhead	23	
	Cost of Goods Sold		23
c.	Cost of Goods Sold	5	
	Manufacturing Overhead		5
d.	Cost of Goods Sold	23	
	Manufacturing Overhead		23

9. How does Dell's management use product cost information?
   a. to set prices of its products
   b. to decide which products to emphasize
   c. to identify ways to cut production costs
   d. all of the above

10. For which of the following reasons would John Barnett, owner of the Barnett Associates law firm, want to know the total costs of a job (serving a particular client)?
    a. to determine the fees charged to the client
    b. for inventory valuation
    c. for external reporting
    d. all of the above

Quick Check Answers

1. b 2. d 3. c 4. d 5. d 6. a 7. c 8. b 9. d 10. a

For Internet Exercises, Excel in Practice, and additional online activities, go to this book's Web site at www.prenhall.com/bamber.

Assess Your Progress

■ Learning Objectives

1 Distinguish between job costing and process costing

2 Summarize a job's cost and use it to make business decisions

3 Account for manufacturing materials and labor

4 Account for manufacturing overhead

5 Account for completion and sales of finished goods and close manufacturing overhead

6 Use job costing at a service firm as a basis for billing clients

■ Short Exercises

S3-1   Decide on product costing system *(Learning Objective 1)*
Would the following companies use job costing or process costing?

a.   A manufacturer of plywood

b.   A manufacturer of wakeboards

c.   A manufacturer of luxury yachts

d.   A professional services firm, such as H&R Block

e.   A landscape garden contractor

S3-2   Calculate job cost, billing, and profit at a car care center *(Learning Objectives 2, 6)*
Conrad's Car Care Center specializes in providing car tune-ups, brake jobs, and tire replacements for most vehicle makes and models. Conrad's charges customers for materials "at cost" but charges labor at a rate of $84 per hour. The labor rate is high enough to cover actual mechanic wages ($24 per hour), to cover shop overhead (allocated at a cost of $16 per hour), and to provide a profit. Cory recently had a 60,000-mile service performed on his Honda Pilot. Materials used on the job included $9.95 for oil and filter, $60.45 for transmission fluid exchange, $20.86 for the air filter, and $33.02 for the cabin filter. The mechanic spent 1.25 hours on the job.

1.   How much was charged to the customer for this work?

2.   What was Conrad's cost for this job?

3.   How much profit did Conrad's earn on this job?

S3-3   Record purchase and use of materials *(Learning Objective 3)*
Trekker manufactures backpacks. Its plant records include the following materials-related transactions:

Purchases of canvas (on account)	$70,000
Purchases of thread (on account)	1,100
Material requisitions:	
Canvas	63,000
Thread	280

continued . . .   Job Costing   **171**

Make the journal entries to record these transactions. Post these transactions to the Raw Materials Inventory account. If the company had $35,680 of Raw Materials Inventory at the beginning of the period, what is the ending balance of Raw Materials Inventory?

S3-4 **Determine transactions from T-accounts** *(Learning Objective 3)*
Use the following T-accounts to determine the cost of direct materials used and indirect materials used.

Raw Materials Inventory			Work in Process Inventory		
Balance	16		Balance	32	
Purchases	230	X			
Balance	24		Direct materials	Y	Cost of goods manufactured 744
			Direct labor	320	
			Manufacturing overhead	200	
			Balance	8	

S3-5 **Record manufacturing labor costs** *(Learning Objective 3)*
Art Glass reports the following labor-related transactions at its plant in Seattle, Washington.

Plant janitor's wages	600
Plant supervisor's wages...	900
Glassblowers' wages...	76,000

Record the journal entries for the incurrence and assignment of these wages.

S3-6 **Record journal entries** *(Learning Objectives 3, 4)*
The following transactions were incurred by Dutch Fabricators during January, the first month of its fiscal year. Record the proper journal entry for each transaction.
1. $190,000 of materials were purchased on account.
2. $174,000 of materials were used in production; of this amount, $152,000 was used on specific jobs.
3. Manufacturing labor and salaries for the month totaled $225,000.
4. $190,000 of the total manufacturing labor and salaries was traced to specific jobs.
5. The company recorded $20,000 of depreciation on the plant and plant equipment. The company also received a plant utility bill for $10,000.
6. $81,000 of manufacturing overhead was allocated to specific jobs.
7. By the end of January, was manufacturing overhead overallocated or underallocated? By how much?

S3-7 **Identify and accumulate manufacturing overhead costs** *(Learning Objective 4)*
Classic Outdoor Furniture manufactures wood patio furniture. The company reports the following costs for January 2009. What is the balance in the Manufacturing Overhead account at the end of January if no manufacturing overhead has been allocated to jobs?

Wood	$230,000
Nails and glue	12,000
Wood-preserving stain	9,000
Depreciation on saws	5,000
Depreciation on delivery truck	2,200
Assembly-line workers' wages	56,000
Salesperson's auto lease	1,400
Indirect manufacturing labor	39,000

S3-8 **Ramifications of overallocating and underallocating jobs** *(Learning Objective 4)*
Answer the following questions:

1. Why do managers use a *predetermined* manufacturing overhead allocation rate rather than the *actual* rate to cost jobs?

2. Jobs will typically be overcosted or undercosted. Is one worse than the other? Explain your thoughts.

S3-9 **Allocate manufacturing overhead to a job** *(Learning Objective 4)*
In the E-Z-Boy job cost record (Exhibit 3-11), how much manufacturing overhead cost will be allocated to Job 293 if the predetermined manufacturing overhead allocation rate is 70% of direct labor cost rather than 80%? What will be the total cost assigned to Job 293?

S3-10 **Compute various manufacturing overhead rates** *(Learning Objective 4)*
Therrien Pools manufactures swimming pool equipment. Therrien estimates total manufacturing costs next year to be $1,200,000. Therrien also estimates it will use 50,000 direct labor hours and incur $1,000,000 of direct labor cost next year. In addition, the machines are expected to be run for 40,000 hours. Compute the predetermined manufacturing overhead rate for next year under the following independent situations:

1. Assume that Therrien uses direct labor hours as its manufacturing overhead allocation base.

2. Assume that Therrien uses direct labor cost as its manufacturing overhead allocation base.

3. Assume that Therrien uses machine hours as its manufacturing allocation base.

S3-11 **Continuation of S3-10: compute total allocated overhead** *(Learning Objective 4)*
Use your answers from S3-10 to determine the total manufacturing overhead allocated to Therrien's manufacturing jobs in the following independent situations:

1. Assume that Therrien actually used 52,300 direct labor hours.

2. Assume that Therrien actually incurred $1,025,000 of direct labor cost.

3. Assume that Therrien actually ran the machines 39,500 hours.

4. Briefly explain what you have learned about the total manufacturing overhead allocated to production.

S3-12 **Continuation of S3-11: determine over- or underallocation** *(Learning Objective 4)*

Use your answers from S3-11 to determine the total overallocation or underallocation of manufacturing overhead during the year. Actual manufacturing costs for the year totaled $1,225,000.

1. Assume that Therrien used direct labor hours as the allocation base.

2. Assume that Therrien used the direct labor cost as the allocation base.

3. Assume that Therrien used machine hours as the allocation base.

4. Were there any situations in which jobs were costed correctly? If not, when were they overcosted? When were they undercosted?

S3-13 **Calculate rate and analyze year-end results** *(Learning Objective 4)*

Rainbow manufactures wooden backyard playground equipment. Rainbow estimated $1,785,000 of manufacturing overhead and $2,100,000 of direct labor cost for the year. After the year was over, the accounting records indicated that the company had actually incurred $1,700,000 of manufacturing overhead and $2,200,000 of direct labor cost.

1. Calculate Rainbow's predetermined manufacturing overhead rate assuming that the company uses direct labor cost as an allocation base.

2. How much manufacturing overhead would have been assigned to manufacturing jobs during the year?

3. At year-end, was manufacturing overhead overallocated or underallocated? By how much? (*Hint:* Use a T-account to aid in your analysis.)

S3-14 **Analyze Manufacturing Overhead** *(Learning Objectives 4, 5)*

In the E-Z-Boy T-accounts shown on page 147 and 152, actual manufacturing overhead was $210,000. Suppose instead that the actual manufacturing overhead was $225,000. Continue to assume that E-Z-Boy's total direct labor cost for the year was $250,000.

1. Draw a T-account of Manufacturing Overhead. Is Manufacturing Overhead underallocated or overallocated? By how much?

2. What would be the actual manufacturing overhead rate? Does this make sense in light of your answer to question 1?

3. Assuming that all of the jobs have been sold, is Cost of Goods Sold too high or too low? Explain.

4. Make the journal entry to close out E-Z-Boy's Manufacturing Overhead account.

S3-15 **Recompute job cost at a legal firm** *(Learning Objective 6)*

In the Barnett Associates example on pages 160–162, suppose Fox's annual salary is $110,000 rather than $100,000. Also suppose the Barnett's attorneys expected to work a total of 12,000 direct labor hours rather than 10,000 direct labor hours.

1. What would be the hourly (cost) rate to Barnett Associates of employing Fox?

2. What direct labor cost would be traced to Client 367?

3. What is the indirect cost allocation rate?

4. What indirect costs will be allocated to Client 367?

5. What is the total job cost for client 367?

■ Exercises

E3-16 **Understanding key terms** *(Learning Objective 1)*
Listed below are several terms. Complete the following statements with one of these terms. You may use a term more than once, and some terms may not be used at all.

Cost allocation	Cost driver	Job costing	Process costing
Cost tracing	Job cost record	Materials requisition	

a. A _____ shows the accumulation of costs of an individual job.

b. _____ is used by companies that produce small quantities of many different products.

c. A _____ is the primary factor that causes costs.

d. Georgia-Pacific pulverizes wood into pulp to manufacture cardboard. The company would use a _____ system.

e. To record costs of maintaining thousands of identical mortgage files, financial institutions such as Money Tree would use a _____ system.

f. _____ is assigning direct costs to cost objects.

g. Companies that produce large numbers of identical products use _____ systems for product costing.

h. The computer repair service that visits your home and repairs your computer would use a _____ system.

i. A _____ is manufacturing personnel's request that materials be moved to the production floor.

j. _____ is assigning indirect costs to cost objects.

E3-17 **Determine the cost of a job and use it for pricing** *(Learning Objectives 2, 4)*
Jungle Jim Industries manufactures custom-designed playground equipment for schools and city parks. Jungle Jim expected to incur $664,000 of manufacturing overhead cost, 41,500 of direct labor hours, and $830,000 of direct labor cost during the year (the cost of direct labor is $20 per hour). The company allocates manufacturing overhead on the basis of direct labor hours. During May, Jungle Jim completed Job 301. The job used 155 direct labor hours and required $12,700 of direct materials. The City of Westlake has contracted to purchase the playground equipment at a price of 20% over manufacturing cost.

1. Calculate the manufacturing cost of Job 301.

2. How much will the City of Westlake pay for this playground equipment?

E3-18 **Compare bid prices under two different allocation bases** *(Learning Objectives 2, 4)*
Landers Recycling recycles newsprint, cardboard, and so forth, into recycled packaging materials. For the coming year, Landers Recycling estimates total manufacturing overhead to be $360,000. The company's managers are not sure if direct labor hours (estimated to be 10,000) or machine hours (estimated to be 15,000 hours) is the best allocation base to use for allocating manufacturing overhead. Landers Recycling bids for jobs using a 30% markup over total manufacturing cost.

After the new fiscal year began, Mills Paper Supply asked Landers recycling to bid for a job that will take 2,000 machine hours and 1,600 direct labor hours to produce. The direct labor cost for this job will be $12 per hour, and the direct materials will total $25,000.

continued . . .

1. Compute the total job cost and bid price if Landers Recycling decided to use direct labor hours as the manufacturing overhead allocation base for the year.

2. Compute the total job cost and bid price if Landers Recycling decided to use machine hours as the manufacturing overhead allocation base for the year.

3. In addition to the bid from Landers Recycling, Mills Paper Supply received a bid of $125,000 for this job from Webster Recycling. What are the ramifications for Landers Recycling?

E3-19 **Determine the cost of a job and record entries** *(Learning Objectives 2, 3, 4, 5)*
Lounge Lizard started and finished Job 310 during April. The company's records show that the following direct materials were requisitioned for Job 310:

> Lumber: 50 units at $9 per unit
>
> Padding: 15 yards at $20 per yard
>
> Upholstery fabric: 30 yards at $25 per yard

Labor time records show the following employees (direct labor) worked on Job 310:

> Vince Owens: 10 hours at $10 per hour
>
> Patrick Erin: 15 hours at $15 per hour

Lounge Lizard allocates manufacturing overhead at a rate of 80% of direct labor cost.

Requirements

1. Compute the total amount of direct materials, direct labor, and manufacturing overhead that should be shown on Job 310's job cost record.

2. Job 310 consists of five recliners. If each recliner sells for $600, what is the gross profit per recliner?

3. Record the summary journal entries needed to:
   a. record the direct materials requisitioned for the job
   b. record the direct labor used on the job
   c. allocate manufacturing overhead to the job
   d. record the completion of the job
   e. record the sale on account of all five recliners (assume a perpetual inventory system)

E3-20 **Prepare the journal entries for Job 293** *(Learning Objectives 3, 4, 5)*
The chapter followed Job 293 through Ford Furniture's job costing system. The completed job cost record for Job 293 is shown in Exhibit 3-11. Prepare the summary journal entries that would have been recorded in Ford Furniture's accounting records to reflect the costs assigned to Job 293 and the journal entry to record the transfer of Job 293 to the finished goods storage area. Assume that Ford Furniture was able to sell all ten recliners at a markup of 150% over manufactured cost. Prepare the journal entry to record the sale (assume a perpetual inventory system).

E3-21 **Diagram flow of costs through T-accounts** *(Learning Objectives 3, 4, 5)*
For a manufacturer that uses job costing, diagram the flow of costs through T-accounts. Label each transaction. Include the following accounts in your diagram: Finished Goods Inventory, Manufacturing Wages, Cost of Goods Sold, Work in Process Inventory, Raw Materials Inventory, and Manufacturing Overhead.

E3-22 Analyze T-accounts *(Learning Objectives 3, 4, 5)*

LCD Direct produces LCD touch screen products. The company reports the following information at December 31, 2008. LCD Direct began operations on January 30, 2008.

Work in Process Inventory		Manufacturing Wages		Manufacturing Overhead		Finished Goods Inventory		Raw Materials Inventory	
30,000	123,000	70,000	70,000	2,000	48,000	123,000	111,000	52,000	32,000
60,000				10,000					
48,000		Balance 0		37,000					

1. What is the cost of direct materials used? The cost of indirect materials used?
2. What is the cost of direct labor? The cost of indirect labor?
3. What is the cost of goods manufactured?
4. What is the cost of goods sold (before adjusting for any under- or overallocated manufacturing overhead)?
5. What is the actual manufacturing overhead?
6. How much manufacturing overhead was allocated to jobs?
7. What is the predetermined manufacturing overhead rate as a percentage of direct labor cost?
8. Is manufacturing overhead underallocated or overallocated? By how much?

E3-23 Prepare journal entries *(Learning Objectives 3, 4, 5)*

Record the following transactions in Super Speakers' general journal.

a. Received bill for Web site expenses, $3,400.
b. Incurred manufacturing wages, $16,000.
c. Purchased materials on account, $14,750.
d. Used in production: direct materials, $7,000; indirect materials, $3,000.
e. Assigned $15,000 of manufacturing labor to jobs, 70% of which was direct labor and 30% of which was indirect labor.
f. Recorded manufacturing overhead: depreciation on plant, $13,000; prepaid plant insurance expired, $1,700; plant property tax, $4,200 (credit Property Tax Payable).
g. Allocated manufacturing overhead to jobs, 200% of direct labor costs.
h. Cost of jobs completed during the month: $33,000.
i. Sold all jobs (on account) completed during the month for $52,000. Assume a perpetual inventory system.

E3-24 **Determine transactions from T-accounts** *(Learning Objectives 3, 4, 5)*
Describe the lettered transactions in the following manufacturing accounts:

Manufacturing Wages		Manufacturing Overhead		Cost of Goods Sold	
(a)	(b)	(b)	(e)	(g)	
		(c)	(f)	(f)	
		(d)			

Raw Materials Inventory		Work in Process Inventory		Finished Goods Inventory	
(h)	(i)	(i)	(j)	(j)	(g)
	(c)	(b)			
		(e)			

E3-25 **Back into unknown information** *(Learning Objective 4)*
At the end of the 2008 fiscal year, Reid Bike's manufacturing records show the following unadjusted ending account balances (and the manufacturing costs of which they are comprised):

	Work in Process Inventory	Finished Goods Inventory	Cost of Goods Sold
Unadjusted account balance..............................	$250,000	720,000	$1,400,000
Which consisted of:			
Direct materials.............	$100,000	$170,000	$ 360,000
Direct labor..................	80,000	250,000	600,000
Manufacturing overhead	70,000	300,000	440,000

Reid's accountants allocated manufacturing overhead during the year using a predetermined rate of $40 per machine hour. At year-end, they computed the actual rate of $52 per machine hour for manufacturing overhead. The beginning balances of both Work in Process Inventory and Finished Goods Inventory were zero.

Requirements
1. How many machine hours did Reid Bike use in 2008?
2. Was manufacturing overhead overallocated or underallocated for the year? By how much?

E3-26 **Analyze manufacturing overhead** *(Learning Objective 4)*

Metal Foundry in Charleston, South Carolina, uses a predetermined manufacturing overhead rate to allocate overhead to individual jobs based on the machine hours required. At the beginning of 2008, the company expected to incur the following:

Manufacturing overhead costs	$ 600,000
Direct labor cost..	1,500,000
Machine hours	75,000

At the end of 2008, the company had actually incurred:

Direct labor cost..	$1,210,000
Depreciation on manufacturing plant and equipment	480,000
Property taxes on plant	20,000
Sales salaries..	25,000
Delivery drivers' wages..	15,000
Plant janitors' wages	10,000
Machine hours	55,000 hours

Requirements

1. Compute Metal's predetermined manufacturing overhead rate.
2. How much manufacturing overhead was allocated to jobs during the year?
3. How much manufacturing overhead was incurred during the year? Is manufacturing overhead underallocated or overallocated at the end of the year? By how much?
4. Were the jobs overcosted or undercosted? By how much?

E3-27 **Record manufacturing overhead** *(Learning Objectives 4, 5)*

Refer to the data in Exercise 3-26. Metal's accountant found an error in her 2008 expense records. Depreciation on manufacturing plant and equipment was actually $400,000, not the $480,000 she had originally reported. The unadjusted Cost of Goods Sold balance at year-end was $600,000.

Requirements

1. Prepare the journal entry(s) to record manufacturing overhead costs incurred.
2. Prepare the journal entry to record the manufacturing overhead allocated to jobs in production.
3. Use a T-account to determine whether manufacturing overhead is underallocated or overallocated and by how much.
4. Record the entry to close out the underallocated or overallocated manufacturing overhead.
5. What is the adjusted ending balance of Cost of Goods Sold?

E3-28 **Account for manufacturing overhead** *(Learning Objectives 4, 5)*

Selected cost data for David's Drywall are as follows:

Expected manufacturing overhead cost for the year	$ 97,800
Expected direct labor cost for the year	61,125
Actual manufacturing overhead cost for the year	104,600
Actual direct labor cost for the year	63,900

Requirements

1. Compute the predetermined manufacturing overhead rate assuming that David's Drywall uses direct labor cost as an allocation base.
2. Prepare the journal entry to allocate overhead cost for the year.
3. Use a T-account to determine the amount of overallocated or underallocated manufacturing overhead at the end of the year.
4. Prepare the journal entry to close the balance of the Manufacturing Overhead account.

E3-29 **Record completion and sale of jobs** *(Learning Objective 5)*

September production generated the following activity in Oliver Piano's Work in Process Inventory:

Work in Process Inventory		
September 1 Bal.	16,000	
Direct materials used	29,000	
Direct labor assigned to jobs	32,000	
Manufacturing overhead allocated to jobs	12,000	

Completed production in September, not yet recorded; consists of Jobs B-78 and G-65, with total costs of $41,000 and $37,000, respectively.

Requirements

1. Compute the balance of Work in Process Inventory at September 30.
2. Prepare the journal entry for the production completed in September.
3. Prepare the journal entry to record the sale (on credit) of Job G-65 for $45,000. Assume a perpetual inventory system.
4. What is the gross profit of Job G-65? What other costs must this gross profit cover?

E3-30 **Job cost and bid price at a consulting firm** *(Learning Objective 6)*

Young Consulting, a real estate consulting firm, specializes in advising companies on potential new plant sites. Young Consulting uses a job cost system with a predetermined indirect cost allocation rate computed as a percentage of expected direct labor costs.

At the beginning of 2009, managing partner Tony Young prepared the following plan, or budget, for 2009:

Direct labor hours (professionals)	17,000 hours
Direct labor costs (professionals).................................	$2,669,000
Office rent...	350,000
Support staff salaries..	1,194,300
Utilities..	324,000

Curt's Construction is inviting several consulting firms to bid for work. Young estimates that this job will require about 220 direct labor hours.

Requirements

1. Compute Young Consulting's (a) hourly direct labor cost rate and (b) indirect cost allocation rate.

2. Compute the predicted cost of the Curt's Construction job.

3. If Young wants to earn a profit that equals 50% of the job's cost, how much should he bid for the Curt's Construction job?

Problems (Problem Set A)

P3-31A **Determine flow of costs through accounts** *(Learning Objectives 2, 5)*

Roger's Racing reconditions engines. Its job cost records yield the following information. Roger's Racing uses a perpetual inventory system.

Job No.	Date Started	Date Finished	Sold	Total Cost of Job at March 31	Total Manufacturing Cost Added in April
1	2/26	3/7	3/9	$1,400	
2	2/3	3/12	3/13	1,600	
3	3/29	3/31	4/3	1,300	
4	3/31	4/1	4/1	500	$ 400
5	4/8	4/12	4/14		700
6	4/23	5/6	5/9		1,200

Requirements

1. Compute Roger's Racing's cost of (a) work in process inventory at March 31 and April 30, (b) finished goods inventory at March 31 and April 30, and (c) cost of goods sold for March and April.

2. Make summary journal entries to record the transfer of completed jobs from Work in Process Inventory to Finished Goods Inventory for March and April.

3. Record the sale of Job 5 on account for $1,600.

4. Compute the gross profit for Job 5. What costs must the gross profit cover?

P3-32A Determine and record job costs *(Learning Objectives 2, 3, 4, 5)*

Matt's Manufacturing manufactures prefabricated chalets in Colorado. The company uses a perpetual inventory system and a job cost system in which each chalet is a job. The following events occurred during May:

a. Purchased materials on account, $405,000.

b. Incurred manufacturing wages of $111,600. Requisitioned direct materials and used direct labor in manufacturing as follows:

	Direct Materials	Direct Labor
Chalet 13	$41,100	$14,800
Chalet 14	56,800	28,500
Chalet 15	62,100	19,200
Chalet 16	66,000	21,000

c. Depreciation of manufacturing equipment used on different chalets, $20,000.

d. Other overhead costs incurred on Chalets 13 through 16:

Indirect labor	$28,100
Equipment rentals paid in cash...	10,400
Prepaid plant insurance expired	6,000

e. Allocated overhead to jobs at the predetermined rate of 60% of direct labor cost.

f. Chalets completed: 13, 15, and 16.

g. Chalets sold on account: 13 for $99,000 and 16 for $141,900.

Requirements

1. Record the preceding events in the general journal.

2. Open T-accounts for Work in Process Inventory and Finished Goods Inventory. Post the appropriate entries to these accounts, identifying each entry by letter. Determine the ending account balances assuming that the beginning balances were zero.

3. Summarize the job costs of the unfinished chalet and show that this equals the ending balance in Work in Process Inventory.

4. Summarize the job cost of the completed chalet that has not yet been sold and show that this equals the ending balance in Finished Goods Inventory.

5. Compute the gross profit on each chalet that was sold. What costs must the gross profit cover for Matt's Manufacturing?

P3-33A Prepare job cost record and journal entries *(Learning Objectives 2, 3, 4, 5)*

Tom's Tires manufactures tires for all-terrain vehicles. Tom's Tires uses job costing and has a perpetual inventory system.

On September 22, Tom's Tires received an order for 100 TX tires from ATV Corporation at a price of $55 each. The job, assigned number 298, was promised for October 10. After purchasing the materials, Tom's Tires began production on

September 30 and incurred the following direct labor and direct materials costs in completing the order:

Date	Labor Time Record No.	Description	Amount
9/30	1896	12 hours @ $20	$240
10/3	1904	30 hours @ $19	570

Date	Materials Requisition No.	Description	Amount
9/30	437	60 lb. rubber @ $18	$1,080
10/2	439	40 meters polyester fabric @ $12	480
10/3	501	100 meters steel cord @ $10	1,000

Tom's Tires allocates manufacturing overhead to jobs on the basis of the relation between expected overhead costs ($420,000) and expected direct labor cost ($300,000). Job 298 was completed on October 3 and shipped to ATV on October 5.

Requirements

1. Prepare a job cost record for Job 298 similar to Exhibit 3-11 .
2. Journalize in summary form the requisition of direct materials and the assignment of direct labor and manufacturing overhead to Job 298.
3. Journalize completion of the job and sale of the goods on account.

P3-34A Analyze Manufacturing Overhead (*Learning Objectives 4, 5*)

Easy Life Company produces uniforms. The company allocates manufacturing overhead based on the machine hours each job uses. Easy Life Company reports the following cost data for 2008:

	Budget	Actual
Direct labor hours	7,000 hours	6,200 hours
Machine hours	6,920 hours	6,400 hours
Depreciation on salespeople's autos	$22,000	$22,000
Indirect materials	50,000	52,000
Depreciation on trucks used to deliver uniforms to customers	14,000	12,000
Depreciation on plant and equipment	65,000	67,000
Indirect manufacturing labor	40,000	43,000
Customer service hotline	19,000	21,000
Plant utilities	18,000	20,000
Direct labor cost	70,000	85,000

continued . . .

1. Compute the predetermined manufacturing overhead rate.

2. Post actual and allocated manufacturing overhead to the Manufacturing Overhead T-account.

3. Close the underallocated or overallocated Manufacturing Overhead to Cost of Goods Sold.

4. How can managers use accounting information to help control manufacturing overhead costs?

P3-35A **Use job costing at an advertising agency** *(Learning Objective 6)*

Global.com is an Internet advertising agency. The firm uses a job cost system in which each client is a different "job." Global.com traces direct labor, software licensing costs, and travel costs directly to each job (client). The company allocates indirect costs to jobs based on a predetermined indirect cost allocation rate computed as a percentage of direct labor costs.

At the beginning of 2008, managing partner Ricky Buena prepared a budget:

Direct labor hours (professional).....................................	17,500 hours
Direct labor costs (professional).....................................	$1,750,000
Support staff salaries...	305,000
Rent and utilities..	95,000
Supplies...	15,000
Lease payments on computer hardware.........................	285,000

In January 2008, Global.com served several clients. Records for two clients appear here:

	GoVacation.com	Port Armour Golf Resort
Direct labor hours.........................	460 hours	32 hours
Software licensing costs.................	$1,490	$280
Travel costs....................................	$9,000	$0

Requirements

1. Compute Global.com's predetermined indirect cost allocation rate for 2008.

2. Compute the total cost of each job.

3. If Global.com wants to earn profits equal to 20% of sales revenue, how much (what total fee) should it charge each of these two clients?

4. Why does Global.com assign costs to jobs?

■ Problems (Problem Set B)

P3-36B Determine flow of costs through accounts (*Learning Objectives 2, 5*)

Sleek Speakers Manufacturing makes headphones for portable electronic devices. Its job cost records yield the following information:

Job No.	Date Started	Date Finished	Sold	Total Cost of Job at November 30	Total Manufacturing Cost Added in December
1	11/3	11/12	11/13	$1,400	
2	11/3	11/30	12/1	1,900	
3	11/17	12/24	12/27	300	$ 700
4	11/29	12/29	1/3	500	1,600
5	12/8	12/12	12/14		750
6	12/23	1/6	1/9		500

Requirements

1. Compute Sleek Speakers cost of (a) work in process inventory at November 30 and December 31, (b) finished goods inventory at November 30 and December 31, and (c) cost of goods sold for November and December.

2. Record summary journal entries for the transfer of completed units from Work in Process Inventory to Finished Goods Inventory for November and December.

3. Record the sale of Job 3 on account for $1,400.

4. What is the gross profit for Job 3? What other costs must this gross profit cover?

P3-37B Determine and record job costs (*Learning Objectives 2, 3, 4, 5*)

All Wood Construction is a home builder in Hawaii. All Wood uses a perpetual inventory system and a job cost system in which each house is a job. Because it constructs houses, the company uses accounts titled Construction Wages and Construction Overhead. The following events occurred during August:

a. Purchased materials on account, $480,400.

b. Incurred construction wages of $219,800. Requisitioned direct materials and used direct labor in construction as follows:

	Direct Materials	Direct Labor
House 302.....................	$58,400	$42,300
House 303.....................	69,000	32,800
House 304.....................	67,600	50,400
House 305.....................	84,200	52,700

c. Depreciation of construction equipment, $6,400.

continued . . .

d. Other construction overhead costs incurred on Houses 302 through 305:

Indirect labor	$41,600
Equipment rentals paid in cash..	37,300
Prepaid worker liability insurance expired	7,100

e. Allocated overhead to jobs at the predetermined overhead rate of 40% of direct labor cost.

f. Houses completed: 302 and 304.

g. House sold on account: 304 for $189,500.

Requirements

1. Record the events in the general journal.

2. Open T-accounts for Work in Process Inventory and Finished Goods Inventory. Post the appropriate entries to these accounts, identifying each entry by letter. Determine the ending account balances assuming that the beginning balances were zero.

3. Summarize the job costs of the unfinished houses and show that this total amount equals the ending balance in the Work in Process Inventory account.

4. Summarize the job cost of the completed house that has not yet been sold and show that this equals the ending balance in Finished Goods Inventory.

5. Compute gross profit on the house that was sold. What costs must gross profit cover for All Wood Construction?

P3-38B Prepare job cost record and journal entries *(Learning Objectives 2, 3, 4, 5)*
Patel Technology manufactures CDs and DVDs for computer software and entertainment companies. Patel Technology uses job costing and has a perpetual inventory system.

On November 2, Patel Technology began production of 5,000 DVDs, Job 423, for Lion Pictures for $1.10 each. Patel Technology promised to deliver the DVDs to Lion by November 5. Patel Technology incurred the following direct labor and direct material costs:

Date	Labor Time Record No.	Description	Amount
11-2	655	10 hours @ $22	$220
11-3	656	20 hours @ $16	320

Date	Materials Requisition No.	Description	Amount
11-2	63	31 lb. polycarbonate plastic @ $11	$341
11-2	64	25 lb. acrylic plastic @ $28	700
11-3	74	3 lb. refined aluminum @ $48	144

Patel Technology allocates manufacturing overhead to jobs based on the relationship between expected overhead costs ($537,600) and expected direct labor costs ($448,000). Job 423 was completed and shipped on November 3.

Requirements

1. Prepare a job cost record for Job 423 similar to Exhibit 3-11.
2. Journalize in summary form the requisition of direct materials and the assignment of direct labor and manufacturing overhead to Job 423.
3. Journalize completion of the job and the sale of the 5,000 DVDs on account.

P3-39B Analyze manufacturing overhead *(Learning Objectives 4, 5)*
June's Jewelry manufactures jewelry boxes. The primary materials (wood, brass, and glass) and direct labor are traced directly to the products. Manufacturing overhead costs are allocated based on machine hours. Data for 2007 follow:

	Budget	Actual
Machine hours	28,000 hours	32,800 hours
Direct labor hours	42,000 hours	40,000 hours
Wood	$150,000	$148,000
Maintenance labor (repairs to equipment)	9,000	22,500
Plant supervisor's wages	40,000	44,000
Screws, nails, and glue	20,400	41,000
Plant utilities	45,600	90,850
Brass	75,000	70,500
Glass	125,000	126,275
Freight-out	35,000	44,500
Direct labor	65,000	63,000
Depreciation on plant and equipment	81,000	81,000
Advertising expenses	40,000	55,000

Requirements

1. Compute the predetermined manufacturing overhead rate.
2. Post actual and allocated manufacturing overhead to the Manufacturing Overhead T-account.
3. Close the underallocated or overallocated Manufacturing Overhead to Cost of Goods Sold.
4. The predetermined manufacturing overhead rate usually turns out to be inaccurate. Why don't accountants use just the actual manufacturing overhead rate?

P3-40B Use job costing at a consulting firm *(Learning Objective 6)*

Jackson Design is a Web site design and consulting firm. The firm uses a job cost system in which each client is a different "job." Jackson Design traces direct labor, licensing costs, and travel costs directly to each job (client). It allocates indirect costs to jobs based on a predetermined indirect cost allocation rate computed as a percentage of direct labor costs.

At the beginning of 2008, managing partner Mary Milici prepared the following budget:

Direct labor hours (professional).....................................	8,000 hours
Direct labor costs (professional)......................................	$1,000,000
Support staff salaries...	80,000
Computer lease payments..	46,000
Office supplies...	25,000
Office rent..	49,000

In November 2008, Jackson Design served several clients. Records for two clients appear here:

	Organic Foods	SunNow.com
Direct labor hours............	750 hours	50 hours
Licensing costs	$ 1,850	$160
Travel costs......................	$14,150	$0

Requirements

1. Compute Jackson Design's predetermined indirect cost allocation rate for 2008.
2. Compute the total cost of each job.
3. If Milici wants to earn profits equal to 20% of sales revenue, how much (what total fee) should she charge each of these two clients?
4. Why does Jackson Design assign costs to jobs?

Apply Your Knowledge

■ Decision Cases

Case 3-41. Issues with cost of job *(Learning Objective 2)*

Hegy Chocolate is located in Cleveland. The company prepares gift boxes of chocolates for private parties and corporate promotions. Each order contains a selection of chocolates determined by the customer, and the box is designed to the customer's specifications. Accordingly, Hegy Chocolate uses a job cost system and allocates manufacturing overhead based on direct labor cost.

One of Hegy Chocolate's largest customers is the Bailey and Choi law firm. This organization sends chocolates to its clients each Christmas and also provides them to employees at the firm's gatherings. The law firm's managing partner, Peter Bailey, placed the client gift order in September for 500 boxes of cream-filled dark chocolates. But Bailey and Choi did not place its December staff-party order until the last week of November. This order was for an additional 100 boxes of chocolates identical to the ones to be distributed to clients.

Hegy Chocolate budgeted the cost per box for the original 500-box order as follows:

Chocolate, filling, wrappers, box	$14.00
Employee time to fill and wrap the box (10 min.)	2.00
Manufacturing overhead	1.00
Total manufacturing cost	$17.00

Ben Hegy, president of Hegy Chocolate, priced the order at $20 per box.

In the past few months, Hegy Chocolate has experienced price increases for both dark chocolate and direct labor. *All other costs have remained the same.* Hegy budgeted the cost per box for the second order as:

Chocolate, filling, wrappers, box	$15.00
Employee time to fill and wrap the box (10 min.)	2.20
Manufacturing overhead	1.10
Total manufacturing cost	$18.30

1. Do you agree with the cost analysis for the second order? Explain your answer.
2. Should the two orders be accounted for as one or two jobs in Hegy Chocolate's system?
3. What sales price per box should Hegy set for the second order? What are the advantages and disadvantages of this price?

Case 3-42. Issues with the manufacturing overhead rate *(Learning Objective 4)*

All Natural manufactures organic fruit preserves sold primarily through health food stores and on the Web. The company closes for two weeks each December to allow employees to spend time with their families over the holiday season. All Natural's manufacturing overhead is mostly straight-line depreciation on its plant and air-conditioning costs for keeping the berries cool during the summer months. The company uses direct labor hours as the allocation base. President Kara Wise has just approved new accounting software and is telling Controller Melissa Powers about her decision.

"I think this new software will be great," Wise says. "It will save you time in preparing all of those reports."

"Yes, and having so much more information just a click away will help us make better decisions and help control costs," replies Powers. "We need to consider how we can use the new system to improve our business practices."

"And I know just where to start," says Wise. "You complain each year about having to predict the weather months in advance for estimating air-conditioning costs and direct labor hours for the denominator of the predetermined manufacturing overhead rate, when professional meteorologists can't even get tomorrow's forecast right! I think we should calculate the predetermined overhead rate on a monthly basis."

Controller Powers is not so sure this is a good idea.

Requirements

1. What are the advantages and disadvantages of Wise's proposal?
2. Should All Natural compute its predetermined manufacturing overhead rate on an annual basis or a monthly basis? Explain.

■ Team Project

Project 3-43. Finding the cost of flight routes *(Learning Objective 2)*

Major airlines such as American, Delta, and Continental are struggling to meet the challenges of budget carriers such as Southwest and JetBlue. Suppose Delta CFO Edward Bastian has just returned from a meeting on strategies for responding to competition from budget carriers. The vice president of operations suggests doing nothing: "We just need to wait until these new airlines run out of money. They cannot be making money with their low fares." In contrast, the vice president of marketing, not wanting to lose marketing share, suggests cutting Delta's fares to match the competition. "If JetBlue charges only $75 for that flight from New York, so must we!" Others, including CFO Bastian, emphasize the potential for cutting costs. Another possibility is starting a new budget airline within Delta. Imagine that CEO Gerald Grinstein cuts the meeting short and directs Bastian to "get some hard data."

As a start, Bastian decides to collect cost and revenue data for a typical Delta flight and then compare it to the data for a competitor. Assume that he prepares the following schedule:

	Delta	JetBlue
Route: New York to Tampa.....................	Flight 1247	Flight 53
Distance...	1,011 miles	1,011 miles
Seats per plane	142	162
One-way ticket price..............................	$80–$621*	$75
Food and beverage..................................	Meal	Snack

*The highest price is first-class airfare

Excluding food and beverage, Bastian estimates that the cost per available seat mile is $0.084 for Delta, compared to $0.053 for JetBlue. (That is, the cost of flying a seat for one mile—whether or not the seat is occupied—is $0.084 for Delta and $0.053 for JetBlue.) Assume that the average cost of food and beverage is $5 per passenger for snacks and $10 for a meal.

Split your team into two groups. Group 1 should prepare its response to Requirement 1 and Group 2 should prepare its response to Requirement 2 before the entire team meets to consider Requirements 3 through 6.

Requirements

1. Group 1 uses the data to determine the following for Delta:
   a. The total cost of Flight 1247 assuming a full plane (100% load factor)
   b. The revenue generated by Flight 1247 assuming a 100% load factor and average revenue per one-way ticket of $102
   c. The profit per Flight 1247 given the responses to a and b
2. Group 2 uses the data to determine for JetBlue:
   a. The total cost of Flight 53 assuming a full plane (100% load factor)
   b. The revenue generated by Flight 53 assuming a 100% load factor
   c. The profit per Flight 53 given the responses to a and b
3. The entire team meets, and both groups combine their analyses. Based on the responses to Requirements 1 and 2, carefully evaluate each of the four alternative strategies discussed in Delta's executive meeting.
4. CFO Bastian wants additional data before he meets again with Delta's CEO. Each group should repeat the analyses in *both* Requirements 1 and 2 using another Delta route in Requirement 1 and a budget airline other than JetBlue in Requirement 2 (other budget airlines include America West, with a cost per available seat mile of about $0.065, and Southwest Airlines, with a cost per available seat mile of about $0.063). Information on flights, available seats, airfares, and mileage are available on airline Web sites.
5. The analysis in this project is based on several simplifying assumptions. As a team, brainstorm factors that your quantitative evaluation does not include but that may affect a comparison of Delta's operations against budget carriers.

continued . . .

6. Prepare a memo from CFO Bastian addressed to Delta CEO Grinstein summarizing the results of your analyses. Be sure to include the limitations of your analyses identified in Requirement 5. Use the following format for your memo.

Date: _____

    To: CEO Gerald Grinstein

From: CFO Edward Bastian

Subject: Delta's Response to Competition from Budget Airlines

Process Costing

What's your favorite Jelly Belly flavor? Chocolate Pudding? Very Cherry? Lemon Drop? Peanut Butter? Or maybe Piña Colada? Have you ever wondered how these tasty gems are made?

Each tiny Jelly Belly jelly bean spends seven to ten days going through eight different processes:

1. Cooking the centers
2. Shaping hot liquid centers into jelly beans
3. Drying
4. Sugar shower
5. Shell-building
6. Polishing
7. Stamping (name of the company on each bean)
8. Packaging

The family that owns Jelly Belly needs to know how much it costs to make each batch. That helps them set selling prices and measure profits.

They also want to know how efficiently each process is operating. That helps them control costs. The owners use accounting information to answer these questions.

Jelly Belly mass-produces its jelly beans in a sequence of processes and accumulates the costs for each *process*. Then, the company spreads these costs over the pounds of jelly beans passing through each process. This *process costing* approach differs from the job costing approach that Dell uses for its computers. Why the difference? Because Jelly Belly mass-produces its products, while Dell custom-builds each computer to a specific order. It certainly would not be practical to use job cost records to compile the cost of individual jelly beans! ■

Learning Objectives

1 Distinguish between the flow of costs in process costing and job costing

2 Compute equivalent units

3 Use process costing to assign manufacturing costs to units completed and to units in ending work in process inventory in a first department

4 Use process costing to assign manufacturing costs to units completed and to units in ending work in process inventory in a second or later department

As the chapter-opening story explains, managers need to know how much it costs to make their products. Why? So they can control costs, set selling prices, and identify their most profitable products.

Process Costing: An Overview

Let's start by contrasting the two basic types of costing systems: *job costing* and *process costing*.

1 Distinguish between the flow of costs in process costing and job costing

Two Basic Costing Systems: Job Costing and Process Costing

We saw in Chapter 3 that Dell and Boeing use job costing to determine the cost of producing custom goods. Service companies such as law firms and hospitals also use job costing to determine the cost of serving individual clients. Job cost records accumulate the costs of each individual job, like each computer Dell custom-builds to a customer order. In contrast, companies such as Jelly Belly and Shell Oil use a series of steps (called *processes*) to make large quantities of similar products. These companies typically use *process costing* systems.

For the rest of our discussion, we'll simplify Jelly Belly's processes. We'll combine cooking, shaping, and drying the jelly bean centers into a single process called Centers. We'll also combine the sugar shower, shell-building, polishing, and stamping steps into a second process called Shells. The third process is Packaging.

Jelly Belly *accumulates* the costs of each process and then *assigns* these costs to the units (pounds of jelly beans) passing through that process.

Suppose the Centers process incurs $1,350,000 of costs to produce centers for 1,000,000 pounds of jelly beans, the Shells process incurs $800,000, and Packaging incurs $700,000. The total cost to produce a pound of jelly beans is the sum of the cost per pound for each of the three processes.

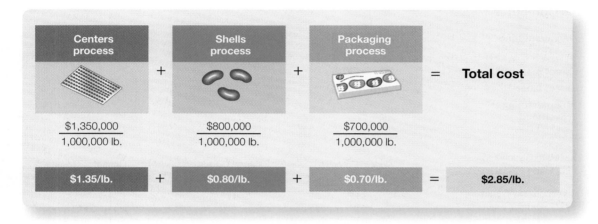

Jelly Belly's owners use the cost per pound of each process to help control costs. For example, they can compare the actual cost of producing centers for a pound of jelly beans (assumed to be $1.35 in our example) to the budget or plan. If the actual cost of the Centers process exceeds the budget, they can look for ways to cut costs in that process. Jelly Belly's owners also consider the total cost of making a pound of jelly beans (assumed to be $2.85 in our example) when setting selling prices. The price should be high enough to cover costs *and* to return a profit. Jelly Belly also uses the total cost of making a pound of jelly beans for financial reporting:

- To value the ending inventory of jelly beans for the balance sheet ($2.85 per pound still in ending inventory)
- To value cost of goods sold for the income statement ($2.85 per pound sold)

The simple computation of the cost to make a pound of jelly beans is correct *only if there are no work in process inventories*, but it takes seven to ten days to complete all of the processes. So, Jelly Belly does have inventories of partially complete jelly beans. These inventories make the costing more complicated. In the rest of this chapter, you'll learn how to do process costing when there are work in process inventories.

How Does the Flow of Costs Differ Between Job and Process Costing?

Exhibit 4-1 compares the flow of costs in

- A job costing system for Dell (Panel A)
- A process costing system for Jelly Belly (Panel B)

Panel A shows that Dell's job costing system has a single Work in Process Inventory control account supported by individual subsidiary job cost records for each job in process (that is, each custom-built computer). Dell assigns direct materials, direct labor, and manufacturing overhead to individual jobs, as explained in Chapter 3. When a job is finished, its costs flow directly into Finished Goods Inventory (*not* from one Work in Process Inventory account into another as illustrated in Panel B for process costing).

EXHIBIT 4-1 **Flow of Costs in Job Costing**

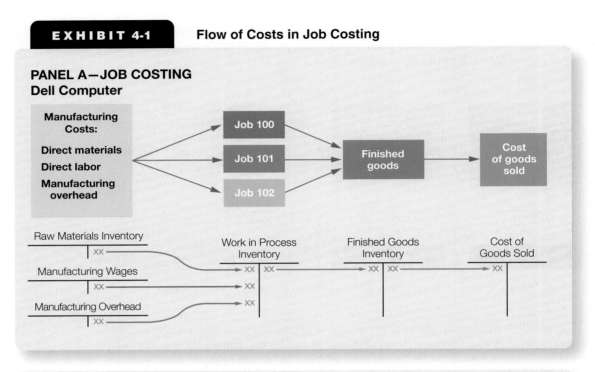

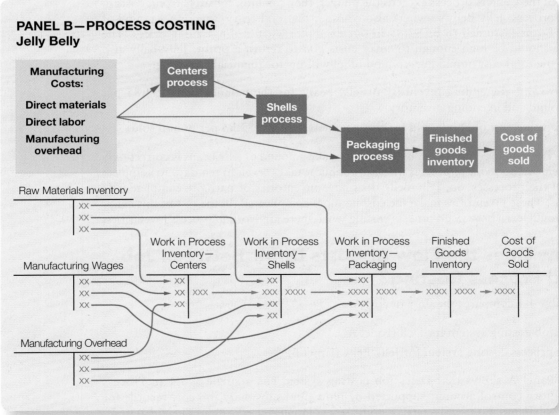

In contrast to Dell's individual jobs, Jelly Belly uses a series of three *manufacturing processes* to produce jelly beans. The movement of jelly beans through these three processes is shown in Exhibit 4-2.

Take a moment to follow along as we describe Exhibit 4-2. In the first process (Centers process), Jelly Belly converts sugar and flavorings (the direct materials) into jelly bean centers using direct labor and manufacturing overhead such as depreciation on the mixing vats. Once the jelly bean centers are made, they are transferred to the Shells process. In the Shells process, Jelly Belly uses different labor and equipment to coat the jelly bean centers with sugar, syrup, and glaze (the direct materials) to form the crunchy shells. Once that process is complete, the finished jelly beans are transferred to the Packaging process. In the Packaging process, Jelly Belly packages the finished jelly beans into various boxes and bags, using other labor and equipment. The boxed and bagged jelly beans are then transferred to finished goods inventory until they are sold.

Now, let's see how Panel B of Exhibit 4-1 summarizes the flow of costs through this process costing system. Study the exhibit carefully, paying particular attention to the following key points:

1. Each process (Centers, Shells, and Packaging) has its own separate Work in Process Inventory account.

2. Direct materials, direct labor, and manufacturing overhead are assigned to *each* processing department's Work in Process Inventory account based on the manufacturing costs incurred by that process. Exhibit 4-2 shows that each of Jelly Belly's processes uses different direct materials, direct labor, and manufacturing overhead costs. These costs are debited to the individual Work in Process Inventory accounts as they are incurred by those processes.

3. Recall from Exhibit 4-2 that when the Centers process is complete, the jelly bean centers are physically *transferred out* of the Centers process and *transferred in* to the Shells process. Likewise, the *cost* of the centers is also *transferred out* of Work in Process Inventory—Centers and *transferred in* to Work in Process Inventory—Shells. The transfer of costs between accounts is pictured in Panel B of Exhibit 4-1 as a series of green *x*'s. As a rule of thumb:

> In process costing, the manufacturing costs assigned to the product must always follow the physical movement of the product. Therefore, when units are physically transferred out of one process and into the next, the *costs* assigned to those units must *also* be transferred out of the appropriate Work in Process Inventory account and into the next.

To simplify the accounting, the journal entry to record this transfer of costs between accounts is generally made once a month to reflect *all* physical transfers that occurred during the month.

4. When the Shells process is complete, the finished jelly beans are transferred out of the Shells process and into the Packaging process. Likewise, the *cost* assigned to the jelly beans thus far (cost of making the centers and adding the shells) is *transferred out* of Work in Process Inventory—Shells and *transferred in* to Work in Process Inventory—Packaging.

5. Finally, when the Packaging process is complete, the finished packages of jelly beans are transferred to finished goods inventory. Likewise, the *cost* assigned to the jelly beans thus far (cost of making and packaging the jelly beans) is transferred out of Work in Process—Packaging and into Finished Goods Inventory. *In process costing, costs are transferred into Finished Goods Inventory only from the Work in Process Inventory of the **last** manufacturing process. The transferred cost includes all costs assigned to the units from every process the units have completed (Centers, Shells, and Packaging).*

EXHIBIT 4-2 **Flow of Costs in Production of Jelly Beans**

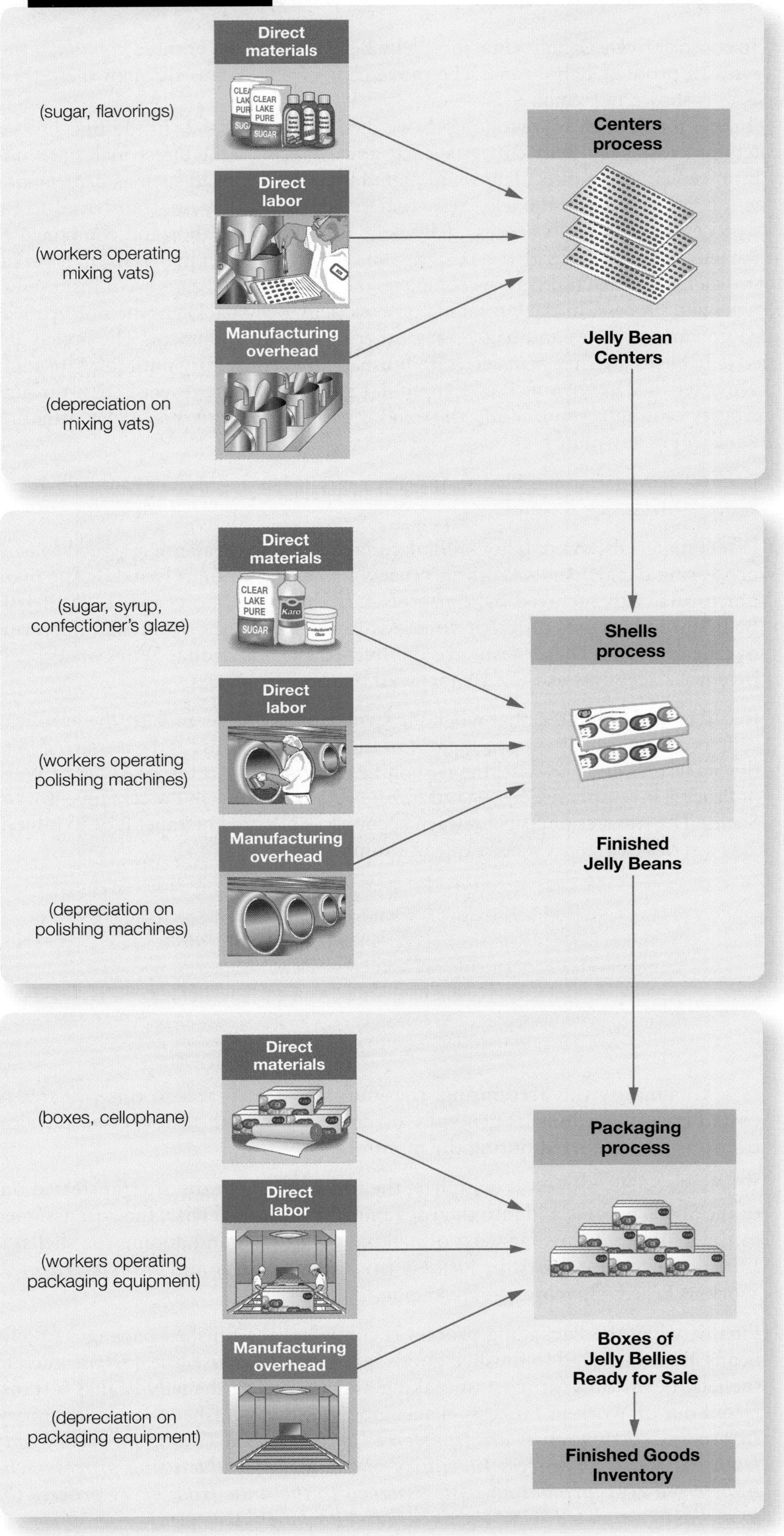

(sugar, flavorings)

Direct materials

CLEAR LAKE PURE SUGAR

(workers operating mixing vats)

Direct labor

(depreciation on mixing vats)

Manufacturing overhead

Centers process

Jelly Bean Centers

(sugar, syrup, confectioner's glaze)

Direct materials

CLEAR LAKE PURE SUGAR Karo Confectioner's Glaze

(workers operating polishing machines)

Direct labor

(depreciation on polishing machines)

Manufacturing overhead

Shells process

Finished Jelly Beans

(boxes, cellophane)

Direct materials

(workers operating packaging equipment)

Direct labor

(depreciation on packaging equipment)

Manufacturing overhead

Packaging process

Boxes of Jelly Bellies Ready for Sale

Finished Goods Inventory

Building Blocks of Process Costing

Before we illustrate process costing in more detail, we must first learn about the three building blocks of process costing: conversion costs, equivalent units, and inventory flow assumptions.

Conversion Costs

Chapter 2 introduced three kinds of manufacturing costs: direct materials, direct labor, and manufacturing overhead. Most companies, like Jelly Belly, that mass-produce a product use automated production processes. Therefore, direct labor is only a small part of total manufacturing costs. Companies that use automated production processes often condense the three manufacturing costs into two categories:

1. Direct materials

2. Conversion costs

   Recall from Chapter 2 that conversion costs are direct labor plus manufacturing overhead. Combining these costs in a single category simplifies the process costing procedures. We call this category *conversion costs* because it is the cost to *convert* direct materials into new finished products.

Equivalent Units

2 Compute equivalent units

When a company has work in process inventories of partially completed goods, we use **equivalent units** to express the amount of work done during a period in terms of fully completed units of output.

   To illustrate equivalent units, let's look at Callaway Golf, a manufacturer of golf balls and golf clubs. See Exhibit 4-3. Assume that Callaway's golf ball production plant has 5,000 partially completed balls in ending work in process inventory. Each ball is 80% of the way through the production process. If conversion costs are incurred evenly throughout the process, then getting each of 5,000 balls 80% of the way through the process takes about the same amount of work as getting 4,000 balls (5,000 × 80%) all the way through the process.

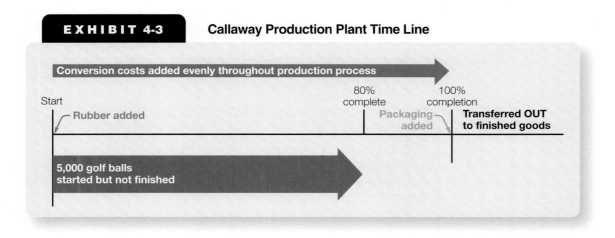

| **EXHIBIT 4-3** | **Callaway Production Plant Time Line** |

Equivalent units are calculated as follows:

Number of partially complete physical units	$\times$	Percentage of process completed	$=$	Number of equivalent units

So, the number of equivalent units of conversion costs in Callaway's ending work in process inventory is calcualted as follows:

5,000	$\times$	80%	$=$	4,000

Conversion cost are usually incurred *evenly* throughout production. However, direct materials are often added at a particular point in the process. For example, Callaway adds rubber at the *beginning* of the production process, but doesn't add packaging materials until the *end*. How many equivalent units of rubber and packaging materials are in the ending inventory of 5,000 balls?

All 5,000 balls are 80% complete, so they all have passed the point at which rubber is added. Each ball has its full share of rubber (100%), so the balls have 5,000 equivalent units of rubber. In contrast, the time line shows that *none* of the 5,000 balls has made it to the end of the process, where the packaging materials are added. The ending inventory, therefore, has *zero* equivalent units of packaging materials.

To summarize, the 5,000 balls in ending work in process inventory have:

- 5,000 equivalent units of rubber (5,000 units $\times$ 100% of rubber)
- 0 equivalent units of packaging materials (5,000 units $\times$ 0% of packaging materials)
- 4,000 equivalent units of conversion costs (5,000 units $\times$ 80% converted)

Be careful to distinguish the *end of the production process* from the *end of the accounting period*. Goods at the end of the production process are transferred to the next process or to finished goods. For example, Callaway's completed golf balls proceed to the finished goods warehouse. By contrast, at the end of the accounting period, goods that are only partway through the production process are the ending work in process inventory. Callaway's ending work in process inventory includes 5,000 golf balls that have their rubber cores but no packaging.

Stop & Think...

Colleges and universities use the equivalent-unit concept to describe the number of faculty as well as the number of students. The University of Georgia has about 2,000 full-time faculty and 400 part-time faculty. Assume the following:

1. A full-time faculty member teaches six courses per year.
2. 100 part-time faculty teach three courses per year.
3. 300 part-time faculty teach two courses per year.

What is the "full-time equivalent" faculty—the number of equivalent units of faculty?

Answer: Compute the full-time equivalent faculty as follows:

Full-time faculty..................................	$2,000 \times 6/6 = 2,000$
Half-time faculty.................................	$100 \times 3/6 = 50$
One-third–time faculty	$300 \times 2/6 = 100$
Full-time equivalent faculty	$\underline{2,150}$

Inventory Flow Assumptions

Firms compute process costing using either the weighted-average or first-in, first-out (FIFO) method. Throughout the rest of the chapter, we will use the **weighted-average method of process costing** rather than the FIFO method because it is simpler and the differences between the two methods' results are usually immaterial. *The two costing methods differ only in how they treat beginning inventory.* The FIFO method requires that any units in beginning inventory be costed *separately* from any units started in the current period. The weighted-average method *combines* any beginning inventory units (and costs) with the current period's units (and costs) to get a weighted-average cost. From a cost-benefit standpoint, many firms prefer to use the weighted-average method because the extra cost of calculating the FIFO method does not justify the additional benefits they gain (if any) from using FIFO information. Therefore, throughout the remainder of the text and throughout all assignment material, we will assume that the weighted-average method is used. The FIFO method is discussed in advanced managerial accounting textbooks.

Illustrating Process Costing in the First Processing Department

Let's see how SeaView, a sporting goods company, uses the weighted-average method of process costing to measure (1) the average cost of producing each swim mask and (2) the cost of the two major processes it uses to make the masks (Shaping and Insertion).

 Use process costing to assign manufacturing costs to units completed and to units in ending work in process inventory in a first department

Exhibit 4-4 illustrates SeaView's production process. The Shaping Department begins with plastic and metal fasteners (direct materials) and uses labor and equipment (conversion costs) to transform the materials into shaped masks. The direct materials are added at the *beginning* of the process, but conversion costs are incurred *evenly* throughout the process. After shaping, the masks move to the Insertion Department, where the shaped masks are polished and then the clear faceplates are inserted.

During October, the Shaping Department incurs the following costs while working on 50,000 masks:

Direct materials...............................		$140,000
Conversion costs:		
Direct labor...................................	$21,250	
Manufacturing overhead..............	46,750	
Total conversion costs..............		68,000
Total costs to account for.................		$208,000

How did SeaView arrive at these costs? SeaView traces direct materials and direct labor to each processing department using materials requisitions and labor time records (just as we used these documents to trace direct materials and direct labor to individual *jobs* in Chapter 3). SeaView allocates manufacturing overhead to each processing department using a predetermined manufacturing overhead rate (just as we allocated manufacturing overhead to individual *jobs* in Chapter 3).

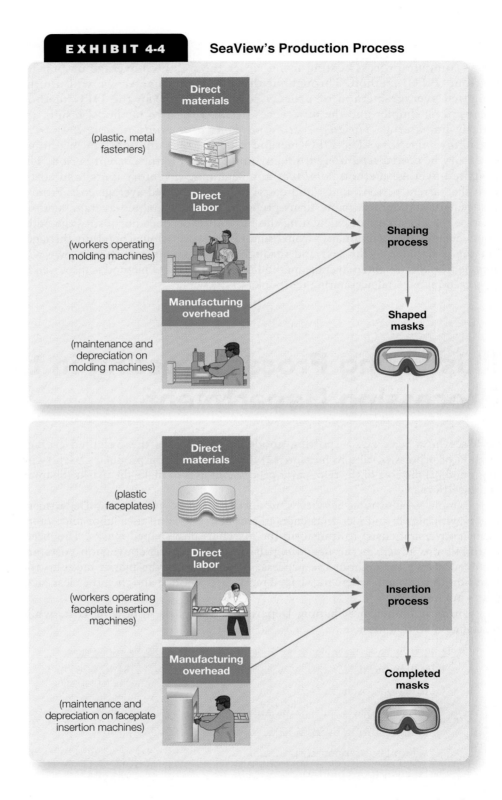

EXHIBIT 4-4 SeaView's Production Process

The summary journal entries to record production costs in October in the Shaping Department are as follows:

Work in Process Inventory—Shaping	140,000	
Raw Materials Inventory		140,000
(*To record direct materials used by the Shaping Department in October.*)		

Work in Process Inventory—Shaping	21,250	
Manufacturing Wages		21,250
(*To record direct labor used in the Shaping Department in October.*)		

Work in Process Inventory—Shaping	46,750	
Manufacturing Overhead		46,750
(*To record manufacturing overhead allocated to the Shaping Department in October.*)		

Let's assume that the Shaping Department has no beginning inventory. After posting these journal entries, the Work in Process Inventory—Shaping Department T-account appears as follows:

Work in Process Inventory—Shaping

Balance, October 1		$ 0
Direct materials		140,000
Direct labor	$208,000	21,250
Manufacturing overhead		46,750

The production costs in the Work in Process Inventory—Shaping account total $208,000. If, at the end of October, all 50,000 masks have been completely shaped and transferred out of the Shaping Department and into the Insertion Department, the entire $208,000 of manufacturing cost associated with these masks should *likewise* be transferred out of Work in Process—Shaping and into Work in Process—Insertion. In this case, the cost for *just* the shaping process is $4.16 per mask ($208,000/50,000 masks).

But what if only 40,000 masks are completely through the shaping process? Let's say that at October 31, the Shaping Department still has 10,000 masks that are only one-quarter of the way through the shaping process. How do we split the $208,000 between the following?

- 40,000 completely shaped masks transferred to the Insertion Department
- 10,000 partially shaped masks remaining in the Shaping Department's ending work in process inventory

In other words, how do we determine the cost of making the *completely* shaped masks versus the cost of making the *partially* shaped masks? We can't simply assign $4.16 to each mask because a partially shaped mask does *not* cost the same to make as a completely shaped mask. We must use the following five-step process costing procedure:

STEP 1: Summarize the flow of physical units
STEP 2: Compute output in terms of equivalent units
STEP 3: Summarize total costs to account for
STEP 4: Compute the cost per equivalent unit
STEP 5: Assign total costs to units completed and to units in ending Work in Process inventory

We'll walk through each of these steps now.

Step 1: Summarize the Flow of Physical Units

Step 1 tracks the physical movement of swim masks into and out of the Shaping Department during the month. Follow along as we walk through this step in the first column of Exhibit 4-5. The first question addressed is this: *How many physical units did the Shaping Department work on during the month?* We assume work began October 1, so there were no masks in the beginning work in process inventory. During the month, the Shaping Department began work on 50,000 masks. Thus, the department needs to account for a *total* of 50,000 masks.

EXHIBIT 4-5   **Step 1: Summarize the Flow of Physical Units**
Step 2: Compute Output in Terms of Equivalent Units

SEAVIEW SHAPING DEPARTMENT
Month Ended October 31

Flow of Production	Step 1 Flow of Physical Units	Step 2 Equivalent Units — Direct Materials	Step 2 Equivalent Units — Conversion Costs
Units to account for:			
Beginning work in process, October 1	0		
Started in production during October	50,000		
Total physical units to account for	50,000		
Units accounted for:			
Completed and transferred out during October	40,000	40,000	40,000
Ending work in process, October 31	10,000	10,000	2,500*
Total physical units accounted for	50,000		
Total equivalent units		50,000	42,500

*10,000 units each 25% complete = 2,500 equivalent units

The second question addressed is this: *What happened to those masks?* The Shaping Department reports that it completed and transferred out 40,000 masks to the Insertion Department during October. The remaining 10,000 partially shaped masks are still in the Shaping Department's ending work in process inventory on October 31. Notice that the *Total physical units to account for* (50,000) must equal the *Total physical units accounted for* (50,000). In other words, the Shaping Department must account for the whereabouts of every mask it worked on during the month.

Step 2: Compute Output in Terms of Equivalent Units

Step 2 computes all of the Shaping Department's output for the month in terms of equivalent units. Step 2 is shown in the last two columns of Exhibit 4-5. First, let's consider the 40,000 masks that were *completed and transferred out* to the Insertion Department during October. These units have been fully completed in the Shaping Department; therefore, these 40,000 completed masks have incurred 40,000 equivalent units of direct materials (40,000 masks × 100% of direct materials) and 40,000 equivalent units of conversion costs (40,000 masks × 100% of conversion costs).

Now, let's consider the 10,000 masks still in ending work in process. These masks are only 25% of the way through the shaping process on October 31. The time line in

Exhibit 4-6 reminds us that all direct materials are added at the *beginning* of the shaping process. Therefore, the partially shaped masks have made it past the point where direct materials are added. As a result, these masks have incurred 10,000 equivalent units of direct materials (10,000 masks × 100% of direct materials).

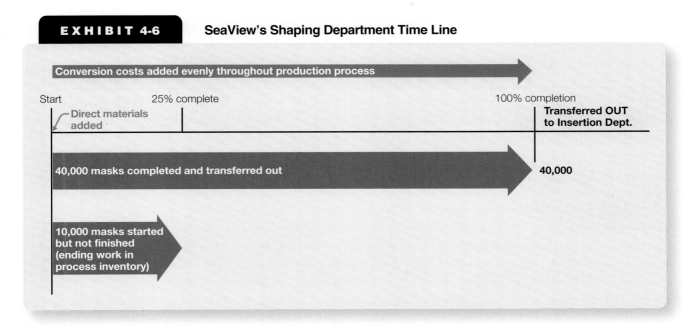

EXHIBIT 4-6   SeaView's Shaping Department Time Line

Unlike direct materials, the conversion costs are added *evenly* throughout the shaping process. For these partially shaped masks, the equivalent units of conversion costs are:

$$10,000 \times 25\% = 2,500 \text{ equivalent units of conversion costs}$$

Our last step is to calculate the Shaping Department's output in terms of *total equivalent units* for the month. We must calculate totals separately for direct materials and conversion costs because they will differ in most circumstances. To find the totals, we simply add the equivalent units of all masks worked on during the month. For example, the *total equivalent units of direct materials* (50,000 as shown in Exhibit 4-5) is simply the sum of the 40,000 equivalent units completed and transferred out *plus* the 10,000 equivalent units still in ending work in process. Likewise, the *total equivalent units of conversion costs* (42,500 shown in Exhibit 4-5) is the sum of the 40,000 equivalent units completed and transferred out plus the 2,500 equivalent units still in ending work in process.

Stop & Think...

Suppose the Shaping Department adds direct materials at the end of the shaping process rather than at the beginning.

1. Draw a new time line similar to Exhibit 4-6.
2. Use the time line to determine the number of equivalent units of direct materials.

continued . . .

Answers

1.

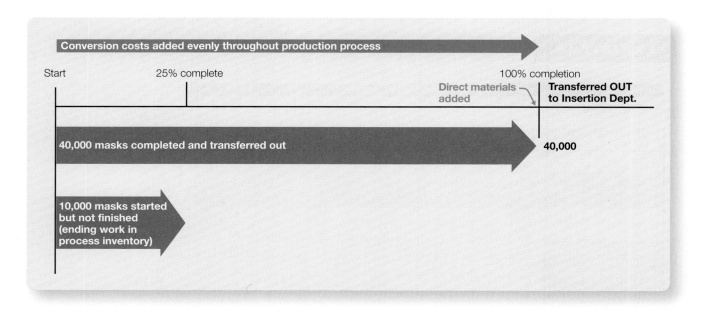

2. The time line shows that the 10,000 masks in ending work in process inventory have not made it to the end of the shaping process where materials are added. Materials have been added *only* to the 40,000 masks completed and transferred out, not to the 10,000 masks in ending work in process. Thus, there are only 40,000 total equivalent units of direct materials.

Step 3: Summarize Total Costs to Account For

Step 3, as shown in Exhibit 4-7, summarizes all of the production costs the Shaping Department must account for. These are the production costs that were associated with beginning inventory (if any existed) plus the production costs that were incurred during the month.[1] *Notice how the total costs to account for ($208,000) is the same dollar amount as we saw in the Work in Process Inventory—Shaping T-account shown on page 203.*

Once again, we must show separate totals for each of the two cost categories: direct materials and conversion costs. Because the Shaping Department did not have any beginning inventory of partially shaped masks, the beginning balance in the Work in Process Inventory—Shaping account is zero. During the month, the Shaping Department used $140,000 of direct material and $68,000 of conversion costs ($21,250 of direct labor plus $46,750 of manufacturing overhead).

We've calculated the Shaping Department's total equivalent units (Step 2) and summarized its total costs to account for (Step 3). Our next step is to calculate the cost per equivalent unit.

---

[1] The Shaping Department did not have a beginning inventory. Summary Problem 1 illustrates a department that does have a beginning inventory. As long as we assume the weighted-average method of process costing, we include the beginning balance to arrive at total costs to account for, as shown in Exhibit 4-7.

EXHIBIT 4-7	Step 3: Summarize Total Costs to Account For

SEAVIEW SHAPING DEPARTMENT
Month Ended October 31

			Direct Materials	Conversion Costs	Total
		Beginning work in process, October 1	$ 0	$ 0	$ 0
		Costs added during October:	140,000	68,000*	208,000
		Total costs to account for	$140,000	$68,000	$208,000

*21,250 of direct labor plus $46,750 of manufacturing overhead = $68,000 of conversion costs

Step 4: Compute the Cost per Equivalent Unit

The word *per* means "divided by," so the *cost per equivalent unit* is the *total costs to account for* (from Step 3) divided by the *total equivalent units* (from Step 2). Because the total equivalent units for direct materials (50,000) and conversion costs (42,500) differ, we must compute a separate cost per equivalent unit for each cost category: direct materials and conversion costs. Exhibit 4-8 shows the computations:

EXHIBIT 4-8	Step 4: Compute the Cost per Equivalent Unit

SEAVIEW SHAPING DEPARTMENT
Month Ended October 31

			Direct Materials	Conversion Costs
		Total costs to account for (from Exhibit 4-7)	$ 140,000	$ 68,000
		Divided by total equivalent units (from Exhibit 4-5)	÷ 50,000	÷ 42,500
		Cost per equivalent unit	$ 2.80	$ 1.60

What do these figures mean? During October, Seaview's Shaping Department incurred an average of $2.80 of direct materials cost and $1.60 of conversion costs to completely shape the equivalent of one mask. In addition to using the cost per equivalent unit in the five-step process costing procedure, managers also use this information to determine how well they have controlled costs. Managers compare the actual cost per equivalent unit to the budgeted cost per equivalent unit (they make separate comparisons for direct materials and conversion costs). If the cost per equivalent unit is the same as or lower than budgeted, the manager has successfully controlled costs.

Step 5: Assign Total Costs to Units Completed and to Units in Ending Work in Process Inventory

The goal of Step 5 (Exhibit 4-9) is to determine how much of the Shaping Department's $208,000 total costs should be assigned to (1) the 40,000 completely shaped masks transferred out to the Insertion Department and (2) the 10,000 partially shaped masks remaining in the Shaping Department's ending work in process inventory. Exhibit 4-9 shows how the equivalent units computed in Step 2 (Exhibit 4-5) are costed at the cost per equivalent unit computed in Step 4 (Exhibit 4-8).

EXHIBIT 4-9	**Step 5: Assign Costs to Units Completed and to Units in Ending Work in Process Inventory**

SEAVIEW SHAPING DEPARTMENT
Month Ended October 31

	Direct Materials	Conversion Costs	Total
Completed and transferred out (40,000)	[40,000 × ($2.80 + $1.60)]		= $176,000
Ending work in process inventory (10,000):			
Direct materials	[10,000 × $2.80]		= $ 28,000
Conversion costs		[2,500 × $1.60]	= 4,000
Total cost of ending work in process inventory			$ 32,000
Total costs accounted for			$208,000

Note: Equivalent units are from Exhibit 4-5; Costs per equivalent are from Exhibit 4-8.

First, consider the 40,000 masks completed and transferred out. Exhibit 4-5 reveals 40,000 equivalent units of work for both direct materials and conversion costs. Thus, the total cost of these completed masks is 40,000 × ($2.80 + $1.60) = $176,000, as shown in Exhibit 4-9. We've accomplished our first goal—now we know how much cost ($176,000) should be assigned to the completely shaped masks transferred to the Insertion Department.

Next, consider the 10,000 masks still in ending work in process. These masks have 10,000 equivalent units of direct materials (at $2.80 per equivalent unit), so the direct material cost is $28,000 (10,000 × $2.80). The 2,500 equivalent units of conversion costs in the ending work in process inventory at $1.60 per equivalent unit yields conversion costs of $4,000 (2,500 × $1.60). As Exhibit 4-9 shows, the total cost of the 10,000 partially completed masks in the Shaping Department's ending work in process inventory is the sum of these direct material and conversion costs: $28,000 + $4,000 = $32,000. Now, we've accomplished our second goal—we know how much cost ($32,000) should be assigned to the partially shaped masks still in ending work in process inventory.

In summary, Exhibit 4-9 has accomplished our goal of splitting the $208,000 *total cost to account for* between the 40,000 masks completed and transferred out and the 10,000 partially shaped masks remaining in Work in Process Inventory.

Recall that the current balance in Work in Process Inventory–Shaping is $208,000. Therefore, SeaView needs to make the following journal entry to transfer the cost of the 40,000 completed masks *out* of the Shaping Department and *into* the Insertion Department (data from Exhibit 4-9):

Work in Process Inventory—Insertion		176,000	
Work in Process Inventory—Shaping			176,000
(*To record transfer of cost out of the Shaping Department and into the Insertion Department.*)			

After this journal entry is posted, the Work in Process Inventory–Shaping account appears as follows. Notice that the new ending balance in the account—$32,000—agrees with the amount assigned to partially shaped masks in Step 5 (Exhibit 4-9).

Work in Process Inventory—Shaping			
Balance, October 1	0	Transferred to Insertion	176,000
Direct materials	140,000		
Direct labor	21,250		
Manufacturing overhead	46,750		
Balance, October 31	32,000		

Average Unit Costs

How does this information relate to unit costs? The average cost of making one *completely shaped* unit is $4.40 ($176,000 transferred to Insertion ÷ 40,000 completely shaped masks transferred to Insertion). This average unit cost ($4.40) is the sum of the direct material cost per equivalent unit ($2.80) and the conversion cost per equivalent unit ($1.60). The average cost of one *partially* shaped unit that is 25% of the way through the production process is $3.20 ($32,000 in ending inventory of Shaping ÷ 10,000 partially shaped masks). We needed the five-step process costing procedure to find these average costs per unit. If the Shaping Department manager ignored the five-step process and simply spread the entire production cost over all units worked on during the period, each unit would be assigned a cost of $4.16 ($208,000 ÷ 50,000 masks)—whether completely shaped or not. That would be wrong. The average cost per unit should be (and is) higher for completely shaped units transferred out to the Insertion Department than it is for partially shaped units remaining in the Shaping Department's ending inventory that workers will finish shaping next month.

Recall that once the masks are shaped, they still need to have the faceplates inserted. In the next section, we will discuss how the second process—Insertion—uses the same five-step procedure to find the *total* unit cost of making a completed mask.

Before continuing, review the Decision Guidelines and complete Summary Problem 1 to make sure you understand equivalent units and the flow of costs in process costing. Summary Problem 1 illustrates the five-step process with a beginning inventory. In the Shaping Department example, there was no beginning inventory. As long as the company uses the weighted-average inventory flow assumption, all steps would be computed in the same fashion even if there were a beginning inventory.

Stop & Think...

Assume that the Shaping Department manager incorrectly assigned all of October's production costs ($208,000) to the completely shaped masks rather than using the five-step process to divide the costs between the completely shaped and partially shaped masks. What would be the results of this error?

Answer: If the manager incorrectly assigned all production costs to the completely shaped masks, the unit cost of completely shaped masks would be too high ($208,000 ÷ 40,000 = $5.20). In addition, the unit cost of the partially shaped masks would be too low ($0.00). In essence, the manager would be saying that the partially shaped units were "free" to make because he assigned all of the production costs to the completely shaped units. To assign production costs properly, managers must use the five-step process.

Decision Guidelines

PROCESS COSTING—FIRST PROCESS

Here are some of the key decisions SeaView made in setting up its process costing system.

Decision	Guidelines
Should SeaView use job or process costing?	SeaView mass-produces large quantities of identical swim masks using two production processes: shaping and insertion. It uses *process costing* to: 1. *Accumulate* the cost of each process. 2. *Assign* these costs to the masks passing through that process.
How do costs flow from Work in Process Inventory to Finished Goods Inventory in SeaView's process costing system?	In SeaView's process costing system, costs flow from: Work in Process Inventory—Shaping ↓ Work in Process Inventory—Insertion ↓ Finished Goods Inventory More generally, costs flow from one Work in Process Inventory account to the next until the last process, after which they flow into Finished Goods Inventory.
How many Work in Process Inventory accounts does SeaView's process costing system have?	SeaView uses a separate Work in Process Inventory account for each of its two major processes: Shaping and Insertion.
How does SeaView account for partially completed products?	SeaView uses equivalent units.
Which costs require separate equivalent-unit computations?	Compute equivalent units separately for each input added at a different point in the production process. SeaView computes equivalent units separately for direct materials and conversion costs because it adds direct materials at a particular point in the production process but incurs conversion costs evenly throughout the process.
How does SeaView compute equivalent units of conversion costs?	SeaView's *conversion costs* are incurred evenly throughout the production process, so the equivalent units are computed as follows: $$\text{Equivalent units} = \text{Number of partially complete units} \times \text{Percentage of process completed}$$

Decision	Guidelines
How does SeaView compute equivalent units of direct materials?	SeaView's *materials* are added at specific points in the production process, so the equivalent units are computed as follows: • If physical units have passed the point at which materials are added, then units are complete with respect to materials; so equivalent units of materials = physical units. • If physical units have *not* passed the point at which materials are added, then units have not incurred any materials; so equivalent units of materials = 0.
How do you compute the cost per equivalent unit?	For each category (direct materials and conversion), divide the total cost to account for by the total equivalent units.
How do you split the costs of the shaping process between the following? • Swim masks completed and transferred out • Partially completed swim masks in ending work in process inventory	Multiply the cost per equivalent unit by the following: • Number of equivalent units completed and transferred out • Number of equivalent units in the ending work in process inventory
How well did the manager of the Shaping Department control the department's costs?	If direct material and conversion cost per equivalent unit is the same or lower than the target unit cost per equivalent unit, the manager has done a good job controlling costs.

Summary Problem 1

Florida Tile produces ceramic tiles using two sequential production departments: Tile-Forming and Tile-Finishing. The following information was found for Florida Tile's first production process, the Tile-Forming Department.

Required: Use the five steps of process costing to calculate the cost that should be assigned to (1) units completed and transferred out and (2) units still in ending work in process inventory. Then prepare the journal entry needed at month-end to transfer the costs associated with the formed tiles to the next department, Tile Finishing.

FLORIDA TILE
TILE-FORMING DEPARTMENT
Month Ended May 31

Information about units:

Beginning work in process, May 1	2,000 units
Started in production during May	18,000 units
Completed and transferred to Finishing Department during May	16,000 units
Ending work in process, May 31 (25% complete as to direct materials, 55% complete as to conversion cost)	4,000 units

Information about costs:

Beginning work in process, May 1 (consists of $800 of direct materials cost and $4,000 of conversion costs)	$ 4,800
Direct materials used in May	$ 6,000
Conversion costs incurred in May	$32,400

Solution

STEP 1: Summarize the flow of physical units.
STEP 2: Compute output in terms of equivalent units.

FLORIDA TILE
TILE-FORMING DEPARTMENT
Month Ended May 31

	Step 1	Step 2: Equivalent Units	
	Flow of Physical	Direct	Conversion
Flow of Production	Units	Materials	Costs
Units to account for:			
Beginning work in process, May 1	2,000		
Started in production during May	18,000		
Total physical units to account for	20,000		
Units accounted for:			
Completed and transferred out in May	16,000	16,000	16,000
Ending work in process, May 31	4,000	1,000*	2,200**
Total physical units accounted for	20,000		
Total equivalent units		17,000	18,200

*Direct materials: 4,000 units each 25% complete = 1,000 equivalent units.
**Conversion costs: 4,000 units each 55% complete = 2,200 equivalent units.

STEP 3: Summarize total costs to account for.

FLORIDA TILE
TILE-FORMING DEPARTMENT
Month Ended May 31

		Direct Materials	Conversion Costs	Total
	Beginning work in process, May 1	$ 800	$ 4,000	$ 4,800
	Costs added during May	6,000	32,400	38,400
	Total costs to account for	$6,800	$36,400	$43,200

Note: All cost information is from the summary problem data set.

STEP 4: Compute the cost per equivalent unit.

FLORIDA TILE
TILE-FORMING DEPARTMENT
Month Ended May 31

		Direct Materials	Conversion Costs
	Total costs to account for (from Step 3)	$ 6,800	$ 36,400
	Divided by total equivalent units (from Step 2)	÷ 17,000	÷ 18,200
	Cost per equivalent unit	$ 0.40	$ 2.00

STEP 5: Assign total costs to units completed and to units in ending work in process inventory.

FLORIDA TILE
TILE-FORMING DEPARTMENT
Month Ended May 31

		Direct Materials	Conversion Costs		Total
	Units completed and transferred out (16,000)	[16,000 × ($0.40 + $2.00)]		=	$38,400
	Units in ending work in process inventory (4,000):				
	Direct materials	[1,000 × $0.40]		=	$ 400
	Conversion costs		[2,200 × $2.00]	=	4,400
	Total cost of ending work in process inventory				$ 4,800
	Total costs accounted for				$43,200

Journal entry needed to transfer costs:

	Work in Process Inventory—Finishing	38,400	
	Work in Process Inventory—Tile Forming		38,400

The cost of making one completely formed tile in the Forming Department is $2.40. This is the sum of the direct materials cost per equivalent unit ($0.40) and the conversion cost per equivalent unit ($2.00). The completely formed tiles must still be finished in the Finishing Department before we will know the final average cost of making one tile from start to finish.

Process Costing in a Second Processing Department

4 Use process costing to assign manufacturing costs to units completed and to units in ending work in process inventory in a second or later department

Most products require a series of processing steps. Recall that Jelly Belly uses eight processing steps to make its jelly beans. In the last section, we saw how much it costs SeaView to *shape* one mask. In this section, we consider a second department, SeaView's Insertion Department. After units pass through the *final* department (Insertion, in SeaView's case), managers can determine the *entire* cost of making one unit—from start to finish.

In the second or later department, we use the same five-step process costing procedure that we used for the Shaping Department, with one major difference: we separately consider the costs *transferred in* to the Insertion Department from the Shaping Department when calculating equivalent units and the cost per equivalent unit. **Transferred-in costs** are incurred in a previous process (the Shaping Department, in the SeaView example) and are carried forward as part of the product's cost when it moves to the next process.

To account for transferred-in costs, we will add one more column to our calculations in Steps 2 through 5. Let's walk through the Insertion Department's process costing to see how this is done.

Process Costing in SeaView's Insertion Department

The Insertion Department receives the shaped masks and polishes them before inserting the faceplates at the end of the process. Exhibit 4-10 shows that:

- Shaped masks are transferred in from the Shaping Department at the beginning of the Insertion Department's process.

EXHIBIT 4-10   SeaView's Insertion Department Time Line

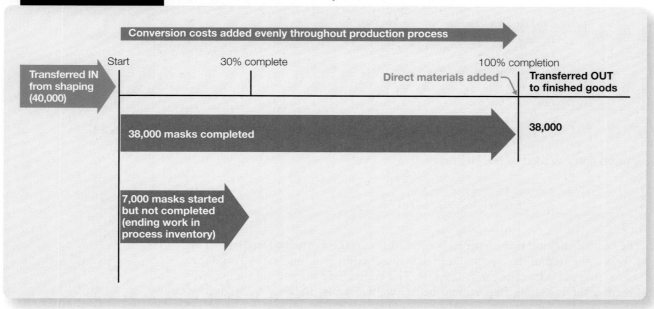

- The Insertion Department's conversion costs are added evenly throughout the process.
- The Insertion Department's direct materials (faceplates) are not added until the *end* of the process.

Keep in mind that *direct materials* in the Insertion Department refer *only* to the faceplates and not to the materials (the plastic and metal fasteners) added in the Shaping Department. Likewise, *conversion costs* in the Insertion Department refer to the direct labor and manufacturing overhead costs incurred *only* in the Insertion Department.

Exhibit 4-11 lists SeaView's Insertion Department data for October. The top portion of the exhibit lists the unit information, while the lower portion lists the costs. Study this information carefully and think about what each item means.

EXHIBIT 4-11	SeaView's Insertion Department Data for October

Information about units:

Beginning work in process, October 1	
(0% complete as to direct materials,	
60% complete as to conversion work)	5,000 masks *
Transferred in from Shaping Department	
during October (from Exhibit 4-6)	40,000 masks
Completed and transferred out to Finished	
Goods Inventory during October	38,000 masks
Ending work in process, October 31	
(0% complete as to direct materials,	
30% complete as to conversion work)	7,000 masks

Information about costs:

Beginning work in process, October 1		
Transferred-in costs	$22,900*	
Conversion costs	1,100*	$ 24,000
Beginning balance		
Transferred in from Shaping Department		176,000
during October (from journal entry on page 208)		
Direct materials added during October in		19,000
Insertion Department		
Conversion costs added during October in		
Insertion Department:		
Direct labor	$ 3,710	
Manufacturing overhead	11,130	14,840
Conversion costs		

*This information would have been obtained from Step 5 of the process costing procedure from September. The September 30 balance in work in process becomes the October 1 balance.

Exhibit 4-11 shows that SeaView's Insertion Department started the October period with 5,000 masks that had made it partway through the insertion process in September. During October, the Insertion Department started work on 40,000 additional masks received from the Shaping Department. By the end of the month, the Insertion Department had completed 38,000 masks, while 7,000 remained partially complete.

Exhibit 4-11 also shows that the Insertion Department started October with a beginning balance of $24,000 in its Work-in Process Inventory account, which is associated with the 5,000 partially completed masks in its beginning inventory. This information is provided here. However, this information is normally obtained from Step 5 of the prior month's process costing procedure (costs assigned to units in ending work in process inventory last month become this month's beginning inventory). During the month, $176,000 was transferred in from the Shaping Department (recall the journal entry on page 208). Additionally, the Insertion Department incurred $19,000 in direct material costs (faceplates) and $14,840 in conversion costs during the month. Just as we did for the Shaping Department, our goal is to split the total cost in the Insertion Department between:

- The 38,000 masks that the Insertion Department completed and transferred out (this time, to Finished Goods Inventory).
- The 7,000 partially complete masks remaining in the Insertion Department's ending work in process inventory at the end of October.

After splitting the total cost, we'll be able to determine the cost of making one complete mask—from start to finish. We use the same five-step process costing procedure that we used for the Shaping Department.

Steps 1 and 2: Summarize the Flow of Physical Units and Compute Output in Terms of Equivalent Units

Step 1: Summarize the Flow of Physical Units

This step is the same as in the Shaping Department—we must track the movement of swim masks into and out of the Insertion Department. Exhibit 4-12 shows that the Insertion Department had a beginning work in process inventory of 5,000 masks that were partway through the insertion process at the start of the period (whereas the Shaping Department had no beginning inventory balance). Recall that during October, the Shaping Department finished 40,000 masks and transferred them *into* the Insertion Department. Thus, Exhibit 4-12 shows that the Insertion Department has 45,000 masks to account for (5,000 + 40,000).

Where did these 45,000 masks go? Exhibits 4-10 and 4-11 show that the Insertion Department completed and transferred 38,000 masks out to Finished Goods Inventory while the remaining 7,000 masks were only partway through the insertion process on October 31. Thus, Exhibit 4-12 shows that the department has accounted for all 45,000 masks (38,000 completed and transferred out + 7,000 in ending work in process inventory).

Step 2: Compute Output in Terms of Equivalent Units

As mentioned earlier, process costing in a second or later department must separately calculate equivalent units for transferred-in costs, much like they separately calculate equivalent units for direct materials and conversion costs. Therefore, Step 2 in Exhibit 4-12 shows *three* columns for the Insertion Department's *three* categories of equivalent units: transferred-in, direct materials, and conversion costs. Let's consider each in turn.

Exhibit 4-10 shows that transferred-in masks are added at the very *beginning* of the insertion process. You might think of the shaped masks transferred in as raw materials added at the very *beginning* of the insertion process. All masks worked on in the Insertion Department—whether completed or not by the end of the month—

| EXHIBIT 4-12 | Step 1: Summarize the Flow of Physical Units |
| | Step 2: Compute Output in Terms of Equivalent Units |

SEAVIEW INSERTION DEPARTMENT
Month Ended October 31

| | Step 1 | Step 2: Equivalent Units | | |
Flow of Production	Flow of Physical Units	Transferred-In	Direct Materials	Conversion Costs
Units to account for:				
Beginning work in process, October 1	5,000			
Transferred in during October	40,000			
Total physical units to account for	45,000			
Units accounted for:				
Completed and transferred out				
during October	38,000	38,000	38,000*	38,000*
Ending work in process, October 31	7,000	7,000	0†	2,100†
Total physical units accounted for	45,000			
Total equivalent units		45,000	38,000	40,100

In the Insertion Department:
*Units completed and transferred out
    Direct materials: 38,000 units each 100% completed = 38,000 equivalent units
    Conversion costs: 38,000 units each 100% completed = 38,000 equivalent units
†Ending inventory
    Direct materials: 7,000 units each 0% completed = 0 equivalent units
    Conversion costs: 7,000 units each 30% completed = 2,100 equivalent units

started in the department as a shaped mask. Therefore, they are *all 100% complete with respect to transferred-in work and costs.* So, the "Transferred-In" column of Exhibit 4-12 shows 38,000 equivalent units completed and transferred out (38,000 physical units × **100%**) and 7,000 equivalent units still in ending inventory (7,000 physical units × **100%**).

> The following rule holds: *All physical units, whether completed and transferred out or still in ending work in process, are considered 100% complete with respect to transferred-in work and costs.*

The Insertion Department calculates equivalent units of direct material the same way as in the Shaping Department. However, in the Insertion Department, the direct materials (faceplates) are added at the *end* of the process rather than at the beginning of the process. The 38,000 masks completed and transferred out contain faceplates (have 100% of the Insertion Department's direct materials). On the other hand, the 7,000 masks in ending work in process inventory have *not* made it to the end of the process, so they *do not* contain faceplates. As we see in Exhibit 4-12, these unfinished masks have zero equivalent units of the Insertion Department's direct materials (7,000 physical units × 0%).

Now, consider the conversion costs. The 38,000 finished masks are 100% complete with respect to the Insertion Department's conversion costs. However, the 7,000 unfinished masks are only 30% converted (see Exhibits 4-10 and 4-11), so the equivalent units of conversion costs equal 2,100 (7,000 × 30%).

Now, the equivalent units in each column are summed to find the *total* equivalent units for each of the three categories: transferred-in (45,000), direct materials (38,000), and conversion costs (40,100). We'll use these equivalent units in Step 4.

Steps 3 and 4: Summarize Total Costs to Account For and Compute the Cost per Equivalent Unit

Exhibit 4-13 accumulates the Insertion Department's total costs to account for based on the data in Exhibit 4-11.

In addition to direct material and conversion costs, the Insertion Department must account for transferred-in costs. Recall that transferred-in costs are incurred in a previous process (the Shaping Department, in the SeaView example) and are carried forward as part of the product's cost when the physical product is transferred to the next process.

If the Insertion Department had bought these shaped masks from an outside supplier, it would have to account for the costs of purchasing the masks. However, the Insertion Department receives the masks from an *internal* supplier—the Shaping Department. Thus, the Insertion Department must account for the costs the Shaping Department incurred to provide the shaped masks (the Insertion Department's transferred-in costs) as well as the Insertion Department's own direct materials (faceplates) and conversion costs (labor and overhead to insert the faceplates).

EXHIBIT 4-13   Step 3: Summarize Total Costs to Account For
Step 4: Compute the Cost per Equivalent Unit

SEAVIEW INSERTION DEPARTMENT Month Ended October 31				
	Transferred-In	Direct Materials	Conversion Costs	Total
Beginning work in process, October 1 (from Exhibit 4-11)	$ 22,900	$ 0	$ 1,100	$ 24,000
Costs added during October (from Exhibit 4-11)	176,000	19,000	14,840	209,840
Total costs to account for	$198,900	$19,000	$15,940	$233,840
Divide by total equivalent units (from Exhibit 4-12)	÷ 45,000	÷ 38,000	÷ 40,100	
Cost per equivalent unit	$ 4.42	$ 0.50	$0.3975*	

*Rounded

Exhibit 4-13 shows that in Step 3, the Insertion Department's total costs to account for ($233,840) is the sum of:

- The cost incurred in September to start the insertion process on the 5,000 masks in the Insertion Department's beginning work in process inventory ($24,000).
- The costs added to Work in Process Inventory—Insertion during October ($209,840 = $176,000 transferred in from the Shaping Department + $19,000 direct materials incurred in the Insertion Department + $14,840 conversion costs incurred in the Insertion Department).

Exhibit 4-13 also shows the results of Step 4—the cost per equivalent unit. For each of the three cost categories, SeaView divides the total cost of that category by the total number of equivalent units in that category.

Step 5: Assign Total Costs to Units Completed and to Units in Ending Work in Process Inventory

Exhibit 4-14 shows how SeaView assigns the Insertion Department's total costs to account for ($233,840, from Exhibit 4-13) to (1) units completed and transferred out to finished goods inventory and (2) units remaining in the Insertion Department's ending work in process inventory. SeaView uses the same approach as it used for the Shaping Department in Exhibit 4-9. SeaView multiplies the number of equivalent units from Step 2 (Exhibit 4-12) by the cost per equivalent unit from Step 4 (Exhibit 4-13).

EXHIBIT 4-14 | **Step 5: Assign Total Costs to Units Completed and to Units in Ending Work in Process Inventory**

SEAVIEW INSERTION DEPARTMENT
Month Ended October 31

	Transferred-In	Direct Materials	Conversion Costs	Total
Units completed and transferred out to				
Finished Goods Inventory (38,000)	[38,000 × ($4.42 + $0.50+ $0.3975)]			$202,065
Ending work in process, October 31 (7,000):				
Transferred-in costs	[7,000 × $4.42]			$ 30,940
Direct materials		[0 × $0.50]		0
Conversion costs			[2,100 × $0.3975]	835*
Total ending work in process, October 31				31,775
Total costs accounted for				$233,840

*Rounded

Exhibit 4-15 illustrates how the costs were assigned in Step 5.

EXHIBIT 4-15 | **Assigning Insertion Department's Costs to Units Completed and Transferred Out and to Ending Work in Process Inventory**

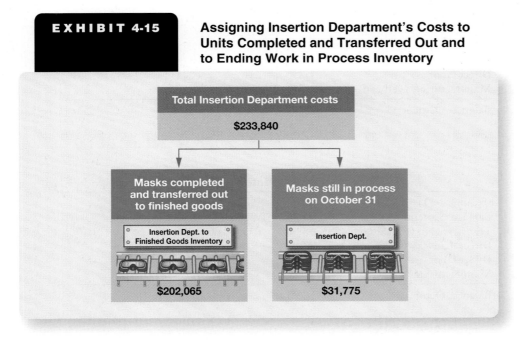

Summary of Journal Entries

The Insertion Department's journal entries are similar to those of the Shaping Department. First, recall the entry we previously made to transfer the cost of shaped swim masks into the Insertion Department (page 208):

Work in Process Inventory—Insertion		176,000	
Work in Process Inventory—Shaping			176,000
(To record the transfer cost out of the Shaping Department and into			
the Insertion Department.)			

The following summary entry records other production costs the Insertion Department incurred during October (data from Exhibit 4-11):

Work in Process Inventory—Insertion	33,840	
Raw Materials Inventory		19,000
Manufacturing Wages		3,710
Manufacturing Overhead		11,130
(To record manufacturing costs incurred in the Insertion Department during October.)		

Finally, we are able to make the journal entry to transfer the cost of completed masks out of the Insertion Department and into Finished Goods Inventory. This journal entry is based on the dollar amount we calculated in Step 5 (in Exhibit 4-14) of the process costing procedure:

Finished Goods Inventory	202,065	
Work in Process Inventory—Insertion		202,065
(To record transfer of cost out of the Insertion Department and into Finished Goods Inventory.)		

After posting, the key accounts appear as follows:

Work in Process Inventory—Shaping

(Exhibit 4-7)		(Exhibit 4-9)	
Balance, September 30	0	Transferred to Insertion	176,000
Direct materials	140,000		
Direct labor	21,250		
Manufacturing overhead	46,750		
Balance, October 31	32,000		

Work in Process Inventory—Insertion

(Exhibit 4-11)		(Exhibit 4-14)	
Balance, September 30	24,000	Transferred to Finished	
Transferred in from Shaping	176,000	Goods Inventory	202,065
Direct materials	19,000		
Direct labor	3,710		
Manufacturing overhead	11,130		
Balance, October 31	31,775		

Finished Goods Inventory

Balance, September 30	0	
Transferred in from Insertion	202,065	

Unit Costs

SeaView's managers can now compute the cost of making one completed mask from start to finish. SeaView transferred $202,065 to the Finished Goods Inventory account for the costs associated with the 38,000 masks finished during the month. SeaView's cost of making one mask was $5.3175 ($202,065 ÷ 38,000). Exhibit 4-14 shows that this cost includes the costs from both processing departments:

- Shaping ($4.42 per unit)[2]
- Insertion ($0.50 for direct materials and $0.3975 for conversion costs)

Stop & Think...

Assume that SeaView sells 36,000 of the masks for $10 each. Assuming that SeaView uses a perpetual inventory system, what journal entries would SeaView make to record the sales transaction?

Answer: The unit cost of making one mask from start to finish is $5.3175 ($202,065 transferred to Finished Goods ÷ 38,000 finished masks). SeaView will make the following entries:

	Accounts Receivable (36,000 × $10.00)		360,000	
	Sales Revenue			360,000

	Cost of Goods Sold (36,000 × $5.3175)		191,430	
	Finished Goods Inventory			191,430

Production Cost Reports

Most companies that use process costing summarize the entire five-step process on one schedule, known as a production cost report. A **production cost report** summarizes a processing department's operations for the month. Notice how the production cost report for the Insertion Department shown in Exhibit 4-16 simply brings together all of the steps that we showed separately in Exhibits 4-12, 4-13, and 4-14. The top half of the schedule focuses on units (Steps 1 and 2), while the bottom half of the schedule focuses on costs (Steps 3, 4, and 5). Each processing department prepares its own production cost report each month. The transferred-in costs, direct materials cost, and conversion costs assigned to the units in ending work in process inventory become the beginning work in process inventory balances on the next month's cost report.

How do managers use the production cost report? When faced with economic uncertainty and falling prices for their products, managers carefully monitor product costs to see what they can cut. For example, as the selling prices for its tools continued to decline, Connecticut-based toolmaker Stanley Works decided to use fewer raw material suppliers. By purchasing more from its remaining suppliers, Stanley had the leverage to negotiate better prices.

---

[2]On page 209, we showed October's shaping cost per unit to be $4.40. Why then is it $4.42 once it has made its way through the Insertion Department? As shown in the transferred-in column of Exhibit 4-13, the weighted-average method of process costing *combines* the current period's costs ($176,000) with any costs in beginning inventory ($22,900) to yield a weighted-average cost per unit ($4.42). If there had been no beginning inventory, the transferred-in cost would have remained at $4.40 per unit.

Similarly, SeaView's managers monitor production costs by comparing the actual direct materials and conversion costs—particularly the equivalent-unit costs in Exhibit 4-16—with expected amounts. If actual unit costs are too high, managers will look for ways to cut costs. If actual costs are less than expected (and assuming quality is maintained), the Insertion Department's managers will likely receive good performance evaluations.

SeaView can use these unit costs for making other decisions. Sales managers must set the mask's selling price high enough to cover the unit manufacturing costs ($5.3175) plus nonmanufacturing costs from the other elements of the value chain, such as marketing and distribution. Armed with selling price and cost information for each of their many products, SeaView's managers can figure out which products are most profitable. Then, they can design sales campaigns to promote those products. Finally, the production cost report supports financial reporting. It provides information for valuing inventory on the balance sheet and cost of goods sold on the income statement.

EXHIBIT 4-16   **Production Cost Report**

SEAVIEW INSERTION DEPARTMENT
Product Cost Report
Month Ended October 31

Flow of Production	Step 1 Flow of Physical Units	Step 2: Equivalent Units Transferred-In	Direct Materials	Conversion Costs	
Units to account for:					
Beginning work in process, Oct. 1	5,000				
Transferred in during October	40,000				
Total physical units to account for	45,000				
Units accounted for:					
Completed and transferred out during Oct.	38,000	38,000	38,000	38,000	
Ending work in process, Oct. 31	7,000	7,000	0	2,100	
Total physical units accounted for	45,000				
Total equivalent units		45,000	38,000	40,100	

Flow of Costs	Steps 3, 4, and 5 Transferred-In	Direct Materials	Conversion Costs	Total
Beginning work in process, Oct. 1	$ 22,900	$ 0	$ 1,100	$ 24,000
Costs added during October	176,000	19,000	14,840	209,840
Total costs to account for	$198,900	$19,000	$15,940	$233,840
÷ Total equivalent units	÷ 45,000	÷ 38,000	÷ 40,100	
Cost per equivalent unit	$ 4.42	$ 0.50	$0.3975	
Assignment of total costs:				
Units completed during October	[38,000 × ($4.42 + $0.50+ $0.3975)]			$202,065
Ending work in process, Oct. 31:				
Transferred-in costs	[7,000 × $4.42]			$ 30,940
Direct materials		[0 × $0.50]		0
Conversion costs			[2,100 × $0.3975*]	835*
Total ending work in process, Oct. 31				31,775
Total costs accounted for				$233,840

*Rounded

Decision Guidelines

PROCESS COSTING—SECOND PROCESS (WITH BEGINNING INVENTORY)

Beginning work in process inventory makes process costing a bit more complicated, and second (or later) departments must account for units and costs transferred in from previous departments. Let's use SeaView's Insertion Department to review some of the key process costing decisions that arise in a second (or later) process that has beginning inventory.

Decision	Guidelines
At what point in the insertion process are transferred-in costs (from the shaping process) incurred?	Transferred-in costs are incurred at the *beginning* of the insertion process. The masks must be completely shaped before the insertion process begins.
What percentage of completion is used to calculate equivalent units in the "Transferred-In" column?	All units, whether completed and transferred out or still in ending work in process, are considered 100% complete with respect to transferred-in work and costs.
What checks and balances does the five-step process costing procedure provide?	The five-step procedure provides two important checks: 1. The total units to account for (beginning inventory + units started or transferred in) *must equal* the total units accounted for (units completed and transferred out + units in ending inventory). 2. The total costs to account for (cost of beginning inventory + costs incurred in the current period) *must equal* the total costs accounted for (cost of units completed and transferred out + cost of ending inventory).
What are the two main goals of the Insertion Department's process costing?	The first goal is to split total costs between swim masks completed and transferred out to finished goods inventory and the masks that remain in the Insertion Department's ending work in process inventory. The second goal is to determine the cost of making each swim mask—from start to finish.
The production cost report summarizes the 5-step process costing procedure. How do managers use the information found on the production cost report?	SeaView's managers use the cost per equivalent unit to determine the cost of producing a swim mask. These costs provide a basis for setting selling prices, doing a profitability analysis to decide which products to emphasize, and so forth. These costs are also the basis for valuing inventory on the balance sheet and cost of goods sold on the income statement. Managers also use the cost per equivalent unit to control material and conversion costs and to evaluate the performance of production department managers. If actual costs per equivalent unit are higher than the budget, managers try to cut costs. If actual costs are lower than the budget while quality is maintained, the department managers have done a good job of controlling costs.

Summary Problem 2

This problem extends the Summary Problem 1 to a second department. During May, Florida Tile Industries reports the following in its Finishing Department:

Finishing Department Data for May	
Information about units:	
Beginning work in process, May 1 (20% complete as to direct materials, 70% complete as to conversion work)	4,000 units
Transferred in from Tile-Forming Department during May	16,000 units
Completed and transferred out to Finished Goods Inventory during May	15,000 units
Ending work in process, May 31 (36% complete as to direct materials, 80% complete as to conversion work)	5,000 units
Information about costs:	
Work in process, May 1 (transferred-in costs, $11,982; direct materials costs, $488; conversion costs, $5,530)	$18,000
Transferred in from Tile-Forming Department during May (page 213)	38,400
Finishing Department direct materials added during May	6,400
Finishing Department conversion costs added during May	24,300

Requirements

1. Assign the Finishing Department's *total costs to account for* to units completed and to units in ending work in process inventory.

   Hint: Don't confuse the Finishing Department with finished goods inventory. The Finishing Department is Florida Tile's second process. The tiles do not become part of finished goods inventory until they have completed the second process, which happens to be called the Finishing Department.

2. Make the journal entry to transfer the appropriate amount of cost to Finished Goods Inventory.

3. What is the cost of making one unit of product from start to finish?

Solution

STEPS 1 AND 2   Summarize the flow of physical units; compute output in terms of equivalent units.

FLORIDA TILE
FINISHING DEPARTMENT
Month Ended May 31

Flow of Production	Step 1 Flow of Physical Units	Step 2: Equivalent Units Transferred-In	Direct Materials	Conversion Costs
Units to account for:				
Beginning work in process, May 1	4,000			
Transferred in from Tile-Forming				
Department during May	16,000			
Total physical units to account for	20,000			
Units accounted for:				
Completed and transferred out during May	15,000	15,000	15,000	15,000
Ending work in process, May 31	5,000	5,000	1,800*	4,000*
Total physical units accounted for	20,000			
Total equivalent units		20,000	16,800	19,000

*Ending inventory:
  Direct materials: 5,000 units each 36% completed = 1,800 equivalent units
  Converted costs: 5,000 units each 80% completed = 4,000 equivalent units

STEPS 3 AND 4   Summarize total costs to account for; compute the cost per equivalent unit.

FLORIDA TILE
FINISHING DEPARTMENT
Month Ended May 31

	Step 1 Transferred-In	Step 2: Equivalent Units Direct Materials	Conversion Costs	Total
Beginning work in process, May 1	$11,982	$ 488	$ 5,530	$18,000
Costs added during May	38,400	6,400	24,300	69,100
Total costs to account for	$50,382	$ 6,888	$29,830	$87,100
Divide by total equivalent units	÷ 20,000	÷ 16,800	÷ 19,000	
Cost per equivalent unit	$2.5191	$ 0.41	$ 1.57	

Step 5 Assign total costs to units completed and to units in ending work in process inventory.

			Transferred-In	Direct Materials	Conversion Costs	Total
		Units completed and transferred out to				
		Finished Goods Inventory:	[15,000 × ($2.5191 + $0.41 + $1.57)]			$67,486*
		Ending work in process, May 31:				
		Transferred-in costs	[5,000 × $2.5191]			12,596*
		Direct materials		[1,800 × $0.41]		738
		Conversion costs			[4,000 × $1.57]	6,280
		Total ending work in process, May 31				19,614
	Total costs accounted for					$87,100

*Rounded

**FLORIDA TILE
FINISHING DEPARTMENT
Month Ended May 31**

Requirement 2

Journal entry:

		Finished Goods Inventory	67,486	
		Work in Process Inventory—Finishing Department		67,486
		(To record the transfer of cost out of the Finishing Department		
		and into Finished Goods Inventory.)		

Requirement 3

The cost of making one unit from start to finish is $4.50 (rounded). This consists of $2.52 (rounded)[3] of cost incurred in the Tile-Forming Department and transferred in and $1.98 of cost incurred in the Finishing Department ($0.41 of direct materials and $1.57 of conversion costs). Another way to find this answer is to divide the total cost assigned to units transferred to Finished Goods Inventory ($67,486) by the number of units transferred (15,000): $67,486 ÷ 15,000 = $4.50 (rounded).

---

[3]In Summary Problem 1, we saw that the average cost per unit in May was $2.40. The weighted-average method combines the current period's costs (May's costs) with any costs in beginning inventory to yield a weighted-average cost of $2.52 per unit.

Review *Process Costing*

■ Accounting Vocabulary

Equivalent Units. (p. 199)
Express the amount of work done during a period in terms of fully completed units of output.

Production Cost Report. (p. 221)
Summarizes a processing department's operations for a period.

Transferred-In Costs. (p. 214)
Costs incurred in a previous process that are carried forward as part of the product's cost when it moves to the next process.

Weighted-Average Method of Process Costing. (p. 201)
A process costing method that *combines* any beginning inventory units (and costs) with the current period's units (and costs) to get a weighted-average cost.

■ Quick Check

1. Which of these companies would use process costing?
   a. Saatchi & Saatchi advertising firm
   b. Pace Foods, producer of Pace picante sauce
   c. Accenture management consultants
   d. Amazon.com

2. Which of the following statements describes Jelly Belly's process costing system?
   a. Direct materials and direct labor are traced to each specific order.
   b. Costs flow directly from a single Work in Process Inventory account to Finished Goods Inventory.
   c. Costs flow through a sequence of Work in Process Inventory accounts and then into Finished Goods Inventory from the final Work in Process Inventory account.
   d. The subsidiary Work in Process Inventory accounts consist of separate records for each individual order, detailing the materials, labor, and overhead assigned to that order.

   Use the following data to answer questions 3 through 7:
   Suppose Jelly Belly's Centers process adds sugar at the beginning of the process and flavorings 75% of the way through the process and conversion costs are incurred evenly throughout the process. Assume that there are no beginning inventories, the company started making centers for 10,000 pounds of jelly beans, and the 2,000 pounds in the Centers ending work in process inventory are 65% through the Centers process.

3. Compute the equivalent units of *sugar* used.
   a. 8,000
   b. 8,700
   c. 9,300
   d. 10,000

4. How many equivalent units of *flavorings* did Jelly Belly use?
   a. 8,000
   b. 8,700
   c. 9,300
   d. 10,000

5. What are the equivalent units of *conversion costs*?
   a. 8,000
   b. 8,700
   c. 9,300
   d. 10,000

6. If the cost per equivalent unit is $0.50 for sugar, $1.00 for flavorings, and $0.40 for conversion costs, what is the cost assigned to the Centers' ending work in process inventory?
   a. $1,520
   b. $1,800
   c. $2,520
   d. $3,800

7. Suppose Jelly Belly's second process, Shells, starts out with 3,000 pounds of jelly beans in its beginning work in process inventory. Assume that the Shells process has 1,500 pounds of jelly beans 70% through the process at the end of the period. Start by using the information preceding question 3 to determine how many pounds of jelly beans started in the Shells process this period. Then, use this result to compute the number of equivalent units of transferred-in costs that the Shells process will use in computing its weighted-average cost per equivalent unit.
   a. 6,500
   b. 8,000
   c. 9,500
   d. 11,000

8. In general, transferred-in costs include:
   a. costs incurred in the previous period
   b. costs incurred in all prior periods
   c. costs incurred in only the previous process
   d. costs incurred in all prior processes

   To answer questions 9 and 10, look at the computation of cost per equivalent unit in SeaView's Insertion Department in Exhibit 4-13.

9. Which of the following describes the $22,900 transferred-in costs in beginning inventory?
   a. costs incurred in October in the Shaping Department
   b. costs incurred prior to October in the Shaping Department
   c. costs incurred in October in the Insertion Department
   d. costs incurred prior to October in the Insertion Department

10. Which of the following best describes the swim masks associated with the $22,900 transferred-in costs in the Insertion Department's beginning work in process inventory?

   a. masks that are partway through the shaping process and have not begun the insertion process by the beginning of October

   b. masks that moved from the Shaping Department to the Insertion Department in September but have not yet begun the insertion process by the beginning of October

   c. masks that moved from the Shaping Department to the Insertion Department during October

   d. masks that moved from the Shaping Department to the Insertion Department in September and are partway through the insertion process by the beginning of October

---

Quick Check Answers

1. b 2. c 3. d 4. a 5. a 6. c 7. a 8. d 9. b 10. d

For Internet Exercises, Excel in Practice, and additional online activities, go to this book's Web site at www.prenhall.com/bamber.

Assess Your Progress

■ Learning Objectives

1 Distinguish between the flow of costs in process costing and job costing

2 Compute equivalent units

3 Use process costing to assign manufacturing costs to units completed and to units in ending work in process inventory in a first department

4 Use process costing to assign manufacturing costs to units completed and to units in ending work in process inventory in a second or later department

■ Short Exercises

S4-1 Compare flow of costs *(Learning Objective 1)*
Use Exhibit 4-1 to help you describe in your own words the major difference in the flow of costs between a job costing system and a process costing system.

S4-2 Flow of costs through Work in Process Inventory *(Learning Objective 1)*
True-Tile produces its product in two processing departments: Forming and Finishing. The following T-account shows the Forming Department's Work in Process Inventory at August 31 prior to completing the five-step process costing procedure:

Work in Process Inventory—Forming Department		
Beginning Balance	$ 53,250	
Direct materials used	78,360	
Direct labor	14,920	
Manufacturing overhead allocated	126,250	

Requirements

1. What is the Forming Department's "Total costs to account for" for the month of August?
2. Assume that after using the five-step process costing procedure, the company determines that the "cost to be assigned to units completed and transferred out" is $243,800. What journal entry is needed to record the transfer of costs to the Finishing Department?
3. After the journal entry is made, what will be the new ending balance in the Forming Department's Work in Process Inventory account?

S4-3 Flow of costs through Work in Process Inventory *(Learning Objective 1)*
As shown in Exhibits 4-1 and 4-2, Jelly Belly produces jelly beans in three sequential processing departments: Centers, Shells, and Packaging. Assume that the Shells processing department began September with $18,340 of unfinished jelly bean centers. During September, the Shells process used $42,600 of direct materials, used $12,130 of direct labor, and was allocated $17,260 of manufacturing overhead. In addition,

$126,400 was transferred out of the Centers processing department during the month and $196,420 was transferred out of the Shells processing department during the month. These transfers represent the cost of the jelly beans transferred from one process to another.

1. Prepare a T-account for the Work in Process Inventory—Shells showing all activity that took place in the account during September.

2. What is the ending balance in the Work in Process Inventory—Shells on September 30? What does this figure represent?

S4-4 **Recompute SeaView's equivalent units** *(Learning Objective 2)*
Look at SeaView's Shaping Department's equivalent-unit computation in Exhibit 4-5. Suppose the ending work in process inventory is 30% of the way through the shaping process rather than 25% of the way through. Compute the total equivalent units of direct materials and conversion costs.

S4-5 **Determine the physical flow of units (process costing Step 1)** *(Learning Objective 2)*
Kunde Winery's bottling department had 20,000 units in the beginning inventory of Work in Process on June 1. During June, 110,000 units were started into production. On June 30, 30,000 units were left in ending work in process inventory. Summarize the physical flow of units in a schedule similar to Exhibit 4-5 (Step 1 column).

S4-6 **Compute equivalent units (process costing Step 2)** *(Learning Objective 2)*
Blumhoff's Packaging Department had the following information at March 31. All direct materials are added at the *end* of the conversion process. The units in ending work in process inventory were only 30% of the way through the conversion process.

				Equivalent Units	
			Physical Units	Direct Materials	Conversion Costs
		Units accounted for:			
		Completed and transferred out	115,000		
		Ending work in process, March 31	15,000		
		Total physical units accounted for:	120,000		
		Total equivalent units			

Requirements
Complete the schedule by computing the total equivalent units of direct materials and conversion costs for the month.

S4-7 **Compute equivalent units (process costing Step 2)** *(Learning Objective 2)*
The Frying Department of Rummel's Potato Chips had 100,000 partially completed units in work in process at the end of August. All of the direct materials had been added to these units, but the units were only 60% of the way through the conversion process. In addition, 1,200,000 units had been completed and transferred out of the Frying Department to the Packaging Department during the month.

continued . . .

1. How many equivalent units of direct materials and equivalent units of conversion costs are associated with the 1,200,000 units completed and transferred out?

2. Compute the equivalent units of direct materials and the equivalent units of conversion costs associated with the 100,000 partially completed units still in ending work in process.

3. What are the total equivalent units of direct materials and the total equivalent units of conversion costs for the month?

S4-8 **Summarize total costs to account for (process costing Step 3)** *(Learning Objective 3)*
McIntyre Industries' Work in Process Inventory account had a $68,000 beginning balance on May 1 ($40,000 of this related to direct materials used during April, while $28,000 related to conversion costs incurred during April). During May, the following costs were incurred in the department:

Direct materials used..	$106,000
Direct labor..	18,000
Manufacturing overhead allocated to the department	154,000

Summarize the department's "Total costs to account for." Prepare a schedule (similar to Exhibit 4-7) that summarizes the department's total costs to account for by direct materials and conversion costs.

S4-9 **Compute the cost per equivalent unit (process costing Step 4)** *(Learning Objective 3)*
At the end of July, Baker's mixing department had "Total costs to account for" of $752,420. Of this amount, $287,045 related to direct materials costs, while the remainder related to conversion costs. The department had 52,190 total equivalent units of direct materials and 45,625 total equivalent units of conversion costs for the month.
Compute the cost per equivalent unit for direct materials and the cost per equivalent unit for conversion costs.

S4-10 **Recompute SeaView's cost per equivalent unit** *(Learning Objective 3)*
Return to the original SeaView example in Exhibits 4-5 and 4-7. Suppose direct labor is $34,000 rather than $21,250. Now what is the conversion cost per equivalent unit? (Use Exhibit 4-8 to format your answer.)

S4-11 **Assign costs (process costing Step 5)** *(Learning Objective 3)*
Tabor Industries produces its product using a *single* production process. For the month of December, Tabor Industries determined its "cost per equivalent unit" to be as follows:

	Direct Materials	Conversion Costs
Cost per equivalent unit:	$4.10	$3.25

During the month, Tabor completed and transferred out 410,000 units to finished goods inventory. At month-end, 80,000 partially complete units remained in ending work in process inventory. These partially completed units were equal to 70,000 equivalent units of direct materials and 50,000 equivalent units of conversion costs.

Requirements

1. Determine the total cost that should be assigned to the following:
   a. units completed and transferred out
   b. units in ending work in process inventory

   (*Hint:* Use Exhibit 4-9 as a guide.)
2. What was the total costs accounted for?
3. What was Tabor's average cost of making one unit of its product?

S4-12 Assign total costs in a second processing department (*Learning Objective 4*)
After completing Steps 1–4 of the process costing procedure, Dale Corp. arrived at the following equivalent units and costs per equivalent unit for its *final* production department for the month of February:

	Equivalent Units		
	Transferred-in	Direct Materials	Conversion Costs
Units completed and transferred out	70,000	70,000	70,000
Units in ending work in process, February 28	10,000	8,000	4,000
Total equivalent units	80,000	78,000	74,000
Cost per equivalent unit	$2.64	$0.15	$1.26

Requirements

1. How much cost should be assigned to the:
   a. units completed and transferred out to Finished Goods Inventory during February?
   b. partially complete units still in ending work in process inventory at the end of February?
2. What was the "Total cost accounted for" during February? What other important figure must this match? What does this figure tell you?
3. What is Dale Corp.'s average cost of making *each unit* of its product from the first production department all the way through the final production department?

S4-13 Find unit cost and gross profit on a final product (*Learning Objective 4*)
BeachCo. produces Formica countertops in two sequential production departments: Forming and Polishing. The Polishing Department calculated the following costs per equivalent unit (square feet) on its April production cost report:

	Transferred-in	Direct Materials	Conversion Costs
Cost per equivalent unit:	$2.64	$0.10	$1.26

During April, 150,000 square feet were completed and transferred out of the Polishing Department to Finished Goods Inventory. The countertops were subsequently sold for $12 per square foot.

continued . . .

Requirements

1. What was the cost per square foot of the finished product?
2. Did most of the production cost occur in the Forming Department or in the Polishing Department? Explain how you can tell.
3. What was the gross profit per square foot?
4. What was the total gross profit on the countertops produced in April?

The following data set is used for S4-14 through S4-18

Polar Springs Data Set: Filtration Department

Polar Springs produces premium bottled water. Polar Springs purchases artesian water, stores the water in large tanks, and then runs the water through two processes:

- Filtration, where workers microfilter and ozonate the water
- Bottling, where workers bottle and package the filtered water

During February, the filtration process incurs the following costs in processing 200,000 liters:

Wages of workers operating the filtration equipment..................	$ 11,100
Wages of workers operating ozonation equipment.......................	12,850
Manufacturing overhead allocated to filtration...........................	24,050
Water...	120,000

Polar Springs has no beginning inventory in the Filtration Department.

S4-14 **Compute cost per liter** *(Learning Objective 1)*

Refer to the Polar Springs Filtration Department Data Set.

Requirements

1. Compute the February conversion costs in the Filtration Department.
2. If the Filtration Department completely processed 200,000 liters, what would be the average filtration cost per liter?
3. Now, assume that the total costs of the filtration process listed in the chart above yield 160,000 liters that are completely filtered and ozonated, while the remaining 40,000 liters are only partway through the process at the end of February. Is the cost per completely filtered and ozonated liter higher, lower, or the same as in Requirement 2? Why?

S4-15 **Summarize physical flow and compute equivalent units** *(Learning Objective 2)*
Refer to the Polar Springs Filtration Department Data Set. At Polar Spring, water is added at the beginning of the filtration process. Conversion costs are added evenly throughout the process, and in February, 160,000 liters have been completed and transferred out of the Filtration Department to the Bottling Department. The 40,000 liters remaining in the Filtration Department's ending work in process inventory are 80% of the way through the filtration process. Recall that Polar Spring has no beginning inventories.

Requirements

1. Draw a time line for the filtration process similar to the one in Exhibit 4-6.

2. Complete the first two steps of the process costing procedure for the Filtration Department: summarize the physical flows of units and then compute the equivalent units of direct materials and conversion costs. Your answer should look similar to Exhibit 4-5.

S4-16 **Continuation of S4-15: summarize total costs to account for and compute cost per equivalent unit** *(Learning Objective 3)*
Refer to the Polar Springs Filtration Department Data Set and your answer to S4-15. Complete Steps 3 and 4 of the process costing procedure: summarize total costs to account for and then compute the cost per equivalent unit for both direct materials and conversion costs.

S4-17 **Continuation of S4-15 and S4-16: assign costs** *(Learning Objective 3)*
Refer to the Polar Springs Filtration Department Data Set and your answer to S4-15 and S4-16. Complete Step 5 of the process costing procedure: assign costs to units completed and to units in ending inventory. Prepare a schedule similar to Exhibit 4-9 that answers the following questions:

Requirements

1. What is the cost of the 160,000 liters completed and transferred out of the Filtration Department?

2. What is the cost of 40,000 liters remaining in the Filtration Department's ending work in process inventory?

S4-18 **Continuation of S4-17: record journal entry and post to T-account** *(Learning Objective 3)*
Refer to the Polar Springs Filtration Department Data Set and your answer to S4-17.

Requirements

1. Record the journal entry to transfer the cost of the 160,000 liters completed and transferred out of the Filtration Department and into the Bottling Department.

2. Record all of the transactions in the Work in Process Inventory—Filtration T-account.

The following data set is used for S4-19 through S4-22

Polar Springs Data Set: Bottling Department

Polar Spring produces premium bottled water. The preceding Short Exercises considered Polar Spring's first process—filtration. We now consider Polar Spring's second process—bottling. In the Bottling Department, workers bottle the filtered water and pack the bottles into boxes. Conversion costs are incurred evenly throughout the bottling process, but packaging materials are not added until the end of the process.

February data from the Bottling Department follow:

Beginning work in process inventory (40% of the way through the process)	8,000 liters
Transferred in from Filtration*	160,000 liters
Completed and transferred out to Finished Goods Inventory in February	154,000 liters
Ending work in process inventory (70% of the way through the bottling process)	14,000 liters

Costs in beginning work in process inventory		Costs added during February	
Transferred in	$1,760	Transferred in*	$136,000
Direct materials	0	Direct materials	30,800
Direct labor	600	Direct labor	33,726
Manufacturing overhead	520	Manufacturing overhead	22,484
Total beginning work in process inventory as of February 1	$2,880	Total costs added during February	$223,010

*S4-17 showed that Polar Spring's Filtration Department completed and transferred out 160,000 liters at a total cost of $136,000.

S4-19 **Compute equivalent units in second department** *(Learning Objectives 2, 4)*
Refer to the Polar Springs Bottling Department Data Set.

Requirements

1. Draw a time line similar to the one in Exhibit 4-10.
2. Complete the first two steps of the process costing procedure for the Bottling Department: summarize the physical flow of units and then compute the equivalent units of direct materials and conversion costs. Your answer should look similar to Exhibit 4-12.

S4-20 **Continuation of S4-19: compute cost per equivalent unit in second department** *(Learning Objective 4)*
Refer to the Polar Springs Bottling Department Data Set and your answer to S4-19. Complete Steps 3 and 4 of the process costing procedure: summarize total costs to account for and then compute the cost per equivalent unit for both direct materials and conversion costs. Your answer should look similar to Exhibit 4-13.

S4-21 **Continuation of S4-19 and S4-20: assign costs in second department** *(Learning Objective 4)*
Refer to the Polar Springs Bottling Department Data Set and your answers to S4-19 and 4-20. Complete Step 5 of the process costing procedure: assign costs to units completed and to units in ending inventory. Your answer should look similar to Exhibit 4-14.

S4-22 **Continuation of S4-21: record journal entry and post to T-account** *(Learning Objective 4)*
Refer to the Polar Springs Bottling Department Data Set and your answer to S4-21.

Requirements

1. Prepare the journal entry to record the cost of units completed and transferred to finished goods.

2. Post all transactions to the Work in Process Inventory—Bottling T-account. What is the ending balance?

■ Exercises

E4-23 **Diagram flow of costs** *(Learning Objective 1)*
Vancor produces kitchen cabinets in a three-stage process that includes milling, assembling, and finishing, in that order. Direct materials are added in the Milling and Finishing departments. Direct labor and overhead are incurred in all three departments. The company's general ledger includes the following accounts:

Cost of Goods Sold	Materials Inventory
Manufacturing Wages	Finished Goods Inventory
Work in Process Inventory—Milling	Manufacturing Overhead
Work in Process Inventory—Assembling	
Work in Process Inventory—Finishing	

Outline the flow of costs through the company's accounts, including a brief description of each flow. Include a T-account for each account title given.

E4-24 **Record journal entries** *(Learning Objective 1)*
Record the following process costing transactions in the general journal:

a. Purchase of raw materials on account, $9,000

b. Requisition of direct materials to
     Assembly Department, $4,000
     Finishing Department, $2,000

c. Incurrence and payment of manufacturing labor, $10,800

d. Incurrence of manufacturing overhead costs:
     Property taxes—plant, $1,900
     Utilities—plant, $4,500
     Insurance—plant, $1,100
     Depreciation—plant, $3,400

continued . . .

e. Assignment of conversion costs to the Assembly Department:

Direct labor, $4,700

Manufacturing overhead, $2,900

f. Assignment of conversion costs to the Finishing Department:

Direct labor, $4,400

Manufacturing overhead, $6,200

g. Cost of goods completed and transferred out of the Assembly Department to the Finishing Department, $10,250

h. Cost of goods completed and transferred out of the Finishing Department into Finished Goods Inventory, $15,600

E4-25 **Analyze flow of costs through inventory T-accounts** *(Learning Objective 1)*
Frizzel Bakery mass-produces bread using three sequential processing departments: Mixing, Baking, and Packaging. The following transactions occurred during January:

1. Direct materials used in the Packaging Department	$ 30,000
2. Costs assigned to units completed and transferred out of Mixing	225,000
3. Direct labor incurred in the Mixing Department......................................	11,000
4. Beginning balance: Work in Process Inventory—Baking	15,000
5. Manufacturing overhead allocated to the Baking Department	75,000
6. Beginning balance: Finished Goods Inventory...	4,000
7. Costs assigned to units completed and transferred out of Baking..............	301,000
8. Beginning balance: Work in Process Inventory—Mixing...........................	12,000
9. Direct labor incurred in the Packaging Department	8,000
10. Manufacturing overhead allocated to the Mixing Department..................	60,000
11. Direct materials used in the Mixing Department......................................	152,000
12. Beginning balance: Raw Materials Inventory	23,000
13. Costs assigned to units completed and transferred out of Packaging........	381,000
14. Beginning balance: Work in Process Inventory—Packaging	8,000
15. Purchases of Raw Materials..	170,000
16. Direct labor incurred in the Baking Department	4,000
17. Manufacturing overhead allocated to the Packaging Department	40,000
18. Cost of goods sold	382,000

Note: No direct materials were used by the Baking Department.

Requirements

1. Post each of these transactions to the company's inventory T-accounts. You should set up separate T-accounts for the following:
   - Raw Materials Inventory
   - Work in Process Inventory—Mixing Department
   - Work in Process Inventory—Baking Department
   - Work in Process Inventory—Packaging Department
   - Finished Goods Inventory

2. Determine the balance at month-end in each of the inventory accounts.

3. Assume that 3,175,000 loaves of bread were completed and transferred out of the Packaging Department during the month. What was the cost per unit of making each loaf of bread (from start to finish)?

E4-26 **Summarize physical units and compute equivalent units (process costing Steps 1 and 2)** *(Learning Objective 2)*

Ralph's Apple Pies collected the following production information relating to June's baking operations:

	Physical Units	Direct Materials (% complete)	Conversion Costs (% complete)
Beginning work in process	200,000	—	—
Ending work in process	150,000	75%	80%
Units started during the month	1,000,000		

Requirements

Complete the first two steps in the process costing procedure:

1. Summarize the flow of physical units.
2. Compute output in terms of equivalent units.

   (*Hint:* Your answer should look similar to Exhibit 4-5.)

E4-27 **Compute equivalent units in a second processing department** *(Learning Objectives 2, 4)*

Marlene's Mayonnaise uses a process costing system to determine its product's cost. The last of the three processes is packaging. The Packaging Department reported the following information for the month of May:

		Equivalent Units		
	Physical Units	Transferred-in	Direct Materials	Conversion Costs
Units to account for:				
Beginning work in process	25,000			
Transferred in during May	225,000			
Total units to account for	(a)			
Units accounted for:				
Completed and transferred out	(b)	(d)	(g)	(j)
Ending work in process	30,000	(e)	(h)	(k)
Total units accounted for:	(c)			
Total equivalent units		(f)	(i)	(l)

The units in ending work in process inventory were 90% complete with respect to direct materials, but only 60% complete with respect to conversion.

Requirements

Summarize the flow of physical units and compute output in terms of equivalent units in order to arrive at the missing figures (a) through (l).

E4-28 **Complete five-step procedure in first department** *(Learning Objective 3)*
Creative World prepares and packages paint products. Creative World has two departments: (1) blending and (2) packaging. Direct materials are added at the beginning of the blending process (dyes) and at the end of the packaging process (cans). Conversion costs are added evenly throughout each process. Data from the month of May for the Blending Department are as follows:

Gallons:	
Beginning work in process inventory...........................	0
Started production	8,000 gallons
Completed and transferred out to Packaging in May..	6,000 gallons
Ending work in process inventory (30% of the way through the blending process)	2,000 gallons
Costs:	
Beginning work in process inventory...........................	$ 0
Costs added during May:	
Direct materials (dyes)...	4,800
Direct labor...	800
Manufacturing overhead...	1,840
Total costs added during May.......................................	$7,440

Requirements

1. Draw a time line for the Blending Department similar to Exhibit 4-6.
2. Summarize the physical flow of units and compute total equivalent units for direct materials and for conversion costs.
3. Summarize total costs to account for and find the cost per equivalent unit for direct materials and conversion costs.
4. Assign total costs to units (gallons):
    a. Completed and transferred out to the Packaging Department.
    b. In the Blending Department ending work in process inventory.
5. What is the average cost per gallon transferred out of the Blending Department to the Packaging Department? Why would Creative World's managers want to know this cost?

E4-29 **Continuation of E4-28: journal entries** *(Learning Objectives 1, 3)*
Return to the Blending Department for Creative World in E4-28.

Requirements

1. Present the journal entry to record the use of direct materials and direct labor and the allocation of manufacturing overhead to the Blending Department. Also, give the journal entry to record the costs of the gallons completed and transferred out to the Packaging Department.
2. Post the journal entries to the Work in Process Inventory—Blending T-account. What is the ending balance?

E4-30 **Compute equivalent units and assign costs** *(Learning Objectives 2, 3)*

The Assembly Department of Whalen Surge Protectors began September with no work in process inventory. During the month, production that cost $39,860 (direct materials, $9,900, and conversion costs, $29,960) was started on 23,000 units. Whalen completed and transferred to the Testing Department a total of 15,000 units. The ending work in process inventory was 37.5% complete as to direct materials and 80% complete as to conversion work.

Requirements

1. Compute the equivalent units for direct materials and conversion costs.

2. Compute the cost per equivalent unit.

3. Assign the costs to units completed and transferred out and ending work in process inventory.

4. Record the journal entry for the costs transferred out of the Assembly Department to the Testing Department.

5. Post all of the transactions in the Work in Process Inventory—Assembly T-account. What is the ending balance?

E4-31 **Complete five-step procedure in first department** *(Learning Objective 3)*

Cogan Winery in Kingston, New York, has two departments: Fermenting and Packaging. Direct materials are added at the beginning of the fermenting process (grapes) and at the end of the packaging process (bottles). Conversion costs are added evenly throughout each process. Data from the month of March for the Fermenting Department are as follows:

Gallons:	
Beginning work in process inventory.........................	2,000 gallons
Started production	6,000 gallons
Completed and transferred out to Packaging in March...	6,550 gallons
Ending work in process inventory (80% of the way through the fermenting process)......................	1,450 gallons
Costs:	
Beginning work in process inventory ($2,800 of direct materials and $2,855 of conversion cost)	$ 5,655
Costs added during March:	
Direct materials...	8,800
Direct labor..	1,600
Manufacturing overhead	2,484
Total costs added during March...............................	$12,884

Requirements

1. Draw a time line for the Fermenting Department similar to Exhibit 4-6.

2. Summarize the flow of physical units and compute the total equivalent units.

3. Summarize total costs to account for and compute the cost per equivalent unit for direct materials and conversion costs.

continued . . .

4. Assign total costs to units (gallons):
   a. Completed and transferred out to the Packaging Department.
   b. In the Fermenting Department ending work in process inventory.
5. What is the average cost per gallon transferred out of Fermenting into Packaging? Why would Cogan's managers want to know this cost?

E4-32 **Continuation of E4-31: journal entries** (*Learning Objectives 1, 3*)
Return to the Fermenting Department for Cogan Winery in E4-31.

Requirements

1. Present the journal entries to record the use of direct materials and direct labor and the allocation of manufacturing overhead to the Fermenting Department. Also, give the journal entry to record the cost of the gallons completed and transferred out to the Packaging Department.
2. Post the journal entries to the Work in Process Inventory—Fermenting T-account. What is the ending balance?

E4-33 **Complete five-step procedure and journalize result** (*Learning Objectives 1, 3*)
The following information was taken from the ledger of Boston Roping:

Work in Process—Forming			
Beginning inventory, October 1	$ 47,820	Transferred to Finishing	$?
Direct materials	193,620		
Conversion costs	168,640		
Ending inventory	?		

The Forming Department had 10,000 partially complete units in beginning work in process inventory. The department started work on 70,000 units during the month and ended the month with 8,000 units still in work in process. These unfinished units were 60% complete as to direct materials but 20% complete as to conversion work. The beginning balance of $47,820 consisted of $21,420 of direct materials and $26,400 of conversion costs.

Requirements

Journalize the transfer of costs to the Finishing Department. (*Hint:* Complete the five-step process costing procedure to determine how much cost to transfer.)

E4-34 **Compute equivalent units in two later departments** *(Learning Objectives 2, 4)*
Selected production and cost data of Larry's Fudge follow for May:

Flow of Production	Flow of Physical Units	
	Mixing Department	Heating Department
Units to account for:		
Beginning work in process, May 1	20,000	6,000
Transferred in during May	70,000	80,000
Total physical units to account for	90,000	86,000
Units accounted for:		
Completed and transferred out during May	80,000	76,000
Ending work in process, May 31	10,000	10,000
Total physical units accounted for	90,000	86,000

On May 31, the Mixing Department's ending work in process inventory was 70% complete as to materials and 20% complete as to conversion costs.

On May 31, the Heating Department's ending work in process inventory was 65% complete as to materials and 55% complete as to conversion costs.

Requirements
Compute the equivalent units for transferred-in costs, direct materials, and conversion costs for both the Mixing and the Heating Departments.

E4-35 **Complete five-step procedure in second department** (*Learning Objective 4*)
Orth Semiconductors experienced the following activity in its Photolithography Department during December. Materials are added at the beginning of the photolithography process.

Units:	
Work in process, December 1 (80% of the way through the process).................................	8,000 units
Transferred in from the Polishing and Cutting Department during December	27,000 units
Completed during December.....................................	? units
Work in process, December 31 (70% of the way through the process)	9,000 units
Costs:	
Work in process, December 1 (transferred-in costs, $20,050; direct materials costs, $20,250; and conversion costs, $19,816)	$60,116
Transferred in from the Polishing and Cutting Department during December	97,200
Direct materials added during December....................	74,250
Conversion costs added during December..................	90,650

Requirements

(Hint: Use Exhibits 4-12, 4-13 and 4-14 as guides if needed.)

1. Summarize flow of physical units and compute total equivalent units for three cost categories: transferred-in, direct materials, and conversion costs.

2. Summarize total costs to account for and compute the cost per equivalent unit for each cost category.

3. Assign total costs to (a) units completed and transferred to Finished Goods Inventory and (b) units in December 31 Work in Process Inventory.

■ Problems (Problem Set A)

P4-36A **Process costing in a single processing department** (*Learning Objectives 1, 2, 3*)
Great Lips produces a lip balm used for cold-weather sports. The balm is manufactured in a single processing department. No lip balm was in process on May 31, and Great Lips started production on 20,400 lip balm tubes during June. Direct materials are added at the beginning of the process, but conversion costs are incurred evenly throughout the process. Completed production for June totaled 15,200 units. The June 30 work in process was 40% of the way through the production process. Direct materials costing $4,080 were placed in production during June, and direct labor of $3,315 and manufacturing overhead of $1,005 were assigned to the process.

Requirements

1. Draw a time line for Great Lips that is similar to Exhibit 4-6.

2. Use the time line to help you compute the total equivalent units and the cost per equivalent unit for June.

3. Assign total costs to (a) units completed and transferred to Finished Goods and (b) units still in process at June 30.

4. Prepare a T-account for Work in Process Inventory to show activity during June, including the June 30 balance.

P4-37A **Process costing in a first department** *(Learning Objectives 1, 2, 3)*

The Albany Furniture Company produces dining tables in a three-stage process: sawing, assembly, and staining. Costs incurred in the Sawing Department during September are summarized as follows:

Work in Process Inventory—Sawing		
September 1 balance	0	
Direct materials	1,860,000	
Direct labor	139,100	
Manufacturing overhead	153,400	

Direct materials (lumber) are added at the beginning of the sawing process, while conversion costs are incurred evenly throughout the process. September activity in the Sawing Department included sawing of 11,000 meters of lumber, which were transferred to the Assembly Department. Also, work began on 1,000 meters of lumber, which on September 30 were 70% of the way through the sawing process.

Requirements

1. Draw a time line for the Sawing Department similar to Exhibit 4-6.

2. Use the time line to help you compute the number of equivalent units and the cost per equivalent unit in the Sawing Department for September.

3. Show that the sum of (a) cost of goods transferred out of the Sawing Department and (b) ending Work in Process Inventory—Sawing equals the total cost accumulated in the department during September.

4. Journalize all transactions affecting the company's sawing process during September, including those already posted.

P4-38A **Five-step process: materials added at different points** *(Learning Objectives 1, 2, 3)*

First Choice produces canned chicken a la king. The chicken a la king passes through three departments: (1) Mixing, (2) Retort (sterilization), and (3) Packing. In the Mixing Department, chicken and cream are added at the beginning of the process, the mixture is partly cooked, and chopped green peppers and mushrooms are added at

continued . . .

the end of the process. Conversion costs are added evenly throughout the mixing process. November data from the Mixing Department are as follows:

Gallons		Costs		
Beginning work in process inventory	0 gallons	Beginning work in process inventory	$	0
Started production	15,000 gallons	Costs added during November:		
Completed and transferred out to Retort in November...	12,900 gallons	Chicken.........................		12,500
		Cream		4,000
Ending work in process inventory (60% of the way through the mixing process)...................	2,100 gallons	Green peppers and mushrooms		11,610
		Direct labor..................		11,108
		Manufacturing overhead		3,052
		Total costs...........................		$42,270

Requirements

1. Draw a time line for the Mixing Department similar to Exhibit 4-6.
2. Use the time line to help you summarize the flow of physical units and compute the equivalent units. (*Hint:* Each direct material added at a different point in the production process requires its own equivalent-unit computation.)
3. Compute the cost per equivalent unit for each cost category.
4. Compute the total costs of the units (gallons):
   a. Completed and transferred out to the Retort Department.
   b. In the Mixing Department's ending work in process inventory.
5. Prepare the journal entry to record the cost of the gallons completed and transferred out to the Retort Department.
6. Post the transactions to the Work in Process Inventory—Mixing T-account. What is the ending balance?
7. What is the primary purpose of the work in requirements 1 through 4?

P4-39A Prepare a Production Cost report and journal entries (*Learning Objectives 1, 4*)
Bria manufactures auto roof racks in a two-stage process that includes shaping and plating. Steel alloy is the basic raw material of the shaping process. The steel is molded according to the design specifications of automobile manufacturers (Ford and General Motors). The Plating Department then adds an anodized finish.

At March 31, before recording the transfer of cost from the Plating Department to Finished Goods Inventory, the Bria general ledger included the following account:

Work in Process Inventory—Plating

March 1 balance	30,480
Transferred-in from Shaping	36,000
Direct materials	24,200
Direct labor	21,732
Manufacturing overhead	35,388

The direct materials (rubber pads) are added at the end of the plating process. Conversion costs are incurred evenly throughout the process. Work in process of the Plating Department on March 1 consisted of 1,200 racks. The $30,480 beginning balance of Work in Process–Plating includes $18,000 of transferred-in cost and $12,480 of conversion cost. During March, 2,400 racks were transferred in from the Shaping Department. The Plating Department transferred 2,200 racks to Finished Goods Inventory in March, and 1,400 were still in process on March 31. This ending inventory was 50% of the way through the plating process.

Requirements

1. Draw a time line for the Plating Department, similar to Exhibit 4-10.
2. Prepare the March production cost report for the Plating Department.
3. Journalize all transactions affecting the Plating Department during March, including the entries that have already been posted.

P4-40A **Complete five-step process in a later department** (*Learning Objectives 2, 4*)
Lum uses four departments to produce plastic handles for screwdrivers: Mixing, Molding, Drying, and Assembly.

Lum's Drying Department requires no direct materials. Conversion costs are incurred evenly throughout the drying process. Other process costing information follows:

Units:	
Beginning work in process..	7,000 units
Transferred-in from the Molding Department during the period..	28,000 units
Completed during the period......................................	16,000 units
Ending work in process (20% complete as to conversion work)	19,000 units
Costs:	
Beginning work in process (transferred-in cost, $140; conversion cost, $231)	$ 371
Transferred-in from the Molding Department during the period...	4,760
Conversion costs added during the period.................	1,947

After the drying process, the screwdrivers are completed by assembling the handles and shanks and packaging for shipment to retail outlets.

continued . . .

Requirements

1. Draw a time line of the Drying Department's process, similar to the one in Exhibit 4-10.

2. Use the time line to compute the number of equivalent units of work performed by the Drying Department during the period, the cost per equivalent unit, and the total costs to account for.

3. Assign total costs to (a) units completed and transferred to the assembly operation and (b) units in the Drying Department's ending work in process inventory.

■ Problems (Problem Set B)

P4-41B Process Costing in a first department *(Learning Objectives 1, 2, 3)*

Fast Calc Company makes electronic personal data assistants (PDAs) in three processes: assembly, programming, and packaging. The Assembly Department had no work in process on June 1. In mid-June, Fast Calc Company started production on 100,000 PDAs. Of this number, 76,400 PDAs were assembled during June. Direct materials are added at the beginning of the assembly process. Conversion costs are incurred evenly throughout the process. The June 30 work in process in the Assembly Department was 60% of the way through the assembly process. Direct materials costing $375,000 were placed in production in the Assembly Department during June, and direct labor of $157,248 and manufacturing overhead of $118,960 were assigned to that department.

Requirements

1. Draw a time line for the Assembly Department, similar to Exhibit 4-6.

2. Use the time line to help you compute the number of equivalent units and the cost per equivalent unit in the Assembly Department for June.

3. Assign total costs in the Assembly Department to (a) units completed and transferred to the Programming Department during June and (b) units still in process at June 30.

4. Prepare a T-account for Work in Process Inventory—Assembly to show its activity during June, including the June 30 balance.

P4-42B Process Costing in a first department *(Learning Objectives 1, 2, 3)*

Webber produces the paper used by wallpaper manufacturers. Webber's four-stage process includes mixing, cooking, rolling, and cutting. In the Mixing Department, wood pulp and chemicals are blended. The resulting mix is heated in the Cooking Department in much the same way as food is prepared. Then the cooked mix is rolled to produce sheets. The final process, cutting, divides the sheets into large rolled units. The Mixing Department incurred the following costs during August:

Work in Process Inventory—Mixing	
Aug. 1 Balance	0
Direct materials	5,520
Direct labor	580
Manufacturing overhead	3,560

During August, the Mixing Department started and completed mixing for 4,500 rolls of paper. The department started but did not finish the mixing for an additional 500 rolls, which were 20% complete with respect to both direct materials and conversion work at the end of August. Direct materials and conversion costs are incurred evenly throughout the mixing process.

Requirements

1. Draw a time line for the Mixing Department, similar to Exhibit 4-6.
2. Use the time line to help you compute the number of equivalent units and the cost per equivalent unit in the Mixing Department for August.
3. Show that the sum of (a) cost of goods transferred out of the Mixing Department and (b) ending Work in Process Inventory—Mixing equals the total cost accumulated in the department during August.
4. Journalize all transactions affecting the company's mixing process during August, including those already posted.

P4-43B Five-step process: materials added at different points *(Learning Objectives 1, 2, 3)*
Batchelder produces exterior siding for homes. The Preparation Department begins with wood, which is chopped into small bits. At the end of the process, an adhesive is added. Then the wood/adhesive mixture goes on to the Compression Department, where the wood is compressed into sheets. Assume conversion costs are added evenly throughout the preparation process. Suppose that April data for the Preparation Department are as follows (in millions):

Sheets		Costs	
Beginning work in process inventory	0 sheets	Beginning work in process inventory	$ 0
Started production	3,000 sheets	Costs added during April:	
Completed and transferred out to Compression in April..........................	1,950 sheets	Wood...............................	2,700
		Adhesive..........................	1,365
		Direct labor......................	629
Ending work in process inventory (40% of the way through the preparation process)......................	1,050 sheets	Manufacturing overhead	1,267
		Total costs..........................	$5,961

Requirements

1. Draw a time line for the Preparation Department, similar to Exhibit 4-6.
2. Use the time line to help you summarize the flow of physical units and compute the equivalent units for direct materials and for conversion costs. (*Hint:* Each direct material added at a different point in the production process requires its own equivalent-unit computation.)
3. Compute the cost per equivalent unit for each cost category.
4. Compute the total costs of the units (sheets)
   a. Completed and transferred out to the Compression Department
   b. In the Preparation Department's ending work in process inventory

continued . . .

5. Prepare the journal entry to record the cost of the sheets completed and transferred out to the Compression Department.

6. Post the journal entries to the Work in Process Inventory—Preparation T-account. What is the ending balance?

7. What is the primary purpose of the work in Requirements 1 through 4?

P4-44B **Prepare a production cost report and journal entries** *(Learning Objectives 1, 4)*

Souda Carpeting manufactures broadloom carpet in seven processes: spinning, dyeing, plying, spooling, tufting, latexing, and shearing. First, fluff nylon purchased from a company such as DuPont or Monsanto is spun into yarn that is dyed the desired color. Then, threads of the yarn are joined together, or plied, for added strength. The plied yarn is spooled for carpet making. Tufting is the process by which yarn is added to burlap backing. After the backing is latexed to hold it together and make it skid-resistant, the carpet is sheared to give it an even appearance and feel.

At March 31, before recording the transfer of costs out of the Dyeing Department, the Souda Carpeting general ledger included the following account for one of its lines of carpet:

Work in Process Inventory—Dyeing	
March 1 Balance	11,174
Transferred in from Spinning	21,000
Direct materials	11,760
Direct labor	8,445
Manufacturing overhead	42,900

In the Dyeing Department, direct materials (dye) are added at the beginning of the process. Conversion costs are incurred evenly throughout the process. Work in process inventory of the Dyeing Department on March 1 consisted of 110 rolls. The $11,174 beginning balance of Work in Process–Dyeing includes $4,400 of transferred-in cost, $1,575 of direct materials cost, and $5,199 of conversion cost. During March, 525 rolls were transferred in from the Spinning Department. The Dyeing Department completed and transferred 500 rolls to the Plying Department in March, and 135 rolls were still in process on March 31. The ending inventory was 80% of the way through the dyeing process.

Requirements

1. Prepare a time line for the Dyeing Department similar to Exhibit 4-10.

2. Prepare the March production cost report for Souda's Dyeing Department.

3. Journalize all transactions affecting the Dyeing Department during March, including the entries that have already been posted.

P4-45B **Complete five-step process in last department** *(Learning Objectives 2, 4)*

Nellaney uses three processes to manufacture lifts for personal watercraft: forming a lift's parts from galvanized steel, assembling the lift, and testing the completed lifts. The lifts are transferred to Finished Goods before shipment to marinas across the country.

Nellaney's Testing Department requires no direct materials. Conversion costs are incurred evenly throughout the testing process. Other information follows:

Units:	
Beginning work in process...	2,000 units
Transferred in from the Assembling Department during the period..	7,000 units
Completed during the period.......................................	4,000 units
Ending work in process (40% complete as to conversion work)	5,000 units
Costs:	
Beginning work in process (transferred-in costs, $93,000; conversion costs, $18,000)	$111,000
Transferred in from the Assembling Department during the period..	672,000
Conversion costs added during the period...................	48,000

The cost transferred into Finished Goods Inventory is the cost of the lifts transferred out of the Testing Department.

Requirements

1. Draw a time line for the Testing Department similar to the one in Exhibit 4-10.
2. Use the time line to compute the number of equivalent units of work performed by the Testing Department during the period, the cost per equivalent unit, and total costs to account for.
3. Assign total costs to (a) units completed and transferred out of the Testing Department and (b) units in the Testing Department's ending work in process inventory.
4. Compute the cost per unit for lifts completed and transferred out to Finished Goods Inventory. Why would management be interested in this cost?

Apply Your Knowledge

▪ Decision Case

Case 4-46. Cost per unit and gross profit *(Learning Objective 4)*

Jimmy Jones operates Jimmy's Cricket Farm in Eatonton, Georgia. Jimmy's raises about 18 million crickets a month. Most are sold to pet stores at $12.60 for a box of 1,000 crickets. Pet stores sell the crickets for $0.05 to $0.10 each as live feed for reptiles.

Raising crickets requires a two-step process: incubation and brooding. In the first process, incubation employees place cricket eggs on mounds of peat moss to hatch. In the second process, employees move the newly hatched crickets into large boxes filled with cardboard dividers. Depending on the desired size, the crickets spend approximately two weeks in brooding before being shipped to pet stores. In the brooding process, Jimmy's crickets consume about 16 tons of food and produce 12 tons of manure.

Jones has invested $400,000 in the cricket farm, and he had hoped to earn a 24% annual rate of return, which works out to a 2% monthly return on his investment. After looking at the farm's bank balance, Jones fears he is not achieving this return. To get more accurate information on the farm's performance, Jones bought new accounting software that provides weighted-average process cost information. After Jones input data, the software provided the following reports. However, Jones needs help interpreting these reports.

Jones does know that a unit of production is a box of 1,000 crickets. For example, in June's report, the 7,000 physical units of beginning work in process inventory are 7,000 boxes (each one of the 7,000 boxes contains 1,000 immature crickets). The finished goods inventory is zero because the crickets ship out as soon as they reach the required size. Monthly operating expenses total $2,000 (in addition to the costs that follow).

JIMMY'S CRICKET FARM
Brooding Department
Production Cost Report (part 1 of 2)
Month Ended June 30

Flow of Production	Flow of Physical Units	Equivalent Units Transferred-In	Direct Materials	Conversion Costs
Units to account for:				
Beginning work in process inventory, June 1	7,000			
Transferred in during June	21,000			
Total units to account for	28,000			
Units accounted for:				
Completed and shipped out during June	19,000	19,000	19,000	19,000
Ending work in process, June 30	9,000	9,000	7,200	3,600
Total physical units accounted for	28,000			
Total equivalent units		28,000	26,200	22,600

JIMMY'S CRICKET FARM
Brooding Department
Production Cost Report (part 2 of 2)
Month Ended June 30

		Transferred-In	Direct Materials	Conversion Costs	Total
	Unit costs:				
	Beginning work in process, June 1	$21,000	$ 39,940	$ 5,020	$ 65,960
	Costs added during June	46,200	156,560	51,480	254,240
	Total costs to account for	$67,200	$196,500	$56,500	$320,200
	Divide by total equivalent units	÷ 28,000	÷ 26,200	÷ 22,600	
	Cost per equivalent unit	$ 2.40	$ 7.50	$ 2.50	
	Assignment of total cost:				
	Units completed and shipped out during June	[19,000 × ($2.40 + $7.50 + $2.50)]			$235,600
	Ending work in process, June 30:				
	Transferred-in costs	[9,000 × $2.40]			21,600
	Direct materials		[7,200 × $7.50]		54,000
	Conversion costs			[3,600 × $2.50]	9,000
	Total ending work in process, June 30				84,600
	Total cost accounted for				$320,200

Requirements

Jimmy Jones has the following questions about the farm's performance during June:

1. What is the cost per box of crickets sold? (*Hint:* This is the cost of the boxes completed and shipped out of brooding.)

2. What is the gross profit per box?

3. How much operating income did Jimmy's Cricket Farm make in June?

4. What is the return on Jones's investment of $400,000 for the month of June? (Compute this as June's operating income divided by Jones' $400,000 investment, expressed as a percentage.)

5. What monthly operating income would provide a 2% monthly rate of return? What price per box would Jimmy's Cricket Farm have had to charge in June to achieve a 2% monthly rate of return?

■ Ethical Issue

Issue 4-47. Ethical dilemma regarding percentage of completion (*Learning Objectives 2, 4*)

Rick Penn and Joe Lopus are the plant managers for Pacific Lumber's particle board division. Pacific Lumber has adopted a JIT management philosophy. Each plant combines wood chips with chemical adhesives to produce particle board to order, and all production is sold as soon as it is completed. Laura Green is Pacific Lumber's regional controller. All of Pacific Lumber's plants and divisions send Green their production and cost information. While reviewing the numbers of the two particle board plants,

continued . . .

she is surprised that both plants estimate their ending work in process inventories at 80% complete, which is higher than usual. Green calls Lopus, whom she has known for some time. He admits that to ensure that their division met its profit goal and that both he and Penn would make their bonus (which is based on division profit), he and Penn agreed to inflate the percentage completion. Lopus explains, "Determining the percentage completion always requires judgment. Whatever the percentage completion, we'll finish the work in process inventory first thing next year."

Requirements

1. How would inflating the percentage completion of ending work in process inventory help Penn and Lopus get their bonus?

2. The particle board division is the largest of Pacific Lumber's divisions. If Green does not correct the percentage completion of this year's ending work in process inventory, how will the misstatement affect Pacific Lumber's financial statements?

3. Evaluate Lopus's justification, including the effect, if any, on next year's financial statements.

4. In considering what Green should do, answer the following questions:
   a. What is the ethical question?
   b. What are the options?
   c. What are the possible consequences?
   d. What should Green do?

■ Team Project

Project 4-48. Calculating costs for a customer order (*Learning Objective 4*)

Hermiston Food Processors in Hermiston, Oregon, processes potatoes into French fries. Production requires two processes: cutting and cooking. The cutting process begins as scalding steam explodes the potatoes' brown skins. Workers using paring knives gouge out black spots before high-pressure water blasts potatoes through a pipe and into blades arranged in a quarter-inch grid. In the cooking process, the raw shoestring fries are cooked in a bleacher, dried, partially fried at 380°F, and immediately flash-frozen at minus 75°F before being dropped into five-pound bags. Direct materials are added at the beginning of the cutting process (potatoes) and at the end of the cooking process (bags). Conversion costs are incurred evenly throughout each process.

Assume that McDonald's offers Hermiston $0.40 per pound to supply restaurants in the Far East. If Hermiston accepts McDonald's offer, the cost (per equivalent unit) that Hermiston will incur to fill the McDonald's order equals the April cost per equivalent unit. J. R. Simlott, manager of the cooking process, must prepare a report explaining whether Hermiston should accept the offer. Simlott gathers the following information from April's cooking operations:

Lola Mendez manages the cutting process. She reports the following data for her department's April operations:

HERMISTON FOOD PROCESSORS
Cooking Department
April Activity and Costs

Beginning work in process inventory, April 1	12,000 pounds
Raw shoestring fries started in April	129,000 pounds
French fries completed and transferred out	130,000 pounds
Ending work in process inventory (30% of way through process), April 30	11,000 pounds
Costs incurred *within* the cooking department in March to start the 12,000 pounds of beginning work in process inventory	$ 576
Costs added during April:	
Direct materials	6,500
Conversion costs	15,420

Split your team into two groups. Each group should meet separately before a meeting of the entire team.

Requirements

1. The first group takes the role of Simlott, manager of the cooking production process. Before meeting with the entire team, determine the maximum transferred-in cost per pound of raw shoestring fries the cooking department can incur from the cutting department if Hermiston is to make a profit on the McDonald's order. (*Hint:* You may find it helpful to prepare a time line and to use Exhibits 4-10 through 4-13 as a guide for your analysis.)

2. The second group takes the role of Mendez, manager of the cutting process. Before meeting with the entire team, determine the April cost per pound of raw shoestring fries in the cutting process. (*Hint:* You may find it helpful to prepare a time line and to use Exhibits 4-10 through 4-13 as a guide for your analysis.)

3. After each group meets, the entire team should meet to decide whether Hermiston should accept or reject the McDonald's offer.

5 Activity-Based Costing and Other Cost Management Tools

After Dell reported its first-ever quarterly loss several years ago, CEO Michael Dell knew he had to focus on the company's most profitable products. But which products were they? The accounting system traced direct materials and direct labor to individual product lines, but it did not do a good job matching indirect costs throughout the value chain with the specific products that caused those costs (Dell wanted to find the full product cost of each product, not just the inventoriable product cost).

Dell needed a more finely tuned cost accounting system: *activity-based costing (ABC)*. Employee teams identified the ten most important indirect activities—for example, purchases of raw materials, indirect assembly labor, and warranty service. *For each activity*, the teams

developed a separate indirect cost allocation rate. The goal was to assign the cost of each activity to the product lines that caused that activity's cost. For example:

- Purchasing costs are assigned based on the number of different parts in a product.
- Indirect assembly labor is assigned based on the number of times the product is "touched."
- Warranty costs are assigned based on the number of service calls for the product line.

ABC assigns costs more accurately than simpler systems that combine the indirect costs of many activities into a single cost pool and then allocate those costs using a single allocation base.

Has ABC worked for Dell? By 2003, Dell was the leader in worldwide PC sales. Given the rapidly changing costs in the computer industry, Dell uses ABC costs for pricing its computers every day. ABC also helps Dell's managers cut costs, especially by highlighting nonvalue-added activities such as inventory storage. As the controller of Dell's American operations says, "Activity-based costing has really allowed Dell to go to the next level of understanding of its profitability for each of the products it sells." ■

Learning Objectives

1 Develop and use departmental overhead rates in place of a traditional plantwide rate

2 Develop activity-based costs (ABC) and use activity-based management (ABM) to make business decisions

3 Explain when ABC is most likely to pass the cost-benefit test

4 Describe a just-in-time (JIT) production system

5 Describe the four costs of quality and use them to make decisions

6 (Appendix) Use JIT costing to record costs in a JIT production environment

To thrive in a globally competitive market, Dell must deliver value to the customer by providing goods or services at an attractive price, while managing costs so the company still earns a profit. This chapter will show you several methods that today's managers use to deliver value to the customer at a profit:

- Refined costing systems such as ABC
- Just-in-time systems
- Costs of quality

Refined Cost Systems

Organizations from Dell to Carolina Power and Light to the U.S. Marine Corps use refined costing systems. Why? Because simple systems that do not match costs with the consumption of resources can assign costs inequitably. The following example shows why.

Why Managers Need More Accurate Cost Systems

David, Matt, and Marc are three college friends who share an apartment. They agree to split the following monthly costs equally:

Rent and utilities	$570
Cable TV	50
High-speed Internet access	40
Groceries	240
Total monthly costs	$900

Each roommate's share is $300 ($900/3).

Things go smoothly for the first few months. But then David calls a meeting. "Since I started having dinner at Amy's each night, I shouldn't have to chip in for the groceries." Matt then pipes in: "I'm so busy studying and using the Internet that I never have time to watch TV. I don't want to pay for the cable TV anymore. And Marc, since your friend Jennifer eats here most evenings, you should pay a double share of the grocery bill." Marc replies, "If that's the way you feel, Matt, then you should pay for the Internet access since you're the only one around here who uses it!"

What happened? The friends originally agreed to share the costs equally. But they are not participating equally in watching cable TV, using the Internet, and using the groceries. Splitting these costs equally is not equitable.

The roommates could use a cost allocation approach that better matches costs with the people who participate in each activity. This means splitting the cable TV costs between David and Marc, assigning the Internet access cost to Matt, and allocating the grocery bill one-third to Matt and two-thirds to Marc. Exhibit 5-1 compares the results of this refined cost allocation system with the original cost allocation system.

EXHIBIT 5-1	More-Refined Versus Less-Refined Cost Allocation System			
	David	Matt	Marc	Total
More-refined cost allocation system:				
Rent and utilities	$190	$190	$190	$570
Cable TV	25	0	25	50
High-speed Internet access	0	40	0	40
Groceries	0	80	160	240
Total costs allocated	$215	$310	$375	$900
Less-refined original cost allocation system	$300	$300	$300	$900
Difference	$ (85)	$ 10	$ 75	$ 0

No wonder David called a meeting! The original cost allocation system charged him $300 a month, but the refined system shows that a more equitable share would be only $215. The new system allocates Marc $375 a month instead of $300. David was paying for resources he did not use (Internet and groceries), while Marc was not paying for all of the resources (groceries) he and his guest consumed. David was "overcosted" and Marc was "undercosted" by the old system.

Total monthly costs are the same ($900) under both systems. The only difference is how that $900 is allocated among the three roommates. The amount by which David was "overcosted" ($85) exactly equals the amounts by which Matt and Marc were "undercosted" ($10 + $75).

As we'll see in the following sections, companies often refine their cost allocation systems to minimize the amount of overcosting and undercosting caused by the simpler traditional cost allocation systems. Overcosting some products while undercosting other products is known as **cost distortion**. By refining their costing systems, companies can more equitably assign indirect costs to their individual products or services, thereby reducing cost distortion.

Sharpening the Focus: From Business Functions to Departments to Activities

1 Develop and use departmental overhead rates in place of a traditional plantwide rate

As the chapter-opening story explained, Dell decided that it needed to refine its costing system so it could better understand which of its products were most profitable. There is little error in assigning direct costs, direct materials and direct labor to computers and servers. So, Dell focused on refining the way it allocated *indirect costs*. The goal was to more accurately reflect the cost of the resources that each product uses. How? By drilling down from the indirect costs incurred in each of the six functions in the value chain to the indirect costs incurred in each individual *department* within each value-chain function and, finally, to the indirect costs of the specific *activities* in each department. Let's look at each step.

The first column of Exhibit 5-2 lists the six value-chain functions: R&D, design, production, marketing, distribution, and customer service. We'll focus on how Dell refined costs in the *production* element of the value chain because that is where most companies, like Dell, begin refining their costing systems.

EXHIBIT 5-2   **Sharpening the Focus from Business Functions to Departments to Activities**

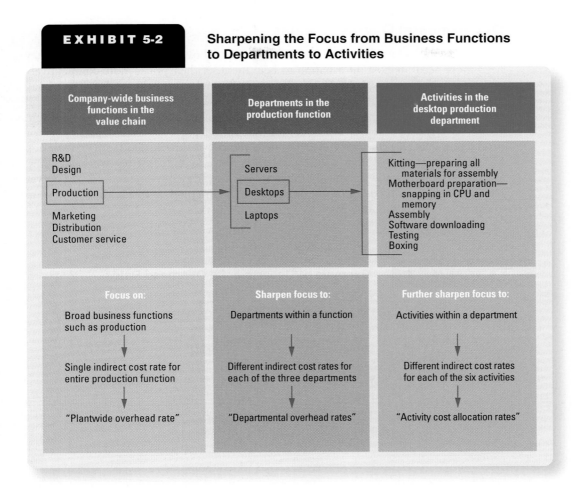

Plantwide Overhead Rate

In the past, simple costing systems were often good enough. Many companies used a single plantwide manufacturing overhead rate, as we did in Chapter 3, to allocate indirect costs within the production function. For example, assume that Dell originally allocated manufacturing overhead costs based on direct labor (DL) hours. If Dell planned to incur $10 million of manufacturing overhead costs and 500,000 direct labor hours in a year, its manufacturing overhead rate was:

$$\$10 \text{ million} \div 500{,}000 \text{ DL hours} = \$20/\text{DL hour}$$

This is called a **plantwide overhead rate** because Dell allocated manufacturing overhead to every product produced in the plant (whether server, desktop, or laptop) using this *same* manufacturing overhead rate. This is also often referred to as a *traditional system* because most manufacturers have traditionally used a plantwide overhead rate for allocating manufacturing overhead costs to their products.

Departmental Overhead Rates

Companies today face incredible competition from all over the globe. As a result, they need more accurate cost information to help them set their prices more competitively and identify their most profitable products. Traditional plantwide overhead rates may no longer provide good enough cost information. If this is the case, managers drill down to focus on the indirect costs incurred by each *department* within the function. Exhibit 5-2 shows that Dell's production function includes separate departments (or production lines) for its three main products: servers, desktops, and laptops. One step in refining a costing system is to establish separate manufacturing overhead rates, known as **departmental overhead rates**, for each department—one rate for the Server Department, another for the Desktop Department, and a third for the Laptop Department, as shown in Exhibit 5-3.

EXHIBIT 5-3 **Example of Departmental Overhead Rates**

Department	Total Departmental Manufacturing Overhead Costs		Total Departmental Direct Labor Hours		Departmental Overhead Rate
Servers	$2 million	÷	50,000 hours	=	$40/DL hour
Desktops	$5 million	÷	250,000 hours	=	$20/DL hour
Laptops	$3 million	÷	200,000 hours	=	$15/DL hour
TOTAL	**$10 million**		**500,000 hours**		

Notice that the *total* manufacturing overhead costs ($10 million) and *total* DL hours (500,000 DL hours) are the same as before. However, the costs and DL hours are now identified with the production department in which they occur. As a result, each production department has its own unique overhead rate. We see that the plantwide overhead rate of $20/DL hour was right for desktops but *too high* for laptops and *too low* for servers. The plantwide overhead rate was causing cost distortion: Laptops were overcosted while servers were undercosted. Just as we saw with the roommate example, the plantwide overhead rate did not fairly distribute indirect costs among products. Departmental overhead rates do a better job matching manufacturing overhead to the products using that overhead.

Our Dell example assumes that all three departments used direct labor hours as the allocation base. However, many firms use different allocation bases for different departments. For example, direct labor hours may be the best allocation base for an "assembly" department, but machine hours may be a better allocation base for a "machining" department. Ideally, companies should identify each department's main cost driver and use that cost driver as the allocation base. Recall from Chapter 3 that a cost driver is the primary factor that causes a cost.

If a product passes through more than one department, the product is allocated overhead in *each* department using each department's unique departmental overhead rate. For example, let's say that a company's Assembly Department overhead rate is based on direct labor hours and its Machining Department overhead rate is based on machine hours. A job passing through *both* the Assembly and Machining Departments is allocated overhead based on the number of direct labor hours it uses in the Assembly Department *and* the number of machine hours it uses in the Machining Department.

Stop & Think...

Wilken Industries produces custom furniture in two production departments: Machining and Assembly. The departmental overhead rates are $150 per machine hour (MH) in the Machining Department and $40 per direct labor (DL) hour in the Assembly Department. Job 101 incurs 2 MH and 1 DL hour in the Machining Department and 10 DL hours in the Assembly Department.

a. How much manufacturing overhead should Wilken Industries allocate to Job 101?

b. If wages and benefits in both departments cost $20/DL hour and Job 101 uses $1,000 of direct material, what is the total cost of the job?

Answer:

a. The company should allocate manufacturing overhead to Job #101 as follows:

Machining department: $150/MH × 2 MH.................... =	$300
Assembly department: $40/DL hour × 10 DL hours...... =	+ $400
Total manufacturing overhead allocated to Job 101 .... =	$700

Notice that Wilken Industries does *not* use the 1 DL hour incurred by Job 101 in the Machining Department for allocating overhead. Why? Because Machining Department overhead is allocated based *only* on machine hours used *in the Machining Department*, while Assembly Department overhead is allocated based *only* on DL hours incurred *in the Assembly Department*.

b. The total cost of Job 101 equals:

Direct labor (11 DL hours in *total* × $20/DL hour) ..... =	$ 220
Direct materials... =	1,000
Manufacturing overhead... =	700
Total job cost... =	$1,920

Activity Cost Allocation Rates

To obtain an even *more* accurate estimate of the resources that each product uses, managers drill down deeper yet to analyze the indirect costs of each *activity* in a department. Exhibit 5-2 shows the six activities in the Desktop Production Department. Rather than using a single departmental overhead rate for the entire Desktop Department, Dell develops separate cost allocation rates for each of these six activities, from kitting to boxing. This is called activity-based costing (ABC).

Think about the three roommates for a moment. The most equitable and accurate cost allocation system for the roommates was one in which the roommates were charged only for the *activities* in which they participated. As shown in Exhibit 5-1, David was not charged for groceries because he no longer ate at the apartment. Furthermore, the roommates were charged for the *extent* to which they used those activities. Marc was charged *twice* as much for groceries as Matt because Marc always had Jennifer over for dinner. Likewise, activity-based costing systems generally cause the *least* amount of cost distortion among products because indirect costs are allocated to the products based on the (1) *type* of activities used by the product and (2) the *extent* to which the activity is used. We'll spend the rest of this half of the chapter discussing activity-based costing in more detail.

Activity-Based Costing

2 Develop activity-based costs (ABC) and use activity-based management (ABM) to make business decisions

Activity-based costing (ABC) focuses on *activities* as the fundamental cost objects. The costs of those activities become building blocks for compiling the indirect costs of products, services, and customers. Companies such as Allied Signal, Coca-Cola, and American Express use ABC to more accurately estimate the cost of resources required to produce different products, to render different services, and to serve different customers.

Companies that use ABC trace direct costs (such as direct materials and direct labor) to cost objects, as described in Chapter 3. The only difference is that ABC systems make more of an effort to allocate *indirect costs*—such as manufacturing overhead—to the products, services, or customers that caused those costs. How? By separately estimating the indirect costs of each activity and then allocating those indirect costs based on what caused them.

Each activity's indirect cost has its own (usually unique) cost driver. For example, Dell allocates indirect assembly costs (such as depreciation on the equipment used in the assembly process) based on the number of times workers touch a computer as it moves through assembly. Computers that require more touches are allocated more costs. Exhibit 5-4 illustrates other common activities and related cost drivers.

| EXHIBIT 5-4 | **Activities and Cost Drivers** |

Data warehouses and other information technology have made detailed ABC systems easier to use. Optical scanning and bar coding reduce the cost of collecting cost-driver information. ERP systems such as SAP, Oracle, and PeopleSoft have ABC modules. Managers can also buy specialized ABC software. But Dell began its ABC system simply using Excel spreadsheets!

Developing an ABC System

The main difference between ABC and traditional systems is that ABC systems have separate indirect cost allocation rates for *each activity*. ABC requires seven steps:

1. Identify the activities.

2. Estimate the total indirect costs associated with each activity.

3. Identify the allocation base for each activity's indirect costs—this is the primary cost driver.

4. Estimate the total quantity of each allocation base.

5. Compute the cost allocation rate for each activity:

$$\text{Activity cost allocation rate} = \frac{\text{Estimated total indirect costs of activity}}{\text{Estimated total quantity of cost allocation base}}$$

6. Obtain the actual quantity of each allocation base used by the cost object (for example, the quantity used by a particular job).

7. Allocate the costs to the cost object:

$$\text{Allocated activity cost} = \text{Activity cost allocation rate} \times \frac{\text{Actual quantity of cost allocation}}{\text{base used by the cost object}}$$

The first step in developing an ABC system is to identify the activities. Analyzing all of the activities required to make a product forces managers to think about how each activity might be improved—or whether the activity is necessary at all. Steps 2 through 7 are the same approach used to allocate manufacturing overhead, as explained in Chapter 3. The only difference is that ABC systems repeat Steps 2 through 7 for *each activity*.

Using ABC for Job Costing

Let's see how Dell would develop an ABC system and use it for job costing. Recall that six key activities occur in Dell's Desktop Production Department (Exhibit 5-2) and the department incurs $5 million of manufacturing overhead (Exhibit 5-3). After identifying the activities, Dell estimates how much of the total $5 million of indirect manufacturing cost is associated with *each* activity. Dell also identifies a cost allocation base, or cost driver, for each activity. Next, Dell computes a unique activity cost allocation rate for each of the activities using the formula shown in Step 5 above. Let's say this process results in the activity cost allocation rates shown in Exhibit 5-5.

EXHIBIT 5-5   **Activity Cost Allocation Rates for Dell's Desktop Production Department**

Activity	Cost Allocation Base	Activity Cost Allocation Rate
Kitting	Number of parts	$0.50 per part
Motherboard preparation	Number of preparations	$1.15 per preparation
Assembly	Number of touches	$0.20 per touch
Software downloading	Number of minutes spent downloading software	$0.25 per minute
Testing	Number of tests performed	$2.50 per test
Boxing	Cubic feet boxed	$0.60 per cubic foot

Just as with a traditional system, these rates are predetermined for the whole year using budgeted information. Once Dell has computed these activity cost allocation rates, it simply allocates manufacturing overhead to each job worked on during the year by multiplying these rates by each job's actual usage of the cost allocation bases (Step 7 above). If a job doesn't use a particular activity, the job isn't charged any indirect cost related to that activity.

Let's use Dell's Job 2690 (an order for one desktop computer) as an example. The amount of manufacturing overhead allocated to Job 2690 is calculated as follows:

Activity	Activity Cost Allocation Rate (from Exhibit 5-5)		Job 2690: Actual Usage of Cost Allocation Base*		Allocated Activity Cost
Kitting	$0.50 per part	×	12 parts	=	$ 6.00
Motherboard preparation	$1.15 per preparation	×	1 preparation	=	1.15
Assembly	$0.20 per touch	×	10 touches	=	2.00
Software downloading	$0.25 per minute	×	12 minutes	=	3.00
Testing	$2.50 per test	×	1 test	=	2.50
Boxing	$0.60 per cubic foot	×	4 cubic feet	=	2.40
Total manufacturing overhead allocated to job					$17.05

*Information would be reported on Job 2690's job cost record.

To find the total inventoriable product cost of Job 2690, Dell adds $17.05 of manufacturing overhead (calculated above) to the direct materials and direct labor traced to the job, just as we did in Chapter 3.[1]

As you can see, the procedure for costing a job using ABC is almost identical to the procedure we used in Chapter 3. The main difference is that the manufacturing overhead allocated to a job involves several activity cost allocation rates rather than one plantwide rate. In addition to using ABC to allocate manufacturing overhead costs in the production function, Dell can extend its use of ABC to the other five functions of the value chain. By doing so, Dell can determine the full cost of each of its products. This helps Dell's managers set prices and determine its most profitable products and customers.

Using ABC to Assess Product Profitability: Chemtech

We just looked at how Dell uses ABC to allocate manufacturing overhead to individual jobs it produces throughout the year. Now, let's see how another company, Chemtech, used ABC to reassess the profitability of its entire product lines. By implementing ABC, Chemtech discovered that its traditional plantwide overhead rate had been causing significant cost distortion between its products.

Keep in mind that our example simplifies the process that would occur in a real company that might identify more than 50 different activities and have hundreds of products.

Chemtech is a chemical development and manufacturing firm. Most of the chemicals the company develops are licensed and sold to other manufacturers. However, Chemtech's Chemical Manufacturing Department continues to produce two types of chemicals: a common chemical (Aldehyde) used for producing plastics and a specialty chemical (Phenylephrine Hydrochloride) used in a blood-pressure medication. Chemtech produces mass quantities of the common chemical for large customers. It produces small batches of the specialty chemical for only one customer (a pharmaceutical company).

Last updated several years ago, the Chemical Manufacturing Department's cost system uses a single plantwide overhead rate that allocates manufacturing overhead ($5 million for the year) at 200% of direct labor cost. Based on this traditional costing system, Chemtech analyzes its products' profitability as shown in Exhibit 5-6.

---

[1]Some companies, especially those that are highly automated, develop activity cost allocation rates for all of their conversion costs combined (direct labor and manufacturing overhead) rather than just for their manufacturing overhead costs. These companies calculate a job's inventoriable product cost by tracing the direct materials to the job and then adding the allocated conversion cost.

EXHIBIT 5-6	**Chemtech's Traditional Costing System: Product Cost and Gross Profit**

	Common Chemical	Specialty Chemical
Sales price per pound	$10.00	$70.00
Less: Manufacturing cost per pound:		
Direct materials	5.00	20.00
Direct labor	1.00	10.00
Manufacturing overhead (at 200% of direct labor cost)	2.00	20.00
Total manufacturing cost per pound	8.00	50.00
Gross profit per pound	$2.00	$20.00
Number of pounds produced and sold	2,000,000	50,000

The gross profit per pound for the specialty chemical ($20) is ten times as high as the gross profit for the common chemical ($2), which surprised Chemtech's CEO. He had expected that the department would be more efficient at producing large batches of the common chemical than producing small batches of the specialty chemical. However, the production supervisor says that it takes no more time to mix a large batch of the common chemical than it does to mix a small batch of the specialty chemical. The CEO is also puzzled because Chemtech's competitors seem to be earning good profits even though they sometimes undercut Chemtech's prices on the common chemical.

Because of the profitability of the specialty chemical, the CEO wonders whether Chemtech should switch its focus to specialty chemicals. Before making such a major shift in operations, the CEO wants to make sure the financial information is correct. Because the cost of direct labor and direct materials is accurate (the company has traced these costs to the products), the only questionable part of the manufacturing cost is the allocation of manufacturing overhead.

Exhibit 5-7 shows how Chemtech's *total* manufacturing overhead ($5 million) is currently allocated between the two products. Since Chemtech allocates overhead at 200% of direct labor cost, it first finds the *total* direct labor cost traced to each product (number of pounds produced × direct labor cost per pound). Then, Chemtech multiplies the total direct labor cost by the 200% plantwide overhead rate.

EXHIBIT 5-7	**Current Allocation of Total Manufacturing Overhead**

	Common Chemical	Specialty Chemical
Number of pounds (from Exhibit 5-6)	2,000,000	50,000
× Direct labor cost per pound (from Exhibit 5-6)	× $1.00	× $10.00
Total Direct labor cost	$2,000,000	$500,000
× Manufacturing overhead rate	× 200% of DL cost	× 200% of DL cost
Total Manufacturing overhead allocated	$4,000,000	$1,000,000

$5,000,000

Because Chemtech allocates overhead based on direct labor cost, it currently assigns four times as much overhead to the common chemical ($4 million) as it does to the specialty chemical ($1 million). This method of allocation makes sense only if direct labor really is the primary cost driver of manufacturing overhead costs. Does the common chemical really use four times as much overhead as the specialty chemical? If not, Chemtech should allocate the $5 million of manufacturing overhead differently.

The CEO wants to better understand manufacturing overhead—what drives it and how it should be allocated. The CEO asks managers to create a cross-functional team (including members from accounting, engineering, and production) to develop a pilot ABC system. A cross-functional team will ensure that the new ABC system incorporates a wide variety of perspectives. In addition, these managers are more likely to believe costs from a costing system they helped build.

Exhibit 5-8 presents a bird's-eye overview that compares Chemtech's traditional manufacturing overhead allocation system based on direct labor (Panel A) to the new ABC system the team developed (Panel B).

EXHIBIT 5-8   **Chemtech's Traditional and ABC Systems**

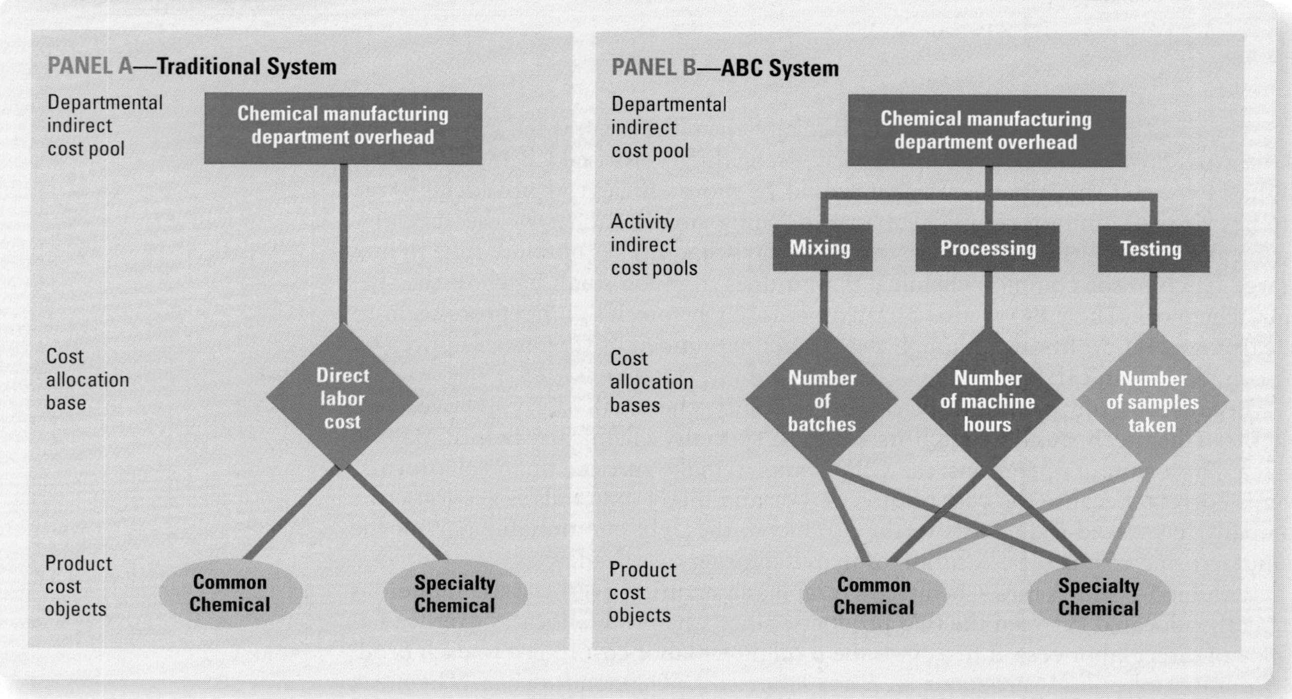

PANEL A—Traditional System

Departmental indirect cost pool → Chemical manufacturing department overhead

Cost allocation base → Direct labor cost

Product cost objects → Common Chemical, Specialty Chemical

PANEL B—ABC System

Departmental indirect cost pool → Chemical manufacturing department overhead

Activity indirect cost pools → Mixing, Processing, Testing

Cost allocation bases → Number of batches, Number of machine hours, Number of samples taken

Product cost objects → Common Chemical, Specialty Chemical

Panel B of Exhibit 5-8 shows that Chemtech's ABC team identifies three manufacturing activities: mixing, processing, and testing. Each activity has its own indirect cost pool and cost driver. But exactly how does this work? The ABC team develops the new system by following the seven steps described earlier. Let's walk through each step.

Step 1: Identify activities

The team identifies three primary activities in the Chemical Manufacturing Department:

- **mixing**
- **processing**
- **testing**

Step 2: Estimate total indirect costs of each activity

The team identifies (or estimates) the total manufacturing overhead costs associated with each activity for the year:

Mixing	$ 825,000
Processing	3,800,000
Testing	375,000
Total manufacturing overhead	$5,000,000

Notice how the total manufacturing overhead is the same as before ($5 million), but now it is divided between the activities according to how much overhead each activity incurs.

Step 3: Identify allocation base for each activity

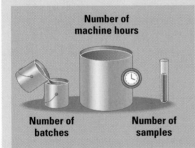

Number of machine hours

Number of batches

Number of samples

The team determines the most appropriate allocation base for each activity. The allocation base should be the activity's cost driver.

Mixing: Workers mix ingredients separately for each batch of chemicals, so the number of batches drives mixing costs.

Processing: Machine depreciation, repairs and maintenance, and utilities make up most of the processing costs; so machine hours (MH) is selected as the cost driver.

Testing: Testing costs are driven by the number of samples collected and tested for quality.

Step 4: Estimate total quantity of each allocation base

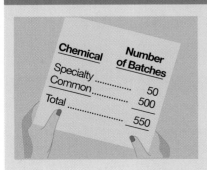

Chemical	Number of Batches
Specialty	50
Common	500
Total	550

The team estimates the total quantity of each cost allocation base Chemtech will use during the year. For example, the team estimates the total number of batches of each chemical it plans to produce and adds them together. The team estimates the total quantities (for both chemicals combined) to be:

Mixing: 550 batches   **Processing:** 15,200 MH   **Testing:** 750 samples

Step 5: Compute cost allocation rates for each activity

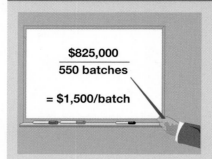

The team calculates a cost allocation rate for *each* activity as follows:

$$\text{Activity cost allocation rate} = \frac{\text{Estimated total indirect costs of activity}}{\text{Estimated total quantity of cost allocation base}}$$

Mixing: $\dfrac{\$825,000}{550 \text{ batches}} = \$1,500$ per batch

Processing: $\dfrac{\$3,800,000}{15,200 \text{ MH}} = \$250$ per MH

Testing: $\dfrac{\$375,000}{750 \text{ samples}} = \$500$ per sample

Step 6: Obtain actual quantity of each allocation base used by each product

During the year, Chemtech collects data on the *actual* number of batches, machine hours, and samples that each product uses:

	Common	Specialty
Mixing: (number of batches)	500	50
Processing: (number of machine hours)	8,000	7,200
Testing: (number of samples)	500	250

Mixing: Chemtech makes about two large batches of the common chemical each work day, but only one small batch of the specialty chemical each week.

Processing: Due to the nature of the chemical, each batch of the specialty chemical requires a far longer processing time than each batch of the common chemical. Over the course of the year, the *total* processing time is only slightly higher for the common chemical than for the specialty chemical.

Testing: One sample per batch of the common chemical is sufficient. However, since the specialty chemical must process for several days, Chemtech must take several samples throughout the processing period.

Step 7: Allocate costs to each cost object

Chemtech allocates costs to each product as follows:
  For each activity, the team allocates manufacturing overhead to the products as follows:

Actual quantity of allocation base used × Activity cost allocation rate = Allocated cost

	Common Chemical			Specialty Chemical		
Mixing:	500 batches × $1,500 per batch	=	$ 750,000	50 batches × $1,500 per batch	=	$ 75,000
Processing:	8,000 MH × $ 250 per MH	=	2,000,000	7,200 MH × $ 250 per MH	=	1,800,000
Testing:	500 samples × $ 500 per sample	=	250,000	250 samples × $ 500 per sample	=	125,000
Total manufacturing overhead allocated:			$3,000,000			$2,000,000

Exhibit 5-9 summarizes the seven steps. Study Exhibit 5-9 carefully, following each of the seven steps to make sure you understand how the activity costs are allocated.

| EXHIBIT 5-9 | Summary of Chemtech's ABC System |

Step 1	Step 2	Step 3	Step 4	Step 5	Step 6		Step 7	
					Actual Quantity of Cost Allocation Base Used By		Allocated Activity Cost	
Activity	Estimated Costs	Cost Allocation Base	Estimated Total Quantity of Cost Allocation Base	Compute Activity Cost Allocation Rate	Common Chemical	Specialty Chemical	Common Chemical	Specialty Chemical
Mixing	$825,000	# batches	550 Batches	$\frac{\$825,000}{550} = \$1,500$/batch	500 batches	50 batches	$1,500 × 500 = $750,000	$1,500 × 50 = $75,000
Processing	$3,800,000	# machine hours (MH)	15,200 MH	$\frac{\$3,800,000}{15,200} = \$250$/MH	8,000 MH	7,200 MH	$250 × 8,000 = $2,000,000	$250 × 7,200 = $1,800,000
Testing	$375,000	# samples	750 Samples	$\frac{\$375,000}{750} = \$500$/sample	500 samples	250 samples	$500 × 500 = $250,000	$500 × 250 = $125,000
	$5,000,000						$3,000,000	$2,000,000

Notice in Step 7 how the *total* manufacturing overhead is the *same* as before ($3 million + $2 million = $5 million). However, the amount of manufacturing overhead allocated to *each* product is *different* from before:

- The ABC system allocates $3 million of manufacturing overhead to the common chemical rather than $4 million (as calculated under the traditional system in Exhibit 5-7). The traditional system had *overcosted* the common chemical by $1 million.

- The ABC system allocates $2 million of manufacturing overhead to the specialty chemical rather than $1 million (as calculated under the traditional system in Exhibit 5-7). The traditional system had *undercosted* the specialty chemical by $1 million.

The ABC system shows that the traditional costing system had resulted in a $1 million cost distortion between Chemtech's two product lines. Just as with the roommates sharing the apartment, the overcosting and the undercosting even out. The *overcosting* of the common chemical exactly equals the *undercosting* of the specialty chemical.

How do we know that the ABC costs are more accurate than the costs assigned by the traditional system? *ABC costs are more accurate because ABC takes into account the resources (mixing costs, processing costs, and testing costs) each product actually uses, and the extent to which they use these resources.* Recall that Chemtech's traditional plantwide overhead rate (based on direct labor) allocated *four times as much* overhead to the common chemical as to the specialty chemical. With more precise allocations, ABC shifts manufacturing overhead costs away from the common chemical to the specialty chemical, where the costs belong. Why? Exhibit 5-9 shows that the common chemical uses more of each activity's resources than the specialty chemical, but *not always four* times as much. Step 6 shows that the common chemical requires ten times as many batches (mixing costs), but only about 11% more machine hours (processing costs) and only twice as many samples (testing costs) as the specialty chemical. ABC captures the differences in resource consumption by each product more accurately than the traditional costing system.

Now that we know that Chemtech should allocate $3 million of overhead to the common chemical and $2 million of overhead to the specialty chemical, let's see how this affects the overhead cost per pound. To determine the manufacturing overhead cost per pound, Chemtech simply divides the total manufacturing overhead allocated to each product by the number of pounds produced (from Exhibit 5-6). Exhibit 5-10 compares the overhead cost per pound under the traditional system and the ABC system.

EXHIBIT 5-10 **Comparison of the Manufacturing Overhead Cost per Pound Under the Traditional and ABC Systems**

	Manufacturing Overhead Cost per Pound (Total manufacturing overhead allocated to product ÷ number of pounds produced)		
	Traditional System	**ABC System**	**Overallocation or (Underallocation)**
Common Chemical	$2.00 ($4,000,000 ÷ 2 million pounds)	$1.50 ($3,000,000 ÷ 2 million pounds)	$0.50 overallocation per pound
Specialty Chemical	$20.00 ($1,000,000 ÷ 50,000 pounds)	$40.00 ($2,000,000 ÷ 50,000 pounds)	($20.00) (underallocation per pound)

Exhibit 5-10 shows that the traditional system had *undercosted* the specialty chemical by $20 per pound. Allocating overhead based on the actual resources used by individual products generally *increases* the unit costs of *low-volume* products such as the specialty chemical that are produced in small batches. Why? Because costs such as mixing and testing are spread over the small number of units (pounds) in that batch, which can dramatically increase unit product costs.

The traditional system had *overcosted* the common chemical by $0.50 per pound. For *high-volume* products produced in large batches, such as the common chemical, mixing and testing costs are spread over the larger number of units (pounds) in the batch. So, ABC often assigns *fewer* costs to each unit of high-volume products than do plantwide overhead rates.

After implementing ABC, companies often realize they were overcosting high-volume products (such as the common chemical) and undercosting low-volume products (such as the specialty chemical), as shown in Exhibit 5-11.

EXHIBIT 5-11 **Typical Result of ABC Costing**

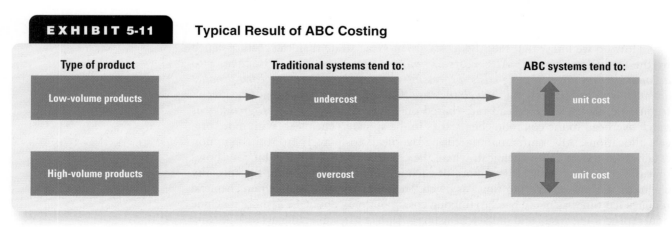

Now that we've seen how ABC revealed cost distortion, let's see how Chemtech's managers *use* this new cost information to reassess the profitability of its two products.

Activity-Based Management: Using ABC for Decision Making

Activity-based management (ABM) refers to using activity-based cost information to make decisions that increase profits while satisfying customers' needs. Chemtech can use ABC information for pricing and product mix decisions, for helping to identify ways of cutting costs, and for routine planning and control decisions.

Pricing and Product Mix Decisions

The information provided by ABC showed the CEO that his suspicions were correct—the traditional overhead allocation system had not properly costed the products. As Exhibit 5-12 shows, the $7.50 total manufacturing cost per pound of the common chemical (shown in Panel A) is *less* than the $8.00 total cost previously computed based on the traditional plantwide overhead rate (shown in Panel B). The cost per pound of the specialty chemical ($70) is *more* than previously computed ($50) based on the traditional plantwide overhead rate. The differences are due *strictly* to the allocation of manufacturing overhead (the cost of direct labor and direct materials was never in question).

EXHIBIT 5-12   **Comparison of Chemtech's Manufacturing Product Costs Under ABC Versus Traditional Systems**

PANEL A: Total Manufacturing Cost and Gross Profit Under ABC

	Common Chemical	Specialty Chemical
Sales price per pound	$10.00	$70.00
Less: Manufacturing cost per pound		
Direct materials	$5.00	$20.00
Direct labor	1.00	10.00
Manufacturing overhead (from Exhibit 5-10)	1.50	40.00
Total manufacturing cost	7.50	70.00
Gross profit per pound	$2.50	$0

PANEL B: Total Manufacturing Cost and Gross Profit Under Traditional Cost System

	Common Chemical	Specialty Chemical
Sales price per pound	$10.00	$70.00
Less: Manufacturing cost per pound		
Direct materials	$5.00	$20.00
Direct labor	1.00	10.00
Manufacturing overhead (from Exhibit 5-10)	2.00	20.00
Total manufacturing cost	8.00	50.00
Gross profit per pound	$2.00	$20.00

The ABC costing system shows that Chemtech had been making more profit on the common chemical ($2.50 per pound) than previously reported ($2.00 per pound). More important, the company had been making *no* profit on the specialty chemical when it previously thought it had been making $20 per pound! When Chemtech considers the nonmanufacturing costs, such as R&D, marketing, and distribution, it has been *losing* money on the production and sale of the specialty chemical.

What should Chemtech do? First, Chemtech may be able to use the ABC analysis to find ways to cut costs. We'll discuss this possibility in the next section. However, if Chemtech cannot cut costs enough to earn a profit on the specialty chemical, it may have to raise the sales price. If Chemtech's specialty chemical customer will not pay more, Chemtech should consider dropping the specialty chemical and using the existing capacity to make more of the common chemical (if demand for it exists). In other words, Chemtech may shift its product mix away from the specialty chemical toward the common chemical. *This is the exact opposite of the strategy suggested by cost data from the traditional system.*

Cutting Costs

Most companies adopt ABC to get more accurate product costs for pricing and product mix decisions, but they often reap even *greater benefits* by using ABM to pinpoint opportunities to cut costs. For example, ABC has allowed Chemtech to better understand what drives its manufacturing overhead costs. The traditional overhead allocation system had not shown Chemtech's managers what was driving manufacturing overhead costs or how to start cutting those costs. However, ABC has shown Chemtech's managers that it costs $1,500 to mix each batch, $250 to process the chemicals each machine hour, and $500 to test each sample. Now, Chemtech's managers have a "starting place" for cutting costs—they can focus their attention on cutting the costs of each of those activities.

Value engineering means reevaluating activities to reduce costs while satisfying customer needs. Value engineering requires cross-functional teams: marketers to identify customer needs, engineers and production personnel to design more efficient processes and products, and accountants to estimate how proposed changes will affect costs. Using value engineering, Chemtech may be able to reduce costs by finding more efficient ways of mixing and processing chemicals. The company may also be able to reduce costs by increasing the size of batches (to decrease the number of batches processed) or by testing fewer samples. Chemtech will undertake these cost-cutting measures only if they do not adversely affect the product quality their customers expect.

Routine Planning and Control Decisions

In addition to pricing, product mix, and cost-cutting decisions, Chemtech can use ABC in routine planning and control. Activity-based budgeting uses the costs of activities to create budgets. Managers can compare actual costs to budgeted costs to determine how well they are achieving their goals. Also, Chemtech's managers can use ABC information to evaluate workers. For example, the production supervisor may receive a bonus if he can cut either of the following:

- The cost per sample tested (that is, cut the cost-allocation rate for the testing activity)
- The number of samples tested (that is, cut the consumption of the activity) *while maintaining product quality.*

Using ABC in Merchandising and Service Companies

Chemtech is a manufacturer that used ABC to more accurately allocate its manufacturing overhead. Merchandising and service companies also find ABC techniques useful. Since merchandising companies already know their inventoriable product costs and service companies have no inventoriable products, how can they use ABC? These firms use ABC to allocate period costs among product or service lines to figure out which are most profitable. For example, Kroger food stores may use ABC to allocate store operating expenses such as ordering and stocking costs among its dairy, bakery, and deli departments. A landscaping company may use ABC to allocate labor, supplies, and other operating costs between commercial customers and residential customers. These firms use the same seven steps but apply them to *operating* (period) costs rather than *manufacturing* overhead costs. Once again, these managers use the ABC data to decide which products or services to emphasize, to set prices, to cut costs, and to make other routine planning and control decisions.

Stop & Think...

Can governmental agencies use ABC/ABM to run their operations more efficiently?

Answer: ABC/ABM is not just for private-sector companies. Several governmental agencies, including the U.S. Postal Service (USPS) and the City of Indianapolis, have successfully used ABC/ABM to run their operations more cost-effectively. For example, the USPS used to accept customer payments only in the form of cash or checks. After using ABC to study the cost of their revenue collection procedures (activities), the USPS found that it would be cheaper to accept debit and credit card sales. Accepting debit and credit card sales also produced higher customer satisfaction, allowing the USPS to better compete with private mail and package carriers.

The City of Indianapolis was able to save its taxpayers millions of dollars after using ABC to study the cost of providing city services (activities) to local citizens. Once the city determined the cost of its activities, it was able to obtain competitive bids for those same services from private businesses. As a result, the city outsourced many activities to private-sector firms for a lower cost.

When Does ABC Pass the Cost-Benefit Test?

Like all other management tools, ABC must pass the cost-benefit test. The system should be refined enough to provide accurate product costs but simple enough for managers to understand. In the Chemtech example, ABC triples the number of allocation bases—from the single allocation base (direct labor) in the original system to three allocation bases (for mixing, processing, and testing). ABC systems are even more complex in real-world companies that have many more activities and cost drivers.

3 Explain when ABC is most likely to pass the cost-benefit test

The Cost-Benefit Test

ABC and ABM pass the cost-benefit test when the benefits of adopting ABC/ABM exceed the costs. Benefits of adopting ABC/ABM are higher for companies in competitive markets because:

- Accurate product cost information is essential for setting competitive sales prices that still allow the company to earn a profit.
- ABM can pinpoint opportunities for cost savings, which increase the company's profit or are passed on to customers in lower prices.

ABC's benefits are higher when ABC reports *different* product costs than costs reported under the old system. This is likely to happen when:

- The company produces many different products that use different amounts of resources. (If all products use similar amounts of resources, a simple single-allocation-base system works fine.)
- The company has high indirect costs. (If the company has few indirect costs, it does not matter how they are allocated.)
- The company produces high volumes of some products and low volumes of other products. (Traditional systems that use a plantwide overhead rate tend to over-cost high-volume products and undercost low-volume products.)

The costs of adopting ABC are lower when the company has:

- Accounting and information system expertise to develop the system.
- Information technology such as bar coding, optical scanning, or data warehouse systems to record and compile cost driver data.

Are real-world companies glad they adopted ABC? Usually, but not always. A survey shows that 89% of the companies using ABC data say that it was worth the cost.[2] Adoption is on the rise among financial companies such as American Express, utilities such as Indianapolis Power and Light, and nonprofits such as the U.S. Marine Corps. But ABC is not a cure-all. As the controller for one Midwest manufacturer said, "ABC will not reduce cost; it will only help you understand costs better to know what to correct."

Signs That the Old Cost System May Be Broken

Broken cars or computers simply stop running. But unlike cars and computers, even broken or outdated product cost systems continue to report "product costs." How can you tell whether a cost system needs repair?

A company's product cost system may need repair when:

Managers don't understand costs and profits:

- In bidding for jobs, managers lose bids they expected to win and win bids they expected to lose.
- Competitors with similar high-volume products price their products below the company's costs but still earn good profits.
- Employees do not believe the cost numbers reported by the accounting system.

The cost system is outdated:

- The company uses a single-allocation-base system developed long ago.
- The company has reengineered its production process but has not changed its accounting system.

---

[2]K. Krumwiede, "ABC: Why It's Tried and How It Succeeds," *Management Accounting*, April 1998, pp. 32–38.

Stop & Think...

Review the Chemtech example on pages 266 through 275. List the symptoms that indicate that the traditional costing system used by Chemtech may be broken.

Answers:

1. The chemical manufacturing department used a plantwide allocation rate based on direct labor cost that was developed several years ago.

2. Competitors that focused on high-volume commodity chemicals earned good profits despite undercutting Chemtech's sales prices. This was puzzling because Chemtech should be especially efficient at producing large batches of commodity chemicals.

3. Cost numbers reported by the accounting system were inconsistent with employees' intuition.

Decision Guidelines

REFINED COSTING SYSTEMS

Several years ago, Dell decided that it needed to refine its costing system. Starting with an Excel spreadsheet, Dell developed a simple ABC system that focused on the ten most critical activities. Here are some of the decisions Dell faced as it began refining its cost system.

Decision	Guidelines
How do we develop an ABC system?	1. Identify the activities. 2. Estimate total indirect costs of each activity. 3. Identify the allocation base (primary cost driver) for each activity's indirect costs. 4. Estimate the total quantity of each allocation base. 5. Compute the cost allocation rate for each activity. 6. Obtain the actual quantity of each allocation base used by cost object. 7. Allocate costs to cost object.
How do we compute an activity cost allocation rate?	$$\dfrac{\text{Estimated total indirect cost of activity}}{\text{Estimated total quantity of cost allocation base}}$$
How do we allocate an activity's cost to the cost object?	$$\begin{array}{c}\text{Activity cost}\\\text{allocation rate}\end{array} \times \begin{array}{c}\text{Actual quantity of cost}\\\text{allocation base used}\\\text{by cost object}\end{array}$$
For what kinds of decisions do managers use ABC?	Managers use ABC data in ABM to make decisions on: • Pricing and product mix. • Cost cutting. • Routine planning and control.
What are the main benefits of ABC?	• More accurate product cost information. • More detailed information on costs of activities and associated cost drivers helps managers control costs.

continued . . .

Decision	Guidelines
When is ABC most likely to pass the cost-benefit test?	• Company is in a competitive environment and needs accurate product costs. • Company makes different products that use different amounts of resources. • Company has high indirect costs. • Company produces high volumes of some products and lower volumes of other products. • Company has accounting and information technology expertise to implement the system. • Old cost system appears "broken."
How do we tell when a cost system needs revision?	• Managers lose bids they expected to win and win bids they expected to lose. • Competitors earn profits despite pricing high-volume products below our costs. • Employees do not believe cost numbers. • Company uses a single-allocation-base system developed long ago. • Company has reengineered the production process but not the accounting system.

Summary Problem 1

Indianapolis Auto Parts (IAP) has a seat manufacturing department that uses ABC. IAP's activity cost allocation rates include all conversion costs (direct labor and manufacturing overhead):

Activity	Allocation Base	Activity Cost Allocation Rate
Purchasing	Number of purchase orders	$60.00 per purchase order
Assembling	Number of parts	0.50 per part
Packaging	Number of finished seats	0.90 per finished seat

Each seat has 20 parts; direct materials cost per seat is $11. Suppose Ford has asked for a bid on 50,000 built-in baby seats that would be installed as an option on some Ford SUVs. IAP will use a total of 200 purchase orders if Ford accepts IAP's bid.

Requirements

1. Compute the total cost IAP will incur to purchase the needed materials and then assemble and package 50,000 baby seats. Also compute the average cost per seat.

2. For bidding, IAP adds a 30% markup to total cost. What price will the company bid for the Ford order?

3. Suppose that instead of an ABC system, IAP has a traditional product costing system that allocates all conversion costs (direct labor and manufacturing overhead) at a plantwide overhead rate of $65 per direct labor hour. The baby-seat order will require 10,000 direct labor hours. What price will IAP bid using this system's total cost?

4. Use your answers to Requirements 2 and 3 to explain how ABC can help IAP make a better decision about the bid price it will offer Ford.

Solution

Requirement 1
Total Cost of Order and Average Cost per Seat:

Direct materials: 50,000 seats × $11.00	$ 550,000
Activity costs:	
Purchasing, 200 purchase orders × $60.00	12,000
Assembling, (50,000 × 20 parts) × $0.50	500,000
Packaging, 50,000 finished seats × $0.90	45,000
Total cost of order	$1,107,000
Divide by number of seats	÷ 50,000
Average cost per seat	$ 22.14

Requirement 2

Bid Price (ABC System):

Bid price ($1,107,000 × 130%)..	**$1,439,100**

Requirement 3

Bid Price (Traditional System):

Direct materials: 50,000 seats × $11.00	$ 550,000
Conversion costs: 10,000 DL hours × $65	650,000
Total cost of order	$1,200,000
Bid price ($1,200,000 × 130%)...	$1,560,000

Requirement 4

IAP's bid would be $120,900 higher using the plantwide overhead rate than using ABC ($1,560,000 versus $1,439,100). Assuming that the ABC system more accurately captures the costs caused by the order, the traditional plantwide overhead system overcosts the order. This leads to a higher bid price that reduces IAP's chance of winning the bid. The ABC system shows that IAP can increase its chance of winning the bid by bidding a lower price and still make a profit.

Traditional Versus Just-in-Time Systems

ABC and ABM often reveal the high costs of (1) buying, storing, and moving inventories and (2) producing poor-quality products and services. So, it is not surprising that a recent study of "best practices" companies revealed that most had linked their ABC/ABM systems to just-in-time (JIT) or quality initiatives. For example, Carrier Corporation adopted JIT after ABC/ABM revealed that the activities relating to handling materials was extremely costly. The rest of this chapter expands on Chapter 1's introduction to JIT and quality.

We begin by contrasting JIT production systems with traditional systems.

Traditional Systems

Traditional businesses keep large inventories of raw materials, work in process, and finished goods. Why? First, poor-quality raw materials lead companies to buy more than they need because some of the materials will not be usable. Also, machine breakdowns and production problems *within* departments prompt managers to keep extra work in process inventory *between* departments. Exhibit 5-13 describes the production of drill bits from bar stock (the raw material). Work in process inventory between the grinding and smoothing operations allows smoothing work to continue even if grinding machines break down.

EXHIBIT 5-13 **Sequence of Operations for Drill-Bit Production**

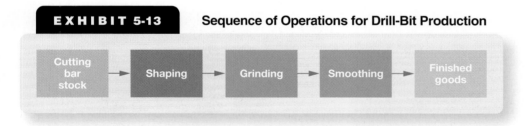

A second reason for large inventories is that companies with products that have long setup times often make products in large batches to spread setup costs over many units. Therefore, they need large quantities of raw materials on hand to prepare the large batches. A third reason for stocking large inventories is uncertainty in deliveries from suppliers and orders from customers. Large raw material inventories protect against delayed deliveries. Large inventories of finished goods protect against lost sales if customer demand is higher than expected.

Why are large inventories a problem? First, inventories tie up cash. Companies incur interest expense or forgo interest revenue on that cash. If a company has to borrow money to pay for inventory, it incurs interest expense on the loan. Even if a company uses its own cash to fund the inventory, it misses the opportunity to earn interest on that cash. In other words, if the cash were not tied up in inventory, the company could invest it and earn a return. Second, large inventories often hide quality problems, production bottlenecks, and obsolescence. Inventory may spoil, be broken or stolen, or become obsolete as it sits in storage and waits to be used in production or sold. Companies in the high-tech and fashion industries are particularly susceptible to inventory obsolescence. What would Dell do with computer chips purchased six months earlier from Intel? The chips would be obsolete and unusable.

Because of the problems associated with large inventories, many companies are now striving to use JIT systems.

Just-in-Time Systems

4 Describe a just-in-time (JIT) production system

Companies with JIT systems buy raw materials *just in time* for production and complete finished goods *just in time* for delivery to customers. For example, workers read orders off a monitor and assemble a Dell desktop every three to five minutes. Most days, workers finish more than 25,000 computers, which ship directly to customers. But the plant rarely holds more than two *hours* of inventory![3] How does Dell do it? By complete commitment to the JIT philosophy.

Many managers regard JIT as a *general philosophy of eliminating waste*. Companies that follow JIT have several common characteristics:

1. **Production activities in self-contained cells.** A traditional drill-bit manufacturer would group all cutting machines in one area, all shaping machines in another area, all grinding machines in a third area, and all smoothing machines in a fourth area, as illustrated in Panel A of Exhibit 5-14. After switching to JIT, the company would group the machines in self-contained production cells, or production lines, as in Panel B of Exhibit 5-14. The goal is continuous production without interruptions or work in process inventories. Arranging machines in sequential production cells slashes production time. Within six years after adopting JIT, Harley-Davidson reduced the time to produce a motorcycle by 77%.

EXHIBIT 5-14   **Equipment Arrangement in Traditional and JIT Production Systems**

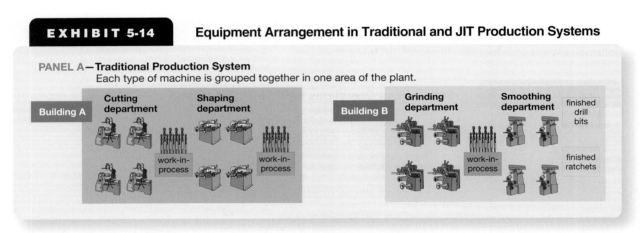

PANEL A—Traditional Production System
Each type of machine is grouped together in one area of the plant.

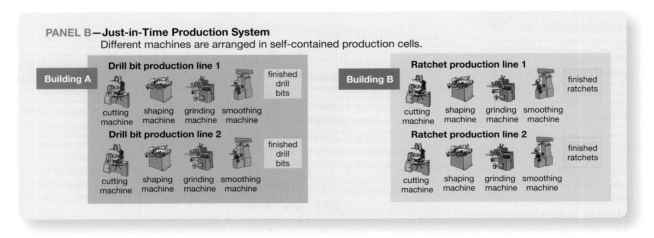

PANEL B—Just-in-Time Production System
Different machines are arranged in self-contained production cells.

---

[3]Kathryn Jones, "The Dell Way," *Business 2.0*, February 2003, www.business2.com.

2. **Short setup times.** JIT companies reduce setup times on machines used for more than one product. Employee training and technology helped Toyota cut setup times from several hours to a few minutes. This increases flexibility in scheduling production to meet customer orders, which, in turn, increases customer satisfaction and company profits.

3. **Broad employee roles.** Employees in JIT systems do more than operate a single machine. They also conduct maintenance, perform setups, inspect their own work, and operate other machines. This cross-training boosts morale and lowers costs. Employees who perform a number of duties rather than one repetitive duty tend to have higher job satisfaction.

4. **Small batches produced just in time.** JIT businesses schedule production in small batches *just in time* to satisfy customer needs. In a JIT "demand-pull system," the customer order—the "demand"—triggers the start of the production process and "pulls" the batch through production. Each order, even if very small, is its own batch. Even raw materials are usually not purchased until a customer order is received. The "demand-pull" system extends back to suppliers of materials who end up making frequent, small deliveries of defect-free raw materials just in time for production. The JIT system replaces the traditional "push" manufacturing system. In a traditional system, large quantities of raw materials are "pushed" through the production process to be stored in finished goods inventory until sold.

    Purchasing and producing only what customers demand reduces inventory. Less inventory frees floor space for more productive use. When HP adopted JIT, the company cut its work in process inventory by 82% and its production floor space by 40%.

5. **Shortened manufacturing cycle times.** Since JIT companies don't produce inventory until they receive a customer order, they must produce their products very quickly. Dell's manufacturing cycle time, as noted, is three to five minutes. GED Integrated Solutions, a window manufacturer, used to take two to three weeks to complete an order. GED has cut manufacturing cycle time to three to five days. Shorter manufacturing times also protect firms from foreign competitors whose cheaper products take longer to ship. Delivery speed has become a competitive weapon.

6. **Emphasis on quality.** JIT companies focus on producing their products right the *first* time, *every* time. Why? First, they have no backup stock to give waiting customers if they run into production problems. Second, defects in materials and workmanship can slow or shut down production. JIT companies cannot afford the time it takes to rework faulty products. JIT companies emphasize "building-in" quality rather than "inspecting-in" quality (that is, hoping to catch defective units through sample inspections).

7. **Supply-chain management.** Because there are no inventory buffers, JIT requires close coordination with suppliers that guarantee on-time delivery of defect-free materials. *Supply-chain management* is the exchange of information with suppliers and customers to reduce costs, improve quality, and speed delivery of goods and services from the company's suppliers, through the company itself, and on to the company's end customers.

    Even the U.S. government uses supply-chain management to implement JIT. A flat tire can ground a $20 million jet fighter, and aircraft carriers don't have room to store many spare parts. How does the U.S. Navy ensure that tires and other parts are available when needed? By contracting with Lockheed Martin to manage the supply chain. Sailors simply fill out an online form, and Lockheed Martin must ensure that the Michelin tires are delivered within four days anywhere in the world.

8. **JIT costing.** Because of the unique characteristics of JIT production described in the last seven points, most JIT producers change their accounting systems to better reflect the production environment. JIT costing, otherwise known as backflush costing, is described and illustrated in the appendix to this chapter.

While companies such as Toyota, Carrier, and Dell credit JIT for saving them millions of dollars, the system is not without problems. With no inventory buffers, JIT users are vulnerable when problems strike suppliers or distributors. For example, Ford cut production of its SUVs in response to the tire shortage resulting from Firestone's tire recall. It also had to shut down five of its U.S. plants when engine deliveries from Canadian suppliers were late due to security-related transportation delays in the wake of the World Trade Center attacks.

Total Quality Management and the Costs of Quality

Companies using JIT strive for high-quality production. Poor-quality materials or defective manufacturing processes can slow down or even shut down production. Because goods are produced only as needed, JIT companies need to make sure their entire production process is able to consistently generate high-quality products.

To meet this challenge, many companies adopt *total quality management (TQM)*. The goal of TQM is to provide customers with superior products and services. Each business function in the value chain continually examines its own activities to improve quality and eliminate defects and waste. Those companies that have already adopted ABC have a head start. They have already identified their primary activities, so now they can concentrate on making those activities more efficient or finding ways to eliminate any activities that do not add value to the final product or service.

Most companies find that if they invest more in the front end of the value chain (R&D and design), they can generate savings in the back end of the value chain (production, marketing, distribution, and customer service). Why? Because carefully designed products and manufacturing processes reduce manufacturing time, inspections, rework, and warranty claims. World-class companies such as Toyota, who have adopted TQM, *design* and *build* quality into their products rather than having to *inspect* and *repair* later, as many traditional manufacturers do.

Costs of Quality

5 Describe the four costs of quality and use them to make decisions

Traditional costing systems such as job costing and process costing do little to help managers identify the costs incurred because of defective products or production processes. Therefore, many companies prepare cost of quality reports. **Cost of quality reports** categorize and list the costs incurred by the company related to quality. Once managers know the extent of their costs of quality, they can start to identify ways for the company to improve quality, while at the same time controlling these costs.

The costs listed on a cost of quality report are generally placed into four different categories: prevention costs, appraisal costs, internal failure costs, and external failure costs. We'll briefly describe each below.

1. **Prevention costs** are costs incurred to *avoid* producing poor-quality goods or services. Many times, poor quality is caused by the variability of the production process or the complexity of the product design. To reduce the variability of the production process, companies often automate as much of the process as possible. Employee training can help decrease variability in nonautomated processes. In addition, reducing the complexity of the product design or manufacturing

process can prevent the potential for error: The fewer parts or processes, the fewer things that can go wrong. Oftentimes, companies need to literally "go back to the drawing board" (the R&D and design stages of the value chain) to make a significant difference in preventing production problems. For example, Dell reengineered its assembly process to cut in half the number of times humans touch the hard drive. As a result, the hard-drive failure rate dropped 40%. Likewise, HP was able to reduce its defect rate by significantly reducing the number of parts that went into a desktop printer.

2. **Appraisal costs** are costs incurred to *detect* poor-quality goods or services. Intel incurs appraisal costs when it tests its products. One procedure, called burn-in, heats circuits to a high temperature. A circuit that fails the burn-in test is also likely to fail in customer use. Nissan tests 100% of the vehicles that roll off the assembly lines at its plant in Canton, Mississippi. Each vehicle is put through the paces on Nissan's all-terrain test track. Any problems are identified before the vehicle leaves the plant.

3. **Internal failure costs** are costs incurred on defective units *before* making delivery to customers. For example, if Nissan does identify a problem, the vehicle is reworked to eliminate the defect before it is allowed to leave the plant. In the worst-case scenario, a product may be so defective that it cannot be reworked and must be completely scrapped. In this case, the entire cost of manufacturing the defective unit, plus any disposal cost, would be an internal failure cost.

4. **External failure costs** are costs incurred because the defective goods or services are not detected until *after* delivery is made to customers. For example, Maytag recently recalled 250,000 washing machines because water leakage onto the electrical connections had the potential to cause an electrical short and ignite the circuit boards. Besides incurring substantial cost for repairing or replacing these recalled washers, the publicity of this defect could cause significant damage to the company's reputation. Reputation damage from selling defective units to end customers can considerably harm the company's future sales. Unsatisfied customers will avoid buying from the same company in the future. Even worse, unsatisfied customers tend to tell their neighbors, family, and friends about any poor experiences with products or services. As a result, a company's reputation for poor quality can grow at an exponential rate. To capture the extent of this problem, external failure costs should include an estimate of how much profit the company is losing because of having a bad reputation for poor quality.

Exhibit 5-15 lists some common examples of the four different costs of quality. Most prevention costs occur in the R&D and design stages of the value chain. In contrast, most appraisal and internal failure costs occur in the production element of the value chain. External failure costs occur in the customer service stage. Managers make trade-offs among these costs. Many prevention costs are incurred only periodically, while internal and external failure costs are ongoing. One expert estimates that $0.08 spent on prevention saves most manufacturers $1.00 in failure costs.

Prevention and appraisal costs are sometimes referred to as "conformance costs" since they are the costs incurred to make sure the product or service conforms to its intended design. In other words, these are the costs incurred to make sure the product is *not* defective. On the other hand, internal and external failure costs are sometimes referred to as "non-conformance costs." These are the costs incurred because the product or service *is* defective.

The costs of quality are not limited to manufacturers. Service firms and merchandising companies also incur costs of quality. For example, CPA firms spend a lot of money providing ongoing professional training to their staff. They also develop standardized audit checklists to minimize the variability of the audit procedures performed for each client. These measures help to *prevent* audit failures. Both audit managers and partners review audit work papers to *appraise* whether the audit

---

EXHIBIT 5-15 Four Types of Quality Costs

Prevention Costs	Appraisal Costs
Training personnel	Inspection of incoming materials
Evaluating potential suppliers	Inspection at various stages of production
Using better materials	Inspection of final products or services
Preventive maintenance	Product testing
Improved equipment	Cost of inspection equipment
Redesigning product or process	

Internal Failure Costs	External Failure Costs
Production loss caused by downtime	Lost profits from lost customers
Rework	Warranty costs
Abnormal quantities of scrap	Service costs at customer sites
Rejected product units	Sales returns and allowances due to
Disposal of rejected units	quality problems
Machine breakdowns	Product liability claims
	Cost of recalls

---

procedures performed and evidence gathered are sufficient on each audit engagement. If audit procedures or evidence is deemed to be lacking (*internal failure*), the audit manager or partner will instruct the audit team to perform additional procedures before the firm will issue an audit opinion on the client's financial statements. This parallels the "rework" a manufacturer might perform on a product that isn't up to par. Finally, recent audit failures, such as those at Enron and WorldCom, illustrate just how expensive and devastating *external failure* can be to a CPA firm. The once prestigious international CPA firm Arthur Andersen & Co. actually went out of business because of the reputation damage caused by its audit failure at Enron.

Now that we have examined the four costs of quality, let's see how they can be presented to management in the form of a Cost of Quality report. Exhibit 5-16 shows Chemtech's Cost of Quality report. Notice how Chemtech identifies, categorizes, and quantifies all of the costs it incurs relating to quality. Although not necessary, Chemtech also calculated the percentage of total costs of quality that are incurred in each cost category. This helps Chemtech's managers see just how little they are spending on conformance costs (prevention and appraisal). Most of their costs are internal and external failure costs. The best way to reduce these failure costs is to invest more in prevention and appraisal. Chemtech's managers can now begin to focus on how they might be able to prevent these failures from occurring.

Using the Costs of Quality to Evaluate Quality Initiatives

After analyzing the Cost of Quality report, the CEO is considering spending the following amounts on a new quality program:

Inspect raw materials	$100,000
Reengineer the production process to improve product quality	750,000
Supplier screening and certification	25,000
Preventive maintenance on plant equipment	75,000
Total costs of implementing quality programs	$950,000

EXHIBIT 5-16	Chemtech's Cost of Quality Report

	Costs Incurred	Total Costs of Quality	Percentage of Total Costs of Quality (rounded)
Prevention Costs:			
Employee training	$ 125,000		
Total prevention costs		$ 125,000	6%*
Appraisal Costs:			
Testing	$ 375,000		
Total appraisal costs		$ 375,000	18%
Internal Failure Costs:			
Rework	$ 300,000		
Cost of rejected units	50,000		
Total internal failure costs		$ 350,000	17%
External Failure Costs:			
Lost profits from lost sales due			
to impaired reputation	$1,000,000		
Sales return processing	65,000		
Warranty costs	135,000		
Total external failure costs		$1,200,000	59%
Total Costs of Quality		$2,050,000	100%

*The percentage of total is computed as the total cost of the category divided by the total costs of quality.
  For example: 6% = $125,000 ÷ $2,050,000.

Although these measures won't completely eliminate internal and external failure costs, Chemtech expects this quality program to *reduce* costs by the following amounts:

Reduction in lost profits from lost sales due to impaired reputation.....	$ 800,000
Fewer sales returns to be processed	50,000
Reduction in rework costs..	250,000
Reduction in warranty costs..	125,000
Total cost savings...	$1,225,000

According to these projections, Chemtech's quality initiative will cost $950,000 but result in total savings of $1,225,000—for a net benefit of $275,000. In performing a cost-benefit analysis, some companies will simply list all of the projected costs ($950,000) and then all of the projected benefits ($1,225,000) as shown above. Other companies like to organize their cost-benefit analysis by cost category so that managers have a better idea of how the quality initiative will affect each cost category. Exhibit 5-17 shows that by increasing prevention costs (by $850,000) and appraisal costs (by $100,000), Chemtech will be able to save $250,000 in internal failure costs and $975,000 in external failure costs. In total, Chemtech expects a net benefit of $275,000 if it undertakes the quality initiative. By spending more on upstream costs (prevention and appraisal costs), Chemtech saves even more on downstream costs (internal and external failure costs).

The analysis shown in Exhibit 5-17 appears very straightforward. However, quality costs can be hard to measure. For example, design engineers may spend only part of their time on quality. Allocating their salaries to various activities is subjective. It is especially hard to measure external failure costs. The biggest external failure cost—profits lost because of the company's reputation for poor quality—does not even appear in the accounting records. This cost must be estimated based on the experiences and judgments of the sales department. Because these estimates may be subjective, TQM programs also emphasize nonfinancial measures such as defect rates, number of customer complaints, and number of warranty repairs that can be objectively measured.

EXHIBIT 5-17 **Cost-Benefit Analysis of Chemtech's Proposed Quality Program**

	Additional Costs and (Cost Savings)	Total New Costs or (Cost Savings)
Prevention Costs:		
Reengineer the production process	$ 750,000	
Supplier screening and certification	25,000	
Preventive maintenance on equipment	75,000	
Total additional prevention costs		$ 850,000
Appraisal Costs:		
Inspect raw materials	$ 100,000	
Total additional appraisal costs		100,000
Internal Failure Costs:		
Reduction of rework costs	$(250,000)	
Total internal failure cost savings		(250,000)
External Failure Costs:		
Reduction of lost profits from lost sales	$(800,000)	
Reduction of sales returns	(50,000)	
Reduction of warranty costs	(125,000)	
Total external failure cost savings		(975,000)
Total costs (savings) from quality program		$(275,000)

Decision Guidelines

JIT AND QUALITY COSTS

Dell, the worldwide leader in PC sales, is famous for its complete commitment to both the JIT and TQM philosophies. The following are several decisions Dell's managers made when adopting these two modern management techniques.

Decision	Guidelines	
How do we change a traditional production system to a JIT system?	**Traditional**	**JIT**
	Like machines grouped together	Production cells
	Longer setup times	Shorter setup times
	Larger batches	Smaller batches
	Higher inventories	Lower inventories
	An individual does fewer tasks	An individual does wider range of tasks
	Longer manufacturing cycle times	Shorter manufacturing cycle times
	Emphasis on using sample inspections to limit the number of defective products sold	Emphasis on "building in" quality to every product
	Many suppliers	Fewer, but well-coordinated, suppliers
What are the four types of quality costs?	1. Prevention costs 2. Appraisal costs 3. Internal failure costs 4. External failure costs	
How do we make trade-offs among the four types of quality costs?	Investment in prevention costs and appraisal costs reduces internal and external failure costs.	

Summary Problem 2

The CEO of IAP is concerned with the quality of its products and the amount of resources currently spent on customer returns. He would like to analyze the costs incurred in conjunction with the quality of the product.

The following information was collected from various departments within the company:

Warranty returns..	$120,000
Training personnel	10,000
Litigation on product liability claims..	175,000
Inspecting 10% of final products	5,000
Rework	10,000
Production loss due to machine breakdowns...............................	45,000
Inspection of raw materials	5,000

Requirements

1. Prepare a Cost of Quality report. In addition to listing the costs by category, determine the percentage of the total costs of quality incurred in each cost category.

2. Do any additional subjective costs appear to be missing from the report?

3. What can be learned from the report?

Solutions

Requirement 1

	Costs Incurred	Total Costs of Quality	Percentage of Total Costs of Quality (rounded)
Prevention Costs:			
Personnel training	$ 10,000		
Total prevention costs		$ 10,000	3%
Appraisal Costs:			
Inspecting raw materials	$ 5,000		
Inspecting 10% of final products	5,000		
Total appraisal costs		$ 10,000	3%
Internal Failure Costs:			
Rework	$ 10,000		
Production loss due to machine breakdown	45,000	$ 55,000	15%
Total internal failure costs			
External Failure Costs:			
Litigation costs from product liability claims	$175,000		
Warranty return costs	120,000		
Total external failure costs		$295,000	79%
Total Costs of Quality		$370,000	100%

Requirement 2

Because the company has warranty returns and product liability litigation, it is very possible that the company suffers from a reputation for poor-quality products. If so, it is losing profits from losing sales. Unsatisfied customers will probably avoid buying from the company in the future. Worse yet, they may tell their friends and family not to buy from the company. This report does not include an estimate of the lost profits arising from the company's reputation for poor-quality products.

Requirement 3

The Cost of Quality report shows that very little is being spent on prevention and maintenance, which is probably why the internal and external failure costs are so high. The CEO should use this information to develop quality initiatives in the areas of prevention and appraisal. Such initiatives should reduce future internal and external failure costs.

Appendix 5A

JIT Costing

6 (Appendix) Use JIT costing to record costs in a JIT production environment

After adopting JIT, many companies simplify their accounting systems. **Just-in-time (JIT) costing**, sometimes called **backflush costing**, is a costing system that starts with output completed and then assigns manufacturing costs to units sold and to finished goods inventories. There are four major differences between JIT costing and the traditional job costing system we described in Chapter 3:

1. JIT systems do not track the cost of products from raw materials inventory to work in process inventory to finished goods inventory. Instead, JIT costing systems wait until the units are completed to record the cost of production. How can companies with JIT systems do this? Recall that JIT requires very short setup and manufacturing cycle times. Often, JIT companies manufacture their product—from start to finish—in less than one day. Instead of making several journal entries in one day to move the costs through the Raw Materials, Work in Process, and Finished Goods inventory accounts, these companies wait until production is *completed* before recording the production costs.

2. Since suppliers deliver raw materials just in time for production to begin, JIT companies have no need for separate Work in Process and Raw Materials Inventory accounts. JIT companies combine raw materials and work in process inventories into a single account called Raw and In Process Inventory.

3. Under the JIT philosophy, workers perform many tasks. The same workers perform both direct labor tasks (such as assembly) and indirect labor tasks (such as machine maintenance and product inspection). Rather than trying to track the direct labor separately, JIT companies combine all production labor and manufacturing overhead costs (all conversion costs) into an account called Conversion Costs. The Conversion Cost account is a temporary account that works just like the Manufacturing Overhead account described in Chapter 3. Actual conversion costs accumulate as debits in the Conversion Cost account, and the account is credited when conversion costs are allocated to completed units. Accountants close any underallocated or overallocated conversion costs to Cost of Goods Sold at the end of the year, just like underallocated or overallocated Manufacturing Overhead in Chapter 3.

4. Standard costs are used to record inventory costs. Think of standard costs as the amount it *should* cost to make one unit. For example, a company may have a supply contract that enables it to obtain direct materials at a cost of $10 per unit. In this case, the standard cost of direct materials is $10 per unit. Many companies also develop standard conversion costs, which are the labor and manufacturing overhead costs they expect to incur to make one unit. For example, the company may plan to incur $15 of labor and manufacturing overhead to convert the direct materials into one finished unit. We'll discuss standard costs in more detail in Chapter 11.

Example of JIT Costing

Consider Mintel, which converts silicon wafers into integrated circuits for computers. Mintel has only one direct-manufacturing product cost: silicon wafers. All other manufacturing costs—including all production, labor, and various chemicals—are indirect costs of converting the silicon wafers into the finished integrated circuits. These indirect costs are accumulated in the Conversion Costs account.

Mintel does not use a separate Work in Process Inventory account. Instead, it uses the following two inventory accounts:

- Raw and In Process Inventory, which combines raw materials with work in process
- Finished Goods Inventory

Mintel has $100,000 of Raw and In Process Inventory and $900,000 of Finished Goods Inventory at July 31, and it uses JIT costing to record the August transactions.

1. Mintel purchases $3,020,000 of direct materials (silicon wafers) on account.

Raw and In Process Inventory	3,020,000	
Accounts Payable		3,020,000

2. Mintel incurs $18,540,000 on labor and overhead costs.

Conversion Costs	18,540,000	
Various Accounts (such as Wages Payable and Accumulated Depreciation on Property, Plant, and Equipment)		18,540,000

3. Mintel completed 3,000,000 circuits. The standard cost of each circuit is $7 ($1 standard direct materials cost and $6 standard conversion cost). The debit to Finished Goods is $21,000,000 (3,000,000 completed circuits × $7). There is no Work in Process inventory in JIT costing, so Mintel credits:

- Raw and In Process Inventory, $3,000,000 (3,000,000 completed circuits × $1 standard direct material cost per circuit) for the silicon wafers.
- Conversion Costs, $18,000,000 (3,000,000 completed circuits × $6 standard conversion cost per completed circuit) for the labor and other indirect costs allocated to the finished circuits.

Finished Goods Inventory	21,000,000	
Raw and In Process Inventory (3,000,000 × $1)		3,000,000
Conversion Costs (3,000,000 × $6)		18,000,000

This is the essence of JIT costing. The system does not track costs as the circuits move through manufacturing. Instead, *completion* of the circuits triggers the accounting system to go back and pull costs from Raw and In Process Inventory and to allocate conversion costs to the finished products.

4. Mintel sold 2,930,000 circuits (2,930,000 circuits × $7 per circuit = $20,510,000). To simplify, we'll leave out of our example the journal entry to record the associated sales revenue and accounts receivable.

Cost of Goods Sold	20,510,000	
Finished Goods Inventory		20,510,000

Exhibit 5-18 shows Mintel's major accounts. Combining the raw materials inventory with work in process inventory to form the single Raw and In Process Inventory account eliminates detail. Although Mintel tracks the number of physical units in process, the company does not use material requisitions or time records to assign costs to circuits as they flow through the production process. Mintel does not assign costs to physical products until the goods are completed.

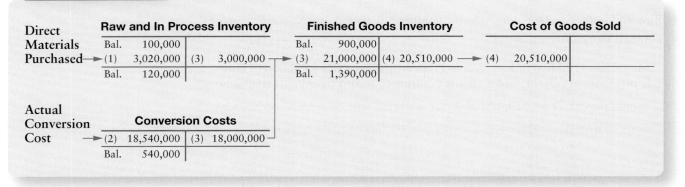

EXHIBIT 5-18   **Mintel's Major JIT Costing Accounts**

5. You can see from Exhibit 5-18 that conversion costs are underallocated by $540,000 ($18,540,000 − $18,000,000). Underallocated and overallocated conversion costs are treated just like underallocated and overallocated manufacturing overhead and closed to Cost of Goods Sold.

Cost of Goods Sold	540,000	
Conversion Costs		540,000

Stop & Think...

ABC is a detailed costing method that provides more accurate product costs. JIT costing is simplified and does not track costs through the sequence of manufacturing operations. Are these two costing systems incompatible? Or can they be used together?

Answer: ABC and JIT costing can be compatible. Mintel's $6 standard conversion cost per circuit used in JIT costing could be provided by an ABC system.

Decision Guidelines

Decision	Guidelines
How do we simplify costing after adopting JIT?	Use JIT costing.
	1. Summary journal entries are not made until units are completed; costs are not separately tracked as units move through production.
	2. Raw materials and work in process are combined into a single Raw and In Process Inventory account.
	3. Labor and overhead costs are combined into a Conversion Cost account.
	4. Standard costs are used to record inventory costs.

Summary Problem 3

The Flores Company manufactures cellular telephones. Flores uses JIT costing. The standard unit cost is $37: $24 of direct materials and $13 of conversion costs. Direct materials purchased on account during June totaled $2,540,000. Actual conversion costs totaled $1,295,000. Flores completed 102,000 telephones in June and sold 98,000.

Requirements

1. Prepare the June journal entries for these transactions.

2. Make the entry to close the underallocated or overallocated conversion costs to Cost of Goods Sold.

Solutions

Requirement 1

Raw and In Process Inventory	2,540,000	
Accounts Payable		2,540,000
Conversion Costs	1,295,000	
Various accounts (such as Payables		
and Accumulated Depreciation)		1,295,000
Finished Goods Inventory	3,774,000	
Raw and In Process Inventory (102,000 × $24)		2,448,000
Conversion Costs (102,000 × $13)		1,326,000
Cost of Goods Sold (98,000 × $37)	3,626,000	
Finished Goods Inventory		3,626,000

Requirement 2

Conversion Costs	
Allocated (102,000 × $13) ..	$1,326,000
Actual incurred	1,295,000
Overallocated..................	$ 31,000

Close overallocated conversion costs as follows:

Conversion Costs	31,000	
Cost of Goods Sold		31,000

Review *Activity-Based Costing and Other Cost Management Tools*

▪ Accounting Vocabulary

Activity-Based Costing (ABC) (p. 263)
Focuses on *activities* as the fundamental cost objects. The costs of those activities become building blocks for compiling the indirect costs of products, services, and customers.

Activity-Based Management (ABM) (p. 273)
Using activity-based cost information to make decisions that increase profits while satisfying customers' needs.

Appraisal Costs (p. 285)
Costs incurred to *detect* poor-quality goods or services.

Cost Distortion (p. 260)
Overcosting some products while undercosting other products.

Cost of Quality Report (p 284)
A report that lists the costs incurred by the company related to quality. The costs are categorized as prevention costs, appraised costs, internal failure costs, and external failure costs.

Departmental Overhead Rates (p. 262)
Separate manufacturing overhead rates established for each department.

External Failure Costs (p. 285)
Costs incurred when the company does not detect poor-quality goods or services until *after* delivery is made to customers.

Internal Failure Costs (p. 285)
Costs incurred when the company detects and corrects poor-quality goods or services *before* making delivery to customers.

Just-in-Time (JIT) Costing (p. 292)
A standard costing system that starts with output completed and then assigns manufacturing costs to units sold and to inventories. Also called backflush costing.

Plantwide Overhead Rate (p. 261)
When overhead is allocated to every product using the same manufacturing overhead rate.

Prevention Costs (p. 284)
Costs incurred to *avoid* poor-quality goods or services.

Value Engineering (p. 274)
Reevaluating activities to reduce costs while satisfying customer needs.

▪ Quick Check

1. Which of the following is *false*?
   a. The distinguishing feature of ABC is that it focuses on allocating indirect costs.
   b. Advances in information technology have made it feasible for more companies to adopt ABC.
   c. ABC is only for manufacturing firms.
   d. A system that uses ABC is more refined than one that uses departmental overhead rates.

   The following data apply to Questions 2 through 4. Two of Dell's primary production activities are *kitting* (assembling raw materials needed for a particular computer or server in one kit) and *boxing* the completed products for shipment to customers. Assume that Dell spends $5 million a month on the kitting activity and $10 million a month on boxing. It allocates kitting activity costs based on the number of parts used in the product and boxing activity costs based on the cubic feet of space the product requires. Suppose Dell estimates it will use 800 million parts a month and ship products with a total volume of 20 million cubic feet.

Assume that each desktop computer requires 100 parts and has a volume of 5 cubic feet. Assume that each server requires 150 parts and has a volume of 7 cubic feet.

2. What is the activity cost allocation rate for kitting and boxing?
   a. $0.00625/part, $0.50/cubic foot
   b. $0.0125/part, $0.25/cubic foot
   c. $0.50/part, $40/cubic foot
   d. $160/part, $2/cubic foot

3. What are the kitting and boxing costs assigned to one desktop computer?
   a. $0.625, $2.50
   b. $0.9375, $3.50
   c. $1.25, $1.25
   d. $50.00, $200.00

4. Dell contracts with its suppliers to pre-kit certain component parts before delivering them to Dell. Assume that this saves $1.5 million of the kitting activity cost and that it reduces the total number of parts by 400 million (because Dell considers each pre-kit as one part). If a server now uses 80 parts, what is the new kitting cost assigned to one server?
   a. $0.35
   b. $0.70
   c. $0.9375
   d. $1.00

5. Dell can use ABC information for what decisions?
   a. pricing
   b. cost cutting
   c. evaluating managers' performance
   d. all of the above

6. Which of the following is *not* a good reason for Dell to use ABC?
   a. The computer industry is highly competitive.
   b. Dell produces many more desktops than servers, and servers are more difficult to assemble.
   c. Most costs are direct; indirect costs are a small proportion of total costs.
   d. Dell has advanced information technology, including bar-coded materials and labor.

7. Dell enjoys many benefits from committing to JIT. Which is *not* a benefit of adopting JIT?

   a. lower inventory carrying costs

   b. more space available for production

   c. ability to respond more quickly to changes in customer demand

   d. ability to continue production despite disruptions in deliveries of raw materials

8. (Appendix:) The following account is not used in JIT costing:

   a. Raw and In Process Inventory

   b. Conversion Costs

   c. Work In Process Inventory

   d. Finished Goods Inventory

9. The cost of lost future sales after a customer finds flaws in a product or service is which of the following quality costs?

   a. external failure cost

   b. internal failure cost

   c. appraisal cost

   d. prevention cost

10. Dell's spending on testing its computers before shipping them to customers helps *reduce* which of the following costs?

    a. prevention cost

    b. appraisal cost

    c. external failure cost

    d. none of the above

Quick Check Answers

1. c 2. a 3. a 4. b 5. d 6. c 7. d 8. c 9. a 10. c

For Internet Exercises, Excel in Practice, and additional online activities, go to this book's Web site at www.prenhall.com/bamber.

Assess Your Progress

■ Learning Objectives

1 Develop and use departmental overhead rates in place of a traditional plantwide rate

2 Develop activity-based costs (ABC) and use activity-based management (ABM) to make business decisions

3 Explain when ABC is most likely to pass the cost-benefit test

4 Describe a just-in-time (JIT) production system

5 Describe the four costs of quality and use them to make decisions

6 (Appendix) Use JIT costing to record costs in a JIT production environment

■ Short Exercises

S5-1 **Use departmental overhead rates to allocate manufacturing overhead** *(Learning Objective 1)*
Quality Furniture uses departmental overhead rates (rather than a plantwide overhead rate) to allocate its manufacturing overhead to jobs. The company's two production departments have the following departmental overhead rates:

> Cutting Department: $10 per machine hour
> Finishing Department: $17 per direct labor hour

Job 392 used the following direct labor hours and machine hours in the two manufacturing departments:

JOB 392	Cutting Department	Finishing Department
Direct labor hours	2	6
Machine hours	8	1

1. How much manufacturing overhead should be allocated to Job 392?
2. Assume that direct labor is paid at a rate of $25/hour and Job 392 used $2,500 of direct materials. What was the total manufacturing cost of Job 392?

S5-2 **Compute departmental overhead rates** *(Learning Objective 1)*
Uncle Bruce's Snacks makes potato chips, corn chips, and cheese puffs using three different production lines within the same manufacturing plant. Currently, Uncle Bruce uses a single plantwide overhead rate to allocate its $3,500,000 of annual manufacturing overhead. Of this amount, $1,800,000 is associated with the potato chip line, $1,000,000 is associated with the corn chip line, and $700,000 is associated with the cheese puff line. Uncle Bruce's plant is currently running a total of 17,500 machine

continued . . .

hours: 11,250 in the potato chip line, 3,450 in the corn chip line, and 2,800 in the cheese puff line. Uncle Bruce considers machine hours to be the cost driver of manufacturing overhead costs.

1. What is Uncle Bruce's plantwide overhead rate?

2. Calculate the departmental overhead rates for Uncle Bruce's three production lines. Round all answers to the nearest cent.

3. Which products had been overcosted by the plantwide rate? Which products had been undercosted by the plantwide rate?

S5-3　**Compute activity cost allocation rates** *(Learning Objective 2)*

Uncle Bruce produces different styles of potato chips (ruffled, flat, thick-cut, gourmet) for different corporate customers. Each style of potato chip requires different preparation time, different cooking and draining times (depending on desired fat content), and different packaging (single serving versus bulk). Therefore, Uncle Bruce has decided to try ABC costing to better capture the manufacturing overhead costs incurred by each style of chip. Uncle Bruce has identified the following activities related to yearly manufacturing overhead costs and cost drivers associated with producing potato chips:

Activity	Manufacturing Overhead	Cost Driver
Preparation	$600,000	Preparation time
Cooking and draining	$900,000	Cooking and draining time
Packaging	$300,000	Units packaged

Compute the activity cost allocation rates for each activity assuming the following total estimated activity for the year: 12,000 preparation hours, 30,000 cooking and draining hours, and 6 million packages.

S5-4　**Continuation of S5-3: Use ABC to allocate overhead** *(Learning Objective 2)*

Uncle Bruce just received an order to produce 12,000 single-serving bags of gourmet, fancy-cut, low-fat potato chips. The order will require 16 preparation hours and 32 cooking and draining hours. Use the activity rates you calculated in S5-3 to compute the following:

1. What is the total amount of manufacturing overhead that should be allocated to this order?

2. How much manufacturing overhead should be assigned to each bag?

3. What other costs will Uncle Bruce need to consider to determine the total manufacturing costs of this order?

S5-5 **Calculate a job cost using ABC** *(Learning Objective 2)*

Berg Industries, a family-run small manufacturer, has adopted an ABC costing system. The following manufacturing activities, indirect manufacturing costs, and usage of cost drivers have been estimated for the year:

Activity	Estimated Total Manufacturing Overhead Costs	Estimated Total Usage of Cost Driver
Machine setup	$150,000	3,000 setups
Machining	$1,000,000	5,000 machine hours
Quality control	$337,500	4,500 tests run

During May, Evan and Stephanie Berg machined and assembled Job 624. Evan worked a total of 10 hours on the job, while Stephanie worked 5 hours on the job. Evan is paid a $25/hour wage rate, while Stephanie is paid $30/hour because of her additional experience level. Direct materials requisitioned for Job 624 totaled $1,050. The following additional information was collected on Job 624: The job required 1 machine setup, 5 machine hours, and 2 quality control tests.

1. Compute the activity cost allocation rates for the year.

2. Complete the following job cost record for Job 624:

Job Cost Record JOB 624	Manufacturing Costs
Direct materials	?
Direct labor	?
Manufacturing overhead	?
Total job cost	$?

S5-6 **Apply activity cost allocation rates** *(Learning Objective 2)*

Narnia Technology uses ABC to allocate all of its conversion costs (direct labor and manufacturing overhead). Narnia's Cell Phone Department, which assembles and tests digital processors, reports the following data regarding processor G27:

Direct materials cost...	$56.00
Activity costs allocated..	?
Manufacturing product cost..	$?

continued . . .

The activities required to build the processors are as follows:

Activity	Allocation Base		Cost Allocated to Each Board	
Start station	Number of processor boards	1	× $ 0.90 =	$0.90
Dip insertion	Number of dip insertions	20	× $ 0.25 =	?
Manual insertion	Number of manual insertions	5	× $? =	2.00
Wave solder	Number of processor boards soldered	1	× $ 4.50 =	4.50
Backload	Number of backload insertions	?	× $ 0.70 =	2.80
Test	Standard time each processor board is in test activity (hr.)	0.15	× $90.00 =	?
Defect analysis	Standard time for defect analysis and repair (hr.)	0.16	× $? =	8.00
Total				$?

Requirements

1. Fill in the blanks in both the opening schedule and the list of activities.
2. Why might managers favor this ABC system instead of the older system that allocated all conversion costs on the basis of direct labor?

S5-7 **Determine the usefulness of refined costing systems in various situations** *(Learning Objective 3)*

In each of the following situations, determine whether the company would be (1) more likely or (2) less likely to benefit from refining its costing system.

1. The company has reengineered its production process but has not changed its accounting system.
2. The company produces few products, and the products consume resources in a similar manner.
3. The company operates in a very competitive industry.
4. The company has very few indirect costs.
5. The company produces high volumes of some of its products and low volumes of other products.
6. In bidding for jobs, managers lost bids they expected to win and won bids they expected to lose.

Mission, Inc. Data Set for S5-8 through S5-14

Mission, Inc., is a technology consulting firm focused on Web site development and integration of Internet business applications. President Susan Nelson's ear is ringing after an unpleasant call from client Jerry Webb. Webb was irate after opening his bill for Mission's redesign of his company's Web site. Webb said that Mission's major competitor, Delta Applications, charged much lower fees to another company for which Webb serves on the board of directors.

Nelson is puzzled for two reasons. First, she is confident that her firm knows Web site design and support as well as any of Mission's competitors. Nelson cannot understand how Delta Applications can undercut Mission's rates and still make a profit. But Delta Applications is reputed to be very profitable. Second, just yesterday Nelson received a call from client Keith Greg. Greg was happy with the excellent service and reasonable fees Nelson charged him for adding a database-driven job-posting feature to his company's Web site. Nelson was surprised by Greg's compliments because this was an unusual job for Mission that required development of complex database management and control applications, and she had felt a little uneasy accepting it.

Like most consulting firms, Mission traces direct labor to individual engagements (jobs). Mission allocates indirect costs to engagements using a budgeted rate based on direct labor hours. Nelson is happy with this system, which she has used since she established Mission in 1995.

Nelson expects to incur $706,000 of indirect costs this year, and she expects her firm to work 5,000 direct labor hours. Nelson and the other systems consultants earn $350 per hour. Clients are billed at 150% of direct labor cost. Last month, Mission's consultants spent 100 hours on Webb's engagement. They also spent 100 hours on Greg's engagement.

S5-8 **Compute and use traditional allocation rate** *(Learning Objective 1)*
Refer to the Mission Data Set.

1. Compute Mission's indirect cost allocation rate.

2. Compute the total costs assigned to the Webb and Greg engagements.

3. Compute the operating income from the Webb and Greg engagements.

S5-9 **Identify clues that old system is broken** *(Learning Objective 3)*
Refer to the Mission Data Set. List all of the signals or clues indicating that Mission's cost system may be "broken."

S5-10 **Explain costs and benfits of ABC** *(Learning Objectives 2, 3)*
Refer to the Mission Data Set. Nelson has employed your consulting firm to help her decide whether to develop an ABC system. Draft a memo to Nelson recommending whether her firm should develop an ABC system. Be sure to explain the

continued . . .

costs and benefits Nelson could expect from adopting ABC. Use the following format for your memo.

Date: _____	
To: Ms. Susan Nelson, President, Mission, Inc.	
From: (Student Name) _____	
Subject: Cost system recommendation	

S5-11 **Compute activity cost allocation rates** *(Learning Objective 2)*

Refer to the Mission Data Set. Nelson suspects that her allocation of indirect costs could be giving misleading results, so she decides to develop an ABC system. She identifies three activities: documentation preparation, information technology support, and training. Nelson figures that documentation costs are driven by the number of pages, information technology support costs are driven by the number of software applications used, and training costs are most closely associated with the number of direct labor hours worked. Estimates of the costs and quantities of the allocation bases follow.

Activity	Estimated Cost	Allocation Base	Estimated Quantity of Cost Driver
Documentation preparation	$100,000	Pages	3,125 pages
Information technology support	156,000	Applications used	780 applications
Training	450,000	Direct labor hours	5,000 hours
Total indirect costs	$706,000		

Compute the cost allocation rate for each activity.

S5-12 **Continuation of S5-11: compute job costs using ABC** *(Learning Objective 2)*

Refer to the Mission Data Set and the activity cost allocation rates you computed in S5-11. The Webb and Greg engagements used the following resources last month:

Cost Driver	Webb	Greg
Direct labor hours	100	100
Pages	50	300
Applications used	1	78

1. Compute the cost assigned to the Webb engagement and to the Greg engagement using the ABC system.
2. Compute the operating income from the Webb engagement and from the Greg engagement using the ABC system.

S5-13   Continuation of S5-8 and S5-12: compare traditional and ABC costs *(Learning Objective 2)*

Refer to the Mission Data Set. Write a memo to Nelson comparing the costs of the Webb and Greg jobs using the original direct labor single-allocation-base system (S5-8) and the ABC system (S5-12). Be sure to explain the following:

- How have the costs changed under the ABC system?
- Why have the costs changed in the direction they changed rather than in the opposite direction?
- Do the ABC results solve Nelson's puzzle from the Mission Data Set? Explain.

  Your memo should follow the format outlined in S5-10.

S5-14   Write ABC memo *(Learning Objective 2)*

Refer to the Mission Data Set. Write a memo to Nelson explaining how she can use the ABC information to make decisions about her consulting firm. Consider how she could use ABC information in:

- setting fees (prices).
- responding to clients' concerns about fees.
- controlling costs.

  Your memo should follow the format outlined in S5-10.

S5-15   Defend ABC *(Learning Objectives 2, 3)*

The vice president of marketing storms into your office exclaiming:

> ABC is worse than useless. It's endangering the future of our company! Because of your ABC cost "information," the CEO is pressuring us to (1) charge customers higher prices for customized products, (2) shift customers from customized products to standard products, and (3) require customers to accept larger deliveries than they would prefer. This completely violates our motto of "delighting the customer." Worse yet, we are being pressured to drop some of the customers we have spent a great deal of effort cultivating. This stupid ABC system will ruin us all!

Reply to your colleague.

S5-16   Identify JIT characteristics *(Learning Objective 4)*

Indicate whether each of the following is characteristic of a JIT production system or a traditional production system.

a. Management works with suppliers to ensure defect-free raw materials.

b. Products are produced in large batches.

c. Large stocks of finished goods protect against lost sales if customer demand is higher than expected.

d. Suppliers make frequent deliveries of small quantities of raw materials.

e. Setup times are long.

f. Employees do a variety of jobs, including maintenance and setups as well as operation of machines.

g. Machines are grouped into self-contained production cells or production lines.

h. Machines are grouped according to function. For example, all cutting machines are located in one area.

i. Suppliers can access the company's intranet.

continued . . .

j. The final operation in the production sequence "pulls" parts from the preceding operation.

k. Each employee is responsible for inspecting his or her own work.

l. There is an emphasis on building in quality.

m. The manufacturing cycle times are longer.

S5-17 **Give examples of costs of quality** *(Learning Objective 5)*

Bombardier manufactures SeaDoo personal watercraft (Jet Skis). Give examples of costs that Bombardier might incur in each of the four categories of quality costs:

1. Prevention costs

2. Appraisal costs

3. Internal failure costs

4. External failure costs

 Be as specific as possible.

S5-18 **Classifying costs of quality** *(Learning Objective 5)*

Classify each of the following quality-related costs as prevention costs, appraisal costs, internal failure costs, or external failure costs.

1. Reworking defective units

2. Litigation costs from product liability claims

3. Inspecting incoming raw materials

4. Training employees

5. Warranty repairs

6. Redesigning the production process

7. Lost productivity due to machine breakdown

8. Inspecting products that are halfway through the production process

9. Incremental cost of using a higher-grade raw material

10. Cost incurred producing and disposing of defective units

S5-19 **Quality initiative decision** *(Learning Objective 5)*

Wharfedale manufactures high-quality speakers. Suppose Wharfedale is considering spending the following amounts on a new quality program:

Additional 20 minutes of testing for each speaker	$ 600,000
Negotiating with and training suppliers to obtain higher-quality materials and on-time delivery	300,000
Redesigning the speakers to make them easier to manufacture	1,400,000

Wharfedale expects this quality program to save costs as follows:

Reduced warranty repair costs	$200,000
Avoid inspection of raw materials	400,000
Rework avoided because of fewer defective units	650,000

It also expects this program to avoid lost profits from:

Lost sales due to disappointed customers	$850,000
Lost production time due to rework	300,000

1. Classify each of these costs into one of the four categories of quality costs (prevention, appraisal, internal failure, external failure).
2. Should Wharfedale implement the quality program? Give your reasons.

S5-20 **Appendix: Prepare JIT costing journal entries** *(Learning Objective 6)*
Hamilton Products uses a JIT system to manufacture trading pins for the 2008 Olympic Games in Beijing, China. The standard cost per pin is $2 for raw materials and $3 for conversion costs. Last month, Hamilton Products recorded the following data:

Number of pins completed	4,000 pins	Raw material purchases	$ 8,800
Number of pins sold	3,500 pins	Conversion costs	$12,660

Use JIT costing to prepare journal entries for the month, including the entry to close the Conversion Cost account.

■ Exercises

E5-21 **Compare traditional and departmental cost allocations** *(Learning Objective 1)*
Bergeron Fine Furnishings manufactures upscale custom furniture. Bergeron Fine Furnishings currently uses a plantwide overhead rate based on direct labor hours to allocate its $1,100,000 of manufacturing overhead to individual jobs. However, Ernie Bergeron, owner and CEO, is considering refining the company's costing system by using departmental overhead rates. Currently, the Machining Department incurs $750,000 of manufacturing overhead while the Finishing Department incurs $350,000 of manufacturing overhead. Ernie has identified machine hours (MH) as the primary manufacturing overhead cost driver in the Machining Department and direct labor (DL) hours as the primary cost driver in the Finishing Department.
Bergeron Fine Furnishings's plant completed Jobs 450 and 455 on May 15. Both jobs incurred a total of 6 DL hours throughout the entire production process. Job 450 incurred 2 MH in the Machining Department and 5 DL hours in the Finishing Department (the other DL hour occurred in the Machining Department). Job 455 incurred 6 MH in the Machining Department and 4 DL hours in the Finishing Department (the other two DL hours occurred in the Machining Department).

Requirements
1. Compute the plantwide overhead rate assuming that Bergeron expects to incur 25,000 total DL hours during the year.
2. Compute departmental overhead rates assuming that Bergeron expects to incur 15,000 MH in the Machining Department and 17,500 DL hours in the Finishing Department during the year.

continued . . .

3. If Bergeron continues to use the plantwide overhead rate, how much manufacturing overhead would be allocated to Job 450 and Job 455?

4. If Bergeron uses departmental overhead rates, how much manufacturing overhead would be allocated to Job 450 and Job 455?

5. Based on your answers to Requirements 3 and 4, does the plantwide overhead rate overcost or undercost either job? Explain. If Bergeron sells his furniture at 125% of cost, will his choice of allocation systems affect product pricing? Explain.

E5-22 Compute activity rates and apply to jobs *(Learning Objective 2)*

Abram uses ABC to account for its chrome wheel manufacturing process. Company managers have identified four manufacturing activities that incur manufacturing overhead costs: materials handling, machine setup, insertion of parts, and finishing. The budgeted activity costs for 2007 and their allocation bases are as follows:

Activity	Total Budgeted Manufacturing Overhead Cost	Allocation Base
Materials handling	$ 12,000	Number of parts
Machine setup	3,400	Number of setups
Insertion of parts	48,000	Number of parts
Finishing	80,000	Finishing direct labor hours
Total	$143,400	

Abram expects to produce 1,000 chrome wheels during the year. The wheels are expected to use 3,000 parts, require 10 setups, and consume 2,000 hours of finishing time.

Job 420 used 150 parts, required 1 setup, and consumed 120 finishing hours.
Job 510 used 425 parts, required 2 setups, and consumed 320 finishing hours.

Requirements

1. Compute the cost allocation rate for each activity.
2. Compute the manufacturing overhead cost that should be assigned to Job 420.
3. Compute the manufacturing overhead cost that should be assigned to Job 510.

E5-23 Apply activity cost allocation rates *(Learning Objective 2)*

The Electronics Manufacturing Department of Southstream uses ABC to allocate all of its conversion costs (direct labor and manufacturing overhead). The company assembles and tests electronic components used in handheld video phones. Consider the following data regarding component T24:

Direct materials cost...	$81.00
Activity costs allocated...	?
Manufacturing product cost..	$?

The activities required to build the component follow.

Activity	Allocation Base			Cost Allocated to Each Unit	
Start station	Number of raw component chassis	2	× $ 1.30 =	$ 2.60
Dip insertion	Number of dip insertions	?	× $ 0.40 =	12.00
Manual insertion	Number of manual insertions	12	× $ 0.80 =	?
Wave solder	Number of components soldered	1	× $ 1.40 =	1.40
Backload	Number of backload insertions	7	× $? =	4.20
Test	Standard time each component is in test activity	0.40	× $80.00 =	?
Defect analysis	Standard time for defect analysis and repair	0.10	× $? =	5.00
Total				$?

Requirements

1. Fill in the blanks in both the opening schedule and the list of activities.

2. Why might managers favor this ABC system instead of the older system, which allocated all conversion costs on the basis of direct labor?

E5-24 Using ABC to bill clients at a service firm *(Learning Objective 2)*
King & Company is an architectural firm specializing in home remodeling for private clients and new office buildings for corporate clients.

King & Company charges customers at a billing rate equal to 135% of the client's total job cost. A client's total job cost is a combination of (1) professional time spent on the client ($65 per hour cost of employing each professional) and (2) operating overhead allocated to the client's job. King allocates operating overhead to jobs based on professional hours spent on the job. King estimates its five professionals will incur a total of 10,000 professional hours working on client jobs during the year.

All operating costs other than professional salaries (travel reimbursements, copy costs, secretarial salaries, office lease, and so forth) can be assigned to the three activities. Total activity costs, cost drivers, and total usage of those cost drivers are estimated as follows:

Activity	Total Activity Cost	Cost Driver	Total Usage by Corporate Clients	Total Usage by Private Clients
Transportation to clients........	$ 9,000	Round-trip mileage to clients......	3,000 miles	12,000 miles
Blueprint copying................	35,000	Number of copies.......	300 copies	700 copies
Office support......................	190,000	Secretarial time...........	2,200 secretarial hours	2,800 secretarial hours
Total operating overhead.....	$234,000			

Amy Lee hired King & Company to design her kitchen remodeling. A total of 24 professional hours were incurred on this job. In addition, Amy's remodeling job required one of the professionals to travel back and forth to her house for a total of 125 miles. The blueprints had to be copied four times because Amy changed the

continued . . .

plans several times. In addition, 18 hours of secretarial time were used lining up the subcontractors for the job.

1. Calculate the current operating overhead allocation rate per professional hour.
2. Calculate the amount that would be billed to Amy Lee given the current costing structure.
3. Calculate the activity cost allocation rates that could be used to allocate operating overhead costs to client jobs.
4. Calculate the amount that would be billed to Amy Lee using ABC costing.
5. Which type of billing system is fairer to clients? Explain.

E5-25 **Reassess product costs using ABC** *(Learning Objective 2)*

Alan, Inc., manufactures only two products, Medium (42-inch) and Large (63-inch) plasma screen TVs. To generate adequate profit and cover its expenses throughout the value chain, Alan prices its TVs at 300% of manufacturing cost. The company is concerned, because the Large model is facing severe pricing competition, whereas the Medium model is the low-price leader in the market. The CEO questions whether the cost numbers generated by the accounting system are correct. He's just learned about ABC and wants to reanalyze this past year's product costs using an ABC system.

Information about the company's products this past year is as follows:

> Medium (42-inch) Plasma TVs:
>   Total direct material cost: $660,000
>   Total direct labor cost: $216,000
>   Production volume: 3,000 units
>
> Large (63-inch) Plasma TVs:
>   Total direct material cost: $1,240,000
>   Total direct labor cost: $384,000
>   Production volume: 4,000 units

Currently, the company applies manufacturing overhead on the basis of direct labor hours. The company incurred $800,000 of manufacturing overhead this year and 25,000 direct labor hours (9,000 direct labor hours making Medium TVs and 16,000 making Large TVs). The ABC team identified three primary production activities that generate manufacturing overhead costs:

> Materials Handling ($150,000); driven by number of material orders handled
> Machine Processing ($560,000); driven by machine hours
> Packaging ($90,000); driven by packaging hours

The company's only two products required the following activity levels during the year:

	Material Orders Handled	Machine Hours	Packaging Hours
Medium	300	20,000	4,000
Large	200	20,000	6,000

1. Use the company's current costing system to find the total cost of producing all Medium (42-inch) TVs and the total cost of producing all Large (63-inch) TVs. What was the average cost of making each unit of each model? Round your answers to the nearest cent.

2. Use ABC to find the total cost of producing all Medium (42-inch) TVs and the total cost of producing all Large (63-inch) TVs. What was the average cost of making each unit of each model? Round your answers to the nearest cent.

3. How much cost distortion was occurring between Alan's two products? Calculate the cost distortion in total and on a per unit basis. Could the cost distortion explain the CEO's puzzle about pricing competition? Explain.

E5-26 **Use ABC to allocate manufacturing overhead** (*Learning Objective 2*)

Several years after reengineering its production process, Donovan Corp. hired a new controller, Natalie Babin. She developed an ABC system very similar to the one used by Donovan's chief rival, Clegg. Part of the reason Babin developed the ABC system was because Donovan's profits had been declining even though the company had shifted its product mix toward the product that had appeared most profitable under the old system. Before adopting the new ABC system, Donovan had used a plantwide overhead rate based on direct labor hours that was developed years ago.

For 2007, Donovan's budgeted ABC manufacturing overhead allocation rates are:

Activity	Allocation Base	Activity Cost Allocation Rate
Materials handling	Number of parts	$ 3.75 per part
Machine setup	Number of setups	300.00 per setup
Insertion of parts	Number of parts	24.00 per part
Finishing	Finishing direct labor hours	50.00 per hour

The number of parts is now a feasible allocation base because Donovan recently purchased bar-coding technology. Donovan produces two wheel models: standard and deluxe. Budgeted data for 2007 are as follows:

	Standard	Deluxe
Parts per wheel..	4.0	6.0
Setups per 1,000 wheels	15.0	15.0
Finishing direct labor hours per wheel....................	1.0	2.5
Total direct labor hours per wheel	2.0	3.0

The company's managers expect to produce 1,000 units of each model during the year.

Requirements

1. Compute the total budgeted manufacturing overhead cost for 2007.

2. Compute the manufacturing overhead cost per wheel of each model using ABC.

3. Compute Donovan's traditional plantwide overhead rate. Use this rate to determine the manufacturing overhead cost per wheel under the traditional system.

E5-27 **Continuation of E5-26: Determine product profitability** *(Learning Objective 2)*
Refer to your answers in E5-26. In addition to the manufacturing overhead costs, the following data are budgeted for the company's standard and deluxe models for 2008:

	Standard	Deluxe
Sales price per wheel	$300.00	$440.00
Direct materials per wheel......................................	30.00	46.00
Direct labor per wheel...	45.00	50.00

Requirements

1. Compute the gross profit per wheel if managers rely on the ABC unit cost data computed in E5-26.

2. Compute the gross profit per wheel if the managers rely on the plantwide allocation cost data.

3. Which product line is more profitable for Donovan?

E5-28 **Continuation of E5-26: identify warning sign** *(Learning Objective 3)*
Refer to E5-26. Why might controller Natalie Babin have expected ABC to pass the cost-benefit test? Were there any warning signs that Donovan's old direct-labor-based allocation system was broken?

E5-29 **Work backward to determine ABC rates** *(Learning Objective 2)*
Clarkson Fabricators completed two jobs in June 2007. Clarkson Fabricators recorded the following costs assigned to the jobs by the company's activity-based costing system:

		Allocated Cost	
Activity	Allocation Base	Job 409	Job 622
Materials handling	Number of parts	$ 500	$ 1,500
Lathe work	Number of lathe turns	5,000	15,000
Milling	Number of machine hours	4,000	28,000
Grinding	Number of parts	300	1,500
Testing	Number of output units	126	2,700

Job 622 required 3,000 parts, 60,000 lathe turns, and 1,400 machine hours. All 300 of the job's output units were tested. All units of Job 409 were tested.

Requirements

1. How do you know that at least one of the costs recorded for the two jobs is inaccurate?

2. Disregard materials handling costs. How many parts were used for Job 409? How many lathe turns did Job 409 require? How many machine hours? How many units were produced in Job 409?

3. A nearby company has offered to test all product units for $13 each. On the basis of ABC data, should Clarkson Fabricators accept or reject the offer? Give your reason.

E5-30   **Differentiate between traditional and JIT production** *(Learning Objective 4)*
Briefly describe how JIT production systems differ from traditional production systems along each of the following dimensions:

1. Inventory levels
2. Batch sizes
3. Setup times
4. Physical layout of plant
5. Roles of plant employees
6. Manufacturing cycle times
7. Quality

E5-31   **Categorize different costs of quality** *(Learning Objective 5)*
O'Neil & Co. makes electronic components. Mike O'Neil, the president, recently instructed Vice President Steve Bensen to develop a total quality control program. "If we don't at least match the quality improvements our competitors are making," he told Bensen, "we'll soon be out of business." Bensen began by listing various "costs of quality" that O'Neil incurs. The first six items that came to mind were as follows:

1. Costs of electronic components returned by customers
2. Costs incurred by O'Neil & Co.'s customer representatives traveling to customer sites to repair defective products
3. Lost profits from lost sales due to reputation for less-than-perfect products
4. Costs of inspecting components in one of O'Neil & Co.'s production processes
5. Salaries of engineers who are designing components to withstand electrical overloads
6. Costs of reworking defective components after discovery by company inspectors

Requirements

Classify each item as a prevention cost, an appraisal cost, an internal failure cost, or an external failure cost.

E5-32   **Prepare a Cost of Quality report** *(Learning Objective 5)*
The CEO of Charlie Snackfoods is concerned about the amount of resources currently spent on customer warranty claims. Each box of snacks is printed with the following logo: "Satisfaction guaranteed, or your money back." Since the claims are so high, she would like to evaluate what costs are being incurred to ensure the quality of

continued . . .

the product. The following information was collected from various departments within the company:

Warranty claims	$420,000
Cost of defective products found at the inspection point	94,000
Training factory personnel	26,000
Recall of Batch #59374	175,000
Inspecting products when halfway through the production process	55,000
Cost of disposing of rejected products	12,000
Preventive maintenance on factory equipment	7,000
Production loss due to machine breakdowns	15,000
Inspection of raw materials	5,000

Requirements

1. Prepare a Cost of Quality report. In addition to listing the costs by category, determine the percentage of the total costs of quality incurred in each cost category.
2. Do any additional subjective costs appear to be missing from the report?
3. What can be learned from the report?

E5-33 **Classify costs and make a quality-initiative decision** *(Learning Objective 5)*
Creighton manufactures radiation-shielding glass panels. Suppose Creighton is considering spending the following amounts on a new TQM program:

Strength-testing one item from each batch of panels	$65,000
Training employees in TQM	30,000
Training suppliers in TQM	40,000
Identifying preferred suppliers who commit to on-time delivery of perfect quality materials	60,000

Creighton expects the new program to save costs through the following:

Avoid lost profits from lost sales due to disappointed customers	$90,000
Avoid rework and spoilage	55,000
Avoid inspection of raw materials	45,000
Avoid warranty costs	15,000

Requirements

1. Classify each item as a prevention cost, an appraisal cost, an internal failure cost, or an external failure cost.
2. Should Creighton implement the new quality program? Give your reason.

E5-34 **(Appendix) Record manufacturing cost using JIT costing** *(Learning Objective 6)*
Lancer produces flat-screen displays. Lancer uses a JIT costing system. One of the company's products has a standard direct materials cost of $8 per unit and a standard conversion cost of $32 per unit.

During 2007, Lancer produced 500,000 units and sold 480,000. It purchased $4,400,000 of direct materials and incurred actual conversion costs totaling $15,280,000.

Requirements

1. Prepare summary journal entries for 2007.

2. The January 1, 2007, balance of the Raw and In Process Inventory account was $80,000. Use a T-account to find the December 31, 2007, balance.

3. Use a T-account to determine whether conversion cost is overallocated or underallocated for the year. By how much? Give the journal entry to close the Conversion Cost account.

E5-35 **(Appendix) Record manufacturing costs using JIT costing** *(Learning Objective 6)*
Refer to the Mission Data Set. Veritek produces digital cameras. Suppose Veritek's standard cost per camera is $24 for materials and $32 for conversion costs. The following data apply to July production:

Materials purchased...	$6,500,000
Conversion costs incurred	$7,420,000
Number of cameras completed...........................	200,000 cameras
Number of cameras sold	196,000 cameras

Veritek uses JIT costing.

Requirements

1. Prepare summary journal entries for July, including the entry to close the Conversion Costs account.

2. The beginning balance of Finished Goods Inventory was $100,000. Use a T-account to find the ending balance of Finished Goods Inventory.

■ Problems (Problem Set A)

P5-36A **Implementation and analysis of departmental rates** *(Learning Objective 1)*
Quintana Products manufactures its products in two separate departments: machining and assembly. Total manufacturing overhead costs for the year are budgeted at $1 million. Of this amount, the Machining Department incurs $600,000 (primarily for machine operation and depreciation) while the Assembly Department incurs $400,000. Quintana Products estimates that it will incur 4,000 machines hours (all in the Machining Department) and 12,500 direct labor hours (2,500 in the Machining Department and 10,000 in the Assembly Department) during the year.

Quintana Products currently uses a plantwide overhead rate based on direct labor hours to allocate overhead. However, the company is considering refining its overhead allocation system by using departmental overhead rates. The Machining Department

continued . . .

would allocate its overhead using machine hours (MH), but the Assembly Department would allocate its overhead using direct labor (DL) hours.

The following chart shows the machine hours (MH) and direct labor (DL) hours incurred by Jobs 500 and 501 in each production department:

	Machining Department	Assembly Department
Job 500	3 MH	12 DL hours
	2 DL hours	
Job 501	6 MH	12 DL hours
	2 DL hours	

Both Jobs 500 and 501 used $1,000 of direct materials. Wages and benefits total $25 per direct labor hour. Quintana Products prices its products at 110% of total manufacturing costs.

1. Compute Quintana Products' current plantwide overhead rate.

2. Compute refined departmental overhead rates.

3. Which job (Job 500 or Job 501) uses more of the company's resources? Explain.

4. Compute the total amount of overhead allocated to each job if Quintana Products uses its current plantwide overhead rate.

5. Compute the total amount of overhead allocated to each job if Quintana Products uses departmental overhead rates.

6. Do both allocation systems accurately reflect the resources that each job used? Explain.

7. Compute the total manufacturing cost and sales price of each job using Quintana Products' current plantwide overhead rate.

8. Based on the current (plantwide) allocation system, how much profit did Quintana Products *think* it earned on each job? Based on the departmental overhead rates and the sales price determined in Requirement 7, how much profit did it *really* earn on each job?

9. Compare and comment on the results you obtained in Requirements 7 and 8.

P5-37A Use ABC to compute full product costs (*Learning Objective 2*)

Prescott's Office Department manufactures computer desks in its Topeka, Kansas, plant. The company uses activity-based costing to allocate all manufacturing conversion costs (direct labor and manufacturing overhead). Its activities and related data follow.

Activity	Budgeted Cost of Activity	Allocation Base	Cost Allocation Rate
Materials handling	$ 300,000	Number of parts	$ 0.60
Assembling	2,500,000	Direct labor hours	15.00
Painting	170,000	Number of painted desks	5.00

Prescott produced two styles of desks in March: the standard desk and unpainted desk. Data for each follow.

Product	Total Units Produced	Total Direct Materials Costs	Total Number of Parts	Total Assembling Direct Labor Hours
Standard desk	6,000	$96,000	120,000	6,000
Unpainted desk	1,500	21,000	30,000	900

Requirements

1. Compute the per-unit manufacturing product cost of standard desks and unpainted desks.

2. Premanufacturing activities, such as product design, were assigned to the standard desks at $5 each and to the unpainted desks at $3 each. Similar analyses were conducted of post manufacturing activities, such as distribution, marketing, and customer service. The post-manufacturing costs were $25 per standard and $22 per unpainted desk. Compute the full product costs per desk.

3. Which product costs are reported in the external financial statements? Which costs are used for management decision making? Explain the difference.

4. What price should Prescott's managers set for standard desks to earn a $42 profit per desk?

P5-38A **Comprehensive ABC implementation** *(Learning Objectives 2, 3)*
Gibson develops software for Internet applications. The market is very competitive, and Gibson's competitors continue to introduce new products at low prices. Gibson offers a wide variety of software—from simple programs that enable new users to create personal Web pages to complex commercial search engines. Like most software companies, Gibson's raw material costs are insignificant.

Gibson has just hired Tom Merrell, a recent graduate of State University's accounting program. Merrell asks Software Department Manager Jeff Gire to join him in a pilot activity-based costing study. Merrell and Gire identify the following activities, related costs, and cost-allocation bases:

Activity	Estimated Indirect Activity Costs	Allocation Base	Estimated Quantity of Allocation Base
Applications development	$1,600,000	New applications	4 new applications
Content production.................	2,400,000	Lines of code	12 million lines
Testing	288,000	Testing hours	1,800 testing hours
Total indirect costs.................	$4,288,000		

Gibson is planning to develop the following new applications:
- X-Page—software for developing personal Web pages
- X-Secure—commercial security and firewall software

continued . . .

X-Page requires 500,000 lines of code and 100 hours of testing, while X-Secure requires 7.5 million lines of code and 600 hours of testing. Gibson expects to produce and sell 30,000 units of X-Page and 10 units of X-Secure.

Requirements

1. Compute the cost allocation rate for each activity.

2. Use the activity-based cost allocation rates to compute the indirect cost of each unit of X-Page and X-Secure. (*Hint:* Compute the total activity costs allocated to each product line and then compute the cost per unit.)

3. Gibson's original single-allocation-based cost system allocated indirect costs to products at $100 per programmer hour. X-Page requires 10,000 programmer hours, while X-Secure requires 15,000 programmer hours. Compute the total indirect costs allocated to X-Page and X-Secure under the original system. Then, compute the indirect cost per unit for each product.

4. Compare the activity-based costs per unit to the costs from the simpler original system. How have the unit costs changed? Explain why the costs changed as they did.

5. What are the clues that Gibson's ABC system is likely to pass the cost-benefit test?

P5-39A JIT features and JIT costing (*Learning Objectives 4, 6*)

Sawyer produces sports watches. The company has a JIT production system and uses JIT costing.

Sawyer has two inventory accounts, Raw and In Process Inventory and Finished Goods Inventory. On August 1, 2007, the account balances were Raw and In Process Inventory, $12,000; Finished Goods Inventory, $2,000.

Sawyer's standard cost per watch is $55: $35 direct materials plus $20 conversion costs. The following data pertain to August manufacturing and sales:

Number of watches completed....	9,000 watches	Raw material purchased.......	$305,000
Number of watches sold..............	8,800 watches	Conversion costs incurred....	$116,000

Requirements

1. What are the major features of a JIT production system such as Sawyer's?

2. (Appendix) Prepare summary journal entries for August. Underallocated and overallocated conversion costs are closed to Cost of Goods Sold at the end of each month.

3. (Appendix) Use a T-account to determine the August 31, 2007, balance of Raw and In Process Inventory.

P5-40A Using ABC in conjunction with quality decisions (*Learning Objectives 2, 5*)

Zeke Toys is using a costs-of-quality approach to evaluate design engineering efforts for a new toy robot. The company's senior managers expect the engineering work to reduce appraisal, internal failure, and external failure activities. The predicted reductions in activities over the two-year life of the toy robot follow. Also shown is the cost allocation rate for each activity.

Activity	Predicted Reduction in Activity Units	Activity Cost Allocation Rate per Unit
Inspection of incoming materials..........	300	$20
Inspection of finished goods.................	300	30
Number of defective units discovered in-house...........................	3,200	15
Number of defective units discovered by customers....................	900	35
Lost sales to dissatisfied customers.......	300	55

Requirements

1. Calculate the predicted quality cost savings from the design engineering work.

2. Zeke Toys spent $60,000 on design engineering for the new toy robot. What is the net benefit of this "preventive" quality activity?

3. What major difficulty would Zeke Toys' managers have had in implementing this costs-of-quality approach? What alternative approach could they use to measure quality improvement?

■ Problems (Problem Set B)

P5-41B Implementation and analysis of departmental rates (Learning Objective 1)

Kane Garage Doors manufactures its products in two separate departments: Machining and Assembly. Total manufacturing overhead costs for the year are budgeted at $1,500,000. Of this amount, the Machining Department incurs $825,000 (primarily for machine operation and depreciation) while the Assembly Department incurs $675,000. Kane estimates that it will incur 6,600 machine hours (all in the Machining Department) and 20,000 direct labor hours (5,000 in the Machining Department and 15,000 in the Assembly Department) during the year.

Kane currently uses a plantwide overhead rate based on direct labor hours to allocate overhead. However, the company is considering refining its overhead allocation system by using departmental overhead rates. The Machining Department would allocate its overhead using machine hours (MH), but the Assembly Department would allocate its overhead using direct labor (DL) hours.

continued . . .

The following chart shows the machine hours (MH) and direct labor (DL) hours incurred by Jobs 400 and 401 in each production department:

	Machining Department	Assembly Department
Job 400	6 MH	10 DL hours
	3 DL hours	
Job 401	12 MH	10 DL hours
	3 DL hours	

Both Jobs 400 and 401 used $1,200 of direct materials. Wages and benefits total $30 per direct labor hour. Kane prices its products at 140% of total manufacturing costs.

1. Compute Kane's current plantwide overhead rate.
2. Compute refined departmental overhead rates.
3. Which job (Job 400 or Job 401) uses more of the company's resources? Explain.
4. Compute the total amount of overhead allocated to each job if Kane uses its current plantwide overhead rate.
5. Compute the total amount of overhead allocated to each job if Kane uses departmental overhead rates.
6. Do both allocation systems accurately reflect the resources that each job used? Explain.
7. Compute the total manufacturing cost and sales price of each job using Kane's current plantwide overhead rate.
8. Based on the current (plantwide) allocation system, how much profit did Kane *think* it earned on each job? Based on the departmental overhead rates and the sales price determined in Requirement 7, how much profit did it *really* earn on each job?
9. Compare and comment on the results you obtained in Requirements 7 and 8.

P5-42B Use ABC to compute full product costs *(Learning Objective 2)*

Cleary manufactures bookcases. The company uses an ABC system to allocate all manufacturing conversion costs (direct labor and manufacturing overhead). Cleary's activity areas and related data follow.

Activity	Budgeted Cost of Activity	Allocation Base	Cost Allocation Rate
Materials handling	$ 200,000	Number of parts	$ 0.80
Assembling	3,000,000	Direct labor hours	15.00
Finishing	160,000	Number of finished units	3.90

Cleary produced two styles of bookcases in April: the standard bookcase and an unfinished bookcase, which has fewer parts per bookcase and requires no finishing. The totals for quantities, direct materials costs, and other data follow.

Product	Total Units Produced	Total Direct Materials Costs	Total Number of Parts	Total Assembling Direct Labor Hours
Standard bookcase	3,000	$26,000	80,000	3,000
Unfinished bookcase	3,600	27,000	84,000	2,000

Requirements

1. Compute the manufacturing product cost per unit of each type of bookcase.

2. Suppose that premanufacturing activities, such as product design, were assigned to the standard bookcases at $4 each and to the unfinished bookcases at $3 each. Similar analyses were conducted of postmanufacturing activities, such as distribution, marketing, and customer service. The postmanufacturing costs were $20 per standard bookcase and $15 per unfinished bookcase. Compute the full product costs per unit.

3. Which product costs are reported in the external financial statements? Which costs are used for management decision making? Explain the difference.

4. What price should Cleary's managers set for unfinished bookcases to earn a unit profit of $16?

P5-43B Comprehensive ABC implementation *(Learning Objectives 2, 3)*

Farrington Pharmaceuticals manufactures an over-the-counter allergy medication called Breathe. Farrington Pharmaceuticals is trying to win market share from Sudafed and Tylenol. Farrington Pharmaceuticals has developed several different Breathe products tailored to specific markets. For example, the company sells large commercial containers of 1,000 capsules to health care facilities and travel packs of 20 capsules to shops in airports, train stations, and hotels.

Farrington Pharmaceuticals' controller, Sandra Dean, has just returned from a conference on ABC. She asks Keith Yeung, supervisor of the Breathe product line, to help her develop an ABC system. Dean and Yeung identify the following activities, related costs, and cost allocation bases:

Activity	Estimated Indirect Activity Costs	Allocation Base	Estimated Quantity of Allocation Base
Materials handling	$190,000	Kilos...........................	19,000 kilos
Packaging.............................	400,000	Machine hours	2,000 hours
Quality assurance.....................	112,500	Samples.....................	1,875 samples
Total indirect costs..................	$702,500		

continued . . .

The commercial-container Breathe product line had a total weight of 8,000 kilos, used 1,200 machine hours, and required 200 samples. The travel-pack line had a total weight of 6,000 kilos, used 400 machine hours, and required 300 samples. Farrington produced 2,500 commercial containers of Breathe and 50,000 travel packs.

Requirements

1. Compute the cost allocation rate for each activity.

2. Use the activity-based cost allocation rates to compute the indirect cost of each unit of the commercial containers and the travel packs. (*Hint:* Compute the total activity costs allocated to each product line and then compute the cost per unit.)

3. Farrington Pharmaceuticals' original single-allocation-based cost system allocated indirect costs to products at $300 per machine hour. Compute the total indirect costs allocated to the commercial containers and to the travel packs under the original system. Then, compute the indirect cost per unit for each product.

4. Compare the activity-based costs per unit to the costs from the original system. How have the unit costs changed? Explain why the costs changed as they did.

5. What clues indicate that Farrington Pharmaceuticals' ABC system is likely to pass the cost-benefit test?

P5-44B JIT features and JIT costing *(Learning Objectives 4, 6)*

Burke produces fleece jackets. The company uses JIT costing for its JIT production system.

Burke has two inventory accounts: Raw and In Process Inventory and Finished Goods Inventory. On October 1, 2007, the account balances were Raw and In Process Inventory, $6,000; Finished Goods Inventory, $1,000.

The standard cost of a jacket is $50: $15 direct materials plus $35 conversion costs. Data for October's activity follow.

Number of jackets completed.......	18,000	Direct materials purchased......	$265,000
Number of jackets sold	17,600	Conversion costs incurred	551,000

Requirements

1. What are the major features of a JIT production system such as Burke?

2. (Appendix) Prepare summary journal entries for October. Underallocated or overallocated conversion costs are closed to Cost of Goods Sold monthly.

3. (Appendix) Use a T-account to determine the October 31, 2007, balance of Raw and In Process Inventory.

P5-45B Using ABC in conjunction with quality decisions *(Learning Objectives 2, 5)*

Blue Sky is using a costs-of-quality approach to evaluate design engineering efforts for a new wakeboard. Blue Sky's senior managers expect the engineering work to reduce appraisal, internal failure, and external failure activities. The predicted reductions in activities over the two-year life of the wakeboards follow. Also shown are the cost allocation rates for each activity.

Activity	Predicted Reduction in Activity Units	Activity Cost Allocation Rate per Unit
Inspection of incoming materials.....................................	400	$ 40
Inspection of work in process...	400	20
Number of defective units discovered in-house...............	1,100	50
Number of defective units discovered by customers	300	70
Lost sales to dissatisfied customers................................	100	110

Requirements

1. Calculate the predicted quality cost savings from the design engineering work.

2. Blue Sky spent $106,000 on design engineering for the new wakeboard. What is the net benefit of this "preventive" quality activity?

3. What major difficulty would Blue Sky's managers have in implementing this costs-of-quality approach? What alternative approach could they use to measure quality improvement?

Apply Your Knowledge

▪ Decision Cases

Case 5-46. Comprehensive ABC *(Learning Objectives 2, 3)*

Axis Systems specializes in servers for work-group, e-commerce, and ERP applications. The company's original job cost system has two direct cost categories: direct materials and direct labor. Overhead is allocated to jobs at the single rate of $22 per direct labor hour.

A task force headed by Axis's CFO recently designed an ABC system with four activities. The ABC system retains the current system's two direct cost categories. Thus, it budgets only overhead costs for each activity. Pertinent data follow.

Activity	Allocation Base	Cost Allocation Rate
Materials handling	Number of parts	$ 0.85
Machine setup	Number of setups	500.00
Assembling	Assembling hours	80.00
Shipping	Number of shipments	1,500.00

Axis Systems has been awarded two new contracts, which will be produced as Job A and Job B. Budget data relating to the contracts follow.

	Job A	Job B
Number of parts..	15,000	2,000
Number of setups.......................................	6	4
Number of assembling hours...................	1,500	200
Number of shipments.............................	1	1
Total direct labor hours	8,000	600
Number of output units	100	10
Direct materials cost...............................	$210,000	$30,000
Direct labor cost.......................................	$160,000	$12,000

Requirements

1. Compute the product cost per unit for each job using the original costing system (with two direct cost categories and a single overhead allocation rate).
2. Suppose Axis Systems adopts the ABC system. Compute the product cost per unit for each job using ABC.
3. Which costing system more accurately assigns to jobs the costs of the resources consumed to produce them? Explain.
4. A dependable company has offered to produce both jobs for Axis for $5,400 per output unit. Axis may outsource (buy from the outside company) Job A only, Job B only, or both jobs. Which course of action will Axis's managers take if they base their decision on (a) the original system? (b) ABC system costs? Which course of action will yield more income? Explain.

Case 5-47. Continues Case 5-46: meeting target costs

To remain competitive, Axis Systems' management believes the company must produce Job B–type servers (from Decision Case 5-46) at a target cost of $5,400. Axis Systems has just joined a B2B e-market site that management believes will enable the firm to cut direct material costs by 10%. Axis's management also believes that a value-engineering team can reduce assembly time.

Requirement

Compute the assembly cost savings per Job B–type server required to meet the $5,400 target cost. (*Hint:* Begin by calculating the direct material, direct labor, and allocated activity cost per server.)

■ Ethical Issue

Issue 5-48. ABC and ethical dilemma *(Learning Objective 2, 3)*

Mary Lipe is assistant controller at Stone Packaging, a manufacturer of cardboard boxes and other packaging materials. Lipe has just returned from a packaging industry conference on ABC. She realizes that ABC may help Stone meet its goal of reducing costs by 5% over each of the next three years.

Stone Packaging's Order Department is a likely candidate for ABC. While orders are entered into a computer that updates the accounting records, clerks manually check customers' credit history and hand-deliver orders to shipping. This process occurs whether the sales order is for a dozen specialty boxes worth $80 or 10,000 basic boxes worth $8,000.

Lipe believes that identifying the cost of processing a sales order would justify (1) further computerizing the order process and (2) changing the way the company processes small orders. However, the significant cost savings would arise from elimination of two positions in the Order Department. The company's sales order clerks have been with the company many years. Lipe is uncomfortable with the prospect of proposing a change that will likely result in terminating these employees.

Requirement

Use the IMA *Statement of Ethical Professional Practice* (Exhibit 1-6) to consider Lipe's responsibility when cost comes at the expense of employees' jobs.

6 Cost Behavior

igh above the rushing waters and mist of Niagara Falls, hundreds of tourists from around the world return to the 512-room Embassy Suites to enjoy a complimentary afternoon refreshment hour, relax in the hotel's pool and spa, and rest in luxurious suites overlooking the Falls. A similar scene occurs across the street at the Sheraton, Marriott, and DoubleTree hotels, as well as at thousands of other travel destinations around the world.

How do hotel managers set prices high enough to cover costs and earn a profit, but low enough to fill most rooms each night? How do they plan for higher occupancy during the busy summer months and lower occupancy during the off-season? They know how their costs behave. Some of the hotel's costs, such as the complimentary morning breakfast and afternoon refreshment hour, vary with the number of

guests staying each night. These *variable* costs rise and fall with the number of guests. But most of the hotel's costs, such as depreciation on the building and furniture, stay the same whether 50 or 2,000 guests stay each night. These costs are *fixed*. Most hotel costs are fixed, so the extra costs to serve each additional guest are low. Once these costs are covered, the revenue from extra guests goes toward profits. ■

Learning Objectives

1 Describe key characteristics and graphs of various cost behaviors

2 Use cost equations to express and predict costs

3 Use account analysis and scatter plots to analyze cost behavior

4 Use the high-low method to analyze cost behavior

5 Use regression analysis to analyze cost behavior

6 Prepare contribution margin income statements for service firms and merchandising firms

7 Use variable costing to prepare contribution margin income statements for manufacturers (Appendix)

Up to this point, we have focused our attention on product costing. We have discussed how managers use job costing, process costing, and ABC to figure out the cost of making a product or providing a service. Product costs are useful for valuing inventory and calculating cost of goods sold. Product costs are also used as a starting place for setting sales prices. However, product costs are not very helpful for planning and some decision making because they contain a mixture of fixed and variable costs. Some of these costs change as volume changes, but other costs do not. To make good decisions and accurate projections, managers must understand **cost behavior**—that is, how costs change as volume changes. In this chapter, we discuss typical cost behaviors and explain methods managers use to determine how their costs behave. The Appendix discusses an alternative product costing system based on cost behavior that manufacturers can use for internal decision making. In the following chapters, we show how managers use cost behavior for planning and decision making.

Cost Behavior: How Do Changes in Volume Affect Costs?

1 Describe key characteristics and graphs of various cost behaviors

The Embassy Suites at Niagara Falls has 512 guest suites that can accommodate between 512 and 2,048 people (four to a room) per night. This means that if every hotel room is booked (100% occupancy rate), the hotel can accommodate between 3,584 and 14,336 guests per week. How do managers plan for such a wide range of volume? They use historic occupancy patterns to determine the most likely range of volume. The room occupancy rate (percentage of rooms booked) varies depending on the season and day of the week. In addition to understanding occupancy patterns, managers must know how changes in volume (number of guests) affect their costs. We first consider three of the most common cost behaviors:

1. **Variable costs** are costs that change in total in direct proportion to changes in volume. For Embassy Suites, complimentary morning breakfast, afternoon refreshments, and in-room toiletries (soap, shampoo, and lotion) are variable costs because these costs increase in total with the number of guests.

2. **Fixed costs** are costs that do not change in total despite wide changes in volume. For Embassy Suites, property taxes, insurance, and depreciation on the hotel building and furnishings are fixed costs that will be the same regardless of the number of hotel guests.

3. **Mixed costs** are costs that change in total, but *not* in direct proportion to changes in volume. Mixed costs have both variable and fixed components. For Embassy Suites, utilities (electricity, gas, water) are mixed costs. Some utility costs will be incurred no matter how many guests stay the night. However, utility costs will also rise as the number of guests turning up the heat or air conditioning, taking showers, and using freshly laundered linens rises.

Variable Costs

Every guest at Embassy Suites is entitled to a complimentary morning breakfast and afternoon refreshment hour (drinks and snacks). In addition, guests receive complimentary toiletries, including shampoo, soap, lotion, and mouthwash, that they typically use or take with them. Let's assume that these toiletries cost the hotel $3 per guest and that the breakfast and refreshment hour costs the hotel $10 per guest. Exhibit 6-1 graphs Embassy Suite's $3-per-guest toiletry cost and the $10-per-guest breakfast and refreshment hour cost. The vertical axis (y-axis) shows total variable costs, while the horizontal axis (x-axis) shows total volume of activity (thousands of guests, in this case).

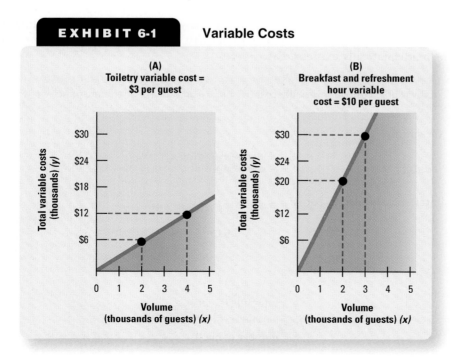

EXHIBIT 6-1 **Variable Costs**

Look at the total variable toiletry costs in Exhibit 6-1(a). If there are no guests, Embassy Suites doesn't incur any costs for the toiletries, so the total variable cost line begins at the bottom left corner. This point is called the *origin*, and it represents zero volume and zero cost. Total variable cost graphs always begin at the origin. The *slope* of the total variable cost line is the *variable cost per unit of activity*. In Exhibit 6-1(a), the slope of the toiletry variable cost line is $3 because the hotel spends an additional $3 on toiletries for each additional guest. If the hotel serves 2,000 guests, it will spend a total of $6,000 on complimentary toiletries. Doubling the number of guests to 4,000 likewise doubles the total variable cost to $12,000. This example illustrates several important points about variable costs—total variable costs change in *direct proportion* to changes in volume. If volume of activity doubles, total variable costs double. If volume triples, total variable costs triple.

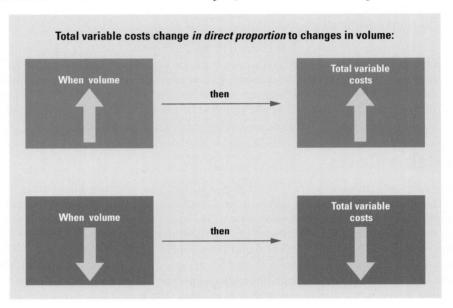

Total variable costs change *in direct proportion* to changes in volume:

When volume ↑   then →   Total variable costs ↑

When volume ↓   then →   Total variable costs ↓

2   Use cost equations to express and predict costs

Managers do not need to rely on graphs to predict total variable costs at different volumes of activity. They can use a **cost equation**, a mathematical equation for a straight line, to express how a cost behaves. On cost graphs like the ones pictured in Exhibit 6-1, the vertical (y-axis) always shows total costs while the horizontal axis (x-axis) shows volume of activity. Therefore, any variable cost line can be mathematically expressed as:

Total variable cost (y) = variable cost per unit of activity (v) × volume of activity (x)

Or simply:

$$y = vx$$

The hotel's total toiletry cost is:

$$y = \$3x$$

where:

y = total toiletry cost
$3 = variable cost per guest
x = number of guests

We can confirm the observations made in Exhibit 6-1(a) using the cost equation. If the hotel has no guests ($x = 0$), total toiletry costs are zero, as shown in the graph. If the hotel has 2,000 guests, total toiletry costs will be:

$$y = \$3 \text{ per guest} \times 2,000 \text{ guests}$$
$$= \$6,000$$

If the hotel has 4,000 guests, managers will expect total toiletry costs to be:

$$y = \$3 \text{ per guest} \times 4,000 \text{ guests}$$
$$= \$12,000$$

Stop & Think...

If the hotel serves 3,467 guests next week, how much will the hotel spend on complimentary toiletries?

Answer: *You would have a hard time answering this question by simply looking at the graph in Exhibit 6-1(a), but cost equations can be used for any volume. We "plug in" the expected volume to our variable cost equation as follows:*

$$y = \$3 \text{ per guest} \times 3,467 \text{ guests}$$
$$= \$10,401$$

Management expects complimentary toiletries next week to cost about $10,401.

Now, look at Exhibit 6-1(b), the total variable costs for the complimentary breakfast and refreshment hour. The slope of the line is $10, representing the cost of providing each guest with the complimentary breakfast and refreshments. We can express the total breakfast and refreshment hour cost as:

$$y = \$10x$$

where:

$$y = \text{total breakfast and refreshment hour cost}$$
$$\$10 = \text{variable cost per guest}$$
$$x = \text{number of guests}$$

The total cost of the breakfast and refreshment hour for 2,000 guests is:

$$y = \$10 \text{ per guest} \times 2,000 \text{ guests}$$
$$= \$20,000$$

This is much higher than the $6,000 toiletry cost for 2,000 guests, so the slope of the line is much steeper than it was for the toiletries. *The higher the variable cost per unit of activity (v), the steeper the slope of the total variable cost line.*

Both graphs in Exhibit 6-1 show how *total* variable costs vary with the number of guests. *But note that the variable cost per guest (v) remains constant in each of the graphs.* That is, Embassy Suites incurs $3 in toiletry costs and $10 in breakfast and refreshment hour costs for each guest no matter how many guests the hotel serves. Some key points to remember about variable costs are shown in Exhibit 6-2.

EXHIBIT 6-2   **Key Characteristics of Variable Costs**

- *Total* variable costs change in *direct proportion* to changes in volume
- The *variable cost per unit of activity* (v) remains constant and is the slope of the variable cost line
- Total variable cost graphs always begin at the origin (if volume is zero, total variable costs are zero)
- Total variable costs can be expressed as:

$$y = vx,$$

where:

y = total variable cost

v = variable cost per unit of activity

x = volume of activity

Fixed Costs

In contrast to total variable costs, total fixed costs do *not* change over wide ranges of volume. Many of Embassy Suites' costs are fixed because the hotel continues to operate daily regardless of the number of guests. Some of the hotel's fixed costs include:

- Property taxes and insurance.
- Depreciation and maintenance on parking ramp, hotel, and room furnishings.
- Pool, fitness room, and spa upkeep.
- Cable TV and wireless Internet access for all rooms.
- Salaries of hotel department managers (housekeeping, food service, special events, etc.).

Most of these costs are **committed fixed costs,** meaning that the hotel is locked in to these costs because of previous management decisions. For example, as soon as the hotel was built, management became locked in to a certain level of property taxes and depreciation, simply because of the location and size of the hotel, and management's choice of furnishings and amenities (pool, fitness room, restaurant, and so forth). Management has little or no control over these committed fixed costs in the short run.

However, the hotel also incurs **discretionary fixed costs,** such as advertising expenses, that are a result of annual management decisions. Companies have more control over discretionary fixed costs because the companies can adjust the costs as necessary in the short run.

Suppose Embassy Suites incurs $100,000 of fixed costs each week. In Exhibit 6-3, the vertical axis (y-axis) shows total fixed costs while the horizontal axis (x-axis) plots volume of activity (thousands of guests). The graph shows total fixed costs as a *flat line* that intersects the y-axis at $100,000 (this is known as the vertical intercept) because the hotel will incur the same $100,000 of fixed costs regardless of the number of guests that stay during the week.

EXHIBIT 6-3	Fixed Costs

Fixed cost = $100,000

The cost equation for a fixed cost is simply:

Total fixed costs (y) = fixed amount over a period of time (f)

Or simply:

$$y = f$$

Embassy Suites' *weekly* fixed cost equation is:

$$y = \$100,000$$

where:

y = total fixed cost per week

In contrast to the *total fixed costs* shown in Exhibit 6-3, the *fixed cost per guest* depends on the number of guests. If the hotel serves 2,000 guests during the week, the fixed cost per guest is:

$$\$100,000 \div 2,000 \text{ guests} = \$50/\text{guest}$$

If the number of guests *doubles* to 4,000, the fixed cost per guest is *cut in half*:

$$\$100,000 \div 4,000 \text{ guests} = \$25/\text{guest}$$

The fixed cost per guest is *inversely proportional* to the number of guests. When volume *increases*, the fixed cost per guest *decreases*. When volume *decreases*, the fixed cost per guest *increases*.

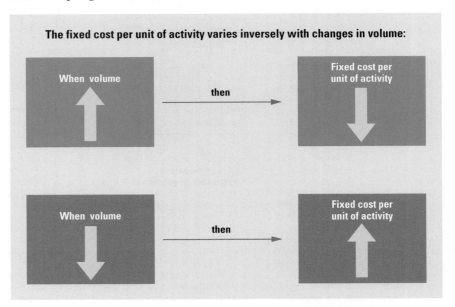

The fixed cost per unit of activity varies inversely with changes in volume:

| When volume ↑ | then → | Fixed cost per unit of activity ↓ |

| When volume ↓ | then → | Fixed cost per unit of activity ↑ |

Key points to remember about fixed costs appear in Exhibit 6-4.

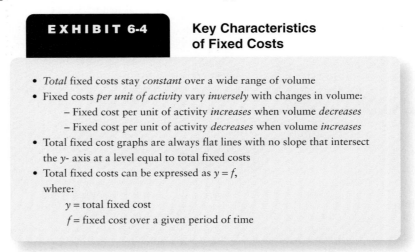

EXHIBIT 6-4   **Key Characteristics of Fixed Costs**

- *Total* fixed costs stay *constant* over a wide range of volume
- Fixed costs *per unit of activity* vary *inversely* with changes in volume:
    - Fixed cost per unit of activity *increases* when volume *decreases*
    - Fixed cost per unit of activity *decreases* when volume *increases*
- Total fixed cost graphs are always flat lines with no slope that intersect the *y*-axis at a level equal to total fixed costs
- Total fixed costs can be expressed as $y = f$,
    where:
    y = total fixed cost
    f = fixed cost over a given period of time

Stop & Think...

Compute the (a) total fixed cost and (b) fixed cost per guest if the hotel reaches full occupancy of 14,336 guests next week (512 rooms booked with four people per room). Compare the fixed cost per guest at full occupancy to the fixed cost per guest when only 2,000 guests stay during the week. Explain why hotels and other businesses like to operate near 100% capacity.

Answer:

a. *Total fixed costs do not react to wide changes in volume; therefore, total fixed costs will still be $100,000.*

b. *Fixed costs per unit decrease as volume increases. At full occupancy, the fixed cost per guest is:*

$100,000 ÷ 14,336 guests = $6.98 (rounded) per guest

When only 2,000 guests stay, the fixed cost per guest is much higher ($50 = $100,000 ÷ 2,000 guests). Businesses like to operate near full capacity because it lowers their fixed cost per unit. A lower cost per unit gives businesses the flexibility to lower their prices to compete more effectively.

Mixed Costs

Mixed costs contain both variable and fixed cost components. Embassy Suites' utilities are mixed costs because the hotel requires a certain amount of utilities just to operate. However, the more guests at the hotel, the more water, electricity, and gas required. Exhibit 6-5 illustrates mixed costs.

For example, let's assume that utilities for the common areas of the hotel and unoccupied rooms cost $2,000 per week. In addition, these costs increase by $8 per guest as they cool or heat their rooms, take showers, turn on the TV and lights, and use freshly laundered sheets and towels.

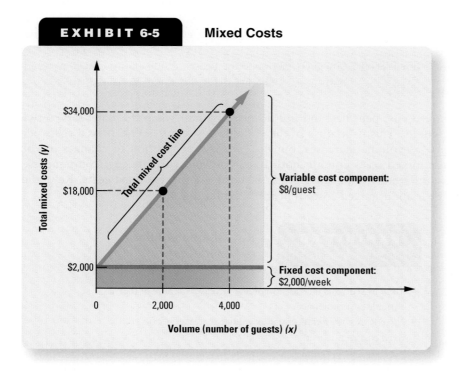

EXHIBIT 6-5   **Mixed Costs**

Notice the two components—variable and fixed—of the mixed cost in Exhibit 6-5. Similar to a variable cost, the total mixed cost line increases as the volume of activity increases. However, *the line does **not** begin at the origin*. Rather, it intersects the y-axis at a level equal to the fixed cost component. Even if no guests stay this week, the hotel will still incur $2,000 of utilities cost.

Managers can once again use a cost equation to express the mixed cost line so that they can predict total mixed costs at different volumes. The mixed cost equation simply *combines* the variable cost and fixed cost equations:

Total mixed costs = Variable cost component + Fixed cost component

$$y \quad = \quad vx \quad + \quad f$$

Embassy Suites' weekly utilities cost equation is:

$$y = \$8x + \$2{,}000$$

where:

$$y = \text{total utilities cost per week}$$
$$x = \text{number of guests}$$

If the hotel serves 2,000 guests this week, they expect utilities to cost:

$$y = (\$8 \text{ per guest} \times 2{,}000 \text{ guests}) + \$2{,}000$$
$$= \$18{,}000$$

If the hotel serves 4,000 guests this week, they expect utilities to cost:

$$y = (\$8 \text{ per guest} \times 4{,}000 \text{ guests}) + \$2{,}000$$
$$= \$34{,}000$$

Total mixed costs increase as volume increases, *but **not** in direct proportion to changes in volume*. The total mixed cost did *not* double when volume doubled. This is because of the fixed cost component. Additionally, consider the mixed cost *per guest*:

If the hotel serves 2,000 guests: $18,000 total cost ÷ 2,000 guests = $9.00 per guest
If the hotel serves 4,000 guests: $34,000 total cost ÷ 4,000 guests = $8.50 per guest

The mixed cost per guest did *not* decrease by half when the hotel served twice as many guests. This is because of the variable cost component. Mixed costs per unit decrease as volume increases, but ***not in direct proportion*** to changes in volume. Because mixed costs contain both fixed cost and variable cost components, they behave differently than purely variable costs and purely fixed costs. Key points to remember about mixed costs appear in Exhibit 6-6.

EXHIBIT 6-6   Key Characteristics of Mixed Costs

- *Total* mixed costs increase as volume increases because of the variable cost component
- Mixed costs *per unit* decrease as volume increases because of the fixed cost component
- Total mixed cost graphs slope upward but do *not* begin at the origin— they intersect the y-axis at the level of fixed costs
- Total mixed costs can be expressed as a *combination* of the variable and fixed cost equations:

  Total mixed costs = variable cost component + fixed cost component
  $$y = vx + f$$
  where:
  y = total mixed cost
  v = variable cost per unit of activity (slope)
  x = volume of activity
  f = fixed cost over a given period of time (vertical intercept)

Stop & Think...

If your cell phone plan charges $10 per month plus $0.15 for each minute you talk, how could you express the monthly cell phone bill as a cost equation? How much will your cell phone bill be if you (a) talk 100 minutes this month or (b) talk 200 minutes this month? If you double your talk time from 100 to 200 minutes, does your total cell phone bill double? Explain.

Answer: *The cost equation for the monthly cell phone bill is:*

$$y = \$0.15x + \$10$$

where:

y = total cell phone bill for the month
x = number of minutes talked

a.   At 100 minutes, the total cost is $25 [= ($0.15 per minute × 100 minutes) + $10]
b.   At 200 minutes, the total cost is $40 [= ($0.15 per minute × 200 minutes) + $10]

The cell phone bill does not double when talk time doubles. The variable portion of the bill doubles from $15 ($0.15 × 100 minutes) to $30 ($0.15 × 200 minutes), but the fixed portion of the bill stays constant ($10).

Relevant Range

Managers always need to keep their **relevant range** in mind when predicting total costs. The relevant range is the band of volume where the following remain constant:

- *Total fixed costs*
- The *variable cost per unit*

A change in cost behavior means a change to a different relevant range.

Let's consider how the concept of relevant range applies to Embassy Suites. As shown in Exhibit 6-3, the hotel's current fixed costs are $100,000 per week. However, since the hotel's popularity continues to grow, room occupancy rates continue to increase. As a result, guests are becoming dissatisfied with the amount of time they have to wait for breakfast tables and elevators. To increase customer satisfaction, management is deciding whether to expand the breakfast facilities and add a 30-passenger elevator to its existing bank of elevators. This expansion, if carried out, will increase the hotel's fixed costs to a new level. Exhibit 6-7 illustrates the hotel's current relevant range and future potential relevant range for fixed costs.

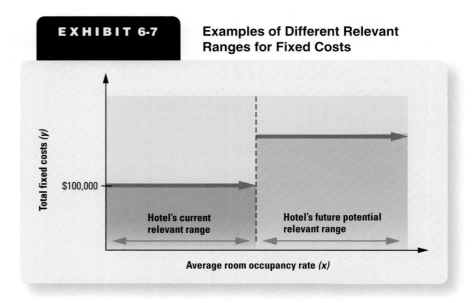

EXHIBIT 6-7

Examples of Different Relevant Ranges for Fixed Costs

Does the concept of relevant range apply only to fixed costs? No, it also applies to variable costs. As shown in Exhibit 6-1, the hotel's current variable cost for toiletries is $3 per guest. However, as room occupancy rates continue to grow, management hopes to negotiate greater volume discounts on the toiletries from its suppliers. These volume discounts will decrease the variable toiletries cost per guest (for example, down to $2.75 per guest). Exhibit 6-8 illustrates the hotel's current relevant range and future potential relevant range for variable toiletries costs.

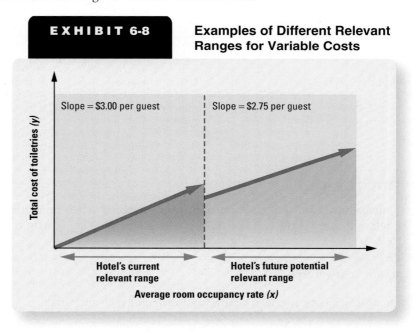

EXHIBIT 6-8

Examples of Different Relevant Ranges for Variable Costs

Why is the concept of relevant range important? Managers can predict costs accurately only if they use cost information for the appropriate relevant range. For example, think about your cell phone plan. Many cell phone plans offer a large block of "free" minutes for a set fee each month. If the user exceeds the allotted minutes, the cell phone company charges an additional per-minute fee. Exhibit 6-9 shows a cell phone plan in which the first 1,000 minutes of call time each month cost $50. After the 1,000 minutes are used, the user must pay an additional $0.30 per minute for every minute of call time. This cell phone plan has two relevant ranges. The first relevant range extends from 0 to 1,000 minutes. In this range, the $50 fee behaves strictly as a

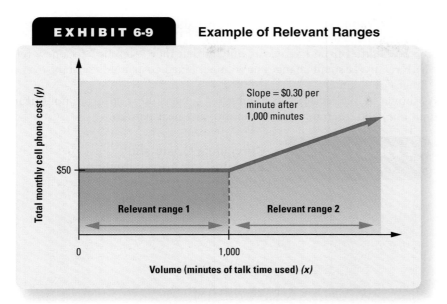

EXHIBIT 6-9   **Example of Relevant Ranges**

Slope = $0.30 per minute after 1,000 minutes

$50

Relevant range 1   Relevant range 2

0   1,000

Total monthly cell phone cost (y)

Volume (minutes of talk time used) *(x)*

fixed cost. You could use 0, 100, or 975 minutes and you would still pay a flat $50 fee that month. The second relevant range starts at 1,001 minutes and extends indefinitely. In this relevant range, the cost is mixed: $50 plus $0.30 per minute. To forecast your cell phone bill each month, you need to know in which relevant range you plan to operate. The same holds true for businesses: To accurately predict costs, they need to know the relevant range in which they plan to operate.

Other Cost Behaviors

While many business costs behave as variable, fixed, or mixed costs, some costs do not neatly fit these patterns. We'll briefly describe other cost behaviors you may encounter.

Step costs resemble stair steps: They are fixed over a small range of activity and then jump up to a new fixed level with moderate changes in volume. Hotels, restaurants, hospitals, and educational institutions typically experience step costs. For example, states usually require day care centers to limit the caregiver-to-child ratio to 1:7—that is, there must be one caregiver for every seven children. As shown in Exhibit 6-10, a day care center that takes on an eighth child must incur the cost of employing another caregiver. The new caregiver can watch the eighth through fourteenth child enrolled at the day care center. If the day care center takes on a fifteenth child, management will once again need to hire another caregiver, costing another $15,000 in salary. The same step cost patterns occur with hotels

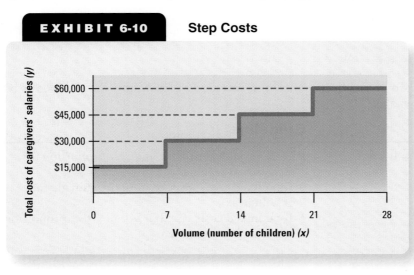

EXHIBIT 6-10   **Step Costs**

$60,000

$45,000

$30,000

$15,000

0   7   14   21   28

Total cost of caregivers' salaries (y)

Volume (number of children) *(x)*

(maid-to-room ratio), restaurants (server-to-table ratio), hospitals (nurse-to-bed ratio), and schools (teacher-to-student ratio).

Step costs differ from fixed costs only in that they "step up" to a new relevant range with relatively small changes in volume. Fixed costs hold constant over much larger ranges of volume.

As shown by the red lines in Exhibit 6-11, **curvilinear costs** are not linear (not a straight line) and, therefore, do not fit into any neat pattern.

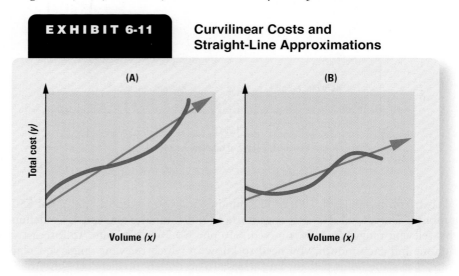

EXHIBIT 6-11   **Curvilinear Costs and Straight-Line Approximations**

As shown by the straight green arrows in Exhibit 6-11, businesses usually *approximate* these types of costs as mixed costs. Sometimes managers also approximate step costs the same way: They simply draw a straight mixed cost line through the steps. If managers need more accurate predictions, they can simply break these types of costs into smaller relevant ranges and make their predictions based on the particular relevant range. For example, the day care center may want to predict total caregiver salaries if it enrolls 26 children. The manager knows this enrollment falls into the relevant range of 21 to 28 children, where she needs to employ four caregivers. She can then predict total caregiver salaries to be $60,000 (4 caregivers × $15,000 salary per caregiver).

We have just described the most typical cost behaviors. In the next part of the chapter, we will discuss methods managers use for determining how their costs behave.

Decision Guidelines

COST BEHAVIOR

Suppose you manage a local fitness club. To be an effective manager, you need to know how the club's costs behave. Here are some decisions you will need to make.

Decision	Guideline
How can you tell if a *total* cost is variable, fixed, or mixed?	• Total variable costs rise in *direct proportion* to increases in volume. • Total fixed costs stay *constant* over a wide range of volumes. • Total mixed costs rise, but *not* in direct proportion to increases in volume.

Decision	Guideline
How can you tell if a *per-unit* cost is variable, fixed, or mixed?	• On a per-unit basis, variable costs stay constant. • On a per-unit basis, fixed costs decrease in proportion to increases in volume (that is to say they are inversely proportional). • On a per-unit basis, mixed costs decrease, but not in direct proportion to increases in volume.
How can you tell by looking at a graph if a cost is variable, fixed, or mixed?	• Variable cost lines slope upward and begin at the origin. • Fixed cost lines are flat (no slope) and intersect the y-axis at a level equal to total fixed costs (this is known as the vertical intercept). • Mixed cost lines slope upward but do *not* begin at the origin. They intersect the y-axis at a level equal to their fixed cost component.
How can you mathematically express different cost behaviors?	• Cost equations mathematically express cost behavior using the equation for a straight line: $$y = vx + f$$ where: y = total cost v = variable cost per unit of activity (slope) x = volume of activity f = fixed cost (the vertical intercept) • For a variable cost, f is zero, leaving: $$y = vx$$ • For a fixed cost, v is zero, leaving: $$y = f$$ • Because a mixed cost has both a fixed cost component and a variable cost component, its cost equation is f: $$y = vx + f$$

Summary Problem 1

The previous manager of Fitness-for-Life started the following schedule, but left before completing it. He wasn't sure but thought the club's fixed operating costs were $10,000 per month and the variable operating costs were $1 per member. The club's existing facilities could serve up to 750 members per month.

Requirements

1. Complete the following schedule for different levels of monthly membership assuming the previous manager's cost behavior estimates are accurate:

Monthly Operating Costs	100 Members	500 Members	750 Members
Total variable costs			
Total fixed costs			
Total operating costs			
Variable cost per member			
Fixed cost per member			
Average cost per member			

2. As the manager of the fitness club, why shouldn't you use the average cost per member to predict total costs at different levels of membership?

Solution

Requirement 1

As volume increases, fixed costs stay constant in total but decrease on a per-unit basis. As volume increases, variable costs stay constant on a per-unit basis but increase in total in direct proportion to increases in volume:

	100 Members	500 Members	750 Members
Total variable costs	$ 100	$ 500	$ 750
Total fixed costs	$10,000	$10,000	$10,000
Total operating costs	$10,100	$10,500	$10,750
Variable cost per member	$ 1.00	$ 1.00	$ 1.00
Fixed cost per member	$100.00	$ 20.00	$ 13.33
Average cost per member	$101.00	$ 21.00	$ 14.33

Requirement 2

The average cost per member should not be used to predict total costs at different volumes of membership because it changes as volume changes. The average cost per member decreases as volume increases due to the fixed component of the club's operating costs. Managers should base cost predictions on cost behavior patterns, not on the average cost per member.

Determining Cost Behavior

In real life, managers need to figure out how their costs behave before they can make predictions and good business decisions. In this section, we discuss the most common ways of determining cost behavior.

3 Use account analysis and scatter plots to analyze cost behavior

Account Analysis

When performing **account analysis**, managers use their judgment to classify each general ledger account as a variable, fixed, or mixed cost. For example, by looking at invoices from his supplier, the hotel manager knows that every guest packet of toiletries costs $3. Because guests use or take these toiletries, the total toiletries cost rises in direct proportion to the number of guests. These facts allow the manager to classify the complimentary toiletries expense account as a variable cost.

Likewise, the hotel manager uses account analysis to determine how the depreciation expense accounts behave. Because the hotel uses straight-line depreciation on the parking ramp, building, and furnishings, the manager would classify the depreciation expense accounts as fixed costs. Thus, the manager can use his knowledge of cost behavior and his judgment to classify many accounts as variable or fixed.

However, the manager also knows that many of the hotel's costs, such as utilities, are mixed. But how does he figure out the portion of the mixed cost that is fixed and the portion that is variable? In other words, how does the manager know from looking at the monthly utility bills that the hotel's utilities cost about $2,000 per week plus $8 more for every guest? Managers figure this out using one of the following methods:

- High-low method
- Regression analysis

Both methods require historical information on costs and volume.

Let's assume that the hotel has the information shown in Exhibit 6-12 about last year's guest volume and utility costs.

EXHIBIT 6-12	**Historical Information on Guest Volume and Utility Costs**

Month	Guest Volume (x)	Utility Costs (y)
January	13,250	$114,000
February	15,200	136,000
March	17,600	135,000
April	18,300	157,000
May	22,900	195,400
June	24,600	207,800
July	25,200	209,600
August	24,900	208,300
September	22,600	196,000
October	20,800	176,400
November	18,300	173,600
December	15,420	142,000

As you can see, the hotel's business is seasonal. More people visit in the summer. However, special events such as the annual Festival of Lights, business conferences, and the nearby casino attract people to the hotel throughout the year. Managers need this type of historical information to determine how much of a mixed cost is fixed and how much is variable. When using historical data to determine a cost's behavior, the first thing managers should do is create a scatter plot of the data. Scatter plots can be done by hand, but they are simpler to create using Microsoft Excel (see the "Technology Makes It Simple" feature).

A scatter plot, which graphs the historical cost data on the y-axis and volume data on the x-axis, helps managers visually determine how strong of a relationship there is between the cost and the volume of the chosen activity base (number of guests, in our example). If there is a fairly strong relationship between the cost and volume, the data points will fall in a linear pattern, meaning they will resemble something close to a straight line. However, if there is little or no relationship between the cost and volume, the data points will appear almost random.

Exhibit 6-13 shows a scatter plot of the data in Exhibit 6-12. Notice how the data points fall in a pattern that resembles something *close* to a straight line. This shows us that there is a strong relationship between the number of guests and the hotel's utility costs. In other words, the number of guests could be considered a cost driver of the hotel's utilities (recall from our discussion of ABC in Chapter 5 that cost drivers are activities that cause costs to be incurred). On the other hand, if there were a *weaker* relationship between the number of guests and the utility costs, the data points would not fall in such a tight pattern. They would be more loosely scattered, but still in a semilinear pattern. If there were *no* relationship between the number of guests and the utility costs, the data points would appear almost random.

EXHIBIT 6-13 **Scatter Plot of Monthly Data**

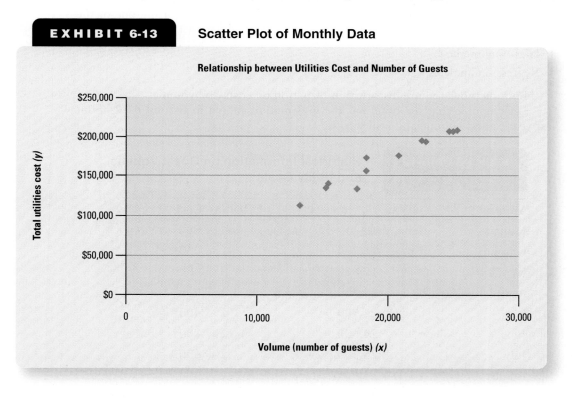

Why is this important? If the data points suggest a fairly weak relationship between the cost and the volume of the chosen activity, any cost equation based on that data will not be very useful for predicting future costs. If this is the case, the manager should consider using a different activity for modeling cost behavior. For example, many hotels use "occupancy rate" (the percentage of rooms rented) rather than number of guests as a basis for explaining and predicting variable and mixed costs.

Scatter plots are also very useful because they allow managers to identify **outliers,** or abnormal data points. Outliers are data points that do not fall in the same general pattern as the other data points. If a manager sees a potential outlier in the data, he should first determine whether the data is correct. Perhaps a clerical error was made when gathering or inputting the data. However, if the data is correct, the manager may need to consider whether he will include that data point when going forward with the high-low method or regression analysis, which will be explained in later sections.

In summary, a scatter plot should be used to establish that a relationship exists between the costs and volume and to screen for potential outliers. The next step is to determine the cost behavior that best describes the historical data points.

Take a moment and pencil in the line that you think best represents the data points in Exhibit 6-13. Where does your line intersect the y-axis? At the origin or above it? In other words, does the utilities cost appear to be a purely variable cost or a mixed cost? If it's a mixed cost, what portion of it is fixed?

Instead of guessing, managers can use either (1) the high-low method or (2) regression analysis to estimate the fixed and the variable components of a mixed cost. The biggest difference between these methods is that the high-low method *uses only two* of the historical data points for this estimate, whereas regression analysis uses *all* of the historical data points. Therefore, regression analysis is theoretically the better of the two methods.

Before continuing, check out the "Technology Makes It Simple" feature. It shows you just how easy it is to make a scatter plot using Microsoft Excel. Two different features are presented: one for Excel 2003 and one for Excel 2007 (on the next page).

Technology
makes it simple   ▶ **Excel 2003**

Scatter Plots

1. In an Excel spreadsheet, type your data as pictured in Exhibit 6-12. Put the volume data in one column and the associated cost data in the next column. Save your spreadsheet because you will probably use this data again.

2. Click on the "Chart Wizard" icon on the tool bar (it looks like a mini bar graph).

3. Follow the four step-by-step instructions:

  i. Select the "XY Scatter" as the type of graph you want. Click "Next."

  ii. Highlight (or type in) the entire data range. Make sure the cost data is displayed on the vertical y-axis and the volume data is displayed on the horizontal x-axis. Click "Next."

  iii. Type in a title for the graph and labels for each axis. Click "Next."

  iv. Finish by selecting where you want the graph displayed (in a separate worksheet or on the same worksheet as your data). Click "Next."

4. That's all. If you want to change the way your graph looks, right-click (use the right button on your mouse) on the graph to check out customizing options. For example, if your data consist of large numbers, the graph may not automatically start at the origin. If you want to see the origin on the graph, simply right-click on either axis line to get the "format axis" menu; then under the "scale" option, set the minimum value to "0." You can also right-click on specific data points to add trend lines and other options. Play around with it and see what happens.

Scatter Plots

1. *In an Excel 2007 spreadsheet, type in your data as pictured in Exhibit 6-12. Put the volume data in one column and the associated cost data in the next column.*

2. *Highlight all of the volume and cost data with your cursor.*

3. *Click on the "Insert" tab on the menu bar and then choose "Scatter" as the chart type. Next, click the plain scatter plot (without any lines). You'll see the scatter plot on your screen. Make sure the volume data is on the x-axis and the cost data is on the y-axis.*

4. *To add labels for the scatter plot and titles for each axis, choose "Layout 1" from the "Chart Layout" menu tab. Customize the titles and labels to reflect your data set.*

5. *If you want to change the way your graph looks, right-click on the graph to check out customizing options. For example, if your data consists of large numbers, the graph may not automatically start at the origin. If you want to see the origin on the graph, right-click on either axis (where the number values are) and choose "Format Axis." Then, fix the minimum value at zero.*

High-Low Method

4 Use the high-low method to analyze cost behavior

The **high-low method** is an easy way to estimate the variable and fixed cost components of a mixed cost. The high-low method basically fits a mixed cost line through the highest and lowest volume data points, as shown in Exhibit 6-14. Hence, the name *high-low*. The high-low method produces the cost equation describing this mixed cost line.

EXHIBIT 6-14   **Mixed Cost Line Using High-Low Method**

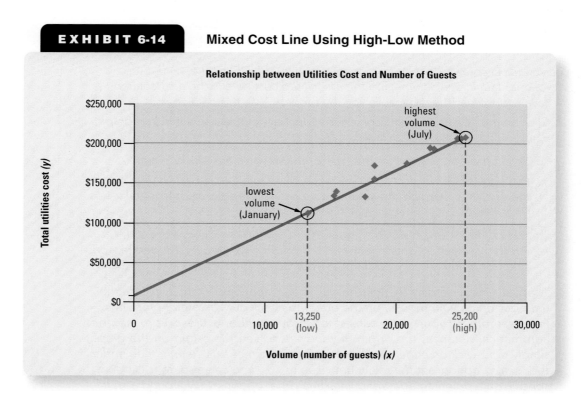

To use the high-low method, we must first identify the months with the highest and lowest volume of activity. Looking at Exhibit 6-12, we see that the hotel served the *most* guests in July and the *fewest* guests in January. *Therefore, we use the data from only these two months in our analysis. We ignore data from all other months.* Even if a month other than July had the highest utility cost, we would still use July. Why? Because we choose the "high" data point based on the month with the highest volume of activity (number of guests)—not the highest cost. We choose the "low" data point in a similar fashion.

STEP 1: The first step is to find *the slope of the mixed cost line* that connects the January and July data points. The slope is the variable cost per unit of activity. We can determine the slope of a line as "rise over run." The *rise* is simply the difference in cost between the high and low data points (July and January in our case), while the *run* is the difference in *volume* between the high and low data points:

$$\text{Slope} = \text{Variable cost per unit of activity } (v) = \frac{\text{Rise}}{\text{Run}} = \frac{\text{Change in cost}}{\text{Change in volume}} = \frac{y\,(\text{high}) - y\,(\text{low})}{x\,(\text{high}) - x\,(\text{low})}$$

Using the data from July (as our high) and January (as our low), we calculate the slope as:

$$\frac{(\$209{,}600 - \$114{,}000)}{(25{,}200 \text{ guests} - 13{,}250 \text{ guests})} = \$8 \text{ per guest}$$

The slope of the mixed cost line, or variable cost per unit of activity, is $8 per guest.

STEP 2: The second step is to find the vertical intercept—the place where the line connecting the January and July data points intersects the y-axis. This is the fixed cost component of the mixed cost. Using a mixed-cost equation, we plug in the slope found in Step 1 and the volume and cost data from *either* our high or low month:

$$\text{Total mixed costs} = \text{Variable cost component} + \text{Fixed cost component}$$
$$y = vx + f$$

Using July's data:

$$\$209{,}600 = (\$8 \text{ per guest} \times 25{,}200 \text{ guests}) + f$$

Solving for f:

$$f = \$8{,}000$$

Or we can use January's data to reach the same conclusion:

$$y = vx + f$$
$$\$114{,}000 = (\$8 \text{ per guest} \times 13{,}250 \text{ guests}) + f$$

Solving for f:

$$f = \$8{,}000$$

Thus, the fixed cost component is $8,000 per month.

STEP 3: Using the variable cost per unit of activity found in Step 1 ($8 per guest) and the fixed cost component found in Step 2 ($8,000), write the equation representing the costs' behavior. This is the equation for the line connecting the January and July data points on our graph.

$$y = \$8x + \$8,000$$

where:

y = total *monthly* utilities cost
x = number of guests

Recall that this equation was based on *monthly* utility bills and *monthly* guest volume. In our discussion of the hotel's mixed costs in the first half of the chapter, we said that the mixed utilities cost was $8 per guest plus $2,000 per *week*. The manager had used the high-low method; but because there are about four weeks in a month, the hotel manager approximated the fixed costs to be about $2,000 *per week* ($8,000 per month ÷ approximately 4 weeks per month).

One major drawback of the high-low method is that it uses only two data points: January and July. Because we ignored every other month, the line might not be representative of those months. In this case, the high-low line is representative of the other data points, but in other situations, it may not be. Despite this drawback, the high-low method is quick and easy to use.

Regression Analysis

5 Use regression analysis to analyze cost behavior

Regression analysis is a statistical procedure for determining the line and cost equation that best fits the data by using *all of the data points, not just the high-volume and low-volume data points*. In fact, some refer to regression analysis as "the line of best fit." Therefore, it is usually more accurate than the high-low method. A statistic (called the R-square) generated by regression analysis also tells us *how well* the line fits the data points. Regression analysis is tedious to complete by hand but simple to do using Microsoft Excel (see the "Technology Makes It Simple" feature on pages 350 and 351). Many graphing calculators also perform regression analysis.

Regression analysis using Microsoft Excel gives us the output shown in Exhibit 6-15. It looks complicated, but for our purposes, we need to consider only three highlighted pieces of information from the output:

1. Intercept coefficient (this refers to the vertical intercept) = 14,538.05

2. X Variable 1 coefficient (this refers to the slope) = 7.85 (rounded)

3. The R-square value (the "goodness-of-fit" statistic) = 0.94726

Let's look at each piece of information, starting with the highlighted information at the bottom of the output:

1. The "Intercept coefficient" is the vertical intercept of the mixed cost line. It's the fixed cost component of the mixed cost. Regression analysis tells us that the fixed component of the monthly utility bill is $14,538 (rounded). Why is this different from the $8,000 fixed component we found using the high-low method? It's because regression analysis considers *every* data point, not just the high- and low-volume data points, when forming the best fitting line.

2. The "X Variable 1 coefficient" is the line's slope, or our variable cost per guest. Regression analysis tells us that the hotel spends an extra $7.85 on utilities for every guest it serves. This is slightly lower than the $8 per guest amount we found using the high-low method.

EXHIBIT 6-15	**Output of Microsoft Excel Regression Analysis**

Regression Statistics

Multiple R	0.973273
R Square	0.94726
Adjusted R Square	0.941986
Standard Error	8053.744
Observations	12

ANOVA

	df	SS	MS	F	Significance F
Regression	1	11650074512	1.17E + 10	179.6110363	1.02696E-07
Residual	10	648627988.2	64862799		
Total	11	12298702500			

	Coefficients	Standard Error	t Stat	P-value	Lower 95%	Upper 95%	Lower 95.0%	Upper 95.0%
Intercept	14538.05	11898.3624	1.221853	0.249783701	-11973.15763	41049.25	-11973.16	41049.25
X Variable 1	7.849766	0.585720166	13.4019	1.02696E-07	6.5446997	9.154831	6.5447	9.154831

Using the regression output, we can write the utilities *monthly* cost equation as:

$$y = \$7.85x + \$14{,}538$$

where:

y = total *monthly* utilities cost
x = number of guests

3. Now, let's look at the R-square statistic highlighted near the top of Exhibit 6-15. The R-square statistic is often referred to as a "goodness-of-fit" statistic because it tells us how well the regression line fits the data points. The R-square can range in value from zero to one, as shown in Exhibit 6-16. If there were no relationship between the number of guests and the hotel's utility costs, the data points would be scattered randomly (rather than being in a linear pattern) and the R-square would be close to zero. If there were a *perfect* relationship between the number of guests and the hotel's utility cost, a *perfectly* straight line would run through *every* data point and the R-square would be 1.00. In our case, the R-square of 0.947 means that the regression line fits the data quite well (it's very close to 1.00). In other words, the data points *almost* fall in a straight line (as you can see in Exhibit 6-13).

The R-square provides managers with very helpful information. The higher the R-square, the stronger the relationship between cost and volume. The stronger the relationship, the more confidence the manager would have in using the cost equation to predict costs at different volumes within the same relevant range. As a rule of thumb, an R-square over .80 generally indicates that the cost equation is very reliable for predicting costs at other volumes within the relevant range. An R-square between .50 and .80 means that the manager should use the

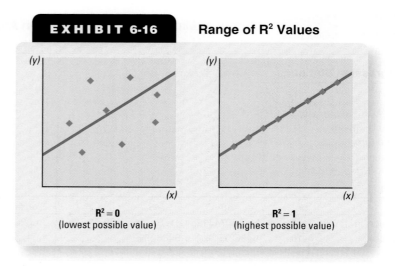

EXHIBIT 6-16 **Range of R² Values**

$R^2 = 0$
(lowest possible value)

$R^2 = 1$
(highest possible value)

cost equation with caution. However, if the R-square is fairly low (for example, less than .50), the manager should try using a different activity base (for example, room occupancy rate) for its cost analysis because the current measure of volume is only weakly related to the costs.

Regression analysis can also help managers implement ABC. Recall from Chapter 5 that managers must choose a cost allocation base for every activity cost pool. The cost allocation base should be the primary cost driver of the costs in that pool. Management will use logic to come up with a short list of potential cost drivers for each activity cost pool. Then, management can run a regression analysis for each potential cost driver to see how strongly related it is to the activity costs in the pool. Managers compare the R-squares from each regression to see which one is highest. The regression with the highest R-square identifies the primary cost driver.

Technology
makes it simple

▶ **Excel 2003**

Regression Analysis

1. *If you created a scatter plot you have already done this first step. In an Excel 2003 spreadsheet, type in your data as shown in Exhibit 6-12. Put the volume data in one column and the cost data in the next column.*

2. *Click on "Tools" on the menu bar.*

3. *Next, click on "Data Analysis" on the pull-down menu. If you don't see it, simply add it to your menu by clicking on "Add-Ins" and check the box labeled "Analysis ToolPak."*

4. *Select "Regression" from the list of analysis tools. Click "OK."*

5. *Follow the two instructions on the screen:*

   i. *Highlight (or type in) the y-axis data range (this is your cost data).*

   ii. *Highlight (or type in) the x-axis data range (this is your volume data).*

   iii *Click "OK."*

6. *That's all. Excel gives you the output shown in Exhibit 6-15.*

| **Technology** | ▶ **Excel 2007** |
| **makes it simple** | |

Regression Analysis

1. *If you created a scatter plot, you have already done this first step. In an Excel spreadsheet, type in your data as pictured in Exhibit 6-12. Put the volume data in one column and the associated cost data in the next column.*
2. *Click on the "Data" tab on the menu bar.*
3. *Next, click on "Data Analysis." If you don't see it on your menu bar, follow the directions for add-ins given below before continuing.*
4. *From the list of data analysis tools, select "Regression," then "OK."*
5. *Follow the two instructions on the screen:*
    - i. *Highlight (or type in) the y-axis data range (this is your cost data).*
    - ii. *Highlight (or type in) the x-axis data range (this is your volume data).*
    - iii. *Click "OK."*
6. *That's all. Excel gives you the output shown in Exhibit 6-15.*

DIRECTIONS FOR ADD-INs: It's easy and free to add the "Data Analysis Toolpak" if it's not already on your menu bar. You'll need to add it only once, and then it will always be on your menu bar. Simply follow these instructions:

1. *While in Excel, click the Microsoft Office button (the colorful button in the upper left-hand corner) and then click on the "Excel Options" box shown at the bottom.*
2. *Click "Add-Ins."*
3. *In the "Manage" box at the bottom of the screen, select "Excel Add-ins" and click "GO."*
4. *In the "Add-Ins available" box, select the "Analysis Toolpak" check box and then click "OK."*
5. *If asked, click "Yes" to install.*

Using the Results of the High-Low Method and Regression Analysis to Predict Costs

Managers use the results of the high-low method or regression analysis to plan for costs at different volumes. Managers should make predictions only for volumes falling in the same relevant range. In other words, they shouldn't use the cost equation to predict costs at a volume that is vastly different from the volumes used to generate the cost equation. Of the two methods, the regression analysis equation usually gives better predictions. Why? Because the regression analysis equation uses more historical data. However, remember that both methods just provide *estimates*. Let's assume that management wants to predict total monthly utility costs if the hotel serves 23,000 guests one month.

Using the high-low method cost equation:	$y = (\$8 \text{ per guest} \times 23{,}000 \text{ guests}) + \$8{,}000$
	$y = \$192{,}000$
Using the regression analysis cost equation:	$y = (\$7.85 \text{ per guest} \times 23{,}000 \text{ guests}) + \$14{,}538$
	$y = \$195{,}088$

The predictions are similar in this situation. However, that won't always be the case, especially if the high- and low-volume data points aren't representative of the other data points.

Data Concerns

Cost equations are only as good as the data on which they are based. For example, if the hotel's utility bills are seasonal, management may want to develop separate cost equations for each season. For example, they might develop a winter utility bill cost equation using historical data from only the winter months. They would do likewise for every other season. Inflation can also affect predictions. If inflation is running rampant, managers should adjust projected costs by the inflation rate. Even if the economy has generally low inflation, certain industries may be experiencing large price changes. For example, the 2005 hurricanes resulted in above-average increases in building supply and fuel costs.

Another cause for concern is outliers, or abnormal data points. Outliers can distort the results of the high-low method and regression analysis. Recall that the high-low method uses only two data points—the data points associated with the highest and lowest volumes of activity. If either of these points is an outlier, the resulting line and cost equation will be skewed. Because regression analysis uses all data points, any outlier in the data will affect the resulting line and cost equation. To find outliers, management should first plot the data like we did in Exhibit 6-13. None of the data points in Exhibit 6-13 appear to be outliers since they all fall in the same general pattern. However, if we saw a data point that was atypical of the others, we would investigate it to see if it was accurate, then possibly exclude it from further analysis—in other words, we would probably not use it in either the high-low method or regression analysis.

The Contribution Margin Income Statement: A Summary of Cost Behavior

6 Prepare contribution margin income statements for service firms and merchandising firms

Almost all businesses, including Embassy Suites, have some fixed costs, some variable costs, and some mixed costs. Companies use account analysis, the high-low method, or regression analysis (or a combination of the three methods) to determine how their costs behave. They may analyze cost behavior on an account-by-account basis, as we did in the previous examples (they prepare separate cost equations for toiletry costs, complimentary breakfast and refreshment costs, utilities costs, and so forth). Or if they do not need so much detail, companies may develop *one* mixed cost equation for *all* operating costs lumped together. Once they have cost behavior information, how do companies communicate it to their managers so that the managers can use it for planning and decision making?

Unfortunately, traditional income statements do not provide managers with any cost behavior information. Traditional income statements are organized by *function*, not by cost behavior. Costs related to the production or purchases function of the value chain appear as cost of goods sold, above the gross profit line, when the manufactured products or merchandise is sold. All other costs (related to all other value-chain functions) appear as operating expenses (period costs), below the gross profit line.

Exhibit 6-17 illustrates this *functional* separation of costs for a retailer specializing in fitness equipment. Notice how the traditional format does not provide managers with much information, if any, on cost behavior. The cost of goods sold is a variable cost for a retailer, but contains a mixture of variable and fixed production costs for manufacturers. Recall from Chapter 2 that manufacturers classify direct materials and direct labor as variable costs, but treat manufacturing overhead as a mixed cost. Likewise, traditional income statements do not distinguish fixed operating costs from variable operating costs. While external users such as investors and creditors find traditional income statements useful, these statements are not very useful for internal managers who need cost behavior information for planning and decision making.

EXHIBIT 6-17	**Traditional Income Statement of a Retailer**

AAA FITNESS EQUIPMENT
Income Statement
Month Ended July 31

Sales revenue	$ 52,500
Less: Cost of goods sold	(27,300)
Gross profit	25,200
Less: Operating expenses	(14,600)
Operating income	$ 10,600

To provide managers with cost behavior information, companies often prepare **contribution margin income statements**. Contribution margin income statements can only be used internally. GAAP does not allow companies to use the contribution margin format for external reporting purposes. Contribution margin income statements organize costs by *behavior* rather than by *function*. Therefore, managers find contribution margin income statements more helpful than traditional income statements for planning and decision making. The contribution margin income statement (shown in Exhibit 6-18) presents *all variable costs*—whether relating to the merchandise sold or selling and administrative activities—*above* the contribution margin line. The contribution margin income statement shows *all fixed costs*—whether relating to the merchandise sold or selling and administrative activities—*below* the contribution margin line. The contribution margin, not the gross profit, is the dividing line. The **contribution margin** is equal to sales revenue minus variable expenses.

EXHIBIT 6-18	**Contribution Margin Income Statement**

AAA FITNESS EQUIPMENT
Contribution Margin Income Statement
Month Ended July 31

Sales revenue	$ 52,500
Less: Variable expenses	(30,900)
Contribution margin	21,600
Less: Fixed expenses	(11,000)
Operating income	$ 10,600

Managers can use contribution margin income statements to predict how changes in volume will affect operating income. Changes in volume will affect total sales revenue and total variable costs (and, therefore, the contribution margin). However, changes in volume will *not* affect fixed costs within the same relevant range. Therefore, the contribution margin income statement distinguishes the financial figures that *will* change from those that *will not* change in response to fluctuations in volume. Traditional income statements do not make this distinction.

In the next chapter, we will discuss many ways managers use the contribution margin to answer business questions, including how changes in volume and costs affect the firm's profits.

The appendix in this chapter is devoted to variable costing. Variable costing is an optional product costing system that *manufacturers* can use for internal purposes. Variable costing results in contribution margin income statements for manufacturers.

Decision Guidelines

COST BEHAVIOR

As the manager of a local fitness club, Fitness-for-Life, you'll want to plan for operating costs at various levels of membership. Before you can make forecasts, you'll need to make some of the following decisions.

Decision	Guidelines
How can I sort out the fixed and the variable components of mixed costs?	• Managers typically use the high-low method or regression analysis. • The high-low method is fast and easy but uses only two data points to form the cost equation and, therefore, may not be very indicative of the costs' true behavior. • Regression analysis uses every data point provided to determine the cost equation that best fits the data. It is simple to do with Excel, but tedious to do by hand.
I've used the high-low method to formulate a cost equation. Can I tell how well the cost equation fits the data?	The only way to determine how well the high-low cost equation fits the data is by (1) plotting the data, (2) drawing a line through the data points associated with the highest and lowest volume, and (3) "visually inspecting" the resulting graph to see if the line is representative of the other plotted data points.
I've used regression analysis to formulate a cost equation. Can I tell how well the cost equation fits the data?	The R-square is a "goodness-of-fit" statistic that tells how well the regression analysis cost equation fits the data. The R-square ranges from 0 to 1, with 1 being a perfect fit. When the R-square is high, the cost equation should render fairly accurate predictions.
Do I need to be concerned about anything before using the high-low method or regression analysis?	Cost equations are only as good as the data on which they are based. Managers should plot the historical data to see if a relationship between cost and volume exists. In addition, scatter plots help managers identify outliers. Managers should remove outliers before further analysis. Managers should also adjust cost equations for seasonal data, inflation, and price changes.
Can I present the club's financial statements in a manner that will help with planning and decision making?	Managers often use contribution margin income statements for internal planning and decision making. Contribution margin income statements organize costs by *behavior* (fixed versus variable) rather than by *function* (product versus period).

Summary Problem 2

As the new manager of a local fitness club, Fitness-for-Life, you have been studying the club's financial data. You would like to determine how the club's costs behave in order to make accurate predictions for next year. Here is information from the last six months:

Month	Club Membership (number of members)	Total Operating Costs	Operating Costs per Member
July	450	$ 8,900	$19.78
August	480	$ 9,800	$20.42
September	500	$10,100	$20.20
October	550	$10,150	$18.45
November	560	$10,500	$18.75
December	525	$10,200	$19.43

Requirements

1. By looking at the "Total Operating Costs" and the "Operating Costs per Member," can you tell whether the club's operating costs are variable, fixed, or mixed? Explain your answer.

2. Use the high-low method to determine the club's monthly operating cost equation.

3. Using your answer from Requirement 2, predict total monthly operating costs if the club has 600 members.

4. Can you predict total monthly operating costs if the club has 3,000 members? Explain your answer.

5. Prepare the club's traditional income statement and its contribution margin income statement for the month of July. Assume that your cost equation from Requirement 2 accurately describes the club's cost behavior. The club charges members $30 per month for unlimited access to its facilities.

6. *Optional:* Perform regression analysis using Microsoft Excel. What is the monthly operating cost equation? What is the R-square? Why is the cost equation different from that in Requirement 2?

Solution

Requirement 1
By looking at "Total Operating Costs," we can see that the club's operating costs are not purely fixed; otherwise, total costs would remain constant. Operating costs appear to be either variable or mixed because they increase in total as the number of members increases. By looking at the "Operating Costs per Member," we can see that the operating costs aren't purely variable; otherwise, the "per-member" cost would remain constant. Therefore, the club's operating costs are mixed.

Requirement 2
Use the high-low method to determine the club's operating cost equation:

continued . . .

STEP 1: The highest volume month is November, and the lowest volume month is July. Therefore, we use *only these two months* to determine the cost equation. The first step is to find the variable cost per unit of activity, which is the slope of the line connecting the November and July data points:

$$\frac{\text{Rise}}{\text{Run}} = \frac{\text{Change in } y}{\text{Change in } x} = \frac{y \text{ (high)} - y \text{ (low)}}{x \text{ (high)} - x \text{ (low)}} = \frac{(\$10,500 - \$8,900)}{(560 - 450 \text{ members})} = \$14.55 \text{ per member (rounded)}$$

STEP 2: The second step is to find the fixed cost component (vertical intercept) by plugging in the slope and either July or November data to a mixed cost equation:

$$y = vx + f$$

Using November data:

$$\$10,500 = (\$14.55/\text{member} \times 560 \text{ guests}) + f$$

Solving for f:

$$f = \$2,352$$

Or we can use July data to reach the same conclusion:

$$\$8,900 = (\$14.55/\text{members} \times 450 \text{ guests}) + f$$

Solving for f:

$$f = \$2,352 \text{ (rounded)}$$

STEP 3: Write the monthly operating cost equation:

$$y = \$14.55x + \$2,352$$

where:

$$x = \text{number of members}$$
$$y = \text{total monthly operating costs}$$

Requirement 3
Predict total monthly operating costs when volume reaches 600 members:

$$y = (\$14.55 \times 600) + \$2,352$$
$$y = \$11,082$$

Requirement 4
Our current data and cost equation are based on 450 to 560 members. If membership reaches 3,000, operating costs could behave much differently. That volume falls outside our current relevant range.

Requirement 5

The club had 450 members in July and total operating costs of $8,900. Thus, its traditional income statement is:

FITNESS-FOR-LIFE
Income Statement
Month Ended July 31

Club membership revenue (450 × $30)	$13,500
Less: Operating expenses (given)	(8,900)
Operating income	$ 4,600

To prepare the club's contribution margin income statement, we need to know how much of the total $8,900 operating costs is fixed and how much is variable. If the cost equation from Requirement 2 accurately reflects the club's cost behavior, fixed costs will be $2,352 and variable costs will be $6,548 (= $14.55 × 450). The 3 contribution margin income statement would look like this:

FITNESS-FOR-LIFE
Contribution Margin Income Statement
Month Ended July 31

Club membership revenue (450 × $30)	$13,500
Less: Variable expenses (450 × $14.55)	(6,548)
Contribution margin	6,952
Less: Fixed expenses	(2,352)
Operating income	$ 4,600

Requirement 6

Regression analysis using Microsoft Excel results in the following cost equation and R-square:

$$y = \$11.80x + \$3,912$$

where:

x = number of members
y = total monthly operating costs

R-square = .8007

The regression analysis cost equation uses all of the data points, not just the data from November and July. Therefore, it better represents all of the data. The high R-square means that the regression line fits the data well and predictions based on this cost equation should be quite accurate.

Appendix 6A

Variable Costing and Absorption Costing

7 Use variable costing to prepare contribution margin income statements for manufacturers

Once they know how their costs behave, managers of *manufacturing* companies can use **variable costing**, which assigns only *variable* manufacturing costs (direct materials, direct labor, and variable manufacturing overhead) to products. They use variable costing to prepare the contribution margin income statements discussed in the preceding section. Managers can use variable costing *and* contribution margin income statements only for *internal management decisions*.

GAAP *requires* managers to use absorption costing, which results in traditional income statements, for *external reporting*. Under **absorption costing**, products "absorb" fixed manufacturing costs as well as variable manufacturing costs. In other words, both fixed and variable manufacturing costs are treated as inventoriable product costs. Supporters of absorption costing argue that companies cannot produce products without fixed manufacturing costs, so these costs are an important part of the inventoriable product costs. In all preceding chapters, we have treated fixed manufacturing costs as an inventoriable product cost; therefore, we have been using absorption costing.

Variable costing assigns only variable manufacturing costs to products. Variable costing treats fixed manufacturing costs as period costs (so they are expensed in the period in which they are incurred). Supporters of variable costing argue that fixed manufacturing costs (such as depreciation on the plant) provide the capacity to produce during a period. Because the company incurs these fixed expenses whether or not it produces any products, they are period costs, not product costs.

All other costs are treated the same way under both absorption and variable costing:

- Variable manufacturing costs are inventoriable products costs.
- All nonmanufacturing costs are period costs.

Exhibit 6-19 summarizes the differences between variable and absorption costing.

Variable Versus Absorption Costing: Sportade

To see how absorption costing and variable costing differ, let's consider the following example. Sportade incurred the following costs for its powdered sports beverage mix in March 2007:

Direct materials cost per case	$ 6.00
Direct labor cost per case	3.00
Variable manufacturing overhead cost per case	2.00
Sales commission per case	2.50
Total fixed manufacturing overhead expenses	50,000
Total fixed marketing and administrative expenses	25,000

EXHIBIT 6-19

Differences Between Absorption Costing and Variable Costing

	Absorption Costing	Variable Costing
Product Costs (Capitalized as Inventory until expensed as Cost of Goods Sold)	Direct materials Direct labor Variable manufacturing overhead Fixed manufacturing overhead	Direct materials Direct labor Variable manufacturing overhead
Period Costs (Expensed in periods incurred)	Variable nonmanufacturing costs Fixed nonmanufacturing costs	Fixed manufacturing overhead Variable nonmanufacturing costs Fixed nonmanufacturing costs
Focus	External reporting—required by GAAP	Internal reporting only
Income Statement Format	Conventional income statement, as in Chapters 1–5	Contribution margin statement

Sportade produced 10,000 cases of powdered mix as planned but sold only 8,000 cases at a price of $30 per case. There were no beginning inventories, so Sportade has 2,000 cases of powdered mix in ending finished goods inventory (10,000 cases produced – 8,000 cases sold).

What is Sportade's inventoriable product cost per case under absorption costing and variable costing?

	Absorption Costing	Variable Costing
Direct materials...	$ 6.00	$ 6.00
Direct labor...	3.00	3.00
Variable manufacturing overhead	2.00	2.00
Fixed manufacturing overhead...........................	5.00*	
Total cost per case	$16.00	$11.00

*$\dfrac{\$50{,}000 \text{ fixed manufacturing overhead}}{10{,}000 \text{ cases}} = \$5 \text{ per case}$

The only difference between absorption and variable costing is that fixed manufacturing overhead is a product cost under absorption costing but a period cost under variable costing. That is why the cost per case is $5 higher under absorption costing (total cost of $16) than under variable costing ($11).

Exhibit 6-20 shows that absorption costing results in a traditional income statement.

EXHIBIT 6-20 **Absorption Costing Income Statement**

SPORTADE
Income Statement (Absorption Costing)
Month Ended March 31, 2007

Sales revenue (8,000 × $30)		$240,000
Deduct: Cost of goods sold:		
Beginning finished goods inventory	$ 0	
Cost of goods manufactured (10,000 × $16)	160,000	
Cost of goods available for sale	160,000	
Ending finished goods inventory (2,000 × $16)	(32,000)	
Cost of goods sold		(128,000)
Gross profit		112,000
Deduct: Operating expenses [(8,000 × $2.50) + $25,000]		(45,000)
Operating income		$ 67,000

Notice that:

- The absorption costing income statement in Exhibit 6-20 groups costs by *function*: manufacturing costs versus nonmanufacturing costs. *We subtract manufacturing costs of goods sold **before** gross profit, whereas we subtract all nonmanufacturing costs (operating expenses) **after** gross profit.*

- Total cost of goods manufactured is the number of cases *produced* multiplied by the $16 total manufacturing cost per case. In contrast, total variable marketing expense (for sales commissions) equals the number of cases *sold* times the sales commission per case.

- Absorption costing holds back as an asset (ending inventory) $32,000 of the manufacturing cost that Sportade incurred this period (2,000 cases × $16 total manufacturing cost per case). This $32,000 is not expensed in the month when Sportade incurred these manufacturing costs. Instead, these manufacturing costs are held back as the asset *Inventory* until the related 2,000 cases are sold.

- The absorption costing income statement does not distinguish between variable and fixed costs. This limits the statement's usefulness for managerial decisions. If the CEO of Sportade wants to predict how a 10% increase in sales will affect operating income, the absorption costing income statement is of little help: It does not separate variable costs (which increase with sales) from fixed costs (which will not change).

The limitations of absorption costing–based income statements lead many manufacturing managers to prefer variable costing and contribution margin income statements *for internal reporting and decision making*. Exhibit 6-21 recasts the Sportade information using variable costing and a contribution margin income statement that groups costs by behavior—variable versus fixed.

Compare the general format of the absorption costing income statement in Exhibit 6-20 with the variable costing contribution margin income statement in Exhibit 6-21. The conventional absorption costing income statement subtracts cost of goods sold (including both variable and fixed manufacturing costs) from sales to obtain *gross profit*. In contrast, the contribution margin income statement subtracts all variable costs (both manufacturing and nonmanufacturing) to obtain *contribution margin*. The following chart highlights the differences between gross profit and contribution margin:

Conventional Income Statement	Contribution Margin Income Statement
Sales revenue	Sales revenue
deduct Cost of Goods Sold:	deduct Variable Expenses:
Variable manufacturing cost of goods sold	Variable manufacturing cost of goods sold
Fixed manufacturing cost of goods sold	Variable nonmanufacturing expenses
= Gross profit	= Contribution margin

The two major differences are as follows:

1. Fixed manufacturing cost of goods sold is subtracted from sales to compute gross profit, but not to compute contribution margin.

2. Variable nonmanufacturing expenses are subtracted from sales to calculate contribution margin, but not to compute gross profit.

Now, let's look more closely at the variable costing contribution margin income statement in Exhibit 6-21. First, notice that the details of the (variable) cost of goods sold computation in Exhibit 6-21 parallel those in the absorption costing income statement *except* that we use the $11 variable costing product cost per case rather than the $16 absorption cost per case. Second, variable costing holds back as an asset (ending inventory) only $22,000 (2,000 cases × $11 variable manufacturing cost per case). Third, the variable costing contribution margin income statement subtracts *all* of the variable costs (*both* the $88,000 manufacturing variable cost of goods sold *and* the $20,000 variable sales commission expense) from sales to get contribution margin. Finally, we subtract fixed costs (both the $50,000 fixed manufacturing overhead and the $25,000 fixed marketing and administrative costs) from contribution margin to get operating income. To summarize, the variable costing contribution margin income statement subtracts all variable costs *before* contribution margin and all fixed costs *after* contribution margin.

EXHIBIT 6-21   **Variable Costing Contribution Margin Income Statement**

SPORTADE
Contribution Margin Income Statement (Variable Costing)
Month Ended March 31, 2007

Sales revenue (8,000 × $30)..		$240,000
Deduct: Variable expenses:		
Variable cost of goods sold:		
Beginning finished goods inventory..........................	$ 0	
Variable cost of goods manufactured (10,000 × $11)	110,000	
Variable cost of goods available for sale	110,000	
Ending finished goods inventory (2,000 × $11).....	(22,000)	
Variable cost of goods sold	88,000	
Sales commission expense (8,000 × $2.50)..................	20,000	(108,000)
Contribution margin		132,000
Deduct: Fixed expenses:		
Fixed manufacturing overhead......................................	50,000	
Fixed marketing and administrative expenses..............	25,000	(75,000)
Operating income...		$ 57,000

By separating variable and fixed costs, the variable costing contribution margin income statement (Exhibit 6-21) allows managers to estimate how changes in sales, costs, or volume will affect profits.

Stop & Think...

Suppose Sportade can increase the number of cases sold by 10% using its existing capacity. Compute the likely effect on operating income.

Answer: *Because Sportade can accommodate the increased production using existing capacity, fixed costs will be unaffected. Thus, the entire increase in contribution margin flows through to operating income. A 10% increase in sales is an extra 800 cases (10% × 8,000).*

Increase in sales revenue (800 cases × $30/case)	$ 24,000
Increase in variable costs (800 cases × $13.50/case*)	(10,800)
Increase in contribution margin...	$ 13,200
Increase in fixed costs..	0
Increase in operating income...	$ 13,200

*Total variable costs per case = $6.00 direct materials + $3.00 direct labor + $2.00 variable manufacturing overhead + $2.50 sales commission. (All variable costs, including the sales commission as well as variable manufacturing costs, must be considered to estimate how the sales increase will affect contribution margin and operating profit.)

Reconciling the Difference in Income

Exhibit 6-20 shows that Sportade's absorption costing operating income is $67,000. Exhibit 6-21 shows that variable costing yields only $57,000 of operating income. Why? To answer this question, we need to understand what happened to the $160,000 ($110,000 variable + $50,000 fixed) total manufacturing costs under each costing method.

Manufacturing costs incurred in March are either:

- Expensed in March, or
- Held back in inventory (an asset)

Exhibit 6-22 shows that of the $160,000 total manufacturing costs incurred during March, absorption costing holds back $32,000 (2,000 × $16) as inventory. This $32,000 assigned to inventory is not expensed until next month, when the units are sold. Thus, only $128,000 ($160,000 – $32,000) of the manufacturing costs are expensed as cost of goods sold during March.

Variable costing holds back in ending inventory only $22,000 (2,000 × $11) of the total manufacturing costs. This is $10,000 ($22,000 – $32,000) *less* than what absorption costing holds back. The difference arises because absorption costing assigns the $5 per case fixed manufacturing overhead costs to the 2,000 cases in ending inventory. In contrast, variable costing does not—it expenses all of the fixed manufacturing overhead in the current month.

Costs that are not held back in inventory are expensed in the current period, so variable costing expenses are $138,000 ($160,000 – $22,000) of manufacturing costs in March. (This $138,000 also equals the $88,000 variable cost of goods sold plus the $50,000 fixed manufacturing overhead.) This is $10,000 *more* than the $128,000 absorption costing manufacturing expenses during March. *Variable costing has $10,000 more expense in March, so its income is $10,000 lower than absorption costing income.*

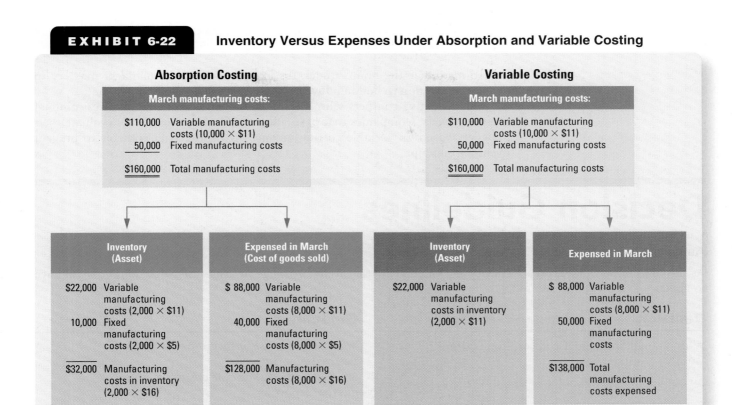

EXHIBIT 6-22 Inventory Versus Expenses Under Absorption and Variable Costing

Stop & Think...

Suppose Sportade has no inventory at the end of the next month, April. Will absorption costing report higher or lower operating income than variable costing for the month of April?

Answer: *Absorption costing will report lower income than variable costing during April. Ending inventory in March becomes the beginning inventory of April. Absorption costing assigns a higher value to beginning inventory in April. When that beginning inventory is sold, the higher beginning inventory costs increase cost of goods sold for April, which, in turn, reduces income.*

Absorption Costing and Manager's Incentives

The general rule is this: When inventories increase (more units are produced than sold), absorption costing income is higher than variable costing income. When inventories decline (when fewer units are produced than sold), absorption costing income is lower than variable costing income. Suppose the Sportade manager receives a bonus based on absorption costing income. Will the manager want to increase or decrease production?

The manager knows that absorption costing assigns each case of Sportade $5 of fixed manufacturing overhead.

- For every case produced but not sold, absorption costing "hides" $5 of fixed overhead in ending inventory (an asset).
- The more cases that are added to inventory, the more fixed overhead that is "hidden" in ending inventory at the end of the month.

- The more fixed overhead in ending inventory, the smaller the cost of goods sold and the higher the operating income.

To maximize the bonus under absorption costing, the manager may try to increase production to build up inventory.

This incentive conflicts with the JIT philosophy, which emphasizes minimal inventory levels. Companies that have adopted JIT should either (1) evaluate their managers based on variable costing income or (2) use strict controls to prevent inventory buildup.

Decision Guidelines

ABSORPTION AND VARIABLE COSTING

As the CEO of Sportade, you are considering whether to use variable costing. Here are some decisions you will have to make.

Decision	Guidelines
When should Sportade use absorption costing? Variable costing?	Sportade must use absorption costing for external reporting. Sportade can use variable costing only for internal reporting.
What is the difference between absorption and variable costing?	Fixed manufacturing costs are treated as: • Inventoriable product costs under absorption costing. • Period costs under variable costing.
How should Sportade compute inventoriable product costs under absorption costing and variable costing?	*Absorption Costing* *Variable Costing* Direct materials Direct materials + Direct labor + Direct labor + Variable overhead + Variable overhead + Fixed overhead = Product cost = Product cost

Will absorption costing income be higher than, lower than, or the same as variable costing income?	If units produced > units sold:
	    Absorption costing income > Variable costing income
	If units produced < units sold:
	    Absorption costing income < Variable costing income
	If units produced = units sold:
	    Absorption costing income = Variable costing income

Why should Sportade use variable costing for internal reporting?	• Managers can use variable costing contribution margin income statements to estimate how changes in sales or costs will affect profits. • Variable costing does not give Sportade's managers incentives to build up inventory.

Summary Problem 3

Continue the Sportade illustration from pages 358–363. In April 2007, Sportade produces 10,000 cases of the powdered sports beverage and sells 12,000 cases (the 2,000 cases of inventory on March 31, 2007, plus the 10,000 cases produced during April). The variable costs per case and the total fixed costs are the same as in March.

Requirements

1. Prepare an income statement for the month ended April 30, 2007, using absorption costing.

2. Prepare an income statement for the month ended April 30, 2007, using variable costing.

3. Reconcile (explain the difference between) operating income under absorption versus variable costing.

Solution

Requirement 1

SPORTADE
Income Statement (Absorption Costing)
Month Ended April 30, 2007

Sales revenue (12,000 × $30)		$360,000
Deduct: Cost of goods sold:		
Beginning finished goods inventory	$ 32,000*	
Cost of goods manufactured (10,000 × $16)	160,000†	
Cost of goods available for sale	192,000	
Ending finished goods inventory	(0)	
Cost of goods sold		192,000
Gross profit		168,000
Deduct: Operating expenses [(12,000 × $2.50) + $25,000]		(55,000)
Operating income		$113,000

*Ending inventory from March 31, 2007 (Exhibit 6-20).
†Absorption costing cost per case = $6 + $3 + $2 + $5.

Requirement 2

SPORTADE
Contribution Margin Income Statement (Variable Costing)
Month Ended April 30, 2007

Sales revenue (12,000 × $30)...		$360,000
Deduct: Variable expenses		
Variable cost of goods sold..		
Beginning finished goods inventory..............................	$ 22,000*	
Variable cost of goods manufactured (10,000 × $11)	110,000†	
Variable cost of goods available for sale.......................	132,000	
Ending finished goods inventory	(0)	
Variable cost of goods sold..	132,000	
Sales commission expense (12,000 × $2.50)...............	30,000	(162,000)
Contribution margin		198,000
Deduct: Fixed expenses		
Fixed manufacturing overhead.....................................	50,000	
Fixed marketing and administrative expenses...............	25,000	(75,000)
Operating income..		$ 123,000

*Ending inventory from March 31, 2007 (Exhibit 6-21).
†Variable costing cost per case = $6 + $3 + $2.

Requirement 3

April 2007 operating income is $10,000 higher under variable costing than under absorption costing. Why? Both methods expense all of April's $160,000 manufacturing costs ($110,000 variable + $50,000 fixed) during April. However, the two methods differ in the amount of March manufacturing cost expensed in April. Absorption costing holds $32,000 of March manufacturing costs in inventory and expenses them in April when the goods are sold. Variable costing holds only $22,000 of March manufacturing costs in inventory and expenses them in April.

Thus, absorption costing operating income is:

- $10,000 higher than variable costing income in March (because absorption costing defers $10,000 more of March costs to April).

- $10,000 lower than variable costing income in April (because absorption costing expenses $10,000 more of March costs in April).

Review Cost Behavior

■ Accounting Vocabulary

Absorption Costing (p. 358)
The costing method where products "absorb" both fixed and variable manufacturing costs.

Account Analysis (p. 343)
A method for determining cost behavior that is based on a manager's judgment in classifying each general ledger account as a variable, fixed, or mixed cost.

Committed Fixed Costs (p. 332)
Fixed costs that are locked in because of previous management decisions; management has little or no control over these costs in the short run.

Contribution Margin (p. 353)
Sales revenue minus variable expenses.

Contribution Margin Income Statement (p. 353)
Income statement that organizes costs by *behavior* (variable costs or fixed costs) rather than by *function*.

Cost Behavior (p. 328)
Describes how costs change as volume changes.

Cost Equation (p. 330)
A mathematical equation for a straight line that expresses how a cost behaves.

Curvilinear Costs (p. 340)
A cost behavior that is not linear (not a straight line).

Discretionary Fixed Costs (p. 332)
Fixed costs that are a result of annual management decisions; fixed costs that are controllable in the short run.

Fixed Costs (p. 329)
Costs that do not change in total despite wide changes in volume.

High-Low Method (p. 346)
A method for determining cost behavior that is based on two historical data points: the highest and lowest volume of activity.

Mixed Cost (p. 329)
Costs that change, but *not* in direct proportion to changes in volume. Mixed costs have both variable cost and fixed cost components.

Regression Analysis (p. 348)
A statistical procedure for determining the line that best fits the data by using *all of the historical data points, not just the high and low data points*.

Relevant Range (p. 337)
The band of volume where total fixed costs remain constant at a certain level and where the variable cost *per unit* remains constant at a certain level.

Step Costs (p. 339)
A cost behavior that is fixed over a small range of activity and then jumps to a different fixed level with moderate changes in volume.

Outliers (p. 345)
Abnormal data points; data points that do not fall in the same general pattern as the other data points.

Variable Costs (p. 329)
Costs that change in total in direct proportion to changes in volume.

Variable Costing (p. 358)
The costing method that assigns only *variable* manufacturing costs to products.

■ Quick Check

1. For most businesses, straight-line depreciation on the company's buildings is a
   a. variable cost
   b. fixed cost
   c. mixed cost
   d. step cost

2. If a *per-unit* cost remains constant over a wide range of volume, the cost is most likely a
   a. variable cost
   b. fixed cost
   c. mixed cost
   d. step cost

3. The following graph indicates which type of cost behavior?

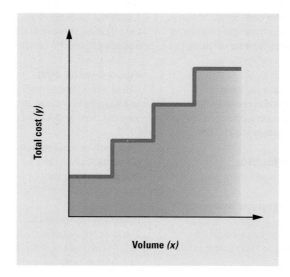

   a. variable cost
   b. fixed cost
   c. mixed cost
   d. step cost

4. In the following mixed cost equation, what amount represents the **total variable cost component**: $y = vx + f$?
   a. y
   b. v
   c. f
   d. vx

5. The cost per unit decreases as volume increases for which of the following cost behaviors?
   a. variable costs and fixed costs
   b. variable costs and mixed costs
   c. fixed costs and mixed costs
   d. only fixed costs

6. Which of the following cost behaviors best explains why companies like to operate at or near full capacity?
   a. variable cost
   b. fixed cost
   c. mixed cost
   d. step cost

7. Each month, a fitness club incurs $7,000 of fixed operating costs plus $6 of operating costs for every club member. If x represents the number of club members, which of the following best describes the club's total monthly operating costs?

   a. $y = \$7{,}000x$

   b. $y = \$6$

   c. $y = \$6x$

   d. $y = \$7{,}000 + \$6x$

8. Manufacturing overhead is usually a

   a. variable cost

   b. fixed cost

   c. mixed cost

   d. step cost

9. (Appendix) The only difference between variable costing and absorption costing lies in the treatment of

   a. fixed manufacturing overhead costs

   b. variable manufacturing overhead costs

   c. direct materials and direct labor costs

   d. variable nonmanufacturing costs

10. (Appendix) When inventories decline, operating income under variable costing is

   a. lower than operating income under absorption costing

   b. the same as operating income under absorption costing

   c. higher than operating income under absorption costing

Quick Check Answers

1. b 2. a 3. d 4. d 5. c 6. b 7. d 8. c 9. a 10. c

For Internet Exercises, Excel in Practice, and additional online activities, go to this book's Web site at www.prenhall.com/bamber.

Assess Your Progress

■ Learning Objectives

1   Describe key characteristics and graphs of various cost behaviors

2   Use cost equations to express and predict costs

3   Use account analysis and scatter plots to analyze cost behavior

4   Use the high-low method to analyze cost behavior

5   Use regression analysis to analyze cost behavior

6   Prepare contribution margin income statements for service firms and merchandising firms

7   Use variable costing to prepare contribution margin income statements for manufacturers (Appendix)

■ Short Exercises

S6-1   **Identify cost behavior** (*Learning Objective 1*)

The chart below shows three different costs: Cost A, Cost B, and Cost C. For each cost, the chart shows the total cost and cost per unit at two different volumes within the same relevant range. Based on this information, identify each cost as fixed, varable, or mixed. Explain your answers.

	At 5,000 units		At 6,000 units	
	Total Cost	**Cost per Unit**	**Total Cost**	**Cost per Unit**
Cost A	$30,000	$6.00	$36,000	$6.00
Cost B	$30,000	$6.00	$30,000	$5.00
Cost C	$30,000	$6.00	$33,000	$5.50

S6-2   **Sketch cost behavior graphs** (*Learning Objective 1*)

Sketch graphs of the following cost behaviors. In each graph, the y-axis should be "total costs" and the x-axis should be "volume of activity."

a.   Step

b.   Fixed

c.   Curvilinear

d.   Mixed

e.   Variable

S6-3   **Computer fixed costs per unit** (*Learning Objective 2*)

Sport-time produces high-quality basketballs. If the fixed cost per basketball is $3 when the company produces 12,000 basketballs, what is the fixed cost per basketball when it produces 15,000 basketballs? Assume that both volumes are in the same relevant range.

S6-4   **Define various cost equations** (*Learning Objective 2*)

Write the cost equation for each of the following cost behaviors. Define the variables in each equation.

a.   Fixed

b. Mixed

c. Variable

S6-5 **Predict total mixed costs** *(Learning Objective 2)*
Ritter Razors produces deluxe razors that compete with Gillette's Mach line of razors. Total manufacturing costs are $100,000 when 20,000 packages are produced. Of this amount, total variable costs are $40,000. What are the total production costs when 25,000 packages of razors are produced? Assume the same relevant range.

S6-6 **Predict and graph total mixed costs** *(Learning Objectives 1, 2)*
Suppose World-Link offers an international calling plan that charges $5.00 per month plus $0.35 per minute for calls outside the United States.

1. Under this plan, what is your monthly international long-distance cost if you call Europe for

    a. 20 minutes?

    b. 40 minutes?

    c. 80 minutes?

2. Draw a graph illustrating your total cost under this plan. Label the axes and show your costs at 20, 40, and 80 minutes.

S6-7 **Classify cost behavior** *(Learning Objective 3)*
Ariel builds innovative loudspeakers for music and home theater. Identify the following costs as variable or fixed:

a. Depreciation on equipment used to cut wood enclosures

b. Wood for speaker enclosures

c. Patents on crossover relays (internal components)

d. Crossover relays

e. Grill cloth

f. Glue

g. Quality inspector's salary

S6-8 **Prepare and analyze a scatter plot** *(Learning Objective 3)*
Lube-for-Less is a car care center specializing in ten-minute oil changes. Lube-for-Less has two service bays, which limits its capacity to 3,600 oil changes per month. The following information was collected over the past six months:

Month	Number of Oil Changes	Operating Expenses
January	3,400	$36,800
February	2,800	$32,300
March	3,000	$33,250
April	2,900	$32,900
May	3,500	$37,400
June	3,100	$34,100

1. Prepare a scatter plot graphing the volume of oil changes (x-axis) against the company's monthly operating expenses (y-axis). Graph by hand or use Excel.

2. How strong of a relationship does there appear to be between the company's operating expenses and the number of oil changes performed each month? Explain. Do there appear to be any outliers in the data? Explain.

continued . . .

3. Based on the graph, do the company's operating costs appear to be fixed, variable, or mixed? Explain how you can tell.

4. Would you feel comfortable using this information to project operating costs for a volume of 4,000 oil changes per month? Explain.

S6-9 **Use the high-low method** *(Learning Objective 4)*
Refer to the Lube-for-Less data in S6-8. Use the high-low method to determine the variable and fixed cost components of Lube-for-Less's operating costs. Use this information to project the monthly operating costs for a month in which the company performs 3,600 oil changes.

S6-10 **Analyze a scatter plot** *(Learning Objectives 3, 4)*
The local Holiday Inn collected seven months of data on the number of room-nights rented per month and the monthly utilities cost. The data was graphed, resulting in the following scatter plot:

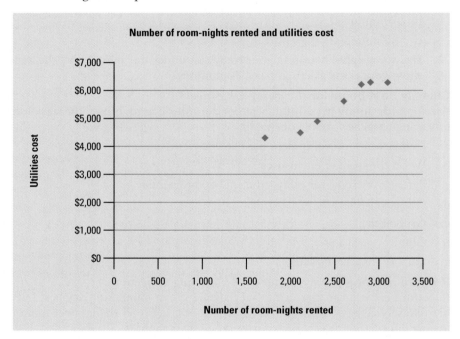

1. Based on this scatter plot, how strong of a relationship does there appear to be between the number of room-nights rented per month and the monthly utilities cost?

2. Do there appear to be any outliers in the data? Explain.

3. Suppose management performs the high-low method using this data. Do you think the resulting cost equation would be very accurate? Explain.

S6-11 **Theoretical comparison of high-low and regression analysis** *(Learning Objectives 4, 5)*
Refer to the Holiday Inn scatter plot in S6-10.

1. Would the high-low method or regression analysis result in a more accurate cost equation for the data pictured in the scatter plot? Explain.

2. A regression analysis of the data revealed an R-squared figure of 0.939. Interpret this figure in light of the lowest and highest possible R-squared values.

Requirement 2
As a manager, would you be confident predicting utilities costs for other room-night volumes within the same relevant range?

S6-12 **Write a cost equation given regression output** *(Learning Objective 5)*
A firm wanted to determine the relationship between its monthly operating costs and a potential cost driver. The output of a regression analysis showed the following information:

> Intercept Coefficient = 21,635
> X variable 1 Coefficient = 62.53
> R-Square = 0.2312

a. Given this output, write the firm's monthly cost equation.

b. Should management use this equation to predict monthly operating costs? Explain your answer.

S6-13 **Prepare a contribution margin income statement** *(Learning Objective 6)*
Pam's Quilt Shoppe sells homemade Amish quilts. Pam buys the quilts from local Amish artisans for $250 each, and her shop sells them for $350 each. Pam also pays a sales commission of 5% of sales revenue to her sales staff. Pam leases her country-style shop for $1,000 per month and pays $1,200 per month in payroll costs in addition to the sales commissions. Pam sold 80 quilts in February. Prepare Pam's traditional income statement and contribution margin income statement for the month.

S6-14 **Prepare income statement using variable costing** *(Learning Objective 7)*
(Appendix) Consider the Sportade example on pages 358–364. Suppose that during April, the company produces 10,000 cases of powdered drink mix and sells 11,000 cases. Sales price, variable cost per case, and total fixed expenses remain the same as in March. Prepare the April income statement using variable costing.

S6-15 **Continuation of S6-14: absorption costing** *(Learning Objective 7)*
(Appendix) Refer to the Sportade example on pages 358–364 and the data and your answer to S6-14.

1. Prepare the April income statement under absorption costing.

2. Is absorption costing income higher or lower than variable costing income? Explain.

■ Exercises

E6-16 **Graph specific costs** *(Learning Objective 1)*
Graph these cost behavior patterns over a relevant range of 0 to 10,000 units:

a. Variable expenses of $8 per unit

b. Mixed expenses made up of fixed costs of $20,000 and variable costs of $3 per unit

c. Fixed expenses of $15,000

E6-17 **Identify cost behavior terms** *(Learning Objectives 1, 2, 3, 4, 5)*
Complete the following statements with one of the terms listed here. You may use a term more than once, and some terms may not be used at all.

Account analysis	Step cost(s)	High-low method
Variable cost(s)	Fixed cost(s)	Regression analysis
Curvilinear cost(s)	Total cost(s)	Average cost per unit
R-square	Mixed cost(s)	Committed fixed costs

continued . . .

a. _____ remain constant in total over a wide range of volume.

b. _____ is often referred to as the "goodness-of-fit" statistic.

c. _____ and _____ increase in total as volume increases.

d. Graphs of _____ always begin at the origin.

e. _____ uses the manager's judgment to determine the cost behavior of various accounts.

f. _____ remain constant in total over small ranges of activity.

g. _____ and _____ increase on a per unit basis as volume decreases.

h. _____ uses only two historical data points to determine the cost line and cost equation.

i. _____ remain constant on a per unit basis.

j. When graphing cost equations, _____ are always shown on the y-axis.

k. The _____ should not be used to predict total costs at various volumes unless it is strictly a/an _____.

l. _____ uses all historical data points provided to determine the cost equation.

m. _____ are the result of previous management decisions and are not usually controllable in the short run.

E6-18 **Forecast costs at different volumes** *(Learning Objectives 1, 2)*
Sam's Sock Shop has capacity to clean up to 5,000 garments per month.

Requirements

1. Complete the following schedule for the three volumes shown:

	2,000 Garments	3,500 Garments	5,000 Garments
Total variable costs		$2,625	
Total fixed costs			
Total operating costs			
Variable cost per garment			
Fixed cost per garment		$ 2.00	
Average cost per garment			

2. Why does the average cost per garment change?

3. Suppose the owner, Sam Perreth, erroneously uses the average cost per unit *at full capacity* to predict total costs at a volume of 2,000 garments. Would he overestimate or underestimate his total costs? By how much?

E6-19 **Prepare income statement in two formats** *(Learning Objective 6)*
Refer to the Sam's Sock Shop in E6-18. Assume that Perreth charges customers $7 per garment for dry cleaning. Prepare Perreth's *projected* income statement if 4,252 garments are cleaned in March. First, prepare the income statement using the traditional format; then, prepare Perreth's contribution margin income statement.

E6-20 **Use unit cost data to forecast total costs** *(Learning Objective 2)*
Acme Mailboxes produces decorative mailboxes. The company's average cost per unit is $26.43 when it produces 1,000 mailboxes.

a. What is the total cost of producing 1,000 mailboxes?

b. If $18,000 of the total costs are fixed, what is the variable cost of producing each mailbox?

c. Write Acme Mailboxes' cost equation.

d. If the plant manager uses the average cost per unit to predict total costs, what would his forecast be for 1,200 mailboxes?

e. If the plant manager uses the cost equation to predict total costs, what would his forecast be for 1,200 mailboxes?

f. What is the dollar difference between your answers to Questions d and e? Which approach to forecasting costs is appropriate? Why?

E6-21 **Use account analysis to determine cost behavior** *(Learning Objective 3)*

Use your judgment (just as a manager would use his judgment for account analysis) to determine the cost behavior of each of the following personal costs:

a. Apartment rental, $500 per month

b. Local phone service with unlimited local calls, $19.99 per month

c. Cell phone plan, the first 700 minutes are included for $39.99 per month and every minute thereafter costs $0.30

d. Utilities, $0.475 per kilowatt hour

e. Car payment, $350 per month

f. Car insurance, $250 per month

g. Gas, $2.59 per gallon and your car averages 25 miles per gallon

h. Cable TV, $50 per month for 120 channels plus $4.99 per pay-per-view movie

i. Commuter rail tickets, $2 per ride

j. Student activity pass, $100 plus $5 per event

k. Campus meal plan, $3 per meal

E6-22 **Create a scatter plot** *(Learning Objective 3)*

Alice Jungemann, owner of Tulip Time, operates a local chain of floral shops. Each shop has its own delivery van. Instead of charging a flat delivery fee, Jungemann wants to set the delivery fee based on the distance driven to deliver the flowers. Jungemann wants to separate the fixed and variable portions of her van operating costs so that she has a better idea how delivery distance affects these costs. She has the following data from the past seven months:

Month	Miles Driven	Van Operating Costs
January	15,800	$5,460
February	17,300	5,748
March	14,600	4,935
April	16,000	5,310
May	17,100	5,830
June	15,400	5,420
July	14,500	5,020

February and May are always Tulip Time's biggest months because of Valentine's Day and Mother's Day, respectively.

1. Prepare a scatter plot of Alice's volume (miles driven) and van operating costs.

continued . . .

2. Does the data appear to contain any outliers? Explain.

3. How strong of a relationship is there between miles driven and van operating costs?

E6-23 **High-low method** *(Learning Objective 4)*
Refer to Alice's Tulip Time data in E6-22. Use the high-low method to determine Tulip Time's cost equation for van operating costs. Use your results to predict van operating costs at a volume of 15,000 miles.

E6-24 **Continuation of E6-23: regression analysis** *(Learning Objective 5)*
Refer to the Tulip Time data in E6-22. Use Microsoft Excel to:

1. Run a regression analysis (use Excel shown on pages 350 or 351).

2. Determine the firm's cost equation (use the output from the Excel Regression shown in Exhibit 6-15).

3. Determine the R-square (use the output from the Excel Regression shown in Exhibit 6-15). What does Flower Power's R-square indicate?

4. Predict van operating costs at a volume of 15,000 miles.

5. Compare your prediction in Question 4 to your prediction in E6-23.

E6-25 **Prepare and interpret a scatter plot** *(Learning Objective 3)*
Dave's "Hot Stacks" Pancake Restaurant features sourdough pancakes made from a strain of sourdough dating back to the Alaskan gold rush. To plan for the future, Dave needs to figure out his cost behavior patterns. He has the following information about his operating costs and the number of pancakes served:

Month	Number of Pancakes	Total Operating Costs
July	3,600	$2,338
August	3,900	$2,390
September	3,200	$2,320
October	3,300	$2,272
November	3,850	$2,562
December	3,620	$2,534

1. Prepare a scatter plot of Dave's pancake volume and operating costs. (*Hint:* If you use Excel, be sure to force the vertical axis to zero. See the "Technology Makes It Simple" feature on pages 345–346.)

2. Does the data appear sound, or do there appear to be any outliers? Explain.

3. Based on the scatter plot, do operating costs appear to be variable, fixed, or mixed costs?

4. How strong of a relationship is there between pancake volume and operating costs?

E6-26 **High-low method** *(Learning Objective 4)*
Refer to Dave's "Hot Stacks" Pancake Restaurant in E6-25.

1. Use the high-low method to determine Dave's operating cost equation.

2. Use your answer from Requirement 1 to predict total monthly operating costs if Dave serves 4,000 pancakes one month.

3. Can you predict total monthly operating costs if Dave serves 10,000 pancakes a month? Explain.

E6-27   **Regression Analysis** *(Learning Objective 5)*
Refer to Dave's "Hot Stacks" Pancake Restaurant in E6-25.

1. Use Microsoft Excel to perform regression analysis on Dave's monthly data. Based on the output, write Dave's monthly operating cost equation.

2. Based on the R-square shown on the regression output, how well does this cost equation fit the data?

E6-28   **Determine cost behavior and predict operating costs** *(Learning Objective 4)*
Shady Apartments is a 500-unit apartment complex. When the apartments are 90% occupied, monthly operating costs total $200,000. When occupancy dips to 80%, monthly operating costs fall to $197,000. The owner of the apartment complex is worried because many of the apartment residents work at a nearby manufacturing plant that has just announced that it will close in three months. The apartment owner fears that occupancy of his apartments will drop to 60% if residents lose their jobs and move away. Assuming the same relevant range, what can the owner expect his operating costs to be if occupancy falls to 60%?

E6-29   **Critique the high-low method** *(Learning Objective 4)*
You have been assigned an intern to help you forecast your firm's costs at different volumes. He thinks he will get cost and volume data from the two most recent months, plug them in to the high-low method equations, and turn in the cost equation results to your boss before the hour is over. As his mentor, explain to him why the process isn't quite as simple as he thinks. Point out some of the concerns he is over-looking, including your concerns about his choice of data and method.

E6-30   **Prepare a contribution margin income statement** *(Learning Objective 6)*
Exotic Pets is a small e-tail business specializing in the sale of exotic pet gifts and accessories over the Web. The business is owned by a sole proprietor and operated out of her home. Results for 2009 are shown below:

EXOTIC PETS		
Income Statement		
Year Ended December 31, 2009		
Sales revenue		$ 987,000
Cost of goods sold		(665,000)
Gross profit		322,000
Operating expenses:		
Selling and marketing expenses	$61,000	
Web site maintenance expenses	56,000	
Other operating expenses	17,000	
Total operating expenses		(134,000)
Operating income		$ 188,000

For internal planning and decision-making purposes, the owner of Exotic Pets would like to translate the company's income statement into the contribution margin format. Since Exotic Pets is an e-tailer, all of its cost of goods sold is variable. A large portion of the selling and marketing expenses consists of freight-out charges ($19,000), which were also variable. Only 20% of the remaining selling and marketing expenses and 25% of the Web site expenses were variable. Of the other operating expenses, 90% were fixed.

Based on this information, prepare Exotic Pets' contribution margin income statement for 2009.

E6-31 Prepare a contribution margin income statement (*Learning Objective 6*)
Colt Carriage Company offers guided horse-drawn carriage rides through historic Charleston, South Carolina. The carriage business is highly regulated by the city. Charleston Carriage Company has the following operating costs during April:

Monthly depreciation expense on carriages and stable...	$2,000
Fee paid to the City of Charleston...	15% of ticket revenue
Cost of souvenir set of postcards given to each passenger	$0.50/set of postcards
Brokerage fee paid to independent ticket brokers (60% of tickets are issued through these brokers; 40% are sold directly by the Charleston Carriage Company)	$1.00/ticket sold by broker
Monthly cost of leasing and boarding the horses..	45,000
Carriage drivers (tour guides) are paid on a per passenger basis.....................................	$3.00 per passenger
Monthly payroll costs of non–tour guide employees	$7,500
Marketing, Web site, telephone, and other monthly fixed costs	$7,000

During April (a month during peak season) Colt Carriage Company had 12,960 passengers. Eighty-five percent (85%) of passengers were adults ($20 fare) while 15% were children ($12 fare).

1. Prepare the company's contribution margin income statement for the month of April. Round all figures to the nearest dollar.

2. Assume that passenger volume increases by 10% in May. Which figures on the income statement would you expect to change, and by what percentage would they change? Which figures would remain the same as in April?

E6-32 Absorption and variable costing income statements (*Learning Objective 7*)
(Appendix) The 2008 data that follow pertain to Sea Down There, a manufacturer of swimming goggles (Sea Down There has no beginning inventories in January 2008):

Sales price	$ 35
Variable manufacturing expense per unit..............................	15
Sales commission expense per unit......................................	5
Fixed manufacturing overhead..	2,000,000
Fixed operating expenses..	250,000
Number of goggles produced	200,000
Number of goggles sold...	185,000

Requirements

1. Prepare both conventional (absorption costing) and contribution margin (variable costing) income statements for Sea Down There for the year ended December 31, 2008.

2. Which statement shows the higher operating income? Why?

3. Sea Down There's marketing vice president believes a new sales promotion that costs $150,000 would increase sales to 200,000 goggles. Should the company go ahead with the promotion? Give your reason.

■ Problems (Problem Set A)

P6-33A Analyze cost behavior (*Learning Objectives 1, 2, 3, 4*)
Orange Industries is in the process of analyzing its manufacturing overhead costs. Orange Industries is not sure if the number of units produced or number of direct

labor (DL) hours is the best cost driver to use for predicting manufacturing overhead (MOH) costs. The following information is available:

Month	Manufacturing Overhead Costs	Direct Labor Hours	Units Produced	MOH Cost per DL Hour	MOH Cost per Unit Produced
July	$460,475	23,000	3,600	$20.02	$127.91
August	515,280	26,400	4,320	19.52	119.28
September	419,010	18,800	4,200	22.29	99.76
October	447,970	21,600	3,400	20.74	131.76
November	543,470	28,600	5,750	19.00	94.52
December	437,020	19,400	3,250	22.53	134.47

1. Are manufacturing overhead costs fixed, variable, or mixed? Explain.
2. Graph Orange Industries' manufacturing overhead costs against DL hours. Use Excel or graph by hand.
3. Graph Orange Industries' manufacturing overhead costs against units produced. Use Excel or graph by hand.
4. Do the data appear to be sound, or do you see any potential data problems? Explain.
5. Use the high-low method to determine Orange Industries' manufacturing overhead cost equation using DL hours as the cost driver. Assume that management believes that all data is accurate and wants to include all of it in the analysis.
6. Estimate manufacturing overhead costs if Orange Industries incurs 24,000 DL hours in January.

P6-34A **Continuation of P6-33A: regression analysis** *(Learning Objective 5)*
Refer to Orange Industries in P6-33A.

1. Use Excel regression analysis to determine Orange Industries' manufacturing overhead cost equation using DL hours as the cost driver. Comment on the R-square. Estimate manufacturing overhead costs if Orange Industries incurs 24,000 DL hours in January.
2. Use Excel regression analysis to determine Orange's manufacturing overhead cost equation using number of units produced as the cost driver. Use all of the data provided. Project total manufacturing overhead costs if Orange Industries produces 5,000 units. Which cost equation is better—this one or the one from Question 1? Why?
3. Use Excel regression analysis to determine Orange Industries' manufacturing overhead cost equation using number of units produced as the cost driver. This time, remove any potential outliers before performing the regression. How does this affect the R-square? Project total manufacturing overhead costs if 5,000 units are produced.
4. In which cost equation do you have the most confidence? Why?

P6-35A **Prepare traditional and contribution margin income statements** *(Learning Objective 6)*
Eddie's Ice Cream Shoppe sold 9,000 servings of ice cream during June for $3 per serving. Eddie purchases the ice cream in large tubs from the Fun Time Ice Cream

continued . . .

Company. Each tub costs Eddie $15 and has enough ice cream to fill 30 ice cream cones. Eddie purchases the ice cream cones for $0.05 each from a local warehouse club. Eddie's Shoppe is located in a local strip mall, and he pays $1,800 a month to lease the space. Eddie expenses $250 a month for the depreciation of the Shoppe's furniture and equipment. During June, Eddie incurred an additional $2,500 of other operating expenses (75% of these were fixed costs).

1. Prepare Eddie's June income statement using a traditional format.

2. Prepare Eddie's June income statement using a contribution margin format.

P6-36A **Determine financial statement components** *(Learning Objective 7)* (Appendix)
Violins-by-Coughlin produces student-grade violins for beginning violin students. The company produced 2,000 violins in its first month of operations. At month-end, 600 finished violins remained unsold. There was no inventory in work in process. Violins were sold for $112.50 each. Total costs from the month are as follows:

Direct materials used	$80,000
Direct labor	50,000
Variable manufacturing overhead	30,000
Fixed manufacturing overhead	40,000
Variable selling and administrative expenses	10,000
Fixed selling and administrative expenses	15,000

The company prepares traditional (absorption costing) income statements for its bankers. Coughlin would also like to prepare contribution margin income statements for her own management use. Compute the following amounts that would be shown on these income statements:

1. Gross Profit

2. Contribution Margin

3. Total Expenses shown **below** the **Gross Profit** line

4. Total Expenses shown **below** the **Contribution Margin** line

5. Dollar value of ending inventory under absorption costing

6. Dollar value of ending inventory under variable costing

Which income statement will have a higher operating income? By how much? Explain.

P6-37A **Absorption and variable costing income statements** *(Learning Objective 7)* (Appendix)
Brian's Foods produces frozen meals, which it sells for $7 each. The company uses the FIFO inventory costing method, and it computes a new monthly fixed manufacturing overhead rate based on the actual number of meals produced that month. All costs and production levels are exactly as planned. The following data are from Brian's Foods' first two months in business:

	January 2007	February 2007
Sales	1,000 meals	1,200 meals
Production	1,400 meals	1,000 meals
Variable manufacturing expense per meal	$ 4	$ 4
Sales commission expense per meal	$ 1	$ 1
Total fixed manufacturing overhead	$ 700	$ 700
Total fixed marketing and administrative expenses	$ 600	$ 600

1. Compute the product cost per meal produced under absorption costing and under variable costing. Do this first for January and then for February.

2. Prepare separate monthly income statements for January and for February, using:

   a. Absorption costing.

   b. Variable costing.

3. Is operating income higher under absorption costing or variable costing in January? In February? Explain the pattern of differences in operating income based on absorption costing versus variable costing.

■ Problems (Problem Set B)

P6-38B Analyze cost behavior *(Learning Objectives 1, 2, 3, 4)*

Battle Microbrewery is in the process of analyzing its manufacturing overhead costs. Battle Microbrewery is not sure if the number of cases or the number of processing hours is the best cost driver of manufacturing overhead (MOH) costs. The following information is available:

Month	Manufacturing Overhead Costs	Direct Labor Hours	Units Produced	MOH Cost per DL Hour	MOH Cost per Unit Produced
July	$460,475	23,000	3,600	$20.02	$127.91
August	515,280	26,400	4,320	19.52	119.28
September	419,010	18,800	4,200	22.29	99.76
October	447,970	21,600	3,400	20.74	131.76
November	543,470	28,600	5,750	19.00	94.52
December	437,020	19,400	3,250	22.53	134.47

1. Are manufacturing overhead costs fixed, variable, or mixed? Explain.

2. Graph Battle Microbrewery's manufacturing overhead costs against processing hours. Use Excel or graph by hand.

3. Graph Battle Microbrewery's manufacturing overhead costs against cases produced. Use Excel or graph by hand.

4. Does the data appear to be sound, or do you see any potential data problems? Explain.

5. Use the high-low method to determine Battle Microbrewery's manufacturing overhead cost equation using processing hours as the cost driver. Assume that management believes all of the data to be accurate and wants to include all of it in the analysis.

6. Estimate manufacturing overhead costs if Battle Microbrewery incurs 550 processing hours in July.

P6-39B Continuation of P6-38B: regression analysis *(Learning Objective 5)*

Refer to Battle Microbrewery in P6-38B.

1. Use Excel regression analysis to determine Battle Microbrewery's manufacturing overhead cost equation using processing hours as the cost driver. Comment on the R-square. Estimate manufacturing overhead costs if Battle Microbrewery incurs 550 processing hours in July.

continued . . .

2. Use Excel regression analysis to determine Battle Microbrewery's manufacturing overhead cost equation using number of cases produced as the cost driver. Use all of the data provided. Project total manufacturing overhead costs if Battle Microbrewery produces 6,000 cases. Which cost equation is better—this one or the one from Question 1? Why?

3. Use Excel regression analysis to determine Battle Microbrewery's manufacturing overhead cost equation using number of cases produced as the cost driver. This time, remove any potential outliers before performing the regression. How does this affect the R-square? Project total manufacturing overhead costs if Battle Microbrewery produces 6,000 cases.

4. In which cost equation do you have the most confidence? Why?

P6-40B Contribution margin income statement (*Learning Objective 6*)

Zippy's Rock Shop is a full-service music store. Zippy's rents and sells instruments, sells sheet music, and hires musicians on an "as-needed" hourly basis to give student lessons. Zippy's also has one full-time employee who helps run the shop. Zippy's general ledger accounts indicate the following for the year:

Instrument rental revenue	$22,000
Cost of sheet music sold	$ 2,000
Instrument sales	$27,000
Straight-line depreciation expense on owned rental equipment	$ 4,000
Sheet music sales	$ 7,000
Music lesson revenue	$40,000
Cost of instruments sold	$ 7,500
Store lease payments	$12,000
Payments to musicians	$25,000
Full-time employee salary	$30,000

Based on this information, prepare Zippy's income statement using two formats: traditional format and contribution margin format. When preparing the income statements, you may combine the sales revenue accounts, but show all other detail. Which income statement will be more useful to Zippy's Rock Shop as it plans for next year? Why?

P6-41B Determine financial statement components (*Learning Objective 7*) (Appendix)

Juda, a budding professional tennis player, was unsatisfied with the tennis racquets currently available at sports stores and pro shops. She decided to produce and sell her own line of high-grade tennis racquets to be sold strictly through pro shops, where she could effectively communicate the advantages of her racquets and use her name as a marketing tool. Juda produced 200 racquets in her **first** month of operations. At month-end, 60 finished racquets remained unsold. There was no inventory in work in process. Racquets were sold for $150 each at pro shops throughout the Southeast (her test market). Total costs from the month are as follows:

Direct materials used..	$ 7,000
Direct labor...	5,000
Variable manufacturing overhead	3,000
Fixed manufacturing overhead..................................	4,200
Variable selling and administrative expenses..........	6,000
Fixed selling and administrative expenses..............	13,000

Juda needs to prepare absorption income statements for her bankers. She would also like to prepare contribution margin income statements for her own management use. Compute the following amounts that would be shown on these income statements:

1. Gross Profit
2. Contribution Margin
3. Total Expenses shown **below** the **Gross Profit** line
4. Total Expenses shown **below** the **Contribution Margin** line
5. Dollar value of ending inventory under absorption costing
6. Dollar value of ending inventory under variable costing

Which income statement will have a higher operating income? By how much? Explain.

P6-42B **Absorption and variable costing income statements** (*Learning Objective 7*) (Appendix) Touch Of A Button Limited manufactures video games, which it sells for $40 each. The company uses the FIFO inventory costing method, and it computes a new monthly fixed manufacturing overhead rate based on the actual number of games produced that month. All costs and production levels are exactly as planned. The following data are from Touch Of A Button Limited's first two months in business during 2007:

	October	November
Sales...	2,000 units	2,200 units
Production	2,500 units	2,000 units
Variable manufacturing expense per game	$ 15	$ 15
Sales commission per game	$ 8	$ 8
Total fixed manufacturing overhead ...	$10,000	$10,000
Total fixed marketing and administrative expenses....................	$ 9,000	$ 9,000

Requirements

1. Compute the product cost per game produced under absorption costing and under variable costing. Do this first for October and then for November.
2. Prepare separate monthly income statements for October and for November, using:
   a. Absorption costing.
   b. Variable costing.
3. Is operating income higher under absorption costing or variable costing in October? In November? Explain the pattern of differences in operating income based on absorption costing versus variable costing.

Apply Your Knowledge

▪ Decision Case

Case 6-43. Appendix *(Learning Objective 7)*

Suppose you serve on the board of directors of American Faucet, a manufacturer of bathroom fixtures that recently adopted JIT production. Part of your responsibility is to develop a compensation contract for Toni Moen, the vice president of manufacturing. To give her the incentive to make decisions that will increase the company's profits, the board decides to give Moen a year-end bonus if American Faucet meets a target operating income.

Write a memo to Chairperson of the Board Herbert Kohler explaining whether the bonus contract should be based on absorption costing or variable costing. Use the following format:

Date: _____

To: _____

From: _____

Subject: _____

7 Cost-Volume-Profit Analysis

The Internet boom of the 1990s led many entrepreneurs to believe that they could earn profits well above those of traditional retail stores by avoiding the high fixed costs of brick-and-mortar retail outlets. Online business flourished for a while, but when the dot.com bubble burst, many of these Internet dreams died. Many, but not all. Consider art.com, an e-tail business that offers over 100,000 different prints, photos, and posters to customers ranging from budget-minded college students to professional decorators searching for high-end art. Founded in 1995, art.com has enjoyed positive cash flows and double-digit revenue growth since 2000. In 2003, Deloitte & Touche named art.com one of the fastest-growing tech companies in America. It attracts more than a million people to its award-winning Web site each month.

Even though art.com doesn't face the fixed costs of traditional retail outlets, it still incurs fixed costs tied to its Web site and its custom-framing facilities. It also incurs variable costs for each piece of art. The bottom line: e-tail or retail, every business faces fixed and variable costs, and

art.com is no exception. Before they launched the company, how did art.com managers figure out what sales volume they had to reach to break even? How did they forecast the volume needed to achieve their target profit levels? And as the company continues to operate, how do managers respond to fluctuating business conditions, changing variable and fixed costs, and pricing pressure from new competitors? Cost-volume-profit (CVP) analysis helps managers answer such questions. ■

Learning Objectives

1 Calculate the unit contribution margin and the contribution margin ratio

2 Use CVP analysis to find breakeven points and target profit volumes

3 Perform sensitivity analysis in response to changing business conditions

4 Find breakeven and target profit volumes for multiproduct companies

5 Determine a firm's margin of safety and operating leverage

In the last chapter, we discussed cost behavior patterns and methods managers use to determine how their costs behave. We showed how managers use the contribution margin income statement to separately display the firm's variable and fixed costs. In this chapter, we show how managers identify the volume of sales necessary to achieve breakeven and target profit levels. We also look at how changes in costs, sales price, and volume affect the firm's profit. Finally, we discuss ways to identify the firm's risk level, including ways to gauge how easily a firm's profits could turn to loss if sales volume declines.

How Does Cost-Volume-Profit Analysis Help Managers?

Cost-volume-profit, or CVP, analysis is a powerful tool that helps managers make important business decisions. **Cost-volume-profit analysis** expresses the relationships among costs, volume, and profit or loss. For example, at art.com, managers need to determine how many pieces of art the company must sell each month just to cover costs or to break even. CVP can provide the answer. CVP also helps art.com's managers determine how many pieces of art the company must sell to earn a target profit, such as $1,000,000 per month. And if costs or sales prices change, CVP can help managers decide how sales volume would need to change to achieve the same profit level.

However, to use CVP, managers need certain data. They must also make sure the data are consistent with the assumptions underlying CVP analysis. In addition, managers need a solid understanding of the contribution margin concept introduced in the last chapter. In this section, we'll take a look at the data requirements, assumptions, and contribution margin in more detail.

Data Required for Effective CVP Analysis

CVP analysis relies on the interdependency of five components, or pieces of information, shown in Exhibit 7-1.

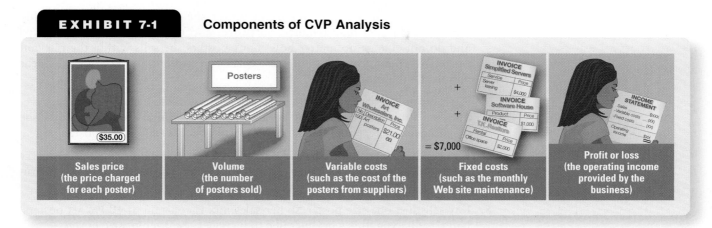

EXHIBIT 7-1   **Components of CVP Analysis**

| Sales price (the price charged for each poster) | Volume (the number of posters sold) | Variable costs (such as the cost of the posters from suppliers) | Fixed costs (such as the monthly Web site maintenance) | Profit or loss (the operating income provided by the business) |

If you know or can estimate four of these five components, you can use CVP analysis to compute the remaining unknown amount. Therefore, CVP helps managers discover how changes in any of these components will affect their business. Because business conditions are always changing, CVP helps managers prepare for and respond to economic changes. Now, let's review the assumptions required for CVP analysis.

CVP Assumptions

CVP analysis assumes that:

1. A change in volume is the only factor that affects costs.

2. Managers can classify each cost (or the components of mixed costs) as either variable or fixed. These costs are linear throughout the relevant range of volume.

3. Revenues are linear throughout the relevant range of volume.

4. Inventory levels will not change.

5. The sales mix of products will not change. **Sales mix** is the combination of products that make up total sales. For example, art.com may sell 15% posters, 25% unframed photographs, and 60% framed prints. If profits differ across products, changes in sales mix will affect CVP analysis.

Let's start by looking at a simple firm that has only one product. Later, we'll expand the firm to include a wider selection of products. Kay Pak, an entrepreneur, has just started an e-tail business selling art posters on the Internet. Kay is a "virtual retailer" and carries no inventory. Kay's software tabulates all customer orders each day and then automatically places the order to buy posters from a wholesaler. Kay buys only what she needs to fill the prior day's sales orders. The posters cost $21 each, and Kay sells them for $35 each. Customers pay the shipping costs, so there are no other variable selling costs. Monthly fixed costs for server leasing and maintenance, software, and office rental total $7,000. Kay's relevant range extends from 0 to 2,000 posters a month. Beyond this volume, Kay will need to hire an employee and upgrade her Web site software in order to handle the increased volume.

Let's see if Kay's business meets the CVP assumptions:

1. Sales volume is the only factor that affects her costs.

2. The $21 purchase cost for each poster is a variable cost. Thus, Kay's *total variable cost* increases in direct proportion to the number of posters she sells (an extra $21 in cost for each extra poster she sells). The $7,000 monthly server leasing and maintenance, software, and office rental costs are fixed and do not change no matter how many posters she sells within the relevant range. We could graph each of these costs as a straight line, so they are linear within the relevant range.

3. Kay's revenue is also linear. She sells each poster for $35, so a graph of her revenues is a straight line beginning at the origin (if she doesn't sell any posters, she won't have any revenue) that slopes upward at a rate of $35 per poster.

4. Kay has no inventory. If she did carry inventory, she wouldn't need to worry about this assumption as long as she didn't allow her inventory levels to fluctuate too much.

5. Kay sells just one size poster, so her sales mix is constant at 100% art posters. Later, we'll expand her product line to include two different size posters—each with a different sales price and variable cost. The resulting CVP modification works for any firm that offers two or more products as long as it assumes that sales mix will remain constant.

Kay's business meets all five assumptions, so her CVP analysis will be accurate. Because most business conditions do not meet these assumptions *perfectly*, managers regard CVP analysis as approximate, not exact.

The Unit Contribution Margin

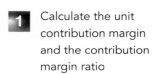
Calculate the unit contribution margin and the contribution margin ratio

The last chapter introduced the **contribution margin income statement,** which separates costs by behavior rather than function. Many managers prefer the contribution margin income statement because it gives them the information for CVP analysis in a "ready-to-use" format. On these income statements, the contribution margin is the "dividing line"—all variable expenses go above the line, and all fixed expenses go below the line. The results of Kay's first month of operations is shown in Exhibit 7-2.

EXHIBIT 7-2	**Contribution Margin Income Statement**

KAY PAK POSTERS
Contribution Margin Income Statement
Month Ended August 31

Sales revenue (550 posters)...	$ 19,250
Less: Variable expenses	(11,550)
Contribution margin	7,700
Less: Fixed expenses..	(7,000)
Operating income...	$ 700

Notice that the **contribution margin** is the excess of sales revenue over variable expenses. The contribution margin tells managers how much revenue is left—after paying variable expenses—for *contributing* toward covering fixed costs and then generating a profit. Hence the name contribution margin.

The contribution margin is stated as a *total* amount on the contribution margin income statement. However, managers often state the contribution margin on a *per unit* basis and as a *percentage,* or *ratio.* A product's **contribution margin per unit**—or **unit contribution margin**—is the excess of the selling price per unit over the variable cost of obtaining *and* selling each unit. Some businesses pay a sales commission on each unit or have other variable costs, such as shipping costs, for each unit sold. However, Kay's variable cost per unit is simply the price she pays for each poster. Therefore, her unit contribution margin is:

Sales price per poster	$35
Less: Variable cost per poster	(21)
Contribution margin per poster	$14

The unit contribution margin indicates how much profit each unit provides *before* fixed costs are considered. Each unit *first* contributes this profit toward covering the firm's fixed costs. Once the company sells enough units to cover its fixed costs, the unit contribution margin contributes *directly* to profit. For example, every poster Kay sells generates $14 of contribution margin that can be used to pay for the monthly $7,000 of fixed costs. After Kay sells enough posters to cover fixed costs, each additional poster she sells will generate $14 of operating income.

Managers can use the unit contribution margin to quickly forecast income at any volume within their relevant range. First, they project the total contribution margin by multiplying the unit contribution margin by the number of units sold. Then, they simply subtract fixed costs. For example, let's assume that Kay hopes to sell 650 posters next month. She can project her operating income as follows:

Contribution margin (650 posters × $14 per poster)	$9,100
Less: Fixed expenses	(7,000)
Operating income	$2,100

If Kay sells 650 posters next month, her operating income should be $2,100.

The Contribution Margin Ratio

In addition to computing the unit contribution margin, managers often compute the **contribution margin ratio,** which is the ratio of contribution margin to sales revenue. Kay can compute her contribution margin ratio at the unit level as follows:

$$\text{Contribution margin ratio} = \frac{\text{Unit contribution margin}}{\text{Sales price per unit}} = \frac{\$14}{\$35} = 40\%$$

Kay could also compute the contribution margin ratio using any volume of sales. Let's use her current sales volume, pictured in Exhibit 7-2:

$$\text{Contribution margin ratio} = \frac{\text{Contribution margin}}{\text{Sales revenue}} = \frac{\$7,700}{\$19,250} = 40\%$$

The 40% contribution margin ratio means that each *$1.00* of sales revenue contributes $0.40 toward fixed expenses and profit, as shown in Exhibit 7-3. The remaining $0.60 of each sales dollar is used to pay for variable costs. *The contribution margin ratio is the percentage of each sales dollar that is available for covering fixed expenses and generating a profit.*

EXHIBIT 7-3   **Breakdown of $1 of Sales Revenue**

Managers can also use the contribution margin ratio to quickly forecast operating income within their relevant range. When using the contribution margin ratio, managers project income based on sales *dollars* rather than sales *units*. For example, what will Kay's income be if sales revenue reaches $70,000 one month? To find out, simply multiply projected sales revenue by the contribution margin ratio to get the total contribution margin. Then, subtract fixed expenses:

Contribution margin ($70,000 sales × 40%) = ...	$28,000
Less: Fixed expenses...	(7,000)
Operating income..	$21,000

Let's verify. If Kay has $70,000 of sales revenue, she has sold 2,000 posters ($70,000 ÷ $35 price per poster). Her complete contribution margin income statement would be calculated as follows:

Sales revenue (2,000 posters × $35/poster)	$70,000
Less: Variable expenses (2,000 posters × $21/poster)	(42,000)
Contribution margin (2,000 posters × $14/poster)	$28,000
Less: Fixed expenses..	(7,000)
Operating income...	$21,000

The contribution margin per unit and contribution margin ratio help managers quickly and easily project income at different sales volumes. However, when projecting profits, managers must keep in mind the relevant range. For instance, if Kay wants to project income at a volume of 5,000 posters, she shouldn't use the existing contribution margin and fixed costs. Her current relevant range extends to only 2,000 posters per month. At a higher volume of sales, her variable cost per unit may be lower than $21 (due to volume discounts from her suppliers) and her monthly fixed costs may be higher than $7,000 (due to upgrading her system and hiring an employee to handle the extra sales volume).

Rather than use individual unit contribution margins on each of their products, large companies that offer hundreds or thousands of products (like art.com) use their contribution margin *ratio* to predict profits. As long as the sales mix remains constant (one of our CVP assumptions), the contribution margin ratio will remain constant.

We've seen how managers use the contribution margin to project income; but managers use the contribution margin for other purposes too, such as motivating the sales force. Salespeople who know the contribution margin of each product can generate more profit by emphasizing high-margin products. This is why many companies base sales commissions on the contribution margins produced by sales rather than on sales revenue alone.

In the next section, we'll see how managers use the contribution margin in CVP analysis to determine their breakeven point and to determine how many units they need to sell to reach target profits.

Using CVP Analysis to Find the Breakeven Point

A company's **breakeven point** is the sales level at which *operating income is zero*. Sales below the breakeven point result in a loss. Sales above the breakeven point provide a profit. Before Kay started her business, she wanted to figure out how many posters she would have to sell just to break even.

There are three ways to calculate the breakeven point. All of the approaches are based on the income statement, so they all reach the same conclusion. The first two methods find breakeven in terms of sales *units*. The last approach finds breakeven in terms of sales *dollars*.

| | 2 | Use CVP analysis to find breakeven points and target profit volumes |

1. The income statement approach

2. The shortcut approach using the *unit* contribution margin

3. The shortcut approach using the contribution margin *ratio*

Let's examine these three approaches in detail.

The Income Statement Approach

The income statement approach simply breaks the income statement equation into smaller components:

$$\left(\begin{array}{c}\text{Sales price}\\\text{per unit}\end{array}\times\text{Units sold}\right)-\left(\begin{array}{c}\text{Variable cost}\\\text{per unit}\end{array}\times\text{Units sold}\right)-\text{Fixed expenses}=\text{Operating income}$$

where SALES REVENUE − VARIABLE EXPENSES − FIXED EXPENSES = OPERATING INCOME.

Let's use this approach to find Kay's breakeven point. Recall that Kay sells her posters for $35 each and that her variable cost is $21 per poster. Kay's fixed expenses total $7,000. At the breakeven point, operating income is zero. We use this information to solve the income statement equation for the number of posters Kay must sell to break even.

SALES REVENUE	−	VARIABLE EXPENSES	− FIXED EXPENSES	= OPERATING INCOME
($35 × Units sold) −		($21 × Units sold) −	$7,000	= $0
($35	−	$21) × Units sold −	$7,000	= $0
		$14 × Units sold		= $7,000
		Units sold		= $7,000/$14
		Sales in units		= 500 posters

Kay must sell 500 posters to break even. Her breakeven point in sales dollars is $17,500 (500 posters × $35).

You can check your answer by substituting the breakeven number of units into the income statement and checking that this level of sales results in zero profit:

Sales revenue (500 posters × $35)...	$17,500
Less: Variable expenses (500 posters × $21).........................	(10,500)
Contribution margin	$ 7,000
Less: Fixed expenses...	(7,000)
Operating income..	$ 0

Notice that at breakeven, a firm's fixed expenses equal its contribution margin. In other words, the firm has generated just enough contribution margin to cover its fixed expenses (but *not* enough to generate a profit).

The Shortcut Approach Using the Unit Contribution Margin

The shortcut method simply rearranges the income statement equation and isolates "Units sold" on the left:

$$\underbrace{\text{Sales revenue} - \text{Variable expenses}}_{\text{Contribution margin}} - \text{Fixed expenses} = \text{Operating income}$$

$$\text{Contribution margin} - \text{Fixed expenses} = \text{Operating income}$$

$$(\text{Contribution margin per unit} \times \text{Units sold}) = \text{Fixed expenses} + \text{Operating income}$$

Dividing both sides of the equation by contribution margin per unit yields the shortcut method:

$$\text{Sales in units} = \frac{\text{Fixed expenses} + \text{Operating income}}{\text{Contribution margin per unit}}$$

Kay can use this shortcut method to find her breakeven point in units. Kay's fixed expenses total $7,000, and her unit contribution margin is $14. At the breakeven point, operating income is zero. Thus, Kay's breakeven point in units is:

$$\text{Sales in units} = \frac{\$7,000 + \$0}{\$14}$$
$$= 500 \text{ posters}$$

Why does this shortcut method work? Recall that each poster provides $14 of contribution margin. To break even, Kay must generate enough contribution margin to cover $7,000 of fixed expenses. At the rate of $14 per poster, Kay must sell 500 posters ($7,000/$14) to cover her $7,000 of fixed expenses. Because the shortcut method simply rearranges the income statement equation, the breakeven point is the same under both methods (500 posters).

Stop & Think...

What would Kay's operating income be if she sold 501 posters? What would it be if she sold 600 posters?

Answer: Every poster sold provides $14 of contribution margin, which first contributes toward covering fixed costs, then profit. Once Kay reaches her breakeven point (500 posters), she has covered all fixed costs. Therefore, each additional poster sold after the breakeven point contributes $14 *directly to profit*. If Kay sells 501 posters, she has sold one more poster than breakeven. Her operating income is $14. If she sells 600 posters, she has sold 100 more posters than breakeven. Her operating income is $1,400 ($14 per poster × 100 posters). We can verify as follows:

Contribution margin (600 posters × $14 per poster)..	$8,400
Less: Fixed expenses...	(7,000)
Operating income	$1,400

Once a company achieves breakeven, each additional unit sold contributes its unique unit contribution margin directly to profit.

The Shortcut Approach Using the Contribution Margin Ratio

It's easy to compute the breakeven point in *units* for a simple business like Kay's that has only one product. But what about companies that have thousands of products such as art.com, Home Depot, and Amazon.com? It doesn't make sense for these companies to determine the number of each various product they need to sell to break even. Can you imagine a Home Depot manager describing breakeven as 100,000 wood screws, 2 million nails, 3,000 lawn mowers, 10,000 gallons of paint, and so forth? It simply doesn't make sense. Therefore, multiproduct companies usually compute breakeven in terms of *sales dollars*.

This shortcut approach differs from the other shortcut we've just seen in only one way: Fixed expenses plus operating income are divided by the contribution margin *ratio* (not by contribution margin *per unit*) to yield sales in *dollars* (not *units*):

$$\text{Sales in dollars} = \frac{\text{Fixed expenses} + \text{Operating income}}{\text{Contribution margin ratio}}$$

Recall that Kay's contribution margin ratio is 40%. At the breakeven point, operating income is $0, so Kay's breakeven point in sales dollars is:

$$\text{Sales in units} = \frac{\$7,000 + \$0}{0.40}$$
$$= \$17,500$$

This is the same breakeven sales revenue we calculated earlier (500 posters ✕ $35 sales price = $17,500).

Why does the contribution margin ratio formula work? Each dollar of Kay's sales contributes $0.40 to fixed expenses and profit. To break even, she must generate enough contribution margin at the rate of $0.40 per sales dollar to cover the $7,000 fixed expenses ($7,000 ÷ 0.40 = $17,500).

> *To recall which shortcut formula gives which result, remember this: Dividing fixed costs by the **unit** contribution margin provides breakeven in sales **units**. Dividing fixed costs by the contribution margin **ratio** provides breakeven in sales dollars.*

Stop & Think...

Suppose Amazon.com's total revenues are $4.5 billion, its variable expenses are $3.15 billion, and its fixed expenses are $1.1 billion. What is the breakeven point in sales dollars?

Answer: We can use the shortcut approach that uses the contribution margin ratio to determine the breakeven point. First, we compute the contribution margin ratio: The contribution margin ratio is 30% [($4.5 − $3.15) ÷ $4.5]. Then, we use the ratio in the shortcut formula:

$$\text{Sales in dollars} = \frac{\text{Fixed expenses} + \text{Operating income}}{\text{Contribution margin ratio}}$$

$$= \frac{\$1.1 \text{ billion} + \$0}{0.30}$$

$$= \$3.667 \text{ billion (rounded)}$$

Amazon.com must achieve sales revenue of $3.667 billion just to break even.

Using CVP to Plan Profits

For established products and services, managers are more interested in the sales level needed to earn a target profit than in the breakeven point. Managers of new business ventures are also interested in the profits they can expect to earn. For example, Kay doesn't want to just break even—she wants her business to be her sole source of income. She would like the business to earn $4,900 of profit each month. How many posters must Kay sell each month to reach her target profit?

How Much Must We Sell to Earn a Target Profit?

The only difference from our prior analysis is that instead of determining the sales level needed for *zero profit* (breakeven), Kay now wants to know how many posters she must sell to earn a $4,900 profit. We can use the income statement approach or the shortcut approach to find the answer. Because Kay wants to know the number of *units*, we'll use the shortcut approach based on the *unit* contribution margin. This time, instead of an operating income of zero (breakeven), we'll insert Kay's target operating income of $4,900:

$$\text{Sales in } units = \frac{\text{Fixed expenses} + \text{Operating income}}{\text{Contribution margin } per\ unit}$$

$$= \frac{\$7,000 + \$4,900}{\$14}$$

$$= \frac{\$11,900}{\$14}$$

$$= 850 \text{ posters}$$

This analysis shows that Kay must sell 850 posters each month to earn profits of $4,900 a month. Notice that this level of sales falls within Kay's current relevant range (0–2,000 posters per month), so the conclusion that she would earn $4,900 of income at this sales volume is valid. If the calculation resulted in a sales volume outside the current relevant range (greater than 2,000 units), we would need to reassess our cost assumptions.

Assume that Kay also wants to know how much sales revenue she needs to earn $4,900 of monthly profit. Because she already knows the number of units needed (850), she can easily translate this volume into sales revenue:

$$850 \text{ posters} \times \$35 \text{ sales price/poster} = \$29,750 \text{ sales revenue}$$

If Kay only wanted to know the sales revenue needed to achieve her target profit rather than the number of units needed, she could have found the answer directly by using the shortcut approach based on the contribution margin *ratio*:

$$\text{Sales in } dollars = \frac{\text{Fixed expenses} + \text{Operating income}}{\text{Contribution margin } ratio}$$

$$= \frac{\$7,000 + \$4,900}{0.40}$$

$$= \frac{\$11,900}{0.40}$$

$$= \$29,750$$

Finally, Kay could have used the income statement approach to find the same answers:

SALES REVENUE	−	VARIABLE EXPENSES	−	FIXED EXPENSES	=	OPERATING INCOME
($35 × Units sold)	−	($21 × Units sold)	−	$7,000	=	$4,900
($35	−	$21) × Units sold	−	$7,000	=	$4,900
		$14 × Units sold			=	$11,900
				Units sold	=	$11,900/$14
				Units sold	=	850 posters

We can prove that our answers (from any of the three approaches) are correct by preparing Kay's income statment for a sales volume of 850 units:

Sales revenue (850 posters × $35)..	$29,750
Less: Variable expenses (850 posters × $21)...............................	(17,850)
Contribution margin	11,900
Less: Fixed expenses..	(7,000)
Operating income..	$ 4,900

Graphing CVP Relationships

By graphing the CVP relationships for her business, Kay can see at a glance how changes in the levels of sales will affect profits. As in the last chapter, the volume of units (posters) is placed on the horizontal *x*-axis; dollars, on the vertical *y*-axis. Then, she follows five steps to graph the CVP relations for her business, as illustrated in Exhibit 7-4.

EXHIBIT 7-4   **Cost-Volume-Profit Graph**

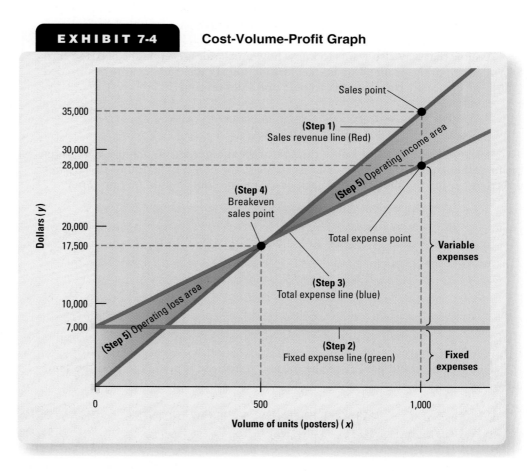

STEP 1: Choose a sales volume, such as 1,000 posters. Plot the point for total sales revenue at that volume: 1,000 posters × $35 per poster = sales of $35,000. Draw the *sales revenue line* from the origin (0) through the $35,000 point. Why does the sales revenue line start at the origin? If Kay does not sell any posters, there is no sales revenue.

STEP 2: Draw the *fixed expense line*, a horizontal line that intersects the *y*-axis at $7,000. Recall that the fixed expense line is flat because fixed expenses are the same ($7,000) no matter how many posters Kay sells within her relevant range (up to 2,000 posters per month).

STEP 3: Draw the *total expense line*. Total expense is the sum of variable expense plus fixed expense. Thus, total expense is a *mixed* cost. So, the total expense line follows the form of the mixed cost line. Begin by computing variable expense at the chosen sales volume: 1,000 posters × $21 per poster = variable expense of $21,000. Add variable expense to fixed expense: $21,000 + $7,000 = $28,000. Plot the total expense point ($28,000) for 1,000 units. Then, draw a line through this point from the $7,000 fixed expense intercept on the dollars axis. This is the *total expense line*. Why does the total expense line start at the fixed expense line? If Kay sells no posters, she still incurs the $7,000 fixed cost for the server leasing, software, and office rental, but she incurs no variable costs.

STEP 4: Identify the *breakeven point*. The breakeven point is the point where the sales revenue line intersects the total expense line. This is the point where sales revenue equals total expenses. Our previous analyses told us that Kay's breakeven point is 500 posters, or $17,500 in sales. The graph shows this information visually.

STEP 5: Mark the *operating income* and the *operating loss* areas on the graph. To the left of the breakeven point, the total expense line lies above the sales revenue line. Expenses exceed sales revenue, leading to an operating loss. If Kay sells only 300 posters, she incurs an operating loss. The amount of the loss is the vertical distance between the total expense line and the sales revenue line:

Sales revenue − Variable expenses − Fixed expenses = Operating income (Loss)
  (300 × $35) −   (300 × $21)   − $7,000   = $(2,800)

To the right of the breakeven point, the business earns a profit. The vertical distance between the sales revenue line and the total expense line equals income. Exhibit 7-4 shows that if Kay sells 1,000 posters, she earns operating income of $7,000 ($35,000 sales revenue − $28,000 total expenses).

Why bother with a graph? Why not just use the income statement approach or the shortcut contribution margin approach? Graphs like Exhibit 7-4 help managers quickly estimate the profit or loss earned at different levels of sales. The income statement and contribution margin approaches indicate income or loss for only a single sales amount.

Decision Guidelines

CVP ANALYSIS

Your friend wants to open her own ice cream parlor after college. She needs help making the following decisions:

Decision	Guidelines
How much will I earn on every ice cream cone I sell?	The unit contribution margin shows managers how much they earn on each unit sold after paying for variable costs *but before considering fixed expenses*. The unit

continued . . .

Decision	Guidelines
	contribution margin is the amount each unit earns that contributes toward covering fixed expenses and generating a profit. It is computed as:

$$\begin{array}{l} \text{Sales price per unit} \\ \underline{\text{Less: Variable cost per unit}} \\ \text{Contribution margin per unit} \end{array}$$

The contribution margin ratio shows managers how much contribution margin is earned on every $1 of sales. It is computed as:

$$\frac{\text{Contribution margin}}{\text{Sales revenue}} = \text{Contribution margin ratio}$$

Decision	Guidelines
Can I quickly forecast my income without creating a full income statement?	The contribution margin concept allows managers to forecast income quickly at different sales volumes. First, find the total contribution margin (by multiplying the forecasted number of units by the unit contribution margin *or* by multiplying the forecasted sales revenue by the contribution margin ratio) and then subtract all fixed expenses.
• How can I compute the *number of ice cream cones* I'll have to sell to break even or earn a target profit?	*Income Statement Approach:*

$$\text{Sales revenue} - \text{Variable expenses} - \text{Total fixed expense} = \text{Operating income}$$

$$\left(\begin{array}{c}\text{Sale price per unit}\\ \times \text{Number of units}\end{array}\right) - \left(\begin{array}{c}\text{Variable cost per unit}\\ \times \text{Number of units}\end{array}\right) - \text{Total fixed expenses} = \text{Operating income}$$

Shortcut Unit Contribution Margin Approach:

$$\text{Sales in } \textit{units} = \frac{\text{Fixed expenses} + \text{Operating income}}{\text{Contribution margin } \textit{per unit}}$$

Decision	Guidelines
• How can I compute the *dollars of sales revenue* I'll have to generate to break even or earn a target profit?	*Shortcut Contribution Margin Ratio Approach:*

$$\text{Sales in } \textit{dollars} = \frac{\text{Fixed expenses} + \text{Operating income}}{\text{Contribution margin } \textit{ratio}}$$

Decision	Guidelines
What will my profits look like over a range of volumes?	CVP graphs show managers, at a glance, how different sales volumes will affect profits.

Summary Problem 1

Fleet Foot buys hiking socks for $6 a pair and sells them for $10. Management budgets monthly fixed expenses of $10,000 for sales volumes between 0 and 12,000 pairs.

Requirements

1. Use the income statement approach and the shortcut unit contribution margin approach to compute monthly breakeven sales in units.

2. Use the shortcut contribution margin ratio approach to compute the breakeven point in sales dollars.

3. Compute the monthly sales level (in units) required to earn a target operating income of $14,000. Use either the income statement approach or the shortcut contribution margin approach.

4. Prepare a graph of Fleet Foot's CVP relationships, similar to Exhibit 7-4. Draw the sales revenue line, the fixed expense line, and the total expense line. Label the axes, the breakeven point, the operating income area, and the operating loss area.

Solution

Requirement 1
Income statement approach:

Sales revenue	−	Variable expenses	−	Fixed expenses	=	Operating income
$\left(\begin{array}{c}\text{Sale price} \\ \text{per unit}\end{array} \times \begin{array}{c}\text{Units} \\ \text{sold}\end{array}\right)$	−	$\left(\begin{array}{c}\text{Variable} \\ \text{cost per unit}\end{array} \times \begin{array}{c}\text{Units} \\ \text{sold}\end{array}\right)$	−	Fixed expenses	=	Operating income
($10 × Units sold)	−	($6 × Units sold)	−	$10,000	=	$0
($10	−	$6) × Units sold			=	$10,000
		$4 × Units sold			=	$10,000
		Units sold			=	$10,000 ÷ $4
		Breakeven sales in units			=	2,500 units

Shortcut unit contribution margin approach:

$$\text{Sales in units} = \frac{\text{Fixed expenses} + \text{Operating income}}{\text{Contribution margin per unit}}$$

$$= \frac{\$10,000 + \$0}{\$10 - \$6}$$

$$= \frac{\$10,000}{\$4}$$

$$= 2,500 \text{ units}$$

Requirement 2

$$\text{Sales in dollars} = \frac{\text{Fixed expenses} + \text{Operating income}}{\text{Contribution margin ratio}}$$

$$= \frac{\$10,000 + \$0}{0.40^*}$$

$$= \$25,000$$

$$^*\text{Contribution margin ratio} = \frac{\text{Contribution margin per unit}}{\text{Sale price per unit}} = \frac{\$4}{\$10} = 0.40$$

Requirement 3

Income statement equation approach:

Sales revenue	−	Variable expenses	−	Fixed expenses	=	Operating income
$\left(\begin{array}{c}\text{Sale price} \\ \text{per unit}\end{array} \times \begin{array}{c}\text{Units} \\ \text{sold}\end{array}\right)$	−	$\left(\begin{array}{c}\text{Variable} \\ \text{cost per unit}\end{array} \times \begin{array}{c}\text{Units} \\ \text{sold}\end{array}\right)$	−	Fixed expenses	=	Operating income
($\$10 \times$ Units sold)	−	($\$6 \times$ Units sold)	−	$\$10,000$	=	$\$14,000$
($\$10	−	$\$6) \times$ Units sold			=	$\$10,000 + \$14,000$
		$\$4 \times$ Units sold			=	$\$24,000$
		Units sold			=	$\$24,000 \div \$4$
		Units sold			=	6,000 units

Shortcut unit contribution margin approach:

$$\text{Sales in units} = \frac{\text{Fixed expenses} + \text{Operating income}}{\text{Contribution margin per unit}}$$

$$= \frac{\$10,000 + \$14,000}{\left(\$10 - \$6\right)}$$

$$= \frac{\$24,000}{\$4}$$

$$= 6000 \text{ units}$$

Requirement 4

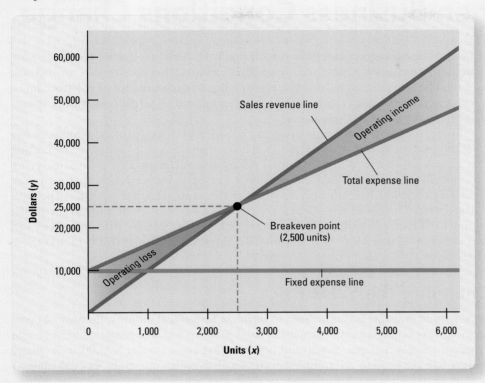

Using CVP When Business Conditions Change

3 Perform sensitivity analysis in response to changing business conditions

In today's fast-changing business world, managers need to quickly estimate how changes in sales price, costs, or volume affect profits. In a recent drive to increase profitability, Starbucks analyzed the profitability of each product at the store level. Then, it realigned prices. For example, coffee mugs and CDs had been money losers, so it raised the prices of these items.

To predict how raising or lowering prices will affect profits, managers use CVP to conduct **sensitivity analysis**. Sensitivity analysis is a "what-if" technique that asks what results will be if actual prices or costs change or if an underlying assumption such as sales mix changes. For example, increased competition may force Kay to lower her sales price, while at the same time her suppliers increase poster costs. How will these changes affect Kay's breakeven and target profit volumes? What will happen if Kay changes her sales mix by offering posters in two different sizes? How will she modify her CVP analysis? We'll tackle these issues next.

Changing the Sales Price

Let's assume that Kay has now been in business for several months. Because of competition, Kay is considering cutting her sales price to $31 per poster. If her variable expenses remain $21 per poster and her fixed expenses stay at $7,000, how many posters will she need to sell to break even? To answer this question, Kay calculates a new unit contribution margin using the new sales price:

New sales price per poster	$31
Less: Variable cost per poster	(21)
New contribution margin per poster	$10

She then uses the new unit contribution margin to compute breakeven sales in units:

$$\text{Sales in units} = \frac{\text{Fixed expenses} + \text{Operating income}}{\text{Contribution margin per unit}}$$

$$= \frac{\$7,000 + \$0}{\$10}$$

$$= 700 \text{ posters}$$

With the original $35 sale price, Kay's breakeven point was 500 posters. If Kay lowers the sales price to $31 per poster, her breakeven point increases to 700 posters. The lower sales price means that each poster contributes *less* toward fixed expenses ($10 versus $14 before the price change), so Kay must sell 200 *more* posters to break even. Each dollar of sales revenue would contribute $0.32 ($10/$31) rather than $0.40 toward covering fixed expenses and generating a profit.

If Kay reduces her sales price to $31, how many posters must she sell to achieve her $4,900 monthly target profit? Kay again uses the new unit contribution margin to determine how many posters she will need to sell to reach her profit goals:

$$\text{Sales in units} = \frac{\$7,000 + \$4,900}{\$10}$$
$$= 1,190 \text{ posters}$$

With the original sales price, Kay needed to sell only 850 posters per month to achieve her target profit level. If Kay cuts her sales price (and, therefore, her contribution margin), she must sell more posters to achieve her financial goals. Kay could have found these same results using the income statement approach. Exhibit 7-5 shows the effect of changes in sales price on breakeven and target profit volumes.

EXHIBIT 7-5   **The Effect of Changes in Sales Price on Breakeven and Target Profit Volumes**

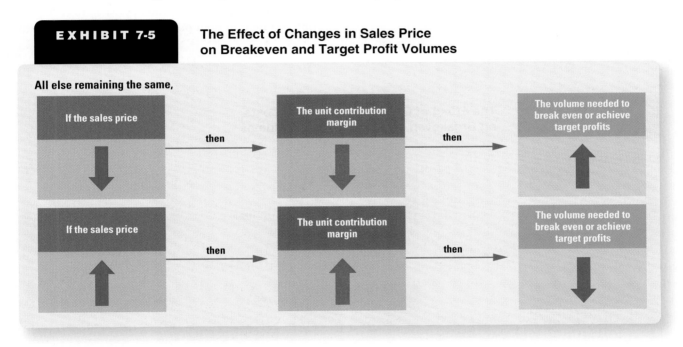

Stop & Think...

Kay believes she could dominate the e-commerce art poster business if she cut the sales price to $20. Is this a good idea?

Answer: No. The variable cost per poster is $21. If Kay sells posters for $20 each, she loses $1 on each poster. Kay will incur a loss if the sales price is less than the variable cost.

Changing Variable Costs

Let's assume that Kay does *not* lower her sales price. However, Kay's supplier raises his price for each poster to $23.80 (instead of the original $21). Kay does not want to pass this increase on to her customers, so she holds her sales price at the original

$35 per poster. Her fixed costs remain $7,000. How many posters must she sell to break even after her supplier raises his prices? Kay's new contribution margin per unit drops to $11.20 ($35 sales price per poster − $23.80 variable cost per poster). So, her new breakeven point is:

$$\text{Sales in units} = \frac{\text{Fixed expenses + Operating income}}{\text{Contribution margin per unit}}$$

$$= \frac{\$7,000 + \$0}{\$11.20}$$

$$= 625 \text{ posters}$$

Higher variable costs per unit have the same effect as lower selling prices per unit—they both reduce the product's unit contribution margin. As a result, Kay will have to sell *more* units to break even and achieve target profits. As shown in Exhibit 7-6, a *decrease* in variable costs would have just the opposite effect. Lower variable costs increase the contribution margin each poster provides and, therefore, lowers the breakeven point.

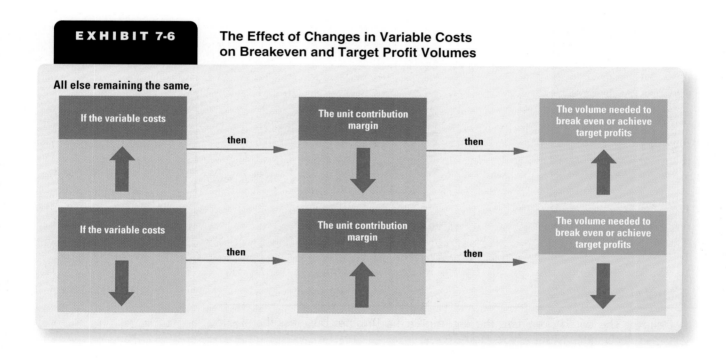

| **EXHIBIT 7-6** | **The Effect of Changes in Variable Costs on Breakeven and Target Profit Volumes** |

All else remaining the same,

If the variable costs ↑ then The unit contribution margin ↓ then The volume needed to break even or achieve target profits ↑

If the variable costs ↓ then The unit contribution margin ↑ then The volume needed to break even or achieve target profits ↓

Stop & Think...

Suppose Kay is squeezed from both sides: Her supply costs have increased to $23.80 per poster, yet she must lower her price to $31 in order to compete. Under these conditions, how many posters will Kay need to sell to achieve her monthly target profit of $4,900? If Kay doesn't think she can sell that many posters, how else might she attempt to achieve her profit goals?

Answer: Kay is now in a position faced by many companies—her unit contribution margin is squeezed by both higher supply costs and lower sales prices:

New sales price per poster..	$31.00
Less: New variable cost per poster	(23.80)
New contribution margin per poster	$ 7.20

Kay's new contribution margin is about half of what it was when she started her business ($14). To achieve her target profit, her volume will have to increase dramatically (yet, it would still fall within her current relevant range for fixed costs—which extends to 2,000 posters per month):

$$\text{Sales in units} = \frac{\text{Fixed expenses} + \text{Operating income}}{\text{Contribution margin per unit}}$$

$$= \frac{\$7,000 + \$4,900}{\$7.20}$$

$$= 1,653 \text{ posters (rounded)}$$

Based on her current volume, Kay may not believe she can sell so many posters. To maintain a reasonable profit level, Kay may need to take other measures. For example, she may try to find a different supplier with lower poster costs. She may also attempt to lower her fixed costs. For example, perhaps she could negotiate a cheaper lease on her office space or move her business to a less expensive location. She could also try to increase her volume by spending *more* on fixed costs, such as advertising. Kay could also investigate selling other products, in addition to her regular-size posters, that would have higher unit contribution margins. We'll discuss these measures next.

Changing Fixed Costs

Let's return to Kay's original data ($35 selling price and $21 variable cost). Kay has decided she really doesn't need a storefront office at the retail strip mall because she doesn't have many walk-in customers. She could decrease her monthly fixed costs from $7,000 to $4,200 by moving her office to an industrial park.

How will this decrease in fixed costs affect Kay's breakeven point? *Changes in fixed costs do not affect the contribution margin.* Therefore, Kay's unit contribution margin is still $14 per poster. However, her breakeven point changes because her fixed costs change:

$$\text{Sales in units} = \frac{\text{Fixed expenses} + \text{Operating income}}{\text{Contribution margin per unit}}$$

$$= \frac{\$4,200 + \$0}{\$14.00}$$

$$= 300 \text{ posters}$$

Because of the decrease in fixed costs, Kay will need to sell only 300 posters, rather than 500 posters, to break even. The volume needed to achieve her monthly $4,900 target profit will also decline. However, if Kay's fixed costs *increase*, she will have to sell *more* units to break even. Exhibit 7-7 shows the effect of changes in fixed costs on breakeven and target profit volumes.

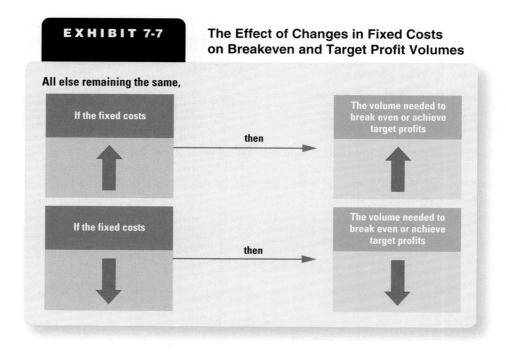

EXHIBIT 7-7   The Effect of Changes in Fixed Costs on Breakeven and Target Profit Volumes

We have seen that changes in sales prices, variable costs, and fixed costs can have dramatic effects on the volume of product that companies must sell to achieve breakeven and target profits. Companies often turn to automation to decrease variable costs (direct labor); but this, in turn, increases their fixed costs (equipment depreciation). Companies often move production overseas to decrease variable and fixed production costs, feeling forced to take these measures to keep their prices as low as their competitors. For example, Charbroil, the maker of gas grills, said that if it didn't move production overseas, profits would decline, or worse yet, the company would go out of business.

Stop & Think...

Kay has been considering advertising as a means to increase her sales volume. Kay could spend an extra $3,500 per month on Web site banner ads. How many *extra* posters would Kay have to sell *just to pay for the advertising?* (Use Kay's original data.)

Answer: Instead of using *all* of Kay's fixed costs, we can isolate *just* the fixed costs relating to advertising. This will allow us to figure out how many *extra* posters Kay would have to sell each month to break even on (or pay for) the advertising cost. Advertising is a fixed cost, so Kay's contribution margin remains $14 per unit.

$$\text{Sales in units} = \frac{\text{Fixed expenses + Operating income}}{\text{Contribution margin per unit}}$$
$$= \frac{\$3,500 + \$0}{\$14.00}$$
$$= 250 \text{ posters}$$

Kay must sell 250 *extra* posters each month just to pay for the cost of advertising. If she sells fewer than 250 extra posters, she'll increase her volume but lose money on the advertising. If she sells more than 250 extra posters, her plan will have worked—she'll increase her volume *and* her profit. Even though investing in the Web banner ads increases Kay's breakeven point to 750 units (500 plus another 250 to cover the advertising costs), Kay may be willing to pay the extra $3,500 if she expects the ads to stimulate enough extra sales to *more than* cover the additional advertising expense. Companies often face this issue. How many *extra* 12-packs of soda do you think Coca-Cola has to sell to pay for one 30-second advertisement during the Super Bowl?

Another way that companies can offset cost and pricing pressures is to expand their product lines to include products with higher contribution margins. In the next section, we'll see what happens when Kay decides to sell higher-margin, large-size posters in addition to regular-size posters.

Effect of Sales Mix on CVP Analysis

So far, we have assumed that Kay sold only one size poster. What would happen if she offered more products? Companies that sell more than one product must consider *sales mix* in figuring CVP relationships. A company earns more income by selling high-contribution margin products than by selling an equal number of low-contribution margin products.

4 Find breakeven and target profit volumes for multiproduct companies

For example, Continental Airlines has focused on attracting more business-people. Business travelers generally pay more for the same flight than leisure travelers, yet the variable costs are the same. By increasing the proportion of higher-paying business fliers, Continental boosted its sales revenue per available seat-mile (available seats × miles flown) from $0.074 to $0.090. Improving sales mix by selling more high-margin tickets reduced Continental's breakeven point. Before the change, Continental had to fill 63% of its seats to break even. By attracting more business travelers, Continental has to fill only 61%.

The same CVP formulas that are used to perform CVP analysis for a company with a single product can be used for any company that sells more than one product. But first, we must compute the *weighted-average contribution margin* of all products. Instead of using the simple average, we *weight* each product's unit contribution margin by the relative number of units sold.

Suppose Kay plans to sell two types of posters. In addition to her regular-size posters, Kay plans to sell large posters. Let's assume that none of Kay's original costs have changed. Recall that the regular posters have a unit contribution margin of $14 ($35 sales price − $21 variable cost). The larger posters will sell for $70 each, yet have variable costs of $40 each. Therefore, the unit contribution margin of each large poster is $30 ($70 − $40). Kay is adding the large-poster line because it carries a higher unit contribution margin. Assume that Kay's fixed expenses remain $7,000.

For every five regular posters sold, Kay expects to sell three large posters. In other words, she expects 5/8 of the sales to be regular posters and 3/8 to be large posters. This is a 5:3 sales mix. To compute breakeven sales in units, Kay first computes the *weighted-average contribution margin* as follows:

	Regular Posters	Large Posters	Total
Sales price per unit	$ 35	$ 70	
Less: Variable cost per unit	(21)	(40)	
Contribution margin per unit	$ 14	$ 30	
Sales mix	× 5	× 3	8
Contribution margin	$ 70	$ 90	$160
Weighted-average contribution margin per unit ($160/8)			$ 20

Notice that the *weighted-average* contribution margin per unit ($20) is lower, in this case, than a *simple average* of the unit contribution margins [$22 = (14 + 30) ÷ 2]. The weighted average is *lower* than the simple average because *more* of the lower-margin regular posters are sold than the higher-margin large posters. If more large posters were sold than regular posters, the weighted-average contribution margin would be *higher* than the simple average.

Once we've computed the weighted-average contribution margin, we use it in the shortcut formula (alternatively, we could use the income statement approach):

$$\text{Sales in total units} = \frac{\text{Fixed expenses} + \text{Operating income}}{\text{Weighted-average contribution margin per unit}}$$

$$= \frac{\$7,000 + \$0}{\$20}$$

$$= 350 \text{ posters}$$

The final step simply "breaks apart" the total number of posters into the regular and large sizes using the sales mix ratios:

Breakeven sales of regular posters (350 × 5/8)	218.75 regular posters
Breakeven sales of large posters (350 × 3/8)	131.25 large posters

As is often the case in real situations, these computations don't yield round numbers. Because Kay cannot sell partial posters, she must sell 219 regular posters and 132 large posters to avoid a loss. Using these rounded numbers would lead to a small rounding error in our check figures, however, so the rest of our computations will use the exact results: 218.75 regular posters and 131.25 large posters.

Kay's overall breakeven point in sales dollars is $16,844 (amounts rounded to the nearest dollar):

218.75 regular posters at $35 each..	$ 7,656
131.25 large posters at $70 each	9,188
Total revenues...	$16,844

We can prove this breakeven point as follows:

	Total
Contribution margin:	
Regular posters (218.75 × $14)...	$ 3,063
Large posters (131.25 × $30)	3,937
Contribution margin	$ 7,000
Less: Fixed expenses..	(7,000)
Operating income...	$ 0

We just found Kay's *breakeven* point, but Kay can also use the same steps to calculate the volume she must sell to achieve a target profit. The only difference, as before, is that she would use *target profit*, rather than *zero*, as the operating income in the shortcut formula.

Stop & Think...

Suppose Kay would still like to earn a monthly profit of $4,900. Recall that she needed to sell 850 posters to achieve this profit level when she was selling only regular posters. If her sales mix is 5:3, as planned, will she need to sell more than or fewer than 850 posters to achieve her target profit? Why?

Answer: Kay will need to sell *fewer* than 850 posters because she is now selling some large posters that have a higher unit contribution margin. We can verify as follows:

$$\text{Sales in total units} = \frac{\text{Fixed expenses} + \text{Operating income}}{\text{Weighted-average contribution margin per unit}}$$

$$= \frac{\$7,000 + \$4,900}{\$20}$$

$$= 595 \text{ posters}$$

Kay would have to sell a *total* of 595 posters: 372 regular posters (595 × 5/8) and 223 large posters (595 × 3/8) to achieve her target profit.

Companies that offer hundreds of products (such as Home Depot and Amazon.com) will not want to find the breakeven point in terms of units. Rather, they'll want to know breakeven (or target profit volumes) in dollars of sales revenue. To find this volume, they'll first need to know their contribution margin ratio. If a company prepares contribution margin income statements, it easily calculates the contribution margin ratio by dividing the total contribution margin by total sales. The contribution margin ratio is *already* weighted by the company's *actual sales mix*! If the company believes that its sales mix will change next year, it can use forecasted contribution margin income statements to compute the contribution margin ratio.

Let's see how this would work for Kay. To use the contribution margin ratio approach to estimate breakeven sales in dollars, Kay must first estimate her contribution margin ratio. Let's assume that Kay expects to sell 500 regular posters and 300 large posters, although she could use *any* total volume of sales as long as it's in the expected sales mix ratio (5:3 in Kay's case).

Total expected contribution margin:		
Regular posters (500 × $14)............................	$ 7,000	
Large posters (300 × $30)	$ 9,000	
Total expected contribution margin		$16,000
Divided by total expected sales revenue:		
Regular posters (500 × $35)............................	$17,500	
Large posters (300 × $70)	21,000	
Total expected sales		÷ 38,500
Contribution margin ratio.........................		= 41.558%

Notice how Kay's contribution margin ratio is higher than it was when she sold only regular posters (40%). That's because she is now selling some large posters that have a 42.9% contribution margin ratio ($30/$70). Because her sales mix changed, she now has a different contribution margin ratio. The contribution margin ratio usually changes when the sales mix changes.

Once Kay knows her contribution margin ratio, she can use the contribution margin ratio approach to estimate breakeven sales in dollars:

$$\text{Sales in units} = \frac{\text{Fixed expenses} + \text{Operating income}}{\text{Contribution margin ratio}}$$

$$= \frac{\$7,000 + \$0}{0.41588}$$

$$= \$16,844 \text{ (rounded)}$$

Notice that this is the same breakeven point in sales dollars we found earlier by first finding breakeven in *units*.

If Kay's actual sales mix is not five regular posters to three large posters, her actual operating income will differ from the planned amount *even if* she sells exactly 800 total posters. The sales mix greatly influences the breakeven point. When companies offer more than one product, they do not have a unique breakeven point. Every sales mix assumption leads to a different breakeven point. In other words, the breakeven point and operating income depend on the sales mix.

Stop & Think...

Suppose Kay plans to sell 800 total posters in the 5:3 sales mix (five regular posters sold for every three large posters). She actually does sell 800 posters—375 regular and 425 large. The sale prices per poster, variable costs per poster, and fixed expenses are exactly as predicted. Without doing any computations, is Kay's actual operating income greater than, less than, or equal to her expected income?

Answer: Kay's actual sales mix did not turn out to be the 5:3 mix she expected. She actually sold *more* of the higher-margin large posters than lower-margin regular posters. This favorable change in the sales mix causes her to earn a higher operating income than she expected.

Information Technology and Sensitivity Analysis

We have just seen that Kay's breakeven point and target profit volumes are very sensitive to changes in her business environment, including changes in sales prices, variable costs, fixed costs, and sales mix assumptions. Information technology allows managers to perform a wide array of sensitivity analyses before committing to decisions. Managers of small- to medium-sized companies use Excel spreadsheets to perform sensitivity analyses like those we just did for Kay. Spreadsheets allow managers to estimate how one change (or several simultaneous changes) affects business operations. Managers also use spreadsheet software to create CVP graphs like the one in Exhibit 7-4.

Many large companies use sophisticated enterprise resource planning software such as SAP, Oracle, and PeopleSoft to provide detailed data for CVP analysis. For example, after Sears stores lock their doors at 9 p.m., records for each individual transaction flow into a massive database. From a Diehard battery sold in Texas to a Trader Bay polo shirt sold in New Hampshire, the system compiles an average of 1.5 million transactions a day. With the click of a mouse, managers access sales price, variable cost, and sales volume for individual products to conduct breakeven or profit planning analyses.

Risk Indicators

A firm's level of risk depends on many factors, including the general health of the economy and the specific industry in which the company operates. In addition, a firm's risk depends on its current volume of sales and the relative amount of fixed and variable costs that make up its total costs. Next, we discuss how a firm can gauge its level of risk, to some extent, by its margin of safety and its operating leverage.

5 Determine a firm's margin of safety and operating leverage

Margin of Safety

The **margin of safety** is the excess of expected sales over breakeven sales. This is the "cushion," or drop in sales, the company can absorb without incurring a loss. The higher the margin of safety, the greater the cushion against loss and the less risky the business plan. Managers use the margin of safety to evaluate the risk of current operations as well as the risk of new plans.

Let's continue to assume that Kay has been in business for several months and that she generally sells 950 posters a month. Kay's breakeven point in our original data is 500 posters. Kay can express her margin of safety in units or in sales dollars:

$$
\begin{aligned}
\textbf{Margin of safety in units} &= \textbf{Expected sales in units} - \textbf{Breakeven sales in units} \\
&= \quad 950 \text{ posters} \quad - \quad 500 \text{ posters} \\
&= \quad 450 \text{ posters}
\end{aligned}
$$

$$
\begin{aligned}
\textbf{Margin of safety in dollars} &= \textbf{Margin of safety in units} \times \textbf{Sale price per unit} \\
&= \quad 450 \text{ posters} \quad \times \quad \$35 \\
&= \quad \$15{,}750
\end{aligned}
$$

Sales can drop by 450 posters, or $15,750 a month, before Kay incurs a loss. This is a comfortable margin.

Managers can also compute the margin of safety as a percentage of sales. Simply divide the margin of safety by sales. We obtain the same percentage whether we use units or dollars.

In units:

$$
\begin{aligned}
\text{Margin of safety as a percentage} &= \frac{\text{Margin of safety in units}}{\text{Expected sales in units}} \\
&= \frac{450 \text{ posters}}{950 \text{ posters}} \\
&= 47.4\% \text{ (rounded)}
\end{aligned}
$$

In dollars:

$$
\begin{aligned}
\text{Margin of safety as a percentage} &= \frac{\text{Margin of safety in dollars}}{\text{Expected sales in dollars}} \\
&= \frac{450 \text{ units} \times \$35}{950 \text{ units} \times \$35} \\
&= \frac{\$15{,}750}{\$33{,}250} \\
&= 47.4\% \text{ (rounded)}
\end{aligned}
$$

The margin of safety percentage tells Kay that sales would have to drop by more than 47.4% before she would incur a loss. If sales fall by less than 47.4%, she would still earn a profit. If sales fall exactly 47.4%, she would break even. This ratio tells Kay that her business plan is not unduly risky.

Operating Leverage

A company's **operating leverage** refers to the relative amount of fixed and variable costs that make up its total costs. Most companies have both fixed and variable costs. However, companies with *high* operating leverage have *relatively more fixed costs* and relatively fewer variable costs. Companies with high operating leverage include golf courses, airlines, and hotels. Because they have fewer variable costs, their contribution margin ratio is relatively high. Recall from the last chapter that Embassy Suites' variable cost of servicing each guest is low, which means that the hotel has a high contribution margin and high operating leverage.

What does high operating leverage have to do with risk? If sales volume decreases, the total contribution margin will drop significantly because each sales dollar contains a high percentage of contribution margin. Yet, the high fixed costs of running the company remain. Therefore, the operating income of these companies can easily turn from profit to loss if sales volume declines. For example, airlines were financially devastated after September 11, 2001, because the number of people flying suddenly dropped, creating large reductions in contribution margin. Yet, the airlines had to continue paying their high fixed costs. High operating leverage companies are at *more* risk because their income declines drastically when sales volume declines.

What if the economy is growing and sales volume *increases*? High operating leverage companies will reap high rewards. Remember that after breakeven, each unit sold contributes its unit contribution margin directly to profit. Because high operating leverage companies have high contribution margin ratios, each additional dollar of sale will contribute more to the firm's operating income. Exhibit 7-8 summarizes these characteristics.

EXHIBIT 7-8   **Characteristics of High Operating Leverage Firms**

- High operating leverage companies have:
    - *Higher* levels of fixed costs and *lower* levels of variable costs
    - *Higher* contribution margin ratios
- For high operating leverage companies, changes in volume significantly affect operating income, so they face:
    - *Higher* risk
    - *Higher* potential for reward

Examples include golf courses, hotels, rental car agencies, theme parks, airlines, cruise lines

However, companies with low operating leverage have relatively *fewer* fixed costs and relatively *more* variable costs. For example, retailers incur significant levels of fixed costs, but more of every sales dollar is used to pay for the merchandise (a variable cost), so less ends up as contribution margin. If sales volume declines, these companies have relatively fewer fixed costs to cover, so they are at *less* risk of incurring a loss. If sales volume increases, their relatively small contribution margins ratios add to the bottom line, but in smaller increments. Therefore, they reap less reward than high operating leverage companies experiencing the same volume increases. *In other words, at low operating leverage companies, changes in sales volume do not have as much impact on operating income as they do at high operating leverage companies.* Exhibit 7-9 summarizes these characteristics.

EXHIBIT 7-9   **Characteristics of Low Operating Leverage Companies**

- Low operating leverage companies have:
    —*Higher* levels of variable costs and *lower* levels of fixed costs
    —*Lower* contribution margin ratios
- For low operating leverage companies, changes in volume do NOT have as significant an effect on operating income, so they face:
    —*Lower* risk
    —*Lower* potential for reward
Examples include merchandising companies.

A company's **operating leverage factor** tells us how responsive a company's operating income is to changes in volume. The greater the operating leverage factors, the greater the impact a change in sales volume has on operating income.

The operating leverage factor, at a given level of sales, is calculated as:

$$\text{Operating leverage factor} = \frac{\text{Contribution margin}}{\text{Operating income}}$$

Why do we say, "at a given level of sales"? A company's operating leverage factor will depend, to some extent, on the sales level used to calculate the contribution margin and operating income. Most companies compute the operating leverage factor at their current or expected volume of sales, which is what we'll do in our examples.

What does the operating leverage factor tell us?

> *The operating leverage factor, at a given level of sales, indicates the percentage change in operating income that will occur from a 1% change in volume. In other words, it tells us how responsive a company's operating income is to changes in volume.*

The *lowest* possible value for this factor is 1, which occurs only if the company has *no* fixed costs (an extremely *low* operating leverage company). *For a minute, let's assume that Kay has no fixed costs.* Given this scenario, her unit contribution margin ($14 per poster) contributes directly to profit because she has no fixed costs to cover. In addition, she has *no* risk. The worst she can do is break even, and that will occur only if she doesn't sell any posters. Let's continue to assume that she generally sells 950 posters a month, so this will be the level of sales at which we calculate the operating leverage factor:

Sales revenue (950 posters × $35/poster)	$ 33,250
Less: Variable expenses (950 posters × $21/poster)	(19,950)
Contribution margin (950 posters × $14/poster)	$ 13,300
Less: Fixed expenses	(0)
Operating income	$ 13,300

Her operating leverage factor is:

$$\text{Operating leverage factor} = \frac{\$13,300}{\$13,300}$$
$$= 1$$

What does this tell us? If Kay's volume changes by 1%, her operating income will change by 1% (her operating leverage factor of 1 multiplied by a 1% change in volume). What would happen to Kay's operating income if her volume changed by 15% rather than 1%? Her operating income would then change by 15% (her operating leverage factor of 1 multiplied by a 15% change in volume).

Let's now see what happens if we assume, as usual, that Kay's fixed expenses are $7,000. We'll once again calculate the operating leverage factor given Kay's current level of sales (950 posters per month):

Contribution margin (950 posters × $14/poster)	$13,300
Less: Fixed expenses..	(7,000)
Operating income...	$ 6,300

Now that we have once again assumed that Kay's fixed expenses are $7,000, her operating leverage factor is:

$$\text{Operating leverage factor} = \frac{\$13,300}{\$6,300}$$
$$= 2.11 \text{ (rounded)}$$

Notice that her operating leverage factor is *larger* (2.11 versus 1) when she has *more* fixed costs ($7,000 versus $0). If Kay's sales volume changes by 1%, her operating income will change by 2.11% (her operating leverage factor of 2.11 multiplied by a 1% change in volume). Again, what would happen to Kay's operating income if her volume changed by 15% rather than 1%? Her operating income would then change by 31.65% (her operating leverage factor of 2.11 multiplied by a 15% change in volume).

Managers use the firm's operating leverage factor to determine how vulnerable their operating income is to changes in sales volume—both positive and negative. The larger the operating leverage factor is, the greater the impact a change in sales volume has on operating income. This is true for both increases *and* decreases in volume. Therefore, companies with higher operating leverage factors are particularly vulnerable to changes in volume. In other words, they have *both* higher risk of incurring losses if volume declines *and* higher potential reward if volume increases. Hoping to capitalize on the reward side, many companies have intentionally increased their operating leverage by lowering their variable costs while at the same time increasing their fixed costs. This strategy works well during periods of economic growth but can be detrimental when sales volume slides.

Stop & Think...

Assume Kay's original data ($14 unit contribution margin, $7,000 fixed costs, and 950 posters per month sales volume). Use Kay's operating leverage factor to determine the percentage impact of a 10% *decrease* in sales volume on Kay's operating income. Prove your results.

continued . . .

Answer: If sales volume decreases by 10%, Kay's operating income will decrease by 21.1% (her operating leverage factor of 2.11 multiplied by a 10% decrease in volume).

Proof:		
	Current volume of posters	950
	Less: Decrease in volume (10% × 950) of posters	(95)
	New volume of posters	855
	Multiplied by: Unit contribution margin	× $14
	New total contribution margin	$11,970
	Less: Fixed expenses	(7,000)
	New operating income	$ 4,970
	versus operating income before change in volume	$ 6,300*
	Decrease in operating income	$ (1,330)
	Percentage change ($1,330/$6,300)	21.1% (rounded)

*(950 posters × $14/unit contribution margin) – $7,000 fixed expenses

In this chapter, we have discussed how managers use the contribution margin and CVP analysis to predict profits, determine breakeven points and target profit levels, and assess how changes in the business environment affect their profits. In the next chapter, we look at several types of short-term decisions managers must make. Cost behavior and the contribution margin will continue to play an important role in these decisions.

Decision Guidelines

CVP ANALYSIS

Your friend did open the ice cream parlor. But now she's facing changing business conditions. She needs help making the following decisions:

Decision	Guidelines
The cost of ice cream is rising, yet my competitors have lowered their prices. How will these factors affect my breakeven and target profit levels?	Increases in variable costs (such as ice cream) and decreases in sales prices both decrease the unit contribution margin and contribution margin ratio. You will have to sell more units in order to achieve breakeven and target profit levels. You can use sensitivity analysis to better pinpoint the actual volume you'll need to sell. Simply compute your new unit contribution margin and use it in the shortcut unit contribution margin formula.
Would it help if I could renegotiate my lease with the landlord?	Decreases in fixed costs do not affect the firm's contribution margin. However, a decrease in fixed costs means that the company will have to sell fewer units to achieve breakeven and target profit levels. Increases in fixed costs have the opposite effect.

continued . . .

Decision	Guidelines
I've been thinking about selling other products in addition to ice cream. Will this affect my target profit levels?	Your contribution margin ratio will change depending on your sales mix. A company earns more income by selling higher-margin products than by selling an equal number of lower-margin products. If you can shift sales toward higher contribution margin products, you will have to sell fewer units to reach breakeven and target profit levels.
If the economy takes a downturn, how much risk do I face of incurring a loss?	The margin of safety indicates how far sales volume can decline before you would incur a loss:

$$\text{Margin of safety} = \text{Expected sales} - \text{Breakeven sales}$$

The operating leverage factor indicates the percentage change in operating income that will occur from a 1% change in volume. It tells you how sensitive your company's operating income is to changes in volume. At a given level of sales, the operating leverage factor is:

$$\text{Operating leverage factor} = \frac{\text{Contribution margin}}{\text{Operating income}}$$

Summary Problem 2

Recall from Summary Problem 1 that Fleet Foot buys hiking socks for $6 a pair and sells them for $10. Monthly fixed costs are $10,000 (for sales volumes between 0 and 12,000 pairs), resulting in a breakeven point of 2,500 units. Assume that Fleet Foot has been selling 8,000 pairs of socks per month.

Requirements

1. What is Fleet Foot's current margin of safety in units, in sales dollars, and as a percentage? Explain the results.

2. At this level of sales, what is Fleet Foot's operating leverage factor? If volume declines by 25% due to increasing competition, by what percentage will the company's operating income decline?

3. Competition has forced Fleet Foot to lower its sales price to $9 a pair. How will this affect Fleet's breakeven point?

4. To compensate for the lower sales price, Fleet Foot wants to expand its product line to include men's dress socks. Each pair will sell for $7.00 and cost $2.75 from the supplier. Fixed costs will not change. Fleet expects to sell four pairs of dress socks for every one pair of hiking socks (at its new $9 sales price). What is Fleet's weighted-average contribution margin? Given the 4:1 sales mix, how many of each type of sock will it need to sell to break even?

Solution

Requirement 1

$$\text{Margin of safety in units} = \text{Expected sales in units} - \text{Breakeven sales in units}$$
$$= 8,000 - 2,500$$
$$= 5,500 \text{ units}$$

$$\text{Margin of safety in sales dollars} = \text{Margin of safety in units} \times \text{sales price per unit}$$
$$= 5,500 \text{ units} \times \$10/\text{unit}$$
$$= \$55,000$$

$$\text{Margin of safety as a percentage} = \frac{\text{Margin of safety in units}}{\text{Expected sales in units}}$$
$$= \frac{5,500 \text{ pairs}}{8,000 \text{ pairs}}$$
$$= 68.75\%$$

Fleet Foot's margin of safety is quite high. Sales have to fall by more than 5,500 units (or $55,000) before Fleet incurs a loss. Fleet will continue to earn a profit unless sales drop by more than 68.75%.

Requirement 2

At its current level of volume, Fleet's operating income is:

Contribution margin (8,000 pairs × $4/pair)	$ 32,000
Less: Fixed expenses	(10,000)
Operating income	$ 22,000

Fleet's operating leverage factor at this level of sales is computed as:

$$\text{Operating leverage factor} = \frac{\text{Contribution margin}}{\text{Operating income}}$$

$$= \frac{\$32,000}{\$22,000}$$

$$= 1.45 \text{ (rounded)}$$

If sales volume declines by 25%, operating income will decline by 36.25% (Fleet's operating leverage factor of 1.45 multiplied by 25%).

Requirement 3

If Fleet drops its sales price to $9 per pair, its contribution margin per pair declines to $3 (sales price of $9 − variable cost of $6). Each sale contributes less toward covering fixed costs. Fleet's new breakeven point *increases* to 3,334 pairs of socks ($10,000 fixed costs ÷ $3 unit contribution margin).

Requirement 4

	Hiking Socks	Dress Socks	Total
Sales price per unit	$ 9.00	$ 7.00	
Deduct: Variable expense per unit	(6.00)	(2.75)	
Contribution margin per unit	$ 3.00	$ 4.25	
Sales mix	× 1	× 4	5
Contribution margin	$ 3.00	$17.00	$20.00
Weighted-average contribution margin per unit ($20/5)			$ 4.00

$$\text{Sales in total units} = \frac{\text{Fixed expenses} + \text{Operating income}}{\text{Weighted-average contribution margin per unit}}$$

$$= \frac{\$10,000 + 0}{\$4}$$

$$= 2,500 \text{ pairs of socks}$$

Breakeven sales of dress socks (2,500 × 4/5)	2,000 pairs dress socks
Breakeven sales of hiking socks (2,500 × 1/5)	500 pairs hiking socks

By expanding its product line to include higher-margin dress socks, Fleet is able to decrease its breakeven point back to its original level (2,500 pairs). However, to achieve this breakeven point, Fleet must sell the planned ratio of four pairs of dress socks to every one pair of hiking socks.

Review Cost-Volume-Profit Analysis

◼ Accounting Vocabulary

Breakeven Point (p. 391)
The sales level at which operating income is zero: Total revenues equal total expenses.

Contribution Margin Per Unit (p. 389)
The excess of the unit sales price over the variable cost per unit. Also called unit contribution margin.

Contribution Margin Income Statement (p. 388)
An income statement that groups costs by behavior rather than function; can be used only by internal management.

Contribution Margin Ratio (p. 389)
Ratio of contribution margin to sales revenue.

Cost-Volume-Profit (CVP) Analysis (p. 386)
Expresses the relationships among costs, volume, and profit or loss.

Margin of Safety (p. 411)
Excess of expected sales over breakeven sales. The drop in sales a company can absorb without incurring an operating loss.

Operating Leverage (p. 412)
The relative amount of fixed and variable costs that make up a firm's total costs.

Operating Leverage Factor (p. 413)
At a given level of sales, the contribution margin divided by operating income. The operating leverage factor indicates the percentage change in operating income that will occur from a 1% change in sales volume.

Sales Mix (p. 387)
The combination of products that make up total sales.

Sensitivity Analysis (p. 402)
A "what-if" technique that asks what results will be if actual prices or costs change or if an underlying assumption changes.

◼ Quick Check

Use the following information for Questions 1 through 10. Grand Canyon Railway operates a turn-of-the-century train that transports passengers from Williams, Arizona, to the Grand Canyon and back every day. Assume that the train tickets sell for $60 per passenger, the railway's variable costs are $10 per passenger, and its fixed expenses are $50,000 each month.

1. What is the contribution margin ratio (rounded)?
   a. 16.67%
   b. 100%
   c. 83.33%
   d. need sales volume to calculate

2. Compute the breakeven point in sales dollars.
   a. $300,000
   b. $60,000
   c. $50,000
   d. $100,000

3. What will the Railway's operating income be if they sell 1,001 tickets in one month?

   a. $50

   b. $10

   c. $60

   d. $60,060

4. If the Grand Canyon Railway wants to earn $100,000 in profit per month, how many tickets must it sell?

   a. 1,000

   b. 31,000

   c. 30,000

   d. 3,000

5. On the Grand Canyon Railway's CVP graph, the total cost line intersects the total revenue line at which of the following points?

   a. the level of the fixed costs

   b. the level of the variable costs

   c. the breakeven point

   d. the origin

6. If the Grand Canyon Railway expects to serve 1,200 passengers next month, what is the margin of safety?

   a. 200 passengers

   b. 1,000 passengers

   c. 1,200 passengers

   d. 2,200 passengers

7. If the Grand Canyon Railway serves 1,200 passengers, what is its operating leverage factor?

   a. 1

   b. 6

   c. 3.27

   d. 0.16

8. If the Grand Canyon Railway's volume decreases by 8%, by what percentage will its operating income decrease?

   a. 48%

   b. 1%

   c. 26.16%

   d. 8%

9. If the Grand Canyon Railway cuts its ticket price to $50 per passenger, what is the new breakeven point?

   a. 100 more passengers than with the original $60 ticket price

   b. 250 more passengers than with the original $60 ticket price

   c. 100 fewer passengers than with the original $60 ticket price

   d. 250 fewer passengers than with the original $60 ticket price

10. The Grand Canyon Railway is thinking about selling souvenirs on the train. The souvenirs will sell for $10 each and have a variable cost of $4 each. The Grand Canyon Railway managers think that they will sell an average of one souvenir to each passenger. Assuming that fixed expenses remain at $50,000, how will the sale of souvenirs affect the number of passengers needed to break even?

    a. It will have no effect.

    b. It will increase the number needed.

    c. It will decrease the number needed.

    d. Not enough information is provided.

Quick Check Answers

1. *c* 2. *b* 3. *a* 4. *d* 5. *c* 6. *a* 7. *b* 8. *a* 9. *b* 10. *c*

For Internet Exercises, Excel in Practice, and additional online activities, go to this book's Web site at www.prenhall.com/bamber.

Assess Your Progress

■ Learning Objectives

1 Calculate the unit contribution margin and the contribution margin ratio

2 Use CVP analysis to find breakeven points and target profit volumes

3 Perform sensitivity analysis in response to changing business conditions

4 Find breakeven and target profit volumes for multiproduct companies

5 Determine a firm's margin of safety and operating leverage

■ Short Exercises

Bay Cruiseline Data Set used for S7-1 through S7-12

Bay Cruiseline offers nightly dinner cruises off the coast of Miami, San Francisco, and Seattle. Dinner cruise tickets sell for $60 per passenger. Bay Cruiseline's variable cost of providing the dinner is $20 per passenger, and the fixed cost of operating the vessels (depreciation, salaries, docking fees, and so forth) is $275,000 per month. The company's relevant range extends to 10,000 monthly passengers.

S7-1 **Compute unit contribution margin and contribution margin ratio** *(Learning Objective 1)*
Use the information from the Bay Cruiseline Data Set to compute the following:
a. What is the contribution margin per passenger?
b. What is the contribution margin ratio (round to five digits)?
c. Use the unit contribution margin to project operating income if monthly sales total 10,000 passengers.
d. Use the contribution margin ratio to project operating income if monthly sales revenue totals $500,000.

S7-2 **Project change in income** *(Learning Objective 1)*
Use the information from the Bay Cruiseline Data Set. If Bay Cruiseline sells an additional 500 tickets, by what amount will its operating income increase (or operating loss decrease)?

S7-3 **Find breakeven** *(Learning Objective 2)*
Use the information from the Bay Cruiseline Data Set to compute the number of dinner cruise tickets it must sell to break even.
a. Use the income statement equation approach.
b. Using the shortcut *unit* contribution margin approach, perform a numerical proof to ensure that your answer is correct.
c. Use your answers from a and b to determine the sales revenue needed to break even.
d. Use the shortcut contribution margin *ratio* approach to verify the sales revenue needed to break even.

S7-4 **Find target profit volume** *(Learning Objective 2)*

Use the information from the Bay Cruiseline Data Set. If Bay Cruiseline has a target operating income of $40,000 per month, how many dinner cruise tickets must the company sell?

S7-5 **Prepare a CVP graph** *(Learning Objective 2)*

Use the information from the Bay Cruiseline Data Set. Draw a graph of Bay Cruiseline's CVP relationships. Include the sales revenue line, the fixed expense line, and the total expense line. Label the axes, the breakeven point, the income area, and the loss area.

S7-6 **Interpret a CVP graph** *(Learning Objective 2)*

Describe what each letter stands for in the CVP graph.

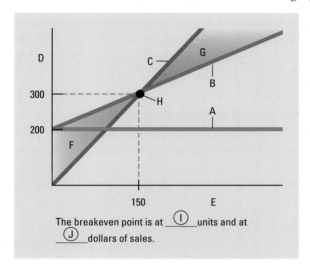

The breakeven point is at ___Ⓘ___ units and at ___Ⓙ___ dollars of sales.

S7-7 **Changes in sales price and variable costs** *(Learning Objective 3)*

Use the information from the Bay Cruiseline Data Set.

1. Suppose Bay Cruiseline cuts its dinner cruise ticket price from $60 to $50 to increase the number of passengers. Compute the new breakeven point in units and in sales dollars. Explain how changes in sales price generally affect the breakeven point.

2. Assume that Bay Cruiseline does *not* cut the price. Bay Cruiseline could reduce its variable costs by no longer serving an appetizer before dinner. Suppose this operating change reduces the variable expense from $20 to $15 per passenger. Compute the new breakeven point in units and in dollars. Explain how changes in variable costs generally affect the breakeven point.

S7-8 **Changes in fixed costs** *(Learning Objective 3)*

Use the information from the Bay Cruiseline Data Set. Suppose Bay Cruiseline embarks on a cost-reduction drive and slashes fixed expenses from $275,000 per month to $200,000 per month.

1. Compute the new breakeven point in units and in sales dollars.

2. Is the breakeven point higher or lower than in S7-3? Explain how changes in fixed costs generally affect the breakeven point.

S7-9   **Compute weighted-average contribution margin** *(Learning Objective 4)*
Use the information from the Bay Cruiseline Data Set. Suppose Bay Cruiseline decides to offer two types of dinner cruises: regular cruises and executive cruises. The executive cruise includes complimentary cocktails and a five-course dinner on the upper deck. Assume that fixed expenses remain at $275,000 per month and that the following ticket prices and variable expenses apply:

	Regular Cruise	Executive Cruise
Sales price per ticket......................	$60	$120
Variable expense per passenger	20	40

Assuming that Bay Cruiseline expects to sell seven regular cruises for every one executive cruise, compute the weighted-average contribution margin per unit. Is it higher or lower than a *simple* average contribution margin? Why? Is it higher or lower than the regular cruise contribution margin calculated in S7-1? Why? Will this new sales mix cause Bay Cruiseline's breakeven point to increase or decrease from what it was when it sold only regular cruises?

S7-10   **Continuation of S7-9: breakeven** *(Learning Objective 4)*
Refer to your answer to S7-9.

a. Compute the total number of dinner cruises that Bay Cruiseline must sell to break even.

b. Compute the number of regular cruises and executive cruises the company must sell to break even.

S7-11   **Compute margin of safety** *(Learning Objective 5)*
Use the information from the Bay Cruiseline Data Set. If Bay Cruiseline sells 7,000 dinner cruises, compute the margin of safety:

a. In units (dinner cruise tickets).

b. In sales dollars.

c. As a percentage of sales.

S7-12   **Compute and use operating leverage factor** *(Learning Objective 5)*
Use the information from the Bay Cruiseline Data Set.

a. Compute the operating leverage factor when Bay Cruiseline sells 10,000 dinner cruises.

b. If volume increases by 10%, by what percentage will operating income increase?

c. If volume decreases by 5%, by what percentage will operating income decrease?

S7-13   **Compute margin of safety** *(Learning Objective 5)*
Consider Kay's e-tail poster business. Suppose Kay expects to sell 800 posters. Use the original data ($35 sales price, $21 variable cost, $7,000 fixed expenses) to compute her margin of safety:

a. In units (posters).

b. In sales dollars.

c. As a percentage of expected sales.

S7-14   **Compute and use operating leverage factor** *(Learning Objective 5)*
Suppose Kay sells 800 posters. Use the original data ($35 sales price, $21 variable cost, $7,000 fixed expenses) to compute her operating leverage factor. If sales volume increases 10%, by what percentage will her operating income change? Prove your answer.

Exercises

E7-15 Prepare contribution margin income statements *(Learning Objective 1)*

Worldwide Travel uses the contribution margin income statement internally. Worldwide's first-quarter results are as follows:

WORLDWIDE TRAVEL Contribution Margin Income Statement Three Months Ended March 31, 2007	
Sales revenue	$ 312,500
Less: Variable expenses	(125,000)
Contribution margin	187,500
Less: Fixed expenses	(170,000)
Operating income	$ 17,500

Worldwide's relevant range is between sales of $250,000 and $360,000.

Requirements

1. Prepare contribution margin income statements at sales levels of $250,000 and $360,000. (*Hint*: Use the contribution margin ratio.)

2. Compute breakeven sales in dollars.

E7-16 Work backward to find missing information *(Learning Objectives 1, 2)*

Aussie Drycleaners has determined the following about their costs: total variable expenses are $40,000, total fixed expenses are $30,000, and the sales revenue needed to break even is $40,000. Use the contribution margin income statement and the shortcut contribution margin approaches to determine Aussie Drycleaners' current (1) sales revenue and (2) operating income. (*Hint*: First, find the contribution margin ratio; then, prepare the contribution margin income statement.)

E7-17 Find breakeven and target profit volume *(Learning Objectives 1, 2)*

Trendy Toes produces sports socks. The company has fixed expenses of $85,000 and variable expenses of $0.85 per package. Each package sells for $1.70.

Requirements

1. Compute the contribution margin per package and the contribution margin ratio.

2. Find the breakeven point in units and in dollars using the contribution margin shortcut approaches.

3. Find the number of packages Trendy Toes needs to sell to earn a $25,000 operating income.

E7-18 Continuation of E7-17: changing costs *(Learning Objective 3)*

Refer to Trendy Toes in E7-17. If Trendy Toes can decrease its variable costs to $0.75 per package by increasing its fixed costs to $100,000, how many packages will it have to sell to generate $25,000 of operating income? Is this more or less than before? Why?

E7-19 **Find breakeven and target profit volume** *(Learning Objectives 1, 2)*

Owner Shan Lo is considering franchising her Happy Garden restaurant concept. She believes people will pay $5 for a large bowl of noodles. Variable costs are $1.50 a bowl. Lo estimates monthly fixed costs for franchisees at $8,400.

Requirements

1. Use the contribution margin ratio shortcut approach to find a franchisee's breakeven sales in dollars.

2. Is franchising a good idea for Lo if franchisees want a minimum monthly operating income of $8,750 and Lo believes that most locations could generate $25,000 in monthly sales?

E7-20 **Continuation of E7-19: changing business conditions** *(Learning Objective 3)*

Refer to Happy Garden in E7-19. Lo did franchise her restaurant concept. Because of Happy Wok's success, Garden Wok has come on the scene as a competitor. To maintain its market share, Happy Garden will have to lower its sales price to $4.50 per bowl. At the same time, Happy Garden hopes to increase each restaurant's volume to 6,000 bowls per month by embarking on a marketing campaign. Each franchise will have to contribute $500 per month to cover the advertising costs. Prior to these changes, most locations were selling 5,500 bowls per month.

Requirements

1. What was the average restaurant's operating income before these changes?

2. Assuming that the price cut and advertising campaign are successful at increasing volume to the projected level, will the franchisees still earn their target profit of $8,750 per month? Show your calculations.

E7-21 **Compute breakeven and project income** *(Learning Objectives 1, 2)*

Grover's Steel Parts produces parts for the automobile industry. The company has monthly fixed expenses of $640,000 and a contribution margin of 80% of revenues.

Requirements

1. Compute Grover's Steel Parts' monthly breakeven sales in dollars. Use the contribution margin ratio shortcut approach.

2. Use the contribution margin ratio to project operating income (or loss) if revenues are $500,000 and if they are $1,000,000.

3. Do the results in Requirement 2 make sense given the breakeven sales you computed in Requirement 1? Explain.

E7-22 **Continuation of E7-21: changing business conditions** *(Learning Objective 3)*

Refer to Grover's Steel Parts in E7-21. Grover feels like he's in a giant squeeze play: The automotive manufacturers are demanding lower prices, and the steel producers have increased raw material costs. Grover's contribution margin has shrunk to 60% of revenues. Grover's monthly operating income, prior to these pressures, was $160,000.

Requirements

1. To maintain this same level of profit, what sales volume (in sales revenue) must Grover now achieve?

2. Grover believes that his monthly sales revenue will go only as high as $1,000,000. He is thinking about moving operations overseas to cut fixed costs. If monthly sales are $1,000,000, by how much will he need to cut fixed costs to maintain his prior profit level of $160,000 per month?

E7-23 **Identify information on a CVP graph** *(Learning Objective 2)*

Chad Brown is considering starting a Web-based educational business, Start Smart MBA. He plans to offer a short-course review of accounting for students entering MBA programs. The materials would be available on a password-protected Web site, and students would complete the course through self-study. Brown would have to grade the course assignments, but most of the work is in developing the course materials, setting up the site, and marketing. Unfortunately, Brown's hard drive crashed before he finished his financial analysis. However, he did recover the following partial CVP chart:

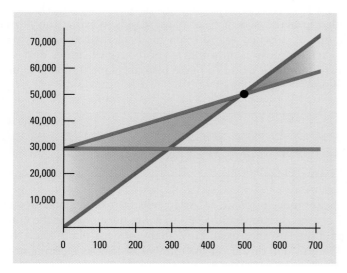

Requirements

1. Label each axis, sales revenue line, total expense line, fixed expense line, operating income area, and operating loss area.
2. If Brown attracts 400 students to take the course, will the venture be profitable?
3. What are the breakeven sales in students and dollars?

E7-24 **Prepare a CVP graph** *(Learning Objective 2)*

Suppose that Turner Field, the home of the Atlanta Braves, earns total revenue that averages $24 for every ticket sold. Assume that annual fixed expenses are $24 million and that variable expenses are $4 per ticket.

Requirements

1. Prepare the ballpark's CVP graph under these assumptions. Label the axes, sales revenue line, fixed expense line, total expense line, operating loss area, and operating income area on the graph.
2. Show the breakeven point in dollars and in tickets.

E7-25 **Work backward to find new breakeven point** *(Learning Objectives 2, 3)*

Empire Industries is planning on purchasing a new piece of equipment that will increase the quality of its production. It hopes the increased quality will generate more sales. The company's contribution margin ratio is 40%, and its current breakeven point is $500,000 in sales revenue. If Empire Industries' fixed expenses increase by $40,000 due to the equipment, what will its new breakeven point be (in sales revenue)?

E7-26 **Find consequence of rising fixed costs** (*Learning Objectives 1, 3*)
DeAnna Braun sells homemade knit scarves for $16 each at local crafts shows. Her contribution margin ratio is 62.5%. Currently, the crafts show entrance fees cost DeAnna $1,000 per year. The crafts shows are raising their entrance fees by 15% next year. How many *extra* scarves will DeAnna have to sell next year just to pay for rising entrance fee costs?

E7-27 **Extension of E7-26: multiproduct firm** (*Learning Objective 4*)
Arlan Braun admired his wife's success at selling scarves at local crafts shows (E7-26), so he decided to make two types of plant stands to sell at the shows. Arlan makes twig stands out of downed wood from his backyard and the yards of his neighbors, so his variable cost is minimal (wood screws, glue, and so forth). However, Arlan has to purchase wood to make his oak plant stands. His unit prices and costs are as follows:

	Twig Stands	Oak Stands
Sales price	$15.00	$35.00
Variable cost	2.50	10.00

The twig stands are more popular, so Arlan sells four twig stands for every one oak stand. DeAnna charges her husband $300 to share her booth at the crafts shows (after all, she has paid the entrance fees). How many of each plant stand does Arlan need to sell to break even? Will this affect the number of scarves DeAnna needs to sell to break even? Explain.

E7-28 **Find breakeven for a multiproduct firm** (*Learning Objective 4*)
Rapid Scooters plans to sell a motorized standard scooter for $54 and a motorized chrome scooter for $78. Rapid Scooters purchases the standard scooter for $36 and the chrome scooter for $50. Rapid Scooters expects to sell two chrome scooters for every three standard scooters. Rapid Scooters' monthly fixed expenses are $9,680. How many of each type of scooter must Rapid Scooters sell monthly to break even? To earn $6,600?

E7-29 **Work backward to find missing data** (*Learning Objective 4*)
Kenisha manufactures two styles of watches—the Digital and the Classic. The following data pertain to the Digital:

Variable manufacturing cost	$120
Variable operating cost	30
Sale price...	200

Kenisha's monthly fixed expenses total $190,000. When Digitals and Classics are sold in the mix of 7:3, respectively, the sale of 2,000 total watches results in an operating income of $60,000. Compute the contribution margin per watch for the Classic.

E7-30 **Breakeven and an advertising decision at a multiproduct company** (*Learning Objectives 3, 4, 5*)
Victor's Sporting Goods is a national retailer of sporting equipment. Last year, Victor's sales revenues totaled $2.62 billion. Total expenses were $2.47 billion. Of this amount, approximately $1.88 billion were variable, while the remainder were fixed. Since

Victor's offers thousands of different products, its managers prefer to calculate the breakeven point in terms of sales dollars rather than units.

1. What is Victor's current operating income?
2. What is Victor's contribution margin ratio (round to the nearest percent)?
3. What is Victor's breakeven point in sales dollars (round to the nearest two decimals)? (*Hint*: The contribution margin ratio calculated in requirement two is already weighted by Victor's actual sales mix.)
4. What is Victor's current margin of safety percentage (round to the nearest percent)? What does it mean?
5. Victor's top management is deciding whether to embark on a $0.05 billion dollar nationwide advertisement campaign. The marketing firm has projected annual sales volume to increase by 15% as a result of this campaign. Assuming that the projections are correct, what effect would this advertising campaign have on Victor's annual operating income?

E7-31 **Compute margin of safety and operating leverage** *(Learning Objective 5)*
Use the Worldwide Travel data in E7-15 to answer the following questions:

1. What is Worldwide Travel's current margin of safety (in dollars)?
2. What is Worldwide Travel's current operating leverage factor?
3. If sales volume increases 5% next quarter, by what percentage will Worldwide's operating income increase? What will the new operating income be?

E7-32 **Work backward through margin of safety** *(Learning Objective 5)*
Bart's Bait Shop had budgeted bait sales for the season at $10,000, with a $2,000 margin of safety. However, due to unseasonable weather, bait sales reached only $9,200. Actual sales exceeded breakeven sales by what amount?

E7-33 **Compute margin of safety and operating leverage** *(Learning Objective 5)*
Carter's Repair Shop has a monthly target operating income of $12,000. *Variable expenses* are 70% of sales, and monthly fixed expenses are $9,000.

Requirements

1. Compute the monthly margin of safety in dollars if the shop achieves its income goal.
2. Express Carter's margin of safety as a percentage of target sales.
3. What is Carter's operating leverage factor at the target level of operating income?
4. Assume that Carter reaches his target. By what percentage will Carter's operating income fall if sales volume declines by 10%?

E7-34 **Use operating leverage factor to find fixed costs** *(Learning Objective 5)*
Guinty Manufacturing had a 1.25 operating leverage factor when sales were $50,000. Guinty Manufacturing's contribution margin ratio was 20%. What were Guinty Manufacturing's fixed expenses?

E7-35 Comprehensive CVP analysis *(Learning Objectives 1, 2, 3, 4, 5)*

SpeeDrive manufactures 1 GB flash drives (jump drives). Price and cost data for a relevant range extending to 200,000 units per month are as follows:

Sales price per unit (current monthly sales volume is 120,000 units)..	$ 20.00
Variable costs per unit:	
Direct materials...	6.40
Direct labor...	5.00
Variable manufacturing overhead	2.20
Variable selling and administrative expenses.........................	1.40
Monthly fixed expenses:	
Fixed manufacturing overhead...	$191,400
Fixed selling and administrative expenses.............................	276,600

Requirements

1. What is the company's contribution margin per unit? Contribution margin percentage? Total contribution margin?

2. What would the company's monthly operating income be if the company sold 150,000 units?

3. What would the company's monthly operating income be if the company had sales of $4,000,000?

4. What is the breakeven point in units? In sales dollars?

5. How many units would the company have to sell to earn a target monthly profit of $260,000?

6. Management is currently in contract negotiations with the labor union. If the negotiations fail, direct labor costs will increase by 10% and fixed costs will increase by $22,500 per month. If these costs increase, how many units will the company have each month to break even?

7. Return to the original data for this question and the rest of the questions. What is the company's current operating leverage factor (round to two decimals)?

8. If sales volume increases by 8%, by what percentage will operating income increase?

9. What is the firm's current margin of safety in sales dollars? What is its margin of safety as a percentage of sales?

10. Say SpeeDrive adds a second line of flash drives (2 GB rather than 1 GB). A package of the 2 GB flash drives will sell for $45 and have variable cost per unit of $20 per unit. The expected sales mix is three of the small flash drives (1 GB) for every one large flash drive (2 GB). Given this sales mix, how many of each type of flash drive will SpeeDrive need to sell to reach its target monthly profit of $260,000? Is this volume higher or lower than previously needed (in Question 5) to achieve the same target profit? Why?

Problems (Problem Set A)

P7-36A Find missing data in CVP relationships *(Learning Objectives 1, 2)*

The budgets of four companies yield the following information:

	Company			
	Q	R	S	T
Target sales................................	$720,000	$300,000	$190,000	$_____
Variable expenses......................	216,000	_____		270,000
Fixed expenses		156,000	100,000	
Operating income (loss)	$ 30,000	$_____	$_____	80,000
Units sold..................................		112,000	12,000	15,750
Contribution margin per unit....	$ 6		$ 9.50	$ 40
Contribution margin ratio.........		0.60		

Requirements

1. Fill in the blanks for each company.
2. Compute breakeven, in sales dollars, for each company. Which company has the lowest breakeven point in sales dollars? What causes the low breakeven point?

P7-37A Find breakeven and target profit and prepare income statements *(Learning Objectives 1, 2)*

A traveling production of *The Phantom of the Opera* performs each year. The average show sells 800 tickets at $50 a ticket. There are 100 shows each year. The show has a cast of 40, each earning an average of $260 per show. The cast is paid only after each show. The other variable expense is program printing costs of $6 per guest. Annual fixed expenses total $942,400.

Requirements

1. Compute revenue and variable expenses for each show.
2. Use the income statement equation approach to compute the number of shows needed annually to break even.
3. Use the shortcut unit contribution margin approach to compute the number of shows needed annually to earn a profit of $1,438,400. Is this goal realistic? Give your reason.
4. Prepare *The Phantom of the Opera's* contribution margin income statement for 100 shows each year. Report only two categories of expenses: variable and fixed.

P7-38A Comprehensive CVP problem *(Learning Objectives 1, 2, 5)*

Pintnox imprints calendars with college names. The company has fixed expenses of $1,035,000 each month plus variable expenses of $3.60 per carton of calendars. Of the variable expense, 70% is Cost of Goods Sold, while the remaining 30% relates to variable operating expenses. Pintnox sells each carton of calendars for $10.50.

Requirements

1. Use the income statement equation approach to compute the number of cartons of calendars that Pintnox must sell each month to break even.

continued . . .

2. Use the contribution margin ratio shortcut formula to compute the dollar amount of monthly sales Pintnox needs in order to earn $285,000 in operating income (round the contribution margin ratio to two decimal places).

3. Prepare Pintnox's contribution margin income statement for June for sales of 450,000 cartons of calendars.

4. What is June's margin of safety (in dollars)? What is the operating leverage factor at this level of sales?

5. By what percentage will operating income change if July's sales volume is 13% higher? Prove your answer.

P7-39A **Compute breakeven, prepare CVP graph, and respond to change** *(Learning Objectives 1, 2, 3)*

Universal Investors is opening an office in Lexington, Kentucky. Fixed monthly expenses are office rent ($2,500), depreciation on office furniture ($260), utilities ($280), special telephone lines ($600), a connection with an online brokerage service ($640), and the salary of a financial planner ($3,400). Variable expenses include payments to the financial planner (10% of revenue), advertising (5% of revenue), supplies and postage (2% of revenue), and usage fees for the telephone lines and computerized brokerage service (3% of revenue).

Requirements

1. Use the contribution margin ratio CVP formula to compute the investment firm's breakeven revenue in dollars. If the average trade leads to $400 in revenue for Personal Investors, how many trades must it make to break even?

2. Use the income statement equation approach to compute dollar revenues needed to earn monthly operating income of $3,840.

3. Graph Universal Investors' CVP relationships. Assume that an average trade leads to $400 in revenue for Universal Investors. Show the breakeven point, sales revenue line, fixed expense line, total expense line, operating loss area, operating income area, and sales in units (trades) and dollars when monthly operating income of $3,840 is earned. The graph should range from 0 to 40 units (trades).

4. Assume that the average revenue that Universal Investors earns decreases to $300 per trade. How does this affect the breakeven point in number of trades?

P7-40A **CVP analysis at a multiproduct firm** *(Learning Objectives 4, 5)*

The contribution margin income statement of Crosby Coffee for February 2008 follows:

CROSBY COFFEE
Contribution Margin Income Statement
For the Month Ended February 29, 2008

Sales revenue		$90,000
Variable expenses:		
Cost of goods sold	$32,000	
Marketing expense	10,000	
General and administrative expense	3,000	45,000
Contribution margin		45,000
Fixed expenses:		
Marketing expense	16,500	
General and administrative expense	3,500	20,000
Operating income		$25,000

Crosby Coffee sells three small coffees for every large coffee. A small coffee sells for $2, with a variable expense of $1. A large coffee sells for $4, with a variable expense of $2.

Requirements

1. Determine Crosby Coffee's monthly breakeven point in the numbers of small coffees and large coffees. Prove your answer by preparing a summary contribution margin income statement at the breakeven level of sales. Show only two categories of expenses: variable and fixed.

2. Compute Crosby Coffee's margin of safety in dollars.

3. Use Crosby Coffee's operating leverage factor to determine its new operating income if sales volume increases 15%. Prove your results using the contribution margin income statement format. Assume that sales mix remains unchanged.

■ Problems (Problem Set B)

P7-41B Find missing data in CVP relationships (*Learning Objectives 1, 2*)

The budgets of four companies yield the following information:

| | Company | | | |
	A	B	C	D
Target sales	$680,000	$_____	$550,000	$_____
Variable expenses......................	_____	150,000	275,000	156,000
Fixed expenses		123,000	143,000	
Operating income (loss)	$120,000	$_____	$_____	$ 35,000
Units sold.................................	187,000	10,000		
Contribution margin per unit....	$ 2	_____	$ 100	$ 12
Contribution margin ratio.........	_____	0.20	_____	0.20

Requirements

1. Fill in the blanks for each company.

2. Compute breakeven, in sales dollars, for each company. Which company has the lowest breakeven point in sales dollars? What causes the low breakeven point?

P7-42B Find breakeven and target profit and prepare income statement (*Learning Objectives 1, 2*)

Countrywide Productions performs *Cats*, the play. The average show sells 1,000 tickets at $60 a ticket. There are 120 shows a year. *Cats* has a cast of 60, each earning an average of $320 a show. The cast is paid only after each show. The other variable expense is program printing costs of $8 per guest. Annual fixed expenses total $295,200.

Requirements

1. Compute revenue and variable expenses for each show.

2. Use the income statement equation approach to compute the number of shows *Cats* must perform each year to break even.

continued . . .

3. Use the shortcut contribution margin approach to compute the number of shows needed each year to earn a profit of $4,264,000. Is this profit goal realistic? Give your reason.

4. Prepare the *Cats* contribution margin income statement for 120 shows for the year. Report only two categories of expenses: variable and fixed.

P7-43B Comprehensive CVP problem *(Learning Objectives 1, 2, 5)*

Trendy Ten sells flags with team logos. Trendy Ten has fixed expenses of $678,600 per year plus variable expenses of $4.20 per flag. Of this variable expense, 60% relates to the cost of goods sold, while 40% relates to operating expenses. Each flag sells for $12.

Requirements

1. Use the income statement equation approach to compute the number of flags that Trendy Ten must sell each year to break even.

2. Use the contribution margin ratio shortcut formula to compute the dollar sales Trendy Ten needs in order to earn $32,500 in operating income.

3. Prepare Trendy Ten's contribution margin income statement for the year ended December 31, 2008, for sales of 100,000 flags.

4. What is December's margin of safety (in dollars)? What is the operating leverage factor at this level of sales?

5. By what percentage will operating income change if January's sales volume is 5% higher? Prove your answer.

P7-44B Compute breakeven, prepare CVP graph, and respond to change *(Learning Objectives 1, 2, 3)*

Jero Investment Group is opening an office in Atlanta. Fixed monthly expenses are office rent ($9,100), depreciation on office furniture ($700), utilities ($1,400), special telephone lines ($1,600), a connection with an online brokerage service ($2,000), and the salary of a financial planner ($4,800). Variable expenses include payments to the financial planner (8% of revenue), advertising (12% of revenue), supplies and postage (4% of revenue), and usage fees for the telephone lines and computerized brokerage service (6% of revenue).

Requirements

1. Use the contribution margin ratio CVP formula to compute Jero Investment Group's breakeven revenue in dollars. If the average trade leads to $700 in revenue for Jero Investment Group, how many trades must it make to break even?

2. Use the income statement equation approach to compute the dollar revenues needed to earn a target monthly operating income of $9,800.

3. Graph Jero Investment Group's CVP relationships. Assume that an average trade leads to $700 in revenue for Jero Investment Group. Show the breakeven point, sales revenue line, fixed expense line, total expense line, operating loss area, operating income area, and sales in units (trades) and dollars when monthly operating income of $9,800 is earned. The graph should range from 0 to 80 units (trades).

4. Assume that the average revenue that Jero Investment Group earns decreases to $560 per trade. Compute the new breakeven point in trades. How does this affect the breakeven point?

P7-45B CVP analysis at a multiproduct firm *(Learning Objectives 4, 5)*

The contribution margin income statement of Curly's Ice Cream Shoppe for July 2008 follows:

ISABELLE'S ICE CREAM SHOPPE
Contribution Margin Income Statement
For the Month Ended July 31, 2008

Sales revenue		$12,000
Variable expenses:		
Cost of goods sold	$4,000	
Marketing expense	500	
General and administrative expense	1,500	6,000
Contribution margin		6,000
Fixed expenses:		
Marketing expense	500	
General and administrative expense	1,900	2,400
Operating income		$ 3,600

Curly's sells four sugar cones for every one large waffle cone. A regular sugar cone sells for $2, with a variable expense of $1. A large waffle cone sells for $4, with a variable expense of $2.

Requirements

1. Determine Curly's monthly breakeven point in the numbers of regular sugar cones and large waffle cones. Prove your answer by preparing a summary contribution margin income statement at the breakeven level of sales. Show only two categories of expenses: variable and fixed.

2. Compute Curly's margin of safety in dollars.

3. Use Curly's operating leverage factor to determine her new operating income if sales volume increases by 15%. Prove your results using the contribution margin income statement format. Assume that sales mix remains unchanged.

Apply Your Knowledge

Decision Cases

Case 7-46. Determine feasibility of business plan *(Learning Objective 2)*

Brian and Nui Soon live in Macon, Georgia. Two years ago, they visited Thailand. Nui, a professional chef, was impressed with the cooking methods and the spices used in the Thai food. Macon does not have a Thai restaurant, and the Soons are contemplating opening one. Nui would supervise the cooking, and Brian would leave his current job to be the maitre d'. The restaurant would serve dinner Tuesday through Saturday.

Brian has noticed a restaurant for lease. The restaurant has seven tables, each of which can seat four. Tables can be moved together for a large party. Nui is planning two seatings per evening, and the restaurant will be open 50 weeks per year.

The Soons have drawn up the following estimates:

Average revenue, including beverages and dessert	$	40 per meal
Average cost of the food..............................	$	12 per meal
Chef's and dishwasher's salaries................................	$50,400 per *year*	
Rent (premises, equipment)..	$ 4,000 per month	
Cleaning (linen and premises)...................................	$ 800 per month	
Replacement of dishes, cutlery, glasses......................	$ 300 per month	
Utilities, advertising, telephone................................	$ 1,900 per month	

Requirements

Compute *annual* breakeven number of meals and sales revenue for the restaurant. Also, compute the number of meals and the amount of sales revenue needed to earn operating income of $75,600 for the year. How many meals must the Soons serve each night to earn their target income of $75,600? Should the couple open the restaurant? Support your answer.

Ethical Issue

Issue 7-47. Ethical dilemma with CVP analysis error *(Learning Objective 2)*

You have just begun your summer internship at Tmedic. The company supplies sterilized surgical instruments for physicians. To expand sales, Tmedic is considering paying a commission to its sales force. The controller, Jane Hewitt, asks you to compute (1) the new breakeven sales figure and (2) the operating profit if sales increase 15% under the new sales commission plan. She thinks you can handle this task because you learned CVP analysis in your accounting class.

You spend the next day collecting information from the accounting records, performing the analysis, and writing a memo to explain the results. The company president is pleased with your memo. You report that the new sales commission plan will lead to a significant increase in operating income and only a small increase in breakeven sales.

The following week, you realize that you made an error in the CVP analysis. You overlooked the sales personnel's $2,500 monthly salaries, and you did not include this fixed marketing expense in your computations. You are not sure what to do. If you tell Hewitt of your mistake, she will have to tell the president. In this case, you are afraid Tmedic might not offer you permanent employment after your internship.

Requirements

1. How would your error affect breakeven sales and operating income under the proposed sales commission plan? Could this cause the president to reject the sales commission proposal?

2. Consider your ethical responsibilities. Is there a difference between (a) initially making an error and (b) subsequently failing to inform the controller?

3. Suppose you tell Hewitt of the error in your analysis. Why might the consequences not be as bad as you fear? Should Hewitt take any responsibility for your error? What could Hewitt have done differently?

4. After considering all of the factors, should you inform Hewitt or simply keep quiet?

■ Team Project

Project 7-48. Advertising campaign and production level decisions
(Learning Objectives 1, 3)

EZPAK Manufacturing produces filament packaging tape. In 2008, EZPAK Manufacturing produced and sold 15 million rolls of tape. The company has recently expanded its capacity, so it can now produce up to 30 million rolls per year. EZPAK Manufacturing's accounting records show the following results from 2008:

Sale price per roll	$ 3.00
Variable manufacturing expenses per roll..........................	$ 2.00
Variable marketing and administrative expenses per roll	$ 0.50
Total fixed manufacturing overhead costs........................	$8,400,000
Total fixed marketing and administrative expenses...........	$ 600,000
Sales...	15 million rolls
Production	15 million rolls

There were no beginning or ending inventories in 2008.

In January 2009, EZPAK Manufacturing hired a new president, Kevin McDaniel. McDaniel has a one-year contract specifying that he will be paid 10% of EZPAK Manufacturing's 2009 operating income (based on traditional absorption costing) instead of a salary. In 2009, McDaniel must make two major decisions:

1. Should EZPAK Manufacturing undertake a major advertising campaign? This campaign would raise sales to 25 million rolls. This is the maximum level of sales that EZPAK Manufacturing can expect to make in the near future. The ad campaign would add an additional $3.5 million in marketing and administrative costs. Without the campaign, sales will be 15 million rolls.

2. How many rolls of tape will EZPAK Manufacturing produce?

At the end of the year, EZPAK Manufacturing's board of directors will evaluate McDaniel's performance and decide whether to offer him a contract for the following year.

continued . . .

Requirements

Within your group, form two subgroups. The first subgroup assumes the role of Kevin McDaniel, EZPAK Manufacturing's new president. The second subgroup assumes the role of EZPAK Manufacturing's board of directors. McDaniel will meet with the board of directors shortly after the end of 2009 to decide whether he will remain at EZPAK Manufacturing. Most of your effort should be devoted to advance preparation for this meeting. Each subgroup should meet separately to prepare for the meeting between the board and McDaniel. [*Hint:* Keep computations (other than per-unit amounts) in millions.]

Kevin McDaniel should:

1. Compute EZPAK Manufacturing's 2008 operating income.

2. Decide whether to adopt the advertising campaign by calculating the projected increase in operating income from the advertising campaign. Do not include the executive bonus in this calculation. Prepare a memo to the board of directors explaining this decision. Use the memo format outlined in Case 6-43. Give this memo to the board of directors as soon as possible (before the joint meeting).

3. Assume that EZPAK Manufacturing adopts the advertising campaign. Decide how many rolls of tape to produce in 2009. Assume that no safety stock is considered necessary to EZPAK's business.

4. Given your response to Question 3, prepare an absorption costing income statement for the year ended December 31, 2009, ending with operating income before bonus. Then, compute your bonus separately. The variable cost per unit and the total fixed expenses (with the exception of the advertising campaign) remain the same as in 2008. Give this income statement and your bonus computation to the board of directors as soon as possible (before your meeting with the board).

5. Decide whether you want to remain at EZPAK Manufacturing for another year. You currently have an offer from another company. The contract with the other company is identical to the one you currently have with EZPAK Manufacturing—you will be paid 10% of absorption costing operating income instead of a salary.

The board of directors should:

1. Compute EZPAK Manufacturing's 2008 operating income.

2. Determine whether EZPAK Manufacturing should adopt the advertising campaign by calculating the projected increase in operating income from the advertising campaign. Do not include the executive bonus in this calculation.

3. Determine how many rolls of tape EZPAK Manufacturing should produce in 2009. Assume that no safety stock is considered necessary to EZPAK's business.

4. Evaluate McDaniel's performance based on his decisions and the information he provided to the board. (*Hint:* You may want to prepare a variable costing income statement.)

5. Evaluate the contract's bonus provision. Are you satisfied with this provision? If so, explain why. If not, recommend how it should be changed.

After McDaniel has given the board his memo and income statement and after the board has had a chance to evaluate McDaniel's performance, McDaniel and the board should meet. The purpose of the meeting is to decide whether it is in their mutual interest for McDaniel to remain with EZPAK Manufacturing and, if so, the terms of the contract EZPAK Manufacturing will offer McDaniel.

8 Short-Term Business Decisions

Most major airlines, including Delta, outsource work. In 2002, Delta announced plans to save over $15 million a year by outsourcing its reservation work to call centers in the Philippines and India. In 2005, Delta revealed plans to cut maintenance costs 34% a year by outsourcing much of its airplane maintenance to Miami- and Canadian-based firms. But why would Delta outsource so much of its work? Primarily to cut costs. Most of the major airlines are experiencing financial difficulties due to rising fuel costs and tight competition, so they need to find ways to cut costs. One way is through outsourcing. Companies can save 20% or more by outsourcing call center work to English-speaking workers in developing countries.

Outsourcing also enables companies to concentrate on their core competencies—the operating activities in which they are experts. When

companies focus on just their core competencies, they often outsource the activities that do not give them a competitive advantage. For example, heavy maintenance of aircraft, which can take two to three weeks per plane, requires specialized expertise. This expertise is provided by members of the outside airline maintenance industry, which performs over half of all airline maintenance. Delta's strategy is to focus on its core competency—flying passengers—and outsource other operating activities, such as reservations and airplane maintenance, to companies who excel at those activities. ■

Learning Objectives

1 Describe and identify information relevant to short-term business decisions

2 Make special order decisions

3 Make pricing decisions

4 Make dropping a product, department, or territory decisions

5 Make product mix decisions

6 Make outsourcing (make-or-buy) decisions

7 Make sell as is or process further decisions

In the last chapter, we saw how managers use cost behavior to determine the company's breakeven point and to estimate the sales volume needed to achieve target profits. In this chapter, we'll see how managers use their knowledge of cost behavior to make six special business decisions, such as whether to outsource operating activities. The decisions we'll discuss in this chapter pertain to short periods of time, so managers do not need to worry about the time value of money. In other words, they do not need to compute the present value of the revenues and expenses relating to the decision. In Chapter 9, we will discuss longer-term decisions (such as buying equipment and undertaking plant expansions) in which the time value of money becomes important. Before we look at the six business decisions in detail, let's consider a manager's decision-making process and the information managers need to evaluate their options.

How Managers Make Decisions

Exhibit 8-1 illustrates how managers decide among alternative courses of action. Management accountants help gather and analyze *relevant information* to compare alternatives. Management accountants also help with the follow-up: comparing the actual results of a decision to those originally anticipated. This feedback helps management as it faces similar types of decisions in the future. It also helps management adjust current operations if actual results of its decision are markedly different from those anticipated.

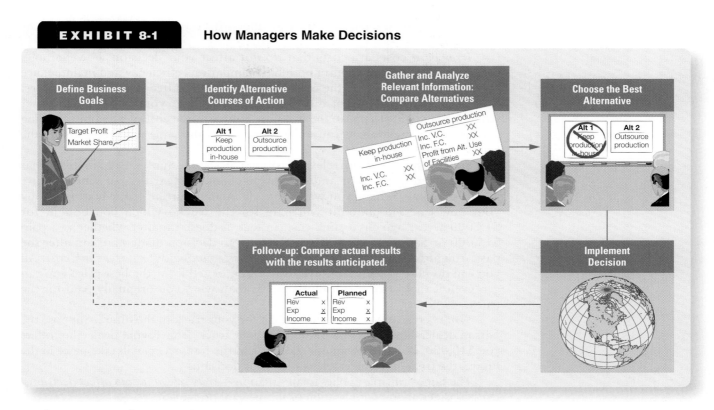

EXHIBIT 8-1   **How Managers Make Decisions**

Relevant Information

When managers make decisions, they focus on costs and revenues that are relevant to the decisions. Exhibit 8-2 shows that **relevant information**:

1. Is expected *future* data.

2. *Differs* among alternatives.

1 Describe and identify information relevant to short-term business decisions

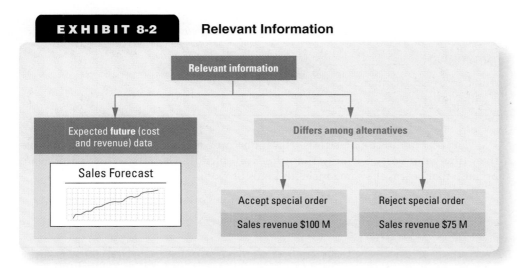

EXHIBIT 8-2   **Relevant Information**

Recall our discussion of relevant costs in Chapter 2. In deciding whether to purchase a Toyota Corolla or Nissan Sentra, the cost of the car, the sales tax, and the insurance premium are relevant because these costs:

• Are incurred in the *future* (after you decide to buy the car).

• *Differ between alternatives* (each car has a different invoice price, sales tax, and insurance premium).

These costs are *relevant* because they affect your decision of which car to purchase.

Irrelevant costs are costs that *do not* affect your decision. For example, because the Corolla and Sentra both have similar fuel efficiency and maintenance ratings, we do not expect the car operating costs to differ between alternatives. Because these costs do not differ, they do not affect your decision. In other words, they are *irrelevant* to the decision. Similarly, the cost of a campus parking sticker is also irrelevant because the sticker costs the same whether you buy the Sentra or the Corolla.

Sunk costs are also irrelevant to your decision. Sunk costs are costs that were incurred in the *past* and cannot be changed regardless of which future action is taken. Perhaps you want to trade in your current truck when you buy your new car. The amount you paid for the truck—which you bought for $15,000 a year ago—is a sunk cost. In fact, it doesn't matter whether you paid $15,000 or $50,000—it's still a sunk cost. No decision made *now* can alter the past. You already bought the truck, so *the price you paid for it is a sunk cost*. All you can do *now* is keep the truck, trade it in, or sell it for the best price you can get, even if that price is substantially less than what you originally paid for the truck.

What *is* relevant is what you can get for your truck in the future. Suppose the Nissan dealership offers you $8,000 for your truck. The Toyota dealership offers you $10,000. Because the amounts differ and the transaction will take place in the future, the trade-in value is relevant to your decision.

The same principle applies to all situations—*only relevant data affect decisions*. Let's consider another application of this general principle.

Suppose Pendleton Woolen Mills is deciding whether to use pure wool or a wool blend in a new line of sweaters. Assume that Pendleton Woolen Mills predicts the following costs under the two alternatives:

	Expected Materials and Labor Cost per Sweater		
	Wool	Wool Blend	Cost Difference
Direct materials........................	$10	$6	$4
Direct labor..............................	2	2	0
Total cost of direct materials and direct labor.....................	$12	$8	$4

The cost of direct materials is relevant because this cost differs between alternatives (the wool costs $4 more than the wool blend). The labor cost is irrelevant because that cost is the same for both kinds of wool.

Stop & Think...

You are considering replacing your Pentium IV computer with the latest model. Is the $1,200 you spent (in 2005) on the Pentium relevant to your decision about buying the new model?

Answer: The $1,200 cost of your Pentium is irrelevant. The $1,200 is a *sunk* cost that you incurred in the past, so it is the same whether or not you buy the new computer.

Relevant Nonfinancial Information

Nonfinancial, or qualitative factors, also play a role in managers' decisions. For example, closing manufacturing plants and laying off employees can seriously hurt employee morale. Outsourcing can reduce control over delivery time and product quality. Offering discounted prices to select customers can upset regular customers and tempt them to take their business elsewhere. Managers must think through the likely quantitative *and* qualitative effects of their decisions.

Managers who ignore qualitative factors can make serious mistakes. For example, the City of Nottingham, England, spent $1.6 million on 215 solar-powered parking meters after seeing how well the parking meters worked in countries along the Mediterranean Sea. However, the city did not consider that British skies are typically overcast. The result? The meters didn't always work because of the lack of sunlight. The city *lost* money because people ended up parking for free! Relevant qualitative information has the same characteristics as relevant financial information: The qualitative factor occurs in the *future*, and it *differs* between alternatives. The amount of *future* sunshine required *differed* between alternatives: The mechanical meters didn't require any sunshine, but the solar-powered meters needed a great deal of sunshine.

Likewise, in deciding between the Corolla and Sentra, you will likely consider qualitative factors that differ between the cars (legroom, trunk capacity, dashboard design, and so forth) before making your final decision. Since you must live with these factors in the future, they become relevant to your decision.

Keys to Making Short-Term Special Decisions

Our approach to making short-term special decisions is called the *relevant information approach* or the *incremental analysis approach*. Instead of looking at the company's *entire* income statement under each decision alternative, we'll just look at how operating income would *change or differ* under each alternative. Using this approach, we'll leave out irrelevant information—the costs and revenues that won't differ between alternatives.

We'll consider six kinds of decisions in this chapter:

1. Special sales orders
2. Pricing
3. Dropping products, departments, and territories
4. Product mix
5. Outsourcing (make or buy)
6. Selling as is or processing further

As you study these decisions, keep in mind the two keys in analyzing short-term special business decisions shown in Exhibit 8-3:

1. **Focus on relevant revenues, costs, and profits.** Irrelevant information only clouds the picture and creates information overload. That's why we'll use the incremental analysis approach.

2. **Use a contribution margin approach that separates variable costs from fixed costs.** Because fixed costs and variable costs behave differently, they must be analyzed separately. Traditional (absorption costing) income statements, which blend fixed and variable costs, can mislead managers. Contribution margin income statements, which isolate costs by behavior (variable or fixed), help managers gather the cost-behavior information they need. Keep in mind that unit manufacturing costs are mixed costs, too, so they can also mislead managers. If you use unit manufacturing costs in your analysis, make sure you separate the cost's fixed and variable components first.

We'll use these two keys in each decision.

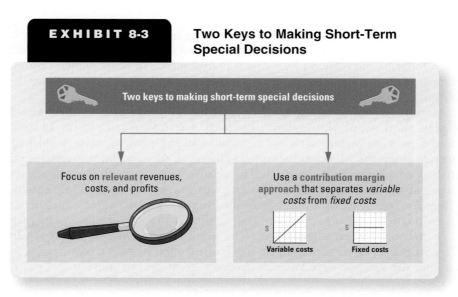

EXHIBIT 8-3 Two Keys to Making Short-Term Special Decisions

Two keys to making short-term special decisions

Focus on **relevant** revenues, costs, and profits

Use a **contribution margin approach** that separates *variable costs* from *fixed costs*

Variable costs | Fixed costs

Special Sales Order and Regular Pricing Decisions

We'll start our discussion on the six business decisions by looking at special sales order decisions and regular pricing decisions. In the past, managers did not consider pricing to be a short-term decision. However, product life cycles are shrinking in most industries. Companies often sell products for only a few months before replacing them with an updated model. The clothing and technology industries have always had short life cycles. Even auto and housing styles change frequently. Pricing has become a shorter-term decision than it was in the past.

Let's examine a special sales order in detail; then we will discuss regular pricing decisions.

Special Sales Order Decisions

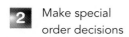

2 Make special order decisions

A special order occurs when a customer requests a one time order at a *reduced* sales price. Often, these special orders are for large quantities. Before agreeing to the special deal, management must consider the questions shown in Exhibit 8-4.

EXHIBIT 8-4 Special Order Considerations

- Do we have excess capacity available to fill this order?

- Will the reduced sales price be high enough to cover the *incremental* costs of filling the order (the variable costs and any additional fixed costs)?

- Will the special order affect regular sales in the long run?

First, managers must consider available capacity. If the company is already making as many units as possible and selling them all at its *regular* sales price, it wouldn't make sense to fill a special order at a *reduced* sales price. Why sell for *less* than the current sales price? Therefore, available excess capacity is a necessity for accepting a special order. This is true for service firms (law firms, caterers, and so forth) as well as manufacturers.

Second, managers need to consider whether the special reduced sales price is high enough to cover the incremental costs of filling the order. The special price *must* exceed the variable costs of filling the order, or the company will lose money on the deal. In other words, the special order must provide a positive contribution margin. Next, the company must consider fixed costs. If the company has excess capacity, fixed costs probably won't be affected by producing more units (or delivering more service). However, in some cases, management may need to hire a consultant or incur some other fixed cost to fill the special order. If so, management will need to consider whether the special sales price is high enough to generate a positive contribution margin *and* cover the additional fixed costs.

Finally, managers need to consider whether the special order will affect regular sales in the long run. Will regular customers find out about the special order and demand a lower price or take their business elsewhere? Will the special order customer come back *again and again*, asking for the same reduced price? Will the special order price start a price war with competitors? Managers must gamble that the answers to these questions are no or consider how customers will respond. Managers may decide that any profit from the special sales order is not worth these risks.

Let's consider a special sales order example. Suppose ACDelco sells oil filters for $3.20 each. Assume that a mail-order company has offered ACDelco $35,000 for 20,000 oil filters, or $1.75 per filter ($35,000 ÷ 20,000 = $1.75). This sale will:

- Use manufacturing capacity that would otherwise be idle.
- Not change fixed costs.
- Not require any variable *nonmanufacturing* expenses (because no extra marketing costs are incurred with this special order).
- Not affect regular sales.

We have addressed every consideration except one: Is the special sales price high enough to cover the variable *manufacturing* costs associated with the order? Let's take a look at the *wrong* way and then the *right* way to figure out the answer to that question.

Suppose ACDelco made and sold 250,000 oil filters before considering the special order. Using the traditional (absorption costing) income statement on the left-hand side of Exhibit 8-5, the manufacturing cost per unit is $2 ($500,000 ÷ 250,000). A manager who does not examine these numbers carefully may believe that ACDelco should *not* accept the special order at a sale price of $1.75 because each oil filter costs $2.00 to manufacture. But appearances can be deceiving! Remember that the unit manufacturing cost of a product ($2) is a *mixed* cost containing both fixed and variable cost components. To correctly answer our question, we need to find only the variable portion of the manufacturing unit cost.

<table>
<tr><td>**EXHIBIT 8-5**</td><td>**Traditional (Absorption Costing) Format and Contribution Margin Format Income Statements**</td></tr>
</table>

INCOME STATEMENT
(at a production and sales level of 250,000 units)
Year Ended December 31, 2007

Traditional (Absorption Costing) Format		Contribution Margin Format		
Sales revenue	$800,000	Sales revenue		$800,000
Less cost of goods sold	(500,000)	Less variable expenses:		
Gross profit	300,000	Manufacturing	$(300,000)	
Less marketing and administrative expenses	(200,000)	Marketing and administrative	(75,000)	(375,000)
		Contribution margin		425,000
		Less fixed expenses:		
		Manufacturing	$(200,000)	
		Marketing and administrative	(125,000)	(325,000)
Operating income	$100,000	Operating income		$100,000

The right-hand side of Exhibit 8-5 shows the contribution margin income statement that separates variable expenses from fixed expenses. The contribution margin income statement shows that the *variable* manufacturing cost per unit is only $1.20 ($300,000 ÷ 250,000). The special sales price of $1.75 is *higher* than the variable manufacturing cost of $1.20. Therefore, the special order will provide a positive contribution margin of $0.55 per unit ($1.75 − $1.20). Since the special order is for 20,000 units, ACDelco's total contribution margin should increase by $11,000 (20,000 units × $0.55 per unit) if it accepts this order.

Remember that in this example, ACDelco's variable marketing expenses are irrelevant because the company will not incur the usual variable marketing expenses on this special order. However, this won't always be the case. Many times, companies will also incur variable operating expenses (such as freight-out) on special orders.

Using an incremental analysis approach, ACDelco compares the additional revenues from the special order with the incremental expenses to see if the special order will contribute to profits. Exhibit 8-6 shows that the special sales order will increase revenue by $35,000 (20,000 × $1.75), but it will also increase variable manufacturing cost by $24,000 (20,000 × $1.20). As a result, ACDelco's contribution margin will increase by $11,000, as previously anticipated.

<table>
<tr><td>**EXHIBIT 8-6**</td><td>**Incremental Analysis of Special Sales Order**</td></tr>
</table>

Expected increase in revenues—sale of 20,000 oil filters × $1.75 each	$ 35,000
Expected increase in expenses—variable manufacturing costs:	
20,000 oil filters × $1.20 each	(24,000)
Expected increase in operating income	$ 11,000

The other costs shown in Exhibit 8-5 are irrelevant. Variable marketing and administrative expenses will be the same whether or not ACDelco accepts the special order because ACDelco made no marketing efforts to get this sale. Fixed manufacturing expenses won't change because ACDelco has enough idle capacity to produce 20,000 extra oil filters without requiring additional facilities. Fixed marketing and administrative expenses won't be affected by this special order either.

Because there are no additional fixed costs, the total increase in contribution margin flows directly to operating income. As a result, the special sales order will increase operating income by $11,000.

Notice that the analysis follows the two keys to making short-term special business decisions discussed earlier: (1) focus on relevant data (revenues and costs that *will change* if ACDelco accepts the special order) and (2) use a contribution margin approach that separates variable costs from fixed costs.

To summarize, for special sales orders, the decision rule is:

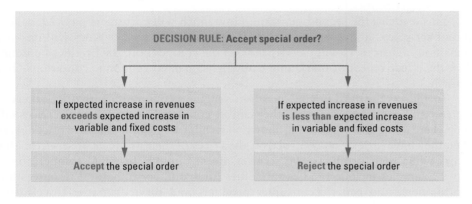

Stop & Think...

The absorption costing income statement on the left-hand side of Exhibit 8-5 shows that the total cost of manufacturing 250,000 filters is $500,000. What is the flaw in reasoning that ACDelco should accept special orders only if the sale price exceeds $2 each?

Answer: The flaw in this analysis arises from treating a mixed cost as though it were variable. Manufacturing one extra oil filter will cost only $1.20—the variable manufacturing cost. Fixed expenses are irrelevant because ACDelco will incur $200,000 of fixed manufacturing overhead expenses whether or not the company accepts the special order. Producing 20,000 more oil filters will not increase *total* fixed expenses, so manufacturing costs increase at the rate of $1.20 per unit, not $2.00 per unit.

Regular Pricing Decisions

In the special order decision, ACDelco decided to sell a limited quantity of oil filters for $1.75 each even though the normal price was $3.20 per unit. But how did ACDelco decide to set its regular price at $3.20 per filter? Exhibit 8-7 shows that managers start with three basic questions when setting regular prices for their products or services.

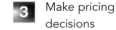 Make pricing decisions

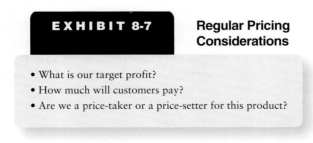

EXHIBIT 8-7   **Regular Pricing Considerations**

- What is our target profit?
- How much will customers pay?
- Are we a price-taker or a price-setter for this product?

The answers to these questions are often complex and ever-changing. Stockholders expect the company to achieve certain profits. Economic conditions, historical company earnings, industry risk, competition, and new business developments all affect the level of profit that stockholders expect. Stockholders usually tie their profit expectations to the amount of assets invested in the company. For example, stockholders may expect a 10% annual return on their investment. A company's stock price tends to decline if the company does not meet target profits, so managers must keep costs low while generating enough revenue to meet target profits.

This leads to the second question: How much will customers pay? Managers cannot set prices above what customers are willing to pay, or sales will decline. The amount customers will pay depends on the competition, the product's uniqueness, the effectiveness of marketing campaigns, general economic conditions, and so forth.

To address the third pricing question, imagine a continuum with price-takers at one end and price-setters at the other end. A company's products and services fall somewhere along this continuum, shown in Exhibit 8-8. Companies are price-takers when they have little or no control over the prices of their products or services. This occurs when their products and services are *not* unique or when competition is heavy. Examples include food commodities (milk and corn), natural resources (oil and lumber), and generic consumer products and services (paper towels, dry cleaning, and banking).

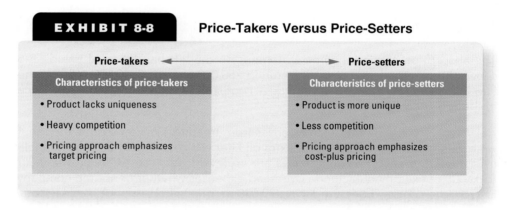

EXHIBIT 8-8   **Price-Takers Versus Price-Setters**

Price-takers ⟵⟶ Price-setters	
Characteristics of price-takers	**Characteristics of price-setters**
• Product lacks uniqueness	• Product is more unique
• Heavy competition	• Less competition
• Pricing approach emphasizes target pricing	• Pricing approach emphasizes cost-plus pricing

Companies are price-setters when they have more control over pricing—in other words, they can "set" the price to some extent. Companies are price-setters when their products are unique, which results in less competition. Unique products such as original art and jewelry, specially manufactured machinery, patented perfume scents, and custom-made furniture can command higher prices.

Obviously, managers would rather be price-setters than price-takers. To gain more control over pricing, companies try to differentiate their products. They want to make their products unique in terms of features, service, or quality—or at least make you *think* their product is unique or somehow better even if it isn't. How do they do this? Primarily through advertising. Consider Nike's tennis shoes, Starbucks' coffee, Hallmark's wrapping paper, Nexus' shampoo, Tylenol's acetaminophen, General Mills' cereal, Capital One's credit cards, Shell's gas, Abercrombie and Fitch's jeans—the list goes on and on. Are these products really better or significantly different from their lower-priced competitors? Possibly. If these companies can make you think so, they've gained more control over their pricing because you are willing to pay *more* for their products or services. The downside? These companies must charge higher prices or sell more just to cover their advertising costs.

A company's approach to pricing depends on whether its product or service is on the price-taking or price-setting side of the spectrum. Price-takers emphasize a target-pricing approach. Price-setters emphasize a cost-plus pricing approach. Keep in mind that many products fall somewhere along the continuum. Therefore, managers tend to use both approaches to some extent. We'll now discuss each approach in turn.

Target Pricing

When a company is a price-taker, it emphasizes a target pricing approach to pricing. Target pricing starts with the market price of the product (the price customers are willing to pay) and subtracts the company's desired profit to determine the product's **target full cost**—the *full* cost to develop, design, produce, market, deliver, and service the product. In other words, the full cost includes every cost incurred throughout the value chain.

Revenue at market price
Less: Desired profit
Target full cost

In this relationship, the market price is "taken." If the product's current cost is higher than the target cost, the company must find ways to reduce costs; otherwise it will not meet its profit goals. Managers often use ABC costing along with value engineering (as discussed in Chapter 5) to find ways to cut costs. Let's look at an example of target pricing.

Let's assume that oil filters are a commodity and that the current market price is $3.00 per filter (not the $3.20 sales price assumed in the earlier ACDelco example). Because the oil filters are a commodity, ACDelco will emphasize a target-pricing approach. Let's assume that ACDelco's stockholders expect a 10% annual return on the company's assets. If the company has $1,000,000 of assets, the desired profit is $100,000 ($1,000,000 × 10%). Exhibit 8-9 calculates the target full cost at the current sales volume (250,000 units). Once we know the target full cost, we can analyze the fixed and variable cost components separately.

EXHIBIT 8-9   **Calculating Target Full Cost**

	Calculations	Total
Revenue at market price	250,000 units × $3.00 price =	$750,000
Less: Desired profit	10% × $1,000,000 of assets	(100,000)
Target full cost		$650,000

Can ACDelco make and sell 250,000 oil filters at a full cost of $650,000? We know from ACDelco's contribution margin income statement (Exhibit 8-5) that the company's variable costs are $1.50 per unit ($375,000 ÷ 250,000 units). This variable cost per unit includes both manufacturing costs ($1.20 per unit) and marketing and administrative costs ($0.30 per unit). We also know that the company incurs $325,000 in fixed costs in its current relevant range. Again, some fixed cost stems from manufacturing and some from marketing and administrative activities. *In setting regular sales prices, companies must cover all of their costs— whether inventoriable or period, fixed or variable.*

Making and selling 250,000 filters currently costs the company $700,000 [(250,000 units × $1.50 variable cost per unit) + $325,000 of fixed costs], which is more than the target full cost ($650,000). So, what are ACDelco's options?

1. Accept a lower profit (an operating income of $50,000, which is a 5% return, not the 10% target return)

2. Cut fixed costs

3. Cut variable costs

4. Use other strategies. For example, ACDelco could attempt to increase sales volume. Recall that the company has excess capacity, so making and selling more units would affect only variable costs. The company could also consider changing or adding to its product mix. Finally, it could attempt to differentiate its oil filters (or strengthen its name brand) to gain more control over sales prices.

Let's look at some of these options. ACDelco may first try to cut fixed costs. As shown in Exhibit 8-10, the company would have to reduce fixed costs to $275,000 to meet its target profit level.

EXHIBIT 8-10   **Calculating Target Fixed Cost**

	Calculations	Total
Target full cost		$650,000
Less: Current variable costs	250,000 units × $1.50	(375,000)
Target fixed cost		$275,000

The company would start by considering whether any discretionary fixed costs could be eliminated without harming the company. Since committed fixed costs are nearly impossible to change in the short run, ACDelco will probably not be able to reduce this type of fixed cost.

If the company can't reduce its fixed costs by $50,000 ($325,000 current fixed costs – $275,000 target fixed costs), it would have to lower its variable cost to $1.30 per unit, as shown in Exhibit 8-11.

EXHIBIT 8-11   **Calculating Target Unit Variable Cost**

	Total
Target full cost	$650,000
Less: Current fixed costs	(325,000)
Target total variable costs	$325,000
Divided by number of units	÷ 250,000
Target variable cost per unit	$ 1.30

Perhaps the company could renegotiate raw materials costs with its suppliers or find a less costly way of packaging or shipping the air filters.

However, if ACDelco can't reduce variable costs to $1.30 per unit, could it meet its target profit through a combination of lowering both fixed costs and variable costs?

Stop & Think...

Suppose ACDelco can reduce its current fixed costs but only by $25,000. If it wants to meet its target profit, by how much will it have to reduce the variable cost of each unit? Assume that sales volume remains at 250,000 units.

Answer: Companies typically try to cut both fixed and variable costs. Because ACDelco can cut its fixed costs only by $25,000, to meet its target profit, it would have to cut its variable costs as well:

Target full cost	$ 650,000
Less: Reduced fixed costs ($325,000 – $25,000)	(300,000)
Target total variable costs	$ 350,000
Divided by number of units	÷ 250,000
Target variable cost per unit	$ 1.40

In addition to cutting its fixed costs by $25,000, the company must reduce its variable costs by $0.10 per unit ($1.50 — $1.40) to meet its target profit at the existing volume of sales.

Another strategy would be to increase sales. ACDelco's managers can use CVP analysis, as you learned in Chapter 7, to figure out how many oil filters the company would have to sell to achieve its target profit. How could the company increase demand for the oil filters? Perhaps it could reach new markets or advertise. How much would advertising cost—and how many extra oil filters would the company have to sell to cover the cost of advertising? These are only some of the questions managers must ask. As you can see, managers don't have an easy task when the current cost exceeds the target full cost. Sometimes, companies just can't compete given the current market price. If that's the case, they may have no other choice than to exit the market for that product.

Cost-Plus Pricing

When a company is a price-setter, it emphasizes a cost-plus approach to pricing. This pricing approach is essentially the *opposite* of the target-pricing approach. **Cost-plus pricing** starts with the product's full costs (as a given) and *adds* its desired profit to determine a cost-plus price.

Full cost
Plus: Desired profit
Cost-plus price

When the product is unique, the company has more control over pricing. However, the company still needs to make sure that the cost-plus price is not higher than what customers are willing to pay. Let's go back to our original ACDelco example. This time, let's assume that the oil filters benefit from brand recognition, so the company has some control over the price it charges for its filters. Exhibit 8-12 takes a cost-plus pricing approach assuming the current level of sales:

EXHIBIT 8-12   Calculating Cost-Plus Price

	Calculations	Total
Current variable costs	250,000 units × $1.50 per unit =	$375,000
Plus: Current fixed costs		+ 325,000
Full product cost		$700,000
Plus: Desired profit	10% × $1,000,000 of assets	+ 100,000
Target revenue		$800,000
Divided by number of units		÷ 250,000
Cost-plus price per unit		$ 3.20

If the current market price for generic oil filters is $3.00, as we assumed earlier, can ACDelco sell its brand-name filters for $3.20 apiece? The answer depends on how well the company has been able to differentiate its product or brand name. The company may use focus groups or marketing surveys to find out how customers would respond to its cost-plus price. The company may find out that its cost-plus price is too high, or it may find that it could set the price even higher without jeopardizing sales.

Stop & Think...

Which costing system (job costing or process costing) do you think price-setters and price-takers typically use?

Answer: Companies tend to be price-setters when their products are unique. Unique products are produced as single items or in small batches. Therefore, these companies use job costing to determine the product's cost. However, companies are price-takers when their products are high-volume commodities. Process costing better suits this type of product.

Notice how pricing decisions used our two keys to decision making: (1) focus on relevant information and (2) use a contribution margin approach that separates variable costs from fixed costs. In pricing decisions, all cost information is relevant because the company must cover *all* costs along the value chain before it can generate a profit. However, we still needed to consider variable costs and fixed costs separately because they behave differently at different volumes.

Our pricing decision rule is:

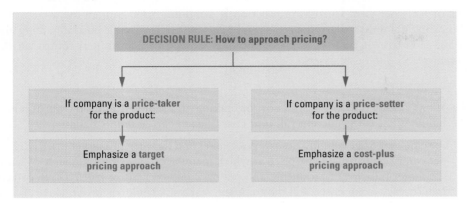

Decision Guidelines

RELEVANT INFORMATION FOR BUSINESS DECISIONS

Nike makes special order and regular pricing decisions. Even though it sells mass-produced tennis shoes and sports clothing, Nike has differentiated its products with advertising. Nike's managers consider both quantitative and qualitative factors as they make pricing decisions. Here are key guidelines that Nike's managers follow in making their decisions.

Decision	Guideline
What information is relevant to a short-term special business decision?	Relevant information: 1. Pertains to the *future* 2. *Differs* between alternatives
What are two key guidelines in making short-term special business decisions?	1. Focus on *relevant* data. 2. Use a *contribution margin* approach that separates variable costs from fixed costs.
Should Nike accept a lower sales price than the regular price for a large order from a customer in São Paulo, Brazil?	If the revenue from the order exceeds the extra variable and fixed costs incurred to fill the order, then accepting the order will increase operating income.
What should Nike consider in setting its regular product prices?	Nike considers: 1. What profit stockholders expect 2. What price customers will pay 3. Whether it is a price-setter or a price-taker
What approach should Nike take to pricing?	Nike has differentiated its products through advertising its brand name. Thus, Nike tends to be a price-setter. Nike's managers can emphasize a cost-plus approach to pricing.
What approach should discount shoe stores such as Payless ShoeSource take to pricing?	Payless ShoeSource sells generic shoes (no-name brands) at low prices. Payless is a price-taker, so managers use a target-pricing approach to pricing.

Summary Problem 1

Szigety Industries makes tennis balls. Szigety's only plant can produce up to 2.5 million cans of balls per year. Current production is 2 million cans. Annual manufacturing, selling, and administrative fixed costs total $700,000. The variable cost of making and selling each can of balls is $1. Stockholders expect a 12% annual return on the company's $3 million of assets.

Requirements

1. What is Szigety's current full cost of making and selling 2 million cans of tennis balls? What is the current full *unit* cost of each can of tennis balls?

2. Assume that Szigety Industries is a price-taker and the current market price is $1.45 per can of balls (this is the price at which manufacturers sell to retailers). What is the *target* full cost of producing and selling 2 million cans of balls? Given Szigety Industries' current costs, will the company reach stockholders' profit goals?

3. If Szigety Industries cannot change its fixed costs, what is the target variable cost per can of balls?

4. Suppose Szigety Industries could spend an extra $100,000 on advertising to differentiate its product so that it could be a price-setter. Assuming the original volume and costs plus the $100,000 of new advertising costs, what cost-plus price will Szigety Industries want to charge for a can of balls?

5. Nike has just asked Szigety Industries to supply 400,000 cans of balls at a special order price of $1.20 per can. Nike wants Szigety Industries to package the balls under the Nike label (Szigety will imprint the Nike logo on each ball and can). Szigety Industries will have to spend $10,000 to change the packaging machinery. Assuming the original volume and costs, should Szigety Industries accept this special order? (Unlike the chapter problem, assume that Szigety will incur variable selling costs as well as variable manufacturing costs related to this order.)

Solution

Requirement 1
The full unit cost is:

Fixed costs	$ 700,000
Plus: Total variable costs (2 million cans × $1 per unit)	+ 2,000,000
Total full costs	$2,700,000
Divided by number of cans...	÷ 2,000,000
Full cost per can...	$ 1.35

Requirement 2
The target full cost is:

Revenue at market price (2,000,000 units × $1.45 price)	$2,900,000
Less: Desired profit (12% × $3,000,000 of assets)	(360,000)
Target *full* cost...	$2,540,000

Szigety Industries' current total full costs ($2,700,000 from Requirement 1) are $160,000 higher than the target full cost ($2,540,000). If Szigety Industries can't cut costs, it won't be able to meet stockholders' profit expectations.

Requirement 3

Assuming that Szigety Industries cannot reduce its fixed costs, the target variable cost per can is:

Target *full* cost (from Requirement 2)	$ 2,540,000
Less: Fixed costs	(700,000)
Target total variable costs	$ 1,840,000
Divided by number of units	÷ 2,000,000
Target variable cost per unit	$ 0.92

Since Szigety Industries cannot reduce its fixed costs, it needs to reduce variable costs by $0.08 per can ($1.00 − $0.92) to meet its profit goals. This would require an 8% cost reduction in variable costs, which may not be possible.

Requirement 4

If Szigety Industries can differentiate its tennis balls, it will gain more control over pricing. The company's new cost-plus price would be:

Current total costs (from Requirement 1)	$2,700,000
Plus: Additional cost of advertising	+ 100,000
Plus: Desired profit (from Requirement 2)	+ 360,000
Target revenue	$3,160,000
Divided by number of units	÷ 2,000,000
Cost-plus price per unit	$ 1.58

Szigety Industries must study the market to determine whether retailers would pay $1.58 per can of balls.

Requirement 5

Nike's special order price ($1.20) is less than the current full cost of each can of balls ($1.35 from Requirement 1). However, this should not influence management's decision. Szigety Industries could fill Nike's special order using existing excess capacity. Szigety Industries takes an incremental analysis approach to its decision: comparing the extra revenue with the incremental costs of accepting the order. Variable costs will increase if Szigety Industries accepts the order, so the variable costs are relevant. Only the *additional* fixed costs of changing the packaging machine ($10,000) are relevant since all other fixed costs will remain unchanged.

Revenue from special order (400,000 × $1.20 per unit)	$480,000
Less: Variable cost of special order (400,000 × $1.00)	(400,000)
Contribution margin from special order	$ 80,000
Less: Additional fixed costs of special order	(10,000)
Operating income provided by special order	$ 70,000

Szigety Industries should accept the special order because it will increase operating income by $70,000. However, Szigety Industries also needs to consider whether its regular customers will find out about the special price and demand lower prices, too.

Other Short-Term Special Business Decisions

In the second part of the chapter, we'll look at other short-term business decisions that managers face, including:

- When to drop a product, department, or territory.
- Which products to emphasize in product mix decisions.
- When to outsource.
- When to sell as is or process further.

Decisions to Drop Products, Departments, or Territories

4 Make dropping a product, department, or territory decisions

Managers often must decide whether to drop products, departments, or territories that are not as profitable as desired. Newell Rubbermaid—maker of Sharpie markers, Graco strollers, and Rubbermaid plastics—recently dropped some of its European products lines. Home Depot closed some of its Expo stores. Kroger food stores replaced some in-store movie rental departments with health food departments. How do managers make these decisions? Exhibit 8-13 shows some questions managers must consider when deciding whether to drop a product line, department, or territory.

> **EXHIBIT 8-13** **Considerations for Dropping Products, Departments, or Territories**
>
> - Does the product provide a positive contribution margin?
> - Will fixed costs continue to exist even if we drop the product?
> - Are there any direct fixed costs that can be avoided if we drop the product?
> - Will dropping the product affect sales of the company's other products?
> - What could we do with the freed capacity?

Once again, we follow the two key guidelines for special business decisions: (1) focus on relevant data and (2) use a contribution margin approach. The relevant financial data are still the changes in revenues and expenses, but now we are considering a *decrease* in volume rather than an *increase*, as we did in the special sales order decision. In the following example, we will consider how managers decide to drop a product. Managers use the same process in deciding whether to drop a department or territory.

Earlier, we assumed that ACDelco offered only one product—oil filters. Now, let's assume that it makes and sells air cleaners, too. Exhibit 8-14 shows the company's contribution margin income statement by product line. Because the air cleaner product line has an operating loss of $19,074, management is considering dropping it.

The first question management should ask is, does the product provide a positive contribution margin? If the product line has a negative contribution margin, the product is not even covering its variable costs. Therefore, the company should drop the product line. However, if the product line has a positive contribution margin, it is

| **EXHIBIT 8-14** | **Contribution Margin Income Statements by Product Line** | | |

| | | Product Line | |
| | Total | Oil Filters | Air Cleaners |
	(270,000 units)	(250,000 units)	(20,000 units)
Sales revenue..	$835,000	$800,000	$ 35,000
Less: Variable expenses	(405,000)	(375,000)	(30,000)
Contribution margin	430,000	425,000	5,000
Less: Fixed expenses:			
Manufacturing	(200,000)	(185,185)*	(14,815)*
Marketing and administrative.....	(125,000)	(115,741)†	(9,259)†
Total fixed expenses	(325,000)	(300,926)	(24,074)
Operating income (loss)	$105,000	$124,074	$(19,074)

* $200,000 ÷ 270,000 units = $0.74074 per unit; 250,000 units × $0.74074 = $185,185; 20,000 units × $0.74074 = $14,815
† $125,000 ÷ 270,000 units = $0.462963 per unit; 250,000 units × $0.462963 = $115,741; 20,000 units × $0.462963 = $9,259

helping to cover at least some of the company's fixed costs. In ACDelco's case, the air cleaners provide a $5,000 positive contribution margin. ACDelco's managers now need to consider fixed costs.

Suppose ACDelco allocates fixed expenses between product lines in proportion to the number of units sold. Dividing the fixed manufacturing expense of $200,000 by 270,000 total units (oil filters, 250,000; air cleaners, 20,000) yields a fixed manufacturing cost of $0.74074 per unit. Allocating this unit cost to the 250,000 oil filters assigns fixed manufacturing cost of $185,185 to this product, as shown in Exhibit 8-14. The same procedure allocates $14,815 to the 20,000 air cleaners. Fixed marketing and administrative expenses are allocated in the same manner.

It is important to note that this allocation method is arbitrary. ACDelco could allocate fixed costs in many different ways, and each way would have allocated a different amount of fixed costs to each product line. Since the amount of fixed costs allocated to each product line will differ depending on the allocation method used, we need to look at fixed costs in a different light. What matters is this:

1. Will the total fixed costs continue to exist *even if* the product line is dropped?

2. Can any *direct* fixed costs of the air cleaners be avoided if the product line is dropped?

Fixed Costs Continue to Exist (Unavoidable Fixed Costs)

Fixed costs that will continue to exist even after a product is dropped are often called unavoidable fixed costs. Unavoidable fixed costs are irrelevant to the decision because they *will not* differ between alternatives — they will be incurred regardless of whether the product line is dropped. Let's assume that all of ACDelco's fixed costs ($325,000) will continue to exist even if the company drops the air cleaners. Perhaps ACDelco makes the air cleaners in the same manufacturing facilities as the oil filters and uses the same administrative overhead. If that is the case, only the contribution margin the air cleaners provide is relevant. If ACDelco drops the air cleaners, it will lose the $5,000 contribution margin that they provide.

The incremental analysis shown in Exhibit 8-15 verifies the loss. If ACDelco drops the air cleaners, revenue will decrease by $35,000; but variable expenses will decrease by only $30,000, resulting in a net $5,000 decrease in operating income. Because the company's total fixed costs are unaffected, they aren't included in the analysis. This analysis suggests that management should *not* drop the air cleaners.

EXHIBIT 8-15 | **Incremental Analysis for Dropping a Product When Fixed Costs Continue to Exist**

Expected decrease in revenues:	
Sale of air cleaners (20,000 × $1.75)	$35,000
Expected decrease in expenses:	
Variable manufacturing expenses (20,000 × $1.50)	30,000
Expected *decrease* in operating income	$ (5,000)

We could also verify that our analysis is correct by looking at what would *remain* if the air cleaners were dropped:

Contribution margin from oil filters..	$ 425,000
Less: Company's fixed expenses (all unavoidable)......................	(325,000)
Remaining operating income..	$ 100,000

The company's operating income after dropping the air cleaners ($100,000) would be $5,000 less than before ($105,000). This verifies our earlier conclusion: ACDelco's income would decrease by $5,000 if it dropped the air cleaners. Keep in mind that most companies have many product lines. Therefore, analyzing the decision to drop a particular product line is accomplished more easily by performing an incremental analysis (as we did in Exhibit 8-15) rather than adding up all of the revenues and expenses that would remain after dropping one product line. We simply show this second analysis as a means of proving our original result.

Direct Fixed Costs That Can Be Avoided

Even though ACDelco allocates its fixed costs between product lines, some of the fixed costs might *belong* strictly to the air cleaner product line. These would be direct fixed costs of the air cleaners.[1] For example, suppose ACDelco employs a part-time supervisor to oversee *just* the air cleaner product line. The supervisor's $13,000 salary is a direct fixed cost that ACDelco can *avoid* if it stops producing air cleaners. Avoidable fixed costs, such as the supervisor's salary, *are relevant* to the decision because they differ between alternatives (they will be incurred if the company keeps the product line; they will *not* be incurred if the company drops the product line).

Exhibit 8-16 shows that in this situation, operating income will *increase* by $8,000 if ACDelco drops air cleaners. Why? Because revenues will decline by $35,000 but expenses will decline even more—by $43,000. The result is a net increase to operating income of $8,000. This analysis suggests that management should drop the air cleaners.

Other Considerations

Management must also consider whether dropping the product line, department, or territory would hurt other sales. In the examples given so far, we assumed that dropping the air cleaners would not affect oil filter sales. However, think about a

---

[1]To aid in decision making, companies should separate direct fixed costs from indirect fixed costs on their contribution margin income statements. Companies should *trace direct fixed costs* to the appropriate product line and *allocate only indirect fixed costs* among product lines. As in the ACDelco example, companies do not always make this distinction on the income statement.

EXHIBIT 8-16 — Incremental Analysis for Dropping a Product When Direct Fixed Costs Can Be Avoided

Expected decrease in revenues:		
Sale of air cleaners (20,000 × $1.75)		$35,000
Expected decrease in expenses:		
Variable manufacturing expenses (20,000 × $1.50)	$30,000	
Direct fixed expenses—supervisor's salary	13,000	
Expected decrease in total expenses		43,000
Expected *increase* in operating income		$ 8,000

grocery store. Even if the produce department is not profitable, would managers drop it? Probably not, because if they did, they would lose customers who want one-stop shopping. In such situations, managers must also include the loss of contribution margin from *other* departments affected by the change when performing the financial analysis shown previously.

Management should also consider what they could do with freed capacity. In the ACDelco example, we assumed that the company produces oil filters and air cleaners using the same manufacturing facilities. If ACDelco drops the air cleaners, could it make and sell another product using the freed capacity? Managers should consider whether using the facilities to produce a different product would be more profitable than using the facilities to produce air cleaners.

Stop & Think...

Assume that all of ACDelco's fixed costs are unavoidable. If the company drops air cleaners, they could make spark plugs with the freed capacity. The company expects spark plugs would provide $50,000 of sales, incur $30,000 of variable costs, and incur $10,000 of new direct fixed costs. Should ACDelco drop the air cleaners and use the freed capacity to make spark plugs?

Answer: If all fixed costs are unavoidable, ACDelco would lose $5,000 of contribution margin if it dropped air cleaners. ACDelco should compare this loss with the expected gain from producing and selling spark plugs with the freed capacity:

Sales of spark plugs	$ 50,000
Less: Variable costs of spark plugs	(30,000)
Less: Direct fixed costs of spark plugs	(10,000)
Operating income gained from spark plugs	$ 10,000

The gain from producing spark plugs ($10,000) outweighs the loss from dropping air cleaners ($5,000). This suggests that management should replace air cleaner production with spark plug production.

Special decisions should take into account all costs affected by the choice of action. Managers must ask what total costs—variable and fixed—will change. As Exhibits 8-15 and 8-16 show, the key to deciding whether to drop products, departments, or territories is to compare the lost revenue against the costs that can be saved and to consider what would be done with the freed capacity. The decision rule is:

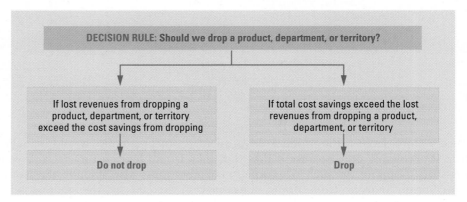

DECISION RULE: Should we drop a product, department, or territory?

If lost revenues from dropping a product, department, or territory exceed the cost savings from dropping	If total cost savings exceed the lost revenues from dropping a product, department, or territory
Do not drop	**Drop**

Product Mix Decisions

5 Make product mix decisions

Companies do not have unlimited resources. **Constraints** that restrict production or sale of a product vary from company to company. For a manufacturer such as Dell, the production constraint is often (because it's not always the case) labor hours, machine hours, or available materials. For a merchandiser such as Wal-Mart, the primary constraint is cubic feet of display space. Other companies are constrained by sales demand. Competition may be stiff, so the company may be able to sell only a limited number of units. In such cases, the company produces only as much as it can sell. However, if a company can sell all of the units it produces, which products should it emphasize, or make more of? Companies facing constraints consider the questions in Exhibit 8-17.

EXHIBIT 8-17 **Product Mix Considerations**

- What constraint(s) stops us from making (or displaying) all of the units we can sell?
- Which products offer the highest contribution margin per unit of the constraint?
- Would emphasizing one product over another affect fixed costs?

Consider Chazz, a manufacturer of shirts and jeans. The company can sell all of the shirts and jeans it produces, but it has only 2,000 machine hours of capacity. The company uses the same machines to produce both jeans and shirts. In this case, machine hours is the constraint. Note that this is a short-term decision, because in the long run, Chazz could expand its production facilities to meet sales demand if it made financial sense to do so. The following data suggest that shirts are more profitable than jeans:

	Per Unit	
	Shirts	**Jeans**
Sale price	$30	$60
Less: Variable expenses	(12)	(48)
Contribution margin	$18	$12
Contribution margin ratio:		
Shirts—$18 ÷ $30	60%	
Jeans—$12 ÷ $60		20%

However, an important piece of information is missing—the time it takes to make each product. Let's assume that Chazz can produce either 20 pairs of jeans *or* 10 shirts per machine hour. *The company will incur the same fixed costs either way, so fixed costs are irrelevant.* Which product should it emphasize?

To maximize profits when fixed costs are irrelevant, follow the decision rule:

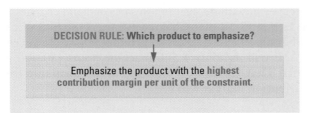

DECISION RULE: Which product to emphasize?

Emphasize the product with the **highest contribution margin per unit of the constraint.**

Because *machine hours* is the constraint, Chazz needs to figure out which product has the *highest contribution margin per machine hour*. Exhibit 8-18 shows the contribution margin per machine hour for each product.

EXHIBIT 8-18   **Product Mix—Which Product to Emphasize**

	Shirts	Jeans
(1) Units that can be produced each machine hour	10	20
(2) Contribution margin per unit	× $18	× $12
Contribution margin per machine hour (1) × (2)	$180	$240
Available capacity—number of machine hours	× 2,000	× 2,000
Total contribution margin at full capacity	$360,000	$480,000

Jeans have a higher contribution margin per machine hour ($240) than shirts ($180). Therefore Chazz will earn more profit by producing jeans. Why? Because even though jeans have a lower contribution margin *per unit*, Chazz can make twice as many jeans as shirts in the available machine hours. Exhibit 8-18 also proves that Chazz earns more total profit by making jeans. Multiplying the contribution margin per machine hour by the available number of machine hours shows that Chazz can earn $480,000 of contribution margin by producing jeans but only $360,000 by producing shirts.

To maximize profit, Chazz should make 40,000 jeans (2,000 machine hours × 20 jeans per hour) and zero shirts. Why zero shirts? Because for every machine hour spent making shirts, Chazz would *give up* $60 of contribution margin ($240 per hour for jeans versus $180 per hour for shirts).

Changing Assumptions: Product Mix When Demand Is Limited

We made two assumptions about Chazz: (1) Chazz's sales of other products, if any, won't be hurt by this decision and (2) Chazz can sell as many jeans and shirts as it can produce. Let's challenge these assumptions. First, how could making only jeans (and not shirts) hurt sales of the company's other products? Using other production equipment, Chazz also makes ties and knit sweaters that coordinate with their shirts. Tie and sweater sales might fall if Chazz no longer offers coordinating shirts.

Let's challenge our second assumption. A new competitor has decreased the demand for Chazz's jeans. Now, the company can sell only 30,000 pairs of jeans. Chazz should make only as many jeans as it can sell and use the remaining machine hours to produce shirts. Let's see how this constraint in sales demand changes profitability.

Recall from Exhibit 8-18 that Chazz will earn $480,000 of contribution margin from using all 2,000 machine hours to produce jeans. However, if Chazz makes only 30,000 jeans, it will use only 1,500 machine hours (30,000 jeans ÷ 20 jeans per machine hour). That leaves 500 machine hours available for making shirts. Chazz's new contribution margin will be:

	Shirts	Jeans	Total
Contribution margin per machine hour (from Exhibit 8-18)..............	$ 180	$ 240	
Machine hours devoted to product	× 500	× 1,500	2,000
Total contribution margin at full capacity.................................	$90,000	$360,000	$450,000

Because of the change in product mix, Chazz's total contribution margin will fall from $480,000 to $450,000, a $30,000 decline. Chazz had to give up $60 of contribution margin per machine hour ($240 – $180) on the 500 hours it spent producing shirts rather than jeans. However, Chazz had no choice—the company would have incurred an *actual loss* from producing jeans that it could not sell. If Chazz had produced 40,000 jeans but sold only 30,000, the company would have spent $480,000 to make the unsold jeans (10,000 jeans × $48 variable cost per pair of jeans) yet would have received no sales revenue from them.

What about fixed costs? In most cases, changing the product mix emphasis in the short run will not affect fixed costs, so fixed costs are irrelevant. However, fixed costs could differ when a different product mix is emphasized. What if Chazz had a month-to-month lease on a zipper machine used only for making jeans? If Chazz made only shirts, it could *avoid* the lease cost. However, if Chazz makes any jeans, it needs the machine. In this case, the fixed costs become relevant because they differ between alternative product mixes (shirts only *versus* jeans only or jeans and shirts).

Stop & Think...

Would Chazz's product mix decision change if it had a $20,000 cancelable lease on a zipper machine needed only for jean production? Assume that Chazz can sell as many units as it makes.

Answer: We would compare the profitability as follows:

	Shirts	Jeans
Total contribution margin at full capacity (from Exhibit 8-18)	$360,000	$480,000
Less: Avoidable fixed costs	-0-	(20,000)
Net benefit	$360,000	$460,000

Even considering the zipper machine lease, producing jeans is more profitable than producing shirts. Chazz would prefer producing jeans over shirts unless demand for jeans drops so low that the net benefit from jeans is less than $360,000 (the benefit gained from solely producing shirts).

Notice that the analysis again follows the two guidelines for special business decisions: (1) focus on relevant data (only those revenues and costs that differ) and (2) use a contribution margin approach, which separates variable from fixed costs.

Outsourcing Decisions (Make-or-Buy)

Recall from the chapter's opening story that Delta outsources much of its reservation work and airplane maintenance. **Outsourcing** decisions are sometimes called **make-or-buy** decisions because managers must decide whether to buy a component product or service or produce it in-house. The heart of these decisions is *how best to use available resources.*

6 Make outsourcing (make-or-buy) decisions

Let's see how managers make outsourcing decisions. DefTone, a manufacturer of music CDs, is deciding whether to make paper liners for CD jewel boxes (the plastic cases in which CDs are sold) in-house or whether to outsource them to Mūz-Art, a company that specializes in producing paper liners. DefTone's cost to produce 250,000 liners is:

	Total Cost (250,000 liners)
Direct materials	$ 40,000
Direct labor	20,000
Variable manufacturing overhead	15,000
Fixed manufacturing overhead	50,000
Total manufacturing cost	$125,000
Number of liners	÷ 250,000
Cost per liner	$ 0.50

Mūz-Art offers to sell DefTone the liners for $0.37 each. Should DefTone make the liners or buy them from Mūz-Art? DefTone's $0.50 cost per unit to make the liner is $0.13 higher than the cost of buying it from Mūz-Art. It first appears that DefTone should outsource the liners. But the correct answer is not so simple. Why? Because manufacturing unit costs contain both fixed and variable components. In deciding whether to outsource, managers must consider fixed and variable costs separately. Exhibit 8-19 shows some of the questions management must consider when deciding whether to outsource.

EXHIBIT 8-19   Outsourcing Considerations

- How do our variable costs compare to the outsourcing cost?
- Are any fixed costs avoidable if we outsource?
- What could we do with the freed capacity?

Let's see how these considerations apply to DefTone. By purchasing the liners, DefTone can avoid all variable manufacturing costs—$40,000 of direct materials, $20,000 of direct labor, and $15,000 of variable manufacturing overhead. In total, the company will save $75,000 in variable manufacturing costs, or $0.30 per liner ($75,000 ÷ 250,000 liners). However, DefTone will have to pay the variable outsourcing cost of $0.37 per unit, or $92,500 for the 250,000 liners. Based only on variable costs, the lower cost alternative is to manufacture the liners in-house. However, managers must still consider fixed costs.

Assume that DefTone cannot avoid any of the fixed costs by outsourcing. In this case, the company's fixed costs are irrelevant to the decision because DefTone would continue to incur $50,000 of fixed costs regardless of whether the company outsources the liners. The fixed costs are irrelevant because they do not differ between alternatives. DefTone should continue to make its own liners because the variable cost of outsourcing the liners ($92,500) exceeds the variable cost of making the liners ($75,000).

However, what if DefTone can avoid some fixed costs by outsourcing the liners? Let's assume that management can reduce fixed overhead cost by $10,000 by outsourcing the liners. DefTone will still incur $40,000 of fixed overhead ($50,000 − $10,000) even if they outsource the liners. In this case, fixed costs become relevant to the decision because they differ between alternatives. Exhibit 8-20 shows the differences in costs between the make and buy alternatives under this scenario.

EXHIBIT 8-20   Incremental Analysis for Outsourcing Decision

Liner Costs	Make Liners	Buy Liners	Difference
Variable costs:			
Direct materials	$ 40,000	—	$40,000
Direct labor	20,000	—	20,000
Variable overhead	15,000	—	15,000
Purchase cost from Mūz-Art			
(250,000 × $0.37)	—	$ 92,500	(92,500)
Fixed overhead	50,000	40,000	10,000
Total cost of liners	$125,000	$132,500	$ (7,500)

Exhibit 8-20 shows that it would still cost DefTone less to make the liners than to buy them from Mūz-Art, even with the $10,000 reduction in fixed costs. The net savings from making 250,000 liners is $7,500.

Exhibit 8-20 also shows that outsourcing decisions follow our two key guidelines for special business decisions: (1) focus on relevant data (differences in costs in this case) and (2) use a contribution margin approach that separates variable costs from fixed costs.

Note how the unit cost—which does not separate costs according to behavior—can be deceiving. If DefTone's managers made their decision by comparing the total manufacturing cost per liner ($0.50) to the outsourcing unit cost per liner ($0.37), they would have incorrectly decided to outsource. Recall that the manufacturing unit cost ($0.50) contains both fixed and variable components whereas the outsourcing cost ($0.37) is strictly variable. To make the correct decision, DefTone had to separate the two cost components and analyze them separately.

Our decision rule for outsourcing is:

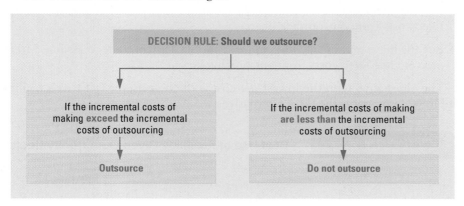

Stop & Think...

Assuming that DefTone could save $10,000 in fixed costs by outsourcing, what is the most the company would be willing to pay per liner to outsource production of 250,000 liners?

Answer: To answer that question, we must find the outsourcing price at which DefTone would be *indifferent* about making the liners or outsourcing the liners. DefTone would be indifferent if the total costs were the *same* either way:

$$\text{Costs if making liners} = \text{Costs if outsourcing liners}$$
$$\text{Variable manufacturing costs} + \text{Fixed costs} = \text{Variable outsourcing costs} + \text{Fixed costs}$$
$$(250{,}000 \text{ units} \times \$0.30 \text{ per unit}) + \$50{,}000 = (250{,}000 \times \text{outsourcing cost per unit}) + \$40{,}000$$
$$\$75{,}000 + \$50{,}000 - \$40{,}000 = (250{,}000 \times \text{outsourcing cost per unit})$$
$$\$85{,}000 = (250{,}000 \times \text{outsourcing cost per unit})$$
$$\$85{,}000 \div 250{,}000 = \text{outsourcing cost per unit}$$
$$\$0.34 = \text{outsourcing cost per unit}$$

DefTone would be indifferent about making or outsourcing the liners if the outsourcing cost price was $0.34 per unit. At that price, DefTone would incur the same cost to manufacture or outsource the liners. DefTone would save money only if the outsourcing price was less than $0.34 per unit. Therefore, the most DefTone would pay to outsource is $0.33 per liner. As shown below, at $0.33 per liner, DefTone would save $2,500 from outsourcing:

Liner Costs	Make Liners	Buy Liners	Difference
Variable costs	$ 75,000 (250,000 units × $0.30 per unit)	$ 82,500 (250,000 × $0.33 per unit)	($7,500)
Plus: Fixed costs	50,000	40,000	10,000
Total costs	$125,000	$122,500	$2,500

We haven't considered what DefTone could do with the freed capacity it would have if it decided to outsource the liners. The analysis in Exhibit 8-20 assumes no other use for the production facilities if DefTone buys the liners from Mūz-Art. But suppose DefTone has an opportunity to use its freed capacity to make more CDs for an additional profit of $18,000. Now, DefTone must consider its **opportunity cost**—the benefit forgone by not choosing an alternative course of action. In this case, DefTone's opportunity cost of making the liners is the $18,000 profit it forgoes if it does not free its production facilities to make the additional CDs.

Let's see how DefTone's managers decide among three alternatives:

1. Use the facilities to make the liners

2. Buy the liners and leave facilities idle (continue to assume $10,000 of avoidable fixed costs from outsourcing liners)

3. Buy the liners and use facilities to make more CDs (continue to assume $10,000 of avoidable fixed costs from outsourcing liners)

The alternative with the lowest *net* cost is the best use of DefTone's facilities. Exhibit 8-21 compares the three alternatives.

EXHIBIT 8-21 Best Use of Facilities Given Opportunity Costs

		Buy Liners	
	Make Liners	Facilities Idle	Make Additional CDs
Expected cost of 250,000 liners (from Exhibit 8-20)	$125,000	$132,500	$132,500
Expected *profit* from additional CDs	—	—	(18,000)
Expected net cost of obtaining 250,000 liners	$125,000	$132,500	$114,500

DefTone should buy the liners from Mūz-Art and use the vacated facilities to make more CDs. If DefTone makes the liners or buys the liners from Mūz-Art but leaves its production facilities idle, it will forgo the opportunity to earn $18,000.

Stop & Think...

How will the $18,000 opportunity cost change the *maximum* amount DefTone is willing to pay to outsource each liner?

Answer: DefTone will now be willing to pay *more* to outsource its liners. In essence, the company is willing to pay for the opportunity to make more CDs.

DefTone's managers should consider qualitative factors as well as revenue and cost differences in making their final decision. For example, DefTone managers may believe they can better control quality or delivery schedules by making the liners themselves. This argues for making the liners.

Outsourcing decisions are increasingly important in today's globally wired economy. In the past, make-or-buy decisions often ended up as "make" because coordination, information exchange, and paperwork problems made buying from suppliers too inconvenient. Now, companies can use the Internet to tap into information systems of suppliers and customers located around the world.

Paperwork vanishes, and information required to satisfy the strictest JIT delivery schedule is available in real time. As a result, companies are focusing on their core competencies and outsourcing more functions.

Sell As Is or Process Further Decisions

At what point in processing should a company sell its product? Many companies, especially in the food processing and natural resource industries, face this business decision. Companies in these industries process a raw material (milk, corn, livestock, crude oil, lumber, and so forth) to a point before it is saleable. For example, Kraft pasteurizes raw milk before it is saleable. Kraft must then decide whether it should sell the pasteurized milk as is or process it further into other dairy products (reduced-fat milk, butter, sour cream, cottage cheese, yogurt, blocks of cheese, shredded cheese, and so forth). Managers consider the questions shown in Exhibit 8-22 when deciding whether to sell as is or process further.

7 | Make sell as is or process further decisions

EXHIBIT 8-22   **Sell As Is or Process Further Considerations**

- How much revenue will we receive if we sell the product as is?
- How much revenue will we receive if we sell the product *after* processing it further?
- How much will it cost to process the product further?

Let's look at one of Chevron's sell or process further decisions. Suppose Chevron spent $125,000 to process crude oil into 50,000 gallons of regular gasoline, as shown in Exhibit 8-23. After processing crude oil into regular gasoline, should Chevron sell the regular gas as is or should it spend more to process the gasoline into premium grade? In making the decision, Chevron's managers consider the following relevant information:

EXHIBIT 8-23   **Sell As Is or Process Further Decision**

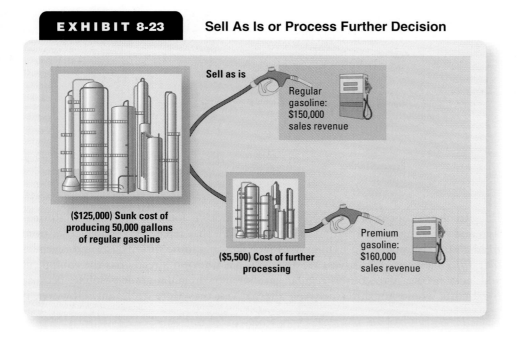

Sell as is

Regular gasoline: $150,000 sales revenue

($125,000) Sunk cost of producing 50,000 gallons of regular gasoline

($5,500) Cost of further processing

Premium gasoline: $160,000 sales revenue

- Chevron could sell regular gasoline for $3 per gallon, for a total of $150,000 (50,000 × $3.00).

- Chevron could sell premium gasoline for $3.20 per gallon, for a total of $160,000 (50,000 × $3.20).

- Chevron would have to spend $0.11 per gallon, or $5,500 (50,000 gallons × $0.11), to further process regular gasoline into premium-grade gas.

Notice that Chevron's managers do *not* consider the $125,000 spent on processing crude oil into regular gasoline. Why? It is a sunk cost. Recall from our previous discussion that a sunk cost is a past cost that cannot be changed regardless of which future action the company takes. Chevron has incurred $125,000 regardless of whether it sells the regular gasoline as is or processes it further into premium gasoline. Therefore, the cost is *not* relevant to the decision.

EXHIBIT 8-24   **Incremental Analysis for Sell As Is or Process Further Decision**

	Sell As Is	Process Further	Difference
Expected revenue from selling 50,000 gallons of regular gasoline at $3.00 per gallon	$150,000		
Expected revenue from selling 50,000 gallons of premium gasoline at $3.20 per gallon		$160,000	$10,000
Additional costs of $0.11 per gallon to convert 50,000 gallons of regular gasoline into premium gasoline		(5,500)	(5,500)
Total net revenue	$150,000	$154,500	$ 4,500

By analyzing only the relevant costs in Exhibit 8-24, managers see that they can increase profit by $4,500 if they convert the regular gasoline into premium gasoline. The $10,000 extra revenue ($160,000 – $150,000) outweighs the incremental $5,500 cost of the extra processing.

Thus, the decision rule is:

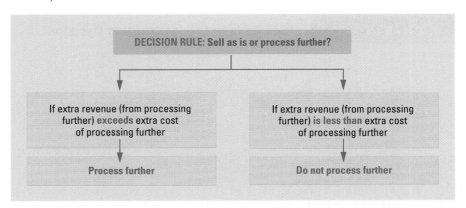

Recall that our keys to decision making include (1) focusing on relevant information and (2) using a contribution margin approach that separates variable costs from fixed costs. The analysis in Exhibit 8-24 includes only those *future* costs and revenues that *differ* between alternatives. We assumed that Chevron already has the equipment and labor necessary to convert regular gasoline into premium-grade gasoline. Because fixed costs would not differ between alternatives, they were irrelevant. However, if

Chevron has to acquire equipment or hire employees to convert the gasoline into premium-grade gasoline, the extra fixed costs would be relevant. Once again, we see that fixed costs are relevant only if they *differ* between alternatives.

Stop & Think...

Suppose one of Chevron's customers wants to buy the 50,000 gallons, but in the form of regular gasoline, not premium gasoline. The customer is willing to pay more than $3 a gallon for the regular gasoline. What is the minimum price Chevron should charge?

Answer: Exhibit 8-24 shows that if Chevron does not process the gasoline into premium grade, it will give up $154,500 of net revenue ($160,000 revenues given up − $5,500 further processing cost not incurred). To obtain at least the same income from selling the gasoline as regular grade, Chevron must sell the regular gasoline for at least $3.09 per gallon ($154,500 ÷ 50,000 gallons of regular gasoline). At $3.09 per gallon, Chevron would be indifferent about the two alternatives. If the customer offers to pay more than $3.09 per gallon, Chevron will be better off selling regular gasoline to this customer. If the customer offers less than $3.09, Chevron will be better off further processing the gasoline into premium-grade gasoline.

Decision Guidelines

SHORT-TERM SPECIAL BUSINESS DECISIONS

Amazon.com has confronted most of the special business decisions we've covered. Here are the key guidelines Amazon.com's managers follow in making their decisions.

Decision	Guideline
Should Amazon.com drop its electronics product line?	If the cost savings exceed the lost revenues from dropping the electronics product line, then dropping will increase operating income.
Given limited warehouse space, which products should Amazon.com focus on selling?	Amazon.com should focus on selling the products with the highest contribution margin per unit of the constraint, which is cubic feet of warehouse space.
Should Amazon.com outsource its warehousing operations?	If the incremental costs of operating its own warehouses exceed the costs of outsourcing, then outsourcing will increase operating income.
How should a company decide whether to sell a product as is or process further?	Process further only if the extra sales revenue (from processing further) exceeds the extra costs of additional processing.

Summary Problem 2

Requirements

1. Aziz produces standard and deluxe sunglasses:

	Per Pair	
	Standard	Deluxe
Sale price	$20	$30
Variable expenses	16	21

The company has 15,000 machine hours available. In one machine hour, Aziz can produce 70 pairs of the standard model or 30 pairs of the deluxe model. Assuming machine hours is a constraint, which model should Aziz emphasize?

2. Just Do It! incurs the following costs for 20,000 pairs of its high-tech hiking socks:

Direct materials..	$ 20,000
Direct labor..	80,000
Variable manufacturing overhead	40,000
Fixed manufacturing overhead...	80,000
Total manufacturing cost	$220,000
Cost per pair ($220,000 ÷ 20,000)..	$ 11

Another manufacturer has offered to sell Just Do It! similar socks for $10 a pair, a total purchase cost of $200,000. If Just Do It! outsources *and* leaves its plant idle, it can save $50,000 of fixed overhead cost. Or the company can use the released facilities to make other products that will contribute $70,000 to profits. In this case, the company will not be able to avoid any fixed costs. Identify and analyze the alternatives. What is the best course of action?

Solution

Requirement 1

	Style of Sunglasses	
	Standard	Deluxe
Sale price per pair...........................	$ 20	$ 30
Variable expense per pair.............................	(16)	(21)
Contribution margin per pair.......................	$ 4	$ 9
Units produced each machine hour	× 70	× 30
Contribution margin per machine hour........	$ 280	$ 270
Capacity—number of machine hours	× 15,000	× 15,000
Total contribution margin at full capacity....	$4,200,000	$4,050,000

Decision: Emphasize the standard model because it has the higher contribution margin per unit of the constraint—machine hours—resulting in a higher contribution margin for the company.

Requirement 2

| | Make Socks | Buy Socks | |
		Facilities Idle	Make Other Products
Relevant costs:			
Direct materials............................	$ 20,000	—	—
Direct labor..................................	80,000	—	—
Variable overhead	40,000	—	—
Fixed overhead............................	80,000	$ 30,000	$ 80,000
Purchase cost from outsider (20,000 × $10)	—	200,000	200,000
Total cost of obtaining socks......	220,000	230,000	280,000
Profit from other products	—	—	(70,000)
Net cost of obtaining 20,000 pairs of socks	$220,000	$230,000	$210,000

Decision: Just Do It! should buy the socks from the outside supplier and use the released facilities to make other products.

Review Short-Term Business Decisions

■ Accounting Vocabulary

Constraint. (p. 460)
A factor that restricts production or sale of a product.

Cost-Plus Pricing. (p. 451)
An approach to pricing that begins with the product's full costs and adds a desired profit to determine a cost-plus price.

Opportunity Cost. (p. 446)
The benefit forgone by not choosing an alternative course of action.

Outsourcing. (p. 463)
A make-or-buy decision: Managers decide whether to buy a component product or service or produce it in-house.

Relevant Information. (p. 441)
Expected *future* data that *differs* among alternatives.

Sunk Cost. (p. 442)
A past cost that cannot be changed regardless of which future action is taken.

Target Full Cost. (p. 449)
The total cost to develop, design, produce, market, deliver, and service a product.

■ Quick Check

1. In making short-term special decisions, you should
   a. focus on total costs
   b. separate variable from fixed costs
   c. use a traditional absorption costing approach
   d. focus only on quantitative factors

2. Which of the following is relevant to Amazon.com's decision to accept a special order at a lower sale price from a large customer in China?
   a. the cost of Amazon.com's warehouses in the United States
   b. Amazon.com's investment in its Web site
   c. the cost of shipping the order to the customer
   d. founder Jeff Bezos's salary

3. In deciding whether to drop its electronics product line, Amazon.com would consider
   a. the costs it could save by dropping the product line
   b. the revenues it would lose from dropping the product line
   c. how dropping the electronics product line would affect sales of its other products, such as CDs
   d. all of the above

4. In deciding which product lines to emphasize, Amazon.com should focus on the product line that has the highest
   a. contribution margin per unit of the constraining factor
   b. contribution margin per unit of product
   c. contribution margin ratio
   d. profit per unit of product

5. When making outsourcing decisions
   a. the manufacturing full unit cost of making the product in-house is relevant
   b. the variable cost of producing the product in-house is relevant
   c. avoidable fixed costs are irrelevant
   d. expected use of the freed capacity is irrelevant

6. When companies are price-setters, their products and services
   a. are priced by managers using a target-pricing emphasis
   b. tend to be unique
   c. tend to have a great many competitors
   d. tend to be commodities

7. When pricing a product or service, managers must consider which of the following?
   a. only variable costs
   b. only period costs
   c. only manufacturing costs
   d. all costs

8. Which of the following costs are irrelevant to business decisions?
   a. sunk costs
   b. costs that differ between alternatives
   c. variable costs
   d. avoidable costs

9. When deciding whether to sell as is or process a product further, managers should ignore which of the following?
   a. the revenue if the product is processed further
   b. the cost of processing further
   c. the costs of processing the product thus far
   d. the revenue if the product is sold as is

10. When making decisions, managers should
    a. consider sunk costs
    b. consider costs that do not differ between alternatives
    c. consider only variable costs
    d. consider revenues that differ between alternatives

Quick Check Answers

1. b 2. c 3. d 4. a 5. b 6. b 7. d 8. a 9. c 10. d

For Internet Exercises, Excel in Practice, and additional online activities, go to this book's Web site at www.prenhall.com/bamber.

Assess Your Progress

■ Learning Objectives

1 Describe and identify information relevant to short-term business decisions

2 Make special order decisions

3 Make pricing decisions

4 Make dropping a product, department, or territory decisions

5 Make product mix decisions

6 Make outsourcing (make-or-buy) decisions

7 Make sell as is or process further decisions

■ Short Exercises

S8-1 **Determine relevance of information** *(Learning Objective 1)*

You are trying to decide whether to trade in your ink-jet printer for a more recent model. Your usage pattern will remain unchanged, but the old and new printers use different ink cartridges. Are the following items relevant or irrelevant to your decision?

a. The price of the new printer

b. The price you paid for the old printer

c. The trade-in value of the old printer

d. Paper costs

e. The difference between the cost of ink cartridges

S8-2 **Special order decision given revised data** *(Learning Objective 2)*

Consider the ACDelco special sales order example on pages 445–447. Suppose ACDelco's variable manufacturing cost is $1.35 per oil filter (instead of $1.20). In addition, ACDelco would have to buy a special stamping machine that costs $9,000 to mark the customer's logo on the special-order oil filters. The machine would be scrapped when the special order is complete.

Would you recommend that ACDelco accept the special order under these conditions? Show your analysis.

S8-3 **Determine pricing approach and target price** *(Learning Objective 3)*

SnowDreams operates a Rocky Mountain ski resort. The company is planning its lift ticket pricing for the coming ski season. Investors would like to earn a 15% return on the company's $100 million of assets. The company incurs primarily fixed costs to groom the runs and operate the lifts. SnowDreams projects fixed costs to be $33,750,000 for the ski season. The resort serves about 750,000 skiers and snowboarders each season. Variable costs are about $10 per guest. Currently, the resort has such a favorable reputation among skiers and snowboarders that it has some control over the lift ticket prices.

1. Would SnowDreams emphasize target pricing or cost-plus pricing. Why?

2. If other resorts in the area charge $70 per day, what price should SnowDreams charge?

S8-4   **Use target pricing to analyze data** (*Learning Objective 3*)

Consider SnowDreams from S8-3. Assume that SnowDreams' reputation has diminished and other resorts in the vicinity are charging only $65 per lift ticket. SnowDreams has become a price-taker and won't be able to charge more than its competitors. At the market price, SnowDreams managers believe they will still serve 750,000 skiers and snowboarders each season.

1. If SnowDreams can't reduce its costs, what profit will it earn? State your answer in dollars and as a percent of assets. Will investors be happy with the profit level? Show your analysis.

2. Assume that SnowDreams has found ways to cut its fixed costs to $30 million. What is its new target variable cost per skier/snowboarder? Compare this to the current variable cost per skier/snowboarder. Comment.

S8-5   **Decide whether to drop a department** (*Learning Objective 4*)

Knight Fashion in New York operates three departments: Men's, Women's, and Accessories. Knight Fashion allocates all fixed expenses (unavoidable building depreciation and utilities) based on each department's square footage. Departmental operating income data for the third quarter of 2007 are as follows:

	Department			
	Men's	**Women's**	**Accessories**	**Total**
Sales revenue	$105,000	$54,000	$100,000	$259,000
Variable expenses............	60,000	30,000	80,000	170,000
Fixed expenses	25,000	20,000	25,000	70,000
Total expenses................	85,000	50,000	105,000	240,000
Operating income (loss)....	$20,000	$4,000	$(5,000)	$19,000

The store will remain in the same building regardless of whether any of the departments are dropped. Should Knight Fashion drop any of the departments? Give your reason.

S8-6   **Drop a department: revised information** (*Learning Objective 4*)

Consider Knight Fashion from S8-5. Assume that the fixed expenses assigned to each department include only direct fixed costs of the department (rather than unavoidable fixed costs as given in S8-5):

- Salary of the department's manager
- Cost of advertising directly related to that department

If Knight Fashion drops a department, it will not incur these fixed expenses. Under these circumstances, should Knight Fashion drop any of the departments? Give your reason.

S8-7   **Replace a department** (*Learning Objective 4*)

Consider Knight Fashion from S8-5. Assume once again that all fixed costs are unavoidable. If Knight Fashion drops one of the current departments, it plans to replace the dropped department with a shoe department. The company expects the shoe department to produce $80,000 in sales and have $50,000 of variable costs. Because the shoe business would be new to Knight Fashion, the company would have to incur an additional $7,000 of fixed costs (advertising, new shoe display racks, and so forth) per quarter related to the department. What should Knight Fashion do now?

S8-8   **Product mix decision: unlimited demand** *(Learning Objective 5)*
StoreAll produces plastic storage bins for household storage needs. The company makes two sizes of bins: large (50 gallon) and regular (35 gallon). Demand for the product is so high that StoreAll can sell as many of each size as it can produce. The company uses the same machinery to produce both sizes. The machinery can be run for only 3,000 hours per period. StoreAll can produce 10 large bins every hour compared to 15 regular bins in the same amount of time. Fixed expenses amount to $100,000 per period. Sales prices and variable costs are as follows:

	Regular	Large
Sales price per unit	$8.00	$10.00
Variable cost per unit	$3.00	$ 4.00

1. Which product should StoreAll emphasize? Why?
2. To maximize profits, how many of each size bin should StoreAll produce?
3. Given this product mix, what will the company's operating income be?

S8-9   **Product mix decision: limited demand** *(Learning Objective 5)*
Consider StoreAll in S8-8. Assume that demand for regular bins is limited to 30,000 units and demand for large bins is limited to 25,000 units.

1. How many of each size bin should StoreAll make now?
2. Given this product mix, what will be the company's operating income?
3. Explain why the operating income is less than it was when StoreAll was producing its optimal product mix.

S8-10   **Outsourcing production decision** *(Learning Objectives 1, 6)*
Suppose an Olive Garden restaurant is considering whether to (1) bake bread for its restaurant in-house or (2) buy the bread from a local bakery. The chef estimates that variable costs of making each loaf include $0.50 of ingredients, $0.25 of variable overhead (electricity to run the oven), and $0.75 of direct labor for kneading and forming the loaves. Allocating fixed overhead (depreciation on the kitchen equipment and building) based on direct labor assigns $1.00 of fixed overhead per loaf. None of the fixed costs are avoidable. The local bakery would charge Olive Garden $1.75 per loaf.

1. What is the unit cost of making the bread in-house (use absorption costing)?
2. Should Olive Garden bake the bread in-house or buy from the local bakery? Why?
3. In addition to the financial analysis, what else should Olive Garden consider when making this decision?

S8-11   **Relevant information for outsourcing delivery function** *(Learning Objectives 1, 6)*
U.S. Food in Lexington, Kentucky, manufactures and markets snack foods. Betsy Gonzalez manages the company's fleet of 200 delivery trucks. Gonzalez has been charged with "reengineering" the fleet-management function. She has an important decision to make.

- Should she continue to manage the fleet in-house with the five employees reporting to her? To do so, she will have to acquire new fleet-management software to streamline U.S. Food's fleet-management process.

- Should she outsource the fleet-management function to Fleet Management Services, a company that specializes in managing fleets of trucks for other companies? Fleet Management Services would take over the maintenance, repair, and scheduling of U.S. Food's fleet (but U.S. Food would retain ownership). This alternative would require Gonzalez to lay off her five employees. However, her own job would be secure, as she would be U.S. Food's liaison with Fleet Management Services.

Assume that Gonzalez's records show the following data concerning U.S. Food's fleet:

Book value of U.S. Food's trucks, with an estimated five-year life....................................	$3,500,000
Annual leasing fee for new fleet-management software	8,000
Annual maintenance of trucks...	145,500
Fleet Supervisor Gonzalez's annual salary	60,000
Total annual salaries of U.S. Food's five other fleet-management employees.............................	150,000

Suppose that Fleet Management Services offers to manage U.S. Food's fleet for an annual fee of $290,000.

Which alternative will maximize U.S. Food's short-term operating income?

S8-12   **Outsourcing qualitative considerations** *(Learning Objectives 1, 6)*

Refer to U.S. Food in S8-11. What qualitative factors should Gonzalez consider before making a final decision?

S8-13   **Scrap or process further decision** *(Learning Objective 7)*

Auto Components has an inventory of 500 obsolete remote entry keys that are carried in inventory at a manufacturing cost of $80,000. Production Supervisor Terri Smith must decide to do one of the following:

- Process the inventory further at a cost of $20,000, with the expectation of selling it for $28,000

- Scrap the inventory for a sale price of $6,000

What should Smith do? Present figures to support your decision.

S8-14   **Determine most profitable final product** *(Learning Objective 7)*

Chocolite processes cocoa beans into cocoa powder at a processing cost of $10,000 per batch. Chocolite can sell the cocoa powder as is, or it can process the cocoa powder further into chocolate syrup or boxed assorted chocolates. Once processed, each batch of cocoa beans would result in the following sales revenue:

Cocoa powder...	$15,000
Chocolate syrup	$100,000
Boxed assorted chocolates..	$200,000

The cost of transforming the cocoa powder into chocolate syrup would be $70,000. Likewise, the company would incur $180,000 to transform the cocoa powder into boxed assorted chocolates. The company president has decided to make boxed assorted chocolates owing to its high sales value and to the fact that the $10,000 cost of processing cocoa beans "eats up" most of the cocoa powder profits. Has the president made the right or wrong decision? Explain your answer. Be sure to include the correct financial analysis in your response.

E8-15 **Determine relevant and irrelevant information** (*Learning Objective 1*)

Joe Roberts, production manager for Chocorua, invested in computer-controlled production machinery last year. He purchased the machinery from Olney Manufacturing at a cost of $2 million. A representative from Olney Manufacturing recently contacted Joe because the company has designed an even more efficient piece of machinery. The new design would double the production output of the year-old machinery but cost Chocorua another $3 million. Roberts is afraid to bring this new equipment to the company president's attention because he persuaded the president to invest $2 million in the machinery last year.

Requirement

Explain what is relevant and irrelevant to Roberts's dilemma. What should he do?

E8-16 **Special order decisions given two scenarios** (*Learning Objective 2*)

Suppose the Baseball Hall of Fame in Cooperstown, New York, has approached Super-Cardz with a special order. The Hall of Fame wants to purchase 50,000 baseball card packs for a special promotional campaign and offers $0.40 per pack, a total of $20,000. Super-Cardz's total production cost is $0.60 per pack, as follows:

Variable costs:	
Direct materials...	$0.14
Direct labor..	0.08
Variable overhead	0.13
Fixed overhead...	0.25
Total cost...	$0.60

Super-Cardz has enough excess capacity to handle the special order.

Requirements

1. Prepare an incremental analysis to determine whether Super-Cardz should accept the special sales order assuming fixed costs would not be affected by the special order.

2. Now, assume that the Hall of Fame wants special hologram baseball cards. Super-Cardz must spend $5,000 to develop this hologram, which will be useless after the special order is completed. Should Super-Cardz accept the special order under these circumstances? Show your analysis.

E8-17 **Special order decision and considerations** *(Learning Objective 2)*

Live It Sunglasses sell for about $150 per pair. Suppose the company incurs the following average costs per pair:

Direct materials...	$40
Direct labor..	12
Variable manufacturing overhead	8
Variable marketing expenses..	4
Fixed manufacturing overhead...	20*
Total costs...	$84

$$* \frac{\$2,000,000 \text{ total fixed manufacturing overhead}}{100,000 \text{ pairs of sunglasses}}$$

Live It Sunglasses has enough idle capacity to accept a one-time-only special order from LensCrafters for 20,000 pairs of sunglasses at $76 per pair. Live It Sunglasses will not incur any variable marketing expenses for the order.

Requirements

1. How would accepting the order affect Live It Sunglasses' operating income? In addition to the special order's effect on profits, what other (longer-term qualitative) factors should Live It Sunglasses' managers consider in deciding whether to accept the order?

2. Live It Sunglasses' marketing manager, Jim Revo, argues against accepting the special order because the offer price of $76 is less than Live It Sunglasses' $84 cost to make the sunglasses. Revo asks you, as one of Live It Sunglasses' staff accountants, to write a memo explaining whether his analysis is correct.

E8-18 **Pricing decisions given two scenarios** *(Learning Objective 3)*

Keane Builders builds 1,500-square-foot starter tract homes in the fast-growing suburbs of Atlanta. Land and labor are cheap, and competition among developers is fierce. The homes are "cookie-cutter," with any upgrades added by the buyer after the sale. Keane Builders' cost per developed sublot are as follows:

Land...	$50,000
Construction	$125,000
Landscaping...	$5,000
Variable marketing costs..	$2,000

Keane Builders would like to earn a profit of 15% of the variable cost of each home sale. Similar homes offered by competing builders sell for $200,000 each.

Requirements

1. Which approach to pricing should Keane Builders emphasize? Why?

2. Will Keane Builders be able to achieve its target profit levels? Show your computations.

continued . . .

3. Bathrooms and kitchens are typically the most important selling features of a home. Keane Builders could differentiate the homes by upgrading bathrooms and kitchens. The upgrades would cost $20,000 per home but would enable Keane Builders to increase the selling prices by $35,000 per home (in general, kitchen and bathroom upgrades typically add at least 150% of their cost to the value of any home). If Keane Builders upgrades, what will the new cost-plus price per home be? Should the company differentiate its product in this manner? Show your analysis.

E8-19 **Decide whether to drop a product line** *(Learning Objective 4)*

Top managers of Preston Video are alarmed by their operating losses. They are considering dropping the VCR-tape product line. Company accountants have prepared the following analysis to help make this decision:

	Total	DVD Discs	VCR Tapes
Sales revenue	$420,000	$300,000	$120,000
Variable expenses	230,000	150,000	80,000
Contribution margin	190,000	150,000	40,000
Fixed expenses:			
Manufacturing	125,000	70,000	55,000
Marketing and administrative	70,000	55,000	15,000
Total fixed expenses	195,000	125,000	70,000
Operating income (loss)	$ (5,000)	$ 25,000	$ (30,000)

Total fixed costs will not change if the company stops selling VCR tapes.

Requirements

1. Prepare an incremental analysis to show whether Preston Video should drop the VCR-tape product line. Will dropping VCR tapes add $30,000 to operating income? Explain.

2. Assume that Preston Video can avoid $30,000 of fixed expenses by dropping the VCR-tape product line (these costs are direct fixed costs of the VCR product line). Prepare an incremental analysis to show whether Preston Video should stop selling VCR tapes.

3. Now, assume that all $70,000 of fixed costs assigned to VCR tapes are direct fixed costs and can be avoided if the company stops selling VCR tapes. However, marketing has concluded that DVD sales would be adversely affected by discontinuing the VCR line (retailers want to buy both from the same supplier). DVD production and sales would decline 10%. What should the company do?

E8-20 Dropping a product line *(Learning Objective 4)*

Suppose Kellogg's is considering dropping its Special-K product line. Assume that during the past year, Special-K's product line income statement showed the following:

Sales	$7,600,000
Cost of goods sold	6,400,000
Gross profit	1,200,000
Operating expenses	1,400,000
Operating loss	$ (200,000)

Fixed manufacturing overhead costs account for 40% of the cost of goods, while only 30% of the operating expenses are fixed. Since the Special-K line is only one of Kellogg's breakfast cereals, only $750,000 of direct fixed costs (the majority of which is advertising) will be eliminated if the product line is discontinued. The remainder of the fixed costs will still be incurred by Kellogg's. If the company decides to drop the product line, what will happen to the company's operating income? Should Kellogg's drop the product line?

E8-21 Identify constraint, then determine product mix *(Learning Objective 5)*

Kirby produces two types of exercise treadmills: Regular and Deluxe. The exercise craze is such that Kirby could use all of its available machine hours producing either model. The two models are processed through the same production department.

	Per Unit	
	Deluxe	Regular
Sale price	$1,000	$ 550
Costs:		
Direct materials	$ 290	$ 100
Direct labor	80	180
Variable manufacturing overhead	240	80
Fixed manufacturing overhead*	120	40
Variable operating expenses	115	65
Total cost	845	465
Operating income	$ 155	$ 85

Allocated on the basis of machine hours.

What product mix will maximize operating income? (*Hint:* Use the allocation of fixed manufacturing overhead to determine the proportion of machine hours used by each product.)

E8-22 **Determine product mix for retailer** *(Learning Objective 5)*
Olivo sells both designer and moderately priced fashion accessories. Top management is deciding which product line to emphasize. Accountants have provided the following data:

	Per Item	
	Designer	Moderately Priced
Average sale price......................................	$200	$84
Average variable expenses..........................	85	24
Average fixed expenses (allocated)............	20	10
Average operating income..........................	$95	$50

The Olivo store in Reno, Nevada, has 10,000 square feet of floor space. If Olivo emphasizes moderately priced goods, it can display 650 items in the store. If Olivo emphasizes designer wear, it can display only 300 designer items to create more of a boutique-like atmosphere. These numbers are also the average monthly sales in units.
Prepare an analysis to show which product to emphasize.

E8-23 **Determine product mix for retailer—two stocking scenarios** *(Learning Objective 5)*
Each morning, Max Imery stocks the drink case at Max's Kool Off in Myrtle Beach, South Carolina. Max's Kool Off has 100 linear feet of refrigerated display space for cold drinks. Each linear foot can hold either six 12-ounce cans or four 20-ounce plastic or glass bottles. Max's Kool Off sells three types of cold drinks:

1. Coca-Cola in 12-oz. cans for $1.50 per can
2. A&W Root Beer in 20-oz. plastic bottles for $1.75 per bottle
3. Mountian Dew in 20-oz. glass bottles for $2.20 per bottle

Max's Kool Off pays its suppliers:

1. $0.25 per 12-oz. can of Coca-Cola
2. $0.40 per 20-oz. bottle of A&W Root Beer
3. $0.75 per 20-oz. bottle of Mountain Dew

Max's Kool Off monthly fixed expenses include:

Hut rental	$ 375
Refrigerator rental...	75
Max's salary...	1,550
Total fixed expenses	$2,000

Max's Kool Off can sell all drinks stocked in the display case each morning.

Requirements

1. What is Max's Beach Hut's constraining factor? What should Max stock to maximize profits? What is the maximum contribution margin he could generate from refrigerated drinks each day?

2. To provide variety to customers, suppose Max refuses to devote more than 60 linear feet and no less than 10 linear feet to any individual product. Under this condition, how many linear feet of each drink should Max stock? How many units of each product will be available for sale each day?

3. Assuming the product mix calculated in Requirement 2, what contribution margin will Max generate from refrigerated drinks each day?

E8-24 Make-or-buy product component *(Learning Objective 6)*

Decoste Manufacturing manufactures an optical switch that it uses in its final product. Decoste Manufacturing incurred the following manufacturing costs when it produced 70,000 units last year:

Direct materials...	$ 630,000
Direct labor...	105,000
Variable overhead	140,000
Fixed overhead..	455,000
Total manufacturing cost for 70,000 units............................	$1,330,000

Decoste Manufacturing does not yet know how many switches it will need this year; however, another company has offered to sell Decoste Manufacturing the switch for $14 per unit. If Decoste Manufacturing buys the switch from the outside supplier, the manufacturing facilities that will be idle cannot be used for any other purpose, yet none of the fixed costs are avoidable.

Requirements

1. Given the same cost structure, should Decoste Manufacturing make or buy the switch? Show your analysis.

2. Now, assume that Decoste Manufacturing can avoid $100,000 of fixed costs a year by outsourcing production. In addition, because sales are increasing, Decoste Manufacturing needs 75,000 switches a year rather than 70,000. What should Decoste Manufacturing do now?

3. Given the last scenario, what is the most Decoste Manufacturing would be willing to pay to outsource the switches?

E8-25 Make-or-buy with alternative use of facilities *(Learning Objective 6)*

Refer to E8-24. Decoste Manufacturing needs 80,000 optical switches next year (assume same relevant range). By outsourcing them, Decoste Manufacturing can use its idle facilities to manufacture another product that will contribute $220,000 to operating income, but none of the fixed costs will be avoidable. Should Decoste Manufacturing make or buy the switches? Show your analysis.

E8-26 Determine maximum outsourcing price *(Learning Objective 6)*

Crank It Up's sales have increased; as a result, the company needs 400,000 jewel-case liners rather than 250,000. Crank It Up has enough existing capacity to make all of the liners it needs. In addition, due to volume discounts, its variable costs of making each liner will decline to $0.28 per liner. Assume that by outsourcing, Crank It Up can reduce its current fixed costs ($50,000) by $10,000. There is no alternative use for the factory space freed through outsourcing, so it will just remain idle. What is the maximum Crank It Up will pay to outsource production of its CD liners?

E8-27 Sell as is or process further *(Learning Objective 7)*

Chill Time processes organic milk into plain yogurt. Chill Time sells plain yogurt to hospitals, nursing homes, and restaurants in bulk, one-gallon containers. Each batch, processed at a cost of $800, yields 500 gallons of plain yogurt. Chill Time sells the one-gallon tubs for $6.00 each and spends $0.10 for each plastic tub. Chill Time has recently begun to reconsider its strategy. Chill Time wonders if it would be more profitable to sell individual-size portions of fruited organic yogurt at local food stores. Chill Time could further process each batch of plain yogurt into 10,667 individual portions (3/4 cup each) of fruited yogurt. A recent market analysis indicates that demand for the product exists. Chill Time would sell each individual portion for $0.50. Packaging would cost $0.08 per portion, and fruit would cost $0.10 per portion. Fixed costs would not change. Should Chill Time continue to sell only the gallon-size plain yogurt (sell as is) or convert the plain yogurt into individual-size portions of fruited yogurt (process further)? Why?

■ Problems (Problem Set A)

P8-28A Special order decision and considerations *(Learning Objective 2)*

Gamma manufactures flotation vests in Tampa, Florida. Gamma contribution margin income statement for the most recent month contains the following data:

Sales in units	31,000
Sales revenue	$434,000
Variable expenses:	
Manufacturing	$ 93,000
Marketing and administrative	107,000
Total variable expenses	200,000
Contribution margin	234,000
Fixed expenses:	
Manufacturing	126,000
Marketing and administrative	90,000
Total fixed expenses	216,000
Operating income	$ 18,000

Suppose Theta wants to buy 5,000 vests from Gamma. Acceptance of the order will not increase Gamma's variable marketing and administrative expenses or any of its fixed expenses. The Gamma plant has enough unused capacity to manufacture the additional vests. Theta has offered $10 per vest, which is below the normal sale price of $14.

Requirements

1. Prepare an incremental analysis to determine whether Gamma should accept this special sales order.

2. Identify long-term factors Gamma should consider in deciding whether to accept the special sales order.

P8-29A Pricing of nursery plants *(Learning Objective 3)*

The Big Fuzzy Spider operates a commercial plant nursery where it propagates plants for garden centers throughout the region. The Big Fuzzy Spider has $5 million in assets. Its yearly fixed costs are $600,000, and the variable costs for the potting soil, container, label, seedling, and labor for each gallon-size plant total $1.25. The Big Fuzzy Spider volume is currently 500,000 units. Competitors offer the same quality plants to garden centers for $3.50 each. Garden centers then mark them up to sell to the public for $8 to $10, depending on the type of plant.

Requirements

1. The Big Fuzzy Spider's owners want to earn a 12% return on the company's assets. What is The Big Fuzzy Spider's target full cost?

2. Given that The Big Fuzzy Spider's current costs, will its owners be able to achieve their target profit? Show your analysis.

3. Assume that The Big Fuzzy Spider has identified ways to cut its variable costs to $1.10 per unit. What is its new target fixed cost? Will this decrease in variable costs allow the company to achieve its target profit? Show your analysis.

4. The Big Fuzzy Spider started an aggressive advertising campaign strategy to differentiate its plants from those grown by other nurseries. Danforth Plants made this strategy work, so The Big Fuzzy Spider has decided to try it, too. The Big Fuzzy Spider doesn't expect volume to be affected, but it hopes to gain more control over pricing. If The Big Fuzzy Spider has to spend $100,000 this year to advertise and its variable costs continue to be $1.10 per unit, what will its cost-plus price be? Do you think The Big Fuzzy Spider will be able to sell its plants to garden centers at the cost-plus price? Why or why not?

P8-30A Prepare and use contribution margin statements for dropping a line decision *(Learning Objective 4)*

Members of the board of directors of Sellars Security have received the following operating income data for the year just ended:

	Product Line		
	Industrial Systems	Household Systems	Total
Sales revenue............................	$300,000	$310,000	$610,000
Cost of goods sold:			
Variable	$ 38,000	$ 42,000	$ 80,000
Fixed...................................	210,000	69,000	279,000
Total cost of goods sold	248,000	111,000	359,000
Gross profit............................	52,000	199,000	251,000
Marketing and administrative expenses:			
Variable	66,000	71,000	137,000
Fixed..............................	40,000	22,000	62,000
Total marketing and administrative expenses..	106,000	93,000	199,000
Operating income (loss)	$ (54,000)	$106,000	$ 52,000

continued . . .

Members of the board are surprised that the industrial systems product line is losing money. They commission a study to determine whether the company should drop the line. Company accountants estimate that dropping industrial systems will decrease fixed cost of goods sold by $80,000 and decrease fixed marketing and administrative expenses by $12,000.

Requirements

1. Prepare an incremental analysis to show whether Sellars Security should drop the industrial systems product line.

2. Prepare contribution margin income statements to show Sellars Security's total operating income under the two alternatives: (a) with the industrial systems line and (b) without the line. Compare the *difference* between the two alternatives' income numbers to your answer to Requirement 1. What have you learned from this comparison?

P8-31A **Product mix decision under constraint** (*Learning Objective 5*)
Keystone, located in St. Cloud, Minnesota, produces two lines of electric toothbrushes: deluxe and standard. Because Keystone can sell all of the toothbrushes it produces, the owners are expanding the plant. They are deciding which product line to emphasize. To make this decision, they assemble the following data:

	Per Unit	
	Deluxe Toothbrush	Standard Toothbrush
Sale price...	$80	$48
Variable expenses...........................	20	18
Contribution margin	$60	$30
Contribution margin ratio..............	75%	62.5%

After expansion, the factory will have a production capacity of 4,500 machine hours per month. The plant can manufacture either 60 standard electric toothbrushes or 24 deluxe electric toothbrushes per machine hour.

Requirements

1. Identify the constraining factor for Keystone.

2. Prepare an analysis to show which product line to emphasize.

P8-32A **Outsourcing decision given alternative use of capacity** (*Learning Objective 6*)
Snow Wonderful manufactures snowboards. Its cost of making 1,800 bindings is:

Direct materials...	$ 20,000
Direct labor..	80,000
Variable manufacturing overhead	40,000
Fixed manufacturing overhead..	80,000
Total manufacturing cost	$220,000
Cost per pair ($220,000 ÷ 20,000)...	$ 11

Suppose Abrahmson will sell bindings to Snow Wonderful for $14 each. Snow Wonderful will pay $1.00 per unit to transport the bindings to its manufacturing plant, where it will add its own logo at a cost of $0.20 per binding.

Requirements

1. Snow Wonderful's accountants predict that purchasing the bindings from Abrahmson will enable the company to avoid $2,200 of fixed overhead. Prepare an analysis to show whether Snow Wonderful should make or buy the bindings.

2. The facilities freed by purchasing bindings from Abrahmson can be used to manufacture another product that will contribute $3,100 to profit. Total fixed costs will be the same as if Snow Wonderful had produced the bindings. Show which alternative makes the best use of Snow Wonderful's facilities: (a) make bindings, (b) buy bindings and leave facilities idle, or (c) buy bindings and make another product.

P8-33A Sell or process further decisions *(Learning Objective 7)*

Rovnovsky Chemical has spent $240,000 to refine 72,000 gallons of acetone, which can be sold for $2.16 a gallon. Alternatively, Rovnovsky Chemical can process the acetone further. This processing will yield a total of 60,000 gallons of lacquer thinner that can be sold for $3.20 a gallon. The additional processing will cost $0.62 per gallon of lacquer thinner. To sell the lacquer thinner, Rovnovsky Chemical must pay shipping of $0.22 a gallon and administrative expenses of $0.10 a gallon on the thinner.

Requirements

1. Diagram Rovnovsky decision, using Exhibit 8-23 as a guide.

2. Identify the sunk cost. Is the sunk cost relevant to Rovnovsky decision? Why or why not?

3. Should Rovnovsky sell the acetone or process it into lacquer thinner? Show the expected net revenue difference between the two alternatives.

■ Problems (Problem Set B)

P8-34B Special order decision and considerations *(Learning Objective 2)*

Dynamo Packaging's contribution margin income statement follows:

Sales in units	360,000
Sales revenue	$432,000
Variable expenses:	
Manufacturing	$108,000
Marketing and administrative	53,000
Total variable expenses	161,000
Contribution margin	271,000
Fixed expenses:	
Manufacturing	156,000
Marketing and administrative	40,000
Total fixed expenses	196,000
Operating income	$ 75,000

continued . . .

Colvin Farms wants to buy 5,000 produce boxes from Dynamo Packaging. Acceptance of the order will not increase any of Dynamo Packaging's variable marketing and administrative expenses or any of its fixed expenses. Dynamo Packaging's plant has enough unused capacity to manufacture the additional boxes. Colvin Farms has offered $0.80 per box, which is considerably below the normal sale price of $1.20.

Requirements

1. Prepare an incremental analysis to determine whether Dynamo Packaging should accept this special sales order.

2. Identify long-term factors that Dynamo Packaging should consider in deciding whether to accept the special sales order.

P8-35B Pricing of facial tissues (*Learning Objective 3*)

Flower Petal produces facial tissues. Flower Petal has $50 million in assets. Its yearly fixed costs are $12 million, and the variable cost of producing and selling each box of tissues is $0.25. Flower Petal currently sells 30 million boxes of tissues. Generic facial tissues such as Flower Petal's product generally sell to retailers for $0.75 per box, while name brands such as Kleenex and Puffs sell to retailers for $1.00 per box.

Requirements

1. Flower Petal's stockholders expect a 10% return on the company's assets. What is Flower Petal's target full cost?

2. Given Flower Petal's current costs, will its owners achieve their target profit? Show your analysis.

3. Flower Petal has identified ways to cut its fixed costs by $500,000. What is its new target variable cost per unit? Will Flower Petal be able to reach its target profit?

4. Flower Petal started an aggressive advertising campaign to transform its product into a name brand able to compete with Kleenex and Puffs. Flower Petal doesn't think volume will be affected, but it hopes to gain more control over pricing. If Flower Petal spends $3 million a year to advertise, what will its cost-plus price be? (Continue to assume that fixed costs have declined by $500,000 but that Flower Petal was unable to reduce its variable cost per unit below $0.25). Do you think Flower Petal will be able to sell its facial tissues to retailers at the cost-plus price? Why or why not?

P8-36B Prepare and use contribution margin statements for dropping a line decision (*Learning Objective 4*)

The following operating income data of Arial Seafood highlight the losses of the fresh seafood product line:

		Product Line	
	Total	Fresh Seafood	Frozen Seafood
Sales revenue............................	$730,500	$190,500	$540,000
Cost of goods sold:			
Variable	$138,000	$ 44,000	$ 94,000
Fixed..................................	61,000	20,000	41,000
Total cost of goods sold	199,000	64,000	135,000
Gross profit.............................	531,500	126,500	405,000
Marketing and administrative expenses:			
Variable	223,000	98,000	125,000
Fixed..................................	93,000	38,000	55,000
Total marketing and administrative expenses...	316,000	136,000	180,000
Operating income (loss)	$215,500	$ (9,500)	$225,000

Arial Seafood is considering discontinuing the fresh seafood product line. The company's accountants estimate that dropping the fresh seafood line will decrease fixed cost of goods sold by $16,000 and decrease fixed marketing and administrative expenses by $10,000.

Requirements

1. Prepare an incremental analysis to show whether Arial Seafood should drop the fresh seafood product line.

2. Prepare contribution margin income statements to compare Arial Seafood's total operating income (a) with the fresh seafood product line and (b) without it. Compare the *difference* between the two alternatives' income numbers to your answer to Requirement 1. What have you learned from this comparison?

P8-37B Product mix under constraint (*Learning Objective 5*)
Fontaine Furniture of Charlotte, North Carolina, specializes in outdoor furniture and spas. Owner Linda Spring is expanding the store. She is deciding which product line to emphasize. To make this decision, she assembles the following data:

	Per Unit	
	Spas	Patio Sets
Sale price..	$1,000	$800
Variable expenses.................................	480	440
Contribution margin	$ 520	$360
Contribution margin ratio...................	52%	45%

continued . . .

After renovation, the store will have 8,000 square feet of floor space. By devoting the new floor space to patio sets, Fontaine Furniture can display 60 patio sets. Alternatively, Fontaine Furniture could display 30 spas. Spring expects monthly sales to equal the maximum number of units displayed.

Requirements

1. Identify the constraining factor for Fontaine Furniture.
2. Prepare an analysis to show which product line to emphasize.

P8-38B Outsourcing: alternative use of capacity *(Learning Objective 6)*

Quality Grain makes organic cereal. Costs of producing 140,000 boxes of cereal each year follow:

Direct materials...	$220,000
Direct labor..	140,000
Variable overhead	60,000
Fixed overhead...	440,000
Total manufacturing costs...	$860,000

Suppose Kellogg's will sell Quality Grain the cereal for $4 a box. Quality Grain would also pay $0.19 a box to transport the cereal to its warehouse.

Requirements

1. Quality Grain's accountants predict that purchasing the cereal from Kellogg's will enable the company to avoid $140,000 of fixed overhead. Prepare an analysis to show whether Quality Grain should make or buy the cereal.
2. Assume that the Quality Grain facilities freed up by purchasing the cereal from Kellogg's can be used to manufacture snack bars that will contribute $180,000 to profit. Total fixed costs will be the same as if Quality Grain used the plant to make cereal. Prepare an analysis to show which alternative makes the best use of Quality Grain's facilities: (a) make cereal, (b) buy cereal and leave facilities idle, or (c) buy cereal and make snack bars.

P8-39B Sell or process further decision *(Learning Objective 7)*

Prime Petroleum has spent $200,000 to refine 60,000 gallons of petroleum distillate. Suppose Prime Petroleum can sell the distillate for $6 a gallon. Alternatively, it can process the distillate further and produce 60,000 gallons of cleaner fluid. The additional processing will cost another $1.75 a gallon, and the cleaner can be sold for $8.50 a gallon. To sell cleaner fluid, Prime Petroleum must pay a sales commission of $0.10 a gallon and a transportation charge of $0.15 a gallon.

Requirements

1. Diagram Prime Petroleum's alternatives, using Exhibit 8-23 (sell as is or process further) as a guide.
2. Identify the sunk cost. Is the sunk cost relevant to Prime Petroleum's decision? Why or why not?
3. Prepare an analysis to indicate whether Prime Petroleum should sell the distillate or process it into cleaner fluid. Show the expected net revenue difference between the two alternatives.

Apply Your Knowledge

■ Decision Case

Case 8-40. Outsourcing e-mail *(Learning Objective 6)*

BKFin.com provides banks access to sophisticated financial information and analysis systems via the Web. The company combines these tools with benchmarking data access, including e-mail and wireless communications, so that banks can instantly evaluate individual loan applications and entire loan portfolios.

BKFin.com's CEO, Jon Wise, is happy with the company's growth. To better focus on client service, Wise is considering outsourcing some functions. CFO Jenny Lee suggests that the company's e-mail may be the place to start. She recently attended a conference and learned that companies such as Continental Airlines, DellNet, GTE, and NBC were outsourcing their e-mail function. Wise asks Lee to identify costs related to BKFin.com's in-house Microsoft Exchange mail application, which has 2,300 mailboxes. This information follows:

Variable costs:	
E-mail license	$7 per mailbox per month
Virus protection license..................................	$1 per mailbox per month
Other variable costs	$8 per mailbox per month
Fixed costs:	
Computer hardware costs	$94,300 per month
$8,050 monthly salary for two information technology staff members who work only on e-mail...	$16,100 per month

Requirements

1. Compute the *total cost* per mailbox per month of BKFin.com's current e-mail function.

2. Suppose Mail.com, a leading provider of Internet messaging outsourcing services, offers to host BKFin.com's e-mail function for $9 per mailbox per month. If BKFin.com outsources its e-mail to Mail.com, BKFin.com will still need the virus protection software; its computer hardware; and one information technology staff member who would be responsible for maintaining virus protection, quarantining suspicious e-mail, and managing content (e.g., screening e-mail for objectionable content). Should CEO Wise accept Mail.com's offer? Why or why not?

3. Suppose for an additional $5 per mailbox per month, Mail.com will also provide virus protection, quarantine, and content-management services. Outsourcing these additional functions would mean that BKFin.com would not need an e-mail information technology staff member or the separate virus protection license. Should CEO Wise outsource these extra services to Mail.com? Why or why not?

■ Ethical Issue

Issue 8-41. Outsourcing and ethics *(Learning Objective 6)*

Mary Tan is the controller for Duck Associates, a property management company in Portland, Oregon. Each year, Tan and payroll clerk Toby Stock meet with the external auditors about payroll accounting. This year, the auditors suggest that Tan consider outsourcing Duck Associates' payroll accounting to a company specializing in payroll processing services. This would allow Tan and her staff to focus on their primary responsibility: accounting for the properties under management. At present, payroll requires 1.5 employee positions—payroll clerk Toby Stock and a bookkeeper who spends half her time entering payroll data in the system.

Tan considers this suggestion, and she lists the following items relating to outsourcing payroll accounting:

a. The current payroll software that was purchased for $4,000 three years ago would not be needed if payroll processing were outsourced.

b. Duck Associates' bookkeeper would spend half her time preparing the weekly payroll input form that is given to the payroll processing service. She is paid $450 a week.

c. Duck Associates would no longer need payroll clerk Toby Stock, whose annual salary is $42,000.

d. The payroll processing service would charge $2,000 a month.

Requirements

1. Would outsourcing the payroll function increase or decrease Duck Associates' operating income?

2. Tan believes that outsourcing payroll would simplify her job, but she does not like the prospect of having to lay off Stock, who has become a close personal friend. She does not believe there is another position available for Stock at his current salary. Can you think of other factors that might support keeping Stock rather than outsourcing payroll processing? How should each of the factors affect Tan's decision if she wants to do what is best for Duck Associates and act ethically?

■ Team Project

Project 8-42. Relevant information to outsourcing decision *(Learning Objective 6)*

John Menard is the founder and sole owner of Menards. Analysts have estimated that his chain of home improvement stores scattered around nine midwestern states generate about $3 billion in annual sales. But how can Menards compete with giant Home Depot?

Suppose Menard is trying to decide whether to invest $45 million in a state-of-the-art manufacturing plant in Eau Claire, Wisconsin. Menard expects the plant would operate for 15 years, after which it would have no residual value. The plant would produce Menards' own line of Formica countertops, cabinets, and picnic tables.

Suppose Menards would incur the following unit costs in producing its own product lines:

	Per Unit		
	Countertops	Cabinets	Picnic Tables
Direct materials..	$15	$10	$25
Direct labor..	10	5	15
Variable manufacturing overhead	5	2	6

Rather than Menard making these products, assume that he can buy them from outside suppliers. Suppliers would charge Menards $40 per countertop, $25 per cabinet, and $65 per picnic table.

Whether Menard makes or buys these products, assume that he expects the following annual sales:

- Countertops—487,200 at $130 each
- Picnic tables—100,000 at $225 each
- Cabinets—150,000 at $75 each

If "making" is sufficiently more profitable than outsourcing, Menard will build the new plant. John Menard has asked your consulting group for a recommendation. Menard uses the straight-line depreciation method.

Requirements

1. Are the following items relevant or irrelevant in Menard's decision to build a new plant that will manufacture his own products?

   a. The unit sale prices of the countertops, cabinets, and picnic tables (the sale prices that Menards charges its customers)

   b. The prices that outside suppliers would charge Menards for the three products if Menards decides to outsource the products rather than make them

   c. The $45 million to build the new plant

   d. The direct materials, direct labor, and variable overhead that Menards would incur to manufacture the three product lines

   e. Menard's salary

2. Determine whether Menards should make or outsource the countertops, cabinets, and picnic tables *assuming that the company has already built the plant and, therefore, has the manufacturing capacity to produce these products*. In other words, what is the annual difference in cash flows if Menards decides to make rather than outsource each of these three products?

3. Write a memo giving your recommendation to Menard. The memo should clearly state your recommendation and briefly summarize the reasons for your recommendation.

9

Capital Investment Decisions and the Time Value of Money

n the slopes of Deer Valley Ski Resort in Park Valley, Utah—site of the 2002 Winter Olympics slalom competition—managerial accounting seems a world away. But the counter where you rent your skis, the chairlift that whisks you up the mountain, and the restaurant that serves you dinner are all part of the resort's recent expansion. How did Deer Valley's developers decide to spend $13 million to expand Snow Park Lodge?

Director of Finance Jim Madsen explains that when the resort reaches a target number of skiers per day and a target level of profit, the owners expand. But each expansion must meet two requirements. First, the project must be profitable. Second, Deer Valley must expect to get its money back on the investment in a relatively short time. To figure out which projects meet those requirements, Deer Valley's

managers compare the amount of the investment needed to expand the resort with the additional revenues expected from expansion. The resort managers make this comparison using two capital budgeting techniques:

1. *Net present value*—to predict whether the investment will be profitable
2. *Payback period*—to predict how long it will take to "get the money back" ■

Learning Objectives

1 Describe the importance of capital investments and the capital budgeting process

2 Use the payback and accounting rate of return methods to make capital investment decisions

3 Use the time value of money to compute the present and future values of single lump sums and annuities

4 Use discounted cash flow models to make capital investment decisions

5 Compare and contrast the four capital budgeting methods

In this chapter, we'll see how companies such as Deer Valley use net present value, payback period, and other capital investment analysis techniques to decide which long-term capital investments to make.

Capital Budgeting

1 Describe the importance of capital investments and the capital budgeting process

The process of making capital investment decisions is often referred to as **capital budgeting.** Companies make capital investments when they acquire *capital assets*—assets used for a long period of time. Capital investments include buying new equipment, building new plants, automating production, and developing major commercial Web sites. In addition to affecting operations for many years, capital investments usually require large sums of money. Deer Valley's decision to spend $13 million to expand Snow Park Lodge will tie up resources for years to come—as will Chrysler's recent decision to spend $419 million revamping its Belvidere, Illinois, manufacturing plant.

Capital investment decisions affect all types of businesses as they try to become more efficient by automating production and implementing new technologies. Grocers and retailers such as Wal-Mart have invested in expensive self-scan check-out machines, while airlines such as Delta and Continental have invested in self-check-in kiosks. These new technologies cost money. How do managers decide whether these expansions in plant and equipment will be good investments? They use capital budgeting analysis. Some companies, such as Georgia Pacific, employ staff dedicated solely to capital budgeting analysis. They spend thousands of hours a year determining which capital investments to pursue.

Four Popular Methods of Capital Budgeting Analysis

In this chapter, we discuss four popular methods of analyzing potential capital investments:

1. Payback period

2. Accounting rate of return (ARR)

3. Net present value (NPV)

4. Internal rate of return (IRR)

The first two methods, payback period and accounting rate of return, are fairly quick and easy to calculate and work well for capital investments that have a relatively short life span, such as computer equipment and software that may have a useful life of only three to five years. Management often uses the payback period and accounting rate of return to screen potential investments from those that are less desirable. The payback period provides management with valuable information on how fast the cash invested will be recouped. The accounting rate of return shows the effect of the investment on the company's accrual-based income. However, these two methods are inadequate if the capital investments have a longer life span. Why? Because these methods do not consider the time value of money. The last two methods, net present value and internal rate of return, factor in the time value of money, so they are more appropriate for longer-term capital investments such as Deer Valley's expansion of its lodge, ski runs, and chairlifts. Management often uses a combination of methods to make final capital investment decisions.

Capital budgeting is not an exact science. Although the calculations these methods require may appear precise, remember that they are based on predictions about an uncertain future. These predictions must consider many unknown factors, such as changing consumer preferences, competition, and government regulations. The further into the future the decision extends, the more likely actual results will differ from predictions. Long-term decisions are riskier than short-term decisions.

Focus on Cash Flows

Generally accepted accounting principles (GAAP) are based on accrual accounting, but capital budgeting focuses on cash flows. The desirability of a capital asset depends on its ability to generate *net cash inflows*—that is, inflows in excess of outflows—over the asset's useful life. Recall that operating income based on accrual accounting contains noncash expenses such as depreciation expense and bad-debt expense. The capital investment's *net cash inflows*, therefore, will differ from its operating income. Of the four capital budgeting methods covered in this chapter, only the accounting rate of return method uses accrual-based accounting income. The other three methods use the investment's projected *net cash inflows*.

What do the projected net cash inflows include? Cash *inflows* include future cash revenue generated from the investment, any future savings in ongoing cash operating costs resulting from the investment, and any future residual value of the asset. To determine the investment's *net* cash inflows, the inflows are *netted* against the investment's future cash *outflows*, such as the investment's ongoing cash operating costs and refurbishment, repairs, and maintenance costs. The initial investment itself is also a significant cash outflow. However, in our calculations, *we refer to the amount of the investment separately from all other cash flows related to the investment*. The projected net cash inflows are "given" in our examples and in the assignment material. In reality, much of capital investment analysis revolves around projecting these figures as accurately as possible using input from employees throughout the organization (production, marketing, and so forth, depending on the type of capital investment).

Capital Budgeting Process

The first step in the capital budgeting process is to identify potential investments—for example, new technology and equipment that may make the company more efficient, competitive, and profitable. Employees, consultants, and outside sales vendors often offer capital investment proposals to management. After identifying potential capital investments, managers project the investments' net cash inflows and then analyze the investments using one or more of the four methods listed previously. Sometimes the analysis involves a two-stage process: In the first stage, managers screen the investments using one or both of the methods that do *not* incorporate the time value of money: payback period or accounting rate of return. These simple methods quickly weed out undesirable investments. Potential investments that "pass the initial test" go on to a second stage of analysis. In the second stage, managers further analyze the potential investments using the net present value or internal rate of return method. Because these methods consider the time value of money, they provide more accurate information about the potential investment's profitability. Since each method evaluates the potential investment from a different angle, some companies use all four methods to get the most "complete picture" they can about the investment.

Some companies can pursue all of the potential investments that meet or exceed their decision criteria. However, because of limited resources, other companies must engage in **capital rationing** and choose among alternative capital investments. Based on the availability of funds, managers determine if and when to make specific capital investments. For example, management may decide to wait three years to buy a certain piece of equipment because they consider other investments to be more important. In the intervening three years, the company will reassess whether it should still invest in the equipment. Perhaps technology has changed and even better equipment is available. Perhaps consumer tastes have changed, so the company no longer needs the equipment. Because of changing factors, long-term capital budgets are rarely "set in stone."

Most companies perform **post-audits** of their capital investments. After investing in the assets, they compare the actual net cash inflows generated from the investment to the projected net cash inflows. Post-audits help companies determine whether the investments are going as planned and deserve continued support or whether they should abandon the project and sell the assets. Managers also use feedback from post-audits to better estimate net cash inflow projections for future projects. If managers expect routine post-audits, they will more likely submit realistic net cash inflow estimates with their capital investment proposals.

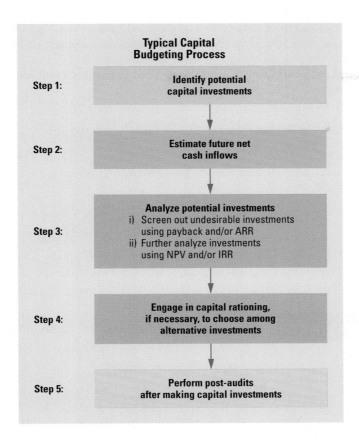

Typical Capital
Budgeting Process

Step 1: Identify potential
capital investments

Step 2: Estimate future net
cash inflows

Step 3: Analyze potential investments
i) Screen out undesirable investments
using payback and/or ARR
ii) Further analyze investments
using NPV and/or IRR

Step 4: Engage in capital rationing,
if necessary, to choose among
alternative investments

Step 5: Perform post-audits
after making capital investments

Using Payback and Accounting Rate of Return to Make Capital Investment Decisions

Payback Period

Payback is the length of time it takes to recover, in net cash inflows, the cost of the capital outlay. The payback model measures how quickly managers expect to recover their investment dollars. The shorter the payback period, the more attractive the asset, *all else being equal*. Why? The quicker an investment pays itself back, the less inherent risk that the investment will become unprofitable. Computing the payback period depends on whether net cash inflows are equal each year or whether they differ over time. We consider each in turn.

2 Use the payback and accounting rate of return methods to make capital investment decisions

Payback with Equal Annual Net Cash Inflows

Tierra Firma makes camping gear. The company is considering investing $240,000 in hardware and software to develop a business-to-business (B2B) portal. Employees throughout the company will use the B2B portal to access company-approved suppliers. Tierra Firma expects the portal to save $60,000 each year for the six years of its useful life. The savings will arise from a reduction in the number of purchasing personnel the company employs and from lower prices on the goods and services purchased. Net cash inflows arise from an increase in revenues, a decrease in expenses, or both. In Tierra Firma's case, the net cash inflows result from lower expenses.

When net cash inflows are equal each year, managers compute the payback period as follows:

$$\text{Payback period} = \frac{\text{Amount invested}}{\text{Expected annual net cash inflow}}$$

Tierra Firma computes the investment's payback as follows:

$$\text{Payback period for B2B portal} = \frac{\$240,000}{\$60,000} = 4 \text{ years}$$

Exhibit 9-1 verifies that Tierra Firma expects to recoup the $240,000 investment in the B2B portal by the end of Year 4, when the accumulated net cash inflows total $240,000.

EXHIBIT 9-1   **Payback—Equal Annual Net Cash Inflows**

| | | Net Cash Inflows | | | |
| | | B2B Portal | | Web Site Development | |
Year	Amount Invested	Annual	Accumulated	Annual	Accumulated
0	$240,000	—	—	—	—
1	—	$60,000	$ 60,000	$80,000	$ 80,000
2	—	60,000	120,000	80,000	160,000
3	—	60,000	180,000	80,000	240,000
4	—	60,000	240,000		
5	—	60,000	300,000		
6	—	60,000	360,000		

Tierra Firma is also considering investing $240,000 to develop a Web site. The company expects the Web site to generate $80,000 in net cash inflows each year of its three-year life. The payback period is computed as follows:

$$\text{Payback period for Web site development} = \frac{\$240,000}{\$80,000} = 3 \text{ years}$$

Exhibit 9-1 verifies that Tierra Firma will recoup the $240,000 investment for Web site development by the end of Year 3, when the accumulated net cash inflows total $240,000.

Payback with Unequal Net Cash Inflows

The payback equation works only when net cash inflows are the same each period. When periodic cash flows are unequal, you must accumulate net cash inflows until the amount invested is recovered. Assume that Tierra Firma is considering an alternate investment, the Z80 portal. The Z80 portal differs from the B2B portal and Web site in two respects: (1) it has *unequal* net cash inflows during its life, and (2) it has a $30,000 residual value at the end of its life. The Z80 portal will generate net cash inflows of $100,000 in Year 1, $80,000 in Year 2, $50,000 each year in Years 3 through 5, $30,000 in Year 6, and $30,000 when it is sold at the end of its life. Exhibit 9-2 shows the payback schedule for these unequal annual net cash inflows.

EXHIBIT 9-2   **Payback—Unequal Annual Net Cash Inflows**

		Net Cash Inflows Z80 Portal		
Year	Amount Invested	Annual		Accumulated
0	$240,000	—		—
1	—	100,000	*Useful Life*	$100,000
2	—	80,000		180,000
3	—	50,000		230,000
4	—	50,000		280,000
5	—	50,000		330,000
6	—	30,000		360,000
Residual Value		30,000		390,000

By the end of Year 3, the company has recovered $230,000 of the $240,000 initially invested and are only $10,000 short of payback. Because the expected net cash inflow in Year 4 is $50,000, by the end of Year 4, the company will have recovered *more* than the initial investment. Therefore, the payback period is somewhere between three and four years. Assuming that the cash flow occurs evenly throughout the fourth year, the payback period is calculated as follows:

$$\text{Payback} = 3 \text{ years} + \frac{\$10,000 \text{ (amount needed to complete recovery in Year 4)}}{\$50,000 \text{ (projected net cash inflow in Year 4)}}$$

$$= 3.2 \text{ years}$$

Criticism of the Payback Period Method

A major criticism of the payback method is that it focuses only on time, not on profitability. The payback period considers only those cash flows that occur *during* the payback period. This method ignores any cash flows that occur *after* that period, including any residual value. For example, Exhibit 9-1 shows that the B2B portal will continue to generate net cash inflows for two years after its payback period. These additional net cash inflows amount to $120,000 ($60,000 × 2 years), yet the payback method ignores this extra cash. A similar situation occurs with the Z80 portal. As shown in Exhibit 9-2, the Z80 portal will provide an additional $150,000 of net cash inflows, including residual value, after its payback period of 3.2 years. In contrast, the Web site's useful life, as shown in Exhibit 9-1, is the *same* as its payback period (three years). Since no additional cash flows occur after the payback period, the Web site will merely cover its cost and provide no profit. Because this is the case, the company has little or no reason to invest in the Web site even though its payback period is the shortest of all three investments.

Exhibit 9-3 compares the payback period of the three investments. As the exhibit illustrates, the payback method does not consider the asset's profitability. *The method only tells management how quickly they will recover their cash.* Even though the Web site has the shortest payback period, both the B2B portal and the Z80 portal are better investments because they provide profit. The key point is that

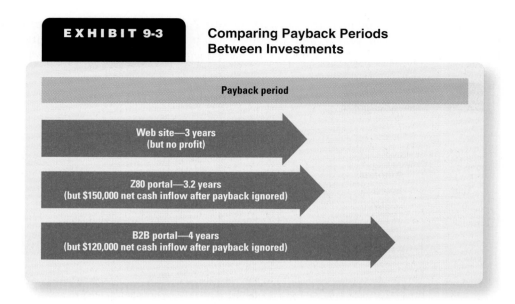

EXHIBIT 9-3   **Comparing Payback Periods Between Investments**

the investment with the shortest payback period is best *only when all other factors are the same.* Therefore, managers usually use the payback method as a screening device to "weed out" investments that will take too long to recoup. They rarely use payback period as the sole method for deciding whether to invest in the asset.

When using the payback period method, managers are guided by the following decision rule:

DECISION RULE: Payback Period

Investments with **shorter** payback periods are more desirable, *all else being equal.*

Accounting Rate of Return (ARR)

Companies are in business to earn profits. One measure of profitability is the **accounting rate of return (ARR)** on an asset:

$$\frac{\text{Accounting}}{\text{rate of return}} = \frac{\text{Average annual operating income from asset}}{\text{Initial investment}^1}$$

The ARR focuses on the *operating income, not the net cash inflow,* that an asset generates. The ARR measures the average annual rate of return over the asset's life. Recall that operating income is based on *accrual accounting.* Therefore, any noncash expenses such as depreciation expense must be subtracted from the asset's net cash inflows to arrive at its operating income. Assuming that depreciation expense is the only noncash expense relating to the investment, we can rewrite the ARR formula as follows:

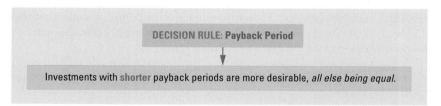

$$\text{ARR} = \frac{\text{Average annual net cash inflow} - \text{Annual depreciation expense}}{\text{Initial investment}}$$

---

[1]Some managers prefer to use the average investment rather than the initial investment as the denominator. For simplicity, we will use the initial investment.

Exhibit 9-4 reviews how to calculate annual depreciation expense using the straight-line method.

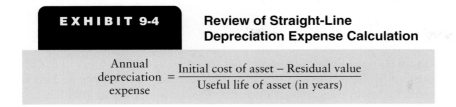

EXHIBIT 9-4   **Review of Straight-Line Depreciation Expense Calculation**

$$\text{Annual depreciation expense} = \frac{\text{Initial cost of asset} - \text{Residual value}}{\text{Useful life of asset (in years)}}$$

Investments with Equal Annual Net Cash Inflows

Recall that the B2B portal, which costs $240,000, has equal annual net cash inflows of $60,000, a six-year useful life, and no residual value.

First, we must find the B2B portal's annual depreciation expense:

$$\text{Annual depreciation expense} = \frac{\$240,000 - 0}{6 \text{ years}} = \$40,000$$

Now, we can complete the ARR formula:

$$\text{ARR} = \frac{\$60,000 - \$40,000}{\$240,000} = \frac{\$20,000}{\$240,000} = 8.33\% \text{ (rounded)}$$

The B2B portal will provide an average annual accounting rate of return of 8.33%.

Investments with Unequal Net Cash Inflows

Now, consider the Z80 portal. Recall that the Z80 portal would also cost $240,000 but it had unequal net cash inflows during its life (as pictured in Exhibit 9-2) and a $30,000 residual value at the end of its life. Since the yearly cash inflows vary in size, we need to first calculate the Z80's *average* annual net cash inflows:

Total net cash inflows *during* operating life of asset (does not include the residual value at end of life)[2] (Year 1 + Year 2, and so forth) from Exhibit 9-2	$360,000
Divide by: Asset's operating life (in years)	÷ 6 years
Average annual net cash inflow from asset	$ 60,000

Now, let's calculate the asset's annual depreciation expense:

$$\text{Annual depreciation expense} = \frac{\$240,000 - \$30,000}{6 \text{ years}} = \$35,000$$

---

[2]The residual value is not included in the net cash inflows *during* the asset's operating life because we are trying to find the asset's average *annual operating* income. We assume that the asset will be sold for its expected residual value ($30,000) at the *end* of its life, resulting in no additional accounting gain or loss.

Finally, we can complete the ARR calculation:

$$\text{ARR} = \frac{\$60,000 - \$35,000}{\$240,000} = \frac{\$25,000}{\$240,000} = 10.42\% \text{ (rounded)}$$

Notice that the Z80 portal's average annual operating ($25,000) income is higher than the B2B portal's average operating income ($20,000). Since the Z80 asset has a residual value at the end of its life, less depreciation is expensed each year, leading to a higher average annual operating income and a higher ARR.

Companies that use the ARR model set a minimum required accounting rate of return. If Tierra Firma required an ARR of at least 10%, its managers would not approve an investment in the B2B portal but would approve an investment in the Z80 portal.

The decision rule is:

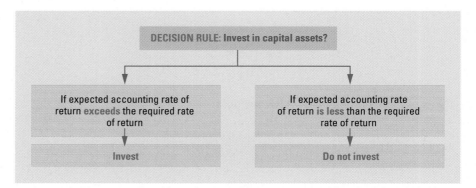

In summary, the payback period focuses on the time it takes for the company to recoup its cash investment but ignores all cash flows occurring after the payback period. Because it ignores any additional cash flows (including any residual value), the method does not consider the profitability of the project.

The ARR, however, measures the profitability of the asset over its entire life using accrual accounting figures. It is the only method that uses accrual accounting rather than net cash inflows in its computations. As we will discuss in Chapter 12, company divisions are often evaluated based on accounting income. Therefore, the investment's ARR helps managers see how the investment will impact their division's profitability. The payback period and ARR methods are simple and quick to compute, so managers often use them to screen out undesirable investments and to gain a more complete picture of the investment's desirability. However, both methods ignore the time value of money.

Decision Guidelines

CAPITAL BUDGETING

Amazon.com started as a virtual retailer. It held no inventory. Instead, it bought books and CDs only as needed to fill customer orders. As the company grew, its managers decided to invest in their own warehouse facilities. Why? Owning warehouse facilities allows Amazon.com to save money by buying in bulk. Also, shipping all items in the customer's order in one package from one location saves shipping costs. Here are some of the guidelines Amazon.com's managers used as they made the major capital budgeting decision to invest in building warehouses.

Decision	Guideline
Why is this decision important?	Capital budgeting decisions typically require large investments and affect operations for years to come.
What method shows us how soon we will recoup our cash investment?	The payback method shows how quickly managers will recoup their investment. The method highlights investments that are too risky due to long payback periods. However, it doesn't reveal any information about the investment's profitability.
Does any method consider the impact of the investment on accrual accounting income?	The accounting rate of return is the only capital budgeting method that shows how the investment will affect accrual accounting income, which is important to financial statement users. All other methods of capital investment analysis focus on the investment's net cash inflows.
How do we compute the payback period if cash flows are *equal*?	$$\text{Payback period} = \frac{\text{Amount invested}}{\text{Expected annual net cash inflow}}$$
How do we compute the payback period if cash flows are *unequal*?	Accumulate net cash inflows until the amount invested is recovered.
How do we compute the ARR?	$$\frac{\text{Accounting}}{\text{rate of return}} = \frac{\text{Average annual operating income from asset}}{\text{Initial investment}}$$ We can also write this formula as follows: $$\text{ARR} = \frac{\text{Average annual net cash inflow} - \text{Annual depreciation expense}}{\text{Initial investment}}$$

Summary Problem 1

Zetamax is considering buying a new bar-coding machine for its Austin, Texas, plant. The company screens its potential capital investments using the payback period and accounting rate of return methods. If a potential investment has a payback period of less than four years and a minimum 7% accounting rate of return, it will be considered further. The data for the machine follow:

Cost of machine	$48,000
Estimated residual value	$ 0
Estimated annual net cash inflow (each year for five years)	$13,000
Estimated useful life	5 years

Requirements

1. Compute the bar-coding machine's payback period.

2. Compute the bar-coding machine's ARR.

3. Should Zetamax turn down this investment proposal or consider it further?

Solution

Requirement 1

$$\text{Payback period} = \frac{\text{Amount invested}}{\text{Expected annual net cash inflow}} = \frac{\$48,000}{\$13,000} = 3.7 \text{ years (rounded)}$$

Requirement 2

$$\text{Accounting rate of return} = \frac{\text{Average annual net cash inflow} - \text{Annual depreciation expense}}{\text{Initial investment}}$$

$$= \frac{\$13,000 - \$9,600^*}{\$48,000}$$

$$= \frac{\$3,400}{\$48,000}$$

$$= 7.08\%$$

*Depreciation expense = $48,000 ÷ 5 years = $9,600

Requirement 3

The bar-coding machine proposal passes both initial screening tests. The payback period is slightly less than four years, and the accounting rate of return is slightly higher than 7%. Zetamax should further analyze the proposal using a method that incorporates the time value of money.

A Review of the Time Value of Money

A dollar received today is worth more than a dollar to be received in the future. Why? Because you can invest today's dollar and earn extra income. The fact that invested money earns income over time is called the **time value of money**, and this explains why we would prefer to receive cash sooner rather than later. The time value of money means that the timing of capital investments' net cash inflows is important. Two methods of capital investment analysis incorporate the time value of money: the NPV and IRR. This section reviews time value of money concepts to make sure you have a firm foundation for discussing these two methods.

 Use the time value of money to compute the present and future values of single lump sums and annuities

Factors Affecting the Time Value of Money

The time value of money depends on several key factors:

1. The principal amount (p)

2. The number of periods (n)

3. The interest rate (i)

The principal (p) refers to the amount of the investment or borrowing. Because this chapter deals with capital investments, we'll primarily discuss the principal in terms of investments. However, the same concepts apply to borrowings (which you probably discussed in your financial accounting course when you studied bonds payable). We state the principal as either a single lump sum or an annuity. For example, if you want to save money for a new car after college, you may decide to invest a single lump sum of $10,000 in a certificate of deposit (CD). However, you may not currently have $10,000 to invest. Instead, you may invest funds as an annuity, depositing $2,000 at the end of each year in a bank savings account. An **annuity** is a stream of *equal installments* made at *equal time intervals*.[3]

The number of periods (n) is the length of time from the beginning of the investment until termination. All else being equal, the shorter the investment period, the lower the total amount of interest earned. If you withdraw your savings after four years rather than five years, you will earn less interest. If you begin to save for retirement at age 22 rather than age 45, you will earn more interest before you retire (you let time do the work). In this chapter, the number of periods is stated in years.[4]

The interest rate (i) is the annual percentage earned on the investment. **Simple interest** means that interest is calculated *only* on the principal amount. **Compound interest** means that interest is calculated on the principal *and* on all interest earned to date. *Compound interest assumes that all interest earned will remain invested at the same interest rate, not withdrawn and spent.* Exhibit 9-5 compares simple interest (6%) on a five-year, $10,000 CD with interest compounded yearly (rounded to the nearest dollar). As you can see, the amount of compound interest earned yearly grows as the base on which it is calculated (principal plus cumulative interest to date) grows. Over the life of this particular investment, the total amount of compound interest is about 13% more than the total amount of simple interest. Most investments yield compound interest, so we assume compound interest rather than simple interest for the rest of this chapter.

---

[3]An *ordinary annuity* is an annuity in which the installments occur at the *end* of each period. An *annuity due* is an annuity in which the installments occur at the *beginning* of each period. Throughout this chapter, we use ordinary annuities since they are better suited to assumptions about capital budgeting cash flow.

[4]The number of periods can also be stated in days, months, or quarters. If so, the interest rate needs to be adjusted to reflect the number of time periods in the year.

	EXHIBIT 9-5		Simple Versus Compound Interest for a Principal Amount of $10,000 at 6% over Five Years	

Year	Simple Interest Calculation	Simple Interest	Compound Interest Calculation	Compound Interest
1	$10,000 × 6% =	$ 600	$10,000 × 6% =	$ 600
2	$10,000 × 6% =	600	($10,000 + 600) × 6% =	636
3	$10,000 × 6% =	600	($10,000 + 600 + 636) × 6% =	674
4	$10,000 × 6% =	600	($10,000 + 600 + 636 + 674) × 6% =	715
5	$10,000 × 6% =	600	($10,000 + 600 + 636 + 674 + 715) × 6% =	758
	Total interest	$3,000	Total interest	$3,383

Fortunately, time value calculations involving compound interest do not have to be as tedious as shown in Exhibit 9-5. Formulas and tables (or proper use of business calculators programmed with these formulas) simplify the calculations. In the next sections, we will discuss how to use these tools to perform time value calculations.

Future Values and Present Values: Points Along the Time Continuum

Consider the time line in Exhibit 9-6. The future value or present value of an investment simply refers to the value of an investment at different points in time.

	EXHIBIT 9-6	Present Value and Future Value Along the Time Continuum

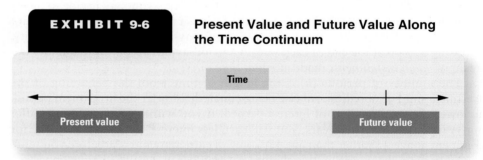

We can calculate the future value or the present value of any investment by knowing (or assuming) information about the three factors listed earlier: (1) the principal amount, (2) the period of time, and (3) the interest rate. For example, in Exhibit 9-5, we calculated the interest that would be earned on (1) a $10,000 principal (2) invested for five years (3) at 6% interest. The future value of the investment is its worth at the end of the five-year time frame—the original principal *plus* the interest earned. In our example, the future value of the investment is:

$$\text{Future value} = \text{Principal} + \text{Interest earned}$$
$$= \$10,000 + \$3,383$$
$$= \$13,383$$

If we invest $10,000 *today*, its *present value* is simply the $10,000 principal amount. So, another way of stating the future value is:

$$\text{Future value} = \text{Present value} + \text{Interest earned}$$

We can rearrange the equation as follows:

Present value = Future value – Interest earned
$10,000 = $13,383 – $3,383

The only difference between present value and future value is the amount of interest that is earned in the intervening time span.

Future Value and Present Value Factors

Calculating each period's compound interest, as we did in Exhibit 9-5, and then adding it to the present value to figure the future value (or subtracting it from the future value to figure the present value) is tedious. Fortunately, mathematical formulas simplify future value and present value calculations. Mathematical formulas have been developed that specify future values and present values for unlimited combinations of interest rates (*i*) and time periods (*n*). Separate formulas exist for single lump-sum investments and annuities.

The formulas have been calculated using various interest rates and time periods. The results are displayed in tables. The formulas and resulting tables are shown in this chapter's Appendix 9A:

1. Present Value of $1 (Table A, p. 543)—*used for lump-sum amounts*

2. Present Value of Annuity of $1 (Table B, p. 544)—*used for annuities*

3. Future Value of $1 (Table C, p. 545)—*used for lump-sum amounts*

4. Future Value of Annuity of $1 (Table D, p. 546)—*used for annuities*

Take a moment to look at these tables because we are going to use them throughout the rest of the chapter. Note that the columns are interest rates (*i*) and the rows are periods (*n*).

The data in each table, known as future value factors (FV factors) and present value factors (PV factors), are for an investment (or loan) of $1. To find the future value of an amount other than $1, you simply multiply the FV factor found in the table by the principal amount. To find the present value of an amount other than $1, you multiply the PV factor found in the table by the principal amount.

Rather than using these tables, you may want to use a business calculator or scientific calculator that has been programmed with time value of money functions. Programmed calculators such as Texas Instruments' BAII-Plus, TI-83 (Plus), and TI-84 (Plus) make time value of money computations much easier because you do not need to find the correct PV and FV factors in the tables. Rather, you simply enter the principal amount, interest rate, and number of time periods in the calculator and instruct the calculator to solve for the unknown value.

The appendices to this chapter show step-by-step directions for performing basic time value of money computations and for performing NPV and IRR computations:

Instructions for TI-83 and TI-84 (or TI-83 Plus and TI-84 Plus): Appendix 9B, beginning on p. 547

Instructions for BAII Plus: Appendix 9C, beginning on p. 555

Instructions for operating other programmed calculators can usually be found on the manufacturer's Web site. In addition, Web sites such as atomiclearning.com offer free online video tutorials for some calculators.

The appendices also show step-by-step use of these calculators for every problem illustrated throughout the rest of the chapter. As you will see in these appendices, using a programmed calculator results in slightly different answers than those presented in the text when using the tables. The differences are due to the fact that the PV and FV factors found in the tables have been rounded to three digits. Finally, all end-of-chapter material has been solved using both the tables and programmed calculators so that you will have the exact solution for the method you choose to use.

Calculating Future Values of Single Sums and Annuities Using FV Factors

Let's go back to our $10,000 lump-sum investment. If we want to know the future value of the investment five years from now at an interest rate of 6%, we determine the FV factor from the table labeled Future Value of $1 (Appendix 9A, Table C). We use this table for lump-sum amounts. We look down the 6% column and across the 5 periods row and find that the future value factor is 1.338. We finish our calculations as follows:

$$\text{Future value} = \text{Principal amount} \times (\text{FV factor for } i = 6\%, n = 5)$$
$$= \$10,000 \times (1.338)$$
$$= \$13,380$$

This figure agrees with our earlier calculation of the investment's future value ($13,383) in Exhibit 9-5. (The difference of $3 is due to two facts: (1) the tables round the FV and PV factors to three decimal places, and (2) we rounded our earlier yearly interest calculations in Exhibit 9-5 to the nearest dollar.)

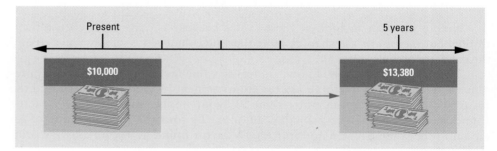

Let's also consider our alternative investment strategy, investing $2,000 at the end of each year for five years. The procedure for calculating the future value of an annuity is similar to calculating the future value of a lump-sum amount. This time, we use the Future Value of Annuity of $1 table (Appendix 9A, Table D). Assuming 6% interest, we once again look down the 6% column. Because we will be making five annual installments, we look across the row marked 5 periods. The Annuity FV factor is 5.637. We finish the calculation as follows:

$$\text{Future value} = \text{Amount of each cash installment} \times (\text{Annuity FV factor for } i = 6\%, n = 5)$$
$$= \$2,000 \times (5.637)$$
$$= \$11,274$$

This is considerably less than the future value ($13,380) of the lump sum of $10,000 even though we invested $10,000 out of pocket either way.

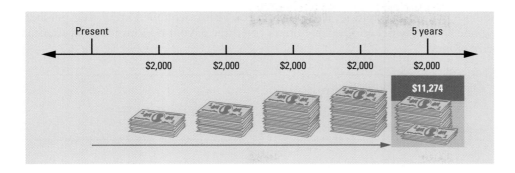

Stop & Think...

Explain why the future value of the annuity ($11,274) is less than the future value of the lump sum ($13,380). Prove that the $11,274 future value is correct by calculating interest using the "longhand" method shown earlier.

Answer: Even though you invested $10,000 out of pocket under both investments, the timing of the investment significantly affects the amount of interest earned. The $10,000 lump sum invested immediately earns interest for the full five years. However, the annuity doesn't begin earning interest until Year 2 (because the first installment isn't made until the *end* of Year 1). In addition, the amount invested begins at $2,000 and doesn't reach a full $10,000 until the end of Year 5. Therefore, the base on which the interest is earned is smaller than the lump-sum investment for the entire five-year period. As shown here, the $11,274 future value of a $2,000 annuity for five years is correct.

Year	Interest Earned During Year (6%) (rounded)	Investment Installment (end of year)	Cumulative Balance at End of Year (investments plus interest earned to date)*
1	$ 0	$2,000	$2,000
2	120	2,000	4,120
3	247	2,000	6,367
4	382	2,000	8,749
5	525	2,000	11,274

*This is the base on which the interest is earned the next year.

Calculating Present Values of Single Sums and Annuities Using PV Factors

The process for calculating present values—often called discounting cash flows—is similar to the process for calculating future values. The difference is the point in time at which you are assessing the investment's worth. Rather than determining its value at a future date, you are determining its value at an earlier point in time (today). For our example, let's assume that you've just won the lottery after purchasing one $5 lottery ticket. The state offers you three payout options for your after-tax prize money:

Option #1: $1,000,000 now

Option #2: $150,000 at the end of each year for the next 10 years

Option #3: $2,000,000 10 years from now

Which alternative should you take? You might be tempted to wait ten years to "double" your winnings. You may be tempted to take the money now and spend it. However, let's assume that you plan to prudently invest all money received—no matter when you receive it—so that you have financial flexibility in the future (for example, for buying a house, retiring early, and taking vacations). How can you choose among the three payment alternatives when the *total amount* of each option varies ($1,000,000 versus $1,500,000 versus $2,000,000) and the *timing* of the cash flows varies (now versus some each year versus later)? Comparing these three options is like comparing apples to oranges—we just can't do it—unless we find some common basis for comparison. Our common basis for comparison will be the prize money's worth at a certain point in time—namely, today. In other words, if we convert each payment option to its *present value*, we can compare apples to apples.

We already know the principal amount and timing of each payment option, so the only assumption we'll have to make is the interest rate. The interest rate will vary depending on the amount of risk you are willing to take with your investment. Riskier investments (such as stock investments) command higher interest rates; safer investments (such as FDIC-insured bank deposits) yield lower interest rates. Let's assume that after investigating possible investment alternatives, you choose an investment contract with an 8% annual return.

We already know that the present value of Option #1 is $1,000,000. Let's convert the other two payment options to their present values so that we can compare them. We'll need to use the Present Value of Annuity of $1 table (Appendix 9A, Table B) to convert payment Option #2 (since it's an annuity) and the Present Value of $1 table (Appendix 9A, Table A) to convert payment Option #3 (since it's a single lump sum). To obtain the PV factors, we look down the 8% column and across the 10 period row. Then, we finish the calculations as follows:

Option #1

Present value = $1,000,000

Option #2

Present value = Amount of each cash installment × (Annuity PV factor for $i = 8\%$, $n = 10$)
Present value = $150,000 × (6.710)
Present value = $1,006,500

Option #3

Present value = Principal amount × (PV factor for $i = 8\%$, $n = 10$)
Present value = $2,000,000 × (0.463)
Present value = $926,000

Exhibit 9-7 shows that we have converted each payout option to a common basis—its worth today—so we can make a valid comparison of the options.

Based on this comparison, we should choose Option #2 because its worth, in today's dollars, is the highest of the three options.

EXHIBIT 9-7   **Comparing Present Values of Lottery Payout Options at $i = 8\%$**

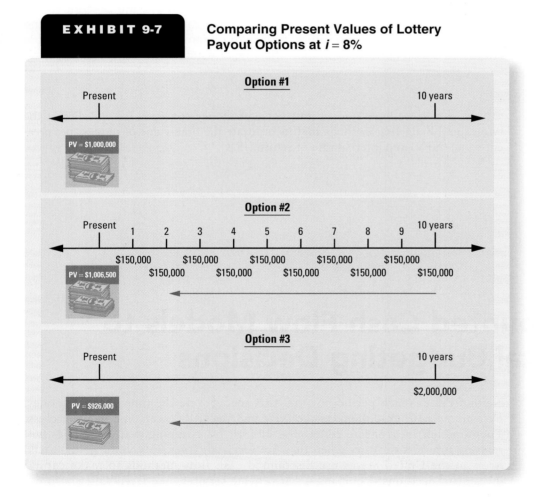

Suppose you decide to invest your lottery winnings very conservatively. You decide to invest in a risk-free investment that earns only 3%. Would you still choose payout Option #2? Explain your decision.

Answer: Using a 3% interest rate, the present values of the payout options are:

Payment Options	Present Value of Lottery Payout (Present value calculation, $i = 3\%$, $n = 10$)
Option #1	$1,000,000 (already stated at its present value)
Option #2	$1,279,500 (= $150,000 × 8.530)
Option #3	$1,488,000 (= $2,000,000 × .744)

When the lottery payout is invested at 3% rather than 8%, the present values change. Option #3 is now the best alternative because its present value is the highest. Present values and future values are extremely sensitive to changes in interest rate assumptions, especially when the investment period is relatively long.

Now that we have studied time value of money concepts, we will discuss the two capital budgeting methods that incorporate the time value of money: net present value (NPV) and internal rate of return (IRR).

Using Discounted Cash Flow Models to Make Capital Budgeting Decisions

Neither the payback period nor the ARR incorporate the time value of money. *Discounted cash flow models*—the NPV and the IRR—overcome this weakness. These models incorporate compound interest by assuming that companies will reinvest future cash flows when they are received. Over 85% of large industrial firms in the United States use discounted cash flow methods to make capital investment decisions. Companies that provide services, like Deer Valley, also use these models.

The NPV and IRR methods rely on present value calculations to *compare* the amount of the investment (the investment's initial cost) with its expected net cash inflows. Recall that an investment's *net cash inflows* includes all future cash flows related to the investment, such as *future* increased sales and cost savings netted against the investment's future cash operating costs. Because the cash outflow for the investment occurs *now* but the net cash inflows from the investment occur in the *future*, companies can make valid "apple-to-apple" comparisons only when they convert the cash flows to the *same point in time*—namely, the present value. Companies use the present value rather than the future value to make the comparison because the investment's initial cost is already stated at its present value.[5]

As shown in Exhibit 9-8, in a favorable investment, the present value of the investment's net cash inflows exceeds the initial cost of the investment. In terms of our earlier lottery example, the lottery ticket turned out to be a "good investment" because the present value of its net cash inflows (the present value of the lottery payout under *any* of the three payout options) exceeded the cost of the investment (the $5 lottery ticket). Let's begin our discussion by taking a closer look at the NPV method.

 Use discounted cash flow models to make capital investment decisions

EXHIBIT 9-8   **Comparing the Present Value of an Investment's Net Cash Inflows Against the Investment's Initial Cost**

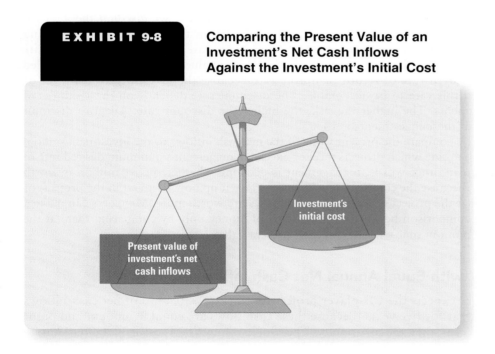

Net Present Value (NPV)

Allegra is considering producing CD players and digital video recorders (DVRs). The products require different specialized machines, each costing $1 million. Each

[5]If the investment is to be purchased through lease payments rather than a current cash outlay, we would still use the current cash price of the investment as its initial cost. If no current cash price is available, we would discount the future lease payments back to their present value to estimate the investment's current cash price.

machine has a five-year life and zero residual value. The two products have different patterns of predicted net cash inflows:

	Annual Net Cash Inflows	
Year	CD Players	DVRs
1	$ 305,450	$ 500,000
2	305,450	350,000
3	305,450	300,000
4	305,450	250,000
5	305,450	40,000
Total	$1,527,250	$1,440,000

The CD-player project generates more net cash inflows, but the DVR project brings in cash sooner. To decide how attractive each investment is, we find its **net present value (NPV)**. The NPV is the *difference* between the present value of the investment's net cash inflows and the investment's cost. We *discount* the net cash inflows to their present value—just as we did in the lottery example—using Allegra's minimum desired rate of return. This rate is called the **discount rate** because it is the interest rate used for the present value calculations. It's also called the **required rate of return** or **hurdle rate** because the investment must meet or exceed this rate to be acceptable. The discount rate depends on the riskiness of investments. The higher the risk, the higher the discount rate. Allegra's discount rate for these investments is 14%.

We compare the present value of the net cash inflows to the investment's initial cost to decide which projects meet or exceed management's minimum desired rate of return. In other words, management is deciding whether the $1 million is worth more (because the company would have to give it up now to invest in the project) or whether the project's future net cash inflows are worth more. Managers can make a valid comparison between the two sums of money only by comparing them at the *same* point in time—namely, at their present value.

NPV with Equal Annual Net Cash Inflows (Annuity)

Allegra expects the CD-player project to generate $305,450 of net cash inflows each year for five years. Because these cash flows are equal in amount and occur every year, they are an annuity. Therefore, we use the Present Value of Annuity of $1 table (Appendix 9A, Table B) to find the appropriate Annuity PV factor for $i = 14\%$, $n = 5$.

The present value of the net cash inflows from Allegra's CD-player project is:

Present value = Amount of each cash inflow × (Annuity PV factor for $i = 14\%$, $n = 5$)
= $305,450 × (3.433)
= $1,048,610

Next, we subtract the investment's initial cost ($1 million) from the present value of the net cash inflows ($1,048,610). The difference of $48,610 is the net present value (NPV), as shown in Exhibit 9-9.

EXHIBIT 9-9	NPV of Equal Net Cash Inflows—CD-Player Project		

	Annuity PV Factor ($i = 14\%$, $n = 5$)	Net Cash Inflow	Present Value
Present value of annuity of equal annual net cash inflows for 5 years at 14%	3.433* ×	\$305,450 =	\$ 1,048,610
Investment			(1,000,000)
Net present value of the CD-player project			\$ 48,610

*Annuity PV factor is found in Appendix 9A, Table B.

A *positive* NPV means that the project earns *more* than the required rate of return. A *negative* NPV means that the project fails to earn the required rate of return. This leads to the following decision rule:

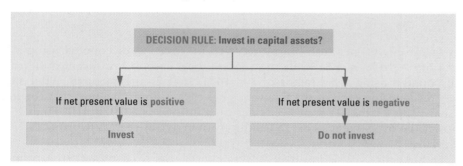

In Allegra's case, the CD-player project is an attractive investment. The \$48,610 positive NPV means that the CD-player project earns *more than* Allegra's 14% target rate of return. In other words, management would prefer to give up \$1 million today to receive the CD-player project's future net cash inflows. Why? Because those future net cash inflows are worth more than \$1 million in today's dollars (they are worth \$1,048,610).

Another way managers can use present value analysis is to start the capital budgeting process by computing the total present value of the net cash inflows from the project to determine the *maximum* the company can invest in the project and still earn the target rate of return. For Allegra, the present value of the net cash inflows is \$1,048,610. This means that Allegra can invest a maximum of \$1,048,610 and still earn the 14% target rate of return. Because Allegra's managers believe they can undertake the project for \$1 million, the project is an attractive investment.

NPV with Unequal Annual Net Cash Inflows

In contrast to the CD-player project, the net cash inflows of the DVR project are unequal—\$500,000 in Year 1, \$350,000 in Year 2, and so forth. Because these amounts vary by year, Allegra's managers *cannot* use the annuity table to compute the present value of the DVR project. They must compute the present value of each individual year's net cash inflows *separately (as separate lump sums received in different years)* using the Present Value of \$1 table (Appendix 9A, Table A). Exhibit 9-10 shows

EXHIBIT 9-10	NPV with Unequal Net Cash Inflows—DVR Project

	PV Factor $(i = 14\%)$		Net Cash Inflow		Present Value
Present value of each year's net cash inflows discounted at 14%:					
Year 1 ($n = 1$)	0.877*	×	$500,000	=	$ 438,500
Year 2 ($n = 2$)	0.769	×	350,000	=	269,150
Year 3 ($n = 3$)	0.675	×	300,000	=	202,500
Year 4 ($n = 4$)	0.592	×	250,000	=	148,000
Year 5 ($n = 5$)	0.519	×	40,000	=	20,760
Total present value of net cash inflows					1,078,910
Investment					(1,000,000)
Net present value of the DVR project					$ 78,910

*PV factors are found in Appendix 9A, Table A.

that the $500,000 net cash inflow received in Year 1 is discounted using a PV factor of $i = 14\%$, $n = 1$, while the $350,000 net cash inflow received in Year 2 is discounted using a PV factor of $i = 14\%$, $n = 2$, and so forth. After separately discounting each of the five year's net cash inflows, we find that the *total* present value of the DVR project's net cash inflows is $1,078,910. Finally, we subtract the investment's cost ($1 million) to arrive at the DVR project's NPV: $78,910.

Because the NPV is positive, Allegra expects the DVR project to earn more than the 14% target rate of return, making this an attractive investment.

Capital Rationing and the Profitability Index

Exhibits 9-9 and 9-10 show that both the CD-player and DVR projects have positive NPVs. Therefore, both are attractive investments. Because resources are limited, companies are not always able to invest in all capital assets that meet their investment criteria. For example, Allegra may not have the funds to invest in both the DVR and CD-player projects at this time. In this case, Allegra should choose the DVR project because it yields a higher NPV. The DVR project should earn an additional $78,910 beyond the 14% required rate of return, while the CD-player project returns an additional $48,610.

This example illustrates an important point. The CD-player project promises more *total* net cash inflows. But the *timing* of the DVR cash flows—loaded near the beginning of the project—gives the DVR investment a higher NPV. The DVR project is more attractive because of the time value of money. Its dollars, which are received sooner, are worth more now than the more distant dollars of the CD-player project.

If Allegra had to choose between the CD and DVR project, it would choose the DVR project because that project yields a higher NPV ($78,910). However, comparing the NPV of the two projects is valid *only* because both projects require the same initial cost—$1 million. In contrast, Exhibit 9-11 summarizes three capital investment options that Raycor, a sporting goods manufacturer, faces. Each capital project requires a different initial investment. All three projects are attractive because each yields a positive NPV. Assuming that Raycor can invest in only one project at this time, which one should it choose? Project B yields the highest NPV, but it also requires a larger initial investment than the alternatives.

| **EXHIBIT 9-11** | **Raycor's Capital Investment Options** |

	Project A	Project B	Project C
Present value of net cash inflows	$150,000	$238,000	$182,000
Investment	(125,000)	(200,000)	(150,000)
Net present value (NPV)	$ 25,000	$ 38,000	$ 32,000

To choose among the projects, Raycor computes the **profitability index** (also known as the **present value index**). The profitability index is computed as follows:

Profitability index = Present value of net cash inflows ÷ Investment

The profitability index computes the number of dollars returned for every dollar invested, *with all calculations performed in present value dollars*. It allows us to compare alternative investments in present value terms (like the NPV method) but also considers differences in the investments' initial cost. Let's compute the profitability index for all three alternatives.

Present value of net cash inflows ÷ Investment = Profitability index
Project A:	$150,000	÷	$125,000	=	1.20
Project B:	$238,000	÷	$200,000	=	1.19
Project C:	$182,000	÷	$150,000	=	1.21

The profitability index shows that Project C is the best of the three alternatives because it returns $1.21 (in present value dollars) for every $1.00 invested. Projects A and B return slightly less.

Let's also compute the profitability index for Allegra's CD-player and DVR projects:

Present value of net cash inflows ÷ Investment = Profitability index
Project A:	$1,048,610	÷	$1,000,000	=	1.049
DVR:	$1,078,910	÷	$1,000,000	=	1.079

The profitability index confirms our prior conclusion that the DVR project is more profitable than the CD-player project. The DVR project returns $1.079 (in present value dollars) for every $1.00 invested. This return is beyond the 14% return already used to discount the cash flows. We did not need the profitability index to determine that the DVR project was preferable because both projects required the same investment ($1 million).

NPV of a Project with Residual Value

Many assets yield cash inflows at the end of their useful lives because they have residual value. Companies discount an investment's residual value to its present value when determining the *total* present value of the project's net cash inflows. The residual value is discounted as a single lump sum—not an annuity—because it will be received only once, when the asset is sold.

Suppose Allegra expects the CD project equipment to be worth $100,000 at the end of its five-year life. This represents an additional future cash inflow from the CD-player project. To determine the CD-player project's NPV, we discount the residual value ($100,000) using the Present Value of $1 table ($i = 14\%$,

$n = 5$) (see Appendix 9A, Table A). We then *add* its present value ($51,900) to the present value of the CD project's other net cash inflows ($1,048,610) as shown in Exhibit 9-12:

EXHIBIT 9-12   **NPV of a Project with Residual Value**

	PV Factor ($i = 14\%$, $n = 5$)	Net Cash Inflow	Present Value
Present value of annuity	3.433 ×	$305,450 =	$ 1,048,610
Present value of residual value (single lump sum)	0.519 ×	100,000 =	51,900
Total present value of net cash inflows			$ 1,100,510
Investment			$(1,000,000)
Net present value (NPV)			$ 100,510

Because of the expected residual value, the CD-player project is now more attractive than the DVR project. If Allegra could pursue only the CD or DVR project, it would now choose the CD project because its NPV ($100,510) is higher than the DVR project ($78,910) and both projects require the same investment ($1 million).

Sensitivity Analysis

Capital budgeting decisions affect cash flows far into the future. Allegra's managers might want to know whether their decision would be affected by any of their major assumptions. For example:

- Changing the discount rate from 14% to 12% or to 16%
- Changing the net cash flows by 10%
- Changing an expected residual value

After entering the basic information for NPV analysis into spreadsheet software or programmed calculators, managers perform sensitivity analyses with just a few keystrokes. The software quickly recalculates and displays the results.

Internal Rate of Return (IRR)

The NPV method only tells management whether the investment exceeds the hurdle rate. Since both the CD-player and DVR projects yield positive NPVs, we know they provide *more* than a 14% rate of return. But what exact rate of return would these investments provide? The IRR method answers that question.

The **internal rate of return (IRR)** is the rate of return, based on discounted cash flows, that a company can expect to earn by investing in the project. *It is the interest rate that makes the NPV of the investment equal to zero:*

$$NPV = 0$$

Let's look at this concept in another light by inserting the definition of NPV:

$$\text{Present value of the investment's net cash inflows} - \text{Investment's cost} = 0$$

Or if we rearrange the equation:

$$\text{Investment's cost} = \text{Present value of the investment's net cash inflows}$$

In other words, the IRR is the *interest rate* that makes the cost of the investment equal to the present value of the investment's net cash inflows. The higher the IRR, the more desirable the project. Like the profitability index, the IRR can be used in the capital rationing process.

IRR computations are very easy to perform on programmed calculators. (See Appendices 9B and 9C.) However, IRR computations are much more cumbersome to perform using the tables.

IRR with Equal Annual Net Cash Inflows (Annuity)

When the investment is an annuity, we can develop a formula that will tell us the Annuity PV factor associated with the investment's IRR. We start with the equation given above and then substitute in as follows:

Investment's cost = Present value of the investment's net cash inflows

Investment's cost = Amount of each equal net cash inflow × Annuity PV factor (i = ?, n = given)

Finally, we rearrange the equation to obtain the following formula:

$$\frac{\text{Investment's cost}}{\text{Amount of each equal net cash inflow}} = \text{Annuity PV factor } (i = ?, n = \text{given})$$

Let's use this formula to find the Annuity PV factor associated with Allegra's CD-player project. Recall that the project would cost $1 million and result in five equal yearly cash inflows of $305,450:

$$\frac{\$1,000,000}{\$305,450} = \text{Annuity PV factor } (i = ?, n = 5)$$
$$3.274 = \text{Annuity PV factor } (i = ?, n = 5)$$

Next, we find the interest rate that corresponds to this Annuity PV factor. Turn to the Present Value of Annuity of $1 table (Appendix 9A, Table B). Scan the row corresponding to the project's expected life—five years, in our example. Choose the column(s) with the number closest to the Annuity PV factor you calculated using the formula. The 3.274 annuity factor is in the 16% column.

Therefore, the IRR of the CD-player project is 16%.

Allegra expects the project to earn an internal rate of return of 16% over its life. Exhibit 9-13 confirms this result: Using a 16% discount rate, the project's NPV is zero. In other words, 16% is the discount rate that makes the investment cost equal to the present value of the investment's net cash inflows.

EXHIBIT 9-13   IRR–CD-Player Project

	Annuity PV Factor (i = 16%, n = 5)		Net Cash Inflow		Total Present Value
Present value of annuity of equal annual					
net cash inflows for 5 years at 16%	3.274	×	$305,450	=	$ 1,000,000†
Investment					(1,000,000)
Net present value of the CD-player project					$ 0‡

†Slight rounding error.
‡The zero difference proves that the IRR is 16%.

To decide whether the project is acceptable, compare the IRR with the minimum desired rate of return. The decision rule is:

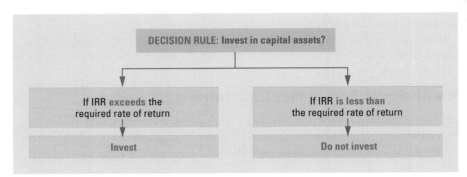

Recall that Allegra's hurdle rate is 14%. Because the CD project's IRR (16%) is higher than the hurdle rate (14%), Allegra would invest in the project.

In the CD-player project, the exact Annuity PV factor (3.274) appears in the Present Value of an Annuity of $1 table (Appendix 9A, Table B). Many times, the exact factor will not appear in the table. For example, let's find the IRR of Tierra Firma's B2B Portal. Recall that the B2B portal had a six-year life with annual net cash inflows of $60,000. The investment cost $240,000. We find its Annuity PV factor using the formula given previously:

$$\frac{\text{Investment's cost}}{\text{Amount of each equal net cash inflow}} = \text{Annuity PV factor } (i = ?, n = \text{given})$$

$$\frac{\$240,000}{\$60,000} = \text{Annuity PV factor } (i = ?, n = 6)$$

$$4.00 = \text{Annuity PV factor } (i = ?, n = 6)$$

Now, look in the Present Value of Annuity of $1 table in the row marked 6 periods (Appendix 9A, Table B). You will not see 4.00 under any column. The closest two factors are 3.889 (at 14%) and 4.111 (at 12%).

Thus, the B2B portal's IRR is somewhere between 12% and 14%.

If we used a calculator programmed with the IRR function, we would find the exact IRR is 12.98%. If Tierra Firma had a 14% hurdle rate, it would *not* invest in the B2B portal because the portal's IRR is less than 14%.

IRR with Unequal Annual Net Cash Inflows

Because the DVR project has unequal cash inflows, Allegra cannot use the Present Value of Annuity of $1 table to find the asset's IRR. Rather, Allegra must use a trial-and-error procedure to determine the discount rate that makes the project's NPV equal to zero. Recall from Exhibit 9-10 that the DVR's NPV using a 14% discount rate is $78,910. Since the NPV is *positive*, the IRR must be *higher* than 14%. Allegra performs the trial-and-error process using *higher* discount rates until it finds the rate that brings the net present value of the DVR project to *zero*. Exhibit 9-14 shows that at 16%, the DVR has an

NPV of $40,390; therefore, the IRR must be higher than 16%. At 18%, the NPV is $3,980, which is very close to zero. Thus, the IRR must be slightly higher than 18%. If we use a calculator programmed with the IRR function rather than the trial-and-error procedure, we would find that the IRR is 18.23%.

EXHIBIT 9-14   Finding the DVR's IRR Through Trial and Error

	Net Cash Inflow		PV Factor (for $i = 16\%$)		Present Value at 16%	Net Cash Inflow		PV Factor (for $i = 18\%$)		Present Value at 18%
Year 1 ($n = 1$)	$500,000	×	0.862*	=	$ 431,000	$500,000	×	0.847*	=	$ 423,500
Year 2 ($n = 2$)	350,000	×	0.743	=	260,050	350,000	×	0.718	=	251,300
Year 3 ($n = 3$)	300,000	×	0.641	=	192,300	300,000	×	0.609	=	182,700
Year 4 ($n = 4$)	250,000	×	0.552	=	138,000	250,000	×	0.516	=	129,000
Year 5 ($n = 5$)	40,000	×	0.476	=	19,040	40,000	×	0.437	=	17,480
Total present value of net cash inflows					$ 1,040,390					$ 1,003,980
Investment					(1,000,000)					(1,000,000)
Net present value (NPV)					$ 40,390					$ 3,980

*PV factors are found in Appendix 9A, Table A.

The DVR's internal rate of return is higher than Allegra's 14% hurdle rate, so the DVR project is attractive.

Comparing Capital Budgeting Methods

We have discussed four capital budgeting methods commonly used by companies to make capital investment decisions. Two of these methods do not incorporate the time value of money: payback period and ARR. Exhibit 9-15 summarizes the similarities and differences between these two methods.

 5 Compare and contrast the four capital budgeting methods

EXHIBIT 9-15   Capital Budgeting Methods That *Ignore* the Time Value of Money

Payback Period	ARR
• Simple to compute	• The only method that uses accrual accounting figures
• Focuses on the time it takes to recover the company's cash investment	• Shows how the investment will affect operating income, which is important to financial statement users
• Ignores any cash flows occurring after the payback period, including any residual value	• Measures the average profitability of the asset over its entire life
• Highlights risks of investments with longer cash recovery periods	• Ignores the time value of money
• Ignores the time value of money	

The discounted cash flow methods are superior because they consider both the time value of money and profitability. These methods compare an investment's initial cost (cash outflow) with its future net cash inflows—all converted to the *same point in time*—the present value. Profitability is built into the discounted cash flow methods because they consider *all* cash inflows and outflows over the project's life. Exhibit 9-16 considers the similarities and differences between the two discounted cash flow methods.

EXHIBIT 9-16 Capital Budgeting Methods That *Incorporate the Time Value of Money*

NPV	IRR
• Incorporates the time value of money and the asset's net cash flows over its entire life	• Incorporates the time value of money and the asset's net cash flows over its entire life
• Indicates whether the asset will earn the company's minimum required rate of return	• Computes the project's unique rate of return
• Shows the excess or deficiency of the asset's present value of net cash inflows over its initial investment cost	• No additional steps needed for capital rationing decisions
• The profitability index should be computed for capital rationing decisions when the assets require different initial investments	

Managers often use more than one method to gain different perspectives on risks and returns. For example, Deer Valley's owners could decide to pursue capital projects with positive NPV provided those projects have a payback of four years or less.

Stop & Think...

A pharmaceutical company is considering two research projects that require the same initial investment. Project A has an NPV of $232,000 and a 3-year payback period. Project B has an NPV of $237,000 and a payback period of 4.5 years. Which project would you choose?

Answer: Many managers would choose Project A even though it has a slightly lower NPV. Why? The NPV is only $5,000 lower, yet the payback period is significantly shorter. The uncertainty of receiving operating cash flows increases with each passing year. Managers often forgo small differences in expected cash inflows to decrease the risk of investments.

Decision Guidelines

CAPITAL BUDGETING

Here are more of the guidelines Amazon.com's managers used as they made the major capital budgeting decision to invest in building warehouses.

Decision	Guideline
Which capital budgeting methods are best?	No one method is best. Each method provides a different perspective on the investment decision.
Why do the NPV and IRR models calculate the present value of an investment's net cash flows?	Because an investment's cash inflows occur in the future, yet the cash outlay for the investment occurs now, all of the cash flows must be converted to a common point in time. These methods use the *present* value as the common point in time.
How do we know if investing in warehouse facilities will be worthwhile?	Investment in warehouse facilities may be worthwhile if the NPV is positive or the IRR exceeds the required rate of return.
How do we compute the net present value (NPV) if the investment has equal annual cash inflows?	Compute the present value of the investment's net cash inflows using the Present Value of an Annuity of $1 table and then subtract the investment's cost.
How do we compute the net present value (NPV) if the investment has unequal annual cash inflows?	Compute the present value of each year's net cash inflows using the Present Value of $1 (lump sum) table, sum the present value of the inflows, and then subtract the investment's cost.
How do we compute the internal rate of return (IRR) if the investment has equal annual cash inflows?	Find the interest rate that yields the following Annuity PV factor: $$\text{Annuity PV factor} = \frac{\text{Investment's cost}}{\text{Amount of each equal net cash inflow}}$$
How do we compute the internal rate of return (IRR) if the investment has unequal annual cash inflows?	Use trial and error, a business calculator, or spreadsheet software to find the IRR.

Summary Problem 2

Recall from Summary Problem 1 that Zetamax is considering buying a new bar-coding machine. The investment proposal passed the initial screening tests (payback period and accounting rate of return), so the company now wants to analyze the proposal using the discounted cash flow methods. Recall that the bar-coding machine costs $48,000, has a five-year life, and has no residual value. The estimated net cash inflows are $13,000 per year over its life. The company's hurdle rate is 16%.

Requirements

1. Compute the bar-coding machine's NPV.

2. Find the bar-coding machine's IRR (exact percentage not required).

3. Should Zetamax buy the bar-coding machine? Why or why not?

Solution

Requirement 1

Present value of annuity of equal annual net cash inflows at 16% ($13,000 × 3.274*)	$ 42,562
Investment	(48,000)
Net present value	$ (5,438)

*Annuity PV factor ($i = 16\%$, $n = 5$).

Requirement 2

$$\frac{\text{Investment's cost}}{\text{Amount of each equal net cash inflow}} = \text{Annuity PV factor } (i = ?, n = \text{given})$$

$$\frac{\$48,000}{\$13,000} = \text{Annuity PV factor } (i = ?, n = 5)$$

$$3.692 = \text{Annuity PV factor } (i = ?, n = 5)$$

Because the cash inflows occur for five years, we look for the PV factor 3.692 in the row marked $n = 5$ on the Present Value of Annuity of $1 table (Appendix 9A, Table B). The PV factor is 3.605 at 12% and 3.791 at 10%. Therefore, the bar-coding machine has an IRR that falls between 10% and 12%. (*Optional:* Using a programmed calculator, we find an 11.038% internal rate of return.)

Requirement 3
Decision: Do not buy the bar-coding machine. It has a negative NPV, and its IRR falls below the company's required rate of return. Both methods show that this investment does not meet management's minimum requirements for investments of this nature.

Review Capital Investment Decisions and the Time Value of Money

■ Accounting Vocabulary

Accounting Rate of Return. (p. 502)
A measure of profitability computed by dividing the average annual operating income from an asset by the initial investment in the asset.

Annuity. (p. 507)
A stream of equal installments made at equal time intervals.

Capital Budgeting. (p. 496)
The process of making capital investment decisions. Companies make capital investments when they acquire *capital assets*—assets used for a long period of time.

Capital Rationing. (p. 498)
Choosing among alternative capital investments due to limited funds.

Compound Interest. (p. 507)
Interest computed on the principal *and* all interest earned to date.

Discount Rate. (p. 516)
Management's minimum desired rate of return on an investment. Also called the hurdle rate and required rate of return.

Internal Rate of Return (IRR). (p. 520)
The rate of return (based on discounted cash flows) that a company can expect to earn by investing in a capital asset. The interest rate that makes the NPV of the investment equal to zero.

Net Present Value (NPV). (p. 516)
The *difference* between the present value of the investment's net cash inflows and the investment's cost.

Payback. (p. 499)
The length of time it takes to recover, in net cash inflows, the cost of a capital outlay.

Post-Audits. (p. 498)
Comparing a capital investment's actual net cash inflows to its projected net cash inflows.

Profitability Index. (p. 519)
An index that computes the number of dollars returned for every dollar invested, *with all calculations performed in present value dollars*. Computed as present value of net cash inflows divided by investment. Also called present value index.

Simple Interest. (p. 507)
Interest computed *only* on the principal amount.

Time Value of Money. (p. 507)
The fact that money can be invested to earn income over time.

■ Quick Check

1. Which of the following methods uses accrual accounting rather than net cash flows as a basis for calculations?
   a. payback
   b. ARR
   c. NPV
   d. IRR

2. Which of the following methods does not consider the investment's profitability?
   a. payback
   b. ARR
   c. NPV
   d. IRR

3. Which of the following is true regarding capital rationing decisions?
   a. Companies should always choose the investment with the shortest payback period.
   b. Companies should always choose the investment with the highest NPV.
   c. Companies should always choose the investment with the highest ARR.
   d. None of the above.

4. Your rich aunt has promised to give you $3,000 a year at the end of each of the next four years to help you pay for college. With a discount rate of 10%, the present value of the gift can be stated as:
   a. PV = $3,000 (PV factor, $i = 4\%$, $n = 10$)
   b. PV = $3,000 \times 10\% \times 5$
   c. PV = $3,000 \times$ (Annuity PV factor, $i = 10\%$, $n = 4$)
   d. PV = $3,000 \times$ (Annuity FV factor, $i = 10\%$, $n = 4$)

5. Which of the following affects the present value of an investment?
   a. the interest rate
   b. the number of time periods (length of the investment)
   c. the type of investment (annuity versus single lump sum)
   d. all of the above

6. When making capital rationing decisions, the size of the initial investment required may differ between alternative investments. The profitability index can be used in conjunction with which of the following methods, to help managers choose between alternatives?
   a. IRR
   b. ARR
   c. Payback Period
   d. NPV

7. The IRR is
   a. the same as the ARR
   b. the firm's hurdle rate
   c. the interest rate at which the NPV of the investment is zero
   d. none of the above

8. Suppose Amazon.com is considering investing in warehouse-management software that costs $500,000, has $50,000 residual value, and should lead to cost savings of $120,000 per year for its five-year life. In calculating the ARR, which of the following figures should be used as the equation's denominator?
   a. $225,000
   b. $500,000
   c. $250,000
   d. $275,000

9. Using the information from Question 8, which of the following figures should be used in the equation's numerator (average annual operating income)?
   a. $120,000
   b. $20,000
   c. $30,000
   d. $10,000

10. Which of the following is the most reliable method for making capital budgeting decisions?

  a. NPV method
  b. ARR method
  c. payback method
  d. post-audit method

Quick Check Answers

1. b 2. a 3. d 4. c 5. d 6. d 7. c 8. b 9. c 10. a

For Internet Exercises, Excel in Practice, and additional online activities, go to this book's Web site at www.prenhall.com/bamber.

Assess Your Progress

■ Learning Objectives

1 Describe the importance of capital investments and the capital budgeting process

2 Use the payback and accounting rate of return methods to make capital investment decisions

3 Use the time value of money to compute the present and future values of single lump sums and annuities

4 Use discounted cash flow models to make capital investment decisions

5 Compare and contrast the four capital budgeting methods

■ Short Exercises

S9-1 **Order the capital budgeting process** *(Learning Objective 1)*
Place the following activities in sequence to illustrate the capital budgeting process:
a. Budget capital investments
b. Project investments' cash flows
c. Perform post-audits
d. Make investments
e. Use feedback to reassess investments already made
f. Identify potential capital investments
g. Screen/analyze investments using one or more of the methods discussed

Allegra Data Set used for S9-2 through S9-5

Allegra is considering producing CD players and digital video recorders (DVRs). The products require different specialized machines, each costing $1 million. Each machine has a five-year life and zero residual value. The two products have different patterns of predicted net cash inflows:

Year	Annual Net Cash Inflows	
	CD Players	**DVRs**
1	$ 305,450	$ 500,000
2	305,450	350,000
3	305,450	300,000
4	305,450	250,000
5	305,450	40,000
Total	$1,527,250	$1,440,000

Allegra will consider making capital investments only if the payback period of the project is less than 3.5 years and the ARR exceeds 8%.

S9-2 **Compute payback period—equal cash inflows** (*Learning Objective 2*)

Refer to the Allegra Data Set. Calculate the CD-player project's payback period. If the CD project had a residual value of $100,000, would the payback period change? Explain and recalculate if necessary. Does this investment pass Allegra's payback period screening rule?

S9-3 **Compute payback period—unequal cash inflows** (*Learning Objective 2*)

Refer to the Allegra Data Set. Calculate the DVR project's payback period. If the DVR project had a residual value of $100,000, would the payback period change? Explain and recalculate if necessary. Does this investment pass Allegra's payback period screening rule?

S9-4 **Compute ARR—equal cash inflows** (*Learning Objective 2*)

Refer to the Allegra Data Set. Calculate the CD-player project's ARR. If the CD project had a residual value of $100,000, would the ARR change? Explain and recalculate if necessary. Does this investment pass Allegra's ARR screening rule?

S9-5 **Compute ARR—unequal cash inflows** (*Learning Objective 2*)

Refer to the Allegra Data Set. Calculate the DVR project's ARR. If the DVR project had a residual value of $100,000, would the ARR change? Explain and recalculate if necessary. Does this investment pass Allegra's ARR screening rule?

S9-6 **Compute annual cash savings** (*Learning Objective 2*)

Suppose Allegra is deciding whether to invest in a DVD-HD project. The payback period for the $5 million investment is four years, and the project's expected life is seven years. What equal annual net cash inflows are expected from this project?

S9-7 **Find the present values of future cash flows** (*Learning Objective 3*)

Your grandfather would like to share some of his fortune with you. He offers to give you money under one of the following scenarios (you get to choose):

1. $8,000 a year at the end of each of the next eight years
2. $50,000 (lump sum) now
3. $100,000 (lump sum) eight years from now

Calculate the present value of each scenario using a 6% interest rate. Which scenario yields the highest present value? Would your preference change if you used a 12% interest rate?

S9-8 **Show how timing affects future values** (*Learning Objective 3*)

Assume that you make the following investments:

a. You invest a lump sum of $5,000 for four years at 12% interest. What is the investment's value at the end of four years?

b. In a different account earning 12% interest, you invest $1,250 at the end of each year for four years. What is the investment's value at the end of four years?

c. What general rule of thumb explains the difference in the investments' future values?

S9-9 **Compare payout options at their future values** (*Learning Objective 3*)

Refer to the lottery payout options on page 486. Rather than compare the payout options at their present values (as is done in the chapter), compare the payout options at their future value ten years from now.

a. Using an 8% interest rate, what is the future value of each payout option?

b. Rank your preference of payout options.

c. Does computing the future value rather than the present value of the options change your preference of payout options? Explain.

S9-10 **Relationship between the PV tables** *(Learning Objective 3)*
Use the Present Value of $1 table (Appendix 9A, Table A) to determine the present value of $1 received one year from now. Assume a 14% interest rate. Use the same table to find the present value of $1 received two years from now. Continue this process for a total of five years.

a. What is the *total* present value of the cash flows received over the five-year period?

b. Could you characterize this stream of cash flows as an annuity? Why or why not?

c. Use the Present Value of Annuity of $1 table (Appendix 9A, Table B) to determine the present value of the same stream of cash flows. Compare your results to your answer in Part a.

d. Explain your findings.

S9-11 **Compute NPV—equal net cash inflows** *(Learning Objective 4)*
Skyline Music is considering investing $750,000 in private lesson studios that will have no residual value. The studios are expected to result in annual net cash inflows of $100,000 per year for the next ten years. Assuming that Skyline Music uses an 8% hurdle rate, what is net present value (NPV) of the studio investment? Is this a favorable investment?

S9-12 **Compute IRR—equal net cash inflows** *(Learning Objective 4)*
Refer to Skyline Music in S9-11. What is the approximate internal rate of return (IRR) of the studio investment?

S9-13 **Compute NPV—unequal net cash inflows** *(Learning Objective 4)*
The local Giant Eagle supermarket is considering investing in self-check-out kiosks for its customers. The self-check-out kiosks will cost $45,000 and have no residual value. Management expects the equipment to result in net cash savings over three years as customers grow accustomed to using the new technology: $14,000 the first year; $19,000 the second year; $24,000 the third year. Assuming a 10% discount rate, what is the NPV of the kiosk investment? Is this a favorable investment? Why or why not?

S9-14 **Compute IRR—unequal net cash inflows** *(Learning Objective 4)*
Refer to Giant Eagle in S9-13. What is the approximate internal rate of return (IRR) of the kiosk investment?

■ Exercises

E9-15 **Write a memo to employees about capital budgeting** *(Learning Objectives 1, 5)*
You have just started a business and want your new employees to be well informed about capital budgeting. Write a memo to your employees (1) explaining why capital budgeting is important, (2) briefly describing the four methods of analyzing capital investments along with some of their strengths and weaknesses, and (3) explaining why your company will post-audit all capital investments.

E9-16 **Compute payback period—equal cash inflows** *(Learning Objective 2)*
Malkind is considering acquiring a manufacturing plant. The purchase price is $1,236,100. The owners believe the plant will generate net cash inflows of $309,025 annually. It will have to be replaced in eight years. To be profitable, the investment payback must occur before the investment's replacement date. Use the payback method to determine whether Malkind should purchase this plant.

E9-17 **Compute payback period—unequal cash inflows** *(Learning Objective 2)*
Preston Hardware is adding a new product line that will require an investment of $1,454,000. Managers estimate that this investment will have a ten-year life and generate net cash inflows of $310,000 the first year, $280,000 the second year, and $240,000 each year thereafter for eight years. The investment has no residual value. Compute the payback period.

E9-18 **ARR with unequal cash inflows** *(Learning Objective 2)*
Refer to the Preston Hardware information in E9-17. Compute the ARR for the investment.

E9-19 **Compute and compare ARR** *(Learning Objective 2)*
Transport Products is shopping for new equipment. Managers are considering two investments. Equipment manufactured by Stenback costs $1,000,000 and will last five years and have no residual value. The Stenback equipment will generate annual operating income of $160,000. Equipment manufactured by Kyler costs $1,200,000 and will remain useful for six years. It promises annual operating income of $240,500, and its expected residual value is $100,000.
    Which equipment offers the higher ARR?

E9-20 **Compare retirement savings plans** *(Learning Objective 3)*
Assume that you want to retire early at age 52. You plan to save using one of the following two strategies: (1) save $3,000 a year in an IRA beginning when you are 22 and ending when you are 52 (30 years) or (2) wait until you are 40 to start saving and then save $7,500 per year for the next 12 years. Assume that you will earn the historic stock market average of 10% per year.

Requirements

1. How much out-of-pocket cash will you invest under the two options?
2. How much savings will you have accumulated at age 52 under the two options?
3. Explain the results.
4. If you let the savings continue to grow for ten more years (with no further out-of-pocket investments), under each scenario, what will the investment be worth when you are age 62?

E9-21 **Show the effect of interest rate on future values** *(Learning Objective 3)*
Your best friend just received a gift of $5,000 from his favorite aunt. He wants to save the money to use as starter money after college. He can (1) invest it risk-free at 3%, (2) take on moderate risk at 8%, or (3) take on high risk at 16%. Help your friend project the investment's worth at the end of four years under each investment strategy and explain the results to him.

E9-22 **Fund future cash flows** *(Learning Objective 3)*
Janet wants to take the next five years off work to travel around the world. She estimates her annual cash needs at $30,000 (if she needs more, she'll work odd jobs). Janet believes she can invest her savings at 8% until she depletes her funds.

Requirements

1. How much money does Janet need now to fund her travels?
2. After speaking with a number of banks, Janet learns she'll be able to invest her funds only at 6%. How much does she need now to fund her travels?

E9-23   Choosing a lottery payout option *(Learning Objective 3)*
Congratulations! You've won a state lotto. The state lottery offers you the following (after-tax) payout options:

> Option #1: $12,000,000 five years from now
>
> Option #2: $2,250,000 at the end of each year for the next five years
>
> Option #3: $10,000,000 three years from now

Assuming that you can earn 8% on your funds, which option would you prefer?

E9-24   Solve various time value of money scenarios *(Learning Objective 3)*

1. Suppose you invest a sum of $2,500 in an account bearing interest at the rate of 14% per year. What will the investment be worth six years from now?

2. How much would you need to invest now to be able to withdraw $5,000 at the end of every year for the next 20 years? Assume a 12% interest rate.

3. Assume that you want to have $150,000 saved seven years from now. If you can invest your funds at a 6% interest rate, how much do you currently need to invest?

4. Your aunt Betty plans to give you $1,000 at the end of every year for the next ten years. If you invest each of her yearly gifts at a 12% interest rate, how much will they be worth at the end of the ten-year period?

5. Suppose you want to buy a small cabin in the mountains four years from now. You estimate that the property will cost $52,500 at that time. How much money do you need to invest each year in an account bearing interest at the rate of 6 percent per year to accumulate the $52,500 purchase price?

E9-25   Calculate NPV—equal annual cash inflows *(Learning Objective 4)*
Use the NPV method to determine whether Resort Products should invest in the following projects:

- *Project A*: Costs $272,000 and offers eight annual net cash inflows of $60,000. Resort Products requires an annual return of 14% on projects like A.

- *Project B*: Costs $380,000 and offers nine annual net cash inflows of $70,000. Resort Products demands an annual return of 12% on investments of this nature.

What is the NPV of each project? What is the maximum acceptable price to pay for each project?

E9-26   Calculate IRR—equal cash inflows *(Learning Objective 4)*
Refer to Resort Products in E9-25. Compute the IRR of each project and use this information to identify the better investment.

E9-27 **Calculate NPV—unequal cash flows** *(Learning Objective 4)*

Cole Industries is deciding whether to automate one phase of its production process. The manufacturing equipment has a six-year life and will cost $900,000. Projected net cash inflows are as follows:

Year 1	$260,000
Year 2	$250,000
Year 3	$225,000
Year 4	$210,000
Year 5	$200,000
Year 6	$175,000

Requirements

1. Compute this project's NPV using Cole Industries's 14% hurdle rate. Should Cole Industries invest in the equipment? Why or why not?

2. Cole Industries could refurbish the equipment at the end of six years for $100,000. The refurbished equipment could be used one more year, providing $75,000 of net cash inflows in Year 7. In addition, the refurbished equipment would have a $50,000 residual value at the end of Year 7. Should Cole Industries invest in the equipment and refurbish it after six years? Why or why not? (*Hint*: In addition to your answer to Requirement 1, discount the additional cash outflow and inflows back to the present value.)

E9-28 **Compute IRR—unequal cash flows** *(Learning Objective 4)*

Ronnie Razors is considering an equipment investment that will cost $950,000. Projected net cash inflows over the equipment's three-year life are as follows: Year 1: $500,000; Year 2: $400,000; and Year 3: $300,000. Ronnie wants to know the equipment's IRR.

Requirements

Use trial and error to find the IRR within a 2% range. (*Hint*: Use Ronnie's hurdle rate of 10% to begin the trial-and-error process.)

Optional: Use a business calculator to compute the exact IRR.

E9-29 **Capital rationing decision** *(Learning Objective 4)*

Sykes Manufacturing is considering three capital investment proposals. At this time, Sykes Manufacturing has funds available to pursue only one of the three investments. Which investment should Sykes Manufacturing pursue at this time? Why?

	Equipment A	Equipment B	Equipment C
Present value of net cash inflows	$1,695,000	$1,960,000	$2,200,000
Investment	($1,500,000)	($1,750,000)	($2,000,000)
NPV	$ 195,000	$ 210,000	$ 200,000

E9-30 **Compare the capital budgeting methods** *(Learning Objective 5)*

Fill in each statement with the appropriate capital budgeting method: payback period, ARR, NPV, or IRR.

a. _____ and _____ incorporate the time value of money.

b. _____ focuses on time, not profitability.

c. _____ uses accrual accounting income.

d. _____ finds the discount rate that brings the investment's NPV to zero.

e. In capital rationing decisions, the profitability index must be computed to compare investments requiring different initial investments when the _____ method is used.

f. _____ ignores salvage value.

g. _____ uses discounted cash flows to determine the asset's unique rate of return.

h. _____ highlights risky investments.

i. _____ measures profitability but ignores the time value of money.

Deer Valley Expansion Data Set used for E9-31 through E9-35

Consider how Deer Valley (from the chapter-opening story) could use capital budgeting to decide whether the $13 million Snow Park Lodge expansion would be a good investment.

Assume that Deer Valley's managers developed the following estimates concerning the expansion (all numbers assumed):

Number of additional skiers per day	120
Average number of days per year that weather conditions allow skiing at Deer Valley	150
Useful life of expansion (in years)..................................	10
Average cash spent by each skier per day	$ 245
Average variable cost of serving each skier per day	$ 85
Cost of expansion	$13,000,000
Discount rate...	12%

Assume that Deer Valley uses the straight-line depreciation method and expects the lodge expansion to have a residual value of $1 million at the end of its ten-year life.

E9-31 **Compute payback and ARR with residual value** *(Learning Objective 2)*

Refer to the Deer Valley Expansion Data Set.

1. Compute the average annual net cash inflow from the expansion.

2. Compute the average annual operating income from the expansion.

3. Compute the payback period.

4. Compute the ARR.

E9-32 **Continuation of E9-31: Compute payback and ARR with no residual value**
(Learning Objective 2)
Refer to the Deer Valley Expansion Data Set. *Assume that the expansion has zero residual value.*

Requirements

1. Will the payback period change? Explain and recalculate if necessary.
2. Will the project's ARR change? Explain and recalculate if necessary.
3. Assume that Deer Valley screens its potential capital investments using the following decision criteria:

Maximum payback period	five years
Minimum accounting rate of return	10%

Will Deer Valley consider this project further or reject it?

E9-33 **Calculate NPV with and without residual value** *(Learning Objective 4)*
Refer to the Deer Valley Expansion Data Set.

1. What is the project's NPV? Is the investment attractive? Why or why not?
2. *Assume that the expansion has no residual value.* What is the project's NPV? Is the investment still attractive? Why or why not?

E9-34 **Calculate IRR with no residual value** *(Learning Objective 4)*
Refer to the Deer Valley Expansion Data Set. *Assume that the expansion has no residual value.* What is the project's IRR? Is the investment attractive? Why or why not?

E9-35 **Continuation of E9-32, E9-33, E9-34: memo** *(Learning Objective 5)*
Use your results from E9-32, E9-33, and E9-34 to write a memo to Deer Valley's Director of Finance Jim Madsen recommending whether Deer Valley should undertake the expansion, *assuming no residual value.* Cover the strengths and weaknesses of each capital budgeting method cited in your memo. Use the following format:

Date: _____

 To: Mr. Jim Madsen, Director of Finance

From: _____

Subject: _____

Problems (Problem Set A)

P9-36A Apply capital budgeting to a current event (*Learning Objective 1*)

Look through the business section of the newspaper. Find a company that has recently made a capital investment. Summarize the company's decision and then answer the following questions: Why is this a capital investment decision? What effect will the decision have on the company? What methods might the company have used to make its decision? What information would the company have used in making its decision?

P9-37A Solve various time value of money scenarios (*Learning Objectives 3, 4*)

1. Jeff just hit the jackpot in Las Vegas and won $25,000! If he invests it now at a 12% interest rate, how much will it be worth in 20 years?

2. Evan would like to have $2,000,000 saved by the time he retires in 40 years. How much does he need to invest now at a 10% interest rate to fund his retirement goal?

3. Assume that Stephanie accumulates savings of $1 million by the time she retires. If she invests this savings at 8%, how much money will she be able to withdraw at the end of each year for 20 years?

4. Katelyn plans to invest $2,000 at the end of each year for the next seven years. Assuming a 14% interest rate, what will her investment be worth seven years from now?

5. Assuming a 6% interest rate, how much would Danielle have to invest now to be able to withdraw $10,000 at the end of each year for the next nine years?

6. Jim is considering a capital investment that costs $485,000 and will provide the following net cash inflows:

Year	Net Cash Inflow
1	$300,000
2	200,000
3	100,000

Using a hurdle rate of 12%, find the NPV of the investment.

7. What is the IRR of the capital investment described in Question 6?

P9-38A Retirement planning in two stages (*Learning Objective 3*)

You are planning for a very early retirement. You would like to retire at age 40 and have enough money saved to be able to draw $225,000 per year for the next 40 years (based on family history, you think you'll live to age 80). You plan to save for retirement by making 15 equal annual installments (from age 25 to age 40) into a fairly risky investment fund that you expect will earn 12% per year. You will leave the money in this fund until it is completely depleted when you are 80 years old. To make your plan work:

1. How much money must you accumulate by retirement? (*Hint:* Find the present value of the $225,000 withdrawals. You may want to draw a time line showing the savings period and the retirement period.)

2. How does this amount compare to the total amount you will draw out of the investment during retirement? How can these numbers be so different?

3. How much must you pay into the investment each year for the first 15 years? (*Hint:* Your answer from Requirement 1 becomes the future value of this annuity.)

4. How does the total out-of-pocket savings compare to the investment's value at the end of the 15-year savings period and the withdrawals you will make during retirement?

P9-39A Evaluate an investment using all four methods *(Learning Objectives 2, 4)*

River Wild is considering purchasing a water park in San Antonio, Texas, for $1,850,000. The new facility will generate annual net cash inflows of $520,000 for eight years. Engineers estimate that the facility will remain useful for eight years and have no residual value. The company uses straight-line depreciation. Its owners want payback in less than five years and an ARR of 10% or more. Management uses a 12% hurdle rate on investments of this nature.

Requirements

1. Compute the payback period, the ARR, the NPV and the approximate IRR of this investment. (If you use the tables to compute the IRR, answer with the closest interest rate shown in the tables.)

2. Recommend whether the company should invest in this project.

P9-40A Compare investments with different cash flows and residual values *(Learning Objectives 2, 4)*

Gyros operates a chain of sandwich shops. The company is considering two possible expansion plans. Plan A would open eight smaller shops at a cost of $8,440,000. Expected annual net cash inflows are $1,600,000 with zero residual value at the end of ten years. Under Plan B, Gyros would open three larger shops at a cost of $8,340,000. This plan is expected to generate net cash inflows of $1,100,000 per year for ten years, the estimated life of the properties. Estimated residual value is $1,000,000. Gyros uses straight-line depreciation and requires an annual return of 8%.

Requirements

1. Compute the payback period, the ARR, and the NPV of these two plans. What are the strengths and weaknesses of these capital budgeting models?

2. Which expansion plan should Gyros choose? Why?

3. Estimate Plan A's IRR. How does the IRR compare with the company's required rate of return?

■ Problems (Problem Set B)

P9-41B Apply capital budgeting to a current event *(Learning Objective 1)*

Look through a recent copy of a business magazine, such as *Forbes* or *Fortune*. Find a company that has recently made a capital investment. Summarize the company's decision and then answer the following questions: Why is this a capital investment decision? What effect will the decision have on the company? What methods might the company have used to make its decision? What information would the company have used in making its decision?

P9-42B Solve various time value of money scenarios *(Learning Objectives 3, 4)*

1. Curt just hit the jackpot in Las Vegas and won $50,000! If he invests it now at a 10% interest rate, how much will it be worth in 15 years?

continued . . .

2. Nathan would like to have $1 million saved by the time he retires in 20 years. How much does he need to invest now at a 14% interest rate to fund his retirement goal?

3. Assume that Lydia accumulates savings of $1,500,000 by the time she retires. If she invests this savings at 8%, how much money will she be able to withdraw at the end of each year for 15 years?

4. Pam plans to invest $3,000 at the end of each year for the next ten years. Assuming a 6% interest rate, what will her investment be worth ten years from now?

5. Assuming a 12% interest rate, how much would Carol have to invest now to be able to withdraw $20,000 at the end of each year for the next ten years?

6. Roger is considering a capital investment that costs $1,145,000 and will provide the following net cash inflows:

Year	Net Cash Inflow
1	$600,000
2	500,000
3	400,000

Using a hurdle rate of 14%, find the NPV of the investment.

7. What is the IRR of the capital investment described Question 6?

P9-43B **Retirement planning in two stages** (*Learning Objective 3*)
You are planning for an early retirement. You would like to retire at age 50 and have enough money saved to be able to draw $225,000 per year for the next 30 years (based on family history, you think you'll live to age 80). You plan to save for retirement by making 25 equal annual installments (from age 25 to age 50) into a fairly risky investment fund that you expect will earn 12% per year. You will leave the money in this fund until it is completely depleted when you are 80 years old. To make your plan work:

1. How much money must you accumulate by retirement? (*Hint*: Find the present value of the $225,000 withdrawals. You may want to draw a time line showing the savings period and the retirement period.)

2. How does this amount compare to the total amount you will draw out of the investment during retirement? How can these numbers be so different?

3. How much must you pay into the investment each year for the first 25 years? (*Hint*: Your answer from Question 1 becomes the future value of this annuity.)

4. How does the total out-of-pocket savings compare to the investment's value at the end of the 25-year savings period and the withdrawals you will make during retirement?

P9-44B **Evaluate an investment using all four methods** (*Learning Objectives 2, 4*)
Davio manufactures motorized scooters in Oakland, California. The company is considering an expansion. The plan calls for a construction cost of $5,200,000. The expansion will generate annual net cash inflows of $675,000 for ten years. Engineers estimate that the new facilities will remain useful for ten years and have no residual value. The company uses straight-line depreciation. Its owners want payback in less than five years and an ARR of 8% or more. Management uses a hurdle rate of 10% on investments of this nature.

Requirements

1. Compute the payback period, the ARR, the NPV, and the IRR of this investment.
2. Recommend whether the company should invest in this project.

P9-45B Compare investments with different cash flows and residual values *(Learning Objectives 2, 4)*

Chocolate Café is considering two possible expansion plans. Plan A is to open eight cafés at a cost of $4,180,000. Expected annual net cash inflows are $780,000 with residual value of $820,000 at the end of seven years. Under Plan B, Chocolate Café would open 12 cafés at a cost of $4,200,000. This investment is expected to generate net cash inflows of $994,000 each year for seven years, which is the estimated useful life of the properties. Estimated residual value of the Plan B cafés is zero. Chocolate Café uses straight-line depreciation and requires an annual return of 14%.

Requirements

1. Compute the payback period, the ARR, and the NPV of each plan. What are the strengths and weaknesses of these capital budgeting models?
2. Which expansion plan should Chocolate Café adopt? Why?
3. Estimate the IRR for Plan B. How does Plan B's IRR compare with Chocolate Café's required rate of return?

Apply Your Knowledge

▪ Decision Case

Case 9-46. Apply time value of money to a personal decision *(Learning Objective 3)*

Ted Christensen, a second-year business student at the University of Utah, will graduate in two years with an accounting major and a Spanish minor. Christensen is trying to decide where to work this summer. He has two choices: work full-time for a bottling plant or work part-time in the accounting department of a meat-packing plant. He probably will work at the same place next summer as well. He is able to work 12 weeks during the summer.

The bottling plant would pay Christensen $380 per week this year and 7% more next summer. At the meat-packing plant, he would work 20 hours per week at $8.75 per hour. By working only part-time, he would take two accounting courses this summer. Tuition is $225 per hour for each of the four-hour courses. Christensen believes that the experience he gains this summer will qualify him for a full-time accounting position with the meat-packing plant next summer. That position will pay $550 per week.

Christensen sees two additional benefits of working part-time this summer. First, he could reduce his studying workload during the fall and spring semesters by one course each term. Second, he would have the time to work as a grader in the university's accounting department during the 15-week fall term. Grading pays $50 per week.

Requirements

1. Suppose that Christensen ignores the time value of money in decisions that cover this short of a time period. Suppose also that his sole goal is to make as much money as possible between now and the end of next summer. What should he do? What nonquantitative factors might Ted consider? What would *you* do if you were faced with these alternatives?

2. Now, suppose that Christensen considers the time value of money for all cash flows that he expects to receive one year or more in the future. Which alternative does this consideration favor? Why?

Appendix 9A

Present Value Tables and Future Value Tables

Table A   Present Value of $1

Present Value of $1														
Periods	1%	2%	3%	4%	5%	6%	8%	10%	12%	14%	16%	18%	20%
1	0.990	0.980	0.971	0.962	0.952	0.943	0.926	0.909	0.893	0.877	0.862	0.847	0.833
2	0.980	0.961	0.943	0.925	0.907	0.890	0.857	0.826	0.797	0.769	0.743	0.718	0.694
3	0.971	0.942	0.915	0.889	0.864	0.840	0.794	0.751	0.712	0.675	0.641	0.609	0.579
4	0.961	0.924	0.888	0.855	0.823	0.792	0.735	0.683	0.636	0.592	0.552	0.516	0.482
5	0.951	0.906	0.863	0.822	0.784	0.747	0.681	0.621	0.567	0.519	0.476	0.437	0.402
6	0.942	0.888	0.837	0.790	0.746	0.705	0.630	0.564	0.507	0.456	0.410	0.370	0.335
7	0.933	0.871	0.813	0.760	0.711	0.665	0.583	0.513	0.452	0.400	0.354	0.314	0.279
8	0.923	0.853	0.789	0.731	0.677	0.627	0.540	0.467	0.404	0.351	0.305	0.266	0.233
9	0.914	0.837	0.766	0.703	0.645	0.592	0.500	0.424	0.361	0.308	0.263	0.225	0.194
10	0.905	0.820	0.744	0.676	0.614	0.558	0.463	0.386	0.322	0.270	0.227	0.191	0.162
11	0.896	0.804	0.722	0.650	0.585	0.527	0.429	0.350	0.287	0.237	0.195	0.162	0.135
12	0.887	0.788	0.701	0.625	0.557	0.497	0.397	0.319	0.257	0.208	0.168	0.137	0.112
13	0.879	0.773	0.681	0.601	0.530	0.469	0.368	0.290	0.229	0.182	0.145	0.116	0.093
14	0.870	0.758	0.661	0.577	0.505	0.442	0.340	0.263	0.205	0.160	0.125	0.099	0.078
15	0.861	0.743	0.642	0.555	0.481	0.417	0.315	0.239	0.183	0.140	0.108	0.084	0.065
20	0.820	0.673	0.554	0.456	0.377	0.312	0.215	0.149	0.104	0.073	0.051	0.037	0.026
25	0.780	0.610	0.478	0.375	0.295	0.233	0.146	0.092	0.059	0.038	0.024	0.016	0.010
30	0.742	0.552	0.412	0.308	0.231	0.174	0.099	0.057	0.033	0.020	0.012	0.007	0.004
40	0.672	0.453	0.307	0.208	0.142	0.097	0.046	0.022	0.011	0.005	0.003	0.001	0.001

The factors in the table were generated using the following formula:

$$\text{Present Value of \$1} = \frac{1}{(1 + i)^n}$$

where:

  i = annual interest rate

  n = number of periods

Table B   Present Value of Annuity of $1

Present Value of Annuity of $1													

Periods	1%	2%	3%	4%	5%	6%	8%	10%	12%	14%	16%	18%	20%
1	0.990	0.980	0.971	0.962	0.952	0.943	0.926	0.909	0.893	0.877	0.862	0.847	0.833
2	1.970	1.942	1.913	1.886	1.859	1.833	1.783	1.736	1.690	1.647	1.605	1.566	1.528
3	2.941	2.884	2.829	2.775	2.723	2.673	2.577	2.487	2.402	2.322	2.246	2.174	2.106
4	3.902	3.808	3.717	3.630	3.546	3.465	3.312	3.170	3.037	2.914	2.798	2.690	2.589
5	4.853	4.713	4.580	4.452	4.329	4.212	3.993	3.791	3.605	3.433	3.274	3.127	2.991
6	5.795	5.601	5.417	5.242	5.076	4.917	4.623	4.355	4.111	3.889	3.685	3.498	3.326
7	6.728	6.472	6.230	6.002	5.786	5.582	5.206	4.868	4.564	4.288	4.039	3.812	3.605
8	7.652	7.325	7.020	6.733	6.463	6.210	5.747	5.335	4.968	4.639	4.344	4.078	3.837
9	8.566	8.162	7.786	7.435	7.108	6.802	6.247	5.759	5.328	4.946	4.607	4.303	4.031
10	9.471	8.983	8.530	8.111	7.722	7.360	6.710	6.145	5.650	5.216	4.833	4.494	4.192
11	10.368	9.787	9.253	8.760	8.306	7.887	7.139	6.495	5.938	5.553	5.029	4.656	4.327
12	11.255	10.575	9.954	9.385	8.863	8.384	7.536	6.814	6.194	5.660	5.197	4.793	4.439
13	12.134	11.348	10.635	9.986	9.394	8.853	7.904	7.103	6.424	5.842	5.342	4.910	4.533
14	13.004	12.106	11.296	10.563	9.899	9.295	8.244	7.367	6.628	6.002	5.468	5.008	4.611
15	13.865	12.849	11.938	11.118	10.380	9.712	8.559	7.606	6.811	6.142	5.575	5.092	4.675
20	18.046	16.351	14.878	13.590	12.462	11.470	9.818	8.514	7.469	6.623	5.929	5.353	4.870
25	22.023	19.523	17.413	15.622	14.094	12.783	10.675	9.077	7.843	6.873	6.097	5.467	4.948
30	25.808	22.396	19.600	17.292	15.373	13.765	11.258	9.427	8.055	7.003	6.177	5.517	4.979
40	32.835	27.355	23.115	19.793	17.159	15.046	11.925	9.779	8.244	7.105	6.234	5.548	4.997

The factors in the table were generated using the following formula:

Present value of annuity of $1 $= \dfrac{1}{i}\left[1 - \dfrac{1}{(1+i)^n}\right]$

where:

i = annual interest rate

n = number of periods

Table C   Future Value of $1

Periods	1%	2%	3%	4%	5%	6%	8%	10%	12%	14%	16%	18%	20%
1	1.010	1.020	1.030	1.040	1.050	1.060	1.080	1.100	1.120	1.140	1.160	1.180	1.200
2	1.020	1.040	1.061	1.082	1.103	1.124	1.166	1.210	1.254	1.300	1.346	1.392	1.440
3	1.030	1.061	1.093	1.125	1.158	1.191	1.260	1.331	1.405	1.482	1.531	1.643	1.728
4	1.041	1.082	1.126	1.170	1.216	1.262	1.360	1.464	1.574	1.689	1.811	1.939	2.074
5	1.051	1.104	1.159	1.217	1.276	1.338	1.469	1.611	1.762	1.925	2.100	2.288	2.488
6	1.062	1.126	1.194	1.265	1.340	1.419	1.587	1.772	1.974	2.195	2.436	2.700	2.986
7	1.072	1.149	1.230	1.316	1.407	1.504	1.714	1.949	2.211	2.502	2.826	3.185	3.583
8	1.083	1.172	1.267	1.369	1.477	1.594	1.851	2.144	2.476	2.853	3.278	3.759	4.300
9	1.094	1.195	1.305	1.423	1.551	1.689	1.999	2.358	2.773	3.252	3.803	4.435	5.160
10	1.105	1.219	1.344	1.480	1.629	1.791	2.159	2.594	3.106	3.707	4.411	5.234	6.192
11	1.116	1.243	1.384	1.539	1.710	1.898	2.332	2.853	3.479	4.226	5.117	6.176	7.430
12	1.127	1.268	1.426	1.601	1.796	2.012	2.518	3.138	3.896	4.818	5.936	7.288	8.916
13	1.138	1.294	1.469	1.665	1.886	2.133	2.720	3.452	4.363	5.492	6.886	8.599	10.669
14	1.149	1.319	1.513	1.732	1.980	2.261	2.937	3.798	4.887	6.261	7.988	10.147	12.839
15	1.161	1.346	1.558	1.801	2.079	2.397	3.172	4.177	5.474	7.138	9.266	11.974	15.407
20	1.220	1.486	1.806	2.191	2.653	3.207	4.661	6.728	9.646	13.743	19.461	27.393	38.338
25	1.282	1.641	2.094	2.666	3.386	4.292	6.848	10.835	17.000	26.462	40.874	62.669	95.396
30	1.348	1.811	2.427	3.243	4.322	5.743	10.063	17.449	29.960	50.950	85.850	143.371	237.376
40	1.489	2.208	3.262	4.801	7.040	10.286	21.725	45.259	93.051	188.884	378.721	750.378	1,469.772

The factors in the table were generated using the following formula:
Future Value of $1 $= (1 + i)^n$

where:

i = annual interest rate

n = number of periods

Table D   Future Value of Annuity of $1

Future Value of Annuity of $1													
Periods	1%	2%	3%	4%	5%	6%	8%	10%	12%	14%	16%	18%	20%
1	1.000	1.000	1.000	1.000	1.000	1.000	1.000	1.000	1.000	1.000	1.000	1.000	1.000
2	2.010	2.020	2.030	2.040	2.050	2.060	2.080	2.100	2.120	2.140	2.160	2.180	2.200
3	3.030	3.060	3.091	3.122	3.153	3.184	3.246	3.310	3.374	3.440	3.506	3.572	3.640
4	4.060	4.122	4.184	4.246	4.310	4.375	4.506	4.641	4.779	4.921	5.066	5.215	5.368
5	5.101	5.204	5.309	5.416	5.526	5.637	5.867	6.105	6.353	6.610	6.877	7.154	7.442
6	6.152	6.308	6.468	6.633	6.802	6.975	7.336	7.716	8.115	8.536	8.977	9.442	9.930
7	7.214	7.434	7.662	7.898	8.142	8.394	8.923	9.487	10.089	10.730	11.414	12.142	12.916
8	8.286	8.583	8.892	9.214	9.549	9.897	10.637	11.436	12.300	13.233	14.240	15.327	16.499
9	9.369	9.755	10.159	10.583	11.027	11.491	12.488	13.579	14.776	16.085	17.519	19.086	20.799
10	10.462	10.950	11.464	12.006	12.578	13.181	14.487	15.937	17.549	19.337	21.321	23.521	25.959
11	11.567	12.169	12.808	13.486	14.207	14.972	16.645	18.531	20.655	23.045	25.733	28.755	32.150
12	12.683	13.412	14.192	15.026	15.917	16.870	18.977	21.384	24.133	27.271	30.850	34.931	39.581
13	13.809	14.680	15.618	16.627	17.713	18.882	21.495	24.523	28.029	32.089	36.786	42.219	48.497
14	14.947	15.974	17.086	18.292	19.599	21.015	24.215	27.975	32.393	37.581	43.672	50.818	59.196
15	16.097	17.293	18.599	20.024	21.579	23.276	27.152	31.772	37.280	43.842	51.660	60.965	72.035
20	22.019	24.297	26.870	29.778	33.066	36.786	45.762	57.275	72.052	91.025	115.380	146.630	186.690
25	28.243	32.030	36.459	41.646	47.727	54.865	73.106	98.347	133.330	181.870	249.210	342.600	471.980
30	34.785	40.568	47.575	56.085	66.439	79.058	113.280	164.490	241.330	356.790	530.310	790.950	1,181.900
40	48.886	60.402	75.401	95.026	120.800	154.760	259.060	442.590	767.090	1,342.000	2,360.800	4,163.200	7,343.900

The factors in the table were generated using the following formula:

Future Value of Annuity of $1 $= \dfrac{(1 + i)^n - 1}{i}$

where:

i = annual interest rate

n = number of periods

Appendix 9B

Using a TI-83, TI-83 Plus, TI-84, or TI-84 Plus Calculator to Perform Time Value of Money Calculations

Time Value of Money Calculations

USING A **TI-83, TI-83 PLUS, TI-84,** OR **TI-84 PLUS** CALCULATOR TO PERFORM TIME VALUE OF MONEY CALCULATIONS:

Steps to perform basic present value and future value calculations:

1. On the TI-83 Plus or TI-84 Plus: Press [APPS] *to show the applications menu* On the TI-83 or TI-84: Press [2nd] [X⁻¹] [ENTER] *to show the applications menu.*
2. Choose **Finance** *to see the finance applications menu.*
3. Choose **TVM solver** *to obtain the list of time value of money (TVM) variables:*
    > N = *number of periods (years)*
    > I% = *interest rate per year (**do not convert percentage to a decimal**)*
    > PV = *present value*
    > PMT = *amount of each annuity installment*
    > FV = *future value*
    > P/Y = *number of compounding periods per year (**leave setting at 1**)*
    > C/Y = *number of coupons per year (**leave setting at 1**)*
    > PMT: **End** or Begin *(leave setting on **End** to denote an ordinary annuity)*
4. **Enter the known variables** and **set all unknown variables to zero** (except P/Y and C/Y, which need to be left set at 1).
5. To compute the unknown variable, scroll to the line for the variable you want to solve and then press [ALPHA] [ENTER].
6. The answer will now appear on the calculator.
7. Press [2nd] [QUIT] *to exit the TVM solver when you are finished.* **If you would like to do more TVM calculations, you do not need to exit. Simply repeat Steps 4 and 5 using the new data.**

Comments:

i. The order in which you input the variables does not matter.
ii. The answer will be shown as a negative number unless you input the original cash flow data as a negative number. **Use the [(-)] key to enter a negative number, not the minus key; otherwise you will get an error message.** The calculator

continued . . .

follows a cash flow sign convention that assumes that all positive figures are cash inflows and all negative figures are cash outflows.

iii. The answers you get will vary slightly from those found using the PV and FV tables in Appendix A. Why? Because the PV and FV factors in the tables have been rounded to three digits.

Example 1: Future value of a lump sum

Let's use our lump-sum investment example from the text. Assume that you invest $10,000 for five years at an interest rate of 6%. Use the following procedures to finds its future value five years from now:

1. On the TI-83 Plus or TI-84 Plus: Press [APPS] *to show the applications menu.*

   On the TI-83 or TI-84: Press [2nd] [X⁻¹] [ENTER] *to show the applications menu.*

2. Choose Finance *to see the finance applications menu.*

3. Choose TVM solver *to obtain the list of time value of money (TVM) variables.*

4. Fill in the variables as follows:

   N = 5

   I% = 6

   PV = –10000 *(Be sure to use the negative number (-) key, not the minus sign.)*

   PMT = 0

   FV = 0

   P/Y = 1

   C/Y = 1

   PMT: **End** or Begin

5. To compute the unknown future value, scroll down to FV and press [ALPHA] [ENTER].

6. The answer will now appear as **FV = 13,382.26** (rounded).

If you forgot to enter the $10,000 principal as a negative number (in Step 4), the FV will be displayed as a negative.

Example 2: Future value of an annuity

Let's use the annuity investment example from the text. Assume that you invest $2,000 at the end of each year for five years. The investment earns 6% interest. Use the following procedures to finds the investment's future value five years from now:

1. On the TI-83 Plus or TI-84 Plus: Press [APPS] *to show the applications menu.*

   On the TI-83 or TI-84: Press [2nd] [X⁻¹] [ENTER] *to show the applications menu.*

2. Choose Finance *to see the finance applications menu.*

3. Choose TVM solver *to obtain the list of time value of money (TVM) variables.*

4. Fill in the variables as follows:

N = 5

I% = 6

PV = 0

PMT = –2000 *(Be sure to use the negative number (-) key, not the minus sign.)*

FV = 0

P/Y = 1

C/Y = 1

PMT: **End** or Begin

5. To compute the unknown future value, scroll down to FV and press [ALPHA] [ENTER].

6. The answer will now appear as **FV = 11,274.19 (rounded)**.

If you forgot to enter the $2,000 annuity as a negative number (in Step 4), the FV will be displayed as a negative.

Example 3: Present value of an annuity—Lottery Option #2

Let's use the lottery payout Option #2 from the text for our example. Option #2 was to receive $150,000 at the end of each year for the next ten years. The interest rate was assumed to be 8%. Use the following procedure to find the present value of this payout option:

1. On the TI-83 Plus or TI-84 Plus: Press [APPS] *to show the applications menu.*

   On the TI-83 or TI-84: Press [2nd] [X⁻¹] [ENTER] *to show the applications menu.*

2. Choose Finance *to see the finance applications menu.*

3. Choose TVM solver *to obtain the list of time value of money (TVM) variables.*

4. Fill in the variables as follows:

N = 10

I% = 8

PV = 0

PMT = –150000 *(Be sure to use the negative number (-) key, not the minus sign.)*

FV = 0

P/Y = 1

C/Y = 1

PMT: **End** or Begin

5. To compute the unknown future value, scroll down to PV and press [ALPHA] [ENTER].

6. The answer will now appear as **PV = 1,006,512.21 (rounded)**.

Had we not entered the annuity as a negative figure, the present value would have been shown as a negative.

Example 4: Present value of a lump sum—Lottery Option #3

Let's use the lottery payout Option #3 from the text as our example. Option #3 was to receive $2 million ten years from now. The interest rate was assumed to be 8%. Use the following procedure to find the present value of this payout option:

1. On the TI-83 Plus or TI-84 Plus: Press [APPS] *to show the applications menu.*

   On the TI-83 or TI-84: Press [2nd] [X⁻¹] [ENTER] *to show the applications menu.*

2. Choose Finance *to see the finance applications menu.*

3. Choose TVM solver *to obtain the list of time value of money (TVM) variables.*

4. Fill in the variables as follows:

   $N = 10$

   $I\% = 8$

   $PV = 0$

   $PMT = 0$

   $FV = -2000000$ *(Be sure to use the negative number (-) key, not the minus sign.)*

   $P/Y = 1$

   $C/Y = 1$

   PMT: **End** or Begin

5. To compute the unknown future value, scroll down to PV and press [ALPHA] [ENTER].

6. The answer will now appear as **PV = 926,386.98** (rounded).

Had we not entered the $2 million future cash flow as a negative, the present value would have been shown as a negative.

Technology
makes it simple

NPV Calculations

USING A TI-83, TI-83 PLUS, TI-84, OR TI-84 PLUS CALCULATOR TO PERFORM NPV CALCULATIONS

Steps to performing NPV calculations:

If you are currently in the TVM solver mode, exit by pressing [2nd] [Quit].

1. On the TI-83 Plus or TI-84 Plus: Press [APPS] *to show the applications menu.*

   On the TI-83 or TI-84: Press [2nd] [X⁻¹] [ENTER] *to show the applications menu.*

2. Choose **Finance** *to see the finance applications menu.*

3. Choose **npv** *to obtain the NPV prompt:* **npv(.**

4. Fill in the following information, paying close attention to using the correct symbols:

   npv (hurdle rate, initial investment*, {cash flow in year 1, cash flow in year 2, etc.})

   *the initial investment must be entered as a negative number

5. To compute the NPV, press [ENTER].

6. The answer will now appear on the calculator.

7. To exit the worksheet, press [CLEAR]. Alternatively, if you would like to change any of the assumptions for sensitivity analysis, you may press [2nd] [ENTER] to recall the formula, edit any of the values, and then recompute the new NPV by pressing [ENTER].

Note: If you would like to find just the present value (not the NPV) of a stream of unequal cash flows, use a zero (0) for the initial investment.

Example 1: NPV of Allegra's CD-player project—an annuity

Recall that the CD-player project required an investment of $1 million and was expected to generate equal net cash inflows of $305,450 each year for five years. The company's discount, or hurdle rate, was 14%.

1. On the TI-83 Plus or TI-84 Plus: Press [APPS] *to show the applications menu.*

   On the TI-83 or TI-84: Press [2nd] [X⁻¹] [ENTER] *to show the applications menu.*

2. Choose Finance *to see the finance applications menu.*

3. Choose npv *to obtain the NPV prompt:* **npv(.**

4. Fill in the following information, paying close attention to using the correct symbols:

   npv (14, –1000000, {305450, 305450, 305450, 305450, 305450}) *(Be sure to use the negative number (-) key, not the minus sign.)*

5. To compute the NPV, press [ENTER].

6. The answer will now appear on the calculator: **48,634.58** (rounded).

7. [CLEAR] the worksheet or recall it [2nd] [ENTER] for sensitivity analysis.

Example 2: NPV of Allegra's DVD project—unequal cash flows

Recall that the DVD project required an investment of $1 million and was expected to generate the unequal periodic cash inflows shown in Exhibit 9-14.

1. On the TI-83 Plus or TI-84 Plus: Press [APPS] *to show the applications menu.*

   On the TI-83 or TI-84: Press [2nd] [X⁻¹] [ENTER] *to show the applications menu.*

2. Choose Finance *to see the finance applications menu.*

3. Choose npv *to obtain the NPV prompt:* **npv(.**

4. Fill in the following information, paying close attention to using the correct symbols:

   npv (14, –1000000, {500000, 350000, 300000, 250000, 40000}) *(Be sure to use the negative number (-) key, not the minus sign.)*

5. To compute the NPV, press [ENTER].

6. The answer will now appear on the calculator: **79,196.40** (rounded).

7. [CLEAR] the worksheet or recall it [2nd] [ENTER] for sensitivity analysis.

Example 3: Investment with a residual value

If an investment has a residual value, simply add the residual value as an additional cash inflow in the year in which it is to be received. For example, assume as we did in Exhibit 9-12 that the CD project equipment will be worth $100,000 at the end of its five-year life. This represents an additional expected cash inflow to the company in Year 5, so we'll show the cash inflow in Year 5 to be $405,450 (= $305,450 + $100,000).

1. On the TI-83 Plus or TI-84 Plus: Press [APPS] *to show the applications menu.*

   On the TI-83 or TI-84: Press [2nd] [X⁻¹] [ENTER] *to show the applications menu.*

2. Choose Finance *to see the finance applications menu.*

3. Choose npv *to obtain the NPV prompt:* **npv(.**

4. Fill in the following information, paying close attention to using the correct symbols:

   npv (14, –1000000, {305450, 305450, 305450, 305450, 405450}) *(Be sure to use the negative number (-) key, not the minus sign.)*

5. To compute the NPV, press [ENTER].

6. The answer will now appear on the calculator: **100,571.45** (rounded).

7. [CLEAR] the worksheet or recall it [2nd] [ENTER] for sensitivity analysis.

Technology
makes it simple

IRR Calculations

USING A TI-83, TI-83 PLUS, TI-84, OR TI-84 PLUS CALCULATOR TO PERFORM IRR CALCULATIONS

The procedure for finding the IRR is virtually identical to the procedure used to find the NPV. The only differences are that we choose IRR rather than NPV from the Finance menu and we don't insert a given hurdle rate.

Steps to performing IRR calculations:

If you are currently in the TVM solver mode, exit by pressing [2nd] [Quit].

1. On the TI-83 Plus or TI-84 Plus: Press [APPS] *to show the applications menu.*

   On the TI-83 or TI-84: Press [2nd] [X⁻¹] [ENTER] *to show the applications menu.*

2. Choose **Finance** *to see the finance applications menu.*

3. Choose **irr** *to obtain the IRR prompt:* **irr(.**

4. Fill in the following information, paying close attention to using the correct symbols:

   irr (initial investment*, {cash flow in year 1, cash flow in year 2, etc.})

   *the initial investment must be entered as a negative number

5. To compute the IRR press [ENTER].

6. The answer will now appear on the calculator.

7. To exit the worksheet, press [CLEAR]. Alternatively, if you would like to change any of the assumptions for sensitivity analysis, you may press [2nd] [ENTER] to recall the formula, edit any of the values, and then recompute the new IRR by pressing [ENTER].

Example 1: IRR of Allegra's CD-player project—an annuity

Recall that the CD-player project required an investment of $1 million and was expected to generate equal net cash inflows of $305,450 each year for five years. Use the following procedures to find the investment's IRR:

1. On the TI-83 Plus or TI-84 Plus: Press [APPS] *to show the applications menu.*

    On the TI-83 or TI-84: Press [2nd] [X⁻¹] [ENTER] *to show the applications menu.*

2. Choose Finance *to see the finance applications menu.*

3. Choose irr *to obtain the IRR prompt:* **irr(.**

4. Fill in the following information, paying close attention to using the correct symbols:

    irr (–1000000, {305450, 305450, 305450, 305450, 305450}) *(Be sure to use the negative number (-) key, not the minus sign.)*

5. To compute the IRR, press [ENTER].

6. The answer will now appear on the calculator: **16.01** (rounded).

7. [CLEAR] the worksheet or recall it [2nd] [ENTER] for sensitivity analysis.

Example 2: IRR of Allegra's DVD project—unequal cash flows

Recall that the DVD project required an investment of $1 million and was expected to generate the unequal periodic cash inflows shown in Exhibit 9-14. Use the following procedures to find the investment's IRR:

1. On the TI-83 Plus or TI-84 Plus: Press [APPS] *to show the applications menu.*

    On the TI-83 or TI-84: Press [2nd] [X⁻¹] [ENTER] *to show the applications menu.*

2. Choose Finance *to see the finance applications menu.*

3. Choose irr *to obtain the IRR prompt:* **irr(.**

4. Fill in the following information, paying close attention to using the correct symbols:

    irr (–1000000, {500000, 350000, 300000, 250000, 40000}) *(Be sure to use the negative number (-) key, not the minus sign.)*

5. To compute the IRR, press [ENTER].

6. The answer will now appear on the calculator: **18.23** (rounded).

7. [CLEAR] the worksheet or recall it [2nd] [ENTER] for sensitivity analysis.

Example 3: Investment with a residual value

If an investment has a residual value, simply add the residual value as an additional cash inflow in the year in which it is to be received. For example, assume as we did in Exhibit 9-12 that the CD project equipment will be worth $100,000 at the end of its five-year life. This represents an additional expected cash inflow to the company in Year 5, so we'll show the cash inflow in Year 5 to be $405,450 (= $305,450 + $100,000).

1. On the TI-83 Plus or TI-84 Plus: Press [APPS] *to show the applications menu.*

    On the TI-83 or TI-84: Press [2nd] [X⁻¹] [ENTER] *to show the applications menu.*

continued . . .

2. Choose Finance *to see the finance applications menu.*

3. Choose irr *to obtain the IRR prompt:* ***irr(.***

4. Fill in the following information, paying close attention to using the correct symbols:

   irr (–1000000, {305450, 305450, 305450, 305450, 405450}) *(Be sure to use the negative number (-) key, not the minus sign.)*

5. To compute the IRR, press [ENTER].

6. The answer will now appear on the calculator: **17.95** (rounded).

7. [CLEAR] the worksheet or recall it [2nd] [ENTER] for sensitivity analysis.

Using the BAII Plus Calculator to Perform Time Value of Money Calculations

Technology
makes it simple

USING A TEXAS INSTRUMENTS BAII PLUS CALCULATOR TO PERFORM TIME VALUE OF MONEY CALCULATIONS

Before you start, you need to make a change to a factory-installed setting. The BAII Plus comes from the factory assuming monthly, not yearly, compounding of interest. To reset the calculator, press [2nd] and then [I/Y]. Enter **1** (in place of the factory setting P/Y = 12) and press [ENTER]. Your calculator will now assume yearly compounding of interest. Press [2nd] [QUIT] to return to a blank screen.

Steps to perform basic present value and future value calculations:

1. Press [2nd] [QUIT] *to return to standard-calculator mode.*
2. Press [2nd] [CLR TVM] *to clear the TVM (time value of money) worksheet.*
3. To enter the TVM value, **key in a value** and **press the associated key**:

    [N] *to enter number of periods*

    [I/Y] *to enter interest rate per year (do not convert percentage to decimals)*

    [PV] *to enter the present value*

    [FV] *to enter the future value*

    [PMT] *to enter the amount of each annual cash installment of an annuity*

4. To compute the unknown TVM value, press [CPT] and then press the key associated with the missing value (e.g., press FV if you are trying to find the future value).
5. The answer will now appear on the calculator.

Comments:

i. The order in which you input the variables does not matter.
ii. The answer will be shown as a negative number unless you input the original cash flow data as a negative number. **Use the [+/−] key to change signs after you have input the number.** The calculator follows a cash flow sign convention that assumes that all positive figures are cash inflows and all negative figures are cash outflows.
iii. The answers you get will vary slightly from those found using the PV and FV factors found in Appendix A. Why? Because the PV and FV factors in the tables have been rounded to the nearest three digits, whereas the calculators do not truncate the PV and FV factors.
iv. Free, short online video tutorials for the use of this calculator can be found at atomiclearning.com/ti_ba2.

Example 1: Future value of a lump sum

Let's use our lump-sum investment example from the text. Assume that you invest $10,000 for five years at an interest rate of 6%. Use the following procedures to finds its future value five years from now:

1. Press [2nd] [QUIT] *to return to standard-calculator mode.*

2. Press [2nd] [CLR TVM] *to clear the TVM worksheet.*

3. Enter −10,000; then press [PV] *to enter the current cash outflow for the investment.*

   Enter 5; then press [N] *to enter the number of periods (years).*

   Enter 6; then press [I/Y] *to enter the interest rate per year.*

4. Press [CPT] [FV] *to find the future value.*

5. The answer appears as **FV = 13,382.26** (rounded).

If you forgot to enter 10,000 as a negative number in Step 3 (a cash outflow for the investment), the FV will be displayed as a negative.

Example 2: Future value of an annuity

Let's use the annuity investment example from the text. Assume that you invest $2,000 at the end of each year for five years. The investment earns 6% interest. Use the following procedures to find the investment's future value five years from now:

1. Press [2nd] [QUIT] *to return to standard-calculator mode.*

2. Press [2nd] [CLR TVM] *to clear the TVM worksheet.*

3. Enter −2,000; then press [PMT] *to enter the amount of each annuity installment.*

   Enter 5; then press [N] *to enter the number of periods (years).*

   Enter 6; then press [I/Y] *to enter the interest rate per year.*

4. Press [CPT] [FV] *to find the future value.*

5. The answer appears as **FV = 11,274.19** (rounded).

If you forgot to input the investment as a cash outflow, the FV will appear as a negative number.

Example 3: Present value of an annuity—Lottery Option #2

Let's use the lottery payout Option #2 from the text for our example. The lottery payout Option #2 was to receive $150,000 at the end of each year for the next ten years. The interest rate was assumed to be 8%. Use the following procedures to find the present value of the lottery winnings:

1. Press [2nd] [QUIT] *to return to standard-calculator mode.*

2. Press [2nd] [CLR TVM] *to clear the TVM worksheet.*

3. Enter −150,000; then press [PMT] *to enter the amount of each annuity installment.*

   Enter 10; then press [N] *to enter the number of periods (years).*

   Enter 8; then press [I/Y] *to enter the interest rate per year.*

4. Press [CPT] [PV] *to find the present value.*

5. The answer appears as **PV = 1,006,512.21**

Had we not entered the annuity as a negative figure, the present value would have been shown as a negative figure to indicate that one would normally have to pay $1,006,512 to receive the ten future installments of $150,000.

Example 4: Present value of a lump sum—Lottery Option #3

Let's use the lottery payout Option #3 from the text as our example. The lottery payout Option #3 was to receive $2 million ten years from now. The interest rate was assumed to be 8%. Use the following procedures to find the present value of the lottery winnings:

1. Press [2nd] [QUIT] *to return to standard-calculator mode.*

2. Press [2nd] [CLR TVM] *to clear the TVM worksheet.*

3. Enter –2,000,000; then press [FV] *to enter the future value of the cash flow.*

   Enter 10; then press [N] *to enter the number of periods (years).*

   Enter 8; then press [I/Y] *to enter the interest rate per year.*

4. Press [CPT] [PV] *to find the present value.*

5. The answer appears as **PV = 926,386.98** (rounded).

Again, the present value is positive because we showed the future cash flow as negative.

Technology
makes it simple

NPV Calculations

Using a Texas Instruments BAII Plus calculator to perform NPV calculations

1. Press [CF] [2nd] [CLR Work] *to clear the worksheet of all prior information.*
2. Press [CF], enter the **investment's initial cost as a negative number**, and press [ENTER] *to enter the cost of the investment as a cash* **outflow (CFo).**
3. Press [↓] *to scroll down to the net cash inflow (C01) information.*
4. Enter the **net cash inflow that will occur in the first year**; then press [ENTER] *to enter the first net cash inflow from the investment.*
5. Press [↓] *to scroll down to the frequency (F01) of this cash flow.*
6. Enter the **number of years** that the net cash inflow (CO1 that you entered in Step 4) will occur; then press [ENTER] *to enter the number of years the net cash inflow will occur.*
7. *Repeat Steps 3 through 6* **only if** *you are finding the NPV of an investment with unequal periodic net cash inflows.*
8. Press [NPV].
9. Enter the interest rate at the prompt I =; then press [ENTER].
10. Press [↓] *to scroll down to the NPV prompt.*
11. Press [CPT] *to compute the NPV.*
12. The answer will appear momentarily.

Example 1: NPV of Allegra's CD-player project—an annuity

Recall that the CD-player project required an investment of $1 million and was expected to generate equal net cash inflows of $305,450 each year for five years. The company's discount, or hurdle rate, is 14%. Use the following procedures to find the investment's NPV:

1. Press [CF] [2nd] [CLR Work] *to clear the worksheet of all prior information.*

2. Press [CF], enter −1,000,000, and press [ENTER] *to enter the cost of the investment as a cash outflow.*

3. Press [↓] *to scroll down to the net cash inflow (C01) information.*

4. Enter 305,450; then press [ENTER] *to enter the first net cash inflow from the investment.*

5. Press [↓] *to scroll down to the frequency (F01) information.*

6. Enter 5; then press [ENTER] *to enter the number of years the first net cash inflow will occur.*

7. *Since the CD-player project is an annuity, all information has been entered and Steps 3 through 6 do not need to be repeated.*

8. Press [NPV].

9. Enter the interest rate at the prompt I = 14; then press [ENTER].

10. Press [↓] *to scroll down to the NPV prompt.*

11. Press [CPT] *to compute the NPV.*

12. The answer will appear as **NPV = 48,634.58** (rounded).

Example 2: NPV of Allegra's DVD project—unequal cash flows

Recall that the DVD project required an investment of $1 million and was expected to generate the unequal periodic cash inflows shown in Exhibit 9-14. The company's discount, or hurdle rate, is 14%. Use the following procedures to find the investment's NPV:

1. Press [CF] [2nd] [CLR Work] *to clear the worksheet of all prior information.*

2. Press [CF], enter −1,000,000, and press [ENTER] *to enter the cost of the investment as a cash outflow.*

3. Press [↓] *to scroll down to the net cash inflow (C01) information.*

4. Enter 500,000; then press [ENTER] *to enter the first net cash inflow from the investment.*

5. Press [↓] *to scroll down to the frequency (F01) information.*

6. Leave as **1** *to show that the $500,000 cash inflow will occur only once.*

7. *Since the DVD project will generate different net cash inflows each year, we must repeat Steps 3 through 6 separately for each year.*

For Year 2:

3. Press [↓] *to scroll down to the cash inflow (C02) information.*

4. Enter 350,000; *then press [ENTER] to enter the cash inflow in Year 2.*

5. Press [↓] *to scroll down to the frequency (F02) information.*

6. Leave as **1** *to show that the $350,000 will be received only once.*

For Year 3:

3. Press [↓] *to scroll down to the cash inflow (C03) information.*
4. Enter 300,000; *then press [ENTER] to enter the cash inflow in Year 3.*
5. Press [↓] *to scroll down to the frequency (F03) information.*
6. Leave as **1** *to show that the $300,000 will be received only once.*

For Year 4:

3. Press [↓] *to scroll down to the cash inflow (C04) information.*
4. Enter 250,000; *then press [ENTER] to enter the cash inflow in Year 4.*
5. Press [↓] *to scroll down to the frequency (F04) information.*
6. Leave as **1** *to show that the $250,000 will be received only once.*

For Year 5:

3. Press [↓] *to scroll down to the cash inflow (C05) information.*
4. Enter 40,000; *then press [ENTER] to enter the cash inflow in Year 5.*
5. Press [↓] *to scroll down to the frequency (F05) information.*
6. Leave as **1** *to show that the $40,000 will be received only once.*

8. Press [NPV].
9. Enter the interest rate at the prompt I = 14; then press [ENTER].
10. Press [↓] *to scroll down to the NPV prompt.*
11. Press [CPT] *to compute the NPV.*
12. The answer will appear as **NPV = 79,196.40** (rounded).

Example 3: Investment with a residual value

If an investment has a residual value, simply add the residual value as an additional cash inflow in the year in which it is to be received. For example, assume as we did in Exhibit 9-12 that the CD project equipment will be worth $100,000 at the end of its five-year life. This represents an additional expected cash inflow to the company in Year 5 so we'll show the cash inflow in Year 5 to be $405,450 (= $305,450 + $100,000) whereas the cash inflows in Years 1 through 4 are still $305,450. Because the yearly cash inflows are no longer equal, we must enter each year's cash inflows separately:

1. Press [CF] [2nd] [CLR Work] *to clear the worksheet of all prior information.*
2. Press [CF], enter –1,000,000, and press [ENTER] *to enter the cost of the investment as a cash outflow.*
3. Press [↓] *to scroll down to the net cash inflow (C01) information.*
4. Enter 305,450; *then press [ENTER] to enter the first net cash inflow from the investment.*
5. Press [↓] *to scroll down to the frequency (F01) information.*
6. Leave as **1** *to show that the $305,450 cash inflow will occur once in year 1.*

continued . . .

7. *Since the CD project will generate different net cash inflows each year, we must repeat Steps 3 through 6 separately for each year:*

For Year 2:

    3. Press [↓] *to scroll down to the cash inflow (C02) information.*

    4. Enter 305,450; *then press [ENTER] to enter the cash inflow in Year 2.*

    5. Press [↓] *to scroll down to the frequency (F02) information.*

    6. Leave as **1** *to show that the $305,450 will occur once in Year 2.*

For Year 3:

    3. Press [↓] *to scroll down to the cash inflow (C03) information.*

    4. Enter 305,450; *then press [ENTER] to enter the cash inflow in Year 3.*

    5. Press [↓] *to scroll down to the frequency (F03) information.*

    6. Leave as **1** *to show that the $305,450 will occur once in Year 3.*

For Year 4:

    3. Press [↓] *to scroll down to the cash inflow (C04) information.*

    4. Enter 305,450; *then press [ENTER] to enter the cash inflow in Year 4.*

    5. Press [↓] *to scroll down to the frequency (F04) information.*

    6. Leave as **1** *to show that the $305,450 will occur once in Year 4.*

For Year 5:

    3. Press [↓] *to scroll down to the cash inflow (C05) information.*

    4. Enter 405,450; *then press [ENTER] to enter the cash inflow in Year 5.*

    5. Press [↓] *to scroll down to the frequency (F05) information.*

    6. Leave as **1** *to show that the $405,450 will occur once in Year 5.*

  8. Press [NPV].

  9. Enter the interest rate at the prompt I = 14; then press [ENTER].

 10. Press [↓] *to scroll down to the NPV prompt.*

 11. Press [CPT] *to compute the NPV.*

 12. The answer will appear as **NPV = 100,571.45** (rounded).

Technology
makes it simple

IRR Calculations

USING A TEXAS INSTRUMENTS BAII PLUS CALCULATOR TO PERFORM IRR CALCULATIONS

The procedure for finding the IRR is virtually identical to the procedure used to find the NPV. The only difference is that in Step 8, we press the [IRR] key rather than the [NPV] key and don't enter a discount rate.

1. Press [CF] [2nd] [CLR Work] *to clear the worksheet of all prior information.*

   You do not need to clear the worksheet if you want to find the IRR for a set of data you have already entered for an NPV calculation. Just reuse the data already stored in the worksheet.

2. Press [CF], enter the **investment's initial cost as a negative number**, and press [ENTER] *to enter the cost of the investment as a cash* **outflow (CFo).**

3. Press [↓] *to scroll down to the net cash inflow (C01) information.*

4. Enter the **net cash inflow that will occur in the first year**; then press [ENTER] *to enter the first net cash inflow from the investment.*

5. Press [↓] *to scroll down to the frequency (F01) information.*

6. Enter the **number of years** that the net cash inflow (CO1 that you entered in Step 4) will occur; then press [ENTER] *to enter the number of years the net cash inflow will occur.*

7. *Repeat Steps 3 through 6* **only if** *you are finding the IRR of an investment with unequal periodic net cash inflows.*

8. Press [IRR]; then press [CPT] *to compute the IRR.*

9. The answer will appear momentarily.

Example 1: IRR of Allegra's CD-player project—an annuity

Recall that the CD-player project required an investment of $1 million and was expected to generate equal net cash inflows of $305,450 each year for five years. Use the following procedures to find the investment's IRR:

1. Press [CF] [2nd] [CLR Work] *to clear the worksheet unless you want to reuse the information already stored in the worksheet.*

2. Press [CF], enter –1,000,000, and press [ENTER] *to enter the cost of the investment as a cash outflow.*

3. Press [↓] *to scroll down to the net cash inflow (C01) information.*

4. Enter 305,450; then press [ENTER] *to enter the first net cash inflow from the investment.*

5. Press [↓] *to scroll down to the frequency (F01) information.*

6. Enter 5; then press [ENTER] *to enter the number of years the first net cash inflow will occur.*

7. *Since the CD-player project is an annuity, all information has been entered and Steps 3 through 6 do not need to be repeated.*

8. Press [IRR]; then press [CPT] *to compute the IRR.*

9. The answer appears as **IRR = 16.01** (rounded).

Example 2: IRR of Allegra's DVD project—unequal cash flows

Recall that the DVD project required an investment of $1 million and was expected to generate the unequal periodic cash inflows shown in Exhibit 9-14. Use the following procedures to find the investment's IRR:

1. Press [CF] [2nd] [CLR Work] *to clear the worksheet unless you want to reuse the information already stored in the worksheet.*

2. Press [CF], enter –1,000,000, and press [ENTER] *to enter the cost of the investment as a cash outflow.*

3. Press [↓] *to scroll down to the net cash inflow (C01) information.*

4. Enter 500,000; then press [ENTER] *to enter the first net cash inflow from the investment.*

continued . . .

5. Press [↓] *to scroll down to the frequency (F01) information.*

6. Enter **1**; then press [ENTER] *to show that the $500,000 cash inflow will occur only once.*

7. *Since the DVD project will generate different net cash inflows each year, we must repeat Steps 3 through 6 separately for each year.*

For Year 2:

3. Press [↓] *to scroll down to the cash inflow (C02) information.*

4. Enter 350,000; *then press [ENTER] to enter the cash inflow in Year 2.*

5. Press [↓] *to scroll down to the frequency (F02) information.*

6. Leave as **1** *to show that the $350,000 will be received only once.*

For Year 3:

3. Press [↓] *to scroll down to the cash inflow (C03) information.*

4. Enter 300,000; *then press [ENTER] to enter the cash inflow in Year 3.*

5. Press [↓] *to scroll down to the frequency (F03) information.*

6. Leave as **1** *to show that the $300,000 will be received only once.*

For Year 4:

3. Press [↓] *to scroll down to the cash inflow (C04) information.*

4. Enter 250,000; *then press [ENTER] to enter the cash inflow in Year 4.*

5. Press [↓] *to scroll down to the frequency (F04) information.*

6. Leave as **1** *to show that the $250,000 will be received only once.*

For Year 5:

3. Press [↓] *to scroll down to the cash inflow (C05) information.*

4. Enter 40,000; *then press [ENTER] to enter the cash inflow in Year 5.*

5. Press [↓] *to scroll down to the frequency (F05) information.*

6. Leave as **1** *to show that the $40,000 will be received only once.*

8. Press [IRR]; then press [CPT] *to compute the IRR.*

9. The answer appears as **IRR = 18.23** (rounded).

Example 3: Investment with a residual value

Use almost the same procedures as we did for finding the NPV. Simply add the residual value as an additional cash inflow in the year in which it is to be received. For example, assume as we did in Exhibit 9-12 that the CD project equipment will be worth $100,000 at the end of its five-year life. This represents an additional expected cash inflow to the company in Year 5, so we'll show the cash inflow in Year 5 to be $405,450 (= $305,450 + $100,000), whereas the cash inflows in Years 1 through 4 are still $305,450. Because the yearly cash inflows are no longer equal, we must enter each year's cash inflows separately. After completing Steps 1–7:

8. Press [IRR]; then press [CPT] *to compute the IRR.*

9. The answer appears as **IRR = 17.95** (rounded).

10

The Master Budget and Responsibility Accounting

ver 20% of sales of books, music, and electronics occur online. If you're one of the millions of customers worldwide who points and clicks to buy your books and CDs on Amazon.com, then you're part of Amazon.com's strategy to "get big fast." This strategy increased Amazon.com's sales, but at a cost. Spending was out of control. There was no budget, and managers spared no expense to help the company grow. As a result, Amazon.com lost more than $860 *million* in 2000.

Founder and CEO Jeff Bezos had to turn this sea of red ink into income. Bezos set up a *budget* for Amazon.com's plan of action. Now, each division budgets both sales and expenses. In weekly meetings, managers compare actual results to the budget, which helps them correct problems quickly.

The result? Between 2000 and 2002, Amazon.com's sales increased 42%. With such an increase in sales, you'd expect expenses also to increase. But Amazon.com's new budget helped managers *cut* operating expenses. How did the company decrease expenses when sales were increasing so dramatically? The budget helped Amazon.com reduce order-filling and distribution costs by 5%. Switching to lower-cost computer systems reduced "technical and content" operating costs by 20%. The result? Amazon.com reported its first-ever income from operations in 2002. By 2004, income from operations had risen to over $588 million.

Sources: Katrina Brooker, "Beautiful Dreamer," *Fortune*, December 18, 2000, pp. 234–239; Fred Vogelstein, "Bezos," *Fortune*, September 2, 2002, pp. 186–187; Fred Vogelstein, "What Went Right 2002," *Fortune*, December 30, 2002, p. 166; Nick Wingfield, "Survival Strategy: Amazon Takes Page from Wal-Mart to Prosper on Web," *Wall Street Journal*, November 22, 2002, p. A1; Fred Vogelstein, "Mighty Amazon," *Fortune*, May 26, 2003, pp. 60–74. ■

Learning Objectives

1 Learn why managers use budgets

2 Prepare an operating budget

3 Prepare a financial budget

4 Use sensitivity analysis in budgeting

5 Prepare performance reports for responsibility centers

Perhaps, like Amazon.com, you've prepared a budget to ensure that you have enough cash to pay your expenses. The budget forces you to plan. If your budgeted cash inflow falls short of expenses, you can do one or both of the following:

- Increase your cash inflow (by taking on a job or a student loan).
- Cut your expenses.

In addition to planning, your personal budget can help you control expenses. To stay within your grocery budget, you may buy macaroni and cheese instead of shrimp. At the end of the month, if your bank balance is less than expected, you can compare your actual cash inflows and expenses to your budget to see why. You need to know whether cash inflows are lower than expected or expenses are higher than expected to know what corrective action to take.

As Amazon.com learned, it's easy for spending to get out of control if you don't have a budget. That's why everyone, from individuals like you to complex international organizations like Amazon.com, uses budgets. Careful budgeting helps both individuals and businesses stay out of trouble by reducing the risk that they will spend more than they earn.

As you'll see throughout this chapter, knowing how costs behave continues to be important in forming budgets. Total fixed costs will not change as volume changes within the relevant range. However, total variable costs must be adjusted when sales volume is expected to fluctuate.

Why Managers Use Budgets

Let's continue our study of budgets by moving from your personal budget to see how a small service business develops a simple budget. Assume that you begin an online service that provides travel itineraries for leisure travelers. You want to earn $550 a month to help with your college expenses. You expect to sell 20 itineraries per month at a price of $30 each. Over the past six months, you paid your Internet service provider an average of $18 a month and you spent an additional $20 per month on reference materials. You expect these monthly costs to remain about the same. These are your monthly fixed costs. Finally, you spend 5% of your sales revenues for banner ads on other travel Web sites. Because advertising costs fluctuate with sales revenue, these costs are variable.

1 Learn why managers use budgets

Exhibit 10-1 shows how to compute budgeted revenues and then subtract budgeted expenses to arrive at budgeted operating income.

EXHIBIT 10-1   **Service Company Budget**

CUSTOM TRAVEL ITINERARIES
Budget for May 2009

Budgeted sales revenue (20 × $30)		$600
Less budgeted expenses:		
Internet access expense	$18	
Reference materials expense	20	
Advertising expense (5% × $600)	30	
Total expenses		68
Budgeted operating income		$532

If business goes according to plan, you will not meet your $550 per month operating income goal. You will have to increase revenue (perhaps through word-of-mouth advertising) or cut expenses (perhaps by finding a less-expensive Internet access provider).

Using Budgets to Plan and Control

Large international for-profit companies such as Amazon.com and nonprofit organizations such as Habitat for Humanity use budgets for the same reasons you do in your personal life or in your small business—to plan and control actions and the related revenues and expenses. Exhibit 10-2 shows how managers use budgets in fulfilling their major responsibilities. First, they develop strategies—overall business goals like Amazon.com's goal to expand its international operations or Gateway's goal to be a value leader in the personal computer market while diversifying into other markets. Then, companies plan and budget for specific actions to achieve those goals. The next step is to act. For example, Amazon.com recently planned for and then added the Marketplace auction feature to its Web sites for the United Kingdom, Germany, and Japan. And Gateway is leaning on its suppliers to cut costs, while at the same time it is pumping out new products such as plasma TVs and audio and video gear.

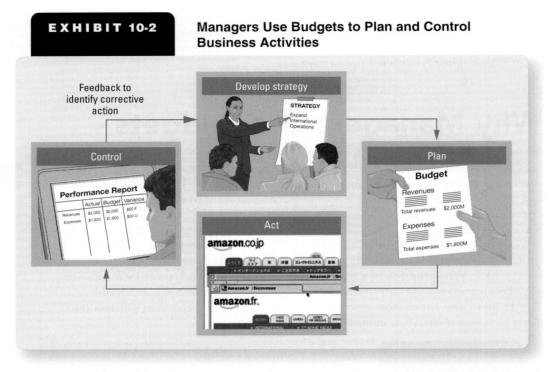

EXHIBIT 10-2   Managers Use Budgets to Plan and Control Business Activities

After acting, managers compare actual results to the budget. This feedback allows them to determine what, if any, corrective action to take. If Amazon.com spent more than expected to add the Marketplace to its international Web sites, managers must cut other costs or increase revenues. These decisions affect the company's future strategies and plans.

Amazon.com has a number of budgets. Each manager develops a budget for his or her division. Software then "rolls up" the division budgets to create an organization-wide budget for the company as a whole. Managers also prepare long-term and short-term budgets. Boeing's long-term budget forecasts demand for planes for the next 20 years.

However, most companies (including Boeing) budget their cash flows monthly, weekly, and even daily to ensure that they have enough cash. They also budget revenues and expenses—and operating income—for months, quarters, and years. This chapter focuses on short-term budgets of one year or less. Chapter 9 explained how companies budget for major capital expenditures on property, plant, and equipment.

Benefits of Budgeting

Exhibit 10-3 summarizes three key benefits of budgeting. Budgeting forces managers to plan, promotes coordination and communication, and provides a benchmark for evaluating actual performance.

Planning

Exhibit 10-1 shows that your expected income from the online travel itinerary business falls short of the target. The sooner you learn of the expected shortfall, the more time you have to plan how to increase revenues or cut expenses. The better your plan and the more time you have to act on the plan, the more likely you will find a way to meet your target. Amazon.com's budget required that managers plan the expansion of the Web sites tailored for customers in Germany, France, and Japan.

| **EXHIBIT 10-3** | **Benefits of Budgeting** |

Budgets force managers to plan.

Budgets promote coordination and communication.

Budgets provide a benchmark that motivates employees and helps managers evaluate performance.

Coordination and Communication

The master budget coordinates a company's activities. It forces managers to consider relations among operations across the entire value chain. For example, Amazon.com stimulates sales by offering free shipping on orders over a specified dollar amount. The budget encourages managers to ensure that the extra profits from increased sales outweigh the revenue lost from not charging for shipping.

Budgets also communicate a consistent set of plans throughout the company. For example, the initial Amazon.com budget communicated the message that all employees should help control costs.

Benchmarking

Budgets provide a benchmark that motivates employees and helps managers evaluate performance. In most companies, part of the manager's performance evaluation depends on how actual results compare to the budget. So, for example, the budgeted expenses for international expansion encourage Amazon.com's employees to increase the efficiency of international warehousing operations and to find less-expensive technology to support the Web sites.

Let's return to your online travel business. Suppose that comparing actual results to the budget in Exhibit 10-1 leads to the performance report in Exhibit 10-4.

| **EXHIBIT 10-4** | **Summary Performance Report** |

	Actual	**Budget**	**Variance (Actual – Budget)**
Sales revenue	$550	$600	$(50)
Less: Total expenses	90	68	(22)
Net income	$460	$532	$(72)

This report should prompt you to investigate why actual sales are $50 less than budgeted ($550 − $600). There are three possibilities:

1. The budget was unrealistic.

2. You did a poor selling job.

3. Uncontrollable factors (such as a sluggish economy) reduced sales.

All three may have contributed to the poor results.

You also want to know why expenses are $22 higher than expected ($90 − $68). Did your Internet service provider increase rates? Did you have to buy more reference materials than planned? Did you spend more than 5% of your revenue on Web banner ads? You need to know the answers to these kinds of questions to decide how to get your business back on track.

Preparing the Master Budget

Now that you know *why* managers go to the trouble of developing budgets, let's consider the steps they take to prepare a budget.

Components of the Master Budget

The **master budget** is the set of budgeted financial statements and supporting schedules for the entire organization. Appendix 10A briefly discusses the similarities and differences between the master budgets for merchandising companies, service companies, and manufacturers. Exhibit 10-5 shows the order in which managers prepare the components of the master budget for a merchandiser such as Amazon.com.

EXHIBIT 10-5   **Master Budget for a Merchandising Company**

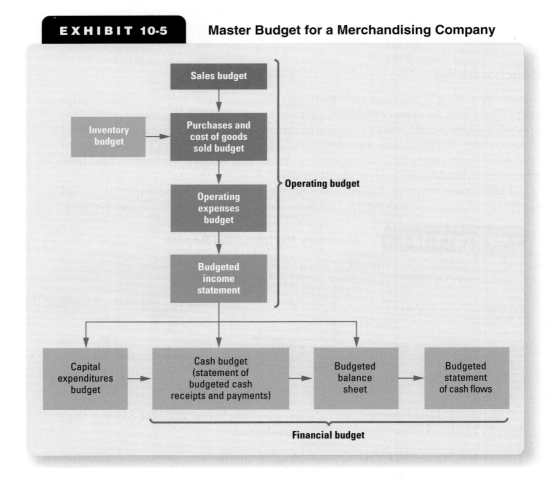

The exhibit shows that the master budget includes three types of budgets:

1. The operating budget
2. The capital expenditures budget
3. The financial budget

Let's consider each in turn.

The first component of the **operating budget** is the sales budget, the cornerstone of the master budget. Why? Because sales affect most other components of the master budget. After projecting sales revenue, cost of goods sold, and operating expenses, management prepares the end result of the operating budget: the budgeted income statement that projects operating income for the period.

The second type of budget is the **capital expenditures budget**. This budget presents the company's plan for purchasing property, plant, equipment, and other long-term assets. Chapter 9 discussed how companies analyze and budget for capital expenditures.

The third type of budget is the **financial budget**. The financial budget has three components:

- Cash budget
- Budgeted balance sheet
- Budgeted statement of cash flows

The cash budget, which projects cash inflows and outflows, feeds into the budgeted period-end balance sheet, which, in turn, feeds into the budgeted statement of cash flows. These budgeted financial statements look like ordinary statements. The only difference is that they list budgeted (projected) rather than actual amounts.

Data Set for Whitewater Sporting Goods' Master Budget

We'll use Whitewater Sporting Goods Store No. 18 to see how managers prepare operating and financial budgets. These budgets are normally prepared for a full 12-month period. However, to simplify, we'll present the budgets over a four-month period. We'll refer to this Data Set by item number as we create the operating and financial budgets, so you may want to bookmark this page.

1. **You manage Whitewater Sporting Goods Store No. 18, which carries a complete line of outdoor recreation gear.** You are to prepare the store's master budget for April, May, June, and July, the main selling season. The division manager and the head of the accounting department will arrive from headquarters next week to review the budget with you.

2. **Your store's budgeted balance sheet at March 31, 2009, appears in Exhibit 10-6.**

3. **Sales in March were budgeted at $40,000.** The sales force predicts these future monthly sales:

April	$50,000
May	80,000
June	60,000
July	50,000

EXHIBIT 10-6   **Balance Sheet**

WHITEWATER SPORTING GOODS STORE NO. 18
Budgeted Balance Sheet
March 31, 2009

Assets		Liabilities	
Current assets:		**Current liabilities:**	
Cash	$ 15,000	Accounts payable	$ 16,800
Accounts receivable	16,000	Salary and commissions	
Inventory...............................	48,000	payable	4,250
Prepaid insurance	1,800	Total liabilities	21,050
Total current assets	80,800		
Plant assets:		**Owners' Equity**	
Equipment and fixtures	32,000	Owners' equity..............................	78,950
Accumulated depreciation	(12,800)		
Total plant assets	19,200	Total liabilities and owners'	
Total assets.....................................	$100,000	equity	$100,000

4. **Cash collections follow sales because some sales are made on account.** Sales are 60% cash and 40% credit. Whitewater collects all credit sales the month *after* the sale. The $16,000 of budgeted accounts receivable at March 31 arose from credit sales in March (40% of $40,000). Uncollectible accounts are immaterial.

5. **Whitewater wants to maintain inventory at a level equal to $20,000 plus 80% of the budgeted cost of goods sold for the following month.** Whitewater prices its product to earn a 30% gross profit on sales revenue. This means that cost of goods sold averages 70% of sales revenue. Therefore, we compute inventory on March 31 as follows:

$$\text{March 31 inventory} = \$20,000 + 0.80 \text{ (cost of goods sold for next month)}$$
$$= \$20,000 + 0.80 \times (0.70 \times \text{April sales of } \$50,000)$$
$$= \$20,000 + (0.80 \times \$35,000)$$
$$= \$20,000 + \$28,000$$
$$= \$48,000$$

See how this agrees with the March 31 inventory shown in Exhibit 10-6. The same procedure is used to calculate budgeted ending inventory every month. Budgeted ending inventory on July 31 is $42,400 (calculated from data not given).

Whitewater *pays* for inventory as follows: 50% during the month of purchase and 50% during the next month. Accounts payable consists of inventory purchases only. Budgeted March purchases were $33,600, so budgeted accounts payable at the end of March totals $16,800 ($33,600 × 0.50).

6. **Monthly payroll has two parts: a salary of $2,500 plus sales commissions equal to 15% of sales.** This is a mixed cost, with both a fixed and variable component. The company pays half this amount during the month and half early the following month. Therefore, at the end of each month, Whitewater reports salary and commissions payable equal to half the month's payroll. The $4,250 liability on the March 31 budgeted balance sheet is half the March payroll of $8,500:

$$\text{March payroll} = \text{Salary of } \$2,500 + \text{Sales commissions of } \$6,000 \ (0.15 \times \$40,000)$$
$$= \$8,500$$

$$\text{March 31 salary and commissions payable} = 0.50 \times \$8,500 = \$4,250$$

7. **Other monthly expenses are as follows:**

Rent expense (fixed cost)............................	$2,000, paid as incurred
Depreciation expense, including truck (fixed cost).....................................	500
Insurance expense (fixed cost).................	200 expiration of prepaid amount
Miscellaneous expenses (variable cost)...	5% of sales, paid as incurred

8. **Whitewater plans to purchase a used delivery truck in April for $3,000 cash.** This information will be recorded on the capital expenditures budget.

9. **Whitewater requires each store to maintain a minimum cash balance of $10,000 at the end of each month.** The store can borrow money on six-month notes payable of $1,000 each at an annual interest rate of 12%. Management borrows no more than the amount needed to maintain the $10,000 minimum. Total interest expense will vary as the amount of borrowing varies from month to month. Notes payable require six equal monthly payments of principal plus monthly interest on the entire unpaid principal. Borrowing and all principal and interest payments occur at the end of the month.

10. **Income taxes are the responsibility of corporate headquarters, so you can ignore tax.**

As you prepare the master budget, remember that you are developing the store's operating and financial plan for the next four months. Normally, managers prepare the budgets for a full 12-month period. However, to simplify, we consider the next four months here. The steps in this process may seem mechanical; but you must think carefully about pricing, product lines, job assignments, needs for additional equipment, and negotiations with banks. Successful managers use this opportunity to make decisions that affect the future course of business.

Preparing the Operating Budget

The first three components of the operating budget, as shown in Exhibit 10-5, are:

1. Sales budget (Exhibit 10-7).

2. Inventory, purchases, and cost of goods sold budget (Exhibit 10-8).

3. Operating expenses budget (Exhibit 10-9).

2 Prepare an operating budget

The results of these three budgets feed into the fourth element of the operating budget: the budgeted income statement (Exhibit 10-10). We consider each in turn.

The Sales Budget

The forecast of sales revenue is the cornerstone of the master budget because the level of sales affects expenses and almost all other elements of the master budget. Budgeted total sales for each product is the sales price multiplied by the expected number of units sold. The overall sales budget in Exhibit 10-7 is the sum of the budgets for the individual products.

EXHIBIT 10-7	Sales Budget

WHITEWATER SPORTING GOODS STORE NO. 18
Sales Budget

	April	May	June	July	April–July Total
Cash sales, 60%	$30,000	$48,000	$36,000	$30,000	
Credit sales, 40%	20,000	32,000	24,000	20,000	
Total sales, 100%	$50,000	$80,000	$60,000	$50,000	$240,000

NOTE: From Data Set items 3 and 4, pages 569–570.

The total sales shown is from Data Set item 3. The breakdown between cash and credit sales is based on Data Set item 4. Trace the April through July total sales ($240,000) to the budgeted income statement in Exhibit 10-10.

The Inventory, Purchases, and Cost of Goods Sold Budget

This budget determines cost of goods sold for the budgeted income statement, ending inventory for the budgeted balance sheet, and purchases for the cash budget. The familiar cost of goods sold computation specifies the relations among these items:

$$\text{Beginning inventory} + \text{Purchases} - \text{Ending inventory} = \text{Cost of goods sold}$$

Beginning inventory is known from last month's budgeted balance sheet, budgeted cost of goods sold is 70% of sales (from Data Set item 5), and budgeted ending inventory is computed as $20,000 + 80\%$ of the cost of goods sold for the next month (from Data Set item 5). You must solve for the budgeted purchases figure. To do this, rearrange the previous equation to isolate purchases on the left side:

$$\text{Purchases} = \text{Cost of goods sold} + \text{Ending inventory} - \text{Beginning inventory}$$

This equation makes sense. How much does Whitewater Sporting Goods have to purchase? Enough to cover its current month's sales and desired ending inventory less the amount of beginning inventory already on hand at the start of the period. Exhibit 10-8 shows Whitewater Sporting Goods' inventory, purchases, and cost of goods sold budget. Remember: Inventory, purchases, and cost of goods sold are all stated at Whitewater's *cost*, not at its sales prices.

Trace the total budgeted cost of goods sold from Exhibit 10-8 ($168,000) to the budgeted income statement in Exhibit 10-10. We will use the budgeted inventory

EXHIBIT 10-8   Inventory, Purchases, and Cost of Goods Sold Budget

WHITEWATER SPORTING GOODS STORE NO. 18
Inventory, Purchases, and Cost of Goods Sold Budget

	April	May	June	July	April–July Total
Cost of goods sold					
(0.70 × sales, from Sales budget in Exhibit 10-7)	$35,000	$56,000	$42,000	$35,000	$168,000
+ Desired ending inventory					
[($20,000 + (0.80 × cost of goods sold for the next month)]	64,800*	53,600	48,000	42,400‡	
= Total inventory required	99,800	109,600	90,000	77,400	
– Beginning inventory	(48,000)†	(64,800)	(53,600)	(48,000)	
= Purchases	$51,800	$44,800	$36,400	$29,400	

*$20,000 + (0.80 × $56,000) = $64,800.
†Balance at March 31 (Exhibit 10-6).
‡Given in Data Set item 5 on page 570.

and purchases amounts later, when we create the budgeted balance sheet and the budgeted cash payments for these four months.

The Operating Expenses Budget

Exhibit 10-9 shows the operating expenses budget. The information used to create the budget is from Data Set items 6 and 7. Study each expense to make sure you know how it is computed. For example, sales commissions fluctuate with sales. Other expenses, such as rent and insurance, are the same each month (fixed).

EXHIBIT 10-9   Operating Expenses Budget

WHITEWATER SPORTING GOODS STORE NO. 18
Operating Expenses Budget

	April	May	June	July	April–July Total
Salary, fixed amount (Data Set item 6)	$ 2,500	$ 2,500	$ 2,500	$ 2,500	
Commission, 15% of sales (Data Set item 6 and Exhibit 10-7)	7,500	12,000	9,000	7,500	
Total salary and commissions	10,000	14,500	11,500	10,000	$46,000
Rent expense, fixed amount (Data Set item 7)	2,000	2,000	2,000	2,000	8,000
Depreciation expense, fixed amount (Data Set item 7)	500	500	500	500	2,000
Insurance expense, fixed amount (Data Set item 7)	200	200	200	200	800
Miscellaneous expenses, 5% of sales (Data Set item 7,					
and Exhibit 10-7)	2,500	4,000	3,000	2,500	12,000
Total operating expenses	$15,200	$21,200	$17,200	$15,200	$68,800

From Data Set items on page 570–571.

Trace the April through July totals from the operating expenses budget in Exhibit 10-9 (salary and commissions of $46,000, rent expense of $8,000, and so forth) to the budgeted income statement in Exhibit 10-10.

The Budgeted Income Statement

We use the sales budget (Exhibit 10-7); the inventory, purchases, and cost of goods sold budget (Exhibit 10-8); and the operating expenses budget (Exhibit 10-9) to prepare the budgeted income statement in Exhibit 10-10. (We explain the computation of interest expense as part of the cash budget in the next section.)

EXHIBIT 10-10 **Budgeted Income Statement**

WHITEWATER SPORTING GOODS STORE NO. 18
Budgeted Income Statement
Four Months Ending July 31, 2009

		Amount	Source
Sales revenue		$240,000	Sales budget (Exhibit 10-7)
Cost of goods sold		168,000	Inventory, purchases, and cost of goods
Gross profit		72,000	sold budget (Exhibit 10-8)
Operating expenses:			
Salary and commissions	$ 46,000		Operating expenses budget (Exhibit 10-9)
Rent expense	8,000		Operating expenses budget (Exhibit 10-9)
Depreciation expense	2,000		Operating expenses budget (Exhibit 10-9)
Insurance expense	800		Operating expenses budget (Exhibit 10-9)
Miscellaneous expenses	12,000	68,800	Operating expenses budget (Exhibit 10-9)
Operating income		3,200	
Interest expense		225*	Cash budget (Exhibit 10-14)
Net income		$ 2,975	

*$90 + $75 + $60

Take this opportunity to solidify your understanding of operating budgets by carefully working out Summary Problem 1.

Summary Problem 1

Review the Whitewater Sporting Goods example. Suppose you now think July sales will be $40,000 instead of the projected $50,000 in Exhibit 10-7. You want to see how this change in sales affects the budget.

Requirement

Revise the sales budget (Exhibit 10-7); the inventory, purchases, and cost of goods sold budget (Exhibit 10-8); and the operating expenses budget (Exhibit 10-9). Prepare a revised budgeted income statement for the four months ended July 31, 2009.

Note: You need not repeat the parts of the revised schedules that do not change. Assume that interest does not change.

Solution

Although not required, this solution repeats the budgeted amounts for April, May, and June. Revised figures appear in color for emphasis.

WHITEWATER SPORTING GOODS STORE NO. 18
Revised—Sales Budget

	April	May	June	July	Total
Cash sales, 60%	$30,000	$48,000	$36,000	$24,000	
Credit sales, 40%	20,000	32,000	24,000	16,000	
Total sales, 100%	$50,000	$80,000	$60,000	$40,000	$230,000

WHITEWATER SPORTING GOODS STORE NO. 18
Revised—Inventory, Purchases, and Cost of Goods Sold Budget

	April	May	June	July	Total
Cost of goods sold (0.70 × sales, from revised sales budget)	$35,000	$56,000	$42,000	$28,000	$161,000
+ Desired ending inventory					
($20,000 + 0.80 × cost of goods sold for next month)	64,800	53,600	42,400	42,400[†]	
= Total inventory required	99,800	109,600	84,400	70,400	
− Beginning inventory	(48,000)*	(64,800)	(53,600)	(42,400)	
= Purchases	$51,800	$44,800	$30,800	$28,000	

*Balance at March 31 (Exhibit 10-6).
[†]Given in Data Set item 5 on page 570.

WHITEWATER SPORTING GOODS STORE NO. 18
Revised—Operating Expenses Budget

	April	May	June	July	Total
Salary, fixed amount	$ 2,500	$ 2,500	$ 2,500	$ 2,500	
Commission, 15% of sales from revised sales budget	7,500	12,000	9,000	6,000	
Total salary and commissions	10,000	14,500	11,500	8,500	$ 44,500
Rent expense, fixed amount	2,000	2,000	2,000	2,000	8,000
Depreciation expense, fixed amount	500	500	500	500	2,000
Insurance expense, fixed amount	200	200	200	200	800
Miscellaneous expenses, 5% of sales from revised sales budget	2,500	4,000	3,000	2,000	11,500
Total operating expenses	$15,200	$21,200	$17,200	$13,200	$ 66,800

WHITEWATER SPORTING GOODS STORE NO. 18
Revised Budgeted Income Statement
Four Months Ending July 31, 2009

		Amount	Source
Sales revenue		$230,000	Revised sales budget
Cost of goods sold		161,000	Revised inventory, purchases, and cost of goods sold budget
Gross profit		69,000	
Operating expenses:			
Salary and commissions	$44,500		Revised operating expenses budget
Rent expense	8,000		Revised operating expenses budget
Depreciation expense	2,000		Revised operating expenses budget
Insurance expense	800		Revised operating expenses budget
Miscellaneous expenses	11,500	66,800	Revised operating expenses budget
Operating income		2,200	
Interest expense		225	Given, Exhibit 10-10
Net income		$ 1,975	

Preparing the Financial Budget

Now that we have prepared the operating budget, we're ready to move on to the financial budget. Recall from Exhibit 10-5 that the financial budget includes the cash budget, the budgeted balance sheet, and the budgeted statement of cash flows. We'll start with the cash budget.

3 Prepare a financial budget

Preparing the Cash Budget

The **cash budget**, or **statement of budgeted cash receipts and payments**, details how the business expects to go from the beginning cash balance to the desired ending balance. The cash budget has five major parts:

- Cash collections from customers (Exhibit 10-11)
- Cash payments for purchases (Exhibit 10-12)
- Cash payments for operating expenses (Exhibit 10-13)
- Cash payments for capital expenditures (for example, the $3,000 capital expenditure to acquire the delivery truck would be shown on the company's capital expenditures budget) less any proceeds from the sale of capital assets
- Cash financing (borrowings, repayments, and interest)

Cash collections and payments depend heavily on revenues and expenses, which appear in the operating budget. This is why you cannot prepare the cash budget until you have finished the operating budget.

Budgeted Cash Collections from Customers

The cash collections budget is all about timing: *When* does Whitewater expect to receive cash from its sales? Of course, Whitewater will receive cash immediately on its cash sales. Whitewater also expects to collect cash for all of its credit sales in the month *after* the sales are made (Data Set item 4). Therefore, Exhibit 10-11 shows two components to each month's cash collections: (1) collections from cash sales and (2) collection of the previous month's credit sales. These components are found on the sales budget shown in Exhibit 10-7.

EXHIBIT 10-11   **Budgeted Cash Collections**

WHITEWATER SPORTING GOODS STORE NO. 18
Budgeted Cash Collections from Customers

	April	May	June	July	April—July Total
Cash sales, from Sales budget (Exhibit 10-7)	$30,000	$48,000	$36,000	$30,000	
Collections of last month's credit sales, from Sales budget (Exhibit 10-7)	16,000*	20,000	32,000	24,000	
Total collections	$46,000	$68,000	$68,000	$54,000	$236,000

*March 31 accounts receivable (Exhibit 10-6).

Take a moment and trace each month's total cash collections in Exhibit 10-11 to the cash budget shown in Exhibit 10-14.

Budgeted Cash Payments for Purchases

The cash payments budget is also about timing: *When* will Whitewater pay for its purchases? Whitewater pays for half of its inventory purchases in the month of purchase and pays for the other half in the month *after* purchase (Data Set item 5). Therefore, Exhibit 10-12 shows two components to each month's cash payments for purchases: (1) 50% of last month's purchases and (2) 50% of this month's purchases. These components are calculated from the purchases shown on the inventory, purchases, and cost of goods sold budget (Exhibit 10-8). For example, May's cash payments for purchases consists of (1) 50% of April's purchases (50% × $51,800 = $25,900) and (2) 50% of May's purchases (50% × $44,800 = $22,400).

EXHIBIT 10-12 **Budgeted Cash Payments for Purchases**

WHITEWATER SPORTING GOODS STORE NO. 18
Budgeted Cash Payments for Purchases

	April	May	June	July	April–July Total
50% of last month's purchases, from Inventory, purchases, and cost of goods sold budget (Exhibit 10-8)	$16,800*	$25,900	$22,400	$18,200	
50% of this month's purchases, from Inventory, purchases, and cost of goods sold budget (Exhibit 10-8)	25,900	22,400	18,200	14,700	
Total payments for purchases	$42,700	$48,300	$40,600	$32,900	$164,500

*March 31 accounts payable (Exhibit 10-6).

Take a moment and trace each month's total cash payments for purchases in Exhibit 10-12 to the cash budget shown in Exhibit 10-14.

Budgeted Cash Payments for Operating Expenses

To budget cash payments for operating expenses, Whitewater must consider the *timing* of when it pays for payroll expenses (Data Set item 6) and other operating expenses (Data Set item 7).

EXHIBIT 10-13 **Budgeted Cash Payments for Operating Expenses**

WHITEWATER SPORTING GOODS STORE NO. 18
Budgeted Cash Payments for Operating Expenses

	April	May	June	July	April–July Total
Salary and commissions:					
50% of last month's expenses, from Operating expenses budget (Exhibit 10-9)	$ 4,250*	$ 5,000	$ 7,250	$ 5,750	
50% of this month's expenses, from Operating expenses budget (Exhibit 10-9)	5,000	7,250	5,750	5,000	
Total salary and commissions	9,250	12,250	13,000	10,750	
Rent expense, from Operating expenses budget (Exhibit 10-9)	2,000	2,000	2,000	2,000	
Miscellaneous expenses, from Operating expenses budget (Exhibit 10-9)	2,500	4,000	3,000	2,500	
Total payments for operating expenses	$13,750	$18,250	$18,000	$15,250	$65,250

*March 31 salary and commissions payable (Exhibit 10-6).

Notice that depreciation and insurance expenses are *not* included in this cash payments budget (See the next Stop & Think).

Take a moment and trace each month's total cash payments for operating expenses in Exhibit 10-13 to the cash budget in Exhibit 10-14.

Stop & Think...

Why are depreciation expense and insurance expense from the operating expenses budget (Exhibit 10-9) *excluded* from the budgeted cash payments for operating expenses in Exhibit 10-13?

Answer: These expenses do not require cash outlays in the current period. Depreciation is the periodic write-off of the cost of the equipment and fixtures that Whitewater Sporting Goods acquired previously. Insurance expense is the expiration of insurance that was prepaid at an earlier date.

The Cash Budget

The top portion of the cash budget shown in Exhibit 10-14 shows all cash collections and payments. We start with the beginning cash balance, then *add* cash collections to determine the cash available. Next, we *subtract* cash payments for purchases (Exhibit 10-12), cash payments for operating expenses (Exhibit 10-13), and cash payments for capital expenditures (from the company's capital expenditures budget). This yields the ending cash balance before financing, shown in blue.

EXHIBIT 10-14   Cash Budget

WHITEWATER SPORTING GOODS STORE NO. 18
Cash Budget
Four Months Ending July 31, 2009

	April	May	June	July
Beginning cash balance	$15,000*	$10,550	$10,410	$18,235
Cash collections (Exhibit 10-11)	46,000	68,000	68,000	54,000
Cash available	$61,000	$78,550	$78,410	$72,235
Cash payments:				
Purchases of inventory (Exhibit 10-12)	$42,700	$48,300	$40,600	$32,900
Operating expenses (Exhibit 10-13)	13,750	18,250	18,000	15,250
Purchase of delivery truck (Data Set item 8)	3,000	—	—	—
Total cash payments	59,450	66,550	58,600	48,150
(1) Ending cash balance before financing	1,550	12,000	19,810	24,085
Less: Minimum cash balance desired	(10,000)	(10,000)	(10,000)	(10,000)
Cash excess (deficiency)	$ (8,450)	$ 2,000	$ 9,810	$14,085
Financing of cash deficiency (see notes *a–c*):				
Borrowing (at end of month)	$ 9,000			
Principal payments (at end of month)		$ (1,500)	$ (1,500)	$ (1,500)
Interest expense (at 12% annually)		(90)	(75)	(60)
(2) Total effects of financing	9,000	(1,590)	(1,575)	(1,560)
Ending cash balance (1) + (2)	$10,550	$10,410	$18,235	$22,525

*March 31 budgeted cash balance (Exhibit 10-6).
Notes
*a*Borrowing occurs in multiples of $1,000 and only for the amount needed to maintain a minimum cash balance of $10,000.
*b*Monthly principal payments: $9,000 ÷ 6 = $1,500.
*c*Interest expense:
  May: $9,000 × (0.12 × 1/12) = $90
  June: ($9,000 – $1,500) × (0.12 × 1/12) = $75
  July: ($9,000 – $1,500 – $1,500) × (0.12 × 1/12) = $60

The lower portion of the cash budget is the financing section. Recall that Whitewater wants to maintain a minimum cash balance of $10,000 at each store (Data Set item 9). April's cash balance before financing ($1,550) falls $8,450 short of this goal, so Whitewater will have to borrow cash. Since Whitewater borrows in increments of $1,000 notes, it will have to borrow a full $9,000 to bring its cash balance above the minimum $10,000 required. After financing, the ending cash balance for April is $10,550.

April's ending cash balance becomes May's beginning cash balance ($10,550). Whitewater follows the same process in May: adding cash collections and subtracting cash payments. In May, Whitewater's ending cash balance before financing ($12,000) is $2,000 greater than the minimum required cash balance. Therefore, Whitewater can start repaying its notes payable.

Data Set item 9 states that Whitewater must repay the notes in six equal installments. Thus, May through July shows principal repayments of $1,500 ($9,000 ÷ 6) per month. Whitewater also pays interest expense on the outstanding notes payable at 12% per year. Interest expense is paid monthly. The June interest expense is $75 [($9,000 principal − $1,500 repayment at the end of May) × 12% × $\frac{1}{12}$]. Interest expense for the four months totals $225 ($90 + $75 + $60). This interest expense appears on the budgeted income statement in Exhibit 10-10.

The cash balance at the end of July ($22,525) is the cash balance in the July 31 budgeted balance sheet in Exhibit 10-15.

The Budgeted Balance Sheet

To prepare the budgeted balance sheet, project each asset, liability, and owners' equity account based on the plans outlined in the previous exhibits.

Study the budgeted balance sheet in Exhibit 10-15 to make certain you understand the computation of each figure. For example, on the budgeted balance sheet as of July 31, 2009, budgeted cash equals the ending cash balance from the cash budget in Exhibit 10-14 ($22,525). Accounts receivable as of July 31 equal July's credit sales of $20,000, shown in the sales budget (Exhibit 10-7). July 31 inventory of $42,400 is July's desired ending inventory in the inventory, purchases, and cost of goods sold budget in Exhibit 10-8. Detailed computations for each of the other accounts appear in Exhibit 10-15.

The Budgeted Statement of Cash Flows

The final step is preparing the budgeted statement of cash flows. Use the information from the schedules of cash collections and payments, the cash budget, and the beginning balance of cash to project cash flows from operating, investing, and financing activities. Take time to study Exhibit 10-16 on page 582 and make sure you understand the origin of each figure.

Getting Employees to Accept the Budget

What is the most important part of Whitewater Sporting Goods' budgeting system? Despite all of the numbers we have crunched, it is not the mechanics. It is getting managers and employees to accept the budget so Whitewater Sporting Goods can reap the planning, coordination, and control benefits illustrated in Exhibit 10-3.

EXHIBIT 10-15   **Budgeted Balance Sheet**

WHITEWATER SPORTING GOODS STORE NO. 18
Budgeted Balance Sheet
July 31, 2009

Assets		
Current assets:		
Cash (Exhibit 10-14)	$22,525	
Accounts receivable (Sales budget, Exhibit 10-7)	20,000	
Inventory (Inventory, purchases, and cost of goods sold budget,		
Exhibit 10-8)	42,400	
Prepaid insurance (beginning balance of $1,800 − $800* for		
four months' expiration; Operating expenses budget, Exhibit 10-9)	1,000	
Total current assets		$ 85,925
Plant assets:		
Equipment and fixtures (beginning balance of $32,000* + $3,000		
truck acquisition; Data Set item 8)	$35,000	
Accumulated depreciation (beginning balance of $12,800* + $2,000		
for four months' depreciation; Operating expenses budget,		
Exhibit 10-9)	(14,800)	
Total plant assets		20,200
Total assets		$106,125
Liabilities		
Current liabilities:		
Account payable (0.50 × July purchases of $29,400; Inventory,		
purchases, and cost of goods sold budget, Exhibit 10-8)	$14,700	
Short-term note payable ($9,000 − $4,500 paid back;		
Exhibit 10-14)	4,500	
Salary and commissions payable (0.50 × July expenses of $10,000;		
Operating expenses budget, Exhibit 10-9)	5,000	
Total liabilities		$ 24,200
Owners' Equity		
Owners' equity (beginning balance of $78,950* + $2,975 net income;		
Exhibit 10-10)		81,925
Total liabilities and owners' equity		$106,125

*March 31, 2009, Balance Sheet (Exhibit 10-6).

Few people enjoy having their work monitored and evaluated. So, if managers use the budget as a benchmark to evaluate employees' performance, managers must motivate employees to accept the budget's goals. Here's how managers can do it:

- Support the budget themselves, or no one else will.
- Show employees how budgets can help them achieve better results.
- Have employees participate in developing the budget.

But these principles alone are not enough. As the manager of Store No. 18, your performance is evaluated by comparing actual results to the budget. When you develop your store's budget, you may be tempted to build in *slack*. For example, you might want to budget fewer sales and higher purchases than you expect. This increases the chance that actual performance will be better than the budget and that you will receive a good evaluation. But adding slack into the budget makes it less accurate—and less useful for planning and control. When the division manager and the head of the accounting department arrive from headquarters next week, they will scour your budget to find any slack that you may have inserted.

EXHIBIT 10-16   Budgeted Statement of Cash Flows

WHITEWATER SPORTING GOODS STORE NO. 18
Budgeted Statement of Cash Flows
Four Months Ending July 31, 2009

Cash flows from operating activities:		
Receipts:		
Collections from customers (Exhibit 10-11)	$ 236,000	
Total cash receipts		$236,000
Payments:		
Purchases of inventory (Exhibit 10-12)	$(164,500)	
Operating expenses (Exhibit 10-13)	(65,250)	
Payment of interest expense (Exhibits 10-14 and 10-10)	(225)	
Total cash payments		(229,975)
Net cash inflow from operating activities		6,025
Cash flows from investing activities:		
Acquisition of delivery truck (Data Set item 8)	$ (3,000)	
Net cash outflow from investing activities		(3,000)
Cash flows from financing activities:		
Proceeds from issuance of notes payable (Exhibit 10-14)	$ 9,000	
Payment of notes payable (Exhibit 10-14)	(4,500)	
Net cash inflow from financing activities		4,500
Net increase in cash		$ 7,525
Cash balance, April 1, 2009 (Exhibits 10-6 and 10-14)		15,000
Cash balance, July 31, 2009 (Exhibits 10-14 and 10-15)		$ 22,525

Using Information Technology for Sensitivity Analysis and Rolling Up Unit Budgets

Exhibits 10-7 through 10-16 show that the manager must prepare many calculations to develop the master budget for just one of the retail stores in the Whitewater Sporting Goods merchandising chain. No wonder managers embrace information technology to help prepare budgets! Let's see how advances in information technology make it more cost-effective for managers to:

- Conduct sensitivity analysis on their own unit's budget.
- Roll up individual unit budgets to create the company-wide budget.

Sensitivity Analysis

The master budget models the company's *planned* activities. Top management pays special attention to ensure that the results of the budgeted income statement (Exhibit 10-10), the cash budget (Exhibit 10-14), and the budgeted balance sheet (Exhibit 10-15) support key strategies.

But actual results often differ from plans, so management wants to know how budgeted income and cash flows would change if key assumptions turned out to be incorrect. Chapter 7 defined *sensitivity analysis* as a *what-if* technique that asks *what* a result will be *if* a predicted amount is not achieved or *if* an underlying assumption changes. *What if* the stock market crashes? How will this affect Amazon.com's sales? Will it have to postpone the planned expansion in Asia and Europe? *What* will be Whitewater Sporting Goods Store No. 18's cash balance on July 31 *if* the period's sales are 45% cash, not 60% cash? Will Whitewater Sporting Goods have to borrow more cash?

Most companies use computer spreadsheet programs (or special budget software) to prepare master budget schedules and statements. One of the earliest spreadsheet programs was developed by graduate business students who realized that computers could take the drudgery out of hand-computed master budget sensitivity analyses. Today, managers answer what-if questions simply by changing a number. At the press of a key, the computer screen flashes a revised budget that includes all of the effects of the change.

Technology makes it cost effective to perform more comprehensive sensitivity analyses. Armed with a better understanding of how changes in sales and costs are likely to affect the company's bottom line, today's managers can react quickly if key assumptions underlying the master budget (such as sales price or quantity) turn out to be wrong.

4 Use sensitivity analysis in budgeting

Stop & Think...

Consider two budget situations: (1) Whitewater Sporting Goods' marketing analysts produce a near-certain forecast for four-month sales of $4,500,000 for the company's 20 stores. (2) Much uncertainty exists about the period's sales. The most likely amount is $4,500,000, but marketing considers any amount between $3,900,000 and $5,100,000 to be possible. How will the budgeting process differ in these two circumstances?

Answer: Whitewater Sporting Goods will prepare a master budget for the expected sales level of $4,500,000 in either case. Because of the uncertainty in the second situation, executives will want a set of budgets covering the entire range of volume rather than a single level. Whitewater's managers may prepare budgets based on sales of, for example, $3,900,000, $4,200,000, $4,500,000, $4,800,000, and $5,100,000. These budgets will help managers plan for sales levels throughout the forecasted range.

Rolling Up Individual Unit Budgets into the Company-Wide Budget

Whitewater Sporting Goods Store No. 18 is just one of the company's many retail stores. As Exhibit 10-17 shows, Whitewater Sporting Goods' headquarters must roll up the budget data from Store No. 18, along with budgets for each of the other stores, to prepare the company-wide master budget. This roll-up can be difficult for companies whose units use different spreadsheets to prepare the budgets.

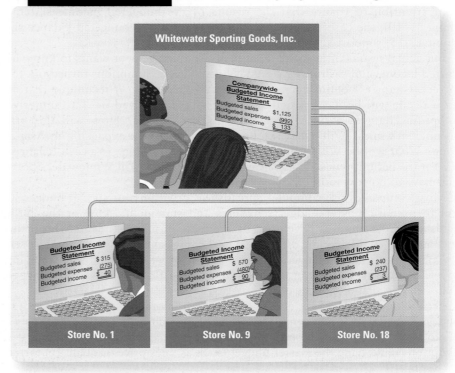

EXHIBIT 10-17 Rolling Up Individual Unit Budgets into the Company-Wide Budget

Companies such as Sunoco turn to budget management software to solve this problem. Often designed as a component of the company's Enterprise Resource Planning (ERP) system (or data warehouse), this software helps managers develop and analyze budgets.

Across the globe, managers sit at their desks, log in to the company's budget system, and enter their numbers. The software allows them to conduct sensitivity analyses on their unit's data. When the manager is satisfied with the budget, he or she can enter it in the company-wide budget with the click of a mouse. The unit's budget automatically rolls up with budgets from all of the other units around the world.

Before the store's budget is officially accepted, it will most likely go through a corporate review process involving division managers and corporate accountants. This review process helps to ensure that the budget is realistic.

Whether at headquarters or on the road, top executives can log in to the budget system and conduct their own sensitivity analyses on individual units' budgets or on the company-wide budget. Managers can spend less time compiling and summarizing data and more time analyzing the information to ensure that the budget leads the company to achieve its key strategic goals.

Responsibility Accounting

Prepare performance reports for responsibility centers

You've seen how managers set strategic goals and develop plans and budget resources for activities that help reach those goals. Let's look more closely at how managers *use* budgets to control operations.

Each manager is responsible for planning and controlling some part of the firm's activities. A **responsibility center** is a part or subunit of an organization whose manager is accountable for specific activities. Lower-level managers are often responsible for budgeting and controlling costs of a single value-chain function. For example, one manager is responsible for planning and controlling the *production* of Pace picante sauce at the plant, while another is responsible for planning and controlling the *distribution* of the product to customers. Lower-level managers report to higher-level managers, who have broader responsibilities. Managers in charge of production and distribution report to senior managers responsible for profits (revenues minus costs) earned by an entire product line.

Four Types of Responsibility Centers

Responsibility accounting is a system for evaluating the performance of each responsibility center and its manager. Responsibility accounting performance reports compare plans (budgets) with actions (actual results) for each center. Superiors then evaluate how well each manager (1) used the budgeted resources to achieve the responsibility center's goals and thereby (2) controlled the operations for which he or she was responsible.

Exhibit 10-18 illustrates four types of responsibility centers.

1. **In a cost center, managers are accountable for costs (expenses) only.** Manufacturing operations, such as the Pace picante sauce production lines, are cost centers. The line supervisor controls costs by ensuring that employees work efficiently. The supervisor is *not* responsible for generating revenues because he or she is not involved in selling the product. The plant manager evaluates the supervisor on his or her ability to control *costs* by comparing actual costs to budgeted costs. All else being equal (for example, holding quality constant), the supervisor is likely to receive a more favorable evaluation when actual costs are less than budgeted costs.

2. **In a revenue center, managers are accountable primarily for revenues.** Examples include the Midwest and Southeast sales regions of businesses such as Pace Foods. These managers of revenue centers may also be responsible for the costs of their own sales operations. Revenue center performance reports compare actual with budgeted revenues and may include the costs incurred by the revenue center itself. All else being equal, the manager is likely to receive a more favorable evaluation when actual revenues exceed the budget.

EXHIBIT 10-18   **Four Types of Responsibility Centers**

In a **cost center**, such as a production line for Pace picante sauce, managers are responsible for costs.

In a **revenue center**, such as the Midwest sales region, managers are responsible for generating sales revenue.

In a **profit center**, such as a line of products, managers are responsible for generating income.

In an **investment center**, such as Campbell Soups and Sauces division, managers are responsible for income and invested capital.

3. **In a profit center, managers are accountable for both revenues and costs (expenses) and, therefore, profits.** The (higher-level) manager responsible for the entire Pace product line is accountable for increasing sales revenue *and* controlling costs to achieve the profit goals. Profit center reports include both revenues and expenses to show the profit center's income. Superiors evaluate the manager's performance by comparing actual revenues, expenses, and profits to the budget. All else being equal, the manager is likely to receive a more favorable evaluation when actual profits exceed the budget.

4. **In an investment center, managers are accountable for investments, revenues, and costs (expenses).** Investment centers are generally large divisions of a corporation. For example, the North American Sauces and Beverages Division (which includes Pace Foods) of Campbell Soup is considered an investment center. Managers of investment centers are responsible for (1) generating sales, (2) controlling expenses, and (3) managing the amount of investment (assets) required to earn the income. Investment centers are treated almost as if they were stand-alone companies. Managers have decision-making authority over how all of the division's assets are used. As a result, managers are held responsible for generating as much income as they can with those assets.

   Top management often evaluates investment center managers based on performance measures such as return on investment (ROI), residual income, and economic value added (EVA). Chapter 12 explains how these measures are calculated and used. All else being equal, the manager will receive a more favorable evaluation if the division's actual ROI, residual income, or EVA exceeds the amount budgeted.

Responsibility Accounting Performance Reports

Exhibit 10-19 shows how an organization such as Campbell Soup Company assigns responsibility.

At the top level, the CEO oversees each of the four divisions. Division managers generally have broad responsibility, including deciding how to use assets to maximize ROI. Most companies consider divisions as *investment centers.*

Each division manager supervises all of the product lines in that division. Exhibit 10-19 shows that the VP of North American Sauces and Beverages oversees the Prego Italian sauces, Pace Mexican sauces, V8 juice, and Franco-American canned pasta product lines. Product lines are generally considered *profit centers.* Thus, the manager of the Pace Foods product line is responsible for evaluating lower-level managers of both of the following:

- *Cost centers* (such as plants that make Pace Foods products)
- *Revenue centers* (such as managers responsible for selling Pace Foods products)

Exhibit 10-20 illustrates responsibility accounting performance reports for each level of management shown in Exhibit 10-19. Exhibit 10-20 uses assumed numbers to illustrate reports like those:

- The CEO may use to evaluate divisions.
- The divisional VPs may use to evaluate individual product lines.
- The product line managers may use to evaluate the development, production, marketing, and distribution of their products.

At each level, the reports compare actual results with the budget.

Start with the lowest level and move to the top. Follow the $25 million budgeted operating income from the Mexican sauces product line report to the report of the VP—North American Sauces and Beverages. The VP's report summarizes the budgeted and actual operating incomes for each of the four product lines he or she supervises.

EXHIBIT 10-19 **Partial Organization Chart**

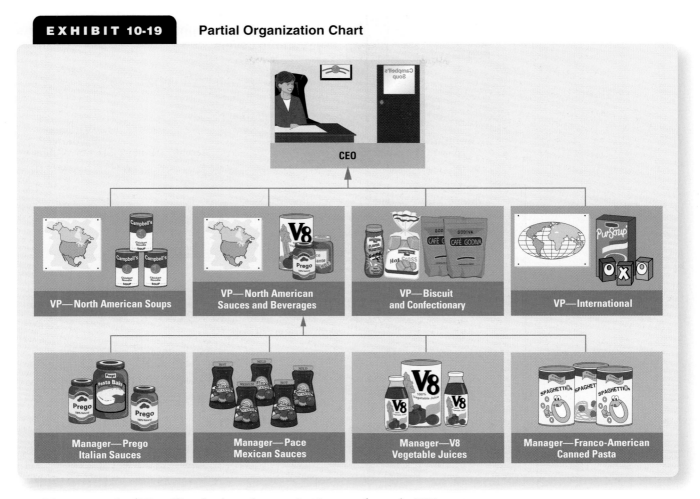

Now, trace the $70 million budgeted operating income from the VP's report to the CEO's report. The CEO's report includes a summary of each division's actual and budgeted profits, as well as the costs incurred by corporate headquarters, which are not assigned to any of the divisions.

Management by Exception

The variances reported in Exhibit 10-20 aid **management by exception**, which directs executives' attention to important differences between actual and budgeted amounts. Look at the CEO's report. The International Soups and Sauces Division's actual operating income of $34 million is very close to the budgeted $35 million. Unless there are other signs of trouble, the CEO will not waste time investigating such a small variance.

In contrast, the North American Sauces and Beverages Division earned a great deal more profit than budgeted. The CEO will want to know why. Suppose the VP of the division believes that a national sales promotion was especially effective. That promotion may be repeated or adapted by other divisions. One reason managers investigate large, favorable variances (not just large, unfavorable ones) is to identify the reason for exceptional results so that other parts of the organization may benefit. Another is to ensure that employees are not skimping on ingredients, marketing, or R&D, which could hurt the company's long-term success. Also, it's possible that large variances are the result of unrealistic budgets.

A CEO who received the report at the top of Exhibit 10-20 would likely concentrate on improving the North American Soups Division because its actual income fell $9 million below budget. The CEO would want to see which product lines

EXHIBIT 10-20 Responsibility Accounting Performance Reports at Various Levels

CEO'S QUARTERLY RESPONSIBILITY REPORT
(in millions of dollars)

Operating Income of Divisions and Corporate Headquarters Expense	Actual	Budget	Variance Favorable/ (Unfavorable)
North American Soups	$209	$218	$ (9)
North American Sauces and Beverages	84	70	14
Biscuits and Confectionary	87	79	8
International Soups and Sauces	34	35	(1)
Corporate Headquarters Expense	(29)	(33)	4
Operating Income	$385	$369	$16

VP—NORTH AMERICAN SAUCES AND BEVERAGES QUARTERLY RESPONSIBILITY REPORT
(in millions of dollars)

Operating Income of Product Lines	Actual	Budget	Variance Favorable/ (Unfavorable)
Italian Sauces	$18	$20	$ (2)
Mexican Sauces	38	25	13
Vegetable Juices	15	10	5
Canned Pastas	13	15	(2)
Operating Income	$84	$70	$14

MANAGER—MEXICAN SAUCES QUARTERLY RESPONSIBILITY REPORT
(in millions of dollars)

Revenue and Expenses	Actual	Budget	Variance Favorable/ (Unfavorable)
Sales revenue	$ 84	$ 80	$ 4
Cost of goods sold	(30)	(36)	6
Gross profit	54	44	10
Marketing expenses	(9)	(12)	3
Research and development expenses	(3)	(2)	(1)
Other expenses	(4)	(5)	1
Operating income	$ 38	$ 25	$13

caused the shortfall so that he or she and the VP of the division could work together to correct any problems.

Exhibit 10-20 also shows how summarized data can hide problems. Although as a whole, the North American Sauces and Beverages Division performed well, the Italian sauces and canned pasta lines did not. If the CEO received only the condensed report at the top of the exhibit, he or she would rely on division managers to spot and correct problems in individual product lines.

Not a Question of Blame

Responsibility accounting assigns managers responsibility for their unit's actions and provides a way to evaluate both the managers and their unit's performance. But superiors should not misuse responsibility accounting to find fault or place blame. The question is not who is to blame for an unfavorable variance. Instead, the question is who can best explain why a specific variance occurred. Consider the North American Soups Division in Exhibit 10-20. Suppose a tornado devastated the primary production plant. The remaining plants may have operated very efficiently, and this efficiency kept the income variance down to $9 million. If so, the North American Soups Division and its VP actually did a good job.

Other Performance Measures

Top management uses responsibility accounting performance reports to assess each responsibility center's *financial* performance. Top management also often assesses each responsibility center's nonfinancial *operating* performance. Typical nonfinancial performance measures include customer satisfaction ratings, delivery time, product quality, and employee expertise. Chapter 12 discusses the broader view of performance evaluation, known as the "balanced scorecard." In that chapter, we will look at how managers use both financial and nonfinancial performance measures to form a "balanced view" of each responsibility center's performance.

The following Decision Guidelines review budgets and the way managers use them in responsibility accounting. Study these guidelines before working on Summary Problem 2.

Decision Guidelines

THE MASTER BUDGET AND RESPONSIBILITY ACCOUNTING

Amazon.com's initial strategy was to "get big fast." But without a budget, spending got out of control. So, founder and CEO Jeff Bezos added a second strategic goal—to become the world's most cost-efficient, high-quality e-tailer. Today, Amazon.com's managers use budgets to help reach growth and cost-efficiency goals. Let's consider some of the decisions Amazon.com made as it set up its budgeting process.

Decision	Guidelines
What benefits should Amazon.com expect to obtain from developing a budget?	Requires managers to *plan* how to increase sales and how to cut costs.
	Promotes *coordination and communication*, such as communicating the importance of the cost-efficiency goal.
	Provides a *benchmark* that motivates employees and helps managers evaluate how well employees contributed to the sales growth and cost-efficiency goals.
In what order should Amazon.com's managers prepare the components of the master budget?	1. Begin with the *operating budget*: • Start with the *sales budget*, which feeds into all other budgets.

continued . . .

Decision	**Guidelines**

	• Then, determine the inventory, purchases, and cost of goods sold budget.
	• Next, prepare the operating expenses budget.
	• From these three budgets, create the *budgeted income statement*.
	
	2. Next, prepare the *capital expenditures budget*.
	
	3. Finally, prepare the *financial budget*.
	  • Start with the *cash budget*.
	  • The cash budget provides the ending cash balance for the *budgeted balance sheet* and the details for the *budgeted statement of cash flows*.

What extra steps should Amazon.com take given the uncertainty of Internet-based sales forecasts?	Prepare a *sensitivity analysis* by projecting budgeted results at different sales levels.
How does Amazon.com compute budgeted purchases?	$$\text{Beginning inventory} + \text{Purchases} - \text{Ending inventory} = \text{Cost of goods sold}$$ so $$\text{Purchases} = \text{Cost of goods sold} + \text{Ending inventory} - \text{Beginning inventory}$$
What kind of a responsibility center does each manager supervise?	**Cost center:** Manager is responsible for costs. **Revenue center:** Manager is responsible for revenues. **Profit center:** Manager is responsible for both revenues and costs and, therefore, profits. **Investment center:** Manager is responsible for revenues, costs, and the amount of the investment required to earn the income.
How should Amazon.com evaluate managers?	Compare actual performance with the budget for the manager's responsibility center. *Management by exception* focuses on large differences between budgeted and actual results. The emphasis should be on information, not blame.

Summary Problem 2

Continue the revised Whitewater Sporting Goods illustration from Summary Problem 1. Now that you think July sales will be $40,000 instead of $50,000, as projected in Exhibit 10-7, how will this affect the financial budget?

Requirements

Revise the schedule of budgeted cash collections (Exhibit 10-11), the schedule of budgeted cash payments for purchases (Exhibit 10-12), and the schedule of budgeted cash payments for operating expenses (Exhibit 10-13). Prepare a revised cash budget; a revised budgeted balance sheet at July 31, 2009; and a revised budgeted statement of cash flows for the four months ended July 31, 2009. *Note:* You need not repeat the parts of the revised schedule that do not change.

Hint: You will need to refer to the revised budgets created in Summary Problem 1.

Solution

Although not required, this solution repeats the budgeted amounts for April, May, and June. Revised figures appear in color for emphasis.

WHITEWATER SPORTING GOODS STORE NO. 18
Revised—Budgeted Cash Collections from Customers

	April	May	June	July	Total
Cash sales, from revised sales budget	$30,000	$48,000	$36,000	$24,000	
Collections of last month's credit sales, from revised sales budget	16,000*	20,000	32,000	24,000	
Total collections	$46,000	$68,000	$68,000	$48,000	$230,000

*March 31 accounts receivable (Exhibit 10-6)

WHITEWATER SPORTING GOODS STORE NO. 18
Revised—Budgeted Cash Payments for Purchases

	April	May	June	July	Total
50% of last month's purchases, from revised inventory, purchases, and cost of goods sold budget	$16,800*	$25,900	$22,400	$15,400	
50% of this month's purchases, from revised inventory, purchases, and cost of goods sold budget	25,900	22,400	15,400	14,000	
Total payments for purchases	$42,700	$48,300	$37,800	$29,400	$158,200

*March 31 accounts payable (Exhibit 10-6).

WHITEWATER SPORTING GOODS STORE NO. 18
Revised—Budgeted Cash Payments for Operating Expenses

	April	May	June	July	Total
Salary and commissions:					
50% of last month's expenses, from revised operating expenses budget	$ 4,250*	$ 5,000	$ 7,250	$ 5,750	
50% of this month's expenses, from revised operating expenses budget	5,000	7,250	5,750	4,250	
Total salary and commissions	9,250	12,250	13,000	10,000	
Rent expense, from revised operating expenses budget	2,000	2,000	2,000	2,000	
Miscellaneous expenses, from revised operating expenses budget	2,500	4,000	3,000	2,000	
Total payments for operating expenses	$13,750	$18,250	$18,000	$14,000	$ 64,000

*March 31 salary and commissions payable (Exhibit 10-6).

WHITEWATER SPORTING GOODS STORE NO. 18
Revised Cash Budget
Four Months Ending July 31, 2009

	April	May	June	July
Beginning cash balance	$15,000*	$10,550	$10,410	$21,035
Cash collections (revised budgeted cash collections)	46,000	68,000	68,000	48,000
Cash available	$61,000	$78,550	$78,410	$69,035
Cash payments:				
Purchases of inventory (revised budgeted cash payments for purchases)	$42,700	$48,300	$37,800	$29,400
Operating expenses (revised budgeted cash payments for operating expenses)	13,750	18,250	18,000	14,000
Purchase of delivery truck (Data Set item 8)	3,000	—	—	—
Total cash payments	59,450	66,550	55,800	43,400
(1) Ending cash balance before financing	1,550	12,000	22,610	25,635
Less: Minimum cash balance desired	(10,000)	(10,000)	(10,000)	(10,000)
Cash excess (deficiency)	$ (8,450)	$ 2,000	$12,610	$15,635
Financing of cash deficiency (see notes a–c):				
Borrowing (at end of month)	$ 9,000			
Principal payments (at end of month)		$ (1,500)	$ (1,500)	$ (1,500)
Interest expense (at 12% annually)		(90)	(75)	(60)
(2) Total effects of financing	9,000	(1,590)	(1,575)	(1,560)
Ending cash balance (1) + (2)	$10,550	$10,410	$21,035	$24,075

*March 31 cash balance (Exhibit 10-6).
Notes
[a]Borrowing occurs in multiples of $1,000 and only for the amount needed to maintain a minimum cash balance of $10,000.
[b]Monthly principal payments: $9,000 ÷ 6 = $1,500.
[c]Interest expense:
  May: $9,000 × (0.12 × 1/12) = $90
  June: ($9,000 − $1,500) × (0.12 × 1/12) = $75
  July: ($9,000 − $1,500 − $1,500) × (0.12 × 1/12) = $60

WHITEWATER SPORTING GOODS STORE NO. 18
Revised Budgeted Balance Sheet
July 31, 2009

Assets		
Current assets:		
Cash (revised cash budget)	$24,075	
Accounts receivable (revised sales budget)	16,000	
Inventory	42,400	
Prepaid insurance	1,000	
Total current assets		$ 83,475
Plant assets:		
Equipment and fixtures	$35,000	
Accumulated depreciation	(14,800)	
Total plant assets		20,200
Total assets		$103,675
Liabilities		
Current liabilities:		
Accounts payable (0.50 × July purchases of $28,000; revised		
inventory, purchases, and cost of goods sold budget)	$14,000	
Short-term note payable	4,500	
Salary and commissions payable (0.50 × July expenses of $8,500;		
revised operating expenses budget)	4,250	
Total liabilities		$ 22,750
Owners' Equity		
Owners' equity (beginning balance of $78,950* + $1,975 net income,		
revised budgeted income statement)		80,925
Total liabilities and owners' equity		$103,675

*March 31, 2009, balance sheet (Exhibit 10-6).

Cash flows from operating activities:		
Receipts:		
Collections (revised budgeted cash collections)	$ 230,000	
Total cash receipts		$230,000
Payments:		
Purchases of inventory (revised budgeted cash payments for purchases)	$(158,200)	
Operating expenses (revised budgeted cash payments for operating expenses)	(64,000)	
Payment of interest expense	(225)	
Total cash payments		(222,425)
Net cash inflow from operating activities		7,575
Cash flows from investing activities:		
Acquisition of delivery truck	$ (3,000)	
Net cash outflow from investing activities		(3,000)
Cash flows from financing activities:		
Proceeds from issuance of notes payable	$ 9,000	
Payment of notes payable	(4,500)	
Net cash inflow from financing activities		4,500
Net increase in cash		$ 9,075
Cash balance, April 1, 2009 (Exhibit 10-6)		15,000
Cash balance, July 31, 2009 (revised cash budget)		$ 24,075

Appendix 10A

The Master Budget for Service and Manufacturing Companies

In the chapter, we presented the master budget for a merchandising company. The components of the master budget for a merchandising company are summarized in Exhibit 10-5. The master budgets for service companies and manufacturers vary somewhat from those of a merchandising company:

- *Service companies:* The master budget of a service company is less complex than that of a merchandising company. Since service companies have no merchandise inventory, they do not have an Inventory, Purchases, and Cost of Goods Sold budget. As a result, they won't have to schedule cash payments for inventory purchases, either. All other components of a service company master budget are the same as those for a merchandising company (see Exhibit 10-5).

- *Manufacturing companies:* The master budget of a manufacturing company is slightly more complex than that of a merchandising company. Why? Because they produce rather than purchase their finished inventory. As a result, a production budget replaces the purchases budget used by merchandising firms. The production budget follows the same general format as the merchandiser's purchases budget except that it is calculated in units rather than dollars:

Units needed for curent month's sales	xxx	
Plus: Units needed for desired ending inventory	xxx	
= Total units needed..	xxxx	(what we need)
Less: Units in beginning inventory............................	(xxx)	(what we have)
= Number of units to produce..................................	xxxx	(what we need to make)

Once the production requirements have been budgeted, the manufacturer will develop three additional budgets for the three manufacturing cost components: direct materials, direct labor, and manufacturing overhead:

- The direct materials budget also follows the same general format of the production or purchases budget. Usually, the direct materials budget is formulated in terms of the quantity of raw materials that need to be purchased; then it is translated into the cost of buying those direct materials from suppliers.

- The direct labor budget forecasts the cost of the direct labor that will be needed to meet production requirements.

- The manufacturing overhead budget estimates all manufacturing overhead costs that will be incurred during the year (indirect materials, indirect labor, and other indirect manufacturing costs). This budget is extremely dependent upon cost behavior since many manufacturing overhead costs are fixed while others are variable.

All other components of the manufacturing master budget are the same as those for a merchandising company (see Exhibit 10-5).

Review The Master Budget and Responsibility Accounting

Accounting Vocabulary

Capital Expenditures Budget. (p. 569)
A company's plan for purchases of property, plant, equipment, and other long-term assets.

Cash Budget. (p. 577)
Details how the business expects to go from the beginning cash balance to the desired ending balance. Also called the statement of budgeted cash receipts and payments.

Financial Budget. (p. 569)
The cash budget (cash inflows and outflows), the budgeted period-end balance sheet, and the budgeted statement of cash flows.

Management by Exception. (p. 587)
Directs management's attention to important differences between actual and budgeted amounts.

Master Budget. (p. 568)
The set of budgeted financial statements and supporting schedules for an entire organization. Includes the operating budget, the capital expenditures budget, and the financial budget.

Operating Budget. (p. 569)
Projects sales revenue, cost of goods sold, and operating expenses, leading to the budgeted income statement that projects operating income for the period.

Responsibility Accounting. (p. 585)
A system for evaluating the performance of each responsibility center and its manager.

Responsibility Center. (p. 584)
A part or subunit of an organization whose manager is accountable for specific activities.

Quick Check

1. Amazon.com expected to receive which of the following benefits when it started its budgeting process?
   a. The planning required to develop the budget helps managers foresee and avoid potential problems before they occur.
   b. The budget helps motivate employees to achieve Amazon.com's sales growth and cost reduction goals.
   c. The budget provides Amazon.com's managers with a benchmark against which to compare actual results for performance evaluation.
   d. All of the above.

2. Which of the following is the cornerstone (or most critical element) of the master budget?
   a. the sales budget
   b. the inventory budget
   c. the purchases and cost of goods sold budget
   d. the operating expenses budget

3. The income statement is part of which element of Amazon.com's master budget?
   a. the operating budget
   b. the capital expenditures budget
   c. the financial budget
   d. none of the above

Use the following information to answer Questions 4 through 6. Suppose Amazon.com sells 1 million hardcover books a day at an average price of $30 and 1.5 million paperback books a day at an average price of $15. Assume that Amazon.com's purchase price for the books is 60% of the selling price it charges retail customers. Amazon.com has no beginning inventory, but it wants to have a three-day supply of ending inventory. Assume that operating expenses are $0.5 million per day.

4. Compute Amazon.com's budgeted sales for the next (seven-day) week.
   a. $52.5 million
   b. $210 million
   c. $220.5 million
   d. $367.5 million

5. Determine Amazon.com's budgeted purchases for the next (seven-day) week.
   a. $220.5 million
   b. $315 million
   c. $367.5 million
   d. $525 million

6. What is Amazon.com's budgeted operating income for a (seven-day) week?
   a. $52.5 million
   b. $56 million
   c. $143.5 million
   d. $147 million

7. Which of the following expenses would *not* appear in Amazon.com's cash budget?
   a. depreciation expense
   b. wages expense
   c. interest expense
   d. marketing expense

8. IT has made it easier for Amazon.com's managers to perform all of the following tasks *except*
   a. sensitivity analyses
   b. rolling up individual units' budgets into the company-wide budget
   c. removing slack from the budget
   d. preparing responsibility center performance reports that identify variances between actual and budgeted revenues and costs

9. Which of the following managers is at the highest level of the organization?
   a. cost center manager
   b. revenue center manager
   c. profit center manager
   d. investment center manager

10. Suppose Amazon.com budgets $5 million for customer service costs but actually spends $4 million. Which of the following is true?

a. Because this $1 million variance is favorable, management does not need to investigate further.

b. Management will investigate this $1 million favorable variance to ensure that the cost savings do not reflect skimping on customer service.

c. Management will investigate this $1 million unfavorable variance to try to identify and then correct the problem that led to the unfavorable variance.

d. Management should investigate every variance, especially unfavorable ones.

Quick Check Answers

1. *d* 2. *a* 3. *a* 4. *d* 5. *b* 6. *c* 7. *a* 8. *a* 9. *d* 10. *b*

For Internet Exercises, Excel in Practice, and additional online activities, go to this book's Web site at www.prenhall.com/bamber.

Assess Your Progress

■ Learning Objectives

1 Learn why managers use budgets

2 Prepare an operating budget

3 Prepare a financial budget

4 Use sensitivity analysis in budgeting

5 Prepare performance reports for responsibility centers

■ Short Exercises

S10-1 **Explain benefits of budgeting** *(Learning Objective 1)*
Consider the budget for your travel itinerary business (page 565). Explain how you benefit from preparing the budget.

S10-2 **Order of preparation and components of master budget** *(Learning Objectives 2, 3)*
In what order should you prepare the following components of the master budget?

Budgeted income statement	Operating expense budget	Cash budget
Budgeted statement of cash flows	Purchases and cost of goods sold budget	Capital expenditures budget
Budgeted balance sheet	Sales budget	Inventory budget

Which are components of the operating budget? Which are components of the financial budget?

S10-3 **Sales Budget** *(Learning Objective 2)*
In a series of Short Exercises, you will prepare parts of the master budget for Grippers, which sells its rock-climbing shoes worldwide. We will concentrate on Grippers' budget for January and February.

Grippers expects to sell 4,000 pairs of shoes for $185 each in January and 3,500 pairs of shoes for $220 each in February. All sales are cash only. Prepare the sales budget for January and February.

S10-4 **Continuation of S10-3: inventory, purchases, and cost of goods sold** *(Learning Objective 2)*
In S10-3, Grippers expects cost of goods sold to average 65% of sales revenue and the company expects to sell 4,300 pairs of shoes in March for $240 each. Grippers' target ending inventory is $10,000 plus 50% of the next month's cost of goods sold. Use this information and the sales budget from S10-3 to prepare Grippers' inventory, purchases, and cost of goods sold budget for January and February.

S10-5   **Continuation of S10-3: cash collections** *(Learning Objective 3)*
You prepared Grippers' sales budget in S10-3. Now, assume that Grippers' sales are 25% cash and 75% credit. Grippers' collection history indicates that credit sales are collected as follows:

> 30% in the month of the sale
>
> 60% in the month after the sale
>
> 6% two months after the sale
>
> 4% are never collected

November sales totaled $391,500, and December sales were $398,250. Prepare a schedule for the budgeted cash collections for January and February.

S10-6   **Continuation of S10-5: cash budget** *(Learning Objective 3)*
Refer to S10-5. Grippers has $8,300 cash on hand on January 1. The company requires a minimum cash balance of $7,500. January cash collections are $548,330 (as you calculated in S10-5). Total cash payments for January are $583,200. Prepare a cash budget for January. Will Grippers need to borrow cash by the end of January?

S10-7   **Revise sales budget** *(Learning Objective 4)*
Turn to the original Whitewater Sporting Goods Data Set item 3. Suppose June sales are expected to be $40,000 rather than $60,000. Revise Whitewater Sporting Goods' sales budget. What other components of Whitewater Sporting Goods' master budget would be affected by this change in the sales budget?

S10-8   **Revise inventory, purchases, and cost of goods sold budget** *(Learning Objective 4)*
Refer to the original Whitewater Sporting Goods Data Set item 5. Suppose cost of goods sold averages 75% of sales rather than 70%. Revise Whitewater Sporting Goods' inventory, purchases, and cost of goods sold budget for April and May. What other components of Whitewater Sporting Goods' master budget would be affected by the change in the budgeted cost of goods sold?

S10-9   **Revise cash collections budget** *(Learning Objective 4)*
Turn to the original Whitewater Sporting Goods Data Set item 4. Suppose 70% of sales are cash and 30% are credit. Revise Whitewater's sales budget and budgeted cash collections from customers for April and May.

S10-10   **Revise cash payments for purchases** *(Learning Objective 4)*
Refer to the original Whitewater Sporting Goods Data Set item 5. Suppose Whitewater Sporting Goods pays for 60% of inventory purchases in the month of the purchase and 40% during the next month. Revise Whitewater Sporting Goods' budgeted cash payments for purchases of inventory for April and May. (*Hint:* Assume that these new percentages also apply to March purchases of $33,600 given in Data Set item 5.)

S10-11 **Identify responsibility centers** *(Learning Objective 5)*
Fill in the blanks with the phrase that best completes the sentence.

A cost center	A responsibility center	Lower
An investment center	A revenue center	Higher
A profit center		

a. The maintenance department at the San Diego Zoo is _____.

b. The concession stand at the San Diego Zoo is _____.

c. The menswear department at Bloomingdale's, which is responsible for buying and selling merchandise, is _____.

d. A production line at a PalmPilot plant is _____.

e. _____ is any segment of the business whose manager is accountable for specific activities.

f. Gatorade, a division of Quaker Oats, is _____.

g. The sales manager in charge of Nike's northwest sales territory oversees _____.

h. Managers of cost and revenue centers are at _____ levels of the organization than are managers of profit and investment centers.

S10-12 **Corporate headquarters expenses** *(Learning Objective 5)*
In Exhibit 10-20, the next to last line of the CEO's report consists entirely of expenses. Describe the kinds of expenses that would be included in this category.

S10-13 **Management by exception** *(Learning Objective 5)*
Look at the performance report in Exhibit 10-20. According to the management by exception principle, on which variances should the manager of the Mexican sauces product line focus his or her efforts? For these variances, compute the variance as a percent of the budgeted amount and suggest some questions the manager may want to investigate.

S10-14 **Interpret favorable variance** *(Learning Objective 5)*
Exhibit 10-20 shows that the Mexican sauces product line had a favorable marketing expense variance. Does this favorable variance necessarily mean that the manager of the Mexican sauces line is doing a good job? Explain.

■ Exercises

E10-15 **Prepare summary performance report** *(Learning Objective 1)*
Hanna White owns a chain of travel goods stores. Last year, her sales staff sold 10,000 suitcases at an average sales price of $150. Variable expenses were 80% of sales revenue, and the total fixed expense was $100,000. This year, the chain sold more expensive product lines. Sales were 8,000 suitcases at an average price of $200. The variable expense percentage and the total fixed expense were the same both years. White evaluates the chain manager by comparing this year's income with last year's income.

   Prepare a performance report for this year, similar to Exhibit 10-4. How would you improve White's performance evaluation system to better analyze this year's results?

E10-16 **Prepare inventory, purchases, and cost of goods sold budget** *(Learning Objective 2)*

Car First sells tire rims. Its sales budget for the nine months ended September 30 follows:

	Quarter Ended			Nine-Month Total
	March 31	June 30	Sept. 30	
Cash sales, 30%	$ 30,000	$ 45,000	$ 37,500	$112,500
Credit sales, 70%	70,000	105,000	87,500	262,500
Total sales, 100%	$100,000	$150,000	$125,000	$375,000

In the past, cost of goods sold has been 60% of total sales. The director of marketing and the financial vice president agree that each quarter's ending inventory should not be below $20,000 plus 10% of cost of goods sold for the following quarter. The marketing director expects sales of $220,000 during the fourth quarter. The January 1 inventory was $19,000.

Prepare an inventory, purchases, and cost of goods sold budget for each of the first three quarters of the year. Compute cost of goods sold for the entire nine-month period (use Exhibit 10-8 as a model).

E10-17 **Prepare a cash collections budget** *(Learning Objective 3)*

Refer to the sales budget presented in E10-16. Credit sales are typically collected as follows: 60% in the quarter of the sale, 30% in the quarter after the sale, 7% in the second quarter after the sale, and 3% uncollectible. Prepare the cash collections budget for the third quarter (the quarter ended September 30).

E10-18 **Prepare a sales budget for a not-for-profit organization** *(Learning Objective 2)*

Pretty Place Preschool operates a not-for-profit morning preschool. Each family pays a nonrefundable registration fee of $120 per child per school year. Monthly tuition for the nine-month school year varies depending on the number of days per week that the child attends preschool. The monthly tuition is $115 for the two-day program, $130 for the three-day program, $145 for the four-day program, and $160 for the five-day program. The following enrollment has been projected for the coming year:

two-day program:	56 children
three-day program:	32 children
four-day program:	48 children
five-day program:	16 children

In addition to the morning preschool, Pretty Place Preschool offers a Lunch Bunch program where kids have the option of staying an extra hour for lunch and playtime. Pretty Place charges an additional $3 per child for every Lunch Bunch attended. Historically, half the children stay for Lunch Bunch an average of ten times a month.

Requirement

Calculate Pretty Place Preschool's budgeted revenue for the school year.

E10-19 **Continuation of E10-18: prepare an operating expenses budget** *(Learning Objectives 1, 2)*

Refer to Pretty Place Preschool's data in E10-18. Pretty Place's primary expense is payroll. The state allows a student-to-teacher ratio of no more than eight children to each teacher. Teachers are paid a flat salary each month as follows:

Teachers of two-day program:	$432 per month
Teachers of three-day program:	$648 per month
Teachers of four-day program:	$864 per month
Teachers of five-day program:	$1,080 per month
Preschool director's salary:	$1,500 per month

In addition to the salary expense, Pretty Place must pay federal payroll taxes (FICA taxes) in the amount of 7.65% of salary expense. Pretty Place leases its facilities from a local church, paying $2,000 per month plus 10% of monthly tuition revenue. Fixed operating expenses (telephone, Internet access, bookkeeping services, and so forth) amount to $850 per month over the nine-month school year. Variable monthly expenses (over the nine-month school year) for art supplies and other miscellaneous supplies are $12 per child.

Requirements

1. Prepare Pretty Place Preschool's monthly operating budget. Round all amounts to the nearest dollar.

2. Using your answer from E10-18 and Requirement 1, create Pretty Place Preschool's budgeted income statement for the entire nine-month school year. You may group all revenues together and all operating expenses together.

3. Pretty Place is a not-for-profit preschool. What might Pretty Place do with their projected income for the year?

E10-20 **Prepare an inventory, purchases, and cost of goods sold budget** *(Learning Objective 2)*

Cool Logos buys logo-imprinted merchandise and then sells it to university bookstores. Sales are expected to be $2,000,000 in September, $2,160,000 in October, $2,376,000 in November, and $2,500,000 in December. Cool Logos sets its prices to earn an average 30% gross profit on sales revenue. The company does not want inventory to fall below $400,000 plus 15% of the next month's cost of goods sold.

Prepare an inventory, purchases, and cost of goods sold budget for the months of October and November.

E10-21 **Prepare budgeted income statement** *(Learning Objective 2)*

Radical is an exotic car dealership. Suppose its Miami office projects that 2009 quarterly sales will increase by 3% in Quarter 1, by another 4% in Quarter 2, by another 6% in Quarter 3, and by another 5% in Quarter 4. Management expects operating expenses to be 80% of revenues during each of the first two quarters, 79% of revenues during the third quarter, and 81% during the fourth quarter. The office manager expects to borrow $100,000 on July 1, with quarterly principal payments of $10,000 beginning on September 30 and interest paid at an annual rate of 13%. Assume that fourth-quarter 2008 sales were $4,000,000.

continued . . .

Prepare a budgeted income statement for each of the four quarters of 2009 and for the entire year. Present the 2009 budget as follows:

Quarter 1	Quarter 2	Quarter 3	Quarter 4	Full Year

E10-22 **Compute cash receipts and payments** *(Learning Objective 3)*

Wonderland is a distributor of bottled water. For each of the items a through c, compute the amount of cash receipts or payments Wonderland will budget for September. The solution to one item may depend on the answer to an earlier item.

a. Management expects to sell equipment that costs $14,000 at a gain of $2,000. Accumulated depreciation on this equipment is $7,000.

b. Management expects to sell 7,500 cases of water in August and 9,200 in September. Each case sells for $12. Cash sales average 30% of total sales, and credit sales make up the rest. On average, three-fourths of credit sales are collected in the month of sale, with the balance collected the following month.

c. The company pays rent and property taxes of $4,200 each month. Commissions and other selling expenses average 25% of sales. Wonderland pays two-thirds of commissions and other selling expenses in the month incurred, with the balance paid the following month.

E10-23 **Prepare sales and cash collections budgets** *(Learning Objectives 2, 3)*

Potsie Reeds, a manufacturer of saxophone, oboe, and clarinet reeds, has projected sales to be $890,000 in October, $950,000 in November, $1,025,000 in December, and $920,000 in January. Potsie's sales are 25% cash and 75% credit. Potsie's collection history indicates that credit sales are collected as follows:

> 25% in the month of the sale
> 65% in the month after the sale
> 8% two months after the sale
> 2% are never collected

Requirements

1. Prepare a sales budget for all four months, showing the breakdown between cash and credit sales.

2. Prepare a cash collections budget for December and January. Round all answers up to the nearest dollar.

E10-24 **Prepare cash budget, then revise** *(Learning Objectives 3, 4)*

Unique Power, a family-owned battery store, began October with $10,500 cash. Management forecasts that collections from credit customers will be $11,000 in October and $15,000 in November. The store is scheduled to receive $6,000 cash on a business note receivable in October. Projected cash payments include inventory purchases ($13,000 in October and $13,900 in November) and operating expenses ($3,000 each month).

Unique Power's bank requires a $10,000 minimum balance in the store's checking account. At the end of any month when the account balance dips below $10,000, the bank automatically extends credit to the store in multiples of $1,000. Unique Power borrows as little as possible and pays back loans in quarterly installments of $2,000 plus 4% interest on the entire unpaid principal. The first payment occurs three months after the loan.

Requirements

1. Prepare Unique Power's cash budget for October and November.

2. How much cash will Unique Power borrow in November if collections from customers that month total $12,000 instead of $15,000?

E10-25 **Finish an incomplete cash budget** *(Learning Objective 3)*

You recently began a job as an accounting intern at Big Valley Adventures. Your first task was to help prepare the cash budget for February and March. Unfortunately, the computer with the budget file crashed, and you did not have a backup or even a hard copy. You ran a program to salvage bits of data from the budget file. After entering the following data in the budget, you may have just enough information to reconstruct the budget.

Big Valley Adventures eliminates any cash deficiency by borrowing the exact amount needed from Riverside Bank, where the current interest rate is 8%. Big Valley Adventures pays interest on its outstanding debt at the end of each month. The company also repays all borrowed amounts at the end of the month as cash becomes available.

Complete the following cash budget:

BIG VALLEY ADVENTURES LTD.
Cash Budget
February and March

	February	March
Beginning cash balance	$ 16,900	$?
Cash collections	?	79,600
Cash from sale of plant assets	0	1,800
Cash available	106,900	?
Cash payments:		
Purchase of inventory	$?	$41,000
Operating expenses	47,200	?
Total payments	98,000	?
(1) Ending cash balance before financing	?	25,100
Minimum cash balance desired	20,000	20,000
Cash excess (deficiency)	$?	$?
Financing of cash deficiency:		
Borrowing (at end of month)	$?	$?
Principal repayments (at end of month)	?	?
Interest expense	?	?
(2) Total effects of financing	?	?
Ending cash balance (1) + (2)	$?	$?

E10-26 **Prepare budgeted balance sheet** *(Learning Objective 3)*

Use the following information to prepare a budgeted balance sheet for Ocean.com at March 31, 2009. Show computations for the cash and owners' equity amounts.

a. March 31 inventory balance, $15,000

b. March payments for inventory, $4,600

c. March payments of accounts payable and accrued liabilities, $8,200

d. March 31 accounts payable balance, $4,300

continued . . .

e.   February 28 furniture and fixtures balance, $34,800; accumulated depreciation balance, $29,870

f.   February 28 owners' equity, $26,700

g.   March depreciation expense, $600

h.   Cost of goods sold, 60% of sales

i.   Other March expenses, including income tax, total $5,000; paid in cash

j.   February 28 cash balance, $11,400

k.   March budgeted sales, $12,200

l.   March 31 accounts receivable balance, one-fourth of March sales

m.   March cash receipts, $14,300

E10-27   **Identify types of responsibility centers** *(Learning Objective 5)*

Identify each responsibility center as a cost center, a revenue center, a profit center, or an investment center.

a.   The bakery department of a Publix supermarket reports income for the current year.

b.   Pace Foods is a subsidiary of Campbell Soup Company.

c.   The personnel department of State Farm Insurance Companies prepares its budget and subsequent performance report on the basis of its expected expenses for the year.

d.   The shopping section of Burpee.com reports both revenues and expenses.

e.   Burpee.com's investor relations Web site provides operating and financial information to investors and other interested parties.

f.   The manager of a BP service station is evaluated based on the station's revenues and expenses.

g.   A charter airline records revenues and expenses for each airplane each month. Each airplane's performance report shows its ratio of operating income to average book value.

h.   The manager of the southwest sales territory is evaluated based on a comparison of current period sales against budgeted sales.

E10-28   **Prepare performance reports at different organizational levels**
(Learning Objective 5)

Symphonic is a Seattle company that sells cell phones and PDAs on the Web. Symphonic has assistant managers for its digital and video cell phone operations. These assistant managers report to the manager of the total cell phone product line, who, with the manager of PDAs, reports to the manager for all sales of handheld devices, Beth Beverly. Beverly received the following data for November operations:

| | Cell Phones | | |
	Digital	Video	PDAs
Revenues, budget	$204,000	$800,000	$300,000
Expenses, budget..........	140,000	390,000	225,000
Revenues, actual............	214,000	840,000	290,000
Expenses, actual............	135,000	400,000	230,000

Arrange the data in a performance report similar to Exhibit 10-20. Show November results, in thousands of dollars, for digital cell phones, for the total cell phone product line, and for all devices. Should Beverly investigate the performance of digital cell phone operations? Why or why not?

▪ Problems (Problem Set A)

P10-29A **Prepare budgeted income statement** *(Learning Objective 2)*
The budget committee of Big Eagle Office Supply has assembled the following data. As the business manager, you must prepare the budgeted income statements for May and June 2009.

a. Sales in April were $42,100. You forecast that monthly sales will increase 2.0% in May and 2.4% in June.

b. Big Eagle Office Supply maintains inventory of $9,000 plus 25% of sales budgeted for the following month. Monthly purchases average 50% of sales revenues in that same month. Actual inventory on April 30 is $14,000. Sales budgeted for July are $42,400.

c. Monthly salaries amount to $4,000. Sales commissions equal 4% of sales for that month. Combine salaries and commissions into a single figure.

d. Other monthly expenses are:

Rent expense	$3,000, paid as incurred
Depreciation expense	$600
Insurance expense	$200, expiration of prepaid amount
Income tax	20% of operating income

Prepare Big Eagle Office Supply's budgeted income statements for May and June. Show cost of goods sold computations. Round *all* amounts to the nearest $100. (Round amounts ending in $50 or more upward and amounts ending in less than $50 downward.) For example, budgeted May sales are $42,900 ($42,100 × 1.02) and June sales are $43,900 ($42,900 × 1.024).

P10-30A **Continuation of P10-29A: cash budgets**
Refer to P10-29A. Big Eagle Office Supply's sales are 70% cash and 30% credit (use the rounded sales on the last line of P10-29A). Credit sales are collected in the month after sale. Inventory purchases are paid 50% in the month of purchase and 50% the following month. Salaries and sales commissions are also paid half in the month earned and half the next month. Income tax is paid at the end of the year.

The April 30, 2009, balance sheet showed the following balances:

Cash	$11,000
Accounts payable	7,400
Salary and commissions payable	2,850

continued . . .

Requirements

1. Prepare schedules of (a) budgeted cash collections, (b) budgeted cash payments for purchases, and (c) budgeted cash payments for operating expenses. Show amounts for each month and totals for May and June. Round your computations to the nearest dollar.

2. Prepare a cash budget similar to Exhibit 10-14. If no financing activity took place, what is the budgeted cash balance on June 30, 2009?

P10-31A **Prepare budgeted balance sheet and statement of cash flows** *(Learning Objective 3)*

State Printing of Baltimore has applied for a loan. Bank of America has requested a budgeted balance sheet at April 30, 2009, and a budgeted statement of cash flows for April. As State Printing's controller, you have assembled the following information:

a. March 31 equipment balance, $52,400; accumulated depreciation, $41,300.
b. April capital expenditures of $42,800 budgeted for cash purchase of equipment.
c. April depreciation expense, $900.
d. Cost of goods sold, 60% of sales.
e. Other April operating expenses, including income tax, total $13,200, 25% of which will be paid in cash and the remainder accrued at April 30.
f. March 31 owners' equity, $93,700.
g. March 31 cash balance, $40,600.
h. April budgeted sales, $90,000, 70% of which is for cash. Of the remaining 30%, half will be collected in April and half in May.
i. April cash collections on March sales, $29,700.
j. April cash payments of March 31 liabilities incurred for March purchases of inventory, $17,300.
k. March 31 inventory balance, $29,600.
l. April purchases of inventory, $10,000 for cash and $36,800 on credit. Half of the credit purchases will be paid in April and half in May.

Requirements

1. Prepare the budgeted balance sheet for State Printing at April 30, 2009. Show separate computations for cash, inventory, and owners' equity balances.

2. Prepare the budgeted statement of cash flows for April.

3. Suppose State Printing has become aware of more efficient (and more expensive) equipment than it budgeted for purchase in April. What is the total amount of cash available for equipment purchases in April, before financing, if the minimum desired ending cash balance is $21,000? (For this requirement, disregard the $42,800 initially budgeted for equipment purchases.)

P10-32A **Continuation of P10-31A: revised sales** *(Learning Objective 4)*

Refer to P10-31A. Before granting a loan to State Printing, Bank of America asks for a sensitivity analysis assuming that April sales are only $60,000 rather than the $90,000 originally budgeted. (While the cost of goods sold will change, assume that purchases, depreciation, and the other operating expenses will remain the same as in P10-31A.)

Requirements

1. Prepare a revised budgeted balance sheet for State Printing, showing separate computations for cash, inventory, and owners' equity balances.

2. Suppose State Printing has a minimum desired cash balance of $23,000. Will the company need to borrow cash in April?

3. In this sensitivity analysis, sales declined by 33⅓% ($30,000 ÷ $90,000). Is the decline in expenses and income more or less than 33⅓%? Explain.

P10-33A Identify responsibility centers *(Learning Objective 5)*

Is each of the following most likely a cost center, a revenue center, a profit center, or an investment center?

a. Shipping department of Amazon.com

b. Eastern district of a salesperson's territory

c. Child care department of a church or synagogue

d. Catering operation of Sonny's BBQ restaurant

e. Executive headquarters of the United Way

f. Accounts payable section of the accounting department at Home Depot

g. Proposed new office of Coldwell Banker, a real estate firm

h. Disneyland

i. The Empire State Building in New York City

j. Branch warehouse of Dalton Carpets

k. Information systems department of Habitat for Humanity

l. Service department of Audio Forest stereo shop

m. Investments department of Citibank

n. Assembly-line supervisors at Dell Computer

o. American subsidiary of a Japanese manufacturer

p. Surgery unit of a privately owned hospital

q. Research and development department of Cisco Systems

r. Childrenswear department at a Target store

s. Typesetting department of Northend Press, a printing company

t. Prescription-filling department of Drugstore.com

u. Order-taking department at L.L.Bean

v. Personnel department of Goodyear Tire and Rubber Company

w. Grounds maintenance department at Augusta National Golf Club

P10-34A **Prepare performance reports for various organizational levels** *(Learning Objectives 1, 5)*

Pretty Pups operates a chain of pet stores in the Midwest. The manager of each store reports to the region manager, who, in turn, reports to the headquarters in Milwaukee, Wisconsin. The *actual* income statements for the Dayton store, the Ohio region (including the Dayton store), and the company as a whole (including the Ohio region) for July 2009 are:

	Dayton	Ohio	Company-Wide
Revenue	$148,900	$1,647,000	$4,200,000
Expenses:			
Region manager/ headquarters office	$ —	$ 60,000	$ 116,000
Cost of materials	81,100	871,900	1,807,000
Salary expense	38,300	415,100	1,119,000
Depreciation expense	7,200	91,000	435,000
Utilities expense	4,000	46,200	260,000
Rent expense	2,400	34,700	178,000
Total expenses	133,000	1,518,900	3,915,000
Operating income	$ 15,900	$ 128,100	$ 285,000

Budgeted amounts for July were as follows:

	Dayton	Ohio	Company-Wide
Revenue	$162,400	$1,769,700	$4,450,000
Expenses:			
Region manager/ headquarters office	$ —	$ 65,600	$ 118,000
Cost of materials	86,400	963,400	1,972,000
Salary expense	38,800	442,000	1,095,000
Depreciation expense	7,200	87,800	449,000
Utilities expense	4,400	54,400	271,000
Rent expense	3,600	32,300	174,000
Total expenses	140,400	1,645,500	4,079,000
Operating income	$ 22,000	$ 124,200	$ 371,000

Requirements

1. Prepare a report for July 2009 that shows the performance of the Dayton store, the Ohio region, and the company as a whole. Follow the format of Exhibit 10-20.

2. As the Ohio region manager, would you investigate the Dayton store on the basis of this report? Why or why not?

3. Briefly discuss the benefits of budgeting. Base your discussion on Pretty Pups' performance report.

Problems (Problem Set B)

P10-35B Prepare budgeted income statement *(Learning Objective 2)*

Representatives of the various departments of Have Fun Sports have assembled the following data. As the business manager, you must prepare the budgeted income statements for August and September 2009.

a. Sales in July were $196,000. You forecast that monthly sales will increase 3% in August and 2% in September.

b. Have Fun Sports tries to maintain inventory of $50,000 plus 20% of sales budgeted for the following month. Monthly purchases average 60% of sales revenue in that same month. Actual inventory on July 31 is $90,000. Sales budgeted for October are $220,000.

c. Monthly salaries amount to $15,000. Sales commissions equal 6% of sales for that month. Combine salaries and commissions into a single figure.

d. Other monthly expenses are:

Rent expense.............................	$3,000, paid as incurred
Depreciation expense	$600
Insurance expense	$200, expiration of prepaid amount
Income tax	20% of operating income

Prepare Have Fun Sports' budgeted income statements for August and September. Show cost of goods sold computations. Round *all* amounts to the nearest $1,000. For example, budgeted August sales are $202,000 ($196,000 × 1.03) and September sales are $206,000 ($202,000 × 1.02).

P10-36B Continuation of P10-35B: cash budgets *(Learning Objective 3)*

Refer to P10-35B. Have Fun Sports' sales are 50% cash and 50% credit (use sales on the last two lines of P10-35B). Credit sales are collected in the month after the sale. Inventory purchases are paid 60% in the month of purchase and 40% the following month. Salaries and sales commissions are paid three-fourths in the month earned and one-fourth the next month. Income tax is paid at the end of the year.

The July 31, 2009, balance sheet showed the following balances:

Cash..	$22,000
Accounts payable	52,000
Salaries and commissions payable	6,750

Requirements

1. Prepare schedules of (a) budgeted cash collections from customers, (b) budgeted cash payments for purchases, and (c) budgeted cash payments for operating expenses. Show amounts for each month and totals for August and September. Round your computations to the nearest dollar.

2. Prepare a cash budget similar to Exhibit 10-14. If no financing activity took place, what is the budgeted cash balance on September 30, 2009?

P10-37B **Prepare budgeted balance sheet and statement of cash flows** *(Learning Objective 3)*

Wildwind has applied for a loan. First Central Bank has requested a budgeted balance sheet at June 30, 2009, and a budgeted statement of cash flows for June. As the controller (chief accounting officer) of Wildwind, you have assembled the following information:

a. May 31 equipment balance, $80,800; accumulated depreciation, $12,400.

b. June capital expenditures of $16,400 budgeted for cash purchase of equipment.

c. June depreciation expense, $400.

d. Cost of goods sold, 50% of sales.

e. Other June operating expenses, including income tax, total $34,000, 75% of which will be paid in cash and the remainder accrued at June 30.

f. May 31 owners' equity, $137,500.

g. May 31 cash balance, $50,200.

h. June budgeted sales, $85,000, 40% of which is for cash. Of the remaining 60%, half will be collected in June and half in July.

i. June cash collections on May sales, $15,300.

j. June cash payments of liabilities for May inventory purchases on credit, $8,300.

k. May 31 inventory balance, $11,900.

l. June purchases of inventory, $11,000 for cash and $37,200 on credit. Half the credit purchases will be paid in June and half in July.

Requirements

1. Prepare the budgeted balance sheet for Wildwind at June 30, 2009. Show separate computations for cash, inventory, and owners' equity balances.

2. Prepare the budgeted statement of cash flows for June.

3. On the basis of this data, if you were a First Central Bank loan officer, would you grant Wildwind a loan? Give your reason.

P10-38B **Continuation of P10-37B: revised sales** *(Learning Objective 4)*

Refer to P10-37B. Before granting a loan to Wildwind, First Central Bank asks for a sensitivity analysis, assuming that June sales are only $65,000 rather than the $85,000 originally budgeted. (While cost of goods sold will change, assume that purchases, depreciation, and the other operating expenses will remain the same as in P10-37B.)

Requirements

1. Prepare a revised budgeted balance sheet for Wildwind, showing separate computations for cash, inventory, and owners' equity balances.

2. Suppose Wildwind has a minimum desired cash balance of $35,000. Will the company borrow cash in June?

3. How would this sensitivity analysis affect First Central's loan decision?

P10-39B **Identify responsibility centers** *(Learning Objective 5)*

Is each of the following most likely a cost center, a revenue center, a profit center, or an investment center?

a. Purchasing department of Milliken, a textile manufacturer

b. Quality control department of Mayfield Dairies

c. European subsidiary of Coca-Cola

d. Payroll department at the University of Wisconsin

e. Lighting department in a Sears store

f. Children's nursery in a church or synagogue

g. Personnel department of E*TRADE, the online broker

h. igourmet.com, an e-tailer of gourmet cheeses

i. Service department of an automobile dealership

j. Customer service department of Procter & Gamble

k. Proposed new office of Deutsche Bank

l. Southwest region of Pizza Inns

m. Delta Airlines

n. Order-taking department at Lands' End

o. Editorial department of *The Wall Street Journal*

p. A Ford Motor Company production plant

q. Police department of Boston

r. Century 21 Real Estate

s. A small pet-grooming business

t. Northeast sales territory for Boise-Cascade

u. Different product lines of Broyhill, a furniture manufacturer

v. McDonald's restaurants under the supervision of a regional manager

w. Job superintendents of a home builder

P10-40B **Prepare performance reports for various organizational levels** *(Learning Objectives 1, 5)*

PG is a chain of home electronics stores. Each store has a manager who answers to a city manager, who, in turn, reports to a statewide manager. The actual income statements of Store No. 23, all stores in the Dallas area (including Store No. 23), and all stores in the state of Texas (including all Dallas stores) are summarized as follows for April:

	Store No. 23	Dallas	State of Texas
Sales revenue......................	$43,300	$486,000	$3,228,500
Expenses:			
City/state manager's office expenses	$ —	$ 18,000	$ 44,000
Cost of goods sold..........	15,000	171,300	1,256,800
Salary expense...............	4,000	37,500	409,700
Depreciation expense	3,700	13,100	320,000
Utilities expense	1,900	19,300	245,600
Rent expense.................	700	16,600	186,000
Total expenses..................	25,300	275,800	2,462,100
Operating income.............	$18,000	$210,200	$ 766,400

Budgeted amounts for April were as follows:

	Store No. 23	Dallas	State of Texas
Sales revenue......................	$39,000	$470,000	$3,129,000
Expenses:			
City/state manager's office expenses	$ —	$ 19,000	$ 45,000
Cost of goods sold..........	12,100	160,800	1,209,000
Salary expense................	6,000	37,900	412,000
Depreciation expense	3,200	23,400	320,000
Utilities expense	1,000	15,000	240,000
Rent expense.................	700	15,700	181,000
Total expenses...................	23,000	271,800	2,407,000
Operating income...............	$16,000	$198,200	$ 722,000

Requirements

1. Prepare a report for April that shows the performance of Store No. 23, all of the stores in the Dallas area, and all of the stores in Texas. Follow the format of Exhibit 10-20.

2. As the city manager of Dallas, would you investigate Store No. 23 on the basis of this report? Why or why not?

3. Briefly discuss the benefits of budgeting. Base your discussion on PG's performance report.

Apply Your Knowledge

▪ Decision Cases

Case 10-41. Suggest performance improvements *(Learning Objective 1)*

Donna Tse recently joined Cycle World, a bicycle store in St. Louis, as an assistant manager. She recently finished her accounting courses. Cycle World's manager and owner, Jeff Towry, asks Tse to prepare a budgeted income statement for 2009 based on the information he has collected. Tse's budget follows:

CYCLE WORLD
Budgeted Income Statement
For the Year Ending July 31, 2009

Sales revenue		$244,000
Cost of goods sold		177,000
Gross profit		67,000
Operating expenses:		
Salary and commission expense	$ 46,000	
Rent expense	8,000	
Depreciation expense	2,000	
Insurance expense	800	
Miscellaneous expenses	12,000	68,800
Operating loss		(1,800)
Interest expense		225
Net loss		$ (2,025)

Requirements

Tse does not want to give Towry this budget without making constructive suggestions for steps Towry could take to improve expected performance. Write a memo to Towry outlining your suggestions. Your memo should take the following form:

Date: _____

To: Mr. Jeff Towry, Manager
    Cycle World

From: Donna Tse

Subject: Cycle World's 2009 budgeted income statement

Case 10-42. Prepare cash budgets under two alternatives *(Learning Objectives 2, 3)*

Each autumn, as a hobby, Suzanne De Angelo weaves cotton place mats to sell at a local crafts shop. The mats sell for $20 per set of four. The shop charges a 10% commission and remits the net proceeds to De Angelo at the end of December.

continued . . .

De Angelo has woven and sold 25 sets each of the last two years. She has enough cotton in inventory to make another 25 sets. She paid $7 per set for the cotton. De Angelo uses a four-harness loom that she purchased for cash exactly two years ago. It is depreciated at the rate of $10 per month. The accounts payable relate to the cotton inventory and are payable by September 30.

De Angelo is considering buying an eight-harness loom so that she can weave more intricate patterns in linen. The new loom costs $1,000; it would be depreciated at $20 per month. Her bank has agreed to lend her $1,000 at 18% interest, with $200 principal plus accrued interest payable each December 31. De Angelo believes she can weave 15 linen place mat sets in time for the Christmas rush if she does not weave any cotton mats. She predicts that each linen set will sell for $50. Linen costs $18 per set. De Angelo's supplier will sell her linen on credit, payable December 31.

De Angelo plans to keep her old loom whether or not she buys the new loom. The balance sheet for her weaving business at August 31, 2009, is as follows:

SUZANNE DE ANGELO, WEAVER
Balance Sheet
August 31, 2009

Current assets:			Current liabilities:	
Cash	$ 25		Accounts payable	$ 74
Inventory of cotton	175			
	200			
Fixed assets:				
Loom	500		Owner's equity	386
Accumulated depreciation	(240)			
	260			
Total assets	$460		Total liabilities and owner's equity	$460

Requirements

1. Prepare a cash budget for the four months ending December 31, 2009, for two alternatives: weaving the place mats in cotton using the existing loom and weaving the place mats in linen using the new loom. For each alternative, prepare a budgeted income statement for the four months ending December 31, 2009, and a budgeted balance sheet at December 31, 2009.

2. On the basis of financial considerations only, what should De Angelo do? Give your reason.

3. What nonfinancial factors might De Angelo consider in her decision?

■ Ethical Issue

Issue 10-43. Ethical considerations for padded budgets *(Learning Objectives 1, 5)*
Residence Suites operates a regional hotel chain. Each hotel is operated by a manager and an assistant manager/controller. Many of the staff who run the front desk, clean the rooms, and prepare the breakfast buffet work part-time or have a second job, so turnover is high.

Assistant manager/controller Terry Dunn asked the new bookkeeper to help prepare the hotel's master budget. The master budget is prepared once a year and submitted to company headquarters for approval. Once approved, the master budget is used to evaluate the hotel's performance. These performance evaluations affect hotel managers' bonuses; they also affect company decisions about which hotels deserve extra funds for capital improvements.

When the budget was almost complete, Dunn asked the bookkeeper to increase amounts budgeted for labor and supplies by 15%. When asked why, Dunn responded that hotel manager Clay Murry told her to do this when she began working at the hotel. Murry explained that this budgetary cushion gave him flexibility in running the hotel. For example, because company headquarters tightly controls capital improvement funds, Murry can use the extra money budgeted for labor and supplies to replace broken televisions or to pay "bonuses" to keep valued employees. Dunn initially accepted this explanation because she had observed similar behavior at her previous place of employment.

Put yourself in Dunn's position. In deciding how to deal with the situation, answer the following questions:

1. What is the ethical issue?
2. What are my options?
3. What are the possible consequences?
4. What should I do?

■ Team Project

Project 10-44. Analyzing and discussing budget concerns (*Learning Objectives 1, 2, 5*)

Xellnet provides e-commerce software for the pharmaceuticals industry. Xellnet is organized into several divisions. A company-wide planning committee sets general strategy and goals for the company and its divisions, but each division develops its own budget.

Rick Watson is the new division manager of wireless communications software. His division has two departments: development and sales. Carrie Pronai manages the 20 or so programmers and systems specialists typically employed in the development department to create and update the division's software applications. Liz Smith manages the sales department.

Xellnet considers the divisions to be investment centers. To earn his bonus next year, Watson must achieve a 30% return on the $3 million invested in his division. This amounts to $900,000 of income (30% × $3 million). Within the wireless division, development is a cost center, while sales is a revenue center.

Budgeting is in progress. Pronai met with her staff and is now struggling with two sets of numbers. Alternative A is her best estimate of next year's costs. However, unexpected problems can arise in the writing of software, and finding competent programmers is an ongoing challenge. She knows that Watson was a programmer before he earned an MBA, so he should be sensitive to this uncertainty. Consequently, she is thinking of increasing her budgeted costs (Alternative B). Her department's bonuses largely depend on whether the department meets its budgeted costs.

continued . . .

XELLNET Wireless Division Development Budget 2009	Alternative A	Alternative B
Salaries expense (including overtime and part-time)	$ 2,400,000	$2,640,000
Software expense	120,000	132,000
Travel expense	65,000	71,500
Depreciation expense	255,000	255,000
Miscellaneous expense	100,000	110,000
Total expense	$ 2,940,000	$3,208,500

Liz Smith is also struggling with her sales budget. Companies have made their initial investments in communications software, so it is harder to win new customers. If things go well, she believes her sales team can maintain the level of growth achieved over the last few years. This is Alternative A in the sales budget. However, if Smith is too optimistic, sales may fall short of the budget. If this happens, her team will not receive bonuses. Therefore, Smith is considering reducing the sales numbers and submitting Alternative B.

XELLNET Wireless Division Sales Budget 2009	Alternative A	Alternative B
Sales revenue	$ 5,000,000	$4,500,000
Salaries expense	360,000	360,000
Travel expense	240,000	210,500

Split your team into three groups. Each group should meet separately before the entire team meets.

Requirements

1. The first group plays the role of Development Manager Carrie Pronai. Before meeting with the entire team, determine which set of budget numbers you are going to present to Rick Watson. Write a memo supporting your decision. Use the format shown in Case 10-41. Give this memo to the third group before the team meeting.

2. The second group plays the role of Sales Manager Liz Smith. Before meeting with the entire team, determine which set of budget numbers you are going to present to Rick Watson. Write a memo supporting your decision. Use the format shown in Case 10-41. Give this memo to the third group before the team meeting.

3. The third group plays the role of Division Manager Rick Watson. Before meeting with the entire team, use the memos that Pronai and Smith provided to prepare a division budget based on the sales and development budgets. Your divisional overhead costs (additional costs beyond those incurred by the development and sales departments) are approximately $390,000. Determine whether the wireless division can meet its targeted 30% return on assets given the budgeted alternatives submitted by your department managers.

During the meeting of the entire team, the group playing Watson presents the division budget and considers its implications. Each group should take turns discussing its concerns with the proposed budget. The team as a whole should consider whether the division budget must be revised. The team should prepare a report that includes the division budget and a summary of the issues covered in the team meeting.

11 Flexible Budgets and Standard Costs

How does McDonald's make sure that its 30,000 restaurants deliver quality, service, cleanliness, and value to over 46 million customers worldwide each day? By using budgets, standards, and variances. Managers budget sales for each hour and schedule just enough workers to handle the budgeted level of sales. During the day, the manager computes variances for sales (for example, actual sales minus budgeted sales) and for direct labor. If actual sales fall short of the budget, the manager can send employees home early. This helps control direct labor cost.

McDonald's also sets budgets and standards for direct materials. From Beijing to Miami, the standards for a regular McDonald's hamburger are the same: 1 bun, 1 hamburger patty, 1 pickle slice, 1/8 teaspoon of onion, 1/4 teaspoon of mustard, and 1/2 ounce of ketchup. To control direct materials costs, for example, the manager compares the

number of hamburger patties actually used with the number of patties that should have been used, given the store's actual sales.

McDonald's uses budgets, standards, and variances to control costs so prices remain low enough that customers believe McDonald's provides good *value*. McDonald's also uses standards and variances to motivate employees to focus on:

- Quality—sandwiches unsold within ten minutes are thrown away.
- Service—customers should receive food within 90 seconds of ordering.
- Cleanliness—mystery shoppers score restaurants' cleanliness. ■

Learning Objectives

1 Prepare a flexible budget for planning purposes

2 Use the sales volume variance and flexible budget variance to explain why actual results differ from the master budget

3 Identify the benefits of standard costs and learn how to set standards

4 Compute standard cost variances for direct materials and direct labor

5 Compute manufacturing overhead variances

6 (Appendix) Record transactions at standard cost and prepare a standard cost income statement

This chapter builds on your knowledge of budgeting (from Chapter 10) to show how managers use variances to learn *why* actual results differ from budgets. Why is this important? Because you must know *why* actual costs differ from the budget to identify problems and to decide what, if any, action to take.

In this chapter, you'll learn how you—like managers of companies from McDonald's to Dell—can use flexible budgets, standards, and variances to pinpoint *why* actual results differ from the budget. This is the first step in determining how to correct problems.

How Managers Use Flexible Budgets

In this chapter we'll see how Kool-Time Pools, an installer of in-ground swimming pools, uses flexible budgets and standard costs to help control its operations. Kool-Time uses direct materials, direct labor, and manufacturing overhead (such as the monthly lease on the earth moving equipment) to manufacture the swimming pools directly on the customer's site. In addition to manufacturing costs, the company incurs selling and administrative expenses in conjunction with its marketing and sales efforts. As with most companies, some of these costs are variable, while others are fixed.

What Is a Static Budget?

At the beginning of the year, Kool-Time's managers prepared a master budget like the one in Chapter 10. The master budget is a **static budget**, which means that it is prepared for *one* level of sales volume. Once the master budget is developed, it does not change.

Exhibit 11-1 compares June's actual results with the static (master) budget for June. The difference between actual results and the budget is called a **variance**. In this case, because we are comparing actual results against the static budget, this particular variance is called the static budget variance. Variances are considered favorable (F) when a higher actual amount increases operating income and unfavorable (U) when a higher actual amount decreases operating income. Favorable variances should not necessarily be interpreted as "good." Likewise, unfavorable variances should not be interpreted as "bad." Rather, they simply indicate the variance's effect on operating income. Exhibit 11-1 shows that Kool-Time's revenues were $25,000 higher than expected and its expenses were $21,000 higher than expected. Together, these variances resulted in a $4,000 favorable static budget variance for operating income. However, Kool-Time's managers are still concerned about the $21,000 unfavorable expense variance.

EXHIBIT 11-1	Actual Results Versus Static Budget

KOOL-TIME POOLS
Comparison of Actual Results with Static Budget
Month Ended June 30, 2007

	Actual Results	Static (Master) Budget	Static Budget Variance
Output units (pools installed)	10	8	2 F
Sales revenue	$121,000	$96,000	$25,000 F
Expenses	(105,000)	(84,000)	(21,000) U
Operating income	$ 16,000	$12,000	$ 4,000 F

What Is a Flexible Budget?

The static budget variance in Exhibit 11-1 is hard to analyze because the static budget is based on eight pools, but actual results are for ten pools. Trying to compare actual results against a budget prepared for a different volume is like comparing apples to oranges. Why did the $21,000 unfavorable expense variance occur? Were materials wasted? Did the cost of materials suddenly increase? How much of the additional expense arose because Kool-Time installed ten pools rather than eight? The simple comparison presented in Exhibit 11-1 does not give managers enough information to answer these questions.

However, flexible budgets can help managers answer such questions. Exhibit 11-2 shows that in contrast to the static budget developed for a single level of sales volume, **flexible budgets** are summarized budgets prepared for different levels of volume. Flexible budgets can be used to help managers plan for future periods *and* to evaluate performance after the period has ended. We'll consider both uses and then get back to the question of why the $21,000 unfavorable expense variance occurred.

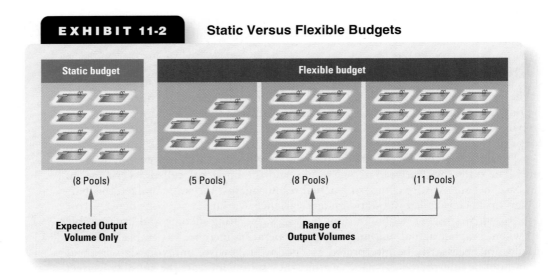

EXHIBIT 11-2   **Static Versus Flexible Budgets**

Using Flexible Budgets for Planning

1 Prepare a flexible budget for planning purposes

Managers can use flexible budgets for planning revenues and expenses at different sales volumes. Even though Kool-Time's managers believe the company will install eight pools in June, company managers know that they might not be correct about this estimate. Pool sales could be higher or lower during the month, and managers need to be prepared for both possibilities. Flexible budgets show how Kool-Time's revenues and expenses *should* vary as the number of pools installed varies.

Let's prepare flexible budgets for Kool-Time, assuming pool sales for the month could be as low as 5 or as high as 11. We'll start with revenues: The budgeted sales price per pool is $12,000, so each additional pool sale should yield another $12,000 of revenue. Exhibit 11-3 shows projected revenues at three possible volumes: 5 pools, 8 pools, and 11 pools.

EXHIBIT 11-3   **Flexible Budget**

KOOL-TIME POOLS
Flexible Budget
Month Ended June 30, 2007

	Flexible Budget per Output Unit	Output Units (Pools Installed)		
		5	8	11
Sales revenue	$12,000	$60,000	$96,000	$132,000
Variable expenses	8,000	40,000	64,000	88,000
Fixed expenses		20,000	20,000	20,000
Total expenses		60,000	84,000	108,000
Operating income		$ 0	$12,000	$ 24,000

To project expenses at different volumes, managers must know how the company's costs behave. Total fixed costs will be the same regardless of volume as long as the volume is within the same relevant range. However, total variable costs will change as volume changes. Managers use a mixed cost equation, such as the one we discussed in Chapter 6, to budget expenses at different volumes. This is sometimes referred to as a flexible budget formula:

$$\text{Flexible budget total cost} = \left(\begin{array}{c} \text{Number of} \\ \text{output units} \end{array} \times \begin{array}{c} \text{Variable cost} \\ \text{per output unit} \end{array} \right) + \text{Total fixed cost}$$

Kool-Time's variable costs are $8,000 per pool. Of this amount, $7,000 is for variable manufacturing costs (direct materials, direct labor, and variable manufacturing overhead such as gasoline to operate the earth moving equipment), while $1,000 is for variable selling and administrative expenses (such as the commission paid to sales staff on every pool sold). It is these variable expenses that put the "flex" in the flexible budget because budgeted total monthly fixed costs remain constant. Kool-Time's monthly fixed costs are $20,000. This includes $12,000 of fixed monthly manufacturing overhead (such as the the monthly lease of earth-moving equipment), while $8,000 relates to fixed selling and administrative expenses (sales and administrative salaries, lease of sales office, telephone and Internet service, and so forth).

Using this information on cost behavior, managers can predict costs at different volumes, just as we did in Chapter 6. For example, the total budgeted cost for five pools is:

$60,000 = (5 pools × $8,000 variable cost per pool) + $20,000 fixed cost

Likewise, the total budgeted cost for 11 pools is:

$108,000 = (11 pools × $8,000 variable cost per pool) + $20,000 fixed cost

Exhibit 11-3 shows the revenues and expenses anticipated if Kool-Time sells 5, 8, or 11 pools during the month. Kool-Time's best estimate is 8 pools, but by acknowledging that sales could be as low as 5 or as high as 11, Kool-Time's managers will be better prepared for any differences in volume that may arise.

Managers develop flexible budgets like Exhibit 11-3 for any number of volumes using a simple Excel spreadsheet or more sophisticated Web-based budget management software. However, managers must be careful: *They must consider the company's relevant range.* Why? Because total monthly fixed costs and the variable cost per pool change outside this range. Kool-Time's relevant range is 0 to 11 pools. If the company installs 12 pools, it will have to lease additional equipment, so fixed monthly costs will exceed $20,000. Kool-Time also will have to pay workers an overtime premium, so the variable cost per pool will be more than $8,000.

Graphing Flexible Budget Costs

Sometimes, it's helpful for managers to see a graph of the flexible budget costs. Exhibit 11-4 shows budgeted total costs for the entire relevant range of 0 to 11 pools. Because Kool-Time has both fixed and variable costs, its total costs are mixed. Kool-Time's flexible budget graph has the same characteristics as the mixed cost graphs we discussed in Chapter 6. The total cost line intersects the vertical axis at the level of total fixed cost ($20,000) that Kool-Time will incur whether it installs 0 pools or 11 pools. The total cost line also slopes upward at the rate of $8,000 per pool, which is Kool-Time's variable cost per pool. Each additional pool, up to 11 pools, should cost Kool-Time an extra $8,000.

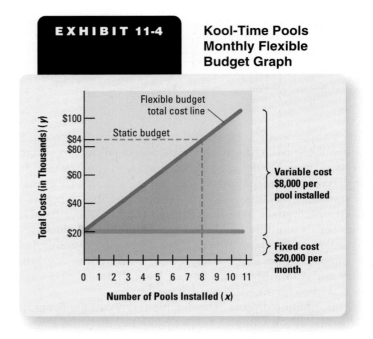

EXHIBIT 11-4

Kool-Time Pools Monthly Flexible Budget Graph

As shown by the dotted line in Exhibit 11-4, Kool-Time expects to install eight pools in June (at a total cost of $84,000). But managers also can use this graph to *plan* costs for anywhere from 0 to 11 pools.

Using Flexible Budgets for Evaluating Performance

We just saw how managers can use flexible budgets for planning purposes. But managers can also use flexible budgets *at the end of the period* to evaluate the company's financial performance and help control costs. Rather than comparing actual revenues and expenses against the static budget (as shown in Exhibit 11-1), managers can compare the actual results against the flexible budget *for the actual volume of output* that occurred during the period.

Consider June, when Kool-Time *actually* installed ten pools. The flexible budget graph in Exhibit 11-5 show that *flexible budgeted* total costs for ten pools are:

Variable costs (10 × $8,000)	$ 80,000
Fixed costs	20,000
Total costs..	$100,000

June's *actual* costs were $105,000 (Exhibit 11-1). Consequently, June's actual costs for ten pools ($105,000) slightly exceed the budget for ten pools ($100,000). Managers can use graphs such as Exhibit 11-5 to see at a glance whether actual costs are either of the following:

- Higher than budgeted for the actual volume of output (as in April, June, and August)
- Lower than budgeted for the actual volume of output (as in May and July)

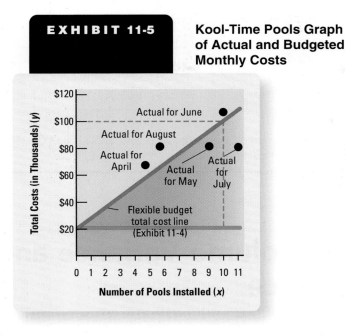

EXHIBIT 11-5   **Kool-Time Pools Graph of Actual and Budgeted Monthly Costs**

We used a simple graph to illustrate how Kool-Time's managers can compare actual costs against flexible budgeted costs. Unlike the apples-to-oranges comparison in Exhibit 11-1, comparing actual costs against flexible budgeted costs allows managers to make an apples-to-apples comparison. Why? Because both the actual costs and the flexible budgeted costs are based on the *same actual volume of activity (ten pools)*. In other words, if management would have had a crystal ball before the month began, they would have budgeted for ten pools rather than eight. By comparing the actual costs with the flexible budgeted costs for ten pools, Kool-Time's managers see that their expenses were only $5,000 higher than anticipated *for this volume*. This explains a portion of the $21,000 unfavorable expense variance shown in Exhibit 11-1. In the next section, we'll see how managers can perform a more in-depth analysis to find out more about why the $21,000 unfavorable expense variance shown in Exhibit 11-1 occurred.

Stop & Think...

Use the graph in Exhibit 11-5 and Kool-Time's flexible budget mixed cost equation to answer the following questions:

1. How many pools did Kool-Time install in July?
2. What were Kool-Time's actual costs in July?
3. Using Kool-Time's flexible budget mixed cost equation, what is the flexible budget total cost for the month of July?
4. Is Kool-Time's variance for total costs favorable or unfavorable in July?

Answer:

1. Exhibit 11-5 shows that Kool-Time installed 11 pools in July.
2. Exhibit 11-5 shows that Kool-Time's actual costs in July were about $80,000.

continued . . .

3. Using Kool-Time's flexible budget mixed cost equation:

Variable costs (11 × $8,000)...	$ 88,000
Fixed costs...	20,000
Total costs...	$108,000

4. Kool-Time's July variance for total costs is $28,000 ($108,000 − $80,000) favorable because actual costs are less than the budget.

Computing the Sales Volume Variance and Flexible Budget Variance

2 Use the sales volume variance and flexible budget variance to explain why actual results differ from the master budget

Managers must know *why* a variance occurred to pinpoint problems and to identify corrective action. Recall that Kool-Time's managers had a hard time understanding why the static budget variances in Exhibit 11-1 occurred because comparing the figures in that exhibit was like comparing apples to oranges: The actual results were based on the ten pools installed, yet the budget was for eight pools. To get more answers as to why the static budget variance occurred, managers often separate the static budget variance into two different parts: (1) the sales volume variance and (2) the flexible budget variance. Exhibit 11-6 shows how the static budget variance can be separated into these two variances. To obtain these variances managers first need to prepare a flexible budget for the actual level of output for the period (ten pools).

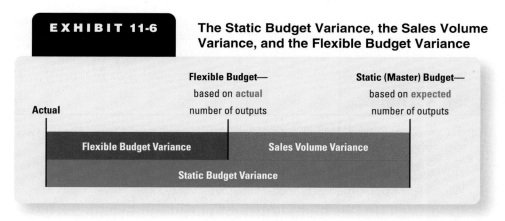

EXHIBIT 11-6 The Static Budget Variance, the Sales Volume Variance, and the Flexible Budget Variance

Exhibit 11-6 shows that:

-   The **sales volume variance** is the difference between the *static* (master) budget and the *flexible* budget (for the actual number of outputs). As the name suggests, this variance arises *only* because the number of units actually sold differs from the volume originally planned for in the static master budget.
-   The **flexible budget variance** is the difference between the *flexible* budget and the *actual* results. This variance arises because the company actually earned more or less revenue or incurred more or less expense than expected *for the actual level of output (ten pools)*. In other words, this variance is due to factors *other than* volume.

Let's see how Kool-Time's managers calculate and interpret these two different variances. Exhibit 11-7 shows Kool-Time's performance report for June. Column 1 shows Kool-Time's actual results for the period. This information is gathered from the general ledger. Now, consider the static master budget amounts presented in column 5. Recall that at the *beginning* of the period, Kool-Time *expected* to sell eight pools. For these eight pools, Kool-Time's:

- Budgeted sales revenue is $96,000 (8 × $12,000).
- Budgeted variable expenses are $64,000 (8 × $8,000).
- Budgeted fixed expenses are $20,000.

Notice that the amounts shown in columns 1 and 5 are the same as those shown in Exhibit 11-1. The only difference is that here we show a little more detail: Variable and fixed costs are shown separately; they are not lumped together.

EXHIBIT 11-7   **Income Statement Performance Report**

KOOL-TIME POOLS
Income Statement Performance Report
Month Ended June 30, 2007

	(1) Actual Results at Actual Prices	(2) (1)–(3) Flexible Budget Variance	(3) Flexible Budget for Actual Number of Output Units*	(4) (3)–(5) Sales Volume Variance	(5) Static (Master) Budget*
Output units (pools installed)	10	–0–	10	2 F	8
Sales revenue	$121,000	$ 1,000 F	$120,000	$ 24,000 F	$ 96,000
Variable expenses	83,000	3,000 U	80,000	16,000 U	64,000
Fixed expenses	22,000	2,000 U	20,000	–0–	20,000
Total expenses	105,000	5,000 U	100,000	16,000 U	84,000
Operating income	$ 16,000	$ 4,000 U	$ 20,000	$ 8,000 F	$ 12,000

Flexible budget variance, $4,000 U   Sales volume variance, $8,000 F

Static budget variance, $4,000 F

*Budgeted sales price is $12,000 per pool, budgeted variable expense is $8,000 per pool, and budgeted total monthly fixed expenses are $20,000.

Finally, consider column 3. In contrast to the static budget, which is developed *before* the period, the flexible budget used in the performance report is not developed until the *end* of the period. Why? Because *flexible budgets used in performance reports are based on the actual number of outputs, which is not known until the end of the period*. For Kool-Time, this flexible budget is based on the *ten pools actually installed*:

- Budgeted sales revenue is $120,000 (10 × $12,000).
- Budgeted variable expenses are $80,000 (10 × $8,000).
- Budgeted fixed expenses are $20,000.

Now that you know how this performance report was developed, let's take a look at the variances in more detail.

Sales Volume Variance

The sales volume variance (shown in column 4 of Exhibit 11-7) is the difference between the static master budget (column 5) and the flexible budget (column 3). The *only difference* between the static and flexible budgets in the performance report is the *number of outputs on which the budget is based* (eight pools versus ten pools). Both budgets use the same

- Budgeted sales price per unit ($12,000 per pool).
- Budgeted variable cost per unit ($8,000 per pool).
- Budgeted total fixed costs ($20,000 per month).

Holding selling price per unit, variable cost per unit, and total fixed costs constant highlights the effects of differences in sales volume—the variance shown in column 4. Exhibit 11-7 shows that by installing two more pools than initially expected, Kool-Time's:

- Sales revenue *should* increase from $96,000 (8 × $12,000) to $120,000 (10 × $12,000)—a $24,000 favorable sales volume variance.
- Variable costs *should* increase from $64,000 (8 × $8,000) to $80,000 (10 × $8,000)—a $16,000 unfavorable sales volume variance.

Budgeted total fixed expenses are unaffected because eight pools and ten pools are within the relevant range where fixed expenses total $20,000. Consequently, installing two more pools should increase operating income by $8,000 ($24,000 F − $16,000 U). So, Kool-Time's June sales volume variance is $8,000 F.

Since the sales volume variance arises *only* because the number of units actually sold differs from the volume originally planned for in the master budget, this variance is typically marketing's responsibility.

Who is responsible for sales volume variance?

Sales Volume	
Actual	10
Budgeted	8

Answer: Marketing

Stop & Think...

When is there a sales volume variance for fixed expenses?

Answer: Only when the number of units actually sold falls within a different relevant range than the static budget sales volume. When actual and expected number of units sold fall in the same relevant range, there is no sales volume variance for fixed expenses.

Flexible Budget Variance

As the name suggests, the flexible budget variance (shown in column 2 of Exhibit 11-7) is the difference between the *flexible* budget (column 3) and the *actual* results (column 1). Recall that the flexible budget is based on the actual level of output (ten pools), so it shows the revenues and expenses that Kool-Time's managers expect for a volume of ten pools. Therefore, the flexible budget *variance* highlights *unexpected* revenues and expenses.

Exhibit 11-7 shows a $1,000 favorable flexible budget variance for sales revenue. Kool-Time actually received $121,000 for installing ten pools rather than the $120,000 expected for ten pools (10 pools × $12,000). This variance means that the average sales price was $12,100 per pool ($121,000 ÷ 10 pools), which is $100 higher than the budgeted sales price of $12,000 per pool. This variance is typically marketing's responsibility.

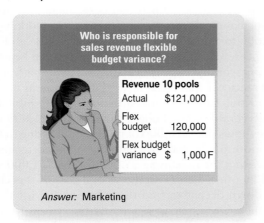

Exhibit 11-7 also shows a $3,000 unfavorable flexible budget variance for variable expenses. Kool-Time actually incurred $83,000 of variable expenses rather than the $80,000 expected for ten pools (ten pools × $8,000 per pool). The company also spent $2,000 more on fixed expenses than was budgeted ($22,000 − $20,000). Consequently, the flexible budget variance for total expenses is $5,000 unfavorable ($3,000 U + $2,000 U). In other words, Kool-Time spent $5,000 more than it would expect to spend for installing ten pools. This is the same $5,000 flexible budget expense variance we saw graphed in Exhibit 11-5. This variance is typically the responsibility of the purchasing, production, and human resources managers.

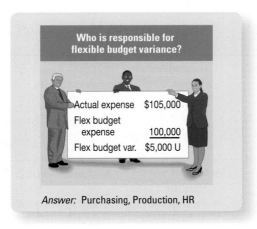

Interpreting the Variances

How would Kool-Time's managers use these variances? The favorable sales volume variance reveals that strong sales should have increased Kool-Time's income by $8,000. In addition, the sales staff increased sales without discounting prices: The favorable $1,000 flexible budget variance for sales revenue shows that the sales price was, on average, *higher* than budgeted. These favorable variances due to the quantity of pools sold (the $8,000 favorable sales volume variance) and the sales price per pool (the $1,000 favorable sales revenue price variance) suggest that Kool-Time's marketing staff did a better-than-expected job in selling pools and maintaining sales prices. Perhaps the high sales commissions paid on each pool sale is doing a good job of motivating the sales staff.

However, higher-than-expected expenses offset much of the favorable sales volume variance. Exhibit 11-7 shows a $5,000 unfavorable flexible budget variance for expenses. Management will want to find out why. The reason might be an uncontrollable increase in the cost of materials. Or higher costs might have resulted from more-controllable factors, such as employees wasting materials or working inefficiently. If so, managers can take action to reduce waste or inefficiency. Although Kool-Time does not have any favorable expense variances, in general, managers can benefit from examining favorable as well as unfavorable expense variances. Favorable variances may be the result of some type of efficiency that could be used in other areas of the company, too.

Let's get back to Kool-Time's original question from Exhibit 11-1: Why did the company have an unfavorable static budget variance of $21,000 for expenses? The *sales volume variance* shows that $16,000 of this amount is due to the fact that Kool-Time installed two more pools than it originally planned to install. The *flexible budget variance* shows that the remaining $5,000 (of the $21,000 variance) is due to cost overruns caused by other factors. In the second part of this chapter, we will see how managers drill down deeper to find the root cause(s) for this $5,000 flexible budget expense variance. Once managers identify the reason for the cost overruns, they can decide what action to take to avoid similar overruns in the future.

Decision Guidelines

FLEXIBLE BUDGETS

You and your roommate have started a business printing T-shirts for special customer requests (for example, including school or student organization logos). How can you use flexible budgets to plan and control your costs?

Decision	Guidelines
How should we estimate sales revenues, costs, and profits over the range of likely sales (output) levels?	Prepare a set of flexible budgets for different sales levels.
How should we prepare a flexible budget for total costs?	Use a mixed cost equation to predict costs at different volumes within the relevant range: $$\text{Flexible budget total cost} = \left(\begin{array}{c} \text{Number} \\ \text{of T-shirts} \end{array} \times \begin{array}{c} \text{Variable cost} \\ \text{per T-shirts} \end{array} \right) + \begin{array}{c} \text{Fixed} \\ \text{cost} \end{array}$$
How should we use budgets to help control costs?	• Graph actual costs versus flexible budget costs, as in Exhibit 11-5. • Prepare an income statement performance report, as in Exhibit 11-7.

Decision	Guidelines
On which output level is the budget based?	Static (master) budget—*expected* number of T-shirts, estimated before the period. Flexible budget—*actual* number of T-shirts, not known until the end of the period.
Why does your actual income differ from budgeted income?	Prepare an income statement performance report comparing actual results, flexible budget for actual number of T-shirts sold, and static (master) budget, as in Exhibit 11-7.
How do we interpret favorable and unfavorable variances?	• Favorable variances increase operating income. • Unfavorable variances decrease operating income.
How much of the difference is because the actual number of T-shirts sold does not equal budgeted sales?	Compute the sales volume variance (SVV) by comparing the flexible budget with the static budget. • Favorable SVV— Actual number of T-shirts sold > Expected number of T-shirts sold • Unfavorable SVV— Actual number of T-shirts sold < Expected number of T-shirts sold
How much of the difference occurs because actual revenues and costs are not what they should have been for the actual number of T-shirts sold?	Compute the flexible budget variance (FBV) by comparing actual results with the flexible budget. • Favorable FBV— Actual sales revenue > Flexible budget sales revenue OR Actual expenses < Flexible budget expenses • Unfavorable FBV— Actual sales revenue < Flexible budget sales revenue OR Actual expenses > Flexible budget expenses
What actions can we take to avoid an unfavorable sales volume variance?	• Design more-attractive T-shirts to increase demand. • Provide marketing incentives to increase number of T-shirts sold.
What actions can we take to avoid an unfavorable flexible budget variance?	• Maintain (do not discount) sales prices. • Control variable expenses, such as the cost of the plain T-shirts, dye, and labor. • Control fixed expenses.

Summary Problem 1

Exhibit 11-7 indicates that Kool-Time installed ten swimming pools during June. Now, assume that Kool-Time installed seven pools (instead of ten) and that the actual sales price averaged $12,500 per pool. Actual variable expenses were $57,400, and actual fixed expenses were $19,000.

Requirements

1. Prepare a revised income statement performance report using Exhibit 11-7 as a guide.

2. Show that the sum of the flexible budget variance and the sales volume variance for operating income equals the static budget variance for operating income.

3. As the company owner, which employees would you praise and which employees would you criticize after you analyze this performance report?

Solution

Requirements 1 and 2

KOOL-TIME POOLS
Income Statement Performance Report—Revised
Month Ended June 30, 2007

	(1) Actual Results at Actual Prices	(2) (1)–(3) Flexible Budget Variance	(3) Flexible Budget for Actual Number of Output Units	(4) (3)–(5) Sales Volume Variance	(5) Static (Master) Budget
Output units	7	–0–	7	1 U	8
Sales revenue	$ 87,500	$ 3,500 F	$ 84,000	$12,000 U	$96,000
Variable expenses	57,400	1,400 U	56,000	8,000 F	64,000
Fixed expenses	19,000	1,000 F	20,000	—	20,000
Total expenses	76,400	400 U	76,000	8,000 F	84,000
Operating income	$ 11,100	$ 3,100 F	$ 8,000	$ 4,000 U	$12,000

Flexible budget variance, $3,100 F

Sales volume variance, $4,000 U

Static budget variance, $900 U

Requirement 3

As the company owner, you should determine the *causes* of the variances before deciding who deserves praise or criticism. It is especially important to determine who is responsible for the variance and whether the variance is due to factors the manager can control. For example, the unfavorable sales volume variance could be due to an ineffective sales staff. Or it could be due to an uncontrollable long period of heavy rain that brought work to a standstill. Similarly, the $1,000 favorable flexible budget variance for fixed expenses could be due to an employee finding a lower-cost source of rented equipment. Or the savings might have come from delaying a needed overhaul of equipment that would increase the company's costs in the long run. Smart managers use variances to raise questions and direct attention, not to fix blame.

Standard Costs

Think of a **standard cost** as a budget for a single unit. In Kool-Time's case, a single unit would be one swimming pool. Most companies use standard costs to develop their flexible budgets. Recall that Kool-Time developed its flexible budget using a *standard variable cost per pool* of $8,000 (see Exhibit 11-3). Of the total standard variable cost per pool, $7,000 relates to the cost of variable manufacturing inputs: the direct materials, direct labor, and variable manufacturing overhead costs necessary to install one pool. The other $1,000 relates to selling and administrative costs associated with *selling* each pool (sales commission, for example). For the rest of this chapter, we are going to concentrate on *standard manufacturing costs*, although the same concepts apply to selling, general, and administrative costs.

In a standard cost system, each manufacturing input (such as direct materials) has a quantity standard and a price standard. For example, McDonald's has a standard for the amount of beef used per hamburger and a standard for the price paid per pound of beef. Likewise, Kool-Time has a standard for the amount of gunite (a concrete-like material) used per pool and a standard for the price it pays per cubic foot of gunite. Let's see how managers set these quantity and price standards.

3 Identify the benefits of standard costs and learn how to set standards

Quantity Standards

Engineers and production managers set direct material and direct labor quantity standards, usually allowing for unavoidable waste and spoilage. For example, each pool that Kool-Time installs requires 975 cubic feet of gunite. As part of the normal installation process, an additional 25 cubic feet of gunite is typically wasted due to unavoidable spoilage from hardened, unusable gunite. Kool-Time calculates the standard quantity of gunite per pool as follows:

Gunite required	975	cubic feet per pool
Unavoidable waste and spoilage	25	cubic feet per pool
Standard quantity of gunite	1,000	cubic feet per pool

Kool-Time also develops quantity standards for direct labor based on time records from past pool installations and current installation requirements. In setting labor standards, managers usually allow for unavoidable work interruptions and normal downtime for which the employee would still be paid. Considering these factors, Kool-Time has set its direct labor quantity standard at 400 direct labor hours per pool.

Price Standards

Now, let's turn our attention to price standards. Accountants help managers set direct material price standards after considering the base purchase price of materials, early-payment discounts, receiving costs, and freight-in. For example, the manager in charge of purchasing gunite for Kool-Time indicates that the purchase price, net of discounts, is $1.90 per cubic foot and that freight-in costs $0.10 per cubic foot. Kool-Time calculates its price standard for gunite as follows:

Purchase price, net of discounts...	$1.90	per cubic foot
Freight-in	0.10	per cubic foot
Standard cost of gunite...	$2.00	per cubic foot

For direct labor, accountants work with personnel or human resources managers to determine standard labor rates, taking into account payroll taxes and fringe benefits as well as the hourly wage rate. Kool-Time's Human Resources Department indicates that the hourly wage rate for production workers is $8.00 and that payroll taxes and fringe benefits total $2.50 per direct labor hour. Kool-Time's direct labor price (or rate) standard is:

Hourly wage rate	$ 8.00	per direct labor hour
Payroll taxes and fringe benefits.............................	2.50	per direct labor hour
Standard direct labor rate..	$10.50	per direct labor hour

Standard Manufacturing Overhead Rates

In addition to direct materials and direct labor price and quantity standards, companies also set standard manufacturing overhead rates. The standard predetermined manufacturing overhead rates are calculated as you learned in Chapter 3 except that *two* rates are calculated: one for fixed overhead and one for variable overhead. Why? Because isolating the variable overhead component helps managers create flexible budgets for different volumes. For setting standard overhead rates, accountants work with production managers to estimate variable and fixed manufacturing overhead expenses. Managers then identify an appropriate allocation base for computing the standard manufacturing overhead rates.

For example, recall that Kool-Time's fixed manufacturing overhead costs are expected to be $12,000 per month (the other $8,000 of fixed costs related to selling and administrative expenses). Production managers also estimate variable manufacturing overhead costs to be $800 per pool, or a total of $6,400 for the eight pools they plan to produce during the month ($800 × 8 = $6,400). Kool-Time has decided to use direct labor hours as its overhead allocation base, so they estimate the total number of direct labor hours they expect to incur during the month:

8 pools × 400 standard direct labor hours per pool = 3,200 direct labor hours

Kool-Time computes the standard variable overhead rate as follows:

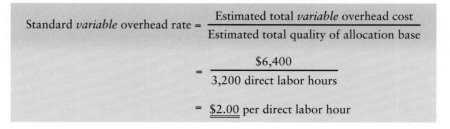

$$\text{Standard } \textit{variable} \text{ overhead rate} = \frac{\text{Estimated total } \textit{variable} \text{ overhead cost}}{\text{Estimated total quality of allocation base}}$$

$$= \frac{\$6,400}{3,200 \text{ direct labor hours}}$$

$$= \underline{\$2.00} \text{ per direct labor hour}$$

Kool-Time computes the standard fixed overhead rate in a similar way:

$$\text{Standard } \textit{fixed} \text{ overhead rate} = \frac{\text{Estimated total } \textit{fixed} \text{ overhead cost}}{\text{Estimated total quality of allocation base}}$$

$$= \frac{\$12,000}{3,200 \text{ direct labor hours}}$$

$$= \underline{\$3.75} \text{ per direct labor hour}$$

The standard total overhead rate is the *sum* of the standard *variable* overhead and the standard *fixed* overhead rates:

Variable overhead rate	+ Fixed overhead rate	= Standard overhead rate
$2.00 per direct labor hour	+ $3.75 per direct labor hour	= $5.75 per direct labor hour

Notice that the standard manufacturing overhead rate ($5.75 per direct labor hour) is the rate we would have computed in Chapter 3 based on all anticipated manufacturing overhead costs, regardless of cost behavior ($5.75 = $18,400 total estimated manufacturing overhead costs ÷ 3,200 total estimated direct labor hours).

Standard Cost of Inputs

Once managers have developed quantity and price standards, they calculate the standard cost of *each input* (such as direct materials, direct labor, and manufacturing overhead) by multiplying the quantity standard by the price standard:

Quantity standard × Price standard = Standard cost of input

For example, Kool-Time's standard direct materials cost per pool is:

1,000 cubic feet of gunite × $2.00 per cubic foot = $2,000 of direct materials per pool

Likewise, Kool-Time's standard direct labor cost per pool is:

400 direct labor hours × $10.50 per direct labor hour = $4,200 of direct labor per pool

Exhibit 11-8 shows Kool-Time's standard costs for variable and fixed overhead. The exhibit also shows that by adding the standard cost of all of the inputs Kool-Time can find the standard cost of *manufacturing* one pool ($8,500). However, this cost can be misleading to managers because it contains a fixed overhead component. It's really only valid when Kool-Time installs exactly eight pools in a month.

Rather than run the risk of misleading managers, it is often more helpful to highlight just the standard *variable* manufacturing cost per pool. Exhibit 11-8 shows that Kool-Time's standard costs for direct materials ($2,000) and direct labor ($4,200) and variable overhead ($800) amount to $7,000 variable manufacturing cost per pool. How does this correspond with variable cost per pool used for flexible budgeting? In addition to variable *manufacturing* costs, recall that Kool-Time expects to incur $1,000 of variable *selling and administrative* expenses per pool (for sales commissions, for example). Added together, these two costs

EXHIBIT 11-8 — Kool-Time's Standard Manufacturing Costs per Pool

Direct Materials Standard Cost		Direct Labor Standard Cost		Variable Overhead Standard Cost		Fixed Overhead Standard Cost		Standard Manufacturing Cost Per Pool
	+		+		+		=	$8,500
1,000 cubic feet × $2.00 per cubic foot = $2,000		400 hours × $10.50 per hour = $4,200		400 hours × $2.00 per hour = $800		400 hours × $3.75 per hour = $1,500		

Standard *variable* manufacturing cost per pool = $7,000

total the $8,000 variable cost per pool that Kool-Time used for flexible budgeting in Exhibit 11-3.

Kool-Time is not alone in its use of standards. U.S. surveys have shown that more than 80% of responding companies use standard costs. International surveys show that over half of responding companies in the United Kingdom, Ireland, Sweden, and Japan use standard costs. Why? Most companies believe that the benefits from using standard costs outweigh the costs of developing the standards and periodically revising them as business conditions change.

For example, companies should reassess their price standards when input prices such as the price of raw materials or labor rates change due to nontemporary market conditions. They should also reassess quantity standards when the product or production process is modified and, as a result, different quantities of materials or labor are required.

Exhibit 11-9 shows five benefits that companies, such as McDonald's, obtain from using standard costs.

EXHIBIT 11-9 — The Benefits of Standard Costs

1 Standards help managers plan by providing unit amounts for budgeting.
2 Standards help managers control operations by setting target levels of performance.
3 Standards motivate employees by serving as performance benchmarks.
4 Standards provide unit costs managers can use to set sale prices of products or services.
5 Standards simplify record keeping and reduce clerical costs.

Now, let's take a look at how Kool-Time uses its standard costs to analyze flexible budget variances.

Using Standard Costs to Analyze Direct Material and Direct Labor Variances

Let's return to our Kool-Time example. Exhibit 11-7 showed that the main cause for concern at Kool-Time is the $5,000 unfavorable flexible budget variance for expenses. The first step in identifying the causes of this variance is to take a more detailed look at what is included in the *expenses*. See Panel A of Exhibit 11-10. Note that this exhibit is different from Exhibit 11-7 in three ways: (1) It shows only expenses (it leaves out all revenue data), (2) it contains only actual and flexible budget data (it leaves out the static master budget and sales volume variance), and (3) it shows the *components* of Kool-Time's variable and fixed expenses (detailed production costs are shown separately from marketing and administrative expenses). Take a moment to see that the total variable expenses ($83,000 actual versus $80,000 budgeted), total fixed expenses ($22,000 actual versus $20,000 budgeted), and total expenses ($105,000 actual versus $100,000 budgeted) agree with Exhibit 11-7. The total $5,000 unfavorable flexible budget variance for expenses also agrees with Exhibit 11-7.

Study Exhibit 11-10 carefully because we will continue to refer to it throughout the rest of the chapter. Panel B (shown on page 640) shows how we used Kool-Time's price and quantity standards to compute the flexible budget amounts shown in Panel A. Panel C (also shown on page 640) shows how we computed the actual direct materials and direct labor costs shown in Panel A.

4 Compute standard cost variances for direct materials and direct labor

---

| **EXHIBIT 11-10** | **Data for Standard Costing Example** |

KOOL-TIME POOLS
Data for Standard Costing Example
Month of June 2007

PANEL A—Comparison of Actual Results with Flexible Budget for 10 Swimming Pools

	(1) Actual Results at Actual Prices	(2) Flexible Budget for 10 Pools	(1) – (2) Flexible Budget Variance
Variable expenses:			
Direct materials	$ 23,100*	$ 20,000†	$3,100 U
Direct labor	41,800*	42,000†	200 F
Variable overhead	9,000	8,000†	1,000 U
Marketing and administrative expenses	9,100	10,000	900 F
Total variable expenses	83,000	80,000	3,000 U
Fixed expenses:			
Fixed overhead	12,300	12,000‡	300 U
Marketing and administrative expenses	9,700	8,000	1,700 U
Total fixed expenses	22,000	20,000	2,000 U
Total expenses	$105,000	$100,000	$5,000 U

*See Panel C.
†See Panel B.
‡Fixed overhead was budgeted at $12,000 per month.

continued...

| EXHIBIT 11-10 | Data for Standard Costing Example |

KOOL-TIME POOLS
Data for Standard Costing Example
Month of June 2007

PANEL B—Computation of Flexible Budget for Direct Materials, Direct Labor, and Variable Overhead for 10 Swimming Pools

	(1) Standard Quantity of Inputs Allowed for 10 Pools	(2) Standard Price per Unit of Input	(1) × (2) Flexible Budget for 10 Pools
Direct materials	1,000 cubic feet per pool × 10 pools = 10,000 cubic feet	× $ 2.00	= $20,000
Direct labor	400 hours per pool × 10 pools = 4,000 hours	× 10.50	= 42,000
Variable overhead	400 hours per pool × 10 pools = 4,000 hours	× 2.00	= 8,000

PANEL C—Computation of Actual Costs for Direct Materials and Direct Labor for 10 Swimming Pools

	(1) Actual Quantity of Inputs Used for 10 Pools	(2) Actual Price per Unit of Input	(1) × (2) Actual Cost for 10 Pools
Direct materials	11,969 cubic feet actually used × $1.93 actual cost/cubic foot		= $23,100
Direct labor	3,800 hours actually used × $11.00 actual cost/hour		= 41,800

Direct Material Variances

The largest single component of the flexible budget variance in Panel A of Exhibit 11-10 is the $3,100 unfavorable variance in direct materials. Recall that the flexible budget variance is the difference between the actual cost incurred and the flexible budget (as shown in Exhibits 11-6 and 11-7). Exhibit 11-11 shows that Kool-Time computes the direct materials flexible budget variance as the difference between (1) the actual amount paid for gunite and (2) the flexible budget amount (*not the static budget amount!*) that Kool-Time should have spent on gunite for the ten pools that it actually installed.

EXHIBIT 11-11 Kool-Time Pools Direct Materials Flexible Budget Variance

The actual amount paid for the direct materials (Panel C of Exhibit 11-10)	The flexible budget for the amount of gunite that *should have been used to install 10 pools* (Panel B of Exhibit 11-10)
Actual quantity of gunite × Actual price per cubic foot of gunite	Standard quantity of gunite for actual number of pools × Standard price per cubic foot of gunite
11,969 cubic feet of gunite used × $1.93 actual price paid per cubic foot of gunite = $23,100	(1,000 cubic feet of gunite per pool × 10 pools) × $2.00 standard price per cubic foot of gunite = $20,000

$3,100 **unfavorable direct materials flexible budget variance**

Now that Kool-Time knows that it spent $3,100 more than it should have on gunite, the next question is why. Did the $3,100 unfavorable variance arise because Kool-Time:

- Did not meet the price standard because it paid too much for each cubic foot of gunite?
- Did not meet the quantity standard because workers used more gunite than they should have used to install ten pools?

To answer those questions, Kool-Time's managers separate the flexible budget variance for direct materials into price and efficiency components, as shown in Exhibit 11-12.

EXHIBIT 11-12 The Relations Among Price, Efficiency, Flexible Budget, Sales Volume, and Static Budget Variances

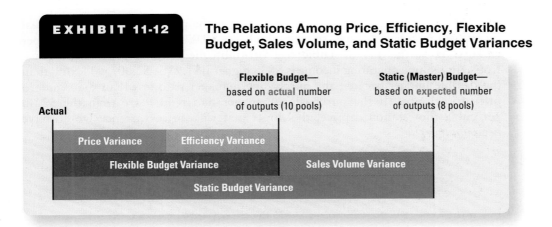

Exhibit 11-12 emphasizes two points. First, the price and efficiency variances sum to the flexible budget variance. Second, *static budgets (like column 5 of Exhibit 11-7) play no role in computing the flexible budget variance or in determining how it is split into price and efficiency variances.* The static budget is used *only* in computing the sales volume variance—never in computing the flexible budget variance or its component price and efficiency variances.

Direct Materials Price Variance

A **price variance** measures how well the business keeps unit prices of material and labor inputs within standards. As the name suggests, the price variance is the *difference in prices* (actual price per unit − standard price per unit) of an input, multiplied by the *actual quantity* of the input:

$$\text{Price variance} = \left(\begin{array}{c}\text{Actual} \\ \text{price per} \\ \text{input unit}\end{array} - \begin{array}{c}\text{Standard} \\ \text{price per} \\ \text{input unit}\end{array}\right) \times \left(\begin{array}{c}\text{Actual quantity} \\ \text{of input}\end{array}\right)$$

For Kool-Time, the direct materials price variance for gunite is:

$$\begin{array}{l}\text{Direct materials} \\ \text{price variance}\end{array} = \left(\begin{array}{c}\$1.93 \text{ per} \\ \text{cubic foot}\end{array} - \begin{array}{c}\$2.00 \text{ per} \\ \text{cubic foot}\end{array}\right) \times 11{,}969 \text{ cubic feet}$$

$$= (\$0.07 \text{ per cubic foot}) \times 11{,}969 \text{ cubic feet}$$

$$= \$838 \text{ F (rounded)}$$

The $838 direct materials price variance is *favorable* because the purchasing manager spent $0.07 *less* per cubic foot of gunite than budgeted ($1.93 actual price − $2.00 standard price).

The purchasing manager is responsible for the price variance on the *actual quantity* of materials he buys, so we multiply the $0.07 favorable price variance per cubic foot by the 11,969 cubic feet of gunite he *actually purchased*. Thus, Kool-Time's June operating income is $838 higher [($1.93 − $2.00) × 11,969] than the flexible budget because the purchasing manager paid less than the standard price for gunite. (If the purchasing manager had paid *more* than the $2.00 per cubic foot standard price, the direct materials price variance would have been *unfavorable*.)

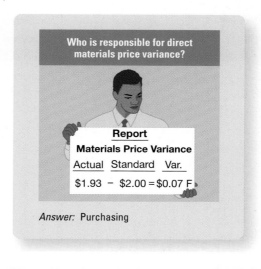

Answer: Purchasing

Direct Materials Efficiency Variance

An **efficiency variance** measures whether the firm meets its quantity standards. In other words, it measures whether the quantity of materials actually used to make the *actual number of outputs* is within the standard allowed for that number of outputs. The efficiency variance is the *difference in quantities* (actual quantity of input used − standard quantity of input allowed for the actual number of outputs) multiplied by the *standard price per unit* of the input.

$$\text{Efficiency variance} = \left(\begin{array}{c} \text{Actual} \\ \text{quantity} \\ \text{of input} \end{array} - \begin{array}{c} \text{Standard quantity of input} \\ \text{allowed for the actual} \\ \text{number of outputs} \end{array} \right) \times \left(\begin{array}{c} \text{Standard price} \\ \text{per input unit} \end{array} \right)$$

The standard quantity of inputs is the *quantity that should have been used*, or the standard quantity of inputs *allowed*, for the actual output. For Kool-Time, the *standard quantity of inputs (gunite) that workers should have used for the actual number of outputs* (ten pools) is:

1,000 cubic feet of gunite per pool × 10 pools installed = 10,000 cubic feet of gunite

Thus, the direct materials efficiency variance is:

$$\begin{aligned} \text{Direct materials efficiency variance} &= \left(\begin{array}{c} 11,969 \\ \text{cubic feet} \end{array} - \begin{array}{c} 10,000 \\ \text{cubic feet} \end{array} \right) \times \begin{array}{c} \$2 \text{ per} \\ \text{cubic foot} \end{array} \\ &= (1,969 \text{ cubic feet}) \times \$2 \text{ per cubic foot} \\ &= \$3,938 \text{ U} \end{aligned}$$

The $3,938 direct materials efficiency variance is *unfavorable* because workers actually used 1,969 *more* cubic feet of gunite than they should have used to install ten pools (11,969 actual cubic feet − 10,000 standard cubic feet).

The manager in charge of installing the pools is responsible for the variance in the quantity of the materials (gunite) used—in this case, the extra 1,969 cubic feet of gunite. However, this manager generally is *not* the person who purchases the gunite. The manager who installs the pools often has no control over the actual price paid for the gunite. Thus, we multiply the extra 1,969 cubic feet of gunite his workers used by the *standard price* of $2 per cubic foot to obtain the direct materials efficiency variance. Kool-Time's operating income is $3,938 lower [(11,969 − 10,000) × $2] than the flexible budget because workers used more gunite than they should have to install the ten pools in June. (If workers had used *less* than the standard 10,000 cubic feet to install the ten pools, the direct materials efficiency variance would have been *favorable*.)

Answer: Pool Installation Manager

Summary of Direct Material Variances

Exhibit 11-13 summarizes how Kool-Time splits the $3,100 unfavorable direct materials flexible budget variance first identified in Panel A of Exhibit 11-10 into price and efficiency variances.

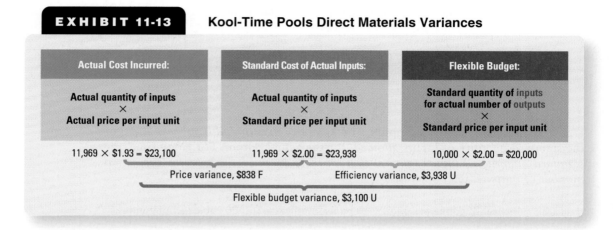

| EXHIBIT 11-13 | Kool-Time Pools Direct Materials Variances |

Actual Cost Incurred:	Standard Cost of Actual Inputs:	Flexible Budget:
Actual quantity of inputs × Actual price per input unit	Actual quantity of inputs × Standard price per input unit	Standard quantity of inputs for actual number of outputs × Standard price per input unit
11,969 × $1.93 = $23,100	11,969 × $2.00 = $23,938	10,000 × $2.00 = $20,000

Price variance, $838 F   Efficiency variance, $3,938 U

Flexible budget variance, $3,100 U

Kool-Time actually spent $3,100 more than it should have for gunite because a good price for the gunite increased profits by $838 but inefficient use of the gunite reduced profits by $3,938.

Let's review who is responsible for each of these variances and consider why each variance may have occurred.

1. *Purchasing managers typically are responsible for direct materials price variances* because they should know why the actual price differs from the standard price. Kool-Time's purchasing manager may have negotiated a good price for gunite, or perhaps the supplier did not increase the price of gunite as much as expected when Kool-Time developed its standard cost. In either case, the purchasing manager is in the best position to explain the favorable price variance.

2. *Production managers typically are responsible for direct materials efficiency variances* because they are responsible for ensuring that workers use materials efficiently and effectively. The manager in charge of installing pools should be able to explain why workers used more gunite than they should have to install the ten pools. Was the gunite of lower quality? Did workers waste materials? Did their equipment malfunction? Kool-Time's top management needs answers to those questions to decide what corrective action to take. Should they require purchasing to buy higher-quality gunite, train and supervise workers more closely to reduce waste, or improve maintenance of equipment?

Smart managers know that these variances raise questions that can help pinpoint problems. But be careful! A favorable variance does not necessarily mean that a manager did a good job, nor does an unfavorable variance mean that a manager did a bad job. Perhaps Kool-Time's purchasing manager obtained a lower price by purchasing inferior-quality gunite, which, in turn, led to waste and spoilage. If so, the purchasing manager's decision hurt the company because the $838 favorable price variance is more than offset by the $3,938 unfavorable efficiency variance. This illustrates why good managers (1) use variances as a guide for investigation rather than as a simple tool to assign blame and (2) investigate favorable as well as unfavorable variances.

Direct Labor Variances

Kool-Time uses a similar approach to analyze the direct labor flexible budget variance. Using the information from Panels B and C of Exhibit 11-10, Exhibit 11-14 shows how Kool-Time computes this variance as the difference between the actual amount paid for direct labor and the flexible budget amount that Kool-Time should have spent on direct labor for ten pools.

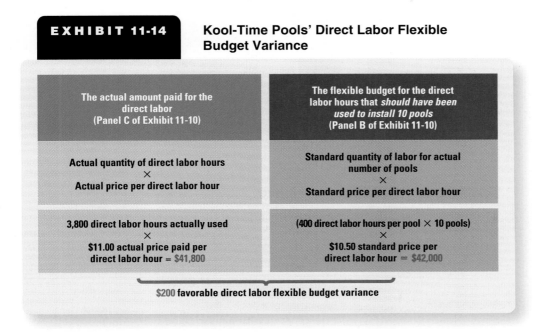

EXHIBIT 11-14   **Kool-Time Pools' Direct Labor Flexible Budget Variance**

The actual amount paid for the direct labor (Panel C of Exhibit 11-10)	The flexible budget for the direct labor hours that *should have been used to install 10 pools* (Panel B of Exhibit 11-10)
Actual quantity of direct labor hours × Actual price per direct labor hour	Standard quantity of labor for actual number of pools × Standard price per direct labor hour
3,800 direct labor hours actually used × $11.00 actual price paid per direct labor hour = $41,800	(400 direct labor hours per pool × 10 pools) × $10.50 standard price per direct labor hour = $42,000

$200 **favorable direct labor flexible budget variance**

Why did Kool-Time spend $200 less on labor than it should have to install ten pools? To answer that question, Kool-Time splits the direct labor flexible budget variance into price and efficiency variances the same way it did for direct materials.

Direct Labor Price Variance

The direct labor price variance is computed the same way as the direct materials price variance, so we use the same formula for price variance shown earlier:

$$\text{Price variance} = \left(\begin{array}{c} \text{Actual} \\ \text{price per} \\ \text{input unit} \end{array} - \begin{array}{c} \text{Standard} \\ \text{price per} \\ \text{input unit} \end{array} \right) \times \begin{array}{c} \text{Actual quantity} \\ \text{of input} \end{array}$$

$$
\begin{aligned}
\text{Direct labor price variance} &= \Big(\$11.00 \text{ per hour} - \$10.50 \text{ per hour} \Big) \times 3{,}800 \text{ hours} \\
&= (\$0.50 \text{ per hour}) \times 3{,}800 \text{ hours} \\
&= \$1{,}900 \text{ U}
\end{aligned}
$$

The $1,900 direct labor price variance is *unfavorable* because the human resources (or personnel) department hired workers at $0.50 *more* per direct labor hour than budgeted ($11.00 actual price − $10.50 standard price).

The human resources manager is responsible for the price variance on the *actual quantity* of labor she hires, so we multiply the $0.50 unfavorable price variance per direct labor hour by the 3,800 hours of labor she *actually purchased*.

Answer: HR Department

Direct Labor Efficiency Variance

The direct labor efficiency variance is computed the same way as the direct materials efficiency variance, so once again, we use the same formula for efficiency variance shown earlier:

$$\text{Efficiency variance} = \left(\begin{array}{c}\text{Actual} \\ \text{quantity} \\ \text{of input}\end{array} - \begin{array}{c}\text{Standard quantity of} \\ \text{input allowed for the} \\ \text{actual number of outputs}\end{array}\right) \times \begin{array}{c}\text{Standard} \\ \text{price per} \\ \text{input unit}\end{array}$$

For Kool-Time, the *standard quantity of direct labor hours that workers should have used for the actual number of outputs* (ten pools) is:

400 direct labor hours per pool × 10 pools installed = 4,000 direct labor hours

Thus, the direct labor efficiency variance is:

$$\begin{aligned}\text{Direct labor} \\ \text{efficiency variance}\end{aligned} \begin{aligned} &= (3{,}800 \text{ hours} - 4{,}000 \text{ hours}) \times \$10.50 \text{ per hour} \\ &= (200 \text{ hours}) \times \$10.50 \text{ per hour} \\ &= \$2{,}100 \text{ F}\end{aligned}$$

The $2,100 direct labor efficiency variance is *favorable* because installers actually worked 200 *fewer* hours than they should have to install ten pools (3,800 actual hours − 4,000 standard hours).

The manager in charge of installing the pools is responsible for the variance in the quantity of direct labor hours used—in this case, the 200 fewer hours used. Assuming that this manager is not also responsible for setting employees' pay rates (which is usually the responsibility of the human resources or personnel department), the manager in charge of installing the pools has little control over the actual price paid per labor hour. Thus, we multiply the 200 fewer direct labor hours by the *standard price* of $10.50 per direct labor hour to obtain the direct labor efficiency variance.

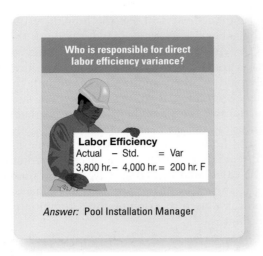

Who is responsible for direct labor efficiency variance?

Labor Efficiency
Actual − Std. = Var
3,800 hr. − 4,000 hr. = 200 hr. F

Answer: Pool Installation Manager

Summary of Direct Labor Variances

Exhibit 11-15 summarizes how Kool-Time splits the $200 favorable direct labor flexible budget variance into price and efficiency variances.

Had they looked only at the $200 favorable direct labor flexible budget variance, Kool-Time's managers might have thought direct labor costs were close to expectations. But this illustrates the danger in ending the analysis after computing only the flexible budget variance. "Peeling the onion" to examine the price and efficiency variances yields more insight:

- The unfavorable direct labor price variance means that Kool-Time's operating income is $1,900 lower than expected because the company paid its employees an average of $11.00 per hour in June instead of the standard rate of $10.50. But this unfavorable variance was more than offset by the favorable direct labor efficiency variance.

EXHIBIT 11-15   **Kool-Time Pools Direct Labor Variances**

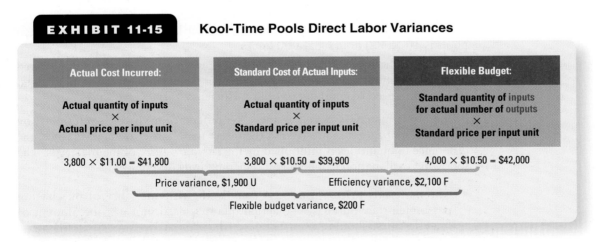

Actual Cost Incurred:	Standard Cost of Actual Inputs:	Flexible Budget:
Actual quantity of inputs × Actual price per input unit	Actual quantity of inputs × Standard price per input unit	Standard quantity of inputs for actual number of outputs × Standard price per input unit
3,800 × $11.00 = $41,800	3,800 × $10.50 = $39,900	4,000 × $10.50 = $42,000

Price variance, $1,900 U   Efficiency variance, $2,100 F

Flexible budget variance, $200 F

- The favorable direct labor efficiency variance means that Kool-Time's operating income is $2,100 higher than expected because workers installed ten pools in 3,800 hours instead of the budgeted 4,000 hours.

Kool-Time's top management will ask the human resources department to explain the unfavorable labor price variance, and it will ask the manager in charge of installing the pools to explain the favorable labor efficiency variance. Once again, there might have been a trade-off. Kool-Time might have hired more-experienced (and thus more highly paid) workers and traded off an unfavorable price variance for a favorable efficiency variance. If so, the strategy was successful—the overall effect on profits was favorable. This possibility reminds us that managers should be careful in using variances to evaluate performance.

You have now seen how Kool-Time analyzes flexible budget variances for direct materials and direct labor. Variances for variable marketing and administrative expenses could be calculated the same way, but for simplicity, we limit our detailed analysis to the variances in the production element of the value chain. Before leaving this topic, we need to examine three common pitfalls in computing price and efficiency variances.

Price and Efficiency Variances: Three Common Pitfalls

Here are three common pitfalls to avoid in computing price and efficiency variances for direct materials and direct labor:

1. *Static budgets like column 5 of Exhibit 11-7 play no role in computing the flexible budget variance or in determining how it is split into the price and efficiency variances.* Exhibit 11-12 shows that the static budget is used *only* in computing the sales volume variance—never in computing the flexible budget variance or its component price and efficiency variances.

2. In the efficiency variance, the standard quantity is the *standard quantity of inputs allowed for the actual number of outputs*—the basis for the flexible budget. To compute the standard quantity of inputs allowed, determine the actual number of outputs. For Kool-Time, the actual number of outputs is ten pools. Next, compute how many inputs should have been used to produce the actual number of outputs (ten pools). For example, each pool should use 400 direct labor hours, so the standard quantity of direct labor hours allowed for ten pools is 10×400 hours = 4,000 hours.

    Notice that the standard quantity of inputs is *not* based on the budgeted number of outputs (eight pools). That number is the basis for the static budget, which is not used to compute price and efficiency variances.

3. In the direct materials price variance, the difference in prices is multiplied by the *actual quantity* of materials. In the direct materials efficiency variance, the difference in quantities is multiplied by the *standard price* of the materials. The following explanation can help you remember this difference:

    - The materials price variance is usually the responsibility of purchasing personnel; they purchase the actual quantity used, not just the amount of materials that should have been used (the standard quantity). So, the price variance is the difference in prices multiplied by the *actual quantity* of materials purchased.

    - The materials efficiency variance is usually the responsibility of production personnel; they have no influence over the actual price paid. So, the efficiency variance is computed as the difference in quantities multiplied by the *standard* price (the price that should have been paid).

Similar logic applies to the direct labor price and efficiency variances.

Using Variances

Let's look at some practical tips for using variances.

How Often to Compute Variances?

Many firms monitor sales volume, direct materials efficiency, and direct labor efficiency variances day to day or even hour to hour. McDonald's restaurants compute variances for sales and direct labor each hour. Material efficiencies are computed for each shift. The Brass Products Division of Parker Hannifin computes efficiency variances for each job the day after workers finish the job. This allows managers to ask questions about any large variances while the job is still fresh in workers' minds.

Technology such as bar coding of materials and even labor and computerized data entry allows McDonald's and Parker Hannifin to compute efficiency variances quickly. In contrast to efficiency variances, monthly computations of material and labor price variances may be sufficient if long-term contracts with suppliers or labor unions make large price variances unlikely.

Using Variances to Evaluate Employees' Performance

Good managers use variances as a way to raise questions, not as simple indicators of whether employees performed well or poorly. Why should you take care in using variances to evaluate performance?

- Some variances are caused by factors that managers cannot control. For example, perhaps Kool-Time used more gunite than budgeted because workers had to repair cracked foundations resulting from an earthquake.
- Sometimes, variances are the result of inaccurate or outdated standards. Management must take care to review and update standards on a regular basis. If the production process changes or if supply prices change, the standards will need to be updated to reflect current operating conditions.
- Managers often make trade-offs among variances. Chrysler intentionally accepted a large order for customized Dodge vans because it expected the favorable sales volume variance to more than offset the unfavorable direct labor price variance from the overtime premium and the unfavorable sales revenue price variance from extra rebates offered to the customer. Similarly, managers often trade off price variances against efficiency variances. Purchasing personnel may decide to buy higher-quality (but more expensive) direct materials to reduce waste and spoilage. The unfavorable price variance may be more than offset by a favorable efficiency variance.
- Evaluations based primarily on one variance can encourage managers to take actions that make the variance look good but hurt the company in the long run. For example, Kool-Time's managers could:
  - Purchase low-quality gunite or hire less-experienced labor to get favorable price variances.
  - Use less gunite or less labor (resulting in lower-quality installed pools) to get favorable efficiency variances.

How can upper management discourage such actions? One approach is to base performance evaluation on *nonfinancial* measures as well, such as quality indicators (for example, variances in the grade of gunite or labor used) or customer satisfaction measures. For instance, McDonald's discourages skimping on labor by evaluating nonfinancial measures, such as the difference between actual and standard time to serve drive-through customers. If the McDonald's shift manager does not have enough workers, drive-through customers may have to wait to get their french fries. They may take their business to Wendy's or Burger King. In Chapter 12, we'll discuss nonfinancial performance evaluation in more detail.

Stop & Think...

Why might an auto assembly plant experience a favorable direct labor efficiency variance? Should managers investigate favorable as well as unfavorable efficiency variances? Why or why not?

Answer:

1. The plant may have redesigned the manufacturing process to avoid wasted motion. For example, a Dodge van plant in Canada significantly reduced direct labor by reorganizing production so employees reach for raw materials as needed rather than carry armloads of materials across the plant floor.
2. Employees may have worked harder or more intensely than budgeted.
3. Employees may have rushed through the work and skimped on quality.

There are two reasons why managers should investigate favorable efficiency variances. First, managers want to maximize improvements that increase profits. For example, can managers capitalize on 1 and 2 to further improve labor efficiency at this or other plants? Second, managers want to prevent employees from achieving favorable variances at the expense of long-run profits through strategies like 3.

Using Standard Costs to Analyze Manufacturing Overhead Variances

5 Compute manufacturing overhead variances

In the last section, we looked at how managers analyze direct materials and direct labor variances. In this section, we look at manufacturing overhead variances. A company's total manufacturing overhead variance *is the difference between the actual overhead incurred and the standard overhead allocated to production.* In other words, this is the amount by which manufacturing overhead has been overallocated or underallocated to production. The total manufacturing overhead variance can be broken into two components: (1) overhead flexible budget variance and (2) production volume variance.

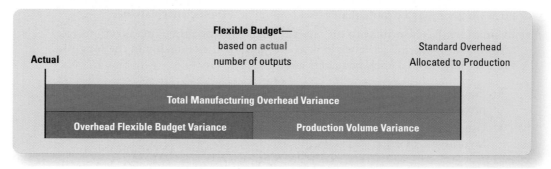

Overhead Flexible Budget Variance

The **overhead flexible budget variance** shows how well management has controlled overhead costs. Therefore, this variance is often referred to as the overhead controllable variance. It is computed *the same way* as the flexible budget variances for direct materials and direct labor. It is the *difference between actual overhead costs and the flexible budget overhead for the actual number of outputs (ten pools).*

The following information about Kool-Time's overhead is taken directly from Exhibit 11-10.

	(1)	(2)	(1) – (2)
	Actual Results	Flexible Budget for 10 Pools	Flexible Budget Variance
Variable overhead ($800 per pool)	$ 9,000	$ 8,000	$1,000 U
Fixed overhead	12,300	12,000	300 U
Total overhead	$21,300	$20,000	$1,300 U

Before continuing, let's quickly review how we arrived at the flexible budget numbers shown above.

The amount of *variable* overhead budgeted for the actual output is calculated as follows:

(400 direct labor hours allowed per pool × $2.00 per direct labor hour variable overhead rate) × 10 pools = $8,000

Since ten pools falls within the relevant range of 0 to 11 pools, *fixed* production overhead for the month is budgeted at $12,000. Therefore, the total flexible budget for overhead is $20,000. Actual overhead for the month is $21,300. Therefore, Kool-Time's calculates the overhead flexible budget variance as follows:

Overhead flexible budget variance = Actual overhead – Flexible budget overhead for actual output

= $21,300 – $20,000

= $1,300 U

Why did Kool-Time spend $1,300 more on overhead items than it should have to install the ten pools in June? You can see that $1,000 ($9,000 − $8,000) of the variance is due to higher-than-expected spending on variable overhead items and that the remaining $300 ($12,300 − $12,000) is due to higher spending on fixed overhead items. Kool-Time will investigate the reason for each of these variances.

Most companies compile actual and budget cost information for the individual component items that make up overhead, such as indirect materials, indirect labor, utilities, and depreciation on plant and equipment. Recall from Chapter 3 that E-Z-Boy Furniture kept subsidiary ledgers for each component of overhead cost. Managers "drill down" by comparing actual costs to budgeted costs for each of these items. For example, Kool-Time's drill-down analysis might reveal that variable overhead costs were higher than expected because the price of gasoline for the earth moving equipment increased. Perhaps spending on fixed overhead increased because Kool-Time's monthly lease on its earth moving equipment expired and it had to negotiate a new lease. Advanced books on cost accounting explain this drill-down variance analysis in more detail.

Production Volume Variance

The second component of the total manufacturing overhead variance is the **production volume variance**. *The production volume variance is the difference between the flexible budget overhead and the standard overhead allocated to production.* As the name suggests, this variance arises when actual production volume differs from expected production volume. The production volume variance arises because companies treat fixed overhead as if it were variable in order to allocate it.

Recall from our discussion on standard costs that Kool-Time allocates overhead at a rate of $5.75 per direct labor hour. The total standard overhead rate consists of $2.00 per direct labor hour for variable overhead and $3.75 per direct labor hour for fixed overhead. Kool-Time computed these standard overhead rates based on the assumption that they would sell eight pools. Because Kool-Time actually installed ten pools, the amount of standard overhead *allocated* to production was:

Standard overhead rate per direct labor hour	$ 5.75
Standard direct labor hours (400 DL hours per pool × 10 pools)	× 4,000
Standard overhead allocated to production	$23,000

Notice that when companies use standard costing, they allocate manufacturing overhead to the units produced using the standard overhead rate multiplied by the *standard quantity of the allocation base allowed* (400 DL hours per pool × 10 pools), *not by the actual quantity* of the allocation base used (3,800 hours for the ten pools), as you did in Chapter 3.

The production volume variance is calculated as follows:

Production volume variance = Flexible budget overhead for actual output − Standard overhead allocated to production

= $20,000 − $23,000

= $3,000 F

The production volume variance is favorable whenever actual output (ten pools for Kool-Time) exceeds expected output (eight pools). By installing ten pools instead of eight, Kool-Time used its production capacity more fully than originally planned. In other words, it used its capacity more efficiently, resulting in a favorable variance. If Kool-Time had installed seven or fewer pools, the production volume variance would have been unfavorable because the company would have used less production capacity than expected.

The production volume variance is due only to *fixed* overhead. Why? Because the amount of *variable* overhead in the flexible budget ($8,000) is the *same* as the variable overhead allocated to production ($8,000 = 10 pools × 400 DL hours/pool × $2/DL hour). *In essence, the production volume variance arises because companies treat fixed overhead ($12,000) as if it were variable ($3.75 per DL hour) to allocate it.* The $3,000 favorable production volume variance arises because Kool-Time budgeted fixed overhead of $12,000 (Exhibit 11-10) but allocated $15,000 of fixed overhead to the ten pools it installed (10 pools × 400 DL hours/pool × $3.75 *fixed* overhead per DL hour).

Another way to see this is by examining the hours used to determine the overhead allocation rate versus the hours used to actually allocate overhead. Since the variance is due *strictly* to the fixed overhead, we multiply the difference in hours by the fixed overhead rate:

Total hours used to determine allocation rate (*8 pools* × 400 direct labor hours)..........	= 3,200
Total hours used to allocate overhead (*10 pools* × 400 direct labor hours)...................	= 4,000
Difference in hours (additional hours of overhead allocated)	800
Fixed overhead rate per hour..	× $3.75
Production volume variance	$3,000

As you can see, the production volume variance is due to the fact that Kool-Time allocated more fixed overhead than it had budgeted.

Overview of Kool-Time's Manufacturing Overhead Variances

Kool-Time's overhead variances are summarized as follows:

Total overhead variance:	
Actual overhead cost ($9,000 variable + $12,300 fixed)............................	$21,300
Standard overhead allocated to production (10 pools × 400 standard direct labor hours per pool × $5.75)	23,000
Total overhead variance..	$ 1,700 F
Overhead flexible budget variance:	
Actual overhead cost (from above)..	$21,300
Flexible budget overhead for actual outputs ($8,000 variable + $12,000 fixed)..	20,000
Overhead flexible budget variance	$ 1,300 U
Production volume variance:	
Flexible budget overhead for actual outputs (from above).........	$20,000
Standard overhead allocated to production (from above)..........	23,000
Production volume variance..	$ 3,000 F

As we have just seen, many companies use standard costs independent of the general ledger accounting system to develop flexible budgets and evaluate performance through variance analysis. Once managers know the causes of the variances, they can use that information to improve operations.

Other companies integrate standards directly into their general ledger accounting. This method of accounting, called standard costing, is discussed in the Appendix to this chapter.

Decision Guidelines

STANDARD COSTS AND VARIANCE ANALYSIS

You've seen how managers use standard costs and variances in actual and budgeted costs to identify potential problems. Variances help managers see *why* actual costs differ from the budget. This is the first step in determining how to correct problems.

Let's review how Kool-Time made some of the key decisions in setting up and using its standard cost system.

Decision	Guidelines
How does Kool-Time set standards?	Historical performance data
	Engineering analysis/time-and-motion studies
How does Kool-Time compute a price variance for materials or labor?	$\text{Price variance} = \left(\begin{array}{c} \text{Actual price} \\ \text{per input unit} \end{array} - \begin{array}{c} \text{Standard price} \\ \text{per input unit} \end{array} \right) \times \begin{array}{c} \text{Actual} \\ \text{quantity of} \\ \text{input} \end{array}$
How does Kool-Time compute an efficiency variance for materials or labor?	$\text{Efficiency variance} = \left(\begin{array}{c} \text{Actual} \\ \text{quantity of} \\ \text{input} \end{array} - \begin{array}{c} \text{Standard quantity} \\ \text{of input for actual} \\ \text{number of outputs} \end{array} \right) \times \begin{array}{c} \text{Standard} \\ \text{price per} \\ \text{input unit} \end{array}$
Who is most likely responsible for:	
Sales volume variance?	Marketing department
Sales revenue flexible budget variance?	Marketing department
Direct materials price variance?	Purchasing department
Direct materials efficiency variance?	Production department
Direct labor price variance?	Human resources or personnel department
Direct labor efficiency variance?	Production department
How does Kool-Time allocate manufacturing overhead in a standard costing system?	$\begin{array}{c} \text{Manufacturing} \\ \text{overhead} \\ \text{allocated} \end{array} = \left(\begin{array}{c} \text{Standard} \\ \text{predetermined} \\ \text{manufacturing} \\ \text{overhead rate} \end{array} \right) \times \left(\begin{array}{c} \text{Standard quantity of} \\ \text{allocation base allowed} \\ \text{for actual outputs} \end{array} \right)$
How does Kool-Time analyze overallocated or underallocated manufacturing overhead?	Split overallocated or underallocated overhead as follows:
	$\text{Flexible budget variance} = \begin{array}{c} \text{Actual} \\ \text{overhead} \end{array} - \begin{array}{c} \text{Flexible budget} \\ \text{overhead} \\ \text{for actual outputs} \end{array}$
	$\begin{array}{c} \text{Production volume} \\ \text{variance} \end{array} = \begin{array}{c} \text{Flexible budget} \\ \text{overhead} \\ \text{for actual outputs} \end{array} - \begin{array}{c} \text{Standard overhead} \\ \text{allocated to} \\ \text{actual outputs} \end{array}$

Summary Problem 2

Exhibit 11-10 indicates that Kool-Time installed ten swimming pools in June. Suppose Kool-Time had installed seven pools instead of ten and that actual expenses were:

Direct materials (gunite).........................	7,400 cubic feet @ $2 per cubic foot
Direct labor...	2,740 hours @ $10 per hour
Variable overhead	$5,400
Fixed overhead.......................................	$11,900

Requirements

1. Given these new data, prepare an exhibit similar to Exhibit 11-10. Ignore marketing and administrative expenses.

2. Compute price and efficiency variances for direct materials and direct labor.

3. Compute the total overhead variance, the overhead flexible budget variance, and the production volume variance. Prepare a summary similar to the one on page 653.

Solution

Requirement 1

KOOL-TIME POOLS
Revised Data for Standard Costing Example
Month of June 2007

PANEL A—Comparison of Actual Results with Flexible Budget for 7 Swimming Pools

	Actual Results at Actual Prices	Flexible Budget for 7 Pools	Flexible Budget Variance
Variable expenses:			
Direct materials	$14,800*	$14,000†	$ 800 U
Direct labor	27,400*	29,400†	2,000 F
Variable overhead	5,400	5,600†	200 F
Total variable expenses	47,600	49,000	1,400 F
Fixed expenses:			
Fixed overhead	11,900	12,000‡	100 F
Total expenses	$59,500	$61,000	$1,500 F

*See Panel C.
†See Panel B.
‡Fixed overhead was budgeted at $12,000 per month.

PANEL B—Computation of Flexible Budget for Direct Materials, Direct Labor, and Variable Overhead for 7 Swimming Pools

	(1) Standard Quantity of Inputs Allowed for 7 Pools	(2) Standard Price per Unit of Input	(1) × (2) Flexible Budget for 7 Pools
Direct materials	1,000 cubic feet per pool × 7 pools = 7,000 cubic feet	× $ 2.00	= $14,000
Direct labor	400 hours per pool × 7 pools = 2,800 hours	× 10.50	= 29,400
Variable overhead	400 hours per pool × 7 pools = 2,800 hours	× 2.00	= 5,600

PANEL C—Computation of Actual Costs for Direct Materials and Direct Labor for 7 Swimming Pools

	(1) Actual Quantity of Inputs Used for 7 Pools	(2) Actual Price per Unit of Input	(1) × (2) Actual Cost for 7 Pools
Direct materials	7,400 cubic feet actually used ×	$2.00 actual cost/cubic foot	$14,800
Direct labor	2,740 hours actually used ×	$10.00 actual cost/hour	27,400

Requirement 2

$$\text{Price variance} = \left(\begin{matrix} \text{Actual price} \\ \text{per input unit} \end{matrix} - \begin{matrix} \text{Standard price} \\ \text{per input unit} \end{matrix} \right) \times \begin{matrix} \text{Actual} \\ \text{quantity of} \\ \text{input} \end{matrix}$$

Direct materials:

$$\text{Price variance} = (\$2.00 - \$2.00) \times 7,400 \text{ cubic feet} = \$0$$

Direct labor:

$$\text{Price variance} = (\$10.00 - \$10.50) \times 2,740 \text{ hours} = \$1,370 \text{ F}$$

$$\text{Efficiency variance} = \left(\begin{matrix} \text{Actual} \\ \text{quantity} \\ \text{of input} \end{matrix} - \begin{matrix} \text{Standard} \\ \text{quantity of} \\ \text{input} \end{matrix} \right) \times \begin{matrix} \text{Standard} \\ \text{price per} \\ \text{input unit} \end{matrix}$$

Direct materials:

$$\text{Efficiency variance} = \left(\begin{matrix} 7,400 \\ \text{cubic feet} \end{matrix} - \begin{matrix} 7,000 \\ \text{cubic feet} \end{matrix} \right) \times \begin{matrix} \$2.00 \text{ per} \\ \text{cubic foot} \end{matrix} = \$800 \text{ U}$$

Direct labor:

$$\text{Efficiency variance} = \left(\begin{matrix} 2,740 \\ \text{hours} \end{matrix} - \begin{matrix} 2,800 \\ \text{hours} \end{matrix} \right) \times \begin{matrix} \$10.50 \text{ per} \\ \text{hours} \end{matrix} = \$630 \text{ F}$$

Requirement 3

Total overhead variance:	
Actual overhead cost ($5,400 variable + $11,900 fixed)...............	$17,300
Standard overhead allocated to production (2,800 standard direct labor hours × $5.75)	16,100
Total overhead variance	$ 1,200 U
Overhead flexible budget variance:	
Actual overhead cost ($5,400 + $11,900)	$17,300
Flexible budget overhead for actual outputs ($5,600 + $12,000)	17,600
Overhead flexible budget variance	$ 300 F
Production volume variance:	
Flexible budget overhead for actual outputs ($5,600 + $12,000)	$17,600
Standard overhead allocated to (actual) production (2,800 standard direct labor hours × $5.75)	16,100
Production volume variance	$ 1,500 U

Appendix 11A

Standard Cost Accounting Systems

6 (Appendix) Record transactions at standard cost and prepare a standard cost income statement

Many companies integrate standards directly into their general ledger accounting by recording inventory-related costs at standard cost rather than actual cost. This method of accounting is called standard costing or standard cost accounting. Standard costing not only saves on bookkeeping costs but also isolates price and efficiency variances as soon as they occur. Before we go through the journal entries, keep the following key points in mind:

1. Each type of variance discussed has its own general ledger account. A debit balance means that the variance is unfavorable since it decreases income (just like an expense). A credit balance means that the variance is favorable since it increases income (just like a revenue).

2. Just as in job costing, the manufacturing costs flow through the inventory accounts in the following order: raw materials → work in process → finished goods → cost of goods sold. The difference is that *standard costs* rather than actual costs are used to record the manufacturing costs put into the inventory accounts.

3. At the end of the period, the variance accounts are closed to cost of goods sold to "correct" for the fact that the standard costs recorded in the accounts were different from actual costs. Assuming that most inventory worked on during the period has been sold, any "error" from using standard costs rather than actual costs is contained in cost of goods sold. Closing the variances to cost of goods sold corrects the account balance.

Journal Entries

We use Kool-Time's June transactions to demonstrate standard costing in a job-costing context.

1. **Recording Raw Materials Purchases**—Kool-Time debits Raw Materials Inventory for the *actual quantity* purchased (11,969 cubic feet) costed at the *standard price* ($2 per cubic foot). It credits Accounts Payable for the *actual quantity* of gunite purchased (11,969 cubic feet) costed at the *actual price* ($1.93 per cubic foot) because this is the amount owed to Kool-Time's suppliers. The difference is the direct material *price* variance. When Kool-Time purchases raw materials, it is immediately able to tell whether it paid more or less than the standard price for the materials; therefore, the direct materials *price* variance "pops out" when the purchase is recorded:

1.	Raw Materials Inventory (11,969 × $2.00)	23,938	
	Direct Materials Price Variance		838
	Accounts Payable (11,969 × $1.93)		23,100
	To record purchases of direct materials.		

Recall that Kool-Time's direct materials price variance was $838 favorable (page 642). So, the variance has a credit balance and increases Kool-Time's June profits.

2. **Recording Use of Direct Materials**—When Kool-Time uses direct materials, it debits Work in Process Inventory for the *standard price × standard quantity* of direct materials that should have been used for the actual output of ten pools. *This maintains Work in Process Inventory at a purely standard cost.* Raw Materials Inventory is credited for the *actual quantity* of materials put into production (11,969 cubic feet) costed at the *standard price* at which journal entry 1 entered them into the Raw Materials Inventory account ($2). The difference is the direct materials *efficiency* variance. The direct materials efficiency variance "pops out" when Kool-Time records the *use* of direct materials:

2.	Work in Process Inventory (10,000 × $2)	20,000	
	Direct Materials Efficiency Variance	3,938	
	Raw Materials Inventory (11,969 × $2)		23,938
	To record use of direct materials.		

Kool-Time's direct materials efficiency variance was $3,938 unfavorable (page 643), which decreases June profits. See how a debit to the variance account corresponds with an unfavorable variance.

3. **Recording the Accumulation of Labor Costs**—Kool-Time accumulates labor costs by debiting Manufacturing Wages at the *standard* price for direct labor ($10.50) multiplied by the *actual* hours worked. Recall from Chapter 3 that Manufacturing Wages is a temporary account used to "hold" labor costs until those costs can be assigned to production. Kool-Time credits Wages Payable for the *actual* hours worked at the *actual* wage rate since this is the amount owed to employees. The difference between the two, the direct labor *price* variance, "pops out" at the time work is performed:

3.	Manufacturing Wages (3,800 × $10.50)	39,900	
	Direct Labor Price Variance	1,900	
	Wages Payable (3,800 × $11.00)		41,800
	To record direct labor costs incurred.		

Again, notice how the debit to this variance account agrees with the unfavorable direct labor price variance calculated on page 645.

4. **Assigning Direct Labor**—Since Work in Process Inventory is maintained at standard cost, Kool-Time debits Work in Process Inventory for the *standard price* of direct labor × *standard quantity* of direct labor that should have been used for the actual output of ten pools (just like it did for direct materials in journal entry 2). Kool-Time credits Manufacturing Wages in the same manner it debited the account in journal entry 3: *standard price × actual hours* worked. Since the difference between the two amounts is due to hours worked, the direct labor *efficiency* variance ($2,100 favorable) "pops out" as a result:

4.	Work in Process Inventory (4,000 × $10.50)	42,000	
	Direct Labor Efficiency Variance		2,100
	Manufacturing Wages (3,800 × $10.50)		39,900
	To assign direct labor costs.		

Notice how the credit to this variance account agrees with the favorable direct labor efficiency variance calculated on page 646.

5. **Recording Manufacturing Overhead Costs Incurred**—Kool-Time Pools records manufacturing overhead costs as usual, debiting the manufacturing overhead account and crediting various accounts:

5.	Manufacturing Overhead	21,300	
	Accounts Payable, Accumulated Depreciation, and so forth		21,300
	To record actual overhead costs incurred (from Exhibit 11-10).		

6. **Allocating Overhead**—In standard costing, the overhead allocated to Work in Process Inventory is computed as the standard overhead rate ($5.75 per DL hour) × standard quantity of the allocation base allowed for the actual output (10 pools × 400 DL hours per pool). As usual, the manufacturing overhead account is credited when assigning overhead:

6.	Work in Process Inventory (4,000 × $5.75)	23,000	
	Manufacturing Overhead		23,000
	To allocate overhead.		

This journal entry corresponds with our calculation, on page 652, of the standard overhead allocated to production.

7. **Recording the Completion of Pools**—So far, Work in Process has been debited with $85,000 of manufacturing cost ($20,000 of direct materials + $42,000 of direct labor + $23,000 of manufacturing overhead). Does this make sense? According to Exhibit 11-8, the standard manufacturing cost of one pool is $8,500 ($2,000 direct material + $4,200 direct labor + $2,300 overhead). The sum of ten pools, costed at *standard* rather than actual cost, is $85,000. As the pools are completed, the standard cost of each is transferred out of Work in Process and into Finished Goods:

7.	Finished Goods Inventory	85,000	
	Work in Process Inventory		85,000
	To record completion of 10 pools.		

8. **Recording the Sale and Release of Inventory**—When the pools are sold, *sales revenue* is recorded at the standard sales price, but accounts receivable is recorded at the actual sales price. The difference between the standard sales price and actual sales price received is the flexible budget sales revenue variance shown in Exhibit 11-7. It is favorable (a credit) because the company sold the pools for a higher price than it anticipated.

8a.	Cash or Accounts Receivable (at actual price)	121,000	
	Flexible Budget Sales Revenue Variance		1,000
	Sales Revenue (at standard)		120,000
	To record the sale of 10 pools.		

Kool-Time must also release inventory for the pools it has sold. Since these pools were recorded at standard cost ($8,500 each), they must be removed from finished goods inventory and go into cost of goods sold at the same (standard) cost:

8b.	Cost of Goods Sold	85,000	
	Finished Goods Inventory		85,000
	To record the cost of sales of 10 pools.		

9. **Closing Manufacturing Overhead**—Kool-Time Pools closes Manufacturing Overhead to the two overhead variance accounts using the calculations performed on pages 651 and 652 ($1,300 unfavorable Overhead Flexible Budget Variance and $3,000 favorable Production Volume Variance).

9.	Manufacturing Overhead	1,700	
	Overhead Flexible Budget Variance	1,300	
	Production Volume Variance		3,000
	To record overhead variances and close the Manufacturing		
	Overhead account.		

Exhibit 11-16 shows selected Kool-Time accounts after posting these entries.

EXHIBIT 11-16   Kool-Time Pools' Flow of Costs in Standard Costing System

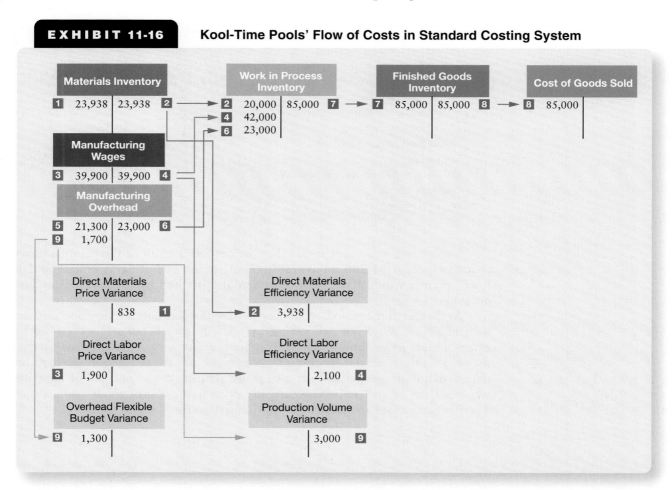

Standard Cost Income Statement for Management

Exhibit 11-17 shows a standard cost income statement that highlights the variances for Kool-Time's management. The statement shows sales revenue at standard and then adds the favorable flexible budget sales revenue variance to yield actual sales revenue. Next, the statement shows the cost of goods sold at standard cost. Then, the statement separately lists each manufacturing cost variance followed by the cost of goods sold at actual cost. (Recall that since Kool-Time had no raw materials, work in process, or finished goods inventories, all of the variances relate to June's sales.)

EXHIBIT 11-17   Standard Cost Income Statement

KOOL-TIME POOLS
Standard Cost Income Statement
Month Ended June 30, 2007

Sales revenue at standard (10 × $12,000)		$120,000
Flexible budget sales revenue variance		1,000
Sales revenue at actual		121,000
Cost of goods sold at standard cost		85,000
Manufacturing cost variances:		
Direct materials price variance	$ (838)	
Direct materials efficiency variance	3,938	
Direct labor price variance	1,900	
Direct labor efficiency variance	(2,100)	
Manufacturing overhead flexible budget variance	1,300	
Production volume variance	(3,000)	
Total manufacturing variances		1,200
Cost of goods sold at actual cost		86,200
Gross profit		34,800
Marketing and administrative expenses*		(18,800)
Operating income		$ 16,000

*$9,100 + $9,700 from Exhibit 11-10.

The income statement shows that the net effect of all of the manufacturing cost variances is $1,200 unfavorable. Thus, June's operating income is $1,200 lower than it would have been if all actual costs had been equal to standard amounts.

At the end of the period, all of the cost variance accounts are closed to zero-out their balances. Why? For two reasons: (1) The financial statements prepared for *external* users never show variances (variances are only for internal management's use) and (2) the general ledger must be "corrected" for the fact that standard rather than actual costs were used to record manufacturing costs. Since all of the pools were sold, the "error" in costing currently exists in the cost of goods sold account. Therefore, the cost variance accounts are closed to cost of goods sold:

10. **Closing the Cost Variance Accounts to Cost of Goods Sold**—To close, or zero-out, the variance accounts, all unfavorable variances (debit balances) must be credited, while all favorable variances (credit balances) must be debited:

10a.	Cost of Goods Sold	1,200	
	Direct Materials Price Variance	838	
	Direct Labor Efficiency Variance	2,100	
	Production Volume Variance	3,000	
	Direct Labor Price Variance		1,900
	Direct Materials Efficiency Variance		3,938
	Overhead Flexible Budget Variance		1,300
	To close cost variance accounts to cost of goods sold.		

Likewise, the favorable flexible budget sales revenue variance (1,000) is closed to sales revenue (to zero-out the variance account and correct the revenue account).

10b.	Flexible Budget Sales Revenue Variance	1,000	
	Sales Revenue		1,000
	To close the revenue variance account.		

Review Flexible Budgets and Standard Costs

■ Accounting Vocabulary

Efficiency Variance. (p. 643)
Measures whether the quantity of materials or labor used to make the actual number of outputs is within the standard allowed for that number of outputs.

Flexible Budget. (p. 623)
A summarized budget prepared for different levels of volume.

Flexible Budget Variance. (p. 628)
The difference arising because the company actually earned more or less revenue or incurred more or less cost than expected for the actual level of output.

Overhead Flexible Budget Variance. (p. 650)
The difference between the actual overhead cost and the flexible budget overhead for the actual number of outputs.

Price Variance. (p. 642)
The difference in prices (actual price per unit minus standard price per unit) of an input multiplied by the actual quantity of the input.

Production Volume Variance. (p. 651)
The difference between the manufacturing overhead cost in the flexible budget for actual outputs and the standard overhead allocated to production.

Sales Volume Variance. (p. 628)
The difference between a static budget amount and a flexible budget amount arising only because the number of units actually sold differs from the static budget units.

Standard Cost. (p. 635)
A budget for a single unit.

Static Budget. (p. 623)
The budget prepared for only one level of sales volume. Also called the master budget.

Variance. (p. 623)
The difference between an actual amount and the budget.

■ Quick Check

Use the following data for Questions 1 through 4. Digital Systems is a start-up company that makes connectors for high-speed Internet connections. The company has budgeted variable costs of $130 for each connector and fixed costs of $8,000 per month.

Digital's static budget predicted production and sales of 100 connectors in January, but the company actually produced and sold only 75 connectors at a total cost of $23,000.

1. Digital Systems' total flexible budget cost for 75 connectors per month is
   a. $17,750
   b. $9,750
   c. $13,000
   d. $8,130

2. Digital Systems' sales volume variance for total costs is
   a. $3,250 F
   b. $5,250 F
   c. $3,250 U
   d. $5,250 U

3. Digital Systems' flexible budget variance for total costs is
   a. $3,250 F
   b. $5,250 F
   c. $3,250 U
   d. $5,250 U

4. Digital Systems' managers could set direct labor standards based on
   a. past actual performance
   b. continuous improvement
   c. benchmarking
   d. time-and-motion studies
   e. any of the above

Use the following data for Questions 5 through 7. Digital Systems has budgeted three hours of direct labor per connector at a standard cost of $15 per hour. During January, technicians actually worked 210 hours completing the 75 connectors. Digital Systems paid the technicians $15.50 per hour.

5. What is Digital Systems' direct labor price variance for January?
   a. $37.50 U
   b. $105.00 U
   c. $112.50 U
   d. $120.00 U

6. What is Digital Systems' direct labor efficiency variance for January?
   a. $75.00 F
   b. $225.00 F
   c. $232.50 F
   d. $1,350.00 F

7. (Appendix) The journal entry to record Digital Systems' *assignment* of direct labor to jobs is
   a. Manufacturing Wages
          Direct Labor Price Variance
          Work in Process Inventory
   b. Manufacturing Wages
          Direct Labor Efficiency Variance
          Work in Process Inventory
   c. Work in Process Inventory
          Direct Labor Price Variance
          Manufacturing Wages
   d. Work in Process Inventory
          Direct Labor Efficiency Variance
          Manufacturing Wages

8. Digital Systems allocates manufacturing overhead based on machine hours. Each connector should require ten machine hours. According to the static budget, Digital Systems is expected to incur:

1,000 machine hours per month (100 connectors × 10 machine hours per connector)

$5,250 in variable manufacturing overhead costs

$8,000 in fixed manufacturing overhead costs

During January, Digital Systems actually used 825 machine hours to make the 75 connectors. Digital Systems' predetermined standard total manufacturing overhead rate is

a. $5.25 per machine hour

b. $8.00 per machine hour

c. $13.25 per machine hour

d. $16.06 per machine hour

9. The total manufacturing overhead variance is composed of

a. price variance and efficiency variance

b. price variance and production volume variance

c. efficiency variance and production volume variance

d. flexible budget variance and production volume variance

10. (Appendix) When Digital Systems *uses* direct materials, the amount of the debit to Work in Process Inventory is based on

a. actual quantity of the materials used × actual price per unit of the materials

b. standard quantity of the materials allowed for the actual production of 75 connectors × actual price per unit of the materials

c. standard quantity of the materials allowed for the actual production of 75 connectors × standard price per unit of the materials

d. actual quantity of the materials used × standard price per unit of the materials

---

Quick Check Answers

1. *a* 2. *a* 3. *d* 4. *e* 5. *b* 6. *b* 7. *d* 8. *c* 9. *d* 10. *c*

For Internet Exercises, Excel in Practice, and additional online activities, go to this book's Web site at www.prenhall.com/bamber.

Assess Your Progress

■ Learning Objectives

1 Prepare a flexible budget for planning purposes

2 Use the sales volume variance and flexible budget variance to explain why actual results differ from the master budget

3 Identify the benefits of standard costs and learn how to set standards

4 Compute standard cost variances for direct materials and direct labor

5 Compute manufacturing overhead variances

6 (Appendix) Record transactions at standard cost and prepare a standard cost income statement

■ Short Exercises

S11-1 **Prepare a flexible budget** *(Learning Objective 1)*
Turn to Kool-Time's flexible budget in Exhibit 11-3.

Requirements

1. Using the data from Exhibit 11-3, develop flexible budgets for four- and nine-pool levels of output.
2. Would Kool-Time's managers use the flexible budgets you developed in Requirement 1 for planning or for controlling? What specific insights can Kool-Time's managers gain from the flexible budgets you prepared in Requirement 1?

S11-2 **Interpret a flexible budget graph** *(Learning Objective 1)*
Look at Kool-Time's graph of actual and budgeted monthly costs in Exhibit 11-5.

1. How many pools did Kool-Time install in May?
2. How much were Kool-Time's actual expenses in May?
3. Using Kool-Time's flexible budget formula, what is the flexible budget total cost for May?
4. What is Kool-Time's flexible budget variance for total costs? Is the variance favorable or unfavorable in May?

S11-3 **Interpret a performance report** *(Learning Objective 2)*
The following is a partially completed performance report for Surf-Side Pools, one of Kool-Time's competitors:

	Actual Results at Actual Prices	Flexible Budget Variance	Flexible Budget for Actual Number of Output Units	Sales Volume Variance	Static (Master) Budget
Output units (pools installed)	6	?	?	?	5
Sales revenue	$102,000	?	$108,000	?	$90,000
Variable expenses	57,000	?	60,000	?	50,000
Fixed expenses	21,000	?	25,000	?	25,000
Total expenses	78,000	?	85,000	?	75,000
Operating income	$24,000	?	$23,000	?	$15,000

SURF-SIDE POOLS
Income Statement Performance Report
Year Ended April 30

Requirements

1. How many pools did Surf-Side originally think it would install in April?
2. How many pools did Surf-Side actually install in April?
3. How many pools is the flexible budget based on? Why?
4. What was the budgeted sales price per pool?
5. What was the budgeted variable cost per pool?
6. Define the sales volume variance. What causes it?
7. Define the flexible budget variance. What causes it?

S11-4 **Complete a performance report** *(Learning Objective 2)*
Complete the performance report shown in S11-3 by filling in all missing values. Be sure to label each variance as favorable (F) or unfavorable (U). Then, answer the following questions:

1. What was the *total* static budget variance?
2. What was the *total* sales volume variance.
3. What was the *total* flexible budget variance?
4. Show that the total sales volume variance and total flexible budget variance sum to the total static budget variance.
5. Interpret the variances and then give one plausible explanation for the variances shown in this performance report.

S11-5 **Interpret the sales volume variance** *(Learning Objective 2)*
Recall that Kool-Time's relevant range is 0 to 11 pools per month.
Explain whether Kool-Time would have a sales volume variance for fixed expenses in Exhibit 11-7 if:
a. Kool-Time installs 14 pools per month.
b. Kool-Time installs 7 pools per month.

S11-6 Understand key terms *(Learning Objectives 1, 2)*

Fill in the blank with the phrase that best completes the sentence.

Actual number of outputs	Beginning of the period	Static budget variance
Expected number of outputs	End of the period	
Sales volume variance	Flexible budget variance	

    a. The static budget is developed at the _____.

    b. The flexible budget used in an income statement performance report is based on the _____.

    c. The master budget is based on the _____.

    d. The flexible budget used in an income statement performance report is developed at the _____.

    e. The difference between actual costs and the costs that should have been incurred for the actual number of outputs is the _____.

S11-7 Explain the benefits of standard costs *(Learning Objective 3)*

Lladró is a Spanish manufacturer of porcelain art objects. Raw materials are mixed to form clay, which is shaped into figurines. The pieces are then glazed and fired at high temperatures.

Explain how the five benefits of standard costs (Exhibit 11-9) apply to Lladró. Be as specific as possible.

McDonald's Data Set: Used for S11-8 through S11-12

As explained in the chapter opening story, the standard direct materials for a regular McDonald's hamburger are:

1 bun	1 pickle slice	1/4 teaspoon of mustard
1 hamburger patty	1/8 teaspoon of onion	1/2 ounce of ketchup

Assume that the company has set the following standard materials prices:

Buns.................................. $0.10 each	Onion............... $0.08 per teaspoon
Hamburger patties .... $0.20 each	Mustard .... $0.04 per teaspoon
Pickle slices .... $0.03 per slice	Ketchup............. $0.10 per ounce

In addition to the direct materials standards, the company sets standards for direct labor. The standard labor wage rate is $6 per hour. Since the griddles are so large, the restaurants cook the hamburgers in batches of 20. The standard time allotted to cook, apply condiments, and wrap each batch of 20 hamburgers is 4 minutes.

Assume that a San Diego, California, McDonald's sold 5,000 hamburgers yesterday and actually used the following materials:

5,150 buns	4,800 pickle slices	1,400 teaspoons of mustard
5,100 hamburger patties	800 teaspoons of onion	2,750 ounces of ketchup

S11-8   Compute standard cost of direct materials *(Learning Objective 3)*
Refer to the McDonald's Data Set on page 669. Compute the standard direct materials cost per hamburger.

S11-9   Compute standard cost of direct labor *(Learning Objective 3)*
Refer to the McDonald's Data Set on page 669. Compute the standard direct labor cost per hamburger. *(Hint:* Find the quantity and price standards in minutes.)

S11-10   Compute direct materials efficiency variances *(Learning Objective 4)*
Refer to the McDonald's Data Set on page 669.

1. Compute the direct materials efficiency variance for buns, hamburger patties, and pickle slices.
2. As a manager, what would you learn from the variances and supporting data?

S11-11   Compute more direct materials efficiency variances *(Learning Objective 4)*
Refer to the McDonald's Data Set on page 669.

1. Compute the direct materials efficiency variance for onion, mustard, and ketchup.
2. As a manager, what would you learn from the variances and supporting data?

S11-12   Compute direct materials price variances *(Learning Objective 4)*
Refer to the McDonald's Data Set on page 669.
Actual prices paid for ingredients purchased during the week were:

Buns	$0.12 each	Onion	$0.07 per teaspoon
Hamburger patties	$0.25 each	Mustard	$0.01 per teaspoon
Pickle slices	$0.02 per slice	Ketchup	$0.12 per ounce

1. Compute the direct materials price variance for each ingredient.
2. As a manager, what would you learn from the variances and supporting data?

S11-13   Compute standard overhead allocation rates *(Learning Objective 3)*
McDonald's supplies its restaurants with many premanufactured ingredients (such as bags of frozen french fries), while other ingredients (such as lettuce and tomatoes) are obtained from local suppliers. Assume that the manufacturing plant processing the fries anticipated incurring a total of $3,080,000 of manufacturing overhead during the year. Of this amount, $1,320,000 is fixed. Manufacturing overhead is allocated based on machine hours. The plant anticipates running the machines 220,000 hours next year.

1. Compute the standard *variable* overhead rate.
2. Compute the *fixed* overhead rate.
3. Compute the standard *total* overhead rate.

S11-14   Compute manufacturing overhead variances *(Learning Objective 5)*
Assume that the McDonald's french fries manufacturing facility actually incurred $2,975,000 of manufacturing overhead for the year. Based on the actual output of french fries, the flexible budget indicated that total manufacturing overhead should have been $3,000,000. Using a standard costing system, the company allocated $2,940,000 of manufacturing overhead to production.

1. Calculate the total manufacturing overhead variance. What does this tell managers?

2. Determine the overhead flexible budget variance. What does this tell managers?

3. Determine the production volume variance. What does this tell managers?

4. Double-check: Do the two variances (computed in Requirements 2 and 3) sum to the total overhead variance computed in Requirement 1?

S11-15 Compute manufacturing overhead variances *(Learning Objective 5)*
Rovnovsky Industries produces high-end flutes for professional musicians across the globe. Actual manufacturing overhead for the year was $1,240,000. The flexible budget indicated that fixed overhead should have been $800,000 and variable overhead should have been $400,000 for the number of flutes actually produced. Using a standard costing system, the company allocated $1,300,000 of overhead to production.

1. Calculate the total overhead variance. What does this tell managers?

2. Determine the overhead flexible budget variance. What does this tell managers?

3. Determine the production volume variance. What does this tell managers?

S11-16 (Appendix) Record direct materials purchase and use *(Learning Objective 6)*
During the week, McDonald's french fry manufacturing facility purchased 10,000 pounds of potatoes at a price of $1.10 per pound. The standard price per pound is $1.05. During the week, 9,760 pounds of potatoes were used. The standard quantity of potatoes that should have been used for the actual volume of output was 9,700 pounds. Record the following transactions using a standard cost accounting system:

1. The purchase of potatoes

2. The use of potatoes

Are the variances favorable, or unfavorable? Explain.

S11-17 (Appendix) Record direct labor purchase and use *(Learning Objective 6)*
During the week, McDonald's french fry manufacturing facility incurred 2,000 hours of direct labor. Direct laborers were paid $12.25 per hour. The standard hourly labor rate is $12. Standards indicate that for the volume of output actually achieved, the factory should have used 2,100 hours. Record the following transactions using a standard cost accounting system:

1. The accumulation of labor costs

2. The assignment of direct labor to production

Are the variances favorable, or unfavorable? Explain.

▪ Exercises

E11-18 Prepare flexible budgets for planning *(Learning Objective 1)*
Comfort Now sells its main product, ergonomic mouse pads, for $11 each. Its variable cost is $5 per pad. Fixed expenses are $200,000 per month for volumes up to 60,000 pads. Above 60,000 pads, monthly fixed expenses are $250,000.

Prepare a monthly flexible budget for the product, showing sales, variable expenses, fixed expenses, and operating income or loss for volume levels of 40,000, 50,000, and 70,000 pads.

E11-19 **Graph flexible budget costs** *(Learning Objective 1)*

Graph the flexible budget total cost line for Comfort Now in Exercise 11-18. Show total costs for volume levels of 40,000, 50,000, and 70,000 pads.

E11-20 **Complete and interpret a performance report** *(Learning Objective 2)*

Joe Boxer Company's managers received the following incomplete performance report:

JOE BOXER COMPANY
Income Statement Performance Report
Year Ended July 31, 2007

	Actual Results at Actual Prices	Flexible Budget Variance	Flexible Budget for Actual Number of Output Units	Sales Volume Variance	Static (Master) Budget
Output units	36,000	?	36,000	4,000 F	?
Sales revenue	$216,000	?	$216,000	$24,000 F	?
Variable expenses	84,000	?	81,000	9,000 U	?
Fixed expenses	106,000	?	100,000	–0–	?
Total expenses	190,000	?	181,000	9,000 U	?
Operating income	$ 26,000	?	$ 35,000	$15,000 F	?

Complete the performance report. Identify the employee group that may deserve praise and the group that may be subject to criticism. Give your reasons.

E11-21 **Prepare an income statement performance report** *(Learning Objective 2)*

Jump In installed nine pools during May. Prepare an income statement performance report for Jump In for May, using Exhibit 11-7 as a guide. Assume that the actual sales price per pool is $12,000, actual variable expenses total $61,000, and actual fixed expenses are $19,000 in May. The master budget was prepared with the following assumptions: variable cost of $8,000 per pool; fixed expenses of $20,000 per month; anticipated sales volume of eight pools at $12,000 per pool.

Compute the sales volume variance and flexible budget variance. Use these variances to explain to Jump In's management why May's operating income differs from operating income shown in the static budget.

E11-22 **Compute sales volume and flexible budget variances** *(Learning Objective 2)*

Top managers of Fretan Industries predicted 2008 sales of 145,000 units of its product at a unit price of $8. Actual sales for the year were 140,000 units at $9.50 each. Variable expenses were budgeted at $2.20 per unit, and actual variable expenses were $2.30 per unit. Actual fixed expenses of $420,000 exceeded budgeted fixed expenses by $20,000. Prepare Fretan Industries' income statement performance report in a format similar to E11-20. What variance contributed most to the year's favorable results? What caused this variance?

E11-23 **Work backward to find missing values** *(Learning Objective 2)*

Kanco has a relative range extending to 30,000 units each month. The following performance report provides information about Kanco's budget and actual performance for April.

KANCO
Income Statement Performance Report
Month Ended April 30, 2007

	Actual Results at Actual Prices	(A)	Flexible Budget for Actual Number of Output Units	(B)	Static (Master) Budget
Output units	25,000		(C)		30,000
Sales revenue	$240,000	$ 5,000 (F)	(D)		
Variable cost			(E)		$187,000
Fixed cost	$ 15,000	(F)			$ 20,000
Operating income					(G)

Requirement

Find the missing data for letters A through F. Be sure to label any variances as favorable or unfavorable. (*Hint:* A and B are titles.)

E11-24 Calculate standard costs *(Learning Objective 3)*

Torrie's Bakery makes desserts for local restaurants. Each pan of gourmet brownies requires 2 cups flour, ½ cup chopped pecans, ¼ cup cocoa, 1 cup sugar, ½ cup chocolate chips, 2 eggs, and ⅓ cup oil. Each pan requires 10 minutes of direct labor for mixing, cutting, and packaging. Each pan must bake for 30 minutes. Restaurants purchase the gourmet brownies by the pan, not by the individual serving. Each pan is currently sold for $12. Standard costs are $1.92 per bag of flour (16 cups in a bag), $6.00 per bag of pecans (3 cups per bag), $2.40 per tin of cocoa (2 cups per tin), $2.40 per 5-pound bag of sugar (16 cups in a bag), $1.80 per bag of chocolate chips (2 cups per bag), $1.08 per dozen eggs, $1.26 per bottle of oil (6 cups per bottle), and $0.50 for packaging materials. The standard wage rate is $12 per hour. Torrie allocates bakery overhead at $7.00 per oven hour.

1. What is the standard cost per pan of gourmet brownies?

2. What is the standard gross profit per pan of gourmet brownies?

3. How often should Torrie reassess her standard quantities and standard prices for inputs?

E11-25 Calculate materials and labor variances *(Learning Objective 4)*

Bergie's manufactures the bags of frozen french fries used at its franchised restaurants. Last week, Bergie's purchased and used 100,000 pounds of potatoes at a price of $0.75 per pound. During the week, 2,000 direct labor hours were incurred in the plant at a rate of $12.25 per hour. The standard price per pound of potatoes is $0.85, and the standard direct labor rate is $12.00 per hour. Standards indicate that for the number of bags of frozen fries produced, the factory should have used 97,000 pounds of potatoes and 1,900 hours of direct labor.

Requirements

1. Determine the direct materials price and efficiency variances. Be sure to label each variance as favorable or unfavorable.

2. Think of a plausible explanation for the variances found in Requirement 1.

3. Determine the direct labor price and efficiency variances. Be sure to label each variance as favorable or unfavorable.

4. Could the explanation for the labor variances be tied to the material variances? Explain.

E11-26 **Compute direct materials variance** *(Learning Objective 4)*
The following direct materials variance computations are incomplete:

> Price variance = ($? − $10) × 9,600 pounds = $4,800
> Efficiency variance = (? − 10,400 pounds) × $10 = ? F
> Flexible budget variance = $?

Fill in the missing values and identify the flexible budget variance as favorable or unfavorable.

E11-27 **Calculate materials and labor variances** *(Learning Objective 4)*
Super Guard, which uses a standard cost accounting system, manufactured 200,000 boat fenders during the year, using 1,450,000 feet of extruded vinyl purchased at $1.05 per foot. Production required 4,500 direct labor hours that cost $14 per hour. The materials standard was 7 feet of vinyl per fender at a standard cost of $1.10 per foot. The labor standard was 0.025 direct labor hour per fender at a standard cost of $13 per hour. Compute the price and efficiency variances for direct materials and direct labor. Does the pattern of variances suggest that Super Guard's managers have been making trade-offs? Explain.

E11-28 **Compute standard manufacturing overhead rates** *(Learning Objective 3)*
Best-Cut processes bags of organic frozen vegetables sold at specialty grocery stores. Best-Cut allocates manufacturing overhead based on direct labor hours. Best-Cut has projected total overhead for the year to be $800,000. Of this amount, $600,000 relates to fixed overhead expenses. Best-Cut expects to process 160,000 cases of frozen organic vegetables this year. The direct labor standard for each case is one-quarter of an hour.

1. Compute the standard *variable* overhead rate.
2. Compute the *fixed* overhead rate.
3. Compute the standard *total* overhead rate.

E11-29 **Continuation of E11-28: compute overhead variances** *(Learning Objective 5)*
Best-Cut actually processed 180,000 cases of frozen organic vegetables during the year and incurred $840,000 of manufacturing overhead. Of this amount, $610,000 was fixed.

Requirements
1. What is the flexible budget (for the actual output) for variable overhead? for fixed overhead? for total overhead?
2. How much overhead would have been allocated to production?
3. Use your answer from Requirement 1 to determine the overhead flexible budget variance. What does this tell managers?
4. Use your answer from Requirements 1 and 2 to determine the production volume variance. What does this tell managers?
5. What is the total overhead variance?

E11-30 Compute manufacturing overhead variances (*Learning Objective 5*)

Scenox manufactures paint. The company charges the following standard unit costs to production on the basis of static budget volume of 30,000 gallons of paint per month:

Direct materials...	$2.50
Direct labor..	2.00
Manufacturing overhead...	1.50
Standard unit cost	$6.00

Scenox allocates overhead based on standard machine hours, and it uses the following monthly flexible budget for overhead:

	Number of Outputs (gallons)		
	27,000	30,000	33,000
Standard machine hours......................	2,700	3,000	3,300
Budgeted manufacturing overhead cost:			
Variable	$13,500	$15,000	$16,500
Fixed..	30,000	30,000	30,000

Scenox actually produced 33,000 gallons of paint using 3,100 machine hours. Actual variable overhead was $16,200, and fixed overhead was $32,500. Compute the total overhead variance, the overhead flexible budget variance, and the production volume variance.

Carrymate Data Set: Used for E11-31 through E11-36

Carrymate is a manufacturer of ceramic bottles. The company has these standards:

Direct materials (clay)	1 pound per bottle, at a cost of $0.40 per pound
Direct labor..	1/5 hour per bottle, at a cost of $14 per hour
Static budget variable overhead......................	$70,000
Static budget fixed overhead	$30,000
Static budget direct labor hours.....................	10,000 hours
Static budget number of bottles......................	50,000

Carrymate allocates manufacturing overhead to production based on standard direct labor hours. Last month, Carrymate reported the following actual results for the production of 70,000 bottles:

Direct materials...	1.1 pound per bottle, at a cost of $0.50 per pound
Direct labor...	1/4 hour per bottle, at a cost of $13 per hour
Actual variable overhead.................................	$104,000
Actual fixed overhead	$28,000

E11-31 **Compute the standard cost of one unit** *(Learning Objective 3)*
Refer to the Carrymate Data Set on page 675.

1. Compute the standard predetermined variable manufacturing overhead rate, the standard predetermined fixed manufacturing overhead rate, and the total standard predetermined overhead rate.

2. Compute the standard cost of each of the following inputs: direct materials, direct labor, variable manufacturing overhead, and fixed manufacturing overhead.

3. Determine the standard cost of one ceramic bottle.

E11-32 **Compute and interpret direct materials variances** *(Learning Objective 4)*
Refer to the Carrymate Data Set on page 675.

1. Compute the direct materials price variance and the direct materials efficiency variance.

2. What is the total flexible budget variance for direct materials?

3. Who is generally responsible for each variance?

4. Interpret the variances.

E11-33 **Compute and interpret direct labor variances** *(Learning Objective 4)*
Refer to the Carrymate Data Set on page 675.

1. Compute the direct labor price variance and the direct labor efficiency variance.

2. What is the total flexible budget variance for direct labor?

3. Who is generally responsible for each variance?

4. Interpret the variances.

E11-34 **Compute and interpret manufacturing overhead variances** *(Learning Objective 5)*
Refer to the Carrymate Data Set on page 675.

1. Compute the total manufacturing overhead variance. What does this tell management?

2. Compute the overhead flexible budget variance. What does this tell management?

3. Compute the production volume variance. What does this tell management?

E11-35 **Record journal entries in a standard costing system** *(Learning Objective 6)*
Refer to the Carrymate Data Set on page 675. Use a standard cost accounting system to:

1. Record Carrymate's direct materials and direct labor journal entries.

2. Record Carrymate's journal entries for manufacturing overhead, including the entry that records the overhead variances and closes the Manufacturing Overhead account.

3. Record the journal entries for the completion and sale of the 70,000 bottles, assuming Carrymate sold (on account) all of the 70,000 bottles at a sales price of $8 each (there were no beginning or ending inventories).

E11-36 **Prepare a standard cost income statement** *(Learning Objective 6)*

Refer to the Carrymate Data Set on page 675. Prepare a standard cost income statement for Carrymate's management, using Exhibit 11-17 as a guide. Assume that sales were $560,000 and actual marketing and administrative expenses were $76,500.

E11-37 **(Appendix) Record materials and labor transactions** *(Learning Objective 6)*

Make the journal entries to record the purchase and use of direct materials and direct labor made by Super GuardF in E11-27.

E11-38 **(Appendix) Interpret a standard cost income statement** *(Learning Objective 6)*

The managers of ViewNow, a contract manufacturer of DVD drives, are seeking explanations for the variances in the following report. Explain the meaning of each of ViewNow's materials, labor, and overhead variances.

VIEWNOW CO. Standard Cost Income Statement Year Ended December 31, 2007		
Sales revenue		$1,200,000
Cost of goods sold at standard cost		700,000
Manufacturing cost variances:		
Direct materials price variance	$ 8,000 F	
Direct materials efficiency variance	32,000 U	
Direct labor price variance	24,000 F	
Direct labor efficiency variance	10,000 U	
Manufacturing overhead flexible budget variance	28,000 U	
Production volume variance	8,000 F	
Total manufacturing variances		30,000
Cost of goods sold at actual cost		730,000
Gross profit		470,000
Marketing and administrative expenses		418,000
Operating income		$ 52,000

E11-39 **(Appendix) Prepare a standard cost income statement** *(Learning Objective 6)*
Northern Outfitters' revenue and expense information for April follows:

Sales revenue..	$560,000
Cost of good sold (standard)...	342,000
Direct materials price variance	2,000 F
Direct materials efficiency variance	6,000 F
Direct labor price variance	4,000 U
Direct labor efficiency variance	2,000 F
Overhead flexible budget variance	3,500 U
Production volume variance..	8,000 F

Prepare a standard cost income statement for management through gross profit. Report all standard cost variances for management's use. Has management done a good or poor job of controlling costs? Explain.

■ Problems (Problem Set A)

P11-40A **Prepare a flexible budget for planning** *(Learning Objective 1)*
Precious Bubbles produces multicolored bubble solution used for weddings and other events. The company's static budget income statement for August 2007 follows. It is based on expected sales volume of 55,000 bubble kits.

PRECIOUS BUBBLES, INC. Static Budget Income Statement Month Ended August 31, 2007	
Sales revenue	$165,000
Variable expenses:	
Cost of goods sold	63,250
Sales commissions	13,750
Utilities expense	6,050
Fixed expenses:	
Salary expense	32,500
Depreciation expense	20,000
Rent expense	11,000
Utilities expense	5,200
Total expenses	151,750
Operating income	$ 13,250

Precious Bubbles' plant capacity is 62,500 kits. If actual volume exceeds 62,500 kits, the company must expand the plant. In that case, salaries will increase by 10%, depreciation by 15%, and rent by $6,000. Fixed utilities will be unchanged by any volume increase.

Requirements

1. Prepare flexible budget income statements for the company, showing output levels of 55,000, 60,000, and 65,000 kits.

2. Graph the behavior of the company's total costs.

3. Why might Precious Bubbles' managers want to see the graph you prepared in Requirement 2 as well as the columnar format analysis in Requirement 1? What is the disadvantage of the graphic approach?

P11-41A **Prepare and interpret a performance report** *(Learning Objective 2)*

Refer to the Precious Bubbles data in P11-40A. The company sold 60,000 bubble kits during August 2007, and its actual operating income was as follows:

PRECIOUS BUBBLES, INC. Income Statement Month Ended August 31, 2007	
Sales revenue	$185,000
Variable expenses:	
Cost of goods sold	$ 69,500
Sales commissions	18,000
Utilities expense	6,600
Fixed expenses:	
Salary expense	34,000
Depreciation expense	20,000
Rent expense	10,000
Utilities expense	5,200
Total expenses	163,300
Operating income	$ 21,700

Requirements

1. Prepare an income statement performance report for August 2007 in a format similar to Exhibit 11-7.

2. What accounts for most of the difference between actual operating income and static budget operating income?

3. What is Precious Bubbles' static budget variance? Explain why the income statement performance report provides Precious Bubbles' managers with more useful information than the simple static budget variance. What insights can Precious Bubbles' managers draw from this performance report?

P11-42A **Comprehensive flexible budget, standards, and variances problem** *(Learning Objectives 2, 3, 4, 5)*

Eagle System assembles PCs and uses flexible budgeting and a standard cost system. Eagle System allocates overhead based on the number of direct materials parts. The company's performance report includes the following selected data:

	Static Budget (20,000 PCs)	Actual Results (22,000 PCs)
Sales (20,000 PCs × $400)	$8,000,000	
(22,000 PCs × $420)...		$9,240,000
Variable manufacturing expenses:		
Direct materials (200,000 parts × $10.00)	2,000,000	
(214,200 parts × $9.80).................................		2,099,160
Direct labor (40,000 hr × $14.00)	560,000	
(42,500 hr × $14.60).....................................		620,500
Variable overhead (200,000 parts × $4.00)	800,000	
(214,200 parts × $4.10).................................		878,220
Fixed manufacturing expenses:		
Fixed overhead...	900,000	930,000
Total cost of goods sold..................................	4,260,000	4,527,880
Gross profit..	$3,740,000	$4,712,120

Requirements

1. Determine the company's standard cost for one unit.
2. Prepare a flexible budget based on the actual number of PCs sold.
3. Compute the price variance for direct materials and for direct labor.
4. Compute the efficiency variances for direct materials and direct labor.
5. For manufacturing overhead, compute the total variance, the flexible budget variance, and the production volume variance.
6. What is the total flexible budget variance for Eagle System's manufacturing costs? Show how the total flexible budget variance is divided into materials, labor, and overhead variances.
7. Have Eagle System's managers done a good job or a poor job controlling material and labor costs? Why?
8. Describe how Eagle System's managers can benefit from the standard costing system.

P11-43A **Work backward through labor variances** *(Learning Objective 4)*

Lily's Music manufactures harmonicas. Lily uses standard costs to judge performance. Recently, a clerk mistakenly threw away some of the records, and Lily has only partial data for October. She knows that the direct labor flexible budget variance for the month was $330 F and that the standard labor price was $10 per hour. A recent pay cut caused a favorable labor price variance of $0.50 per hour. The standard direct labor hours for actual October output were 5,600.

Requirements

1. Find the actual number of direct labor hours worked during October. First, find the actual direct labor price per hour. Then, determine the actual number of direct labor hours worked by setting up the compuation of the direct labor flexible budget variance of $330 F.

2. Compute the direct labor price and efficiency variances. Do these variances suggest that the manager may have made trade-offs? Explain.

P11-44A **Determine all variances** *(Learning Objectives 4, 5)*

McKnight manufactures embroidered jackets. The company prepares flexible budgets and uses a standard cost system to control manufacturing costs. The following standard unit cost of a jacket is based on the static budget volume of 14,000 jackets per month:

Direct materials (3.0 sq. ft × $4.00 per sq. ft)...........		$ 12.00
Direct labor (2 hours × $9.40 per hour)....................		18.80
Manufacturing overhead:		
Variable (2 hours × $0.65 per hour)....................	$1.30	
Fixed (2 hours × $2.20 per hour)........................	4.40	5.70
Total cost per jacket...		$36.50

Data for November of the current year include the following:

a. Actual production was 13,600 jackets.

b. Actual direct materials usage was 2.70 square feet per jacket at an actual cost of $4.15 per square foot.

c. Actual direct labor usage of 24,480 hours cost $235,008.

d. Total actual overhead cost was $79,000.

Requirements

1. Compute the price and efficiency variances for direct materials and direct labor.

2. For manufacturing overhead, compute the total variance, the flexible budget variance, and the production volume variance.

3. McKnight's management intentionally purchased superior materials for November production. How did this decision affect the other cost variances? Overall, was the decision wise? Explain.

P11-45A **(Appendix) Journalize standard cost transactions** *(Learning Objective 6)*

Refer to the data in P11-44A. Journalize the usage of direct materials and the assignment of direct labor, including the related variances.

P11-46A **Compute variances and prepare standard cost income statement** *(Learning Objectives 4, 5, 6)*

Barry and Sons makes ground covers to prevent weed growth. During May, the company produced and sold 44,000 rolls and recorded the following cost data:

	Standard Unit Cost	Actual Total Cost
Direct materials:		
Standard (3 lb × $1.10 per pound)	$3.30	
Actual (136,600 lb × $1.05 per pound)		$143,430
Direct labor:		
Standard (0.1 hr × $9.00 per hr)....................	0.90	
Actual (4,600 hr × $8.80 per hr)....................		40,480
Manufacturing overhead:		
Standard:		
Variable (0.2 machine hr × $9.00 per hr)........... $1.80		
Fixed ($96,000 for static budget volume of 40,000 units and 8,000 machine hours).................................. 2.40		
	4.20	
Actual		168,800
Total manufacturing costs....................................	$8.40	$352,710

Requirements

1. Compute the price and efficiency variances for direct materials and direct labor.
2. For manufacturing overhead, compute the total variance, the flexible budget variance, and the production volume variance.
3. Prepare a standard cost income statement through gross profit to report all variances to management. Sales price was $10.60 per roll.
4. Barry and Sons intentionally purchased cheaper materials during May. Was the decision wise? Discuss the trade-off between the two materials variances.

■ Problems (Problem Set B)

P11-47B **Prepare a flexible budget for planning** *(Learning Objective 1)*

Revolve Technologies manufactures capacitors for cellular base stations and other communications applications. The company's static budget income statement for October 2007 follows. It is based on expected sales volume of 9,000 units.

Revolve Technologies' plant capacity is 9,500 units. If actual volume exceeds 9,500 units, Revolve Technologies must rent additional space. In that case, salaries will increase by 15%, rent will double, and insurance expense will increase by $1,000. Depreciation will be unaffected.

REVOLVE TECHNOLOGIES
Static Budget Income Statement
Month Ended October 31, 2007

Sales revenue	$207,000
Variable expenses:	
Cost of goods sold	90,000
Sales commissions	9,900
Shipping expense	6,300
Fixed expenses:	
Salary expense	30,500
Depreciation expense	12,750
Rent expense	11,500
Insurance expense	3,750
Total expenses	164,700
Operating income	$ 42,300

Requirements

1. Prepare flexible budget income statements for 7,500, 9,000, and 11,000 units.

2. Graph the behavior of the company's total costs.

3. Why might Revolve Technologies' managers want to see the graph you prepared in Requirement 2 as well as the columnar format analysis in Requirement 1? What is the disadvantage of the graphic approach in Requirement 2?

P11-48B **Prepare and interpret a performance report** *(Learning Objective 2)*
Refer to the Revolve Technologies data in P11-47B. The company sold 11,000 units during October 2007, and its actual operating income was as follows:

REVOLVE TECHNOLOGIES
Income Statement
Month Ended October 31, 2007

Sales revenue	$257,000
Variable expenses:	
Cost of goods sold	112,250
Sales commissions	11,800
Shipping expense	8,950
Fixed expenses:	
Salary expense	36,650
Depreciation expense	12,750
Rent expense	22,500
Insurance expense	4,700
Total expenses	209,600
Operating income	$ 47,400

continued . . .

Requirements

1. Prepare an income statement performance report for October in a format similar to Exhibit 11-7.

2. What was the effect on Revolve Technologies' operating income of selling 2,000 units more than the static budget level of sales?

3. What is Revolve Technologies' static budget variance? Explain why the income statement performance report provides more useful information to Revolve Technologies' managers than the simple static budget variance. What insights can Revolve Technologies' managers draw from this performance report?

P11-49B **Comprehensive flexible budget, standards, and variances problem** *(Learning Objectives 2, 3, 4, 5)*

HeadSmart manufactures leather recliners and uses flexible budgeting and a standard cost system. HeadSmart allocates overhead based on yards of direct materials. The company's performance report includes the following selected data:

	Static Budget (1,000 recliners)	Actual Results (980 recliners)
Sales (1,000 recliners × $500)	$500,000	
(980 recliners × $490)		$480,200
Variable manufacturing expenses:		
Direct materials (6,000 yd × $8.90)	53,400	
(6,150 yd × $8.70)		53,505
Direct labor (10,000 hr × $9.00)	90,000	
(9,600 hr × $9.15)		87,840
Variable overhead (6,000 yd × $5.00)	30,000	
(6,150 yd × $6.40)		39,360
Fixed manufacturing expenses:		
Fixed overhead	60,000	66,000
Total cost of goods sold	233,400	246,705
Gross profit	$266,600	$233,495

Requirements

1. Determine the company's standard cost for one unit.
2. Prepare a flexible budget based on the actual number of recliners sold.
3. Compute the price variance for direct materials and for direct labor.
4. Compute the efficiency variances for direct materials and direct labor.
5. For manufacturing overhead, compute the total variance, the flexible budget variance, and the production volume variance.
6. What is the total flexible budget variance for HeadSmart's manufacturing costs? Show how the total flexible budget variance is divided into materials, labor, and overhead variances.
7. Have HeadSmart's managers done a good job or a poor job controlling material and labor costs? Why?
8. Describe how HeadSmart's managers can benefit from the standard costing system.

P11-50B **Work backward through labor variances** *(Learning Objective 4)*

Karen's Shades manufactures lamp shades. The manager uses standard costs to judge performance. Recently, a clerk mistakenly threw away some of the records, and the manager has only partial data for March. The manager knows that the direct labor flexible budget variance for the month was $1,050 U and that the standard labor price was $9 per hour. The shop experienced an unfavorable labor price variance of $0.50 per hour. The standard direct labor hours for actual March output were 4,000.

Requirements

1. Find the actual number of direct labor hours worked during March. First, find the actual direct labor price per hour. Then, determine the actual direct labor hours by setting up the computation of the direct labor flexible budget variance of $1,050 U.

2. Compute the direct labor price and efficiency variances. Do these variances suggest the manager may have made trade-offs? Explain.

P11-51B **Determine all variances** *(Learning Objectives 4, 5)*

Rouse manufactures paperweights that it sells to other companies for customizing with their own logos. Rouse prepares flexible budgets and uses a standard cost system to control manufacturing costs. The standard unit cost of a paperweight is based on static budget volume of 60,000 paperweights per month. The unit cost is computed as follows:

Direct materials (0.2 pounds × $0.25 per pound)		$0.05
Direct labor (3 minutes × $0.12 per minute)............		0.36
Manufacturing overhead:		
Variable (3 minutes × $0.06 per minute).............	$0.18	
Fixed (3 minutes × $0.14 per minute).................	0.42	0.60
Total cost per paperweight..		$1.01

Transactions during May of the current year included the following:

a. Actual production and sales were 62,700 paperweights.

b. Actual direct materials usage was 0.18 pound per paperweight at an actual cost of $0.20 per pound.

c. Actual direct labor usage of 210,000 minutes cost $29,400.

d. Actual overhead cost was $40,800.

Requirements

1. Compute the price and efficiency variances for direct materials and direct labor.

2. For manufacturing overhead, compute the total variance, the flexible budget variance, and the production volume variance. (*Hint:* Remember that the total fixed overhead in the flexible budget equals the total fixed overhead in the static budget.)

3. Rouse intentionally hired more skilled workers during May. How did this decision affect the cost variances? Overall, was the decision wise? Explain.

P11-52B **(Appendix) Journalize standard cost transactions** *(Learning Objective 6)*

Refer to the data in P11-51B. Journalize the usage of direct materials and the assignment of direct labor, including the related variances.

P11-53B Compute variances and prepare standard cost income statement *(Learning Objectives 4, 5, 6)*

Nanco Industries manufactures sunglass cases. During August, the company produced and sold 106,000 cases and recorded the following cost data:

	Standard Unit Cost	Actual Total Cost
Direct materials:		
Standard (2 parts × $0.16 per part)...............	$0.32	
Actual (218,000 parts × $0.20 per part)...........		$43,600
Direct labor:		
Standard (0.02 hr × $8.00 per hr).................	0.16	
Actual (1,650 hr × $8.20 per hr)		13,530
Manufacturing overhead:		
Standard:		
Variable (0.02 machine hr × $8.00 per hr) $0.16		
Fixed ($32,000 for static budget volume of 100,000 units and 2,000 machine hours) 0.32		
	0.48	
Actual		60,500
Total manufacturing costs	$0.96	$117,630

Requirements

1. Compute the price and efficiency variances for direct materials and direct labor.
2. For manufacturing overhead, compute the total variance, the flexible budget variance, and the production volume variance.
3. Prepare a standard cost income statement through gross profit to report all variances to management. Sales price of the sunglass cases was $1.50 each.
4. Nanco Industries' management used more experienced workers during August. Discuss the trade-off between the two direct labor variances.

Apply Your Knowledge

■ Decision Cases

Case 11-54. Compute flexible budget and sales volume variances *(Learning Objective 2)*

ReelTime distributes DVDs to movie retailers, including dot-coms. ReelTime's top management meets monthly to evaluate the company's performance. Controller Terri Lon prepared the following performance report for the meeting.

REELTIME, INC. Income Statement Performance Report Month Ended July 31, 2007	Actual Results	Static Budget	Variance	
Sales revenue	$1,640,000	$1,960,000	$320,000	U
Variable expenses:				
Cost of goods sold	773,750	980,000	206,250	F
Sales commissions	77,375	107,800	30,425	F
Shipping expense	42,850	53,900	11,050	F
Fixed expenses:				
Salary expense	311,450	300,500	10,950	U
Depreciation expense	208,750	214,000	5,250	F
Rent expense	128,250	108,250	20,000	U
Advertising expense	81,100	68,500	12,600	U
Total expenses	1,623,525	1,832,950	209,425	F
Operating income	$ 16,475	$ 127,050	$110,575	U

Lon also revealed that the actual sales price of $20 per movie was equal to the budgeted sales price and that there were no changes in inventories for the month.

Management is disappointed by the operating income results. CEO Lyle Nesbitt exclaims, "How can actual operating income be roughly 13% of the static budget amount when there are so many favorable variances?"

Requirements

1. Prepare a more informative performance report. Be sure to include a flexible budget for the actual number of DVDs bought and sold.

2. As a member of ReelTime's management team, which variances would you want investigated? Why?

3. Nesbitt believes that many consumers are postponing purchases of new movies until after the introduction of a new format for recordable DVD players. In light of this information, how would you rate the company's performance?

Case 11-55. Calculate efficiency variances *(Learning Objective 4)*

Assume that you manage your local Marble Slab Creamery ice cream parlor. In addition to selling ice cream cones, you make large batches of a few flavors of milk shakes to sell throughout the day. Your parlor is chosen to test the company's "Made-for-You" system. The system allows patrons to customize their milk shakes by choosing different flavors.

continued . . .

Customers like the new system, and your staff appears to be adapting, but you wonder whether this new made-to-order system is as efficient as the old system where you made just a few large batches. Efficiency is a special concern because your performance is evaluated in part on the restaurant's efficient use of materials and labor. Assume that your superiors consider efficiency variances greater than 5% unacceptable.

You decide to look at your sales for a typical day. You find that the parlor used 390 pounds of ice cream and 72 hours of direct labor to produce and sell 2,000 shakes. Assume that the standard quantity allowed for a shake is 0.2 pound of ice cream and 0.03 hours (1.8 minutes) of direct labor. Further, assume that standard costs are $1.50 per pound for ice cream and $8.00 an hour for labor.

Requirements

1. Compute the efficiency variances for direct labor and direct materials.

2. Provide likely explanations for the variances. Do you have reason to be concerned about your performance evaluation? Explain.

3. Write a memo to Marble Slab Creamery's national office explaining your concern and suggesting a remedy. Use the following format for your memo:

> **Date:** _____
>
> **To:** Marble Slab Creamery's National Office
>
> **From:** _____
>
> **Subject:** "Made-for-You" System

■ Ethical Issues

Case 11-56. Ethical dilemmas relating to standards (*Learning Objective 3*)
Austin Landers is the accountant for Sun Coast, a manufacturer of outdoor furniture that is sold through specialty stores and Internet companies. Annually, Landers is responsible for reviewing the standard costs for the following year. While reviewing the standard costs for the coming year, two ethical issues arise. Use the IMA's *Statement of Ethical Professional Practice* (in Chapter 1) to identify the ethical dilemma in each situation. Identify the relevant factors in each situation and suggest what Landers should recommend to the controller.

Issue 1
Landers has been approached by Kara Willis, a former colleague who worked with Landers when they were both employed by a public accounting firm. Willis recently started her own firm, Willis Benchmarking Associates, which collects and sells data on industry benchmarks. She offers to provide Landers with benchmarks for the outdoor furniture industry free of charge if he will provide her with the last three

years of Sun Coast's standard and actual costs. Willis explains that this is how she obtains most of her firm's benchmarking data. Landers always has a difficult time with the standard-setting process and believes that the benchmark data would be very useful.

Issue 2

Sun Coast's management is starting a continuous improvement policy that requires a 10% reduction in standard costs each year for the next three years. Dan Jones, manufacturing supervisor of the Teak furniture line, asks Landers to set loose standard costs this year before the continuous improvement policy is implemented. Jones argues that there is no other way to meet the tightening standards while maintaining the high quality of the Teak line.

■ Team Project

Project 11-57. Evaluate standard setting approaches *(Learning Objective 3)*

Pella is the world's second-largest manufacturer of wood windows and doors. In 1992, Pella entered the national retail market with its ProLine windows and doors, manufactured in Carroll, Iowa. Since then, Pella has introduced many new product lines with manufacturing facilities in several states.

Suppose Pella has been using a standard cost system that bases price and quantity standards on Pella's historical long-run average performance. Assume Pella's controller has engaged your team of management consultants to recommend whether Pella should use some basis other than historical performance for setting standards.

1. List the types of variances you recommend that Pella compute (for example, direct materials price variance for glass). For each variance, what specific standards would Pella need to develop? In addition to cost standards, do you recommend that Pella develop any nonfinancial standards? Explain.

2. There are many approaches to setting standards other than simply using long-run average historical prices and quantities.

   a. List three alternative approaches that Pella could use to set standards and explain how Pella could implement each alternative.

   b. Evaluate each alternative method of setting standards, including the pros and cons of each method.

   c. Write a memo to Pella's controller detailing your recommendations. First, should Pella retain its historical data-based standard cost approach? If not, which alternative approach should it adopt? Use the following format for your memo:

Date: _____

   To: Controller, Pella Corporation

From: _____, Management Consultants

Subject: Standard Costs

---

12 Performance Evaluation and the Balanced Scorecard

To deliver over 3.6 billion packages a year in over 200 countries, United Parcel Service (UPS) employs over 370,000 people. But how does management successfully guide the actions of all of these employees? First, it divides—or decentralizes—the company into three segments: domestic packaging, international packaging, and nonpackaging services (such as supply chain and logistics). It further breaks each packaging segment into geographic regions and each region into districts. Management gives each district manager authority to make decisions for his or her district. Because top management wants *every* employee to know how his or her day-to-day job contributes to the company's goals, it implemented a system, called the balanced scorecard, for communicating strategy to all district managers and employees. Management can also use the balanced scorecard to measure whether each district is meeting its goals and to assess where changes should be made. According to one UPS

executive, "The balanced scorecard provided a road map—the shared vision of our future goals—with action elements that let *everyone* contribute to our success."

In 2000, *Forbes* named UPS the "Company of the Year"; and in 2004, *Fortune* rated UPS as the "World's Most Admired Company in its Industry" for the sixth consecutive year. ■

Sources: Robert Kaplan and David Norton, *The Strategy-Focused Organization: How Balanced Scorecard Companies Thrive in the New Business Environment*, Harvard Business School Press, Boston, 2001, pp. 21–22, 239–241; UPS Web site.

Learning Objectives

1 Explain why and how companies decentralize

2 Explain why companies use performance evaluation systems

3 Describe the balanced scorecard and identify key performance indicators for each perspective

4 Use performance reports to evaluate cost, revenue, and profit centers

5 Use ROI, RI, and EVA to evaluate investment centers

Many companies, such as UPS, decentralize their operations into subunits. Decentralization provides large companies with many advantages. Because top management is not directly involved in running the day-to-day operations of each subunit, it needs a system—such as the balanced scorecard—for communicating the company's strategy to subunit managers and for measuring how well the subunits are achieving their goals. Let's first take a look at the advantages and disadvantages of decentralization.

Decentralized Operations

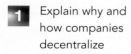

1 Explain why and how companies decentralize

In a small company, the owner or top manager often makes all planning and operating decisions. Small companies can use **centralized** decision making because of the smaller scope of their operations. However, when a company grows, it is impossible for a single person to manage the entire organization's daily operations. Therefore, most companies **decentralize** as they grow.

Companies that decentralize split their operations into different divisions or operating units. Top management delegates decision-making responsibility to the unit managers. Top management determines the type of decentralization that best suits the company's strategy. For example, decentralization may be based on geographic area, product line, customer base, business function, or some other business characteristic. Citizens Bank segments its operations by state (different geographic areas). Sherwin-Williams segments by customer base (commercial and consumer paint divisions). PepsiCo segments by type of product (Pepsi, Gatorade, and Tropicana beverages; Frito-Lay snack foods; and Quaker brand food products). And UPS segmented first by function (domestic packaging, international packaging, and nonpackaging services), then by geographic area.

Advantages of Decentralization

What advantages does decentralization offer large companies? Let's take a look.

Frees Top Management's Time

By delegating responsibility for daily operations to unit managers, top management can concentrate on long-term strategic planning and higher-level decisions that affect the entire company.

Supports Use of Expert Knowledge

Decentralization allows top management to hire the expertise each business unit needs to excel in its specific operations. For example, decentralizing by state allows Citizens Bank to hire managers with specialized knowledge of the banking laws in each state. Such specialized knowledge can help unit managers make better decisions than the company's top managers could make about product and business improvements within the business unit.

Improves Customer Relations

Unit managers focus on just one segment of the company; therefore, they can maintain close contact with important customers. Thus, decentralization often leads to improved customer relations and quicker customer response time.

Provides Training

Decentralization also provides unit managers with training and experience necessary to become effective top managers. For example, in politics, presidential candidates often have experience as senators or state governors. Likewise, companies often choose CEOs based on their past performance as division managers.

Improves Motivation and Retention

Empowering unit managers to make decisions increases managers' motivation and retention and improves job performance and satisfaction.

Disadvantages of Decentralization

As Exhibit 12-1 illustrates, the many advantages of decentralization usually outweigh the disadvantages.

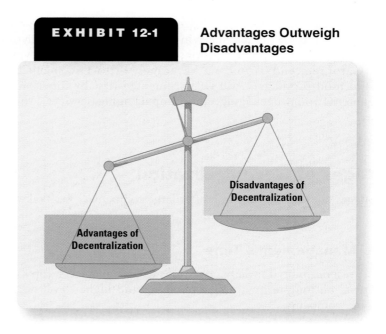

EXHIBIT 12-1 Advantages Outweigh Disadvantages

Despite its advantages, decentralization can also cause potential problems, including those outlined in this section.

Duplication of Costs

Decentralization may cause the company to duplicate certain costs or assets. For example, each business unit may hire its own payroll department and purchase its own payroll software. Companies can often avoid such duplications by providing centralized services. For example, Doubletree Hotels segments its business by property, yet each property shares one centralized reservations office and one centralized Web site.

Problems Achieving Goal Congruence

Goal congruence occurs when unit managers' goals align with top management's goals. Decentralized companies often struggle to achieve goal congruence. Unit managers may not fully understand the big picture of the company. They may make decisions that are good for their division but may harm another division or the rest of the company. For example, the purchasing department may buy cheaper components to decrease product cost. However, cheaper components may hurt the product line's quality, and the company's brand, *as a whole*, may suffer. Later in this chapter, we'll see how management accountants can design performance evaluation systems that foster goal congruence.

Responsibility Centers

Decentralized companies delegate responsibility for specific decisions to each subunit, creating responsibility centers. Recall from Chapter 10 that a **responsibility center** is a part or subunit of an organization whose manager is accountable for specific activities. Exhibit 12-2 reviews the four most common types of responsibility centers.

| EXHIBIT 12-2 | The Four Most Common Types of Responsibility Centers |

Responsibility Center	Manager is responsible for...	Examples
Cost center	Controlling costs	Production line at Dell Computer; legal department and accounting department at Nike
Revenue center	Generating sales revenue	Midwest sales region at Pace Foods; central reservation office at Delta
Profit center	Producing profit through generating sales and controlling costs	Product line at Anheuser-Busch; individual Home Depot stores
Investment center	Producing profit and managing the division's invested capital	Company divisions such as Walt Disney World Resorts and Toon Disney

Performance Measurement

Once a company decentralizes operations, top management is no longer involved in running the subunits' day-to-day operations. Performance evaluation systems provide top management with a framework for maintaining control over the entire organization.

2 Explain why companies use performance evaluation systems

Goals of Performance Evaluation Systems

When companies decentralize, top management needs a system to communicate its goals to subunit managers. In addition, top management needs to determine whether the decisions being made at the subunit level are effectively meeting company goals. We'll now consider the primary goals of performance evaluation systems.

Promoting Goal Congruence and Coordination

As previously mentioned, decentralization increases the difficulty of achieving goal congruence. Unit managers may not always make decisions consistent with the overall goals of the organization. A company will be able to achieve its goals only if each unit moves in a synchronized fashion toward the overall company goals. Like a flock of birds or a school of fish, each individual subunit must move in harmony with the other subunits. The performance measurement system should provide incentives for coordinating the subunits' activities and direct them toward achieving the overall company goals.

Communicating Expectations

To make decisions that are consistent with the company's goals, unit managers must know the goals and the specific part that their units play in attaining those goals. The performance measurement system should spell out the unit's most critical objectives. Without a clear picture of what management expects, unit managers have little to guide their daily operating decisions.

Motivating Unit Managers

Unit managers are usually motivated to make decisions that will help to achieve top management's expectations. For additional motivation, upper management may offer bonuses to unit managers who meet or exceed performance targets. Top management must exercise extreme care in setting performance targets. For example, a manager measured solely by his or her ability to control costs may take whatever actions are necessary to achieve that goal, including sacrificing quality or customer service. But such actions would *not* be in the best interests of the firm as a whole. Therefore, upper management must consider the ramifications of the performance targets it sets for unit managers.

Providing Feedback

In decentralized companies, top management is no longer involved in the day-to-day operations of each subunit. Performance evaluation systems provide upper management with the feedback it needs to maintain control over the entire organization, even though it has delegated responsibility and decision-making authority to unit managers. If targets are not met at the unit level, upper management will take corrective actions, ranging from modifying unit goals (if the targets are unrealistic) to replacing the unit manager (if the targets are achievable but the manager fails to reach them).

Benchmarking

Performance evaluation results are often used for **benchmarking**, which is the practice of comparing the unit's achievements against other units, other companies in the same industry, or the best practices in the industry. Comparing results against industry benchmarks is often more revealing than comparing results against budgets. To survive, a company must keep up with its competitors. Benchmarking helps the company determine whether it is performing at least as well as its competitors.

Stop & Think...

Do companies such as UPS benchmark subunit performance only against competitors and industry standards?

Answer: No. Companies also benchmark performance against the subunit's past performance. Historical trend data (measuring performance over time) helps managers assess whether their decisions are improving, having no effect, or adversely affecting subunit performance. Some companies also benchmark performance against other subunits with similar characteristics.

Limitations of Financial Performance Measurement

In the past, performance evaluation systems revolved almost entirely around *financial* performance. Until 1995, 95% of UPS's performance measures were financial. On the one hand, this focus makes sense because the ultimate goal of a company is to generate profit. On the other hand, *current* financial performance tends to reveal the results of *past* actions rather than indicate *future* performance. For this reason, financial measures tend to be **lag indicators** rather than **lead indicators**. Management needs to know the results of past decisions, but it also needs to know how current decisions may affect the future. To adequately assess the performance of subunits, managers need lead indicators in addition to lag indicators.

Another limitation of financial performance measures is that they tend to focus on the company's short-term achievements rather than on long-term performance. Why is this the case? Because financial statements are prepared on a monthly, quarterly, or annual basis. To remain competitive, top management needs clear signals that assess and predict the company's performance over longer periods of time.

The Balanced Scorecard

In the early 1990s, Robert Kaplan and David Norton introduced the **balanced scorecard**.[1] The balanced scorecard recognizes that management must consider *both* financial performance measures (which tend to measure the results of actions already taken) and operational performance measures (which tend to drive future performance) when judging the performance of a company and its subunits. These measures should be linked with the company's goals and its strategy for achieving those goals. The balanced scorecard represents a major shift in corporate performance measurement: Financial indicators are no longer the sole measure of performance; they are now only one measure among a broader set of performance measures. Keeping score of operating measures *and* traditional financial measures give management a "balanced" view of the organization.

Kaplan and Norton use the analogy of an airplane pilot to illustrate the necessity for a balanced scorecard approach to performance evaluation. The pilot of an airplane cannot rely on only one factor, such as wind speed, to fly a plane. Rather, the pilot must consider other critical factors, such as altitude, direction, and fuel level. Likewise, management cannot rely on only financial measures to guide the company. Management needs to consider other critical factors, such as customer satisfaction, operational efficiency, and employee excellence. Similar to the way a pilot uses cockpit instruments to measure critical factors, management uses *key performance indicators*—such as customer satisfaction ratings and revenue growth—to measure critical factors that affect the success of the company. As shown in Exhibit 12-3, **key performance indicators (KPIs)** are summary performance measures that help managers assess whether the company is achieving its goals.

3 Describe the balanced scorecard and identify key performance indicators for each perspective

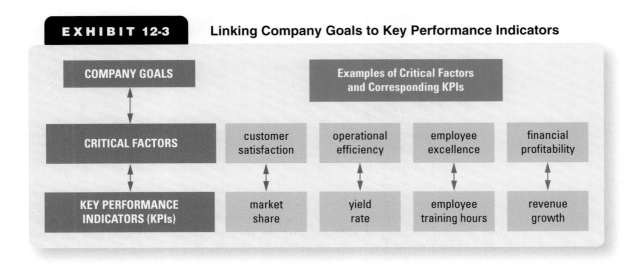

EXHIBIT 12-3 | **Linking Company Goals to Key Performance Indicators**

[1]Robert Kaplan and David Norton, "The Balanced Scorecard—Measures That Drive Performance," *Harvard Business Review on Measuring Corporate Performance*, Boston, 1991, pp. 123–145; Robert Kaplan and David Norton, *Translating Strategy into Action: The Balanced Scorecard*, Boston, Harvard Business School Press, 1996.

The Four Perspectives of the Balanced Scorecard

The balanced scorecard views the company from four different perspectives, each of which evaluates a specific aspect of organizational performance:

1. Financial perspective

2. Customer perspective

3. Internal business perspective

4. Learning and growth perspective

Exhibit 12-4 illustrates how the company's strategy affects, and, in turn, is affected by all four perspectives. In addition, it shows the cause-and-effect relationship linking the four perspectives.

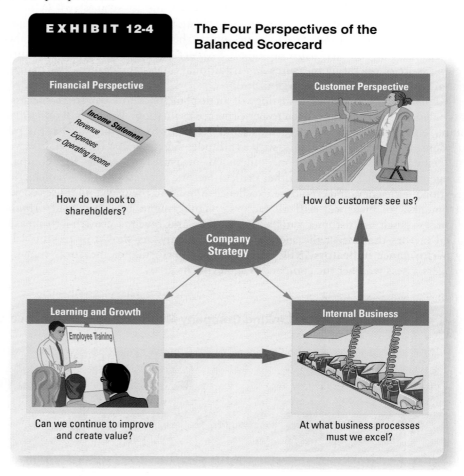

EXHIBIT 12-4   The Four Perspectives of the Balanced Scorecard

Financial Perspective

Income Statement
Revenue
− Expenses
= Operating income

How do we look to shareholders?

Customer Perspective

How do customers see us?

Company Strategy

Learning and Growth

Employee Training

Can we continue to improve and create value?

Internal Business

At what business processes must we excel?

Companies that adopt the balanced scorecard usually have specific objectives they want to achieve within each of the four perspectives. Once management clearly identifies the objectives, it develops KPIs that will assess how well the objectives are being achieved. To focus attention on the most critical elements and prevent information overload, management should use only a few KPIs for each perspective. Let's now look at each of the perspectives and discuss the links between them.

Financial Perspective

The financial perspective helps managers answer the question, how do we look to shareholders? The ultimate goal of a company is to generate income for its owners. Therefore, company strategy revolves around increasing the company's profits through increasing revenue, controlling costs, and increasing productivity. Companies grow revenue through introducing new products, gaining new customers, and increasing sales to existing customers. At the same time, companies must carefully monitor their costs. Companies increase productivity by using the company's assets more efficiently. For example, CVS, the drugstore chain, simply changed the direction of its store aisles and lowered its shelves to create a more user-friendly store layout. As a result, profits increased. Managers may implement seemingly sensible strategies and initiatives, but the test of their judgment is whether these decisions increase company profits.

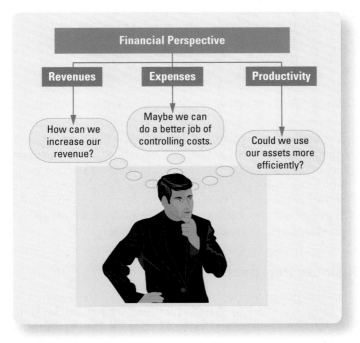

The financial perspective focuses management's attention on KPIs that assess financial objectives such as revenue growth and cost cutting. Some commonly used KPIs include *sales revenue growth*, *gross margin growth*, and *return on investment*. Later in the chapter, the most commonly used financial perspective KPIs will be discussed in detail.

Customer Perspective

The customer perspective helps managers evaluate the question, how do customers see us? Customer satisfaction is a top priority for long-term company success. If customers aren't happy, they won't come back. Therefore, customer satisfaction is critical for the company to achieve its financial goals. Notice in Exhibit 12-4 how the customer perspective influences the financial perspective.

Customers are typically concerned with four specific product or service attributes: (1) the product's price, (2) the product's quality, (3) the sales service quality, and (4) the product's delivery time (the shorter the better). Since each of these attributes is critical to making the customer happy, most companies have specific targets for each of them.

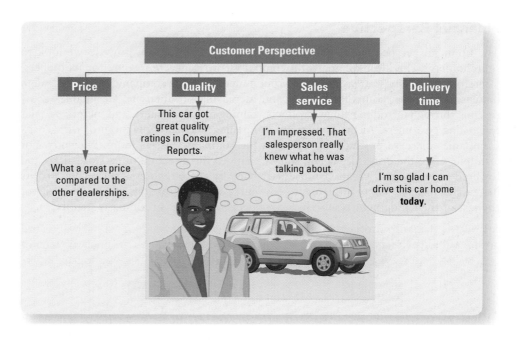

Businesses commonly use *customer satisfaction ratings* to assess how they are performing on these attributes. No doubt, you have filled out a customer satisfaction survey. Because customer satisfaction is crucial, customer satisfaction ratings determine the extent to which bonuses are granted to Bahama Breeze restaurant managers. In addition to customer satisfaction ratings, the customer perspective is often measured using KPIs such as *percentage of market share*, *increase in the number of customers*, *number of repeat customers*, and *rate of on-time deliveries*.

Internal Business Perspective

The internal business perspective helps managers address the question, at what business processes must we excel to satisfy customer and financial objectives? The answer to that question incorporates three factors: (1) innovation, (2) operations, and (3) post-sales service. All three factors critically affect customer satisfaction, which will affect the company's financial success, as shown in Exhibit 12-4.

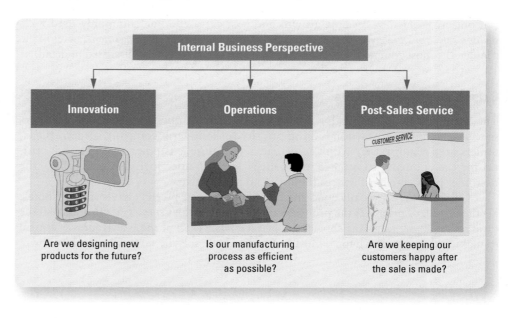

Satisfying customers once does not guarantee future success, which is why the first important factor of the internal business perspective is innovation. Customers' needs and wants change as the world around them changes. Not all that long ago, digital cameras, flat-panel computer monitors, plasma screen televisions, and digital video recorders (DVRs) did not exist. Companies must continually improve existing products (such as the addition of cameras to cell phones) and develop new products (such as iPods and portable DVD players) to succeed in the future. Companies commonly assess innovation using KPIs such as the *number of new products developed* or *new-product development time.*

The second important factor of the internal business perspective is operations. Efficient and effective internal operations allow the company to meet customers' needs and expectations. For example, the time it takes to manufacture a product *(manufacturing cycle time)* affects the company's ability to deliver quickly to meet a customer's demand. Production efficiency *(number of units produced per hour)* and product quality *(defect rate)* also affect the price charged to the customer. To remain competitive, companies must be as good as the industry leader at those internal operations that are essential to their business.

The third factor of the internal business perspective is post-sales service. How well does the company service customers after the sale? Claims of excellent post-sales service help to generate more sales. Management assesses post-sales service through the following typical KPIs: *number of warranty claims received, average repair time,* and *average wait time on the phone for a customer service representative.*

Learning and Growth Perspective

The learning and growth perspective helps managers assess the question, can we continue to improve and create value? The learning and growth perspective focuses on three factors: (1) employee capabilities, (2) information system capabilities, and (3) the company's "climate for action." As shown in Exhibit 12-4, the learning and growth perspective lays the foundation needed to improve internal business operations, sustain customer satisfaction, and generate financial success. Without skilled employees, updated technology, and a positive corporate culture, the company will not be able to meet the objectives of the other perspectives.

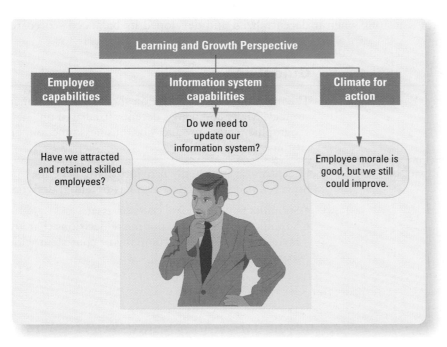

Let's consider each of these factors. First, because most routine work is automated, employees are free to be critical and creative thinkers who help achieve the company's goals. The learning and growth perspective measures employees' skills, knowledge, motivation, and empowerment. KPIs typically include *hours of employee training, employee satisfaction, employee turnover,* and *number of employee suggestions implemented.* Second, employees need timely and accurate information on customers, internal processes, and finances; therefore, other KPIs measure the maintenance and improvement of the company's information system. For example, KPIs might include the *percentage of employees having online access to information about customers* and the *percentage of processes with real-time feedback on quality, cycle time, and cost.* Finally, management must create a corporate culture that supports communication, change, and growth. For example, UPS used the balanced scorecard to communicate strategy to all employees and to show them how their daily work contributed to company success.

In summary, the balanced scorecard focuses performance measurement on progress toward the company's goals in each of the four perspectives. In designing the scorecard, managers start with the company's goals and its strategy for achieving those goals and then identify the *most* important measures of performance that will predict long-term success. Some of these measures are operational lead indicators, while others are financial lag indicators. Managers must consider the linkages between strategy and operations and the way those operations will affect finances now and in the future.

So far, we have looked at why companies decentralize, why they need to measure subunit performance, and how the balanced scorecard can help. In the second half of the chapter, we'll focus on how companies measure the financial perspective of the balanced scorecard.

Decision Guidelines

PERFORMANCE EVALUATION AND THE BALANCED SCORECARD

UPS had to make the following types of decisions when it decentralized and developed its balanced scorecard for performance evaluation.

Decision	Guidelines
How should we decentralize?	The manner of decentralization should fit the company's strategy. Many companies decentralize based on geographic region, product line, business function, or customer type.
Will decentralization have a negative impact on the company?	Decentralization usually provides many benefits; however, decentralization also has potential drawbacks: • Subunits may duplicate costs or assets. • Subunit managers may not make decisions that are favorable to the entire company or consistent with top managers' goals.

Decision	Guidelines
How can responsibility accounting be incorporated at decentralized companies?	Subunit managers are given responsibility for specific activities and are held accountable only for the results of those activities. Subunits generally fall into one of the following four categories according to their responsibilities: 1. **Cost centers**—responsible for controlling costs 2. **Revenue centers**—responsible for generating revenue 3. **Profit centers**—responsible for controlling costs and generating revenue 4. **Investment centers**—responsible for controlling costs, generating revenue, and efficiently managing the division's invested capital (assets)
Is a performance evaluation system necessary?	While not mandatory, most companies will reap many benefits from implementing a well-designed performance evaluation system. Such systems will promote goal congruence, communicate expectations, motivate managers, provide feedback, and enable benchmarking.
Should the performance evaluation system include lag or lead measures?	Better performance evaluation systems include *both* lag and lead measures. Lag measures reveal the results of past actions, while lead measures project future performance.
What are the four balanced scorecard perspectives?	(1) financial perspective, (2) customer perspective, (3) internal business perspective, and (4) learning and growth perspective
Must all four perspectives be included in the company's balanced scorecard?	Every company's balanced scorecard will be unique to its business and strategy. Because each of the four perspectives is causally linked, most companies benefit from developing performance measures for each of the four perspectives.

Summary Problem 1

Requirements

1. Each of the following describes a key performance indicator. Determine which of the balanced scorecard perspectives is being addressed (financial, customer, internal business, learning and growth).

   a. Employee turnover
   b. Earnings per share
   c. Percentage of on-time deliveries
   d. Revenue growth rate
   e. Percentage of defects discovered during manufacturing
   f. Number of warranties claimed
   g. New product development time
   h. Number of repeat customers
   i. Number of employee suggestions implemented

2. Read the following company initiatives and determine which of the balanced scorecard perspectives is being addressed (financial, customer, internal business, learning and growth).

   a. Purchasing efficient production equipment
   b. Providing employee training
   c. Updating retail store lighting
   d. Paying quarterly dividends
   e. Updating the company's information system

Solution

Requirement 1

a. Learning and growth

b. Financial

c. Customer

d. Financial

e. Internal business

f. Internal business

g. Internal business

h. Customer

i. Learning and growth

Requirement 2

a. Internal business

b. Learning and growth

c. Customer

d. Financial

e. Learning and growth

Measuring the Financial Performance of Cost, Revenue, and Profit Centers

In this half of the chapter, we'll take a more detailed look at how companies measure the financial perspective of the balanced scorecard for different subunits of the company. We'll focus on the financial performance measurement of each type of responsibility center.

> **4** Use performance reports to evaluate cost, revenue, and profit centers

Responsibility accounting performance reports capture the financial performance of cost, revenue, and profit centers. Recall from Chapter 10 that responsibility accounting performance reports compare *actual* results with *budgeted* amounts and display a variance, or difference, between the two amounts. Because **cost centers** are responsible only for controlling costs, the only information their performance reports include is the actual versus budgeted *costs*. Likewise, performance reports for **revenue centers** contain only the actual versus budgeted *revenue*. However, **profit centers** are responsible for controlling costs and generating revenue. Therefore, performance reports contain actual and budgeted information on both *revenues and costs*.

Cost Center Performance Reports

Cost center performance reports typically focus on the *flexible budget variance*—the difference between actual results and the flexible budget (as described in Chapter 11). Exhibit 12-5 shows an example of a cost center performance report for a regional payroll processing department of House and Garden Depot, a home improvement warehouse chain. Because the payroll processing department only incurs expenses and does not generate revenue, it is classified as a cost center.

EXHIBIT 12-5   **Example of Cost Center Performance Report**

HOUSE AND GARDEN DEPOT—NORTH FLORIDA REGION
Payroll Processing Department Performance Report
July 2008

	Actual	Flexible Budget	Flexible Budget Variance (U or F)	% Variance* (U or F)
Salary and wages	$18,500	$18,000	$ 500 U	2.8% U
Payroll benefits	6,100	5,000	1,100 U	22.0% U
Equipment depreciation	3,000	3,000	0	0%
Supplies	1,850	2,000	150 F	7.5% F
Other	1,900	2,000	100 F	5.0% F
Total Expenses	$31,350	$30,000	$1,350 U	4.5% U

*Flexible budget variance ÷ flexible budget.

Managers use **management by exception** to determine which variances in the performance report are worth investigating. For example, management may investigate only those variances that exceed a certain dollar amount (for example, over $1,000) or a certain percentage of the budgeted figure (for example, over 10%). Smaller variances signal that operations are close to target and do not require management's immediate attention. For example, in the cost center performance report illustrated in Exhibit 12-5, management might investigate "payroll benefits" because the variance exceeds $1,000 and 10%. As discussed in Chapter 11, management should investigate favorable as well as unfavorable variances that meet their investigation criteria. Companies that use standard costs can compute price and efficiency variances, as described in Chapter 11, to better understand why significant flexible budget variances occurred.

Revenue Center Performance Reports

Revenue center performance reports often highlight both the flexible budget variance and the sales volume variance. The paint department at House and Garden Depot's Tallahassee store might look similar to Exhibit 12-6, with detailed sales volume and revenue shown for each brand and type of paint sold (for simplicity, the exhibit shows volume and revenue for only one item). The cash register bar-coding system provides managment with the sales volume and sales revenue generated by individual products.

EXHIBIT 12-6 **Example of a Revenue Center Performance Report**

HOUSE AND GARDEN DEPOT—Tallahassee Store
Paint Department Performance Report
July 2008

Sales Revenue	Actual Sales	Flexible Budget Variance	Flexible Budget	Sales Volume Variance	Static (Master) Budget
Glidden – Flat:					
Volume (gallons)	2,480	–0–	2,480	155 F	2,325
Revenue	$40,920	$3,720 U	$44,640	$2,790 F	$41,850
Glidden – Semigloss:					
Volume (gallons)					
Revenue					
Glidden – Glossy:					
Volume (gallons)					
Revenue					

Recall from Chapter 11 that the sales volume variance is due strictly to volume differences—selling more or fewer units (gallons of paint) than originally planned. The flexible budget variance, however, is due strictly to differences in the sales price—selling units for a higher or lower price than originally planned. Both the sales volume variance and the flexible budget variance help revenue center managers understand why they have exceeded or fallen short of budgeted revenue.

Profit Center Performance Reports

Managers of profit centers are responsible for generating revenue and controlling costs so their performance reports include both revenues and expenses. Exhibit 12-7 shows an example of a profit center performance report for the Tallahassee House and Garden Depot store.

Notice how this profit center performance report contains the line "Service department charges." Recall that one drawback of decentralization is that subunits may duplicate costs or assets. Many companies avoid this problem by providing centralized service departments where several subunits, such as profit centers, share assets or costs. For example, the payroll processing cost center shown in Exhibit 12-5 serves all of the House and Garden Depot stores in the north Florida region. In addition to centralized payroll departments, companies often provide centralized human resource departments, legal departments, and information systems.

When subunits share centralized services, should those services be "free" to the subunits? If they are free, the subunit's performance report will *not* include any charge for using those services. However, if they are not free, the performance report will show a charge, as you see in Exhibit 12-7. Most companies charge subunits for their

EXHIBIT 12-7   **Example of a Profit Center Performance Report**

HOUSE AND GARDEN DEPOT
Tallahassee Store—Performance Report
July 2008

	Actual	Flexible Budget	Flexible Budget Variance	% Variance
Sales Revenue	$5,243,600	$5,000,000	$243,600 F	4.9% F
Operating expenses	4,183,500	4,000,000	183,500 U	4.6% U
Income from operations before service department charges	1,060,100	1,000,000	60,100 F	6.0% F
Service department charges (allocated)	84,300	75,000	9,300 U	12.4% U
Income from operations	$ 975,800	$ 925,000	$ 50,800 F	5.5% F

use of centralized services because the subunit would otherwise have to buy those services on its own. For example, if House and Garden Depot didn't operate a centralized payroll department, the Tallahassee House and Garden Depot store would have to hire its own payroll department personnel and purchase any computers, payroll software, and supplies necessary to process the store's payroll. As an alternative, it could outsource payroll to a company such as Paychex or ADP. In either event, the store would incur a cost for processing payroll. It only seems fair that the store is charged for using the centralized payroll processing department. In addition, subunits tend to use centralized services more judiciously when they are charged for using the services. The appendix later in this chapter describes how companies allocate service department costs between subunits. Because the charges are the result of allocation rather than a direct cost of the profit center, they are usually shown on a separate line rather than "buried" in the subunit's other operating expenses.

Exhibit 12-8 shows the basic decisions management must make regarding centralized service departments.

EXHIBIT 12-8   **Centralized Services Decision Tree**

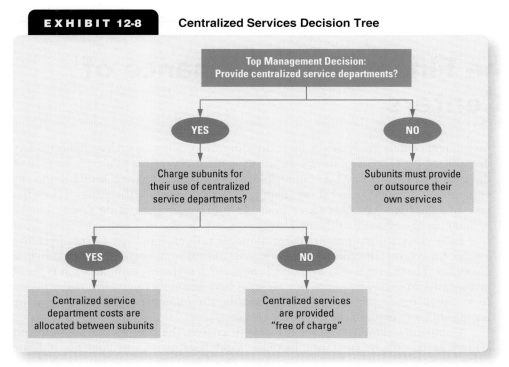

Regardless of the type of responsibility center, performance reports should focus on information, not blame. Analyzing budget variances helps managers understand the underlying reasons for the unit's performance. Once management understands these reasons, it may be able to take corrective actions. But some variances are uncontrollable. For example, the 2005 hurricanes along the Gulf Coast increased the price of gasoline (due to damaged oil refineries) and building materials (as people repaired hurricane-damaged homes). These price increases resulted in unfavorable cost variances for many companies. Managers should not be responsible for conditions they cannot control. Responsibility accounting can help management identify the causes of variances, thus allowing them to determine what was controllable and what was not.

We have just looked at the *detailed* financial information presented in responsibility accounting performance reports. In addition to these detailed reports, upper management often uses *summary* measures—financial KPIs—to assess the financial performance of cost, revenue, and profit centers. Examples include the *cost per unit of output* (for cost centers), *revenue growth* (for revenue centers), and *gross margin growth* (for profit centers). KPIs such as these are used to address the financial perspective of the balanced scorecard for cost, revenue, and profit centers. In the next section, we'll look at the most commonly used KPIs for investment centers.

Stop & Think...

We have just seen that companies such as House and Garden Depot use responsibility accounting performance reports to evaluate the financial performance of cost, revenue, and profit centers. Are these types of performance reports sufficient for evaluating the financial performance of investment centers? Why or why not?

Answer: Investment centers are responsible not only for generating revenue and controlling costs but also for efficiently managing the subunit's invested capital. The performance reports we have just seen address how well the subunits control costs and generate revenue, but they do not address how well the subunits manage their assets. Therefore, these performance reports will be helpful but not sufficient for evaluating investment center performance.

Measuring the Financial Performance of Investment Centers

 Use ROI, RI, and EVA to evaluate investment centers

Investment centers are typically large divisions of a company, such as the Frito-Lay division of PepsiCo. The duties of an investment center manager are similar to those of a CEO. The CEO is responsible for maximizing income in relation to the company's invested capital by using company assets efficiently. Likewise, investment center managers are responsible not only for generating profit but also for making the best use of the investment center's assets.

How does an investment center manager influence the use of the division's assets? An investment center manager has the authority to open new stores or close old stores. The manager may also decide how much inventory to hold, what types of investments to make, how aggressively to collect accounts receivable, and whether to invest in new equipment. In other words, the manager has decision-making responsibility over all of the division's assets.

Companies cannot evaluate investment centers the way they evaluate profit centers based only on operating income. Why? Because income does not indicate how *efficiently* the division is using its assets. The financial evaluation of investment centers must measure two factors: (1) how much income the division is generating and (2) how efficiently the division is using its assets.

Consider House and Garden Depot. In addition to its home improvement warehouse stores, House and Garden Depot operates a Landscaping Division and a Design Division. Operating income, total assets, and sales for the two divisions follow (in thousands of dollars):

House and Garden Depot	Landscaping Division	Design Division
Operating income	$ 450,000	$ 600,000
Total assets	2,500,000	4,000,000
Sales	7,500,000	10,000,000

Based on operating income alone, the Design Division (with operating income of $600,000) appears to be more profitable than the Landscaping Division (with operating income of $450,000). However, this comparison is misleading because it does not consider the assets invested in each division. The Design Division has more assets to use for generating income than does the Landscaping Division.

To adequately evaluate an investment center's financial performance, companies need summary performance measures—or KPIs—that include *both* the division's operating income *and* its assets (see Exhibit 12-9). In the next sections, we discuss three commonly used performance measures: return on investment (ROI), residual income (RI), and economic value added (EVA). All three measures incorporate both the division's assets and its operating income. For simplicity, we will leave the word *divisional* out of the equations. However, keep in mind that all of the equations use divisional data when evaluating a division's performance.

EXHIBIT 12-9   **Summary Performance Measures (KPIs) for Investment Centers**

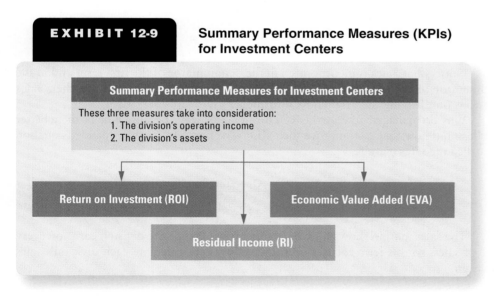

Return on Investment (ROI)

Return on Investment (ROI) is one of the most commonly used KPIs for evaluating an investment center's financial performance. Companies typically define ROI as follows:

$$\text{ROI} = \frac{\text{Operating income}}{\text{Total assets}}$$

ROI measures the amount of income an investment center earns relative to the size of its assets. Let's calculate each division's ROI:

$$\text{Landscaping Division ROI} = \left(\frac{\$450,000}{\$2,500,000} \right) = 18\%$$

$$\text{Design Division ROI} = \left(\frac{\$600,000}{\$4,000,000} \right) = 15\%$$

Although the Design Division has a higher operating income than the Landscaping Division, the Design Division is actually *less* profitable than the Landscaping Division when we consider that the Design Division has more assets from which to generate its profit.

If you had $1,000 to invest, would you rather invest it in the Design Division or Landscaping Division? The Design Division earns a profit of $0.15 on every $1.00 of assets, but the Landscaping Division earns $0.18 on every $1.00 of assets. When top management decides how to invest excess funds, they often consider each division's ROI. A division with a higher ROI is more likely to receive extra funds because it has a track record of providing a higher return.

In addition to comparing ROI across divisions, management also compares a division's ROI across time to determine whether the division is becoming more or less profitable in relation to its assets. In addition, management often benchmarks divisional ROI with other companies in the same industry to determine how each division is performing compared to its competitors.

To determine what is driving a division's ROI, management often restates the ROI equation in its expanded form:

$$\text{ROI} = \frac{\text{Operating income}}{\text{Sales}} \times \frac{\text{Sales}}{\text{Total assets}} = \frac{\text{Operating income}}{\text{Total assets}}$$

Notice that Sales is incorporated in the denominator of the first term and in the numerator of the second term. When the two terms are multiplied together, Sales cancels out, leaving the original ROI formula.

Why do managers rewrite the ROI formula this way? Because it helps them better understand how they can improve their ROI. The first term in the expanded equation is called the **sales margin**:

$$\text{Sales margin} = \frac{\text{Operating income}}{\text{Sales}}$$

The sales margin shows how much operating income the division earns on every $1 of sales, so this term focuses on profitability. Let's calculate each division's sales margin:

$$\text{Landscaping Division's sales margin} = \left(\frac{\$450,000}{\$7,500,000} \right) = 6\%$$

$$\text{Design Division's sales margin} = \left(\frac{\$600,000}{\$10,000,000} \right) = 6\%$$

Both the Landscaping Division and the Design Division have a sales margin of 6%, meaning that both divisions earn a profit of $0.06 on every $1.00 of sales.

If both divisions have identical sales margins, why do their ROIs differ (18% for Landscaping versus 15% for Design)? The answer is found in the second term of the expanded ROI equation, **capital turnover**:

$$\text{Capital turnover} = \frac{\text{Sales}}{\text{Total assets}}$$

Capital turnover shows how efficiently a division uses its assets to generate sales. Rather than focusing on profitability, capital turnover focuses on efficiency. Let's calculate each division's capital turnover:

$$\text{Landscaping Division's capital turnover} = \left(\frac{\$7,500,000}{\$2,500,000}\right) = 3$$

$$\text{Design Division's capital turnover} = \left(\frac{\$10,000,000}{\$4,000,000}\right) = 2.5$$

The Landscaping Division has a capital turnover of 3. This means that the Landscaping Division generates $3 of sales with every $1 of assets. The Design Division's capital turnover is only 2.5. The Design Division generates only $2.50 of sales with every $1.00 of assets. The Landscaping Division uses its assets more efficiently in generating sales than does the Design Division.

Let's put the two terms back together in the expanded ROI equation:

	Sales margin	$\times$	Capital turnover	= ROI
Landscaping Division:	6%	$\times$	3	= 18%
Design Division:	6%	$\times$	2.5	= 15%

As you can see, the expanded ROI equation gives management more insight into the division's ROI. Management can now see that both divisions are equally profitable on their sales (6%), but the Landscaping Division is doing a better job of generating sales with its assets than is the Design Division. Consequently, the Landscaping Division has a higher ROI.

If a manager is not satisfied with the division's capital turnover rate, how can the manager improve it? He or she might try to eliminate nonproductive assets—for example, by being more aggressive in collecting accounts receivables or decreasing inventory levels, as JoAnn Fabrics decided to do. The manager might decide to change the layout of retail stores to generate sales. Recall that CVS successfully increased sales just by lowering shelves and changing the direction of the aisles.

What if management is not satisfied with the current sales margin? To increase the sales margin, management must increase the operating income earned on every dollar of sales. Management may cut product costs or selling and administrative costs, but it needs to be careful when trimming costs. Cutting costs in the short term can hurt long-term ROI. For example, sacrificing quality or cutting back on research and development could decrease costs in the short run but may hurt long-term sales. The balanced scorecard helps management carefully consider the consequences of cost-cutting measures before acting on them.

ROI has one major drawback. Evaluating division managers based solely on ROI gives them an incentive to adopt *only* projects that maintain or increase their current ROI. Assume that top management has set a company-wide target ROI of 16%. Both divisions are considering investing in in-store video display equipment that shows customers how to use featured products. This equipment will increase sales because customers are more likely to buy the products after they see these infomercials. The equipment would cost each division $100,000 and is expected to provide each division with $17,000 of annual income. The *equipment's* ROI is:

$$\text{Equipment ROI} = \frac{\$17,000}{\$100,000} = 17\%$$

Upper management would want the divisions to invest in this equipment since the equipment will provide a 17% ROI, which is higher than the 16% target rate. But what will the managers of the divisions do? Because the Design Division currently has an ROI of 15%, the new equipment (with its 17% ROI) will *increase* the division's *overall* ROI. Therefore, the Design Division manager will buy the equipment. However, the Landscaping Division currently has an ROI of 18%. If the Landscaping Division invests in the equipment, its *overall* ROI will *decrease*. Therefore, the manager of the Landscaping Division will probably turn down the investment. In this case, goal congruence is *not* achieved—only one division will invest in equipment. Yet, top management wants both divisions to invest in the equipment because the equipment return exceeds the 16% target ROI. Next, we discuss a performance measure that overcomes this weakness of ROI.

Residual Income (RI)

Residual income (RI) is another commonly used KPI for evaluating an investment center's financial performance. Essentially, RI looks at whether the division has created any excess (or residual) income above and beyond management's expectations. Similar to ROI, RI incorporates the division's operating income and its total assets, thereby measuring the division's profitability and the efficiency with which it uses its assets. RI also incorporates another piece of information: top management's target rate of return (such as the 16% target return in the previous example). The target rate of return is the minimum acceptable rate of return that top management expects a division to earn with its assets. Management's target rate of return is based on many factors. Some of these factors include the risk level of the division's business, interest rates, investor's expectations, return being earned by other divisions, and general economic conditions. Since these factors change over time, management's target rate of return may also change over time.

RI compares the division's operating income with the minimum operating income that top management expects *given the size of the division's assets*. A positive RI means that the division's operating income exceeds top management's target rate of return. A negative RI means the division is not meeting the target rate of return. Let's look at the RI equation and calculate the RI for both divisions using the 16% target rate of return from the previous example.

$$\text{RI} = \text{Operating income} - \text{Minimum acceptable income}$$

In this equation, the minimum acceptable income is defined as top management's target rate of return multiplied by the division's total assets. Thus,

$$\text{RI} = \text{Operating income} - (\text{Target rate of return} \times \text{Total assets})$$

Let's calculate the residual income for the Landscaping Division:

$$\begin{aligned}\text{Landscaping Division RI} &= \$450,000 - (16\% \times \$2,500,000)\\ &= \$450,000 - \$400,000\\ &= \$50,000\end{aligned}$$

The positive RI indicates that the Landscaping Division exceeded top management's 16% target return expectations. The RI calculation also confirms what we learned about the Landscaping Division's ROI. Recall that the Landscaping Division's ROI was 18%, which is higher than the targeted 16%.

Let's also calculate the RI for the Design Division:

$$\text{Design Division RI} = \$600,000 - (16\% \times \$4,000,000)$$
$$= \$600,000 - \$640,000$$
$$= (\$40,000)$$

The Design Division's RI is negative. This means that the Design Division did not use its assets as effectively as top management expected. Recall that the Design Division's ROI of 15% fell short of the target rate of 16%.

Why would a company prefer to use RI over ROI for performance evaluation? The answer is that RI is more likely to lead to goal congruence than is ROI. Let's once again consider the video display equipment that both divisions could buy. In both divisions, the equipment is expected to generate a 17% return. If the divisions are evaluated based on ROI, the Design Division will buy the equipment because doing so will increase the division's ROI. The Landscaping Division will probably not buy the equipment because doing so will lower the division's ROI.

However, if management evaluates divisions based on RI rather than ROI, what will the divisions do? The answer depends on whether the project yields a positive or negative RI. Recall that the equipment would cost each division $100,000 but would provide $17,000 of operating income each year. The RI provided by *just* the equipment would be:

$$\text{Equipment RI} = \$17,000 - (\$100,000 \times 16\%)$$
$$= \$17,000 - \$16,000$$
$$= \$1,000$$

If purchased, this equipment will *improve* each division's current RI by $1,000. As a result, both divisions will be motivated to invest in the equipment. Goal congruence is achieved because both divisions take the action that top management desires. That is, both divisions invest in the equipment.

Another benefit of RI is that management may set different target returns for different divisions. For example, management might require a higher target rate of return from a division operating in a riskier business environment. If the design industry were riskier than the landscape industry, top management might decide to set a higher target return—perhaps 17%—for the Design Division.

Economic Value Added (EVA)

Economic Value Added (EVA) is a special type of RI calculation. Unlike the RI calculation we've just discussed, EVA looks at a division's RI through the eyes of the company's primary stakeholders: its investors and long-term creditors (such as bondholders). Since these stakeholders provide the company's capital, management often wants to evaluate how efficiently a division is using its assets from these two stakeholders' viewpoints. EVA calculates RI for these stakeholders by specifically considering:

1. The income available to these stakeholders.

2. The assets used to generate income for these stakeholders.

3. The minimum rate of return required by these stakeholders (referred to as the **weighted average cost of capital**, or WACC)

Let's compare the EVA equation with the RI equation and then look at the differences in more detail:

RI = Operating income	– (Total assets	× Target rate of return)

EVA = After-tax operating income – [(Total assets – Current liabilities) × WACC%]

Both equations calculate whether the division created any income above and beyond expectations. They do this by comparing actual income with the minimum acceptable income. But note the differences in the EVA calculation:

1. The EVA calculation uses *after-tax operating income*, which is the income left over after income taxes are subtracted. Why? Because the portion of income paid to the government is not available to investors and long-term creditors.

2. *Total assets is reduced by current liabilities*. Why? Because funds owed to short-term creditors, such as suppliers (accounts payable) and employees (wages payable), will be paid in the immediate future and will not be available for generating income in the long run. The division is not expected to earn a return for investors and long-term creditors on those funds that will soon be paid out to short-term creditors.

3. The *WACC* replaces management's target rate of return. Since EVA focuses on investors and creditors, it's *their* expected rate of return that should be used, not management's expected rate of return. The WACC, which represents the minimum rate of return that *investors and long-term creditors* expect, is based on the company's cost of raising capital from both groups of stakeholders. The riskier the business, the higher the expected return. Detailed WACC computations are discussed in advanced accounting and finance courses.

In summary, EVA incorporates all of the elements of RI from the perspective of investors and long-term creditors. Now that we've walked through the equation's

Effective income tax rate	30%
WACC	13%
Landscaping Division's current liabilities	$150,000
Design Division's current liabilities	$250,000

components, let's calculate EVA for the Landscape and Design Divisions discussed earlier. We'll need the following additional information:

The 30% effective income tax rate means that the government takes 30% of the company's income, leaving only 70% to the company's stakeholders. Therefore, we calculate *after-tax operating income* by multiplying the division's operating income by 70%, or (100% – effective tax rate of 30%).

EVA = After-tax operating income – [(Total assets – Current liabilities) × WACC%]

$$\begin{aligned}
\text{Landscaping Division EVA} &= (\$450,000 \times 70\%) - [(\$2,500,000 - \$150,000) \times 13\%) \\
&= \$315,000 \qquad\quad - (\$2,350,000) \times 13\%) \\
&= \$315,000 \qquad\quad - \$305,500 \\
&= \$9,500
\end{aligned}$$

$$\begin{aligned}
\text{Design Division EVA} &= (\$600,000 \times 70\%) - [(\$4,000,000 - \$250,000) \times 13\%] \\
&= \$420,000 \qquad\quad - (\$3,750,000) \times 13\%) \\
&= \$420,000 \qquad\quad - \$487,500 \\
&= (\$67,500)
\end{aligned}$$

These EVA calculations show that the Landscaping Division has generated income in excess of expectations for its investors and long-term debtholders whereas the Design Division has not.

Many firms, such as Coca-Cola and JCPenney, measure the financial performance of their investment centers using EVA. EVA promotes goal congruence, just as RI does. In addition, EVA looks at the income generated by the division in excess of expectations solely from the perspective of investors and long-term creditors. Therefore, EVA specifically addresses the financial perspective of the balanced scorecard that asks this question: How do we look to shareholders?

Exhibit 12-10 summarizes the three performance measures and some of their advantages.

EXHIBIT 12-10 **Three Investment Center Performance Measures: A Summary**

ROI:

Equation	$\text{ROI} = \dfrac{\text{Operating income}}{\text{Sales}} \times \dfrac{\text{Sales}}{\text{Total assets}} = \dfrac{\text{Operating income}}{\text{Total assets}}$
Advantages	• The expanded equation provides management with additional information on profitability and efficiency • Management can compare ROI across divisions and with other companies • ROI is useful for resource allocation

RI:

Equation	$\text{RI} = \text{Operating income} - (\text{Total assets} \times \text{Target rate of return})$
Advantages	• Promotes goal congruence better than ROI • Incorporates management's minimum required rate of return • Management can use different target rates of return for divisions with different levels of risk

EVA:

Equation	$\text{EVA} = (\text{After-tax operating income}) - [(\text{Total assets} - \text{Current liabilities}) \times \text{WACC\%}]$
Advantages	• Considers income generated for investors and long-term creditors in excess of their expectations • Promotes goal congruence

Limitations of Financial Performance Measures

We have just finished looking at three KPIs (ROI, RI, and EVA) commonly used to evaluate the financial performance of investment centers. As discussed in the following sections, all of these measures have drawbacks that management should keep in mind when evaluating the financial performance of investment centers.

Measurement Issues

The ROI, RI, and EVA calculations appear to be very straightforward; however, management must make some decisions before these calculations can be made. For example, all three equations use the term *total assets*. Recall that total assets is a balance sheet figure, which means that it is a snapshot at any given point in time. Because the total assets figure will be *different* at the beginning of the period than at the end of the period, many companies choose to use a simple average of the two figures in their ROI, RI, and EVA calculations.

Management must also decide if it really wants to include *all* assets in the total asset figure. Many firms, such as Kohls and Aldi, are continually buying land on which to build future retail outlets. Until those stores are built and opened, the land (including any construction in progress) is a nonproductive asset, which is not adding to the company's operating income. Including nonproductive assets in the total asset figure will drive down the ROI, RI, and EVA figures. Therefore, some firms do not include nonproductive assets in these calculations.

Another asset measurement issue is whether to use the gross book value of assets (the historical cost of the assets) or the net book value of assets (historical cost less accumulated depreciation). Many firms use the net book value of assets because the figure is consistent with and easily pulled from the balance sheet. Because depreciation expense factors into the firm's operating income, the net book value concept is consistent with the measurement of operating income. However, using the net book value of assets has a definite drawback. Over time, the net book value of assets decreases because accumulated depreciation continues to grow until the assets are fully depreciated. Therefore, ROI, RI, and EVA get *larger over time simply because of depreciation* rather than from actual improvements in operations. In addition, the rate of this depreciation effect will depend on the depreciation method used.

In general, calculating ROI based on the net book value of assets gives managers incentive to continue using old, outdated equipment because its low net book value results in a higher ROI. However, top management may want the division to invest in new technology to create operational efficiency (internal business perspective of the balanced scorecard) or to enhance its information systems (learning and growth perspective). The long-term effects of using outdated equipment may be devastating as competitors use new technology to produce cheaper products and sell at lower prices. Thus, to create goal congruence, some firms prefer calculating ROI based on the gross book value of assets or even based on their current replacement cost. The same general rule holds true for RI and EVA calculations: All else being equal, using the net book value will increase RI and EVA over time.

Short-Term Focus

One serious drawback of financial performance measures is their short-term focus. Companies usually prepare performance reports and calculate ROI, RI, and EVA figures using a time frame of one year or less. If upper management uses a short time frame, division managers have an incentive to take actions that will lead to an immediate increase in these measures, even if such actions may not be in the company's long-term interest (such as cutting back on R&D or advertising). On the other hand, for some potentially positive actions that subunit managers consider, it may take longer than one year to generate income at the targeted level. Many **product life cycles** start slow, even incurring losses in the early stages, before generating profit. If managers are measured on short-term financial performance only, they may not introduce new products because they are not willing to wait several years for the positive effect to show up in their financial performance measures.

As a potential remedy, management can measure financial performance using a longer time horizon, such as three to five years. Extending the time frame gives subunit managers the incentive to think long-term rather than short-term and make decisions that will positively impact the company over the next several years.

The limitations of financial performance measures confirm the importance of the balanced scorecard. The deficiencies of financial measures can be overcome by taking a broader view of performance—including KPIs from all four balanced scorecard perspectives—rather than concentrating on only the financial measures.

Decision Guidelines

PERFORMANCE EVALUATION AND THE BALANCED SCORECARD

When managers at UPS developed the financial perspective of their balanced scorecard, they had to make decisions such as these.

Decision	Guidelines
How should the financial section of the balanced scorecard be measured for cost, revenue, and profit centers?	Responsibility accounting performance reports measure the financial performance of cost, revenue, and profit centers. These reports typically highlight the variances between budgeted and actual performance.
How should the financial section of the balanced scorecard be measured for investment centers?	Investment centers require measures that take into account the division's operating income *and* the division's assets. Typical measures include: • Return on investment (ROI). • Residual income (RI). • Economic value added (EVA).
How is ROI computed and interpreted?	$$\text{ROI} = \text{Operating income} \div \text{Total assets}$$ ROI measures the amount of income earned by a division relative to the size of its assets. The higher, the better.
Can managers learn more by writing the ROI formula in its expanded form?	In its expanded form, ROI is written as: $$\text{ROI} = \text{Sales margin} \times \text{Capital turnover}$$ where $$\text{Sales margin} = \text{Operating income} \div \text{Sales}$$ $$\text{Capital turnover} = \text{Sales} \div \text{Total assets}$$ Sales margin focuses on profitability (the amount of income earned on every dollar of sales), while capital turnover focuses on efficiency (the amount of sales generated with every dollar of assets).

Decision	Guidelines
How is RI computed and interpreted?	RI = Operating income − (Target rate of return × Total assets)
	If RI is positive, the division is earning income at a rate that exceeds management's minimum expectations.
	EVA is a special type of RI calculation that focuses on the income (in excess of expectations) the division created for two specific stakeholders: investors and long-term creditors.
How does EVA differ from RI?	If the net book value of assets is used to measure total assets, ROI, RI, and EVA will "artificially" rise over time due to the depreciation of the assets. Using gross book value to measure total assets eliminates this measurement issue.
When calculating ROI, RI, or EVA, what, if any, measurement issues are of concern?	Many firms use the average balance of total assets rather than the beginning or ending balance of assets when they calculate ROI, RI, and EVA.

Summary Problem 2

Assume that House and Garden Depot expects each division to earn a 16% target rate of return. House and Garden Depot's weighted average cost of capital (WACC) is 13%, and its effective tax rate is 30%. Assume that the company's original Retail Division had the following results last year (in millions of dollars):

Operating income..	$ 1,450
Total assets	16,100
Current liabilities	3,600
Sales..	26,500

Requirements

1. Compute the Retail Division's sales margin, capital turnover, and ROI. Round your results to three decimal places. Interpret the results in relation to the Landscaping and Design Divisions discussed in the chapter.

2. Compute and interpret the Retail Division's RI.

3. Compute the Retail Division's EVA. What does this tell you?

4. What can you conclude based on all three financial performance KPIs?

Solution

Requirement 1

$$ROI = \quad \text{Sales margin} \quad \times \quad \text{Capital turnover}$$
$$= (\text{Operating income} \div \text{Sales}) \times (\text{Sales} \div \text{Total assets})$$
$$= (\$1,450 \div \$26,500) \qquad \times (\$26,500 \div \$16,100)$$
$$= .055 \qquad\qquad\qquad \times 1.646$$
$$= .091$$

The original Retail Division is far from meeting top management's expectations. Its ROI is only 9.1%. The sales margin (5.5%) is slightly lower than the Landscaping and Design Divisions (6% each), but the capital turnover (1.646) is much lower than the other divisions (3.0 and 2.5). This means that the original Retail Division is not generating sales from its assets as efficiently as the Landscaping and Design Divisions. Division management needs to consider ways to increase the efficiency of their use of divisional assets.

Requirement 2

$$RI = \text{Operating income} - (\text{Target rate of return} \times \text{Total assets})$$
$$= \$1,450 \qquad\qquad - (16\% \times \$16,100)$$
$$= \$1,450 \qquad\qquad - \$2,576$$
$$= (\$1,126)$$

The negative RI confirms the ROI results: The division is not meeting management's target rate of return.

Requirement 3

$$
\begin{aligned}
\text{EVA} &= \text{After-tax operating income} - [(\text{Total assets} - \text{Current liabilities}) \times \text{WACC\%}] \\
&= (\$1,450 \times 70\%) \qquad\quad - [(\$16,100 - \$3,600) \times 13\%] \\
&= \$1,015 \qquad\qquad\qquad\; - (\$12,500 \times 13\%) \\
&= \$1,015 \qquad\qquad\qquad\; - \$1,625 \\
&= (\$610)
\end{aligned}
$$

The negative EVA means that the division is not generating income for investors and long-term creditors at the rate that these stakeholders desire.

Requirement 4

All three investment center performance measures (ROI, RI, and EVA) point to the same conclusion: The original Retail Division is not meeting financial expectations. Either top management and stakeholders' expectations are unrealistic or the division is not *currently* performing up to par. Recall, however, that financial performance measures tend to be lag indicators—measuring the results of decisions made in the past. The division's managers may currently be implementing new initiatives to improve the division's future profitability. Lead indicators should be used to project whether such initiatives are pointing the company in the right direction.

Allocating Service Department Costs

How do companies charge subunits for their use of service departments? For example, suppose House and Garden Depot incurs $30,000 per month to operate the North Florida Region's centralized payroll department. To simplify the illustration, let's assume that the region has only three stores: Tallahassee, Gainesville, and Jacksonville. How should the company split, or allocate, the $30,000 cost among the three stores? Splitting the cost equally—charging each store $10,000—may not be fair, especially if the three units don't use the services equally.

Ideally, the company should allocate the $30,000 based on each subunit's use of centralized payroll services. The company should use the primary activity that drives the cost of central payroll services as the allocation base. As you may recall from Chapter 5, companies identify cost drivers when they implement ABC. Thus, a company that has already implemented ABC should know what cost drivers would be suitable for allocating service department charges. For example, payroll processing cost may be driven by the number of employee payroll checks or direct deposits processed. The cost driver chosen for allocating the $30,000 might be the number of employees employed by each store, as shown in the following table.

Subunits Sharing Central Payroll Services	Number of Employees (allocation base)	Percentage of Total Employees	Service Department Charge ($30,000 × %)
Tallahassee	100	25%	$ 7,500
Gainesville	140	35%	10,500
Jacksonville	160	40%	12,000
Total	400	100%	$30,000

Most companies use some type of usage-related cost driver to allocate service department costs. The following table lists additional centralized services and common allocation bases.

Centralized Service Departments	Typical Allocation Base
Human resources	Number of employees
Legal	Number of hours spent on legal matters
Travel	Number of business trips booked

However, when usage data are not available or are too costly to collect, companies resort to allocating service department costs based on each subunit's ability to bear the cost. In such cases, companies allocate the service department cost based on the relative amount of revenue or operating income each subunit generates. The following table illustrates this type of allocation.

Subunits Sharing Centralized Payroll Services	Unit Operating Income Before Service Department Charges	Percentage of Total Operating Income	Service Department Charge ($30,000 × %)
Tallahassee	$ 320,000	20%	$ 6,000
Gainesville	480,000	30%	9,000
Jacksonville	800,000	50%	15,000
Total	$1,600,000	100%	$30,000

This type of allocation is like a tax: The higher the subunit's income, the higher the charge.

Even usage-related allocation systems have limitations. What if the cost of running the service department is fixed rather than variable? Then, much of the cost cannot be attributed to a specific cost driver. In our payroll example, suppose $20,000 of the total $30,000 is straight-line depreciation on the equipment and software. Should the company still use the number of employees to allocate the entire $30,000 of cost? As another example, suppose the Tallahassee store downsizes and its relative percentage of employees drops from 25% to 10% while the number of employees in each of the other two stores stays constant. If that happens, the Gainesville and Jacksonville stores will be charged higher costs even though they did nothing to cause an increase. These are just two examples of how the best allocation systems are still subject to inherent flaws. More complex service department allocation systems, such as the step-down and reciprocal methods, are discussed in more advanced accounting texts.

Review *Performance Evaluation and the Balanced Scorecard*

■ Accounting Vocabulary

Balanced Scorecard. (p. 697)
Measures that recognize that management must consider financial performance measures and operational performance measures when judging the performance of a company and its subunits.

Benchmarking. (p. 696)
Comparing actual performance to similar companies in the same industry, to other divisions, or to world-class standards.

Capital Turnover. (p. 711)
The amount of sales revenue generated for every dollar of invested assets; a component of the ROI calculation computed as sales divided by total assets.

Centralized. (p. 692)
Refers to companies in which all major planning and operating decisions are made by top management.

Cost Center. (p. 705)
A subunit responsible only for controlling costs.

Decentralized. (p. 692)
Refers to companies that are segmented into smaller operating units; unit managers make planning and operating decisions for their units.

Economic Value Added (EVA). (p. 713)
A residual income measure calculating the amount of income generated by the company or its divisions in excess of stockholders' and long-term creditors' expectations.

Goal Congruence. (p. 694)
Aligning the goals of subunit managers with the goals of top management.

Investment Center. (p. 708)
A subunit responsible for generating profits and efficiently managing the division's invested capital (assets).

Key Performance Indicator (KPI). (p. 697)
Summary performance measures that help managers assess whether the company is achieving its long-term and short-term goals.

Lag Indicators. (p. 696)
Performance measures that indicate past performance.

Lead Indicators. (p. 696)
Performance measures that forecast future performance.

Management by Exception (p. 705)
Directs management's attention to important differences between actual and budgeted amounts.

Product Life Cycle. (p. 716)
The length of time between a product's initial development and its discontinuance in the market.

Profit Center. (p. 705)
A subunit responsible for generating revenue and controlling costs.

Residual Income. (RI) (p. 712)
A measure of profitability and efficiency computed as the excess of actual income over a specified minimum acceptable income.

Responsibility Center. (p. 694)
A part or subunit of an organization whose manager is accountable for specific activities.

Return on Investment (ROI). (p. 709)
A measure of profitability and efficiency computed as operating income divided by total assets.

Revenue Center. (p. 705)
A subunit responsible only for generating revenue.

Sales Margin. (p. 710)
The amount of income earned on every dollar of sales; a component of the ROI calculation computed as operating income divided by sales.

Weighted Average Cost of Capital (WACC). (p. 714)
The company's cost of capital; the target rate of return used in EVA calculations to represent the return that investors and long-term creditors expect.

Quick Check

1. Which is *not* one of the potential advantages of decentralization?
   a. improves customer relations
   b. increases goal congruence
   c. improves motivation and retention
   d. supports use of expert knowledge

2. The Quaker Foods division of PepsiCo is most likely treated as a
   a. cost center
   b. revenue center
   c. profit center
   d. investment center

3. Decentralization is often based on all the following *except*
   a. geographic region
   b. product line
   c. revenue size
   d. business function

4. Manufacturing yield rate (number of units produced per unit of time) would be a typical measure for which of the following balanced scorecard perspectives?
   a. financial
   b. customer
   c. internal business
   d. learning and growth

5. Which of the following balanced scorecard perspectives essentially asks the question, can we continue to improve and create value?
   a. financial
   b. customer
   c. internal business
   d. learning and growth

6. Assume that the Residential Division of Kohler Faucets had the following results last year (in thousands of dollars):

Sales	$4,250,000
Operating income	850,000
Total assets	5,000,000
Current liabilities	250,000

   Further assume that management's target rate of return is 12% and the weighted average cost of capital is 10%. What is the division's sales margin?
   a. 20%
   b. 85%
   c. 17%
   d. 5%

7. Refer to the Kohler data in Question 6. What is the division's capital turnover?
   a. 20%
   b. 17%
   c. 85%
   d. 117%

8. Refer to the Kohler data in Question 6. What is the division's ROI?
   a. 17%
   b. 5.88%
   c. 17.89%
   d. 85%

9. Refer to the Kohler data in Question 6. What is the division's RI?
   a. $375,000
   b. $250,000
   c. $350,000
   d. $280,000

10. The performance evaluation of a cost center is typically based on its
    a. sales volume variance
    b. ROI
    c. flexible budget variance
    d. static budget variance

Quick Check Answers

1. b 2. d 3. c 4. c 5. d 6. a 7. c 8. a 9. b 10. c

For Internet Exercises, Excel in Practice, and additional online activities, go to this book's Web site at www.prenhall.com/bamber.

Assess Your Progress

■ Learning Objectives

1 Explain why and how companies decentralize

2 Explain why companies use performance evaluation systems

3 Describe the balanced scorecard and identify key performance indicators for each perspective

4 Use performance reports to evaluate cost, revenue, and profit centers

5 Use ROI, RI, and EVA to evaluate investment centers

■ Short Exercises

S12-1 **Explain how and why companies decentralize** *(Learning Objective 1)*
Explain why companies decentralize. Describe some typical methods of decentralization.

S12-2 **Describe each type of responsibility center** *(Learning Objective 1)*
Most decentralized subunits can be described as one of four types of responsibility centers. List the four most common types of responsibility centers and describe their responsibilities.

S12-3 **Classify types of subunits** *(Learning Objective 1)*
Each of the following managers has been given certain decision-making authority. Classify each manager according to the type of responsibility center he or she manages.

1. Manager of Holiday Inn's central reservation office
2. Managers of various corporate-owned Holiday Inn locations
3. Manager of the Holiday Inn corporate division
4. Manager of the housekeeping department at a Holiday Inn
5. Manager of the Holiday Inn Express corporate division
6. Manager of the complimentary breakfast buffet at a Holiday Inn Express

S12-4 **Goals of performance evaluation systems** *(Learning Objective 2)*
Well-designed performance evaluation systems accomplish many goals (see pages 695–696). State which goal is being achieved by the following actions:

a. Comparing targets to actual results
b. Providing subunit managers with performance targets
c. Comparing actual results with industry standards
d. Providing bonuses to subunit managers who achieve performance targets

e. Aligning subunit performance targets with company strategy

f. Comparing actual results to the results of competitors

g. Using the adage "you get what you measure" when designing the performance evaluation system

S12-5 **Classify KPIs by balanced scorecard perspective** *(Learning Objective 3)*
Classify each of the following key performance indicators according to the balanced scorecard perspective it addresses. Choose from financial perspective, customer perspective, internal business perspective, or learning and growth perspective.

a. Number of employee suggestions implemented

b. Revenue growth

c. Number of on-time deliveries

d. Percentage of sales force with access to real-time inventory levels

e. Customer satisfaction ratings

f. Number of defects found during manufacturing

g. Number of warranty claims

h. ROI

S12-6 **Classify KPIs by balanced scorecard perspective** *(Learning Objective 3)*
Classify each of the following key performance indicators according to the balanced scorecard perspective it addresses. Choose from financial perspective, customer perspective, internal business perspective, or learning and growth perspective.

a. Variable cost per unit

b. Percentage of market share

c. Number of hours of employee training

d. Number of new products developed

e. Yield rate (number of units produced per hour)

f. Average repair time

g. Employee satisfaction

h. Number of repeat customers

S12-7 **Describe management by exception** *(Learning Objective 4)*
Describe management by exception and how it is used in the evaluation of cost, revenue, and profit centers.

S12-8 **Assess profitability** *(Learning Objective 5)*
Which of the following corporate divisions is more profitable? Explain.

	Domestic	International
Operating income	$6 million	$10 million
Total assets	$20 million	$35 million

continued . . .

Racer Sports Data Set: Used for S12-9 through S12-13

Racer Sports Company makes snowboards, downhill skis, cross-country skis, skateboards, surfboards, and in-line skates. The company has found it beneficial to split operations into two divisions based on the climate required for the sport: snow sports and non-snow sports. The following divisional information is available for the past year:

	Sales	Operating Income	Total Assets	Current Liabilities
Snow sports	$5,000,000	$ 900,000	$4,000,000	$350,000
Non-snow sports	8,000,000	1,440,000	6,000,000	600,000

Racer's management has specified a target 15% rate of return. The company's weighted average cost of capital (WACC) is 12%, and its effective tax rate

S12-9 **Calculate ROI** *(Learning Objective 5)*
Refer to the Racer Sports Data Set.

Requirements

1. Calculate each division's ROI.

2. Top management has extra funds to invest. Which division will most likely receive those funds? Why?

3. Can you explain why one division's ROI is higher? How could management gain more insight?

S12-10 **Compute sales margin** *(Learning Objective 5)*
Refer to the Racer Sports Data Set. Compute each division's sales margin. Interpret your results.

S12-11 **Continuation of S12-9 and S12-10: capital turnover** *(Learning Objective 5)*
Refer to the Racer Sports Data Set.

Requirements

1. Compute each division's capital turnover (round to two decimal places). Interpret your results.

2. Use your answers to Question 1 along with your answers to S12-10 to recalculate ROI using the expanded formula. Do your answers agree with your ROI calculations in S12-9?

S12-12 **Compute RI** *(Learning Objective 5)*
Refer to the Racer Sports Data Set. Compute each division's RI. Interpret your results. Are your results consistent with each division's ROI?

S12-13 **Compute EVA** *(Learning Objective 5)*
Refer to the Racer Sports Data Set. Compute each division's EVA. Interpret your results.

Exercises

E12-14 Give advice about decentralization *(Learning Objective 1)*

Uncle Pete's Cookie Company sells homemade cookies made with organic ingredients. His sales are strictly Web-based. The business is exceeding Uncle Pete's expectations, with orders coming in from consumers and corporate event planners across the country. Even by employing a full-time baker and a Web designer, Uncle Pete can no longer handle the business on his own. He wants your advice on whether he should decentralize and, if so, how he should do it. Explain some of the advantages and disadvantages of decentralization and offer him three ways he might decentralize his company.

E12-15 Differentiate between lag and lead indicators *(Learning Objective 2)*

Explain the difference between lag and lead indicators. Are financial performance measures typically referred to as lag or lead indicators? Explain, using Zelda Outfitters (a catalog clothing merchandiser) as an example. Are operational measures (such as customer satisfaction ratings, defect rate, and number of on-time deliveries) typically referred to as lag or lead indicators? Explain using Zelda Outfitters as an example.

E12-16 Describe goals of performance evaluation systems *(Learning Objective 2)*

Well-designed performance evaluation systems accomplish many goals. Describe the potential benefits that performance evaluation systems offer.

E12-17 Sketch the balanced scorecard *(Learning Objective 3)*

Sketch a diagram depicting each of the four balanced scorecard perspectives and showing how they are linked together. Expand the diagram to include the primary factors underlying each perspective.

E12-18 Continuation of E12-17: develop KPIs *(Learning Objective 3)*

Imagine you are part of the top management team at Racer Sports Company (refer to Racer Sports Data Set). Using your answer to E12-17, develop two key performance indicators for each factor shown on your diagram.

E12-19 Classify KPIs by balanced scorecard perspective *(Learning Objective 3)*

Classify each of the following key performance indicators according to the balanced scorecard perspective it addresses. Choose from financial perspective, customer perspective, internal business perspective, or learning and growth perspective.

a. Number of customer complaints

b. Number of information system upgrades completed

c. Economic Value Added (EVA)

d. New product development time

e. Employee turnover rate

f. Percentage of products with online help manuals

g. Customer retention

h. Percentage of compensation based on performance

i. Percentage of orders filled each week

j. Gross margin growth

k. Number of new patents

l. Employee satisfaction ratings

E12-20 **Classify KPIs by balanced scorecard perspective** *(Learning Objective 3)*
Classify each of the following key performance indicators according to the balanced scorecard perspective it addresses. Choose from financial perspective, customer perspective, internal business perspective, or learning and growth perspective.

a. Manufacturing cycle time (average length of production process)

b. Earnings growth

c. Average machine setup time

d. Number of new customers

e. Employee promotion rate

f. Cash flow from operations

g. Customer satisfaction ratings

h. Machine downtime

i. Finished products per day per employee

j. Percentage of employees with access to upgraded system

k. Wait time per order prior to start of production

l. Capital turnover

E12-21 **Complete and analyze a performance report** *(Learning Objective 4)*
One subunit of Racer Sports Company had the following financial results last month:

Racer—Subunit X	Actual	Flexible Budget	Flexible Budget Variance (U or F)	% Variance* (U or F)
Direct materials	$ 28,100	$ 26,000		
Direct labor	13,500	14,000		
Indirect labor	26,000	23,000		
Utilities	12,000	11,000		
Depreciation	25,000	25,000		
Repairs and maintenance	4,300	5,000		
Total	$108,900	$104,000		

*Flexible budget variance ÷ Flexible budget.

Requirements

1. Complete the performance evaluation report for this subunit (round to four decimals).

2. Based on the data presented, what type of responsibility center is this subunit?

3. Which items should be investigated if part of management's decision criteria is to investigate all variances exceeding $3,000 or 10%?

4. Should only unfavorable variances be investigated? Explain.

E12-22   Complete and analyze a performance report (*Learning Objective 4*)

The accountant for a subunit of Racer Sports Company went on vacation before completing the subunit's monthly performance report. This is as far as she got:

Racer— Subunit X Revenue by Product	Actual	Flexible Budget Variance	Flexible Budget	Sales Volume Variance	Static (Master) Budget
Downhill Model RI	$ 326,000			$20,000 (F)	$ 300,000
Downhill Model RII	155,000		$165,000		150,000
Cross-country Model EXI	283,000	$2,000 (U)	285,000		300,000
Cross-country Model EXII	252,000		245,000	17,500 (U)	262,500
Snowboard Model LXI	425,000	5,000 (F)			400,000
Total	$1,441,000				$1,412,500

Requirements

1. Complete the performance evaluation report for this subunit.
2. Based on the data presented, what type of responsibility center is this subunit?
3. Which items should be investigated if part of management's decision criteria is to investigate all variances exceeding $15,000? Interpret your results. (What could cause these variances? What impact might these variances have on company inventory levels and operations?)

E12-23   Compute and interpret the expanded ROI equation (*Learning Objective 5*)

Toro, a national manufacturer of lawn-mowing and snowblowing equipment, segments its business according to customer type: professional and residential. The following divisional information was available for the past year (in thousands of dollars):

	Sales	Operating Income	Total Assets	Current Liabilities
Residential	$ 555,000	$ 62,000	$188,000	$ 68,000
Professional	1,030,000	173,000	420,000	150,000

Assume that management has a 25% target rate of return for each division. Also, assume that Toro's weighted average cost of capital is 15% and its effective tax rate is 30%.

Requirements

Round all of your answers to four decimal places.

1. Calculate each division's ROI.
2. Calculate each division's sales margin. Interpret your results.
3. Calculate each division's capital turnover. Interpret your results.
4. Use the expanded ROI formula to confirm your results from Requirement 1. What can you conclude?

E12-24   Compute RI and EVA *(Learning Objective 5)*
Refer to the data about Toro in E12-23.

1. Calculate each division's RI. Interpret your results.

2. Calculate each division's EVA. Interpret your results.

3. Describe the conceptual and computational similarities and differences between RI and EVA.

▪ Problems (Problem Set A)

P12-25A   Evaluate subunit performance *(Learning Objectives 3, 4)*
One subunit of Racer Sports Company had the following financial results last month:

Racer—Subunit X	Actual	Flexible Budget	Flexible Budget Variance (U or F)	Percentage Variance* (U or F)
Sales	$480,000	$450,000		
Cost of goods sold	260,000	250,000		
Gross margin	$220,000	$200,000		
Operating expenses	53,000	50,000		
Operating income before service department charges	$167,000	$150,000		
Service department charges (allocated)	35,000	25,000		
Operating income	$132,000	$125,000		

*Flexible budget variance ÷ Flexible budget.

Requirements

1. Complete the performance evaluation report for this subunit (round to three decimal places).

2. Based on the data presented, what type of responsibility center is this subunit?

3. Which items should be investigated if part of management's decision criteria is to investigate all variances equal to or exceeding $10,000 *and* exceeding 10% (both criteria must be met)?

4. Should only unfavorable variances be investigated? Explain.

5. Is it possible that the variances are due to a higher-than-expected sales volume? Explain.

6. Do you think management will place equal weight on each of the $10,000 variances? Explain.

7. Which balanced scorecard perspective is being addressed through this performance report? In your opinion, is this performance report a lead or lag indicator? Explain.

8. Give one key performance indicator for the other three balanced scorecard perspectives. Indicate which perspective is being addressed by the indicators you list. Are they lead or lag indicators? Explain.

P12-26A **Evaluate divisional performance** *(Learning Objective 5)*

Alloy is a national paint manufacturer and retailer. The company is segmented into five divisions: paint stores (branded retail locations), consumer (paint sold through stores such as Centerville, Fine Furnishings, and Maloney's), automotive (sales to auto manufacturers), international, and administration. The following is selected divisional information for their two largest divisions: paint stores and consumer (in thousands of dollars).

	Sales	Operating Income	Total Assets	Current Liabilities
Paint stores	$3,980,000	$480,000	$1,400,000	$350,000
Consumer	1,295,000	190,000	1,595,000	600,000

Assume that management has specified a 20% target rate of return. Further assume that the company's weighted average cost of capital is 15% and its effective tax rate is 32%.

Requirements

Round all calculations to four decimal places.

1. Calculate each division's ROI.

2. Calculate each division's sales margin. Interpret your results.

3. Calculate each division's capital turnover. Interpret your results.

4. Use the expanded ROI formula to confirm your results from Requirement 1. Interpret your results.

5. Calculate each division's RI. Interpret your results and offer recommendations for any division with negative RI.

6. Calculate each division's EVA. Interpret your results.

7. Describe the conceptual and computational similarities and differences between RI and EVA.

8. Total asset data were provided in this problem. If you were to gather this information from an annual report, how would you measure total assets? Describe your measurement choices and some of the pros and cons of those choices.

9. Describe some of the factors that management considers when setting its minimum target rate of return.

10. Explain why some firms prefer to use RI rather than ROI for performance measurement.

11. Explain why budget versus actual performance reports are insufficient for evaluating the performance of investment centers.

P12-27A **Collect and analyze division data from an annual report** *(Learning Objective 5)*

PepsiCo segments its company into four distinct divisions. The net revenues, operating profit, and total assets for these divisions are disclosed in the footnotes to PepsiCo's consolidated financial statements.

continued . . .

1. Use the following steps to find the divisional data in PepsiCo's 2006 annual report:

   a. Go to pepsico.com.

   b. Go to the Investors link.

   c. Go to the Annual Reports link.

   d. Click on "2006 Annual Report."

   e. After downloading the report, look under "Notes to Consolidated Financial Statements, Note 1—Basis of Presentation and Our Divisions."

2. What are Pepsi's four business divisions? Make a table listing each division, its net revenues, operating profit, and total assets.

3. Use the data you collected in Requirement 2 to calculate each division's sales margin. Interpret your results.

4. Use the data you collected in Requirement 2 to calculate each division's capital turnover. Interpret your results.

5. Use the data you collected in Requirement 2 to calculate each division's ROI. Interpret your results.

6. Can you calculate RI and/or EVA using the data presented? Why or why not?

■ Problems (Problem Set B)

P12-28B **Evaluate subunit performance** *(Learning Objectives 3, 4)*
One subunit of Awesome Sporting Goods had the following financial results last month:

Awesome—Subunit X	Actual	Flexible Budget	Flexible Budget Variance (U or F)	Percentage Variance* (U or F)
Sales	$500,000	$520,000		
Cost of goods sold	385,000	400,000	_____	
Gross margin	$115,000	$120,000		
Operating expenses	22,000	30,000	_____	
Operating income before service department charges	$93,000	$90,000		
Service department charges (allocated)	30,000	15,000	_____	
Operating income	$63,000	$75,000		

Flexible budget variance ÷ Flexible budget.

Requirements

1. Complete the performance evaluation report for the subunit (round to three decimal places).

2. Based on the data presented, what type of responsibility center is this subunit?

3. Which items should be investigated if part of management's decision criteria is to investigate all variances equal to or exceeding $5,000 *and* exceeding 10% (both criteria must be met)?

4. Should only unfavorable variances be investigated? Explain.

5. Is it possible that the variances are due to a higher-than-expected sales volume? Explain.

6. Will management place equal weight on each of the $15,000 variances? Explain.

7. Which balanced scorecard perspective is being addressed through this performance report? In your opinion, is this performance report a lead or lag indicator? Explain.

8. List one key performance indicator for the other three balanced scorecard perspectives. Indicate which perspective is being addressed by the indicators you list. Are they lead or lag indicators? Explain.

P12-29B Evaluate divisional performance (*Learning Objective 5*)

Just For Me Company operates a national drugstore chain. The company is segmented into two divisions: retail pharmacy and PBM (pharmaceutical benefit management). The following is selected divisional information (in millions of dollars).

Assume that management has specified a 10% target rate of return. Further assume that the company's weighted average cost of capital is 9% and its effective tax rate is 32%.

	Sales	Operating Income	Total Assets	Current Liabilities
Retail	$29,730	$1,320	$13,120	$4,460
PBM	1,965	135	1,430	485

Requirements

1. Calculate each division's ROI.

2. Calculate each division's sales margin. Interpret your results.

3. Calculate each division's capital turnover. Interpret your results.

4. Use the expanded ROI formula to confirm your results from Requirement 1.

5. Calculate each division's RI. Interpret your results.

6. Calculate each division's EVA. Interpret your results.

7. Describe the conceptual similarities and differences between RI and EVA.

8. Total asset data were provided for this problem. If you were to gather this information from an annual report, how would you measure total assets? Describe your measurement choices and some of the pros and cons of those choices.

9. Describe some of the factors that management considers when setting its minimum rate of return.

continued . . .

10. Explain why some firms prefer to use RI rather than ROI for performance measurement.

11. Explain why budget versus actual performance reports are insufficient for evaluating the performance of investment centers.

P12-30B **Collect and analyze divisional data** *(Learning Objective 5)*
Marriott International, Inc., segments its company into five lodging segments. The revenues, income, and assets for these segments are disclosed in the footnotes to Marriott's consolidated financial statements.

Requirements

1. Use the following steps to find the segment data in Marriott's 2006 annual report:

   a. Go to Marriott.com.

   b. Go to the Company News & Info. link.

   c. Go to the Investor Relations link.

   d. Go to the Corporate Info. & SEC filings link.

   e. Click on the View the 2006 Annual Report (PDF) link.

   f. Look under "Notes to Consolidated Financial Statements, Note 20 (Business Segments)."

2. What are Marriott's five Lodging Segments? Make a table listing each operating segment, its revenues, income, and assets.

3. Use the data you collected in Requirement 2 to calculate each segment's sales margin. Interpret your results.

4. Use the data you collected in Requirement 2 to calculate each segment's capital turnover. Interpret your results.

5. Use the data you collected in Requirement 2 to calculate each segment's ROI. Interpret your results.

6. Can you calculate RI and/or EVA using the data presented? Why or why not?

Apply Your Knowledge

■ Decision Case

Case 12-31. Collect and analyze division data *(Learning Objective 5)*
Colgate-Palmolive operates two product segments. Using the company's Web site, locate segment information for 2006 in the company's 2006 annual report. (*Hint:* Look under investor relations.) Then, look in the financial statement footnotes.

Requirements

1. What are the two segments (ignore geographical subsets of the one product segment)? Gather data about each segment's net sales, operating income, and identifiable assets.
2. Calculate ROI for each segment.
3. Which segment has the highest ROI? Explain why.
4. If you were on the top management team and could allocate extra funds to only one division, which division would you choose? Why?

13 Financial Statement Analysis

Google was "born" in 1998. If it were a person, it would have started elementary school in 2004, and today it would have just about finished the first grade. If Google were a person, it would graduate from high school in 2016. Given a typical life span, it would expect to be around for almost a century. In the words of its top two executives, "We're just getting started."

Source: Adapted from Google Inc. 2004 Annual Report, Founder's Letter.

You probably use Google's Internet search engine daily, as many people do. The company is an amazing success story. On November 17, 2005, Google's stock price topped $400—one of only four companies listed on a major U.S. stock exchange with a stock price that high.

To show you how to analyze financial statements, we'll be using Google Inc. in the first half of this chapter. Then, in the second part of the chapter, we'll shift to a different type of company—Palisades Furniture—to round out your introduction to financial statement analysis.

To get started, take a look at Google's comparative income statement, which follows.

GOOGLE INC. Income Statement (Adapted) Year Ended December 31,		
(In millions)	**2004**	**2003**
Revenues (same as Net sales)	$3,189	$1,466
Expenses:		
Cost of revenues (same as Cost of goods sold)	1,458	626
Sales and marketing expense	246	120
General and administrative expense	140	57
Research and development expense	225	91
Other expense	470	225
Income before income tax	650	347
Income tax expense	251	241
Net income	$ 399	$ 106

You can see that 2004 was an incredible year for the company. Net income was over three times the net income of 2003, and Wall Street was very happy. ■

Learning Objectives

1 Perform a horizontal analysis of financial statements

2 Perform a vertical analysis of financial statements

3 Prepare and use common-size financial statements

4 Compute the standard financial ratios

Investors and creditors can't evaluate a company by examining only one year's data. This is why most financial statements cover at least two periods, like the Google Inc. income statement. In fact, most financial analysis covers trends of three to five years. This chapter shows you how to use some of the analytical tools for charting a company's progress through time.

The graphs in Exhibit 13-1 show some important data about Google's progress. They depict a three-year trend of revenues and research and development (R&D). Revenues (sales) and R&D are important drivers of profits.

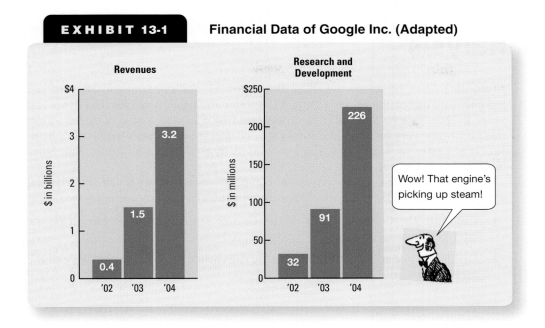

EXHIBIT 13-1   **Financial Data of Google Inc. (Adapted)**

For Google, both revenues and R&D grew dramatically during 2002–2004. These are good signs for the future. But how can we decide what we really think about Google's performance? We need some way to compare a company's performance:

- From year to year
- With a competing company, like Yahoo! Inc.
- With the Internet-information industry

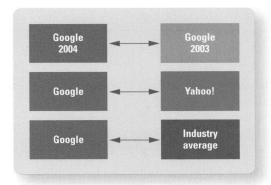

Then, we will have a better idea of how to judge Google's present situation and predict what might happen in the near future.

Methods of Analysis

There are two main ways to analyze financial statements:

- Horizontal analysis provides a year-to-year comparison of a company's performance in different periods.
- Another technique, vertical analysis, is the standard way to compare different companies. Let's begin with horizontal analysis.

Horizontal Analysis

Many decisions hinge on whether the numbers—in sales, expenses, and net income—are increasing or decreasing. Have sales and other revenues risen from last year? By how much? Sales may have increased by $20,000, but considered alone, this fact is not very helpful. The *percentage change* in sales over time is more helpful. It is better to know that sales increased by 20% than to know that sales increased by $20,000.

The study of percentage changes in comparative statements is called **horizontal analysis**. Computing a percentage change in comparative statements requires two steps:

1. Compute the dollar amount of the change from the earlier period to the later period.

2. Divide the dollar amount of change by the earlier period amount. We call the earlier period the base period.

Illustration: Google Inc.

Google reports *revenues*, not sales, because Google sells services rather than a product. You can think of revenues and net sales as the same thing. Horizontal analysis is illustrated for Google Inc. as follows (dollar amounts in millions):

	2004	2003	Increase (Decrease) Amount	Increase (Decrease) Percentage
Revenues (same as net sales)............	$3,189	$1,466	$1,723	117.5%

Sales increased by an incredible 117.5% during 2004, computed as follows:

STEP 1: Compute the dollar amount of change in sales from 2003 to 2004:

2004	2003	Increase
$3,189 −	$1,466 =	$1,723

STEP 2: Divide the dollar amount of change by the base-period amount. This computes the percentage change for the period:

$$\text{Percentage change} = \frac{\text{Dollar amount of change}}{\text{Base-year amount}}$$

$$= \frac{\$1,723}{\$1,466} = 1.175 = 117.5\%$$

Detailed horizontal analyses of Google's financial statements are shown in Exhibit 13-2 (Income Statement) and Exhibit 13-3 (Balance Sheet).

Horizontal Analysis of the Income Statement

Google's comparative income statement reveals exceptional growth during 2004. An increase of 100% occurs when an item doubles, so Google's 117.5% increase in revenues means that revenues more than doubled.

The item on Google's income statement with the slowest growth rate is income tax expense. Income taxes increased by 4.1%. On the bottom line, net income grew by an astounding 276.4%. That's real progress!

EXHIBIT 13-2   **Comparative Income Statement—Horizontal Analysis**

GOOGLE INC.
Income Statement (Adapted)
Year Ended December 31, 2004 and 2003

(Dollar amounts in millions)	2004	2003	Increase (Decrease) Amount	Increase (Decrease) Percentage
Revenues	$3,189	$1,466	$1,723	117.5%
Cost of revenues	1,458	626	832	132.9
Gross profit	1,731	840	891	106.1
Operating expenses:				
Sales and marketing expense	246	120	126	105.0
General and administrative expense	140	57	83	145.6
Research and development expense	225	91	134	147.3
Other expense	470	225	245	108.9
Income before income tax	650	347	303	87.3
Income tax expense	251	241	10	4.1
Net income	$ 399	$ 106	$ 293	276.4

EXHIBIT 13-3   **Comparative Balance Sheet—Horizontal Analysis**

GOOGLE INC.
Balance Sheet (Adapted)
December 31, 2004 and 2003

(Dollar amounts in millions)	2004	2003	Increase (Decrease) Amount	Increase (Decrease) Percentage
Assets				
Current Assets:				
Cash and cash equivalents	$ 427	$149	$ 278	186.6%
Other current assets	2,266	411	1,855	451.3
Total current assets	2,693	560	2,133	380.9
Property, plant, and equipment, net	379	188	191	101.6
Intangible assets, net	194	106	88	83.0
Other assets	47	17	30	176.5
Total assets	$3,313	$871	$2,442	280.4
Liabilities				
Current Liabilities:				
Accounts payable	$ 33	$ 46	$ (13)	(28.3)%
Other current liabilities	307	189	118	62.4
Total current liabilities	340	235	105	44.7
Long-term liabilities	44	47	(3)	(6.4)
Total liabilities	384	282	102	36.2
Stockholders' Equity				
Capital stock	1	45	(44)	(97.8)
Retained earnings and other equity	2,928	544	2,384	438.2
Total stockholders' equity	2,929	589	2,340	397.3
Total liabilities and equity	$3,313	$871	$2,442	280.4

Horizontal Analysis of the Balance Sheet

Google's comparative balance sheet also shows rapid growth in assets, with total assets increasing by 280.4%. That means total assets almost tripled in one year. Very few companies grow that fast.

Google's liabilities grew more slowly. Total liabilities increased by 36.2%, and Accounts Payable actually decreased, as indicated by the liability figures in parentheses. Here's how to compute the percentage decrease in Google's accounts payable:

STEP 1	Increase (Decrease)	2004		2003
	$(13)	= $33	–	$46

STEP 2	Percentage Change	$=$	$\dfrac{\text{Dollar amount of change}}{\text{Base-year amount}}$
	$(28.3)\% =$		$\dfrac{\$(13)}{\$46}$

Trend Percentages

Trend percentages are a form of horizontal analysis. Trends indicate the direction a business is taking. How have sales changed over a five-year period? What trend does net income show? Those questions can be answered by trend percentages over a period, such as three to five years.

Trend percentages are computed by selecting a base year. The base-year amounts are set equal to 100%. The amounts for each following year are expressed as a percentage of the base amount. To compute trend percentages, divide each item for following years by the base-year amount.

$$\text{Trend}\% = \frac{\text{Any year \$}}{\text{Base year \$}}$$

Google Inc.'s total revenues were $19 million in 2000 and rose to $3,189 million in 2004. The company's trend of revenues is so dramatic that percentages in the thousands are hard to interpret.

To illustrate trend analysis, we use a more representative company, Caterpillar Inc., which is famous for its CAT earth moving machinery. Caterpillar's trend of net sales during 2000–2004 follows, with dollars in millions. The base year is 2000, so that year's percentage is set equal to 100.

(in millions)	2004	2003	2002	2001	Base 2000
Net sales..................	$30,251	$22,763	$20,152	$20,450	$20,175
Trend percentages......	150%	113%	99.9%	101%	100%

We want trend percentages for the five-year period 2000 through 2004. Trend percentages are computed by dividing each year's amount by the 2000 amount.

Net sales increased a little in 2001 and took a dip in 2002. The rate of growth increased in 2003 and took off in 2004.

You can perform a trend analysis on any item you consider important. Trend analysis is widely used to predict the future.

Vertical Analysis

As we have seen, horizontal analysis and trend percentages highlight changes in an item over time. But no single technique gives a complete picture of a business, so we also need vertical analysis.

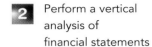

2 Perform a vertical analysis of financial statements

Vertical analysis of a financial statement shows the relationship of each item to its base amount, which is the 100% figure. Every other item on the statement is then reported as a percentage of that base. For an income statement, net sales is the base. Suppose under normal conditions that a company's gross profit is 50% of revenues. A drop to 40% may cause the company to suffer a loss. Investors view a large decline in gross profit with alarm.

Illustration: Google Inc.

Exhibit 13-4 shows the vertical analysis of Google's income statement. In this case:

$$\text{Vertical analysis } \% = \frac{\text{Each income-statement item}}{\text{Revenues (net sales)}}$$

EXHIBIT 13-4 **Comparative Income Statement—Vertical Analysis**

GOOGLE INC.
Income Statement (Adapted)
Year Ended December 31, 2004

(Dollar amounts in millions)	Amount	Percent of Total
Revenues	$3,189	100.0%
Cost of revenues	1,458	45.7
Gross profit	1,731	54.3
Operating expenses:		
Sales and marketing expense	246	7.7
General and administrative expense	140	4.4
Research and development expense	225	7.1
Other expense	470	14.7
Income before income tax	650	20.4
Income tax expense	251	7.9
Net income	$ 399	12.5%

For Google, the vertical-analysis percentage for cost of revenues is 45.7% ($1,458/$3,189 = 0.457). On the bottom line, Google's net income is 12.5% of revenues. That is very good.

Exhibit 13-5 shows the vertical analysis of Google's balance sheet. The base amount (100%) is total assets.

EXHIBIT 13-5	Comparative Balance Sheet— Vertical Analysis

GOOGLE INC.
Balance Sheet (Adapted)
December 31, 2004

(Dollar amount in millions)	Amount	Percent of Total
Assets		
Current Assets:		
Cash and cash equivalents	$ 427	12.9%
Other current assets	2,266	68.4
Total current assets	2,693	81.3
Property, plant, and equipment, net	379	11.4
Intangible assets, net	194	5.9
Other assets	47	1.4
Total assets	$3,313	100.0%
Liabilities		
Current Liabilities:		
Accounts payable	$ 33	1.0%
Other current liabilities	307	9.3
Total current liabilities	340	10.3
Long-term liabilities	44	1.3
Total liabilities	384	11.6
Stockholders' Equity		
Common stock	1	0.0
Retained earnings and other equity	2,928	88.4
Total stockholders' equity	2,929	88.4
Total liabilities and equity	$3,313	100.0%

The vertical analysis of Google's balance sheet reveals several interesting things:

- Current assets make up 81.3% of total assets. For most companies, this percentage is closer to 30%.

- Property, plant, and equipment make up only 11.4% of total assets. This percentage is low because of the nature of Google's business. Google's Web-based operations don't require many buildings and equipment.

- Total liabilities are only 11.6% of total assets, and stockholders' equity makes up 88.4% of total assets. Most of Google's equity is additional paid-in capital and retained earnings—signs of a strong company.

How Do We Compare One Company with Another?

3 Prepare and use common-size financial statements

Horizontal analysis and vertical analysis provide a great deal of useful data about a company. As we have seen, Google's percentages depict a very successful company. But the Google data apply to only one business.

To compare Google Inc. to another company, we can use a common-size statement. A **common-size statement** reports only percentages—the same percentages that appear in a vertical analysis. For example, Google's common-size income statement comes directly from the percentages in Exhibit 13-4.

We can use a common-size income statement to compare Google Inc. and Yahoo! Inc. on profitability. Google and Yahoo! compete in the Internet service industry. Which company earns a higher percentage of revenues as profits for its shareholders? Exhibit 13-6 gives both companies' common-size income statements for 2004.

EXHIBIT 13-6	Common-Size Income Statement Google Versus Yahoo!

GOOGLE INC.
Common-Size Income Statement
Google Versus Yahoo!

	Google Inc.	Yahoo! Inc.
Revenues	100.0%	100.0%
Cost of revenues	45.7	36.3
Gross profit	54.3	63.7
Sales and marketing expense	7.7	21.8
General and administrative expense	4.4	7.3
Research and development expense	7.1	10.3
Other expense (income)	14.7	(11.5)
Income before income tax	20.4	35.8
Income tax expense	7.9	12.3
Net income	12.5%	23.5%

Exhibit 13-6 shows that Yahoo! Inc. is more profitable than Google. Yahoo!'s gross profit percentage is 63.7%, compared to Google's 54.3%. And, most important, Yahoo!'s percentage of net income to revenues is 23.5%. That means almost one-fourth of Yahoo!'s revenues end up as profits for the company's stockholders.

Benchmarking

Benchmarking is the practice of comparing a company with other leading companies. There are two main types of benchmarks in financial statement analysis.

Benchmarking Against a Key Competitor

Exhibit 13-6 uses a key competitor, Yahoo! Inc., to measure Google's profitability. The two companies compete in the same industry, so Yahoo! serves as an ideal benchmark for Google. The graphs in Exhibit 13-7 highlight the profitability difference between Google and Yahoo!. Focus on the segment of the graphs showing net income. Yahoo! is clearly more profitable than Google.

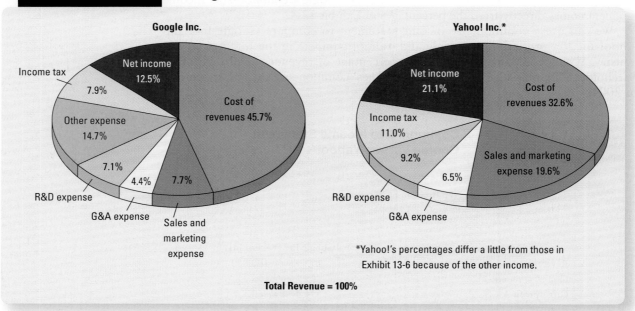

EXHIBIT 13-7   Graphical Analysis of Common-Size Income Statement
Google Versus Yahoo!

Benchmarking Against the Industry Average

The industry average can also serve as a useful benchmark for evaluating a company. An industry comparison would show how Google is performing alongside the average for its industry. *Annual Statement Studies*, published by The Risk Management Association, provides common-size statements for most industries. To compare Google Inc. to the industry average, simply insert the industry-average common-size income statement in place of Yahoo! Inc. as shown in Exhibit 13-6.

Now, let's put your learning to practice. Work the summary problem, which reviews the concepts from the first half of this chapter.

Summary Problem 1

Requirement

Perform a horizontal analysis and a vertical analysis of the comparative income statement of Kimball Corporation, which makes **iPod** labels. State whether 2008 was a good year or a bad year and give your reasons.

KIMBALL CORPORATION
Comparative Income Statement
Years Ended December 31, 2008 and 2007

	2008	2007
Net sales	$275,000	$225,000
Expenses:		
Cost of goods sold	$194,000	$165,000
Engineering, selling, and administrative expenses	54,000	48,000
Interest expense	5,000	5,000
Income tax expense	9,000	3,000
Other expense (income)	1,000	(1,000)
Total expenses	263,000	220,000
Net income	$ 12,000	$ 5,000

Solution

Requirement 1

KIMBALL CORPORATION
Horizontal Analysis of Comparative Income Statement
Years Ended December 31, 2008 and 2007

	2008	2007	Increase (Decrease) Amount	Increase (Decrease) Percent
Net sales	$275,000	$225,000	$50,000	22.2%
Expenses:				
Cost of goods sold	$194,000	$165,000	$29,000	17.6
Engineering, selling, and administrative expenses	54,000	48,000	6,000	12.5
Interest expense	5,000	5,000	—	—
Income tax expense	9,000	3,000	6,000	200.0
Other expense (income)	1,000	(1,000)	2,000	—*
Total expenses	263,000	220,000	43,000	19.5
Net income	$ 12,000	$ 5,000	$ 7,000	140.0%

*Percentage changes are typically not computed for shifts from a negative to a positive amount, and vice versa.

The horizontal analysis shows that total revenues increased 22.2%. Total expenses increased by 19.5%, and net income rose by 140%.

KIMBALL CORPORATION
Vertical Analysis of Comparative Income Statement
Years Ended December 31, 2008 and 2007

	2008		2007	
	Amount	Percent	Amount	Percent
Net sales	$275,000	100.0%	$225,000	100.0%
Expenses:				
Cost of goods sold	$194,000	70.5	$165,000	73.3
Engineering, selling, and administrative expenses	54,000	19.6	48,000	21.3
Interest expense	5,000	1.8	5,000	2.2
Income tax expense	9,000	3.3	3,000	1.3
Other expense (income)	1,000	0.4	(1,000)	(0.4)
Total expenses	263,000	95.6	220,000	97.7
Net income	$ 12,000	4.4%	$ 5,000	2.2%**

**Total expenses (97.8%) and net income (2.2%) equals 99.9% rather than 100% due to rounding.

The vertical analysis shows decreases in the percentages of net sales consumed by:

- Cost of goods sold (from 73.3% to 70.5%).
- Engineering, selling, and administrative expenses (from 21.3% to 19.6%).

These two items are Kimball's largest dollar expenses, so their percentage decreases are important.

2008 net income rose to 4.4% of sales, compared with 2.2% the preceding year. The analysis shows that 2008 was significantly better than 2007.

Using Ratios to Make Decisions

Online financial databases such as Lexis/Nexis and the Dow Jones News Retrieval Service provide data on thousands of companies. Suppose you want to compare some companies' recent earnings histories. You might have the computer compare companies' returns on stockholders' equity. The computer could then give you the names of the 20 companies with the highest return on equity. You can use any ratio that is relevant to a particular decision.

4 Compute the standard financial ratios

The ratios we discuss in this chapter may be classified as follows:

1. Measuring ability to pay current liabilities

2. Measuring ability to sell inventory and collect receivables

3. Measuring ability to pay long-term debt

4. Measuring profitability

5. Analyzing Stock Investments

Measuring Ability to Pay Current Liabilities

Working capital is defined as

$$\text{Working capital} = \text{Current assets} - \text{Current liabilities}$$

Working capital measures the ability to meet short-term obligations with current assets. Two decision tools based on working-capital data are the *current ratio* and the *acid-test ratio*.

Current Ratio

The most widely used ratio is the **current ratio,** which is current assets divided by current liabilities. The current ratio measures the ability to pay current liabilities with current assets.

Exhibit 13-8 gives the comparative income statement and balance sheet of Palisades Furniture Co., which we'll be using in the remainder of the chapter.

The current ratios of Palisades Furniture at December 31, 2008 and 2007, follow, along with the average for the retail furniture industry.

Formula	Palisades' Current Ratio 2008	Palisades' Current Ratio 2007	Industry Average
Current ratio $= \dfrac{\text{Current assets}}{\text{Current liabilities}}$	$\dfrac{\$262,000}{\$142,000} = 1.85$	$\dfrac{\$236,000}{\$126,000} = 1.87$	1.50

While the company's current ratio declined slightly in 2008, the high current ratio indicates that the business has sufficient current assets to maintain normal business operations. Compare Palisades Furniture's current ratio of 1.85 with the industry average of 1.50 and with the current ratios of some well-known companies:

Company	Current Ratio
Walgreen Co.	1.90
Amazon.com	1.57
FedEx	1.05

EXHIBIT 13-8 Comparative Financial Statements

PALISADES FURNITURE CO.
Comparative Income Statement
Years Ended December 31, 2008 and 2007

	2008	2007
Net sales	$858,000	$803,000
Cost of goods sold	513,000	509,000
Gross profit	345,000	294,000
Operating expenses:		
Selling expenses	126,000	114,000
General expenses	118,000	123,000
Total operating expenses	244,000	237,000
Income from operations	101,000	57,000
Interest revenue	4,000	—
Interest (expense)	(24,000)	(14,000)
Income before income taxes	81,000	43,000
Income tax expense	33,000	17,000
Net income	$ 48,000	$ 26,000

PALISADES FURNITURE CO.
Comparative Balance Sheet
December 31, 2008 and 2007

	2008	2007
Assets		
Current Assets:		
Cash	$ 29,000	$ 32,000
Accounts receivable, net	114,000	85,000
Inventories	113,000	111,000
Prepaid expenses	6,000	8,000
Total current assets	262,000	236,000
Long-term investments	18,000	9,000
Property, plant, and equipment, net	507,000	399,000
Total assets	$787,000	$644,000
Liabilities		
Current Liabilities:		
Notes payable	$ 42,000	$ 27,000
Accounts payable	73,000	68,000
Accrued liabilities	27,000	31,000
Total current liabilities	142,000	126,000
Long-term notes payable	289,000	198,000
Total liabilities	431,000	324,000
Stockholders' Equity		
Common stock, no par	186,000	186,000
Retained earnings	170,000	134,000
Total stockholders' equity	356,000	320,000
Total liabilities and equity	$787,000	$644,000

What is an acceptable current ratio? The answer depends on the industry. The norm for companies in most industries is around 1.50, as reported by The Risk Management Association. Palisades Furniture's current ratio of 1.85 is strong. In most industries, a current ratio of 2.0 is very strong.

Acid-Test Ratio

The **acid-test** (or **quick**) **ratio** tells us whether the entity could pay all of its current liabilities if they came due immediately. That is, could the company pass this *acid test*?

To compute the acid-test ratio, we add cash, short-term investments, and net current receivables (accounts and notes receivable, net of allowances) and divide this sum by current liabilities. Inventory and prepaid expenses are *not* included in the acid test because they are the least liquid current assets. Palisades Furniture's acid-test ratios for 2008 and 2007 follow.

		Palisades' Acid-Test Ratio		Industry
	Formula	2008	2007	Average
$\dfrac{\text{Acid-test}}{\text{ratio}} =$	$\dfrac{\begin{array}{c}\text{Cash + Short-term}\\ \text{investments}\\ \text{+ Net current}\\ \text{receivables}\end{array}}{\text{Current liabilities}}$	$\dfrac{\begin{array}{c}\$29,000 + \$0\\ + \$114,000\end{array}}{\$142,000} = 1.01$	$\dfrac{\begin{array}{c}\$32,000 + \$0\\ + \$85,000\end{array}}{\$126,000} = 0.93$	0.40

The company's acid-test ratio improved during 2008 and is significantly better than the industry average. Palisades Furniture's 1.01 acid-test ratio also compares favorably with the acid-test values of some well-known companies.

Company	Acid-Test Ratio
Procter & Gamble	0.49
Wal-Mart	0.15
General Motors	0.91

The norm for the acid-test ratio ranges from 0.20 for shoe retailers to 1.00 for manufacturers of equipment, as reported by The Risk Management Association. An acid-test ratio of 0.90 to 1.00 is acceptable in most industries.

Measuring Ability to Sell Inventory and Collect Receivables

The ability to sell inventory and collect receivables is fundamental to business. In this section, we discuss three ratios that measure the company's ability to sell inventory and collect receivables.

Inventory Turnover

Inventory turnover measures the number of times a company sells its average level of inventory during a year. A high rate of turnover indicates ease in selling inventory; a low rate indicates difficulty. A value of 6 means that the company sold its average level of inventory six times—every two months—during the year.

To compute inventory turnover, we divide cost of goods sold by the average inventory for the period. We use the cost of goods sold—not sales—because both cost of goods sold and inventory are stated *at cost*. Sales at *retail* are not comparable with inventory at *cost*.

Palisades Furniture's inventory turnover for 2008 is:

Formula	Palisades' Inventory Turnover	Industry Average
Inventory turnover $= \dfrac{\text{Cost of goods sold}}{\text{Average inventory}}$	$\dfrac{\$513,000}{\$112,000} = 4.6$	3.4

Cost of goods sold comes from the income statement (Exhibit 13-8). Average inventory is figured by averaging the beginning inventory ($111,000) and ending inventory ($113,000). (See the balance sheet, Exhibit 13-8.)

Inventory turnover varies widely with the nature of the business. For example, Google has no inventory turnover because the company carries no inventory. Most manufacturers of farm machinery have an inventory turnover close to three times a year. In contrast, companies that remove natural gas from the ground hold their inventory for a very short period of time and have an average turnover of 30. Palisades Furniture's turnover of 4.6 times a year is high for its industry, which has an average turnover of 3.4 times per year.

Accounts Receivable Turnover

Accounts receivable turnover measures the ability to collect cash from credit customers. The higher the ratio, the faster the cash collections. But a receivable turnover that's too high may indicate that credit is too tight, causing the loss of sales to good customers.

To compute accounts receivable turnover, divide net credit sales by average net accounts receivable. Palisades Furniture's accounts receivable turnover ratio for 2008 is computed as follows:

Formula	Palisades' Accounts Receivable Turnover	Industry Average
Accounts receivable turnover $= \dfrac{\text{Net credit sales}}{\text{Average net accounts receivable}}$	$\dfrac{\$858,000}{\$99,500} = 8.6$	51.0

Average net accounts receivable is figured by adding the beginning accounts receivable balance ($85,000) and the ending balance ($114,000), then dividing by 2: [($85,000 + $114,000)/2 = $99,500].

Palisades Furniture's receivable turnover of 8.6 times per year is much slower than the industry average. Why the difference? Palisades Furniture is a hometown store that sells to local people who pay their accounts over time. Many furniture stores sell their receivables to other companies called *factors*. That keeps receivables low and receivable turnover high. Palisades Furniture follows a different strategy.

Days' Sales in Receivables

The **days'-sales-in-receivables** ratio also measures the ability to collect receivables. Days' sales in receivables tell us how many days' sales remain in Accounts Receivable. To compute the ratio, we can follow a logical two-step process:

1. Divide net sales by 365 days to figure average sales for one day.

2. Divide this average day's sales amount into average net accounts receivable.

The data to compute this ratio for Palisades Furniture for 2008 are taken from the income statement and the balance sheet (Exhibit 13-8):

Formula	Palisades' Days' Sales in Accounts Receivable	Industry Average
Days' Sales in *average* Accounts Receivable:		
1. One day's sales $= \dfrac{\text{Net sales}}{365 \text{ days}}$	$\dfrac{\$858,000}{365 \text{ days}} = \$2,351$	
2. Days' sales in average accounts receivable $= \dfrac{\text{Average net accounts receivable}}{\text{One day's sales}}$	$\dfrac{\$99,500}{\$2,351} = 42 \text{ days}$	7 days

Average accounts receivable of $99,500 = ($85,000 + $114,000)/2.

Palisades Furniture's ratio tells us that 42 average days' sales remain in accounts receivable and need to be collected. Palisades' days'-sales-in-receivables ratio is much higher (worse) than the industry average because Palisades Furniture collects its own receivables. Palisades Furniture remains competitive because of its personal relationship with customers. Without their good paying habits, the company's cash flow would suffer.

Measuring Ability to Pay Long-Term Debt

The ratios discussed so far yield insight into current assets and current liabilities. They help us measure ability to sell inventory, collect receivables, and pay current liabilities. Most businesses also have long-term debt. Two key indicators of a business's ability to pay long-term liabilities are the *debt ratio* and the *times-interest-earned ratio*.

Debt Ratio

A loan officer at Metro Bank is evaluating loan applications from two companies. Both companies have asked to borrow $500,000 and have agreed to repay the loan over a five-year period. The first firm already owes $600,000 to another bank. The second owes only $100,000. Other things equal, you are more likely to lend money to Company 2 because that company owes less than Company 1.

This relationship between total liabilities and total assets—called the **debt ratio**—shows the proportion of assets financed with debt. When the debt ratio is 1, all of the assets are financed with debt. A debt ratio of 0.50 means that debt finances half the assets; the owners of the business have financed the other half. The higher the debt ratio, the higher the company's financial risk. The debt ratios for Palisades Furniture at the ends of 2008 and 2007 follow.

Formula	Palisades' Debt Ratio		Industry Average
	2008	2007	
Debt ratio $= \dfrac{\text{Total liabilities}}{\text{Total assets}}$	$\dfrac{\$431,000}{\$787,000} = 0.55$	$\dfrac{\$324,000}{\$644,000} = 0.50$	0.64

Palisades Furniture's debt ratio increased slightly in 2008, yet a debt ratio of 0.55 is not very high. The Risk Management Association reports that the average debt ratio for most companies ranges from 0.57 to 0.67, with relatively little variation from company to company. Palisades' debt ratio indicates a fairly low-risk position compared with the industry average debt ratio of 0.64.

Times-Interest-Earned Ratio

The debt ratio says nothing about ability to pay interest expense. Analysts use the **times-interest-earned-ratio** to relate income to interest expense. This ratio is also called the **interest-coverage ratio**. It measures the number of times operating income can cover interest expense. A high interest-coverage ratio indicates ease in paying interest expense; a low ratio suggests difficulty.

To compute this ratio, we divide income from operations (operating income) by interest expense. Calculation of Palisades Furniture times-interest-earned ratio follows.

Formula	Palisades' Times-Interest-Earned Ratio		Industry Average
	2008	2007	
Times-interest-earned ratio $= \dfrac{\text{Income from operations}}{\text{Interest expense}}$	$\dfrac{\$101,000}{\$24,000} = 4.21$	$\dfrac{\$57,000}{\$14,000} = 4.07$	2.80

The company's times-interest-earned ratio of about 4.00 is significantly better than the average for furniture retailers. The norm for U.S. business, as reported by The Risk Management Association, falls in the range of 2.0 to 3.0. Based on its debt ratio and its times-interest-earned ratio, Palisades Furniture appears to have little difficulty *servicing its debt*, that is, paying liabilities.

Measuring Profitability

The fundamental goal of business is to earn a profit. Ratios that measure profitability are reported in the business press and discussed on *Money Line*. We examine four profitability measures.

Rate of Return on Net Sales

In business, the term *return* is used broadly as a measure of profitability. Consider a ratio called the **rate of return on net sales**, or simply **return on sales**. (The word *net* is usually omitted for convenience even though net sales is used to compute the ratio.) This ratio shows the percentage of each sales dollar earned as net income. Palisades Furniture's rate of return on sales follows.

Formula	Palisades' Rate of Return on Sales		Industry Average
	2008	2007	
Rate of return on sales $= \dfrac{\text{Net income}}{\text{Net sales}}$	$\dfrac{\$48,000}{\$858,000} = 5.6\%$	$\dfrac{\$26,000}{\$803,000} = 3.2\%$	0.8%

Companies strive for a high rate of return on sales. The higher the rate of return, the more sales dollars end up as profit. The increase in Palisades Furniture's return on sales is significant and identifies the company as more successful than the average furniture store. Compare Palisades Furniture's rate of return on sales to the rates of return for some leading companies in other industries:

Company	Rate of Return on Sales
Google Inc.	12.5%
Texas Instruments	4.5%
Walgreens	3.6%

Rate of Return on Total Assets

The **rate of return on total assets**, or simply **return on assets**, measures success in using assets to earn a profit. Two groups finance a company's assets:

1. Creditors have loaned money to the company, and they earn interest.

2. Shareholders have invested in stock, and their return is net income.

The sum of interest expense and net income is the return to the two groups that have financed the company's assets. Computation of the return-on-assets ratio for Palisades Furniture follows.

Formula	Palisades' 2008 Rate of Return on Total Assets	Industry Average
$\text{Rate of return on assets} = \dfrac{\text{Net income} + \text{Interest expense}}{\text{Average total assets}}$	$\dfrac{\$48,000 + \$24,000}{\$715,500} = 10.1\%$	7.8%

Average total assets is the average of beginning and ending total assets from the comparative balance sheet: ($644,000 + $787,000)/2 = $715,500. Compare Palisades Furniture's rate of return on assets with the rates of some other companies:

Company	Rate of Return on Assets
Amazon.com..	25.6%
FedEx..	5.6%
Procter & Gamble..	13.6%

Rate of Return on Common Stockholders' Equity

A popular measure of profitability is **rate of return on common stockholders' equity**, often shortened to **return on equity**. This ratio shows the relationship between net income and common stockholders' equity—how much income is earned for each $1 invested by the common shareholders.

To compute this ratio, we subtract preferred dividends from net income to get net income available to the common stockholders. Then, we divide net income available to common stockholders by average common equity during the year. Common equity is total stockholders' equity minus preferred equity. The 2008 rate of return on common stockholders' equity for Palisades Furniture follows.

Formula	Palisades' 2008 Rate of Return on Common Stockholders' Equity	Industry Average
$\text{Rate of return on common stockholders' equity} = \dfrac{\text{Net income} - \text{Preferred dividends}}{\text{Average common stockholders' equity}}$	$\dfrac{\$48,000 - \$0}{\$338,000} = 14.2\%$	12.1%

Average equity is the average of the beginning and ending balances [($356,000 + $320,000)/2 = $338,000].

Palisades Furniture return on equity (14.2%) is higher than its return on assets (10.1%). This difference results from borrowing at one rate—for example, 8%—and investing the money to earn a higher rate, such as the firm's 14.2% return on equity.

This practice is called **trading on the equity**, or using **leverage**. It is directly related to the debt ratio. The higher the debt ratio, the higher the leverage. Companies that finance operations with debt are said to *leverage* their positions.

During good times, leverage increases profitability. But leverage can have a negative impact on profitability. Therefore, leverage is a double-edged sword, increasing profits during good times but compounding losses during bad times. Compare Palisades Furniture's return on equity with the rates of some leading companies.

Company	Rate of Return on Common Equity
Walgreens	17.6%
Procter & Gamble..	41.0%
FedEx...	10.9%

Palisades Furniture is not as profitable as these leading companies. A return on equity of 15% to 20% year after year is considered good in most industries.

Earnings per Share of Common Stock

Earnings per share of common stock, or simply **earnings per share (EPS)**, is perhaps the most widely quoted of all financial statistics. EPS is the only ratio that must appear on the face of the income statement. EPS is the amount of net income earned for each share of the company's outstanding *common* stock. Recall that:

Outstanding stock = Issued stock − Treasury stock

Earnings per share is computed by dividing net income available to common stockholders by the number of common shares outstanding during the year. Preferred dividends are subtracted from net income because the preferred stockholders have a prior claim to dividends. Palisades Furniture has no preferred stock outstanding and no preferred dividends.

The firm's EPS for 2008 and 2007 follow (Palisades had 10,000 shares of common stock outstanding throughout 2007 and 2008).

Formula	Palisades' Earnings per Share	
	2008	2007
Earnings per share of common stock $=\dfrac{\text{Net income} - \text{Preferred dividends}}{\text{Number of shares of common stock outstanding}}$	$\dfrac{\$48,000-\$0}{10,000}=\$4.80$	$\dfrac{\$26,000-\$0}{10,000}=\$2.60$

Palisades Furniture's EPS increased 85%. Its stockholders should not expect this big of a boost in EPS every year. Most companies strive to increase EPS by 10% to 15% annually, and leading companies do so. But even the most successful companies have an occasional bad year.

Analyzing Stock Investments

Investors purchase stock to earn a return on their investment. This return consists of two parts: (1) gains (or losses) from selling the stock at a price above (or below) the purchase price and (2) dividends. The ratios we examine in this section help analysts evaluate stock investments.

Price/Earnings Ratio

The **price/earnings ratio** is the ratio of the market price of a share of common stock to the company's earnings per share. It shows the market price of $1 of earnings. This ratio, abbreviated P/E, appears in the stock listings of *The Wall Street Journal*.

Calculations for the P/E ratios of Palisades Furniture Co. follow. The market price of its common stock was $60 at the end of 2008 and $35 at the end of 2007. These prices can be obtained from a financial publication, a stockbroker, or the company's Web site.

Palisades Furniture's P/E ratio of 12.5 means that the company's stock is selling at 12.5 times earnings. The decline from the 2007 P/E ratio of 13.5 is no cause for alarm because the market price of the stock is not under Palisades Furniture's control. Net income is more controllable, and net income increased during 2008.

	Formula	Palisades' Price/Earnings Ratio	
		2008	2007
P/E ratio =	$\dfrac{\text{Market price per share of common stock}}{\text{Earnings per share}}$	$\dfrac{\$60.00}{\$4.80} = 12.5$	$\dfrac{\$35.00}{\$2.60} = 13.5$

Dividend Yield

Dividend yield is the ratio of dividends per share to the stock's market price per share. This ratio measures the percentage of a stock's market value that is returned annually as dividends. *Preferred* stockholders, who invest primarily to receive dividends, pay special attention to dividend yield.

Palisades Furniture paid annual cash dividends of $1.20 per share of common stock in 2008 and $1.00 in 2007, and market prices of the company's common stock were $60 in 2008 and $35 in 2007. The firm's dividend yields on common stock follow.

	Formula	Dividend Yield on Palisades' Common Stock	
		2008	2007
Dividend yield on common stock* =	$\dfrac{\text{Dividend per share of common stock}}{\text{Market price per share of common stock}}$	$\dfrac{\$1.20}{\$60.00} = 2.0\%$	$\dfrac{\$1.00}{\$35.00} = 2.9\%$

*Dividend yields may also be calculated for preferred stock.

An investor who buys Palisades Furniture common stock for $60 can expect to receive 2% of the investment annually in the form of cash dividends.

Book Value per Share of Common Stock

Book value per share of common stock is common equity divided by the number of common shares outstanding. Common equity equals total stockholders' equity less preferred equity. Palisades Furniture has no preferred stock outstanding. Its book-value-per-share-of-common-stock ratios follow (10,000 shares of common stock were outstanding).

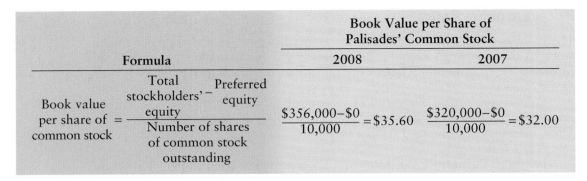

	Formula		Book Value per Share of Palisades' Common Stock	
			2008	2007
Book value per share of common stock	$=$	$\dfrac{\text{Total stockholders' equity} - \text{Preferred equity}}{\text{Number of shares of common stock outstanding}}$	$\dfrac{\$356,000 - \$0}{10,000} = \$35.60$	$\dfrac{\$320,000 - \$0}{10,000} = \$32.00$

Many experts argue that book value is not useful for investment analysis. It bears no relationship to market value and provides little information beyond stockholders' equity reported on the balance sheet. But some investors base their investment decisions on book value. For example, some investors rank stocks on the basis of the ratio of market price to book value. To these investors, the lower the ratio, the more attractive the stock, as this implies that the stock might be undervalued.

Red Flags in Financial Statement Analysis

Analysts look for *red flags* that may signal financial trouble. Recent accounting scandals highlight the importance of these red flags. The following conditions may reveal that the company is too risky.

- **Movement of Sales, Inventory, and Receivables.** Sales, receivables, and inventory generally move together. Increased sales lead to higher receivables and require more inventory to meet demand. Strange movements among sales, inventory, and receivables make the financial statements look suspect.
- **Earnings Problems.** Has net income decreased significantly for several years in a row? Has income turned into a loss? Most companies cannot survive years of consecutive loss.
- **Decreased Cash Flow.** Cash flow validates net income. Is cash flow from operations consistently lower than net income? If so, the company is in trouble. Are the sales of plant assets a major source of cash? If so, the company may face a cash shortage.
- **Too Much Debt.** How does the company's debt ratio compare to that of major competitors? If the debt ratio is too high, the company may be unable to pay its debts.
- **Inability to Collect Receivables.** Are days' sales in receivables growing faster than those of competitors? A cash shortage may be looming.
- **Buildup of Inventories.** Is inventory turnover too slow? If so, the company may be unable to sell goods or it may be overstating inventory.

Do any of these red flags apply to Google Inc.? No, Google's financial statements depict a strong and growing company. Will Google continue to grow at its present breakneck pace? Stay tuned. Time will tell.

The Decision Guidelines summarize the most widely used ratios.

Decision Guidelines

USING RATIOS IN FINANCIAL STATEMENT ANALYSIS

Mike and Roberta Robinson operate a financial services firm. They manage other people's money and do most of their own financial statement analysis. How do they measure companies' ability to pay bills, sell inventory, collect receivables, and so forth? They use the standard ratios discussed in this chapter.

Ratio	Computation	Information Provided
Measuring ability to pay current liabilities:		
1. Current ratio	$$\frac{\text{Current assets}}{\text{Current liabilities}}$$	Measures ability to pay current liabilities with current assets
2. Acid-test (quick) ratio	$$\frac{\text{Cash} + \frac{\text{Short-term}}{\text{investments}} + \frac{\text{Net current}}{\text{receivables}}}{\text{Current liabilities}}$$	Shows ability to pay all current liabilities if they come due immediately
Measuring ability to sell inventory and collect receivables:		
3. Inventory turnover	$$\frac{\text{Cost of goods sold}}{\text{Average inventory}}$$	Indicates saleability of inventory— the number of times a company sells its average inventory during a year
4. Accounts receivable turnover	$$\frac{\text{Net credit sales}}{\text{Average net accounts receivable}}$$	Measures ability to collect cash from customers
5. Days' sales in receivables	$$\frac{\text{Average net accounts receivable}}{\text{One day's sales}}$$	Shows how many days' sales remain in Accounts Receivable—how many days it takes to collect the average level of receivables
Measuring ability to pay long-term debt:		
6. Debt ratio	$$\frac{\text{Total liabilities}}{\text{Total assets}}$$	Indicates percentage of assets financed with debt
7. Times-interest-earned ratio	$$\frac{\text{Income from operation}}{\text{Interest expense}}$$	Measures the number of times operating income can cover interest expense

continued . . .

Ratio	Computation	Information Provided
Measuring profitability:		
8. Rate of return on net sales	$$\frac{\text{Net income}}{\text{Net sales}}$$	Shows the percentage of each sales dollar earned as net income
9. Rate of return on total assets	$$\frac{\text{Net income} + \text{Interest expense}}{\text{Average total assets}}$$	Measures how profitably a company uses its assets
10. Rate of return on common stockholders' equity	$$\frac{\text{Net income} - \text{Preferred dividends}}{\text{Average common stockholders' equity}}$$	Gauges how much income is earned for each dollar invested by common shareholders
11. Earnings per share of common stock	$$\frac{\text{Net income} - \text{Preferred dividends}}{\text{Number of shares of common stock outstanding}}$$	Gives the amount of net income earned for each share of the company's common stock
Analyzing stock as an investment:		
12. Price/earnings ratio	$$\frac{\text{Market price per share of common stock}}{\text{Earnings per share}}$$	Indicates the market price of $1 of earnings
13. Dividend yield	$$\frac{\text{Annual dividend per share of common (or preferred) stock}}{\text{Market price per share of common (or preferred) stock}}$$	Shows the percentage of a stock's market value returned as dividends to stockholders each year
14. Book value per share of common stock	$$\frac{\text{Total stockholders' equity} - \text{Preferred equity}}{\text{Number of shares of common stock outstanding}}$$	Indicates the recorded accounting amount for each share of common stock outstanding

Summary Problem 2

Operating Results*	2007	2006	2005	2004
JAVA INC. Five-Year Selected Financial Data (adapted) Years Ended January 31, 2007, 2006, 2005, and 2004				
Net sales	$13,848	$13,673	$11,635	$ 9,054
Cost of goods sold	9,704	8,599	6,775	5,318
Interest expense	109	75	45	46
Income from operations	338	1,455	1,817	1,333
Net income (net loss)	(8)	877	1,127	824
Cash dividends	76	75	76	77
Financial Position				
Merchandise inventory	1,677	1,904	1,462	1,056
Total assets	7,591	7,012	5,189	3,963
Current ratio	1.48:1	0.95:1	1.25:1	1.20:1
Stockholders' equity	3,010	2,928	2,630	1,574
Average number of shares of common stock outstanding (in thousands)	860	879	895	576

*Dollar amounts are in thousands.

Requirements

Compute the following ratios for 2005 through 2007 and evaluate Java's operating results. Are operating results strong or weak? Did they improve or deteriorate during this period? Your analysis will reveal a clear trend.

1. Gross profit percentage

2. Net income as a percentage of sales

3. Earnings per share

4. Inventory turnover

5. Times-interest-earned ratio

6. Rate of return on stockholders' equity

Solution

	2007	2006	2005
1. Gross profit percentage	$\dfrac{\$13,848-\$9,704}{\$13,848}=29.9\%$	$\dfrac{\$13,673-\$8,599}{\$13,673}=37.1\%$	$\dfrac{\$11,635-\$6,775}{\$11,635}=41.8\%$
2. Net income as a percentage of sales	$\dfrac{\$(8)}{\$13,848}=(.06\%)$	$\dfrac{\$877}{\$13,673}=6.4\%$	$\dfrac{\$1,127}{\$11,635}=9.7\%$
3. Earnings per share	$\dfrac{\$(8)}{860}=\$(0.01)$	$\dfrac{\$877}{879}=\$1.00$	$\dfrac{\$1,127}{895}=\$1.26$
4. Inventory turnover	$\dfrac{\$9,704}{(\$1,677+\$1,904)/2}=5.4 \text{ times}$	$\dfrac{\$8,599}{(\$1,904+\$1,462)/2}=5.1 \text{ times}$	$\dfrac{\$6,775}{(\$1,462+\$1,056)/2}=5.4 \text{ times}$
5. Times-interest-earned ratio	$\dfrac{\$338}{\$109}=3.1 \text{ times}$	$\dfrac{\$1,455}{\$75}=19.4 \text{ times}$	$\dfrac{\$1,817}{\$45}=40.4 \text{ times}$
6. Rate of return on stockholders' equity	$\dfrac{\$(8)}{(\$3,010+\$2,928)/2}=(0.3\%)$	$\dfrac{\$877}{(\$2,928+\$2,630)/2}=31.6\%$	$\dfrac{\$1,127}{(\$2,630+\$1,574)/2}=53.6\%$

Evaluation: During this period, Java's operating results deteriorated on all of these measures except inventory turnover. The gross profit percentage is down sharply, as are the times-interest-earned ratio and return on equity. From these data, it is clear that Java could sell its coffee, but not at the markups the company enjoyed in the past. The final result in 2007 was a net loss for the year.

Review Financial Statement Analysis

■ Accounting Vocabulary

Accounts Receivable Turnover. (p. 754)
Measures a company's ability to collect cash from credit customers. To compute accounts receivable turnover, divide net credit sales by average net accounts receivable.

Acid-Test Ratio. (p. 753)
Ratio of the sum of cash plus short-term investments plus net current receivables to total current liabilities. Tells whether the entity can pay all of its current liabilities if they come due immediately. Also called the **quick ratio.**

Benchmarking. (p. 747)
The practice of comparing a company with other companies that are leaders.

Book Value per Share of Common Stock. (p. 759)
Common stockholders' equity divided by the number of shares of common stock outstanding. The recorded amount for each share of common stock outstanding.

Common-Size Statement. (p. 746)
A financial statement that reports only percentages (no dollar amounts).

Current Ratio. (p. 751)
Current assets divided by current liabilities. Measures ability to pay current liabilities with current assets.

Days' Sales in Receivables. (p. 754)
Ratio of average net accounts receivable to one day's sale. Indicates how many days' sales remain in Accounts Receivable awaiting collection.

Debt Ratio. (p. 755)
Ratio of total liabilities to total assets. Shows the proportion of a company's assets that is financed with debt.

Dividend Yield. (p. 759)
Ratio of dividends per share of stock to the stock's market price per share. Tells the percentage of a stock's market value that the company returns to stockholders annually as dividends.

Earnings per Share (EPS). (p. 758)
Amount of a company's net income for each share of its outstanding common stock.

Horizontal Analysis. (p. 742)
Study of percentage changes in comparative financial statements.

Interest-Coverage Ratio. (p. 756)
Ratio of income from operations to interest expense. Measure the number of times that operating income can cover interest expense. Also called the **times-interest earned ratio.**

Inventory Turnover. (p. 753)
Ratio of cost of goods sold to average inventory. Indicates how rapidly inventory is sold.

Leverage. (p. 758)
Earning more income on borrowed money than the related interest expense, thereby increasing the earnings for the owners of the business. Also called **trading on equity.**

Price/Earnings (P/E) Ratio. (p. 759)
Ratio of the market price of a share of common stock to the company's earnings per share. Measures the value that the stock market places on $1 of a company's earnings.

Quick Ratio. (p. 753)
Ratio of the sum of cash plus short-term investments plus net current receivables to total current liabilities. Tells whether the entity can pay all its current liabilities if they come due immediately. Also called the **acid-test ratio.**

Rate of Return on Common Stockholders' Equity. (p. 757)
Net income minus preferred dividends divided by average common stockholders' equity. A measure of profitability. Also called **return on equity.**

Rate of Return on Net Sales. (p. 756)
Ratio of net income to net sales. A measure of profitability. Also called **return on sales.**

Rate of Return on Total Assets. (p. 757)
Net income plus interest expense divided by average total assets. This ratio measures a company's success in using its assets to earn income for the people who finance the business. Also called **return on assets.**

Return on Assets. (p. 757)
Net income plus interest expense, divided by average total assets. This ratio measures a company's success in using its assets to earn income for the people who finance the business. Also called **rate of return on total assets.**

Return on Equity. (p. 757)
Net income minus preferred dividends, divided by average common stockholders' equity. A measure of profitability. Also called **rate of return on common stockholders' equity.**

Return on Sales. (p. 756)
Ratio of net income to net sales. A measure of profitability. Also called **rate of return on net sales.**

Times-Interest-Earned Ratio. (p. 756)
Ratio of income from operations to interest expense. Measures the number of times operating income can cover interest expense. Also called the **interest-coverage ratio.**

Trading on Equity. (p. 758)
Earning more income on borrowed money than the related interest expense, thereby increasing the earnings for the owners of the business. Also called **leverage.**

Trend Percentages. (p. 744)
A form of horizontal analysis in which percentages are computed by selecting a base year as 100% and expressing amounts for following years as a percentage of the base amount.

Vertical Analysis. (p. 745)
Analysis of a financial statement that reveals the relationship of each statement item to a specified base, which is the 100% figure.

Working Capital. (p. 751)
Current assets minus current liabilities; measures a business's ability to meet its short-term obligations with its current assets.

■ Quick Check

Liberty Corporation reported these figures:

	2007	2006		2007
Cash and equivalents......................	$ 2,345	$ 1,934	Sales.....................................	$19,564
Receivables.....................................	2,097	1,882	Cost of sales.......................	7,105
Inventory...	1,294	1,055	Operating expenses............	7,001
Prepaid expenses	1,616	2,300	Operating income...............	5,458
Total current assets	7,352	7,171	Interest expense..................	199
Other assets....................................	17,149	15,246	Other expense	2,209
Total assets	$24,501	$22,417	Net income.........................	$ 3,050
Total current liabilities...................	$ 7,341	$ 8,429		
Long-term liabilities.......................	5,360	2,622		
Common equity	11,800	11,366		
Total liabilities and equity..............	$24,501	$22,417		

1. Horizontal analysis of Liberty's balance sheet for 2007 would report
   a. cash as 9.6% of total assets
   b. 21% increase in cash
   c. current ratio of 1.00
   d. inventory turnover of six times

2. Vertical analysis of Liberty's balance sheet for 2007 would report
   a. 21% increase in Cash
   b. current ratio of 1.00
   c. cash as 9.6% of total assets
   d. inventory turnover of six times

3. A common-size income statement for Liberty would report (amounts rounded)
   a. net income of 16%
   b. cost of sales at 36%
   c. sales of 100%
   d. all of the above

4. Which statement best describes Liberty's acid-test ratio?
   a. less than 1
   b. equal to 1
   c. greater than 1
   d. none of the above

5. Liberty's inventory turnover during 2007 was
   a. six times
   b. seven times
   c. eight times
   d. not determinable from the data given

6. During 2007, Liberty's days' sales in receivables ratio was
   a. 39 days
   b. 37 days
   c. 35 days
   d. 30 days

7. Which measure expresses Liberty's times-interest-earned ratio?
   a. 15 times
   b. 27 times
   c. 20 times
   d. 51.8%

8. Liberty's return on common stockholders' equity can be described as
   a. weak
   b. normal
   c. average
   d. strong

9. The company has 2,500 shares of common stock outstanding. What is Liberty's earnings per share?

   a. 2.04

   b. 3.6 times

   c. $1.22

   d. $3.05

10. Liberty's stock has traded recently around $44 per share. Use your answer to Question 9 to measure the company's price/earnings ratio.

   a. 36

   b. 44

   c. 1.00

   d. 69

Quick Check Answers

1. *b* 2. *c* 3. *d* 4. *a* 5. *a* 6. *b* 7. *b* 8. *d* 9. *c* 10. *a*

For Internet exercises, Excel in Practice, and additional online activities, go to this book's Web site at www.prenhall.com/bamber.

Assess Your Progress

▪ Learning Objectives

1 Perform a horizontal analysis of financial statements

2 Perform a vertical analysis of financial statements

3 Prepare and use common-size financial statements

4 Compute the standard financial ratios

▪ Short Exercises

S13-1 **Horizontal analysis of revenue and cost of sales** *(Learning Objective 1)*
Micatin reported the following on its comparative income statement:

(in millions)	2006	2005	2004
Revenue	$9,993	$9,489	$8,995
Cost of sales	5,905	5,785	5,404

Perform a horizontal analysis of revenues and gross profit—both in dollar amounts and in percentages—for 2006 and 2005.

S13-2 **Find trend percentages** *(Learning Objective 2)*
Micatin reported the following revenues and net income amounts:

(in millions)	2006	2005	2004	2003
Revenues	$9,993	$9,489	$8,995	$8,777
Net income	634	590	579	451

a. Show Micatin's trend percentages for revenues and net income. Use 2003 as the base year and round to the nearest percent.
b. Which measure increased faster during 2004–2006?

S13-3 **Vertical analysis of assets** *(Learning Objective 2)*
TriState Optical Company reported the following amounts on its balance sheet at December 31, 2006:

	2006
Cash and receivables	$ 48,000
Inventory	38,000
Property, plant, and equipment, net	96,000
Total assets	$182,000

Perform a vertical analysis of TriState Optical Company's assets at the end of 2006.

S13-4   **Prepare common-size income statements** *(Learning Objective 3)*

Compare Sanchez and Alioto by converting their income statements to common size.

	Sanchez	Alioto
Net sales............................	$9,489	$19,536
Cost of goods sold.............	5,785	14,101
Other expense	3,114	4,497
Net income.......................	$ 590	$ 938

Which company earns more net income? Which company's net income is a higher percentage of its net sales?

Lowe's Data Set: Used for S13-5 through S13-9

Lowe's Companies, the home-improvement-store chain, reported these summarized figures (in billions:

LOWE'S COMPANIES
Income Statement (Adapted)
Year Ended January 30, 2004

Net sales	$30.8
Cost of goods sold	21.2
Interest expense	.2
All other expenses	7.5
Net income	$ 1.9

LOWE'S COMPANIES
Balance Sheet (Adapted)
January 31,

	2004	2003		2004	2003
Cash	$ 1.4	$ 0.8	Total current liabilities	$ 4.4	$ 3.6
Short-term investments	0.2	0.3	Long-term liabilities	4.3	4.2
Accounts receivable	0.1	0.2	Total liabilities	8.7	7.8
Inventory	4.6	4.0			
Other current assets	0.4	0.3	Common stock	2.6	2.4
Total current assets	6.7	5.6	Retained earnings	7.7	5.9
All other assets	12.3	10.5	Total equity	10.3	8.3
Total assets	$19.0	$16.1	Total liabilities and equity	$19.0	$16.1

S13-5   **Find current ratio** *(Learning Objective 4)*

Refer to the Lowe's Data Set.

a.   Compute Lowe's current ratio at December 31, 2004 and 2003.

b.   Did Lowe's current ratio improve, deteriorate, or hold steady during 2006?

S13-6 **Analyze inventory and receivables** *(Learning Objective 4)*
Use the Lowe's Data Set to compute the following (amounts in billions):

a. The rate of inventory turnover for 2004.

b. Days' sales in average receivables during 2004 (round dollar amounts to three decimal places)

S13-7 **Compute and interpret debt ratio** *(Learning Objective 4)*
Refer to the Lowe's Data Set.

a. Compute the debt ratio at December 31, 2004.

b. Is Lowe's ability to pay its liabilities strong or weak? Explain your reasoning.

S13-8 **Compute profitability ratios** *(Learning Objective 4)*
Use the Lowe's Data Set to compute these profitability measures for 2004.

a. Rate of return on net sales.

b. Rate of return on total assets (interest expense for 2004 was $0.2 billion)

c. Rate of return on common stockholders' equity.

Are these rates of return strong or weak?

S13-9 **Determine earnings per share** *(Learning Objective 4)*
Use the Lowe's Data Set in addition to the following item (in billions):

Number of shares of common stock outstanding	0.8

a. Compute earnings per share (EPS) for Lowe's. Round to the nearest cent.

b. Compute Lowe's price/earnings ratio. The price of a share of Lowe's is $66.50.

S13-10 **Find missing values on income statement** *(Learning Objective 4)*
A skeleton of Heirloom Mills' income statement appears as follows (amounts in thousands):

HEIRLOOM MILLS
Income Statement
Year Ended December 31, 2007

Net sales..	$7,200
Cost of goods sold..	(a)
Selling and administrative expenses.............................	1,710
Interest expense...	(b)
Other expenses..	150
Income before taxes	1,000
Income tax expense...	(c)
Net income...	$ (d)

Use the following ratio data to complete Heirloom Mills' income statement:

a. Inventory turnover was 5.5 (beginning inventory was $790; ending inventory was $750).

b. Rate of return on sales is 0.095.

S13-11 **Find missing values on balance sheet** *(Learning Objective 4)*

A skeleton of Heirloom Mills' balance sheet appears as follows (amounts in thousands):

HEIRLOOM MILLS
Balance Sheet
December 31, 2007

Cash...	$ 50		Total current liabilities............	$2,100
Receivables.............................	(a)		Long-term note	
Inventories	750		payable.............................	(e)
Prepaid expenses	(b)		Other long-term	
Total current assets	(c)		liabilities............................	820
Plant assets, net.......................	(d)		Stockholders' equity...............	2,400
Other assets............................	2,150		Total liabilities and	
Total assets	$6,800		equity.................................	$ (f)

Use the following ratio data to complete Heirloom Mills' balance sheet:

a. Current ratio is 0.70.

b. Acid-test ratio is 0.30.

Exercises

E13-12 **Trend analysis of working capital** *(Learning Objective 1)*

Compute the dollar amount of change and the percentage of change in Arpegio Enterprises working capital each year during 2008 and 2009. Is this trend favorable or unfavorable?

	2009	2008	2007
Total current assets	$330,000	$300,000	$280,000
Total current liabilities...........	160,000	150,000	140,000

E13-13 **Horizontal analysis** *(Learning Objective 1)*

Prepare a horizontal analysis of the following comparative income statement of Big Tiger Designs. Round percentage changes to the nearest one-tenth percent (three decimal places).

BIG TIGER DESIGNS
Comparative Income Statement
Years Ended December 31, 2007 and 2006

	2007	2006
Net sales revenue	$430,000	$373,000
Expenses:		
Cost of goods sold	$202,000	$188,000
Selling and general expenses	98,000	93,000
Other expense	7,000	4,000
Total expenses	307,000	285,000
Net income	$123,000	$ 88,000

Why did net income increase by a higher percentage than net sales revenue during 2007?

E13-14 **Compute trend percentages** *(Learning Objective 1)*
Compute trend percentages for Autumn Realty's net revenue and net income for the following five-year period using 2004 as the base year. Round to the nearest full percent.

(in thousands)	2008	2007	2006	2005	2004
Net revenue..............	$1,318	$1,187	$1,106	$1,009	$1,043
Net income...............	122	114	83	71	85

Which grew faster during the period, net revenue or net income?

E13-15 **Perform vertical analysis** *(Learning Objective 2)*
Skyline Graphics has requested that you perform a vertical analysis of its balance sheet.

SKYLINE GRAPHICS, INC. Balance Sheet December 31, 2006	
Assets	
Total current assets	$ 42,000
Property, plant, and equipment, net	207,000
Other assets	35,000
Total assets	$284,000
Liabilities	
Total current liabilities	$ 48,000
Long-term debt	108,000
Total liabilities	156,000
Stockholders' Equity	
Total stockholders' equity	128,000
Total liabilities and stockholders' equity	$284,000

E13-16 **Prepare common-size income statement** *(Learning Objective 3)*
Prepare a comparative common-size income statement for Big Tiger Designs using the 2007 and 2006 data of Exercise 13-13 and rounding percentages to one-tenth percent (three decimal places). To an investor, how does 2007 compare with 2006? Explain your reasoning.

E13-17 **Calculate ratios** *(Learning Objective 4)*

The financial statements of Harper's Health Foods include the following items:

	Current Year	Preceding Year
Balance sheet:		
Cash..	$ 17,000	$ 22,000
Short-term investments..............	11,000	26,000
Net receivables..........................	54,000	73,000
Inventory....................................	77,000	71,000
Prepaid expenses	16,000	8,000
Total current assets	$175,000	$200,000
Total current liabilities...............	$131,000	$ 91,000
Income statement:		
Net credit sales..........................	$464,000	
Cost of goods sold.....................	317,000	

Requirements

Compute the following ratios for the current year:

a. Current ratio

b. Acid-test ratio

c. Inventory turnover

d. Days' sales in average receivables

E13-18 **More ratio analysis** *(Learning Objective 4)*

Lennox Picture Frames has asked you to determine whether the company's ability to pay current liabilities and total liabilities improved or deteriorated during 2007. To answer that question, compute these ratios for 2007 and 2006:

a. Current ratio

b. Acid-test ratio

c. Debt ratio

d. Times-interest-earned ratio

Summarize the results of your analysis in a written report.

	2007	2006
Cash..	$ 61,000	$ 47,000
Short-term investments..............	28,000	—
Net receivables..........................	122,000	116,000
Inventory....................................	237,000	272,000
Total assets	560,000	490,000
Total current liabilities...............	275,000	202,000
Long-term note payable	40,000	52,000
Income from operations	165,000	158,000
Interest expense.........................	48,000	39,000

E13-19 **Compute profitability ratios** *(Learning Objective 4)*

Compute four ratios that measure Pyrodyne's ability to earn profits. The company's comparative income statement follows. The data for 2004 are given as needed.

PYRODYNE
Comparative Income Statement
Years Ended December 31, 2006 and 2005

Dollars in Thousands	2006	2005	2004
Net sales	$174,000	$158,000	
Cost of goods sold	$ 93,000	$ 86,000	
Selling and general expenses	46,000	41,000	
Interest expense	9,000	10,000	
Income tax expense	10,000	9,000	
Net income	$ 16,000	$ 12,000	
Additional data:			
Total assets	$204,000	$191,000	$171,000
Common stockholders' equity	$ 96,000	$ 89,000	$ 79,000
Preferred dividends	$ 3,000	$ 3,000	$ 0
Common shares outstanding during			
the year	20,000	20,000	18,000

Did the company's operating performance improve or deteriorate during 2006?

E13-20 **Compute stock ratios** *(Learning Objective 4)*

Evaluate the common stock of Personal State Bank as an investment. Specifically, use the three stock ratios to determine whether the common stock has increased or decreased in attractiveness during the past year.

	2008	2007
Net income..	$ 60,000	$ 52,000
Dividends—common..	20,000	20,000
Dividends—preferred	12,000	12,000
Total stockholders' equity at year-end (includes 80,000 shares of common stock)...	780,000	600,000
Preferred stock, 6%...	200,000	200,000
Market price per share of common stock	$16.50	$13

E13-21 **Find missing values** *(Learning Objective 4)*

The following data (dollar amounts in millions) are adapted from the financial statements of Giant Rhino Stores, Inc.

Total current assets	$10,500
Accumulated depreciation	$ 2,000
Total liabilities	$15,000
Preferred stock	$ 0
Debt ratio.......................................	60%
Current ratio	1.50

Requirements

Complete Giant Rhino's condensed balance sheet.

Current assets..	$?
Property, plant, and equipment......................................	$?
Less Accumulated depreciation	(?)
Total assets	$?
Current liabilities	$?
Long-term liabilities	?
Stockholders' equity	?
Total liabilities and stockholders' equity	$?

Problems (Problem Set A)

P13-22A **Prepare trend analysis** *(Learning Objectives 1, 4)*

Net sales revenue, net income, and common stockholders' equity for Rafferty Corporation, a manufacturer of contact lenses, follow for a four-year period.

(in thousands)	2008	2007	2006	2005
Net sales revenue.................................	$761	$704	$641	$662
Net income..	60	40	36	48
Ending common stockholders' equity......	366	354	330	296

Requirements

1. Compute trend percentages for each item for 2006 through 2008. Use 2005 as the base year and round to the nearest whole percent.

2. Compute the rate of return on common stockholders' equity for 2006 through 2008, rounding to three decimal places.

P13-23A Comprehensive analysis (*Learning Objectives 2, 3, 4*)

Carlton Department Stores' chief executive officer (CEO) has asked you to compare the company's profit performance and financial position with the average for the industry. The CEO has given you the company's income statement and balance sheet, as well as the industry average data for retailers.

CARLTON DEPARTMENT STORES, INC.
Income Statement Compared with Industry Average
Year Ended December 31, 2006

		Carlton	Industry Average
	Net sales	$781,000	100.0%
	Cost of goods sold	528,000	65.8
	Gross profit	253,000	34.2
	Operating expenses	163,000	19.7
	Operating income	90,000	14.5
	Other expenses	5,000	0.4
	Net income	$ 85,000	14.1%

CARLTON DEPARTMENT STORES, INC.
Balance Sheet Compared with Industry Average
December 31, 2006

	Carlton	Industry Average
Current assets	$305,000	70.9%
Fixed assets, net	119,000	23.6
Intangible assets, net	4,000	0.8
Other assets	22,000	4.7
Total assets	$450,000	100.0%
Current liabilities	$207,000	48.1%
Long-term liabilities	102,000	16.6
Stockholders' equity	141,000	35.3
Total liabilities and stockholders' equity	$450,000	100.0%

Requirements

1. Prepare a common-size income statement and balance sheet for Carlton Department Stores. The first column of each statement should present Carlton Department Stores' common-size statement; the second column, the industry averages.

2. For the profitability analysis, compute Carlton Department Stores' (a) ratio of gross profit to net sales, (b) ratio of operating income to net sales, and (c) ratio of net income to net sales. Compare these figures with the industry averages. Is Carlton Department Stores' profit performance better or worse than the industry average?

3. For the analysis of financial position, compute Carlton Department Stores' (a) ratio of current assets to total assets and (b) ratio of stockholders' equity to total assets. Compare these ratios with the industry averages. Is Carlton Department Stores' financial position better or worse than the industry averages?

P13-24A Effect of transactions on ratios *(Learning Objective 4)*

Financial statement data of *Eastern Traveler* magazine include the following items (dollars in thousands):

Cash	$ 22,000
Accounts receivable, net	82,000
Inventories	149,000
Total assets	637,000
Short-term notes payable	49,000
Accounts payable	103,000
Accrued liabilities	38,000
Long-term liabilities	191,000
Net income	71,000
Common shares outstanding	50,000

Requirements

1. Compute *Eastern Traveler*'s current ratio, debt ratio, and earnings per share. Round all ratios to two decimal places and use the following format for your answer:

Current Ratio	Debt Ratio	Earnings per Share

2. Compute the three ratios after evaluating the effect of each transaction that follows. Consider each transaction *separately*.
   a. Purchased inventory on account, $46,000
   b. Borrowed $125,000 on a long-term note payable
   c. Issued 5,000 shares of common stock, receiving cash of $120,000
   d. Received cash on account, $19,000

Format your answer as follows:

Transaction	Current Ratio	Debt Ratio	Earnings per Share
a.			

P13-25A **Ratio analysis over two years** *(Learning Objective 4)*
Comparative financial statement data of Coughlin, Inc., follow.

COUGHLIN, INC.
Comparative Income Statement
Years Ended December 31, 2009 and 2008

	2009	2008
Net sales	$462,000	$427,000
Cost of goods sold	240,000	218,000
Gross profit	222,000	209,000
Operating expenses	136,000	134,000
Income from operations	86,000	75,000
Interest expense	11,000	12,000
Income before income tax	75,000	63,000
Income tax expense	25,000	27,000
Net income	$ 50,000	$ 36,000

COUGHLIN, INC.
Comparative Balance Sheet
December 31, 2009 and 2008

	2009	2008	2007*
Current assets:			
Cash	$ 96,000	$ 97,000	
Current receivables, net	112,000	116,000	$103,000
Inventories	147,000	162,000	207,000
Prepaid expenses	16,000	7,000	
Total current assets	371,000	382,000	
Property, plant, and equipment, net	214,000	178,000	
Total assets	$585,000	$560,000	598,000
Total current liabilities	$226,000	$243,000	
Long-term liabilities	119,000	97,000	
Total liabilities	345,000	340,000	
Preferred stock, 6%	100,000	100,000	
Common stockholders' equity, no par	140,000	120,000	90,000
Total liabilities and stockholders' equity	$585,000	$560,000	

*Selected 2007 amounts.

1. Market price of Coughlin's common stock: $49.00 at December 31, 2009, and $32.50 at December 31, 2008
2. Common shares outstanding: 10,000 during 2009 and 9,000 during 2008
3. All sales on credit

Requirements
1. Compute the following ratios for 2009 and 2008:
   a. Current ratio
   b. Times-interest-earned ratio
   c. Inventory turnover

continued . . .

d. Return on common stockholders' equity

e. Earnings per share of common stock

f. Price/earnings ratio

2. Decide (a) whether Coughlin's ability to pay debts and to sell inventory improved or deteriorated during 2009 and (b) whether the investment attractiveness of its common stock appears to have increased or decreased.

P13-26A **Make an investment decision** *(Learning Objective 4)*

Assume that you are purchasing an investment and have decided to invest in a company in the digital phone business. You have narrowed the choice to Global Corp. and Vast Spirit and have assembled the following data:

Selected income statement data for the current year:

	Global	Vast Spirit
Net sales (all on credit).............	$421,000	$497,000
Cost of goods sold...................	209,000	258,000
Interest expense.......................	—	19,000
Net income..............................	50,000	72,000

Selected balance sheet data at the *beginning* of the current year:

	Global	Vast Spirit
Current receivables, net...............................	$ 40,000	$ 48,000
Inventories	83,000	88,000
Total assets	259,000	270,000
Common stock, $1 par (10,000 shares)........	10,000	
$1 par (15,000 shares)........		15,000

Selected balance sheet and market-price data at the *end* of the current year:

	Global	Vast Spirit
Current assets:		
Cash...	$ 26,000	$ 19,000
Short-term investments...........................	40,000	18,000
Current receivables, net..........................	38,000	46,000
Inventories..	67,000	100,000
Prepaid expenses	2,000	3,000
Total current assets.................................	173,000	186,000
Total assets..	265,000	328,000
Total current liabilities...............................	100,000	98,000
Total liabilities...	100,000	131,000
Common stock, $1 par (10,000 shares)	10,000	
$1 par (15,000 shares).......		15,000
Total stockholders' equity...........................	157,000	197,000
Market price per share of common stock....	$ 8	$ 86.40

Your strategy is to invest in companies that have low price/earnings ratios but appear to be in good shape financially. Assume that you have analyzed all other factors and that your decision depends on the results of ratio analysis.

Requirements

Compute the following ratios for both companies for the current year and decide which company's stock better fits your investment strategy.

a. Acid-test ratio

b. Inventory turnover

c. Days' sales in average receivables

d. Debt ratio

e. Earnings per share of common stock

f. Price/earnings ratio

P13-27A **Investment recommendation** *(Learning Objective 4)*

Take the role of an investment analyst at Great Gulch Bank. It is your job to recommend investments for your clients. The only information you have are some ratio values for two companies in the pharmaceuticals industry.

Ratio	Shea Corp.	Hancin
Return on equity	21.5%	32.3%
Return on assets	16.4%	17.1%
Days' sales in receivables	42	36
Inventory turnover	8	6
Gross profit percentage	51%	53%
Net income as a percentage of sales	8.3%	7.2%
Times interest earned	9	16

Write a report to Great Gulch Bank's investment committee. Recommend one company's stock over the other. State the reasons for your recommendation.

Problems (Problem Set B)

P13-28B **Prepare trend analysis** *(Learning Objectives 1, 4)*

Net sales, net income, and total assets for Forte Electronics for a four-year period follow.

(in thousands)	2008	2007	2006	2005
Net sales	$307	$313	$266	$281
Net income	9	21	11	18
Total assets	266	254	209	197

continued . . .

Requirements

1. Compute trend percentages for each item for 2006 through 2008. Use 2005 as the base year and round to the nearest whole percent.

2. Compute the rate of return on net sales for 2006 through 2008, rounding to three decimal places.

P13-29B **Comprehensive analysis** *(Learning Objectives 2, 3, 4)*

Top managers of Crescendo Music Company have asked for your help in comparing the company's profit performance and financial position with the average for the industry. The accountant has given you the company's income statement and balance sheet and the following data for the industry:

CRESCENDO MUSIC COMPANY
Income Statement Compared with Industry Average
Year Ended December 31, 2008

	Crescendo	Industry Average
Net sales	$957,000	100.0%
Cost of goods sold	613,000	65.9
Gross profit	344,000	34.1
Operating expenses	204,000	28.1
Operating income	140,000	6.0
Other expenses	10,000	0.4
Net income	$130,000	5.6%

CRESCENDO MUSIC COMPANY
Balance Sheet Compared with Industry Average
December 31, 2008

	Crescendo	Industry Average
Current assets	$486,000	74.4%
Fixed assets, net	117,000	20.0
Intangible assets, net	24,000	0.6
Other assets	3,000	5.0
Total assets	$630,000	100.0%
Current liabilities	$246,000	45.6%
Long-term liabilities	136,000	19.0
Stockholders' equity	248,000	35.4
Total liabilities and stockholders' equity	$630,000	100.0%

Requirements

1. Prepare a common-size income statement and balance sheet for Crescendo Music Company. The first column of each statement should present Crescendo Music Company's common-size statement, and the second column should show the industry averages.

2. For the profitability analysis, compute Crescendo's (a) ratio of gross profit to net sales, (b) ratio of operating income to net sales, and (c) ratio of net income to net sales. Compare these figures with the industry averages. Is Crescendo's profit performance better or worse than the average for the industry?

3. For the analysis of financial position, compute Crescendo's (a) ratios of current assets and current liabilities to total assets and (b) ratio of stockholders' equity to total assets. Compare these ratios with the industry averages. Is Crescendo's financial position better or worse than average for the industry?

P13-30B Effect of transactions on ratios *(Learning Objective 4)*

Financial statement data on Tran RV Park include the following:

Cash	$ 47,000	Accounts payable	$ 96,000
Accounts receivable, net	123,000	Accrued liabilities	50,000
Inventories	189,000	Long-term liabilities	224,000
Total assets	833,000	Net income	110,000
Short-term notes payable	72,000	Common shares outstanding	20,000

Requirements

1. Compute Tran RV Park's current ratio, debt ratio, and earnings per share. Round all ratios to two decimal places and use the following format for your answer:

Transaction	Current Ratio	Debt Ratio	Earnings per Share

2. Compute the three ratios after evaluating the effect of each transaction that follows. Consider each transaction *separately*.

   a. Borrowed $27,000 on a long-term note payable

   b. Issued 10,000 shares of common stock, receiving cash of $108,000

   c. Purchased inventory of $48,000 on account

   d. Received cash on account, $6,000

Format your answer as follows:

Transaction	Current Ratio	Debt Ratio	Earnings per Share
a.			

P13-31B Ratio analysis over two years (*Learning Objective 4*)
Comparative financial statement data of Perfecto DVDs Inc. follow.

PERFECTO DVDs, INC.
Comparative Income Statement
Years Ended December 31, 2006 and 2005

	2006	2005
Net sales	$667,000	$599,000
Cost of goods sold	378,000	283,000
Gross profit	289,000	316,000
Operating expenses	129,000	147,000
Income from operations	160,000	169,000
Interest expense	37,000	51,000
Income before income tax	123,000	118,000
Income tax expense	34,000	53,000
Net income	$ 89,000	$ 65,000

PERFECTO DVDs INC.
Comparative Balance Sheet
December 31, 2006 and 2005

	2006	2005	2004*
Current assets:			
Cash	$ 37,000	$ 40,000	
Current receivables, net	208,000	151,000	$138,000
Inventories	298,000	286,000	184,000
Prepaid expenses	5,000	20,000	
Total current assets	548,000	497,000	
Property, plant, and equipment, net	287,000	276,000	
Total assets	$835,000	$773,000	707,000
Total current liabilities	$286,000	$267,000	
Long-term liabilities	245,000	235,000	
Total liabilities	531,000	502,000	
Preferred stock, 4%	50,000	50,000	
Common stockholders' equity, no par	308,000	221,000	198,000
Total liabilities and stockholders' equity	$889,000	$773,000	

*Selected 2004 amounts.

Other Information

1. Market price of Perfecto's common stock: $92.80 at December 31, 2006, and $67.50 at December 31, 2005
2. Common shares outstanding: 15,000 during 2006 and 14,000 during 2005
3. All sales on credit

Requirements

1. Compute the following ratios for 2006 and 2005:
   a. Current ratio
   b. Times-interest-earned ratio
   c. Inventory turnover

d. Return on common stockholders' equity

e. Earnings per share of common stock

f. Price/earnings ratio

2. Decide (a) whether Perfecto DVD's ability to pay its debts and to sell inventory improved or deteriorated during 2006 and (b) whether the investment attractiveness of its common stock appears to have increased or decreased.

P13-32B **Make an investment decision** *(Learning Objective 4)*

Assume that you are considering purchasing stock in a company in the music industry. You have narrowed the choice to Harmonic Music Makers (HMM) and Symphonic Sound and have assembled the following data.

Selected income statement data for the current year:

	HMM	Symphonic
Net sales (all on credit)..............	$603,000	$519,000
Cost of goods sold......................	484,000	387,000
Interest expense.........................	—	8,000
Net income................................	75,000	38,000

Selected balance sheet and market-price data at the *end* of the current year:

	HMM	Symphonic
Current assets:		
Cash...	$ 45,000	$ 39,000
Short-term investments................................	76,000	13,000
Current receivables, net...............................	99,000	164,000
Inventories	211,000	183,000
Prepaid expenses	19,000	15,000
Total current assets	450,000	414,000
Total assets	974,000	938,000
Total current liabilities.................................	306,000	338,000
Total liabilities	667,000	691,000
Common stock, $1 par (150,000 shares).........	150,000	
$5 par (20,000 shares)...........		100,000
Total stockholders' equity..............................	307,000	247,000
Market price per share of common stock	$ 8	$ 41.80

continued . . .

Selected balance sheet data at the *beginning* of the current year:

	HMM	Symphonic
Current receivables, net	$102,000	$193,000
Inventories	209,000	197,000
Total assets	842,000	909,000
Common stock, $1 par (150,000 shares)	150,000	
$5 par (20,000 shares)		100,000

Your strategy is to invest in companies that have low price/earnings ratios but appear to be in good shape financially. Assume that you have analyzed all other factors and that your decision depends on the results of ratio analysis.

Requirements
Compute the following ratios for both companies for the current year and decide which company's stock better fits your investment strategy.

a. Acid-test ratio

b. Inventory turnover

c. Days' sales in average receivables

d. Debt ratio

e. Earnings per share of common stock

f. Price/earnings ratio

P13-33B Investment recommendation (*Learning Objective 4*)
Take the role of an investment analyst at E. M. Boone. It is your job to recommend investments for your client. The only data you have are the ratio values for two companies in the graphics software industry.

Ratio	Rally Software Company	Disc Tech, Inc.
Return on equity	36%	29%
Return on assets	21%	20%
Days' sales in receivables	43	51
Inventory turnover	8	9
Gross profit percentage	71%	62%
Net income as a percentage of sales	14%	16%
Times interest earned	18	12

Write a report to the E. M. Boone investment committee. Recommend one company's stock over the other. State the reasons for your recommendation.

Apply Your Knowledge

■ Decision Cases

Case 13-34. Effect of transactions on ratios *(Learning Objective 4)*

General Motors and Ford Motor Company both had a bad year in 2005; the companies' auto units suffered net losses. The loss pushed some return measures into the negative column, and the companies' ratios deteriorated. Assume that top management of GM and Ford are pondering ways to improve their ratios. In particular, management is considering the following transactions:

1. Borrow $100 million on long-term debt
2. Purchase treasury stock for $500 million cash
3. Expense one-fourth of the goodwill carried on the books
4. Create a new auto design division at a cash cost of $300 million
5. Purchase patents from DaimlerChrysler, paying $20 million cash

Requirements

Top management wants to know the effects of these transactions (increase, decrease, or no effect) on the following ratios:

a. Current ratio

b. Debt ratio

c. Return on equity

Case 13-35. Identify affected ratios *(Learning Objective 4)*

Lance Berkman is the controller of Saturn, a dance club whose year-end is December 31. Berkman prepares checks for suppliers in December and posts them to the appropriate accounts in that month. However, he holds on to the checks and mails them to the suppliers in January. What financial ratio(s) are most affected by the action? What is Berkman's purpose in undertaking this activity?

■ Ethical Issue

Issue 13-36. Effect of decisions on ratios *(Learning Objective 4)*

Betsy Ross Flag Company's long-term debt agreements make certain demands on the business. For example, Ross may not purchase treasury stock in excess of the balance of retained earnings. Also, long-term debt may not exceed stockholders' equity, and the current ratio may not fall below 1.50. If Ross fails to meet any of those requirements, the company's lenders have the authority to take over management of the company.

Changes in consumer demand have made it hard for Ross to attract customers. Current liabilities have mounted faster than current assets, causing the current ratio to fall to 1.47. Before releasing financial statements, Ross's management is scrambling to improve the current ratio. The controller points out that an investment can be classified as either long-term or short-term, depending on management's intention. By deciding to convert an investment to cash within one year, Ross can classify the investment as short-term—a current asset. On the controller's recommendation, Ross's board of directors votes to reclassify long-term investments as short-term.

continued . . .

Requirements

1. What effect will reclassifying the investments have on the current ratio? Is Ross's true financial position stronger as a result of reclassifying the investments?

2. Shortly after the financial statements are released, sales improve; so, too, does the current ratio. As a result, Ross's management decides not to sell the investments it had reclassified as short-term. Accordingly, the company reclassifies the investments as long-term. Has management behaved unethically? Give the reasoning underlying your answer.

■ Team Projects

Project 13-37. Ratio analysis *(Learning Objective 4)*

Select an industry you are interested in and use the leading company in that industry as the benchmark. Then, select two other companies in the same industry. For each category of ratios in the Decision Guidelines on pages 761 and 762, compute at least two ratios for all three companies. Write a two-page report that compares the two companies with the benchmark company.

Project 13-38. Comparison of common-size financials *(Learning Objective 3)*

Select a company and obtain its financial statements. Convert the income statement and the balance sheet to common size and compare the company you selected to the industry average. The Risk Management Association's *Annual Statement Studies*, **Dun & Bradstreet's** *Industry Norms & Key Business Ratios*, and Prentice Hall's *Almanac of Business and Industrial Financial Ratios* by Leo Troy publish common-size statements for most industries.

Chapter 3: Demo Doc 1

■ Job Costing for Manufacturers

Learning Objectives 1, 3, 4, 5

Douglas Art manufactures specialized art for customers. Suppose Douglas has the following transactions during the month:

a. Raw materials were purchased on account for $67,000.

b. Materials costing $45,000 were requisitioned for production. Of this total, $5,000 were indirect materials.

c. $32,000 of labor was incurred in the factory.

d. Of the total labor costs, $30,000 was traced to specific jobs worked on during the month. The remainder of the factory labor cost related to indirect labor.

e. Manufacturing overhead is assigned to production using the predetermined overhead rate of 75% of direct labor cost.

f. Jobs costing $67,000 were completed during the month.

g. Douglas sold several jobs during the month for a total price of $106,000. These jobs cost $65,000 to produce. Assume a perpetual inventory system.

Requirements

1. What type of product costing system would Douglas use? Justify your answer.

2. What document would Douglas use to accumulate direct materials, direct labor, and manufacturing overhead costs assigned to each individual job?

3. Prepare journal entries for each transaction.

Demo Doc 1 Solutions

Requirement 1

What type of product costing system would Douglas use?

Job Costing System—companies that manufacture batches of unique or specialized products would use a job costing system to accumulate costs for each job or batch.

Requirement 2

What document would Douglas use to accumulate direct materials, direct labor, and manufacturing overhead costs assigned to each individual job?

Douglas would use a job cost record to accumulate direct materials, direct labor, and manufacturing overhead costs assigned to each individual job. Managers use the job cost record to see how they can use materials and labor more efficiently. For example, if a job's costs exceed its budget, managers must do a better job controlling costs on future jobs, or raise the sale price on similar jobs, to be sure that the company remains profitable.

Requirement 3

Prepare journal entries for each transaction.

a. Raw materials were purchased on account for $67,000.

When materials are purchased on account, you want to record the increase in raw materials inventory, so you would debit Raw Materials Inventory (an asset) for the cost of the materials, $67,000.

You also want to record the liability to your suppliers, so you would credit Accounts Payable (a liability) for $67,000.

Raw Materials Inventory	67,000	
Accounts Payable		67,000

b. Materials costing $45,000 were requisitioned for production. Of this total, $5,000 were indirect materials.

When materials are requisitioned, it means that they moved from raw materials inventory into production. A job costing system records this movement of inventory.

Of the total amount requisitioned ($45,000), only $5,000 was classified as indirect materials. That means that the remaining $40,000 represents the cost of direct materials traced to specific jobs. This cost is debited directly to Work in Process Inventory, increasing the asset by $40,000.

The materials that cannot be traced to a specific job (indirect materials) would be debited to manufacturing overhead (an increase of $5,000).

Because we are taking the materials out of the raw materials inventory, we reduce this asset with a credit for the total amount of the materials requisitioned ($45,000).

Work in Process Inventory	40,000	
Manufacturing Overhead	5,000	
Raw Materials Inventory		45,000

c. $32,000 of labor was incurred in the factory.

First, we debit Manufacturing Wages for the full amount of labor (direct and indirect) to accumulate the total labor cost incurred in the factory. The Manufacturing Wages account is a temporary account that is used to accumulate labor costs until the costs can be properly assigned. We then credit Wages Payable to show the liability to our employees.

Manufacturing Wages	32,000	
Wages Payable		32,000

d. Of the total labor costs, $30,000 was traced to specific jobs worked on during the month. The remainder of the factory labor cost related to indirect labor.

The next step is to assign the labor costs. Some of the labor ($30,000) can be traced to specific jobs. This amount, called direct labor, is assigned to the jobs by debiting Work in Process Inventory. The rest of the labor, $2,000, is for indirect labor, such as maintenance and janitorial services. Indirect labor cannot be traced to specific jobs; therefore, it is debited to Manufacturing Overhead.

Manufacturing Wages is credited for the full amount of the labor cost, bringing its balance to zero. The labor cost is now properly divided between Work in Process Inventory and Manufacturing Overhead.

Work in Process Inventory	30,000	
Manufacturing Overhead	2,000	
Manufacturing Wages		32,000

e. Manufacturing overhead is assigned to production using the predetermined overhead rate of 75% of direct labor cost.

Manufacturing overhead consists of all of the indirect costs of running the manufacturing plant, such as depreciation on the plant and equipment, salaries of the janitors, utilities, and property taxes and insurance on the plant. It is impossible to trace these costs to each job; therefore, manufacturers allocate some of these costs to each job using a predetermined overhead rate. In this case, the amount of overhead allocated to production is equal to 75% of the direct labor cost traced to production. Therefore, the amount of overhead allocated to production for the month is:

75% × $30,000 of direct labor (from part d) = $22,500

All actual manufacturing overhead costs are recorded as debits to the Manufacturing Overhead account. To take cost *out* of the account and assign it to specific jobs in production, we credit the Manufacturing Overhead account:

Manufacturing Overhead	
(Actual Costs)	(Allocated to Jobs)

To record the amount of manufacturing overhead allocated to jobs, we debit Work in Process Inventory. We then take this cost out of the Manufacturing Overhead account through a credit, as shown in the T-account on the previous page.

Work in Process Inventory	22,500	
Manufacturing Overhead		22,500

f. Jobs costing $67,000 were completed during the month.

When jobs are completed, the direct materials, direct labor, and manufacturing overhead costs shown on the job cost records are added to determine the total cost of the jobs. Then the jobs are moved off the plant floor and into the finished goods storage area until they are shipped to customers. In the accounting records, we also show the movement of these completed jobs by transferring the cost of the jobs from one inventory account to the next. Since all inventory accounts are assets, we debit the accounts to increase them and credit the accounts to decrease them. Thus, the following entry shows an increase in the Finished Goods Inventory and a decrease in the Work in Process Inventory:

Finished Goods Inventory	67,000	
Work in Process Inventory		67,000

g. Douglas sold several jobs during the month for a total price of $106,000. These jobs cost $65,000 to produce. Assume a perpetual inventory system.

We need to make two journal entries here. The first journal entry records the sale of the art to customers at a sales price of $106,000. We'll assume that the sales were made on account rather than paid in cash. Therefore, the following entry records an increase in the accounts receivable and an increase in sales revenue for the year:

Accounts Receivable	106,000	
Sales Revenue		106,000

The second entry is made assuming that Douglas has a perpetual inventory system. In a perpetual inventory system, companies show the costs of goods sold at the time they make a sale. They also show that the inventory sold is no longer theirs—it has been sold to the customer. So, they make the following journal entry to increase the Cost of Goods Sold (through a debit) and decrease the amount of inventory they have on hand (through a credit):

Cost of Goods Sold	65,000	
Finished Goods Inventory		65,000

Chapter 4: Demo Doc 1

■ Illustrating Process Costing

Learning Objectives 2, 3

Clear Bottled Water produces bottled water. Clear Bottled Water has two production departments: Blending and Packaging. In the Blending Department, materials are added at the beginning of the process. Conversion costs are added evenly throughout the process for blending. Data for the month of April for the Blending Department are as follows:

Units:	
Beginning work in process..	0
Started in production during April	116,000 units
Completed and transferred out to Packaging in April.........	98,000 units
Ending work in process inventory (70% completed)	18,000 units
Costs:	
Beginning work in process..	0
Costs added during April:	
Direct materials..	$54,520
Conversion costs	32,074
Total costs added during April...	$86,594

Requirement

Use the five-step process to calculate (1) the cost of the units completed and transferred out to the Packaging Department and (2) the total cost of the units in the Blending Department's ending work in process inventory.

Demo Doc 1 Solutions

Requirement

Use the five-step process costing procedure to calculate (1) the cost of the units completed and transferred out to the Packaging Department and (2) the total cost of the units in the Blending Department's ending work in process inventory.

Step 1: Summarize the flow of physical units.

The first step tracks the physical movement of units into and out of the Blending Department during the month. We first ask ourselves, "How many physical units did the Blending Department work on during the month?" That's the total number of units the Blending Department must account for. Total units to account for (116,000) is the sum of the units in beginning work in process (0) plus the units started in production during the month (116,000).

Next we ask ourselves, "What happened to those units?" The Blending Department accounts for the whereabouts of every unit it worked on during the month by showing that the total units accounted for equals the total units to account for. Total units accounted for (116,000) is the sum of units completed and transferred out of the Blending Department in April (98,000) plus the units in ending work in process at April 30 (18,000).

	Step 1
Flow of Production	**Flow of Physical Units**
Units to account for:	
Beginning work in process, April 1	0
Started in production during April	116,000
Total physical units to account for	116,000
Units accounted for:	
Completed and transferred out during April	98,000
Ending work in process, April 30	18,000
Total physical units accounted for	116,000
Total equivalent units	

Step 2: Compute output in terms of equivalent units.

Now that we have analyzed the flow of physical units, we compute the output in terms of equivalent units. First, the units completed and transferred out during April have 100% of their direct material and conversion costs. Therefore, the equivalent units for direct materials and conversion are the same as their physical units (98,000).

Next, consider the physical units (18,000) still in ending work in process. Materials are added at the beginning of the blending process, so 100% of the direct materials have been added. Therefore, the direct materials equivalent units are also 18,000 (18,000 physical units × 100%).

Conversion costs include both direct labor and manufacturing overhead. Conversion costs are added evenly throughout the blending process, so the conversion equivalent units for the ending work in process are the physical units in ending work in process (18,000) $\times$ the percentage complete, (70%), which equals 12,600.

Flow of Production	Step 1 Flow of Physical Units	Step 2 Equivalent Units Direct Materials	Conversion Costs
Units to account for:			
Beginning work in process, April 1	0		
Started in production during April	116,000		
Total physical units to account for	116,000		
Units accounted for:			
Completed and transferred out during April	98,000	98,000	98,000
Ending work in process, April 30	18,000	18,000	12,600
Total physical units accounted for	116,000		
Total equivalent units		116,000	110,600

The total equivalent units for direct materials is 116,000 (98,000 completed units + 18,000 in work in process). The total equivalent units for conversion costs is 110,600 (98,000 completed units + 12,600 in work in process).

Steps 3 and 4: Summarize total costs to account for and compute the cost per equivalent unit.

The next step is to summarize the total costs to account for, which consists of the costs in beginning work in process inventory plus the manufacturing costs incurred during April. The beginning inventory was zero. Direct materials of $54,520 and conversion costs of $32,074 were added during April. The total costs to account for is $86,594:

	Direct Materials	Conversion Costs	Total
Beginning work in process, April 1	$ 0	$ 0	$ 0
Costs added during April	54,520	32,074	86,594
Total costs to account for	$ 54,520	$ 32,074	$ 86,594
Divide by total equivalent units	÷ 116,000	÷ 110,600	
Cost per equivalent unit	$ 0.47	$ 0.29	

The cost per equivalent unit is computed by dividing the total costs to account for by the total equivalent units for each of the cost categories.

To calculate the cost per equivalent unit for direct materials, we divide the total direct materials costs of $54,520 by the equivalent units of direct materials, determined in Step 2 as 116,000 units. The result is $0.47 per equivalent unit for direct materials.

To calculate the cost per equivalent unit for conversion costs, we divide the total conversion cost of $32,074 by the number of equivalent units for conversion (which was determined in Step 2 to be 110,600). Dividing $32,074 by 110,600 gives us $0.29 per equivalent unit for conversion costs.

The cost of completing one unit in the Blending Department is $0.76 ($0.47 for direct materials plus $0.29 for conversion costs).

Step 5: Assign costs to units completed and to units in ending work in process inventory.

Because the units completed and transferred out were finished in the month of April, each unit is assigned the full unit cost of $0.76. Thus, the total cost to be assigned to the units completed and transferred out is $74,480 (98,000 units × $0.76). Shown another way, the total cost to be assigned to the units completed and transferred out is computed by multiplying the number of equivalent units (found in Step 2) by the cost per equivalent unit (found in Step 4):

$$98,000 \times \$0.47 = \$46,060 \text{ (direct materials)}$$
$$98,000 \times \$0.29 = \underline{\$28,420} \text{ (conversion costs)}$$
$$\$74,480$$

The total cost to be assigned to the units still in work in process inventory is computed in a similar manner. The number of equivalent units still in ending work in process (from Step 2) is multiplied by the cost per equivalent unit (found in Step 4):

$$18,000 \times \$0.47 = \$\ 8,460 \text{ (direct materials)}$$
$$12,600 \times \$0.29 = \underline{\$\ 3,654} \text{ (conversion costs)}$$
$$\$12,114$$

The total costs to account for ($86,594) is now properly divided between the units completed and transferred out to the Packaging Department ($74,480) and the units still in the Blending Department ending work in process inventory ($12,114).

	Direct Materials	Conversion Costs		Total
Completed and transferred out (98,000)	98,000 × ($0.47 + $0.29)		=	$74,480
Ending work in process inventory:				
Direct materials	18,000 × $0.47		=	$ 8,460
Conversion costs		12,600 × $0.29	=	3,654
Total cost of ending work in process inventory				$12,114
Total costs accounted for				$86,594

Chapter 7: Demo Doc 1

■ Using CVP for Sensitivity Analysis

Learning Objectives 2, 3, 4

Hacker Golf has developed a unique swing trainer golf club. The company currently pays a production company to produce the golf club at a cost of $22 each. Other variable costs total $6 per golf club, and monthly fixed expenses are $16,000. Hacker Golf currently sells the trainer golf club for $48.

NOTE: Solve each requirement as a separate situation.

Requirements

1. Calculate Hacker Golf's breakeven point in units.

2. Hacker Golf is considering raising the club's selling price to $49.95. Calculate the new breakeven in units.

3. Hacker Golf has found a new company to produce the golf club at a lower cost of $19. Calculate the new breakeven in units.

4. Because many customers have requested a golf glove to go along with the trainer club, Hacker Golf is considering selling gloves. They expect to sell only one glove for every four trainer clubs they sell. Hacker Golf can purchase the gloves for $5 a pair and sell them for $9 a pair. Total fixed costs should remain the same at $16,000 per month. Calculate the breakeven point in units for trainer clubs and golf gloves.

5. Use a contribution margin income statement to prove the breakeven point calculated in Requirement 4.

Demo Doc 1 Solutions

Requirement 1

Calculate Hacker's breakeven point in units.

To determine how changes in sales prices, costs, or volume affect profits, let's first start by calculating the current breakeven point.

To determine the breakeven point, we first must calculate the contribution margin per unit. The contribution margin is calculated by subtracting variable costs from the sales revenue. Therefore:

> Contribution margin per unit = Sales price per unit − Variable cost per unit

Hacker Golf's variable cost per club (unit) is the price it pays for each club ($22) plus its additional variable costs per golf club ($6). Therefore, its unit contribution margin is:

Selling price per club	$48
Variable cost per club ($22 + $6)	(28)
Contribution margin per club	$20

The contribution margin represents the amount from each unit sold that is available to cover fixed expenses. That means Hacker Golf earns $20 per club, which contributes toward fixed expenses until fixed expenses are covered. After fixed expenses are covered, each club sold contributes $20 directly to the company's operating income.

Breakeven is the level of sales at which income is zero. The breakeven point can be calculated as follows:

$$\text{Breakeven in units} = \frac{\text{Fixed expenses} + \text{Operating income}}{\text{Contribution margin per unit}}$$

$$\text{Breakeven in units} = \frac{\$16,000 + \$0}{\$20}$$

$$= 800 \text{ trainer clubs}$$

Requirement 2

Hacker Golf is considering raising the club's selling price to $49.95. Calculate the new breakeven in units.

Even if Hacker Golf raises its sales price per club to $49.95, its variable costs ($28 per unit) and fixed expenses ($16,000) will stay the same. As a result of increasing the sales price, the company will now have a higher contribution margin per unit:

Selling price per club	$49.95
Variable cost per club ($22 + $6)	(28.00)
Contribution margin per club	$21.95

Once again, you can use the breakeven formula to find the new breakeven point:

$$\text{Breakeven in units} = \frac{\text{Fixed expenses} + \text{Operating income}}{\text{Contribution margin per unit}}$$

$$\text{Breakeven in units} = \frac{\$16,000 + \$0}{\$21.95}$$

$$= 728.93 \text{ rounded to } 729 \text{ trainer clubs}$$

With the increased selling price, breakeven has been reduced from 800 clubs to 729 clubs. The higher price means that each club contributes more to fixed expenses.

You can prove the answer by preparing an income statement for a sales volume of 729 units:

Sales revenue (729 × $49.95)......................................	$ 36,412 (rounded)
Less: Variable expenses (729 × $28)...........................	(20,412)
Total contribution margin..	16,000
Less: Fixed expenses...	(16,000)
Operating income...	0

If the selling price increases, the volume required to break even or achieve target profit goals decreases (provided costs do not change). Conversely, if the selling price decreases, the volume required to break even or achieve target profit goals increases.

Requirement 3

Hacker Golf has found a new company to produce the golf club at a lower cost of $19. Calculate the new breakeven in units.

Let's return to Hacker Golf's original sales price ($48). Assuming that Hacker Golf has found a new company to produce the golf club for $19 each, the company's variable costs per club will decrease. However, fixed expenses remain the same ($16,000). Once again, Hacker Golf's contribution margin per unit will increase as a result of this change in business conditions:

Selling price per club	$48
Variable cost per club ($19 + $6)	(25)
Contribution margin per club..	$23

The new breakeven point is found as follows:

$$\text{Breakeven in units} = \frac{\text{Fixed expenses} + \text{Operating income}}{\text{Contribution margin per unit}}$$

$$\text{Breakeven in units} = \frac{\$16,000 + \$0}{\$23}$$

$$= 695.65 \text{ rounded to } 696 \text{ clubs}$$

With the reduced variable cost, Hacker Golf's breakeven in units decreases from 800 clubs to 696 clubs. Using this information, Hacker Golf's management must decide if it is worth the risk to switch to a new producer.

You can also prove this result by preparing an income statement:

Sales revenue (696 × $48)...	$ 33,400 (rounded)
Less: Variable expenses (696 × $25)............................	(17,400)
Total contribution margin..	16,000
Less: Fixed expenses...	(16,000)
Operating income..	$ 0

As variable or fixed expenses increase, so does the volume needed to break even or achieve target profits. Conversely, as these expenses decrease, the volume needed to break even or achieve target profits also decreases.

Requirement 4

Because many customers have requested a golf glove to go along with the trainer club, Hacker Golf is considering selling gloves. They expect to sell only one glove for every four trainer clubs they sell. Hacker Golf can purchase the gloves for $5 a pair and sell them for $9 a pair. Total fixed expenses should remain the same at $16,000 per month. Calculate the breakeven point in units for trainer clubs and golf gloves.

Calculating the breakeven point is fairly straightforward when a company is selling only one product. But Hacker Golf is now considering selling two products. Now, breakeven becomes more complicated. Different products will have different effects on the contribution margins because of different costs and selling prices. So, the company needs to consider the sales mix (a combination of products that make up total sales) in determining CVP relationships.

Finding the breakeven point for multiproduct firms involves a simple three-step process. The first step is to calculate a combined weighted-average contribution margin for all of the products that the company sells.

Step 1: Calculate the weighted-average contribution margin.

Hacker Golf believes that it can sell one glove for every four clubs that it sells. This would give the company a 4:1 sales mix. So, Hacker expects that 1/5 (or 20%) of sales will be gloves and 4/5 (or 80%) of sales will be trainer clubs.

Let's return to Hacker's original selling price and variable costs for the trainer club. Recall that Hacker Golf earns a $20 contribution margin on each golf club that it sells. Hacker will also earn a $4 contribution margin on each golf glove that it sells:

	Clubs	Gloves
Sales price per unit	$ 48	$ 9
Less: Variable cost per unit	(28)	(5)
Contribution margin per unit....................	$ 20	$ 4

The weighted-average contribution margin is calculated by multiplying the contribution margin per unit by the sales mix expected for each product. Once we have a total contribution margin for the bundle of products ($80 + $4 = $84, in this case), we divide it by the total number of units (5) in the sales mix, as follows:

	Clubs	Gloves	Total
Sales price per unit	$ 48	$ 9	
Less: Variable cost per unit	(28)	(5)	
Contribution margin per unit	$ 20	$ 4	
Sales mix in units	× 4	× 1	5
Contribution margin	$ 80	$ 4	$ 84
Weighted-average contribution margin per unit ($84/5)			$16.80

The $16.80 represents a weighted-average contribution margin for all of the products that Hacker Golf sells. The golf clubs are weighted more heavily because Hacker Golf expects to sell four times as many clubs as golf gloves.

The next step is to calculate the breakeven in units for the bundle of products.

Step 2: Calculate the breakeven point in units for the total of both products combined.

This is calculated using the breakeven formula modified for the weighted-average contribution margin in the denominator:

$$\text{Sales in total units} = \frac{\text{Fixed expenses + Operating income}}{\text{Weighted-average contribution margin per unit}}$$

We know from the question that fixed expenses will not be affected, so they should remain at $16,000. The weighted-average contribution margin, as we just calculated, is $16.80 per unit. So, we compute total sales as follows:

$$\text{Sales in total units} = \frac{\$16,000 + \$0}{\$16.80}$$
$$= 952.38 \text{ rounded to } 953$$

Hacker Golf must sell 953 clubs and gloves combined to break even. We round up because Hacker Golf cannot sell a partial unit. Management needs to know how many units of *each* product must be sold to break even. Therefore, the next step is to determine how many of the total sales units (953) need to be clubs and how many need to be gloves in order to break even.

Step 3: Calculate the breakeven in units for each product line.

Because Hacker Golf believes that it will sell four trainer clubs for every one pair of gloves, the total number of units, 953, is multiplied by each product's sales mix percentage:

Breakeven sales of clubs: [953 × (4/5)] = 762.4 rounded to 763

Breakeven sales of gloves: [953 × (1/5)] = 190.6 rounded to 191

From this analysis, we know that Hacker Golf needs to sell 763 trainer clubs and 191 pairs of gloves to break even.

Requirement 5

Use a contribution margin income statement to prove the breakeven point calculated in Requirement 4.

To test the calculation of the breakeven point, you would add the revenue generated from all sales, subtract the variable costs associated with all sales, and subtract the total fixed expenses. The result should balance to zero (or close to zero in cases in which rounding occurs).

	Clubs	Gloves	Total
Sales revenue:			
Trainer clubs (763 × $48)...................	$ 36,624		
Gloves (191 × $9)................................		$1,719	$ 38,343
Variable expenses:			
Trainer clubs (763 × $28)...................	(21,364)		
Gloves (191 × $5)................................		(955)	(22,319)
Contribution margin	$ 15,260	$ 764	$ 16,024
Fixed expenses			(16,000)
Operating income......................................			$ 24

There is a slight $24 profit because of a rounding error.

Chapter 10: Demo Doc 1

■ Master Budget

Learning Objective 2

Joe University sells college sweatshirts. Actual sales for the month ended September 30 were $20,000. Joe expects sales to increase 8% in October and another 4% in November. Cash sales are expected to be 60% of total sales and credit sales about 40% of sales.

Cost of goods sold should be 60% of total sales. Joe doesn't want inventory to fall below $4,000 plus 10% of cost of goods sold for the next month. Sales of $25,000 are expected for December. Inventory on September 30 is $6,000.

Operating expenses include sales commission, 10% of sales; rent expense of $1,000; depreciation expense of $1,200; utility expense of $800; and insurance expense of $400.

Round all figures to the nearest dollar.

Requirement

Prepare the following budgets for October and November:

a. **Sales budget**

b. **Inventory, purchases, and cost of goods sold budget**

c. **Operating expense budget**

d. **Budgeted income statement**

Demo Doc 1 Solutions

Requirement

Prepare the following budgets for October and November:

a. Sales budget

We prepare the sales budget first because sales impact most elements of the other budgets we will be preparing for this period.

To complete the sales budget, we start by calculating the total sales for each month. We then compute the split between cash sales and credit sales for each month based on Joe's estimation that cash sales will be 60% of the total sales for each month and credit sales will be 40% of total sales for each month.

Let's begin by calculating Joe's total sales for October and November. We know that actual sales for the month ended September 30 were $20,000 and that Joe expects sales to increase by 8% over that amount in October and another 4% over October's sales in November:

October total sales = September sales × 108%

October total sales = $20,000 × 108% = $21,600

November total sales = October sales × 104%

November total sales = $21,600 × 104% = $22,464

So, we begin to build our sales budget with this data:

JOE UNIVERSITY
Sales Budget

	October	November	Total
Cash sales, 60%			
Credit sales, 40%			
Total sales	$21,600	$22,464	$44,064

Now, we work backward to calculate the split between cash and credit sales for each month. In this case, cash sales are 60% of total sales and credit sales are 40% of total sales for the current months:

Cash sales = Total sales × 60%

October cash sales = $21,600 × 60% = $12,960

November cash sales = $22,464 × 60% = $13,478.40 (rounded to $13,478)

Credit sales = Total sales × 40%

October credit sales = $21,600 × 40% = $8,640

November credit sales = $22,464 × 40% = $8,985.60 (rounded to $8,986)

The following is the completed sales budget:

JOE UNIVERSITY
Sales Budget

	October	November	Total
Cash sales, 60%	$12,960	$13,478	$26,438
Credit sales, 40%	8,640	8,986	17,626
Total sales	$21,600	$22,464	$44,064

This gives us a total sales budget for October and November of $44,064, with 60% of that ($26,438) from cash and 40% ($17,626) from credit.

Because the sales budget calculates values you will use when preparing other budgets, it's always a good idea to check your work.

b. Inventory, purchases, and cost of goods sold budget

The inventory, purchases, and cost of goods sold budget takes the following format:

Cost of goods sold	(what we need for current month sales)
+ Desired ending inventory	(what we need to have on hand at month-end)
= Total inventory required	(what we need)
− Beginning inventory	(what we have)
= Purchases	(what we need to buy)

First, we calculate the cost of goods sold. We know from the question that cost of goods sold is expected to be 60% of total sales for the period. From the sales budget, we know that total sales for October are expected to be $21,600 and total sales for November are expected to be $22,464. We can calculate cost of goods sold as follows:

Cost of goods sold = 60% of budgeted sales from the sales budget
October = $21,600 × 60% = $12,960
November = $22,464 × 60% = $13,478

Here's our budget so far:

JOE UNIVERSITY
Inventory, Purchases, and Cost of Goods Sold Budget

	October	November	
Cost of goods sold	$12,960	$13,478	
+ Desired ending inventory			
= Total inventory required			
− Beginning inventory			
= Purchases			

Next, we need to add the desired ending inventory for each month. The information states that Joe doesn't want inventory to fall below $4,000 plus 10% of cost of goods sold for the next month. To calculate the desired ending inventory for November, we need to know the cost of goods sold for December. December's sales are expected to be $25,000. Returning to our calculation for cost of goods sold:

Cost of goods sold = 60% of budgeted sales from the sales budget
December = $25,000 × 60% = $15,000

Desired ending inventory is calculated as follows:

Desired ending inventory = [$4,000 + (10% of cost of goods sold for the next month)]
October = $4,000 + (10% × $13,478) = $5,348
November = $4,000 + (10% × $15,000) = $5,500

We can now calculate the total inventory required:

JOE UNIVERSITY
Inventory, Purchases, and Cost of Goods Sold Budget

	October	November	
Cost of goods sold	$12,960	$13,478	
+ Desired ending inventory	5,348	5,500	
= Total inventory required	$18,308	$18,978	
− Beginning inventory			
= Purchases			

Beginning inventory is equal to the previous month's desired ending inventory. We know that the inventory on September 30 is $6,000, so this becomes October's beginning inventory. Once we determine beginning inventory, we subtract it from the total inventory required to determine purchases for the period:

JOE UNIVERSITY
Inventory, Purchases, and Cost of Goods Sold Budget

	October	November	
Cost of goods sold	$12,960	$13,478	
+ Desired ending inventory	5,348	5,500	
= Total inventory required	$18,308	$18,978	
− Beginning inventory	6,000	5,348	
= Purchases	$12,308	$13,630	

c. Operating expense budget

With the exception of the sales commission, which we know to be 10% of sales, all expenses remain constant between October and November, as follows:

JOE UNIVERSITY
Operating Expense Budget

	October	November	Total
Sales commission			
Rent expense	1,000	1,000	2,000
Insurance expense	400	400	800
Depreciation expense	1,200	1,200	2,400
Utility expense	800	800	1,600

The only calculation to perform here is sales commission. We can compute sales commissions for October and November using the respective sales computations ($21,600 and $22,464) from the sales budget:

Sales commission = Expected sales × 10%

October sales commission = $21,600 × 10% = $2,160

November sales commission = $22,464 × 10% = $2,246.40 (rounded to $2,246)

Here's our completed operating expense budget for October and November:

JOE UNIVERSITY
Operating Expense Budget

	October	November	Total
Sales commission	$2,160	$2,246	$4,406
Rent expense	1,000	1,000	2,000
Insurance expense	400	400	800
Depreciation expense	1,200	1,200	2,400
Utility expense	800	800	1,600
Total operating expenses	$5,560	$5,646	$11,206

d. Budgeted income statement

The results of the budgets you've created so far are carried over into the fourth element: the budgeted income statement.

Sales revenue is traced from the sales budget in part a.

Cost of goods sold is traced from the inventory, purchases, and cost of goods sold budget in part b.

We compute gross profit by subtracting the cost of goods sold from sales revenue:

JOE UNIVERSITY
Budgeted Income Statement

	October	November	Total
Sales revenue	$21,600	$22,464	$44,064
Cost of goods sold	12,960	13,478	26,438
Gross profit	8,640	8,986	17,626
Operating expenses			
Operating income			

Operating expenses are traced from the operating expenses budget.

We compute operating income (loss) by subtracting operating expenses from gross profit. Our completed budgeted income statement looks like this:

JOE UNIVERSITY
Budgeted Income Statement

	October	November	Total
Sales revenue	$21,600	$22,464	$44,064
Cost of goods sold	12,960	13,478	26,438
Gross profit	8,640	8,986	17,626
Operating expenses	5,560	5,646	11,206
Operating income	$ 3,080	$ 3,340	$ 6,420

Photo Credits

Chapter 1, *Page 27,* Courtesy of Lon C. Diehl, PhotoEdit Inc.

Chapter 2, *Page 71,* Courtesy of Sergio Piumatti.

Chapter 3, *Page 129,* Courtesy of Greg Smith, Corbis/Bettmann.

Chapter 4, *Page 193,* Courtesy of Jelly Belly Candy Company, used with permission from Jelly Belly Candy Company.

Chapter 5, *Page 257,* Courtesy of AP Wide World Photos.

Chapter 6, *Page 327,* Courtesy of Karen Braun.

Chapter 7, *Page 385,* Reproduced with permission of art.com.™

Chapter 8, *Page 439,* Courtesy of Tim Boyle, Getty Images, Inc.

Chapter 9, *Page 495,* Courtesy of Karl Weatherly, © Karl Weatherly / CORBIS, all rights reserved.

Chapter 10, *Page 563,* Courtesy of Amazon.com.®

Chapter 11, *Page 621,* Courtesy of McDonalds Corp.

Chapter 12, *Page 691,* Courtesy of Myrleen Ferguson Cate, PhotoEdit Inc.

Chapter 13, *Page 739,* Courtesy of Alamy Images.

Company Index

Glindex
A Combined Glossary/Subject

A

ABC. *See* Activity-based costing (ABC)

Absorption costing. The costing method where products "absorb" both fixed and variable manufacturing costs, 358–364

Absorption costing income statement, 360, 446, 447

Account analysis. A method for determining cost behavior that is based on a manager's judgment in classifying each general ledger account as a variable, fixed, or mixed cost, 343–346

Accounting rate of return (ARR). A measure of profitability computed by dividing the average annual operating income from an asset by the initial investment in the asset, 497, 502–504, 523

Accounts receivable turnover. Measure a company's ability to collect cash from credit customers. To compute accounts receivable turnover, divide net credit sales by average net accounts receivable, 754

Accrual accounting, 502

Acid-test ratio. Ratio of the sum of cash plus short-term investments plus net current receivables to total current liabilities. Tells whether the entity can pay all of its current liabilities if they come due immediately. Also called the quick ratio, 753

Activity-based costing (ABC). Focuses on activities as the fundamental cost objects. The costs of those activities become the building blocks for compiling the indirect costs of products, services, and customers, 264–272

assessing product profitability with, 266–272

cost-benefit test, 275–276

development of system for, 264–265

using for decision making, 273–275

using for job costing, 265–266

Activity-based management (ABM). Using activity-based cost information to make decisions that increase profits while satisfying customer's needs, 273–274

Activity cost allocation rates, 263

Advertising, 76

Allocate. To assign an indirect cost to a cost object, 80

Allocation base. A common denominator that links indirect costs to cost objects (such as jobs or production processes). Ideally, the allocation base is the primary cost driver of the indirect cost, 148

Annuities. A stream of equal installments made at equal time intervals, 507

calculating future value of, 510–511

calculating present value of, 511–514

internal rate of return with, 521–522

net present value with, 516–517

Appraisal costs. Costs incurred to detect poor-quality goods or services, 285, 286

Assets

capital, 496

residual value of, 519–520

return on, 757

total, 716, 757

Assign. To attach a cost to a cost object, 80

Audit committee. A subcommittee of the board of directors that is responsible for overseeing both the internal audit function and the annual financial statement audit by CPAs.

Average costs. The total cost divided by the number of units, 98–99

Average unit costs, 209

B

BAII Plus calculator, 555–562

Balanced scorecard. Measures that recognize that management must consider financial performance measures and operational performance measures when judging the performance of a company and its subunits, 697–702

Balance sheets, 93–94. *See also* Financial statements

budgeted, 580

comparative, 743–744, 746

horizontal analysis of, 743–744

vertical analysis of, 746

Benchmarking. The practice of comparing a company with other companies that are leaders, 567–568, 696, 747–748

against industry average, 748

against key competitor, 747

Blame, 589

Board of directors. The body elected by shareholders to oversee the company, 33

Book value per share of common stock. Common stockholders' equity divided by the number of shares of common stock outstanding. The recorded amount for each share of common stock outstanding, 759–760

Breakeven point. The sales level at which operating income is zero: Total revenues equal total expenses.

affect of changes in fixed costs on, 406

affect of changes in sales price on, 403

affect of changes in variable costs on, 404

finding, using CVP analysis, 391–394, 408–410

graphing, 397

Budgeted balance sheet, 580

Budgeted income statement, 574

Budgeted manufacturing overhead rate, 149